CRIMINAL LITIGATION AND SENTENCING

CRIMINAL LITIGATION AND SENTENCING

Inns of Court School of Law

BLACKSTONE PRESS LIMITED

First published in Great Britain 1996 by Blackstone Press Limited,
Aldine Place, London W12 8AA. Telephone (020) 8740 2277
www.blackstonepress.com

First edition 1996
Second edition 1997
Third edition 1998
Fourth edition 1999
Fifth edition 2000

ISBN: 1 84174 058 6

British Library Cataloguing in Publication Data
A CIP catalogue record for this book is available from the British Library.

Typeset by Style Photosetting Ltd, Mayfield, East Sussex
Printed by Ashford Colour Press, Gosport, Hants

FOREWORD

These manuals are designed primarily to support training on the Bar Vocational Course, though they are also intended to provide a useful resource for legal practitioners and for anyone undertaking training in legal skills.

The Bar Vocational Course was designed by staff at the Inns of Court School of Law, where it was introduced in 1989. This course is intended to equip students with the practical skills and the procedural and evidential knowledge that they will need to start their legal professional careers. These manuals are written by staff at the Inns of Court School of Law who have helped to develop the course, and by a range of legal practitioners and others involved in legal skills training. The authors of the manuals are very well aware of the practical and professional approach that is central to the Bar Vocational Course.

The range and coverage of the manuals have grown steadily. All the manuals are updated annually, and regular reviews and revisions of the manuals are carried out to ensure that developments in legal skills training and the experience of our staff are fully reflected in them.

This updating and revision is a constant process and we very much value the comments of practitioners, staff and students. Legal vocational training is advancing rapidly, and it is important that all those concerned work together to achieve and maintain high standards. Please address any comments to the Bar Vocational Course Director at the Inns of Court School of Law.

With the validation of other providers for the Bar Vocational Course it is very much our intention that these manuals will be of equal value to all students wherever they take the course, and we would very much value comments from tutors and students at other validated institutions.

The enthusiasm of the staff at Blackstone Press Ltd and their efficiency in arranging production and publication of the manuals is much appreciated.

The Hon. Mr Justice Elias
Chairman of the Board of Governors
Inns of Court School of Law
August 2000

CONTENTS

PREFACE

Criminal litigation covers the procedural rules which govern a criminal case. It spans the magistrates' and youth court as well as the Crown Court and the various appellate courts. It is crucial for anyone who may practise in the criminal courts (including all barristers, whether that is their primary intention or not) to have the more important of these rules at their fingertips. To be able to deal effectively with a criminal case means that a barrister must have a sound grasp of the main rules of criminal procedure, and must be able to apply them. It also means that where those rules are capable of different interpretations, the practitioner must be able to argue for the interpretation which favours his or her case. To do this, some understanding of the purpose behind the procedural rules is necessary. Rote learning is not enough.

This Manual deals with the rules of criminal litigation in such a way that the reader should be assisted to apply them in a practical context. The complementary subject of sentencing, which in practice is an integral part of criminal litigation, is dealt with in more detail in the second part of the Manual. Attention is devoted both to the process of sentencing and to the factors which may influence what sentence is actually passed. The Manual as a whole is firmly set in a practical context, with examples, questions and problems to help the reader apply the principles of criminal procedure and sentencing to cases as they are encountered in practice.

As a result, the Manual ought to provide assistance not only in acquiring a grasp of the relevant rules, but in performing the tasks associated with the skills of the barrister — including applying for (or opposing) bail, advising in conference on plea and sentence, delivering a plea in mitigation, and making the various procedural submissions and speeches which occur during the criminal process.

This Manual has been updated to include the Youth Justice and Criminal Evidence Act 1999 and the Powers of Criminal Courts (Sentencing) Act 2000.

TABLE OF CASES

TABLE OF STATUTES

CRIMINAL LITIGATION

ONE

INTRODUCTION

1.1 Aims of the Course

The main intention of those responsible for designing both the Criminal Litigation element of the Bar Vocational Course, and this Manual, has been to make the subject both real and practical. The Criminal Litigation Course should instil you with a knowledge of how the criminal justice system actually works; then give you the opportunity to demonstrate that you have assimilated such knowledge and are able to make the decisions which a barrister could find himself or herself making in practice.

1.2 Objectives of the Course

By the end of the course, and having read this Manual, you should be:

(a) Familiar with the progress of a case through the criminal courts, understanding the various stages and what each stage involves.

(b) Able to prepare for a hearing in the magistrates' court or Crown Court, knowing what the procedure will be in court and what matters will need to be covered.

(c) Capable of taking informed decisions (and, if necessary, advising your client on how to act) with regard to the various different paths that a case can take, both as to its final resolution and the intermediate hearings.

(d) Able to decide whether or not a decision taken in criminal proceedings merits an appeal — whether it be in relation to conviction, sentence or some procedural matter.

(e) Able to prepare properly for an appeal and advise your client which is the most suitable method of appeal (where a choice exists).

1.3 The Manual

The Manual is designed primarily for use in conjunction with the Criminal Litigation classes on the Bar Vocational Course. It should prepare you to deal with a particular topic as well as supporting specific classes through the material it contains. It is also designed to stand alone as a practical and sensible guide to legal practice in the criminal courts of England and Wales. It contains most of the 'bare bones' of what anyone needs to know when starting on a career in the criminal courts; it devotes rather less space to the remoter world of the Court of Appeal and the House of Lords.

Throughout the text, references will be found to other sources (see **1.6** below). These include law reports and statutes, and there are also references to relevant chapters in the two main works used by practitioners, *Archbold* and *Blackstone's Criminal Practice*. Occasional reference is also made to *Stone's Justices' Manual* (everything you need to know for the magistrates' court), the excellent book by Christopher Emmins and John

Sprack, *Emmins on Criminal Procedure*, and to articles in periodicals (notably the *Criminal Law Review*). These references are intended to indicate other sources of information either more eloquent, more authoritative or more detailed than this Manual. They should all promote an understanding of the subject. The Manual is a concise and, it is hoped, readable guide, both by way of introduction and as a source of practical knowledge.

1.3.1 THE STRUCTURE OF THE MANUAL

The Criminal Litigation Course starts at the beginning of the process (e.g. an individual being charged with an offence) and works its way through to the possible endings — acquittal, conviction and sentence, appeal. This Manual reflects that pattern because this seems to be the best way to promote an understanding of the various practices and procedures that govern the passage of a case through the criminal courts. The Manual starts with preliminary matters such as powers of arrest, then the commencement of criminal proceedings against an accused person. Having dealt with the subject of bail, the Manual continues by looking at what happens when an accused person first appears in court once proceedings have started. The usual way of disposing of a case — summary trial — is next on the list, followed by a brief examination of the way that young people are treated by the criminal justice system. The focus then shifts to the Crown Court — considering first how cases are sent there (committal for trial), then the drafting of an indictment and the different pleas that might be offered by a defendant. Criminal Litigation ends with chapters on trial in the Crown Court and appeals from that court to the Court of Appeal and beyond. The Manual itself concludes with several chapters on sentencing, which is taught as a separate related subject on the Bar Vocational Course.

1.4 Structure and Relationship of the Courts

All cases begin in the magistrates' court. A youth court is a type of magistrates' court which deals exclusively with juveniles. The vast majority of cases will be tried in the magistrates' court and will end there (unless the accused is committed to the Crown Court for sentence, or appeals to either the Crown Court or the High Court). The remaining cases will begin in the magistrates' court but be transferred for trial to the Crown Court with the possibility of an appeal to the Court of Appeal. From both the Court of Appeal and the High Court it is possible, though rare, to appeal to the House of Lords on matters of law. The interrelationship of the courts is set out in **Figure 1.1**.

1.5 The Civil Jurisdiction of the Magistrates' Court

It is appropriate at this stage to say something about the civil jurisdiction of magistrates. Although the magistrates' court is known primarily as a criminal court, it does have the power to deal with non-criminal cases. The magistrates' court is given such powers as it has by Acts of Parliament — it has no inherent jurisdiction. Numerous Acts establish the jurisdiction of the court to deal with an amazing variety of work, from excluding violent partners from the family home to granting permission to cafes to stay open after midnight. The most significant aspects for a barrister of the magistrates' jurisdiction over civil matters are, perhaps, their role in family or domestic proceedings and their power to grant licences in connection with the sale of alcohol.

1.5.1 FAMILY PROCEEDINGS

The main statute covering this area is the Domestic Proceedings and Magistrates' Courts Act 1978, but frequent reference should also be made to the Children Act 1989. Since October 1991, when dealing with matrimonial matters, magistrates sit as a 'family proceedings court', pursuant to the Children Act 1989. Such courts must be constituted in a similar way to youth courts (which deal with young offenders), in that they should usually have at least one man and one woman magistrate to hear each case. Stipendiary magistrates may sit in the family proceedings court.

Figure 1.1 Structure and Relationship of the Courts

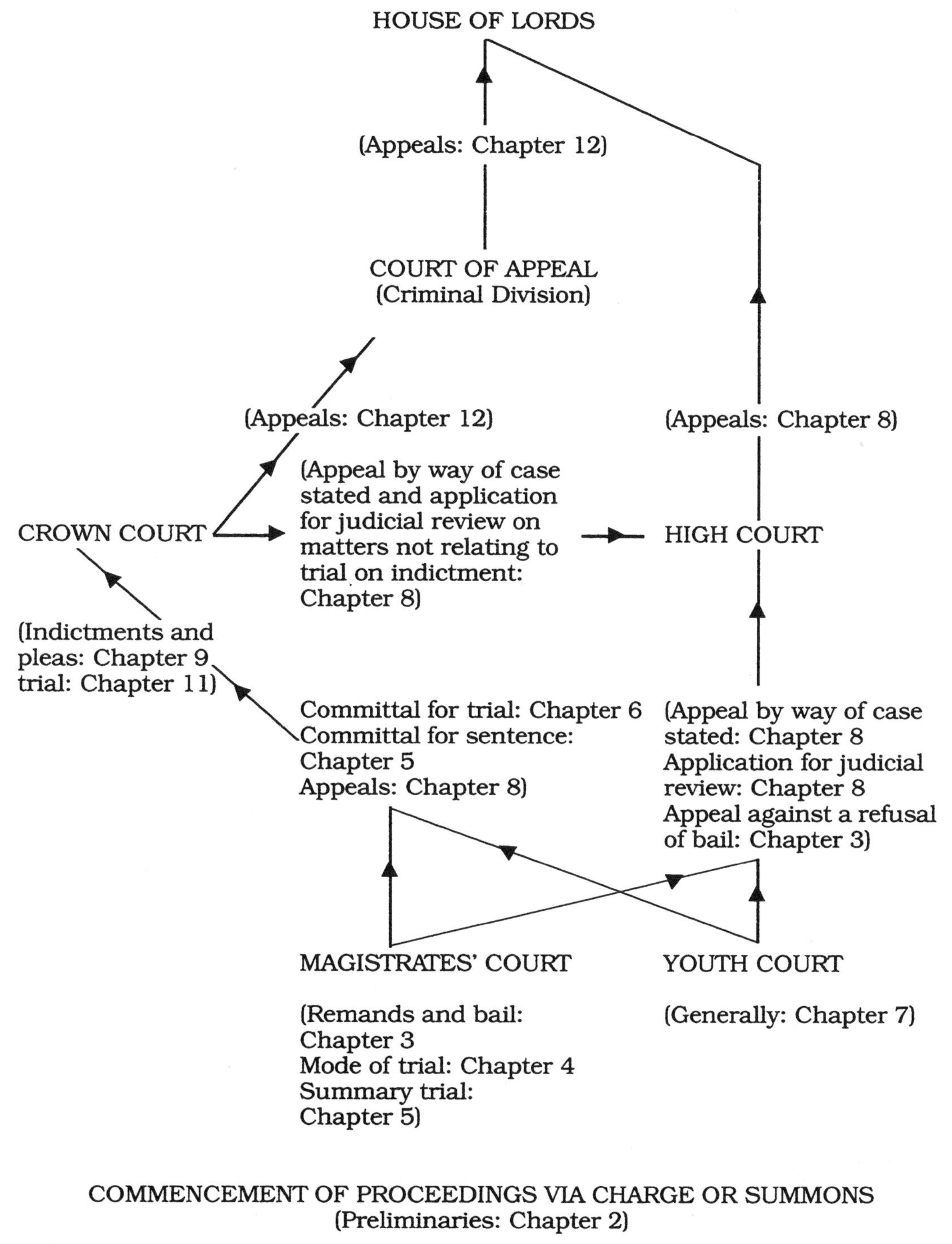

A husband or wife may apply to the family proceedings court for financial provision under the Domestic Proceedings and Magistrates' Courts Act 1978. Such provision may be for themselves or any child of the family. The family proceedings court also has power to order a party to a marriage not to use or threaten violence against their spouse or a child of the family; also, in certain circumstances, to exclude a violent partner from the matrimonial home. Applications for the adoption of children may be made to the family proceedings court, as may other applications concerning children. Following the implementation of the Children Act 1989, the jurisdiction of the family proceedings court is quite similar to that of the County Court and High Court in a number of areas. The choice of court will often depend on the need for urgency, what other proceedings are currently proceeding with regard to the same people, and the complexity or gravity of the case.

Further explanation is beyond the scope of this Manual. Readers are recommended to read *Rayden and Jackson on Divorce and Family Matters*, 17th edn, especially Chapter 49.

1.5.2 LICENSING APPLICATIONS

Magistrates have the power to grant licences to those who wish to sell alcohol — either to the immediate consumer (in a public house, hotel or restaurant) or in a more indirect fashion (in a supermarket or cornershop off-licence). The main statute on this topic is the Licensing Act 1964 (as amended over the intervening years). One may find that a simple licence is sought for the sale of alcohol to be consumed off the premises — an off-licence — or perhaps a licence for alcohol to be sold with bar meals (usually giving longer hours for sale and consumption). The application may be for a single event — for example, the Church fête or a street party if alcohol is to be sold there. Generally there is little difficulty in obtaining the necessary licence so long as the requisite formalities have been observed. These usually relate to giving due notice of the application — to the police, fire brigade, in the newspapers, on the premises — and attending court with the appropriate pieces of paper (and people) to prove it. This Manual is not the proper place for a detailed examination of the licensing laws, but reference should be made (whenever necessary) to *Paterson's Licensing Acts.*

1.6 Research

You are advised to read further about the topics covered in this course in the following books:

(a) Archbold, *Criminal Pleading, Evidence and Practice*, 2000 edn, Sweet and Maxwell.

(b) Sprack, *Emmins on Criminal Procedure*, 8th edn, Blackstone Press.

(c) *Blackstone's Criminal Practice*, 2000, Blackstone Press (also available in CD-rom format).

A thorough work of reference for magistrates' courts is *Stone's Justices' Manual.* Other specialist works exist and are used by practitioners, e.g. *Wilkinson on Road Traffic Offences.*

You will find cross-references to other publications throughout the text which follows but should also refer where necessary to the following Manuals:

(a) ***Advocacy***;

(b) ***Conference Skills***;

(c) ***Negotiation Skills***;

(d) ***Opinion Writing***;

(e) ***Drafting***;

(f) ***Evidence***;

(g) ***Case Preparation***.

Note: In some chapters of ***Criminal Litigation and Sentencing***, statistical tables are reproduced with the kind permission of the Home Office Statistics Department. Due to different recording procedures in some areas of the country and some incomplete data, the figures in these Tables should be taken only as a guide.

1.7 Abbreviations

Abbreviations are often used in the text. Some are probably familiar, e.g. *Archbold, Stone's*, WLR for Weekly Law Reports. Others will become familiar in time. The following list of common abbreviations should help.

BA 1976 (Bail Act 1976);

CAA 1968 or 1995 (Criminal Appeal Act, either 1968 or 1995);

CDA 1998 (Crime and Disorder Act 1998);

CICB (Criminal Injuries Compensation Board);

CJA (Criminal Justice Act, various years but most likely are 1982, 1987, 1988, 1991 and 1993);

CJPOA 1994 (Criminal Justice and Public Order Act 1994);

CLA (Criminal Law Act, various years);

CPIA 1996 (Criminal Procedure and Investigations Act 1996);

CPS (Crown Prosecution Service);

Cr App R (Criminal Appeal Reports. A specialist series, reporting cases from the Divisional Court of the Queen's Bench Division, Court of Appeal (Criminal Division), and the House of Lords);

Cr App R (S) (Criminal Appeal Reports (Sentencing). A companion to the Cr App R but concentrating on sentencing decisions);

Crim LR (Criminal Law Review. A monthly publication with brief, up-to-date reports of cases and useful articles);

C(S)A 1997 (Crime (Sentences) Act 1997);

CSO (Community Service Order);

CYPA 1933 or 1969 (Children and Young Persons Act, either 1933 or 1969);

DTO (Detention and Training Orders);

ECHR (European Convention on Human Rights and Fundamental Freedoms);

HRA 1998 (Human Rights Act 1998);

JA 1974 (Juries Act 1974);

MCA 1980 (Magistrates' Courts Act 1980);

MHA 1983 (Mental Health Act 1983);

PACE 1984 (Police and Criminal Evidence Act 1984);

PCC(S)A 2000 (Powers of Criminal Courts (Sentencing) Act 2000);

ROA 1974 (Rehabilitation of Offenders Act 1974);

SCA 1981 (Supreme Court Act 1981);

t.i.c (taken into consideration);

YJCEA 1999 (Youth Justice and Criminal Evidence Act 1999).

TWO

PRELIMINARIES

Useful article — Ian McKenzie, Rod Morgan and Robert Reiner 'Helping the police with their enquiries' [1990] Crim LR 22.

2.1 Preamble

There are essentially two methods of commencing prosecutions, namely the arrest and charge of the suspect, described at **2.2** below, and the issue of process, described at **2.3** below. Two matters may be conveniently dealt with now by way of preamble.

2.1.1 JURISDICTION AND IMMUNITY

English courts accept jurisdiction to try an accused for an offence committed in England and Wales, regardless of the nationality of the offender. In addition, English courts have jurisdiction over some offences committed abroad in certain circumstances, such as offences of murder and manslaughter where the accused is a British subject, and offences of hijacking regardless of the nationality of the accused. For a complete list of such offences, see *Archbold*, 2000 edn, para. 2–33 et seq and *Blackstone's Criminal Practice*, 2000 edn, sections D1.71 et seq. For the limited jurisdiction of magistrates' courts, see **2.5** below.

Certain persons are entitled to immunity from prosecution. The Queen is immune, as are foreign sovereigns and heads of state, their families and personal servants. Diplomatic agents, their staff and families are also immune. For a complete list of those immune from prosecution, see *Archbold*, 2000 edn, para. 1–82 et seq.

2.1.2 THE RIGHT TO PROSECUTE

The Crown Prosecution Service (CPS) was created by the Prosecution of Offences Act 1985, and is a single, national, prosecution service, with the Director of Public Prosecutions (DPP) at its head, and under the 'superintendence' of the Attorney-General. The main duty of the CPS is to take over and conduct all criminal proceedings commenced by the police, which includes the power to discontinue proceedings or to change or amend any charges originally preferred.

The right of an individual, and of certain statutory bodies such as the Inland Revenue, to institute and conduct criminal proceedings, is expressly preserved by the Act. However, under s. 6(2), the DPP has an unfettered discretion to intervene in any proceedings, and conduct them on his or her own behalf.

2.2 Arrest and Charge

Most police powers of arrest, interviewing and charging a suspect are contained in the Police and Criminal Evidence Act 1984 (PACE 1984) and the Codes of Practice created thereunder. In general terms, the Act provides the overall framework, and the Codes provide the fine detail. There are five Codes of Practice, namely:

Code A: Code of Practice for the Exercise by Police Officers of Statutory Powers of Stop and Search.

Code B: Code of Practice for the Searching of Premises by Police Officers and the Seizure of Property found by Police Officers on Persons and Premises.

Code C: Code of Practice for the Detention, Treatment and Questioning of Persons by Police Officers.

Code D: Code of Practice for the Identification of Persons by Police Officers.

Code E: Code of Practice on Tape Recording.

The Codes contain detailed regulations on the exercise of police powers, and 'notes for guidance'. The notes for guidance are not provisions of the Codes, but are guidance to police officers and others about their application and interpretation.

The Codes of Practice apply to:

(a) police officers (s. 67(8) and (10)); and

(b) persons 'other than police officers who are charged with the duty of investigating offences or charging offenders' (s. 67(9)). This includes local authority officials, post office investigators, officers of the Serious Fraud Office, customs officers and store detectives. Whether a body or person conducting an enquiry is subject to s. 67(9) is a question of fact in each case (*R* v *Seelig* [1992] 1 WLR 148).

While students should be familiar with all five codes, this Manual is mainly concerned with Code C, and any reference to 'the Code' should be understood accordingly. Students should consult the ***Evidence Manual*** and standard texts for a full discussion of this area.

2.2.1 POWERS OF ARREST WITHOUT WARRANT

A police officer has a number of powers of arrest in a number of circumstances, the most important of which are as follows:

(a) if the offence is designated by PACE 1984, s. 24, as an arrestable offence. These are:

   (i) Where the sentence for the offence is fixed by law (e.g. murder).

   (ii) Where the offence carries at least five years' imprisonment (e.g. theft).

   (iii) Specified offences in s. 24(2), for example, taking a motor vehicle without authority or going equipped for stealing under s. 12(1) and s. 25(1) respectively of the Theft Act 1968.

(b) Under PACE 1984, s. 25, if a police officer has reasonable grounds for suspecting that an offence, not included within s. 24, has been committed or attempted, he may arrest the person he suspects of committing the offence, if one of the following conditions, known as general arrest conditions, is satisfied:

   (i) That it is impossible to ascertain accurately the suspect's name and address.

   (ii) That the officer has reasonable grounds for believing that arrest is necessary to prevent the suspect:

   — causing physical injury to himself or herself or any other person; or

— suffering physical injury; or

— causing loss of or damage to property; or

— committing an offence against public decency; or

— causing an unlawful obstruction of the highway.

(iii) That the officer has reasonable grounds for believing that arrest is necessary to protect a child or other vulnerable person from the suspect.

(c) Schedule 2 to PACE 1984 preserves pre-existing powers of arrest created under earlier statutes, for example, where a suspect fails to provide a breath test under the Road Traffic Act 1988, s. 6(5) or is unlikely to comply with the conditions of his bail under the Bail Act 1976 (BA 1976), s. 7 (see further **3.15**).

(d) PACE 1984, s. 46A, inserted by s. 29 of the Criminal Justice and Public Order Act 1994 (CJPOA 1994), provides the police with a power to arrest any person who, having been bailed by police subject to a duty to attend at a police station, fails to do so.

(e) The Public Order Act 1986 contains specific powers of arrest relating to offences of fear or provocation of violence (s. 4(3)), and harassment, alarm or distress (s. 5(4)).

(f) The Criminal Justice and Public Order Act 1994 gives a constable in uniform the power to remove trespassers from land (s. 61), to seize or remove any vehicle after a request to remove has been refused (s. 62), and certain other powers to deal with raves.

2.2.2 SERIOUS ARRESTABLE OFFENCES

PACE 1984 also defines certain offences as being serious arrestable offences. While these offences do not carry any greater power of arrest, the fact that the defendant is charged with a serious arrestable offence gives the police wider powers of detention (see **2.2.4** et seq.) and it is convenient to include them here. Under s. 116 and sch. 5 serious arrestable offences are:

(a) Treason.

(b) Murder.

(c) Manslaughter.

(d) Rape.

(e) Kidnapping.

(f) Incest with a girl under 13.

(g) Buggery with a boy under 16 or a person who has not consented.

(h) Indecent assault which constitutes an act of gross indecency.

(i) Causing explosions likely to endanger life or property contrary to the Explosive Substances Act 1883, s. 2.

(j) Intercourse with a girl under 13 contrary to the Sexual Offences Act 1956, s. 5.

(k) Possession of firearms with intent to injure contrary to the Firearms Act 1968, s. 16.

(l) Use of firearms and imitation firearms to resist arrest contrary to the Firearms Act 1968, s. 17.

(m) Carrying firearms with criminal intent contrary to the Firearms Act 1968, s. 18.

(n) Causing death by dangerous driving contrary to the Road Traffic Act 1988, s. 1.

(o) Hostage-taking contrary to the Taking of Hostages Act 1982, s. 1.

(p) Hijacking contrary to the Aviation Security Act 1982.

(q) Offences under the Prevention of Terrorism (Temporary Provisions) Act 1989, ss. 2, 8, 9, 10 and 11 are always serious offences for the purpose of the rights contained in PACE 1984, s. 56 and s. 58 (note that the 1989 Act will be repealed when the Terrorism Act 2000 comes into force).

(r) An arrestable offence is a serious arrestable offence if its commission has led to, is intended or is likely to lead to, or consists of making a threat which if carried out would lead to:

    (i) Serious harm to the security of the State or to public order.

    (ii) Serious interference with the administration of justice or with the investigation of offences or of a particular offence.

    (iii) The death of any person.

    (iv) Serious injury to any person.

    (v) Substantial financial gain to any person.

    (vi) Serious financial loss to any person. (Loss is serious if it is serious for the person who suffers it. See for example *R* v *McIvor* [1987] Crim LR 409.)

2.2.3 EFFECTING THE ARREST

A person is arrested by:

(a) being informed by a police officer that he or she is under arrest; or

(b) being physically seized by a police officer, in which case he or she must be informed that he or she is under arrest as soon as is practicable after the arrest (PACE 1984, s. 28(1), and see *R* v *Brosch* [1988] Crim LR 743).

The arrested person must be told the reason for the arrest, even if it is obvious (s. 28(3) and (4)). If the reason given renders the arrest unlawful, it is irrelevant that there was a valid reason for the arrest if this was not communicated to the arrested person at the time (*Christie* v *Leachinsky* [1947] AC 573; *Abassy* v *Commissioner of Police of the Metropolis* [1990] 1 WLR 385).

If an officer arrests a person because he or she has reasonable cause to suspect that the person has committed an arrestable offence, but knows that there is no possibility of a charge being made, the arrest is unlawful, because the officer has acted on an irrelevant consideration or for an improper purpose (*Plange* v *Chief Constable of South Humberside Police, The Times*, 23 March 1992).

The arrested person must be taken immediately to a police station, unless it is reasonable to carry out other investigations first (s. 30(1) and (10), and *Dallison* v *Caffery* [1965] 1 QB 348).

In each police area, certain police stations are designated as being suitable for the detention of arrested persons (PACE 1984, s. 35(1)). If it is anticipated that the detention will exceed six hours, the arrested person must be detained in a designated police station (s. 30(2) and (3)).

2.2.4 AT THE POLICE STATION

The following (rather complicated) timetable of the detention of the arrested person (hereafter called 'suspect') is contained in PACE 1984, ss. 34–46.

Stage 1: At the police station, the suspect is taken to the custody officer. Each designated police station has one or more officers, of at least the rank of sergeant, appointed as custody officers. The custody officer is not involved in the investigation. As regards the suspect, the custody officer has several duties:

(a) To inform the suspect of his or her rights to consult a solicitor, to have someone informed, and to examine the Codes of Practice (see **2.2.8.1** to **2.2.8.3**).

(b) To maintain a custody record, being a complete record of the suspect's detention, including matters such as times of meals, interviews, the caution, if given, and the charge.

(c) To oversee the whole of the suspect's detention. As he or she is unconnected with the investigation the custody officer is able to take a more detached view when assessing whether the suspect should be released or detained, or whether there is sufficient evidence to charge the suspect.

(d) To order the release of the suspect, or his or her charge, unless continued detention without charge is necessary:

   (i) to secure or preserve evidence relating to the offence; or

   (ii) to obtain such evidence by questioning him or her.

Stage 2: If the custody officer authorises detention, periodic reviews of the detention must be made by a review officer. If the suspect has not yet been charged, the review officer must be:

(a) an officer of at least the rank of inspector; and

(b) not directly involved in the investigation.

The first review must be held within six hours of the original decision to detain.

Stage 3: A second review of the detention must be held within nine hours of the first review. Reviews must thereafter be held at not more than nine-hourly intervals.

Stage 4: After a maximum of 24 hours after arrival at the police station, the suspect must be released or charged, unless the following conditions are satisfied:

(a) the continued detention is authorised by an officer of at least the rank of superintendent; and

(b) the suspect is under arrest in connection with a serious arrestable offence; and

(c) the authorising officer has reasonable grounds for believing that the suspect's continued detention is necessary to:

   (i) secure or preserve evidence relating to the offence, or

   (ii) obtain such evidence by questioning the suspect; and

(d) the authorising officer has reasonable grounds for believing that the investigation is being conducted diligently and expeditiously.

Stage 5: After a maximum of 36 hours, the suspect must be released or charged unless a warrant of further detention is issued by a magistrates' court. A court may authorise detention for a further 36 hours if:

(a) the court comprises at least two magistrates; and

(b) the application for the warrant is made on oath and supported by written information which is also supplied to the suspect; and

(c) the suspect is present in court; and

(d) the suspect is detained in connection with a *serious* arrestable offence; and

(e) the court is satisfied of the matters in paras. (c) and (d) of Stage 4 above.

Stage 6: After a maximum of 72 hours the court may authorise further detention if all the conditions of Stage 5 above are satisfied. This further detention is for a maximum of 36 hours, and, in any event, the court may not authorise detention for a period of more than 96 hours.

Stage 7: No detention without charge is permitted after 96 hours. Thereafter, the suspect must be charged and/or released.

Note: These time-limits do not apply to those who are detained under the Prevention of Terrorism (Temporary Provisions) Act 1989 (note that the 1989 Act will be repealed when the Terrorism Act 2000 comes into force).

2.2.5 THE CAUTION

Under para. 10 of the Code, a person who has fallen under suspicion must be cautioned before any questions about the offence are put for the purpose of obtaining evidence which may be given to a court at trial. If the answers to questions already put to him or her have given ground for that suspicion, then he or she should be cautioned at that stage.

Because a caution is required only where there are '*grounds to suspect*' the person of an offence, it need not be given where the questions are merely general, preliminary questions, to establish, for example, identity or ownership, or in the furtherance of a proper and effective search, or to obtain verification of any written record of comments made outside the context of an interview.

In addition, para. 10 provides that the caution must be given on arrest unless the suspect has already been cautioned immediately prior to arrest, or it is impracticable to administer the caution by reason of behaviour at the time.

The caution should be re-administered after a break in questioning, but see *R* v *Oni* [1992] Crim LR 183, CA, where it was held to be unnecessary after a break of only two minutes. However, the caution should always be re-administered if there is any doubt as to whether or not it is necessary.

Prior to the CJPOA 1994, the suspect had what was referred to as a 'right to silence'. This meant essentially that no adverse inferences could be drawn from his failure to answer questions during an interview (or to testify in court). The CJPOA 1994, s. 34 now provides that the court may 'draw such inferences from the failure as appear proper' (s. 34(2)), if evidence is given that the defendant:

> *(a) at any time before he was charged with the offence, on being questioned under caution by a constable trying to discover whether or by whom the offence had been committed, failed to mention any fact relied on in his defence in those proceedings; or*
> *(b) on being charged with the offence or officially informed that he might be prosecuted for it, failed to mention any such fact, being a fact which in the*

circumstances existing at the time the accused could reasonably have been expected to mention when so questioned, charged or informed, as the case may be.

The caution is in the following terms:

You do not have to say anything. But it may harm your defence if you do not mention, when questioned, something which you later rely on in court. Anything you do say may be given in evidence.

Provided that the sense of the caution is preserved, minor deviations from the stated form do not constitute a breach of the Code.

You are referred to the text of the CJPOA 1994 and the revised Codes of Practice made thereunder, for the full effect of these provisions.

Note: This is nothing to do with the use of a caution as an alternative to taking criminal proceedings against a suspect. See, e.g. **7.3**.

2.2.6 INTERVIEWS

An interview is defined by Code C, para. 11.1A as:

the questioning of a person regarding his involvement or suspected involvement in a criminal offence or offences which . . . is required to be carried out under caution.

See **2.2.5** above for the circumstances in which a caution must be administered.

Once a person has been arrested, he or she must not be interviewed until he or she is at the police station, unless any delay would be likely to lead to interference with evidence, harm to persons, alerting suspects or hindering the recovery of property (para. 11.1).

Problems occasionally arise where a brief conversation or 'exchange' takes place between police officers and a suspect outside a police station, for example, after a speeding or stolen car has been stopped. If the exchange goes beyond a mere request for information and the suspect is, in effect, questioned about his or her involvement in an offence, then the exchange has become an interview. It is the nature of the questioning rather than the length which is relevant (*R* v *Ward* (1994) 98 Cr App R 337). If the questioning has become an interview, then the defendant is immediately protected by the provisions of the Code, including the requirement to caution, and any breaches will be taken into account by the court at any subsequent trial in determining the reliability of any confession that may have been made. See, for example, *R* v *Cox* (1993) 96 Cr App R 464. For a full discussion of the law relating to confessions, see the ***Evidence Manual***.

Any interview at a police station should take place in an adequately lit, heated and ventilated interview room. At the beginning of the interview the interviewing officer must identify himself or herself and any other officer present. The suspect must not be required to stand during the interview, and should be given breaks at recognised meal times. In addition, there should be short breaks for refreshment every two hours. The Code specifically provides that in any period of 24 hours, the suspect should be provided with one main and two light meals. In addition, he or she should be allowed a continuous period of eight hours' sleep without interruption, normally at night.

All interviews with persons cautioned in respect of an indictable offence or where questions are put to, or a statement of another person is shown to, a person who has been charged should be tape-recorded. Tapes need not be made if it is not reasonably practicable to do so for reasons such as the failure of the equipment, and the custody officer considers that the interview should not be delayed. For detailed provisions on tape recording and tape security, see Code E.

2.2.7 PERSONS AT RISK

Special rules apply when the police are dealing with persons at risk, that is juveniles, the mentally ill, and the mentally handicapped. The reason, according to para. 13B of the notes for guidance, is that, though capable of giving reliable evidence, they may unknowingly or without wishing to do so be prone to providing information which is unreliable, misleading or self-incriminating. Further, the investigating officers should seek corroboration of any facts admitted wherever possible.

Persons at risk should normally be interviewed in the presence of an appropriate adult. An appropriate adult is, for example, the parent or guardian of a juvenile, or the guardian of the person who is mentally ill or mentally handicapped. The appropriate adult is not expected to act simply as an observer. He or she is there first to advise the person being questioned and observe whether or not the interview is being conducted fairly, and secondly, to facilitate communication with the person at risk.

The appropriate adult must be informed of these duties.

The adult must be 'appropriate', that is, capable of understanding what is happening and not someone who is estranged from the suspect (see *R* v *Morse* [1991] Crim LR 195 and *DPP* v *Blake* (1989) 89 Cr App R 179, respectively).

In an emergency, however, a person at risk may be questioned in the absence of an appropriate adult, if Annex C to the Code applies; and it will apply if:

(a) the interview is authorised by an officer of at least the rank of superintendent; and

(b) the officer considers that delay will involve an immediate risk of harm to persons or serious loss of or damage to property.

2.2.8 THE RIGHTS OF THE SUSPECT

The suspect has three important rights in the police station.

2.2.8.1 The right to consult a solicitor

PACE 1984, s. 58(1) provides that a person who has been arrested and is being held in custody is entitled, upon request, to consult privately with a solicitor at any time. He or she must be informed of this right by the custody officer on arrival at the police station, and must sign the custody record indicating whether or not a request was made. The request must be complied with as soon as is practicable.

Note that s. 58 gives the suspect the right to consult a solicitor but not specifically the right to have the solicitor present during the interview. However, para. 6.8 of Code D provides that if the solicitor is available at the time the interview begins or is in progress, the suspect 'must be allowed to have his solicitor present while he is interviewed'.

The right may not be denied, but may be delayed for up to 36 hours after the suspect's arrival at the police station. It may be delayed if:

(a) the suspect is detained in connection with a serious arrestable offence; and

(b) the delay is authorised by an officer of at least the rank of superintendent; and

(c) the authorising officer has reasonable grounds for believing that immediate consultation will lead to:

   (i) interference with or harm to evidence connected with a serious arrestable offence or interference with or physical injury to other persons; or

(ii) the alerting of other persons suspected of having committed the offence but not yet arrested for it; or

(iii) the hindrance of the recovery of any property obtained as a result of such an offence.

The suspect must be told why access to a solicitor has been delayed, and that reason must be entered on the custody record.

Wrongful denial of access to a solicitor may lead to any confession made without having taken legal advice being excluded at any subsequent trial. See, for example, *R* v *Samuel* [1988] 1 WLR 920; *R* v *Alladice* (1988) 87 Cr App R 380. For a full discussion of the cases where a confession has been obtained in such circumstances, students should refer to the ***Evidence Manual***.

2.2.8.2 The right to have someone informed

Under PACE 1984, s. 56(1), the suspect has the right to have a friend or relative, or some other person who is known to him or her or who is likely to take an interest in his or her welfare, told of the arrest. He or she has no right to make personal contact, it being the duty of the police to pass on the information. The request must be complied with as soon as is practicable.

The right to have someone informed may be delayed in the same circumstances as the right to consult a solicitor may be delayed.

2.2.8.3 The right to consult the Codes

The suspect has the right to consult all the Codes of Practice. This does not entitle him or her to delay unreasonably any investigation or administrative action while this is done (para. 3.1, Code C).

2.2.9 THE CHARGE

Under para. 17 of the Code, when the investigating officer considers that there is sufficient evidence upon which to prosecute the suspect, he or she must take him or her before the custody officer who will decide whether he or she should be charged. If charged, he or she should first be cautioned, and any answers made will be recorded.

Once the suspect has been charged, he or she may not be asked any further questions except where it is necessary:

(a) to prevent or minimise harm or loss to some other person or to the public; or

(b) to clear up an ambiguity in a previous answer or statement; or

(c) in the interests of justice that the suspect should have the opportunity of commenting on information that has come to light since he or she was charged.

Before any further questions are put, the suspect should first be cautioned.

2.2.9.1 The decision to release

After the charge the custody officer must order the suspect's release from custody under PACE 1984, s. 38(1) unless one of the situations contained in s. 38(1)(a), as amended by s. 28 of the CJPOA 1994, applies:

(a) The suspect's name or address cannot be ascertained.

(b) The custody officer has reasonable grounds for doubting whether the name and address supplied are genuine.

(c) The custody officer has reasonable grounds for believing that:

(i) the suspect will not surrender to bail; or

(ii) (imprisonable offences) the detention is necessary to prevent him from committing an offence; or

(iii) (non-imprisonable offences) the detention is necessary to prevent him from causing physical injury to any other person or loss or damage to property; or

(iv) the detention is necessary to prevent him from interfering with the administration of justice or with the investigation of any offence or offences; or

(v) the detention is necessary for his own protection.

If the suspect is to be released after charge, he is likely to be bailed to attend at the appropriate magistrates' court to answer to the charge on a specified day. Prior to the passing of the CJPOA 1994, the extent to which the police could impose conditions on bail was not entirely clear. Section 27 of that Act, however, provides that s. 3 of the BA 1976 (power of the court to impose conditions on bail) shall apply with certain modifications (see below) to bail granted by the police.

The bail decision is taken by the custody officer, who may not impose conditions on the grant of bail unless it appears, under s. 3A(5) of the BA 1976 (inserted by s. 27 of the CJPOA 1994) that it is necessary to do so for the purposes of preventing the bailed person from:

(a) failing to surrender to custody; or

(b) committing an offence while on bail; or

(c) interfering with witnesses or otherwise obstructing the course of justice, whether in relation to himself or any other person.

The main differences between conditions imposed by police and those imposed by the court are as follows:

(a) The court, but not the police, has the power to order that reports be compiled on the bailed person (BA 1976, s. 3A(3), as inserted by the CJPOA 1994, s. 27(3)).

(b) The court, but not the police, may require the bailed person to reside in a bail hostel (BA 1976, s. 3A(2), as inserted by the CJPOA 1994, s. 27(3)).

(c) Where the custody officer has granted bail, either he himself or another officer serving at the same police station may vary the conditions of bail, at the request of the bailed person (BA 1976, s. 3A(4), inserted by the CJPOA 1994, s. 27(3)). Further, the bailed person may apply to a magistrates' court to have conditions of bail varied, but should bear in mind that the court has the power to impose more onerous conditions (MCA 1980, s. 43B, inserted by the CJPOA 1994, sch. 3, para. 3).

(Note that a person who is subject to investigation but has not yet been charged, may be bailed, with or without conditions, to attend at the police station on a specified date (CJPOA 1994, s. 37(2)).)

If the suspect is detained after charge, he or she must be brought before a magistrates' court as soon as is practicable, and in any event not later than the first sitting after he or she has been charged with an offence. If no suitable court is sitting, the clerk of the court must be informed, and a special sitting will be arranged. See generally PACE 1984, s. 46.

If release is authorised, the suspect is bailed to appear before the magistrates' court on a specified day to answer the charge (see PACE 1984, s. 47).

A useful article is 'Detention in a police station and false imprisonment' by J. Mackenzie, 142 NLJ 534.

2.3 Issue of Process

The laying of an information, and the subsequent issue of a summons (known as the issue of process) is appropriate where the offence involved is not particularly serious, though in theory there is nothing to prevent all prosecutions beginning in this way. In practice, however, serious offences almost always begin with the arrest and charge of the suspect as detailed in **2.2** above.

The procedure is governed by the MCA 1980 and the Magistrates' Courts Rules 1981 (MCR 1981).

2.3.1 THE INFORMATION

The information is the formal accusation that a certain individual (the 'accused') has committed an offence, and is roughly equivalent to an indictment in the Crown Court (see **Chapter 9**).

An information will contain the following matters:

(a) The name and address of the accused.

(b) The statement of the offence. This need not be in technical language, as long as all the elements of the offence are included, and the statement gives clear information as to the nature of the charge. If the offence is created by statute, the relevant Act and section should be quoted. Each information must charge only one offence — see **Chapter 9** for the rule against duplicity.

(c) The place of the offence.

(d) The date of the offence. Magistrates may only proceed to trial of a purely summary offence if the information was laid within six months of the offence, unless the statute creating the offence provides otherwise (see MCA 1980, s. 127).

Where information is laid through a computer link between police station and magistrates' court, the information is treated as having been laid when it is fed into the computer, regardless of when the information is printed out by the court (*R* v *Pontypridd Juvenile Court, ex parte B* [1988] Crim LR 842).

Further problems as to whether the information was laid in the time arose in *Lawrence* v *MAFF* [1992] Crim LR 874, DC, and *R* v *Thames Metropolitan Stipendiary Magistrate, ex parte Hackney London Borough Council* (1993) 158 JP 305, DC.

In *R* v *Betrus*, 10 July 1998, unreported, the defendant was informed, within the six month time limit, that he faced prosecution in relation to a road traffic accident. He applied for a stay of the summons on the ground that it amounted to an abuse of process in that the police had previously written to him saying that they had decided 'after careful consideration' that no action would be taken, and that the issue of the summons therefore amounted to a 'U-turn'. The summons was stayed.

An occasional problem arises where, the information having been laid within six months, the summons is not served promptly, due to either inefficiency or a deliberate abuse of process (for example, see *R* v *Oxford City Justices, ex parte*

Smith (1982) 75 Cr App R 200). In this situation, the magistrates have a discretion to dismiss the information and acquit the accused without hearing any evidence. In appropriate circumstances, the court may infer prejudice from the mere passage of time (*R* v *Bow Street Stipendiary Magistrate, ex parte DPP* (1989) 91 Cr App R 283). For a recent example, see *R* v *Crawley Justices, ex parte DPP* [1991] COD 365.

It is worth stressing that this is the only situation where the magistrates have such a discretion. Other than this, they may not dismiss an information without trial, for such reasons as the triviality of the charges, the seeming unfairness of the prosecution etc. This principle has been confirmed in *R* v *Dorchester Justices, ex parte DPP* [1990] RTR 369 and *R* v *Watford Justices, ex parte DPP* [1990] RTR 374.

(e) The signature of the prosecutor. This may be the signature either of the individual officer, or the rubber-stamped signature of a senior officer. Practices vary around the country and nothing turns on it. Note that the information must be laid in the name of an individual, and not by an unincorporated body such as 'Thames Valley Police' (see *Rubin* v *DPP* [1990] 2 QB 80). However, a technical defect of this nature is unlikely to be fatal to the proceedings.

As to where the information was signed by a person who had no authority to initiate proceedings, see *R* v *Norwich Justices, ex parte Texas Homecare* [1991] Crim LR 555.

2.3.2 LAYING THE INFORMATION

The vast majority of informations are laid in writing. Large bundles of informations and corresponding summonses are forwarded by the police to the local magistrates' court. The information is treated as having been laid as soon as it is received by the clerk's office of the magistrates' court (see *R* v *Manchester Stipendiary Magistrate, ex parte Hill* [1983] 1 AC 328).

Exceptionally, the information is laid orally. A typical example would be where there has been a dispute between neighbours in which the police do not wish to proceed. If one party goes before the magistrates and relates what happened, he or she has laid an information orally. It will be reduced into writing by the clerk of the court. As to where information is laid via a 'computer link', see *R* v *Pontypridd Juvenile Court, ex parte B* [1988] Crim LR 842. As to where it was laid by letter, see *R* v *Kennett Justices, ex parte Humphrey and Wyatt* [1993] Crim LR 787, DC.

2.3.3 ISSUING THE SUMMONS

The summons is a document issuing from the court, telling the accused that an allegation has been made against him or her and instructing him or her to attend court on a particular date to meet that allegation. The documents must contain:

(a) The name and address of the accused.

(b) The address of the court which he or she is to attend.

(c) The date and the time of the hearing.

(d) The contents of the information laid against him or her.

(e) The name and address of the informant.

The magistrate or the clerk will issue the summons on the basis of the information that has been laid. When deciding whether or not to issue a summons, the magistrate or clerk is exercising a judicial discretion. In theory, therefore, the magistrate has a discretion not to issue the summons if it appears that the prosecution is frivolous or vexatious, or where the charge is not supported by the evidence. In practice, however, the volume of business is so great that the magistrate rarely examines the information (unless it has been laid orally by a member of the public) and the issue of the summons is usually automatic.

Once the summons has been signed, everything is returned to the informant, the court retaining copies. The police will serve the summons, usually by posting it to the accused's last known or usual address.

2.3.4 JURISDICTION TO ISSUE PROCESS

The court has the power to issue process in the manner outlined above, subject to certain territorial limitations contained in MCA 1980, s. 1. These are:

(a) Where the offence is purely summary, the court may issue process if:

  (i) the offence occurred within the county; or

  (ii) the accused is already being tried for an offence by that court (whether indictable or summary). It is irrelevant in this case that the present offence did not occur within the county.

(b) Where the offence is indictable, the court may issue process if the offence was committed within the county, or the accused is believed to be or lives in the county.

(c) In either case, the court may issue process if it is necessary or expedient in the better administration of justice that the accused should be tried jointly with another person who is being proceeded against in that county.

2.3.5 TRYING TWO OR MORE INFORMATIONS

If the accused stands before the court charged with more than one offence, or if several accused stand before the court together, the question arises whether all outstanding matters can be dealt with at once.

(a) Where several accused are jointly charged with an offence, they will almost always be automatically tried together, despite any objection they may make.

(b) Where one accused stands charged with several matters, or several accused stand charged of related offences, then they may be tried together as long as no objection is made. If objection is made, the magistrates will order separate trials unless they are of the opinion that the offences are so connected that the interests of justice would be best served by a single trial. See *Chief Constable of Norfolk* v *Clayton* [1983] 2 AC 473.

If the magistrates decide against a single trial, it would seem those magistrates are debarred from hearing the case at all, as they are supposed to be unaware of any charges outstanding against an accused (see *R* v *Liverpool City Justices, ex parte Topping* [1983] 1 WLR 119). In these circumstances, each case may have to be heard by a different bench. In *R* v *Gough* [1993] AC 646, the House of Lords held that the test in all cases of apparent bias is: Was there a real danger of bias?

2.3.6 AMENDMENT

The court has wide powers to amend the information (or indeed the summons or warrant) as originally laid. Further MCA 1980, s. 123, provides that defects in the information, or any variations between the information and the evidence subsequently adduced, are not grounds upon which objection may be taken.

It has been held that if the defect or variation was trivial, and the accused was not in fact misled, any subsequent conviction will be upheld. See, for example, *R* v *Sandwell*

Justices, ex parte West Midlands Passenger Transport Board [1979] Crim LR 56. On the other hand, if the defect or variation is substantial, the prosecution should seek to amend the information. The magistrates will then consider whether the accused has been misled by the defect, and if so, offer an adjournment so that he or she can prepare for and meet the case now put forward by the prosecution. Failure either to amend, or adjourn, in these circumstances is likely to lead to any subsequent conviction being quashed. See, for example, *Wright* v *Nicholson* [1970] 1 WLR 142.

An information may be amended, even to allege a different offence, including a purely summary offence, more that six months after it was laid, provided that the offence arose from the same incident as the offence originally charged, and the amendment was in the interests of justice. See *R* v *Scunthorpe Justices, ex parte M, The Times*, 10 March 1998, where the information alleging robbery was amended to common assault, a purely summary offence. A similar point was made in *R* v *Newcastle Upon Tyne Magistrates' Court, ex parte Poundstretchers Ltd*, 3 March 1998, unreported.

Late amendments cannot cure an information which discloses no offence known to law (*Garman* v *Plaice* [1969] 1 WLR 19).

2.3.7 DUPLICITY

An information is said to be duplicitous when two offences are charged within it. In such a situation, the prosecution may elect which charge to proceed with (Magistrates' Courts (Miscellaneous Amendments) Rules 1993 (SI 1993 No. 118)).

Students are referred to **Chapter 9** for a full discussion of duplicity.

2.4 Issue of a Warrant

Instead of issuing a summons, a magistrate may issue a warrant for the arrest of the person named therein. A warrant should contain the following information:

(a) The name of the court.

(b) The name and address of the accused.

(c) The offence alleged.

(d) The signature of the magistrate (the signature of the clerk is insufficient).

(e) If the warrant is to be backed for bail, any conditions of bail imposed by the magistrate (see **3.13**).

2.4.1 CONDITIONS FOR THE ISSUE OF A WARRANT

Before the warrant can be issued the following conditions must be met:

(a) The information must be in writing and supported by sworn evidence. In practice, the police officer applying for the warrant will simply swear that all the allegations contained in the information are true, without having to detail what the allegations are.

(b) The offence must be imprisonable (or the accused is a juvenile or resides at an unknown address).

(c) The proceedings must take place before a magistrate, not a clerk.

2.4.2 WARRANTS 'BACKED FOR BAIL'

In most cases a warrant will not be necessary. Less serious offences can be commenced by the issue of a summons, and more serious offences are arrestable in any event.

However, the warrant is important where the accused fails to appear in answer to the summons, or fails to surrender to bail. A warrant issued in these circumstances is often referred to as a 'bench warrant'.

If the magistrates think that the accused's absence is due to an error, they may order that the warrant be 'backed for bail', that is, the conditions of bail upon which the accused may be released once arrested are endorsed on the back of the warrant. After arrest, the accused must be released once the conditions are complied with (see also **Chapter 3**).

2.5 Jurisdiction to Try Offences

The jurisdiction of the magistrates' courts to try offences is similar to their jurisdiction to issue process, described at **2.3.4** above. More specifically:

(a) Where the offence is triable either way: magistrates have the power to try offences which are triable either way wherever they were committed, as long as the accused has consented to summary trial as described at **4.2** (MCA 1980, s. 2(3) and (4)).

(b) Where the offence is triable summarily only: magistrates have the power to try summary offences where:

 (i) The offence was committed within the county for which they act (MCA 1980, s. 2(1)).

 (ii) The offence was committed outside the county, but the court is already trying the accused for another offence (MCA 1980, s. 2(6)). See *Morgan* v *Croydon LBC, The Independent*, 30 June 1997 for an example.

 (iii) The offence was committed outside the county, but it is necessary or expedient in the better administration of justice that the accused should be jointly tried with another person who is being proceeded against in that county (MCA 1980, s. 1(2)(b) and s. 2(2)).

Under MCA 1980, s. 3 an offence committed within 500 yards of the county border may be dealt with by the courts in either county. This is to avoid disputes as to exactly where the offence was committed, and which court, therefore, has jurisdiction.

2.6 Legal Aid

Legal aid may be divided into two categories.

2.6.1 LEGAL ADVICE AND ASSISTANCE

This covers the initial need for legal advice at the very beginning of the criminal justice process, i.e. matters preliminary to the hearing. There are two ways in which such advice can be given:

(a) *The Green Form Scheme:* This is a quick and efficient method of obtaining legal advice and is designed to cover the initial interview between a solicitor and client. A solicitor operating the scheme will be paid out of the Legal Aid Fund in the form of a fixed fee for the interview. The Green Form will be filled in at the interview and signed by the client. Advice under the Green Form Scheme is automatically available for defendants on income support, family credit or disability working allowance. If the defendant's income or capital is above designated levels, it is not available.

(b) *The Duty Solicitor Scheme*: There is no means test for this free advice and assistance. Solicitors taking part in the duty solicitor scheme attend a magistrates' court on a regular basis and are on call day and night to attend at a police station or elsewhere where a suspect is being questioned about an offence. They are also expected to give telephone advice to a suspect who requests it. The duty solicitor who is on the rota for attending at a magistrates' court can give free advice and represent a defendant on his or her first appearance. The scheme is designed to cover matters such as bail applications and simple pleas in mitigation. Should the case be more complicated, it should be adjourned so that the defendant can apply for legal aid and give full instructions to a representative of his or her choice.

2.6.2 LEGAL AID

This is governed by the Legal Aid Act 1988 and by various regulations. The Legal Aid in Criminal and Care Proceedings (General) Regulations (SI 1989 No. 344) as amended, set out the details of obtaining legal aid and the Legal Aid in Criminal and Care Proceedings (Costs) Regulations (SI 1989 No. 343) as amended, deal with remuneration.

Criminal legal aid is available for proceedings before a magistrates' court, the Crown Court, the Court of Appeal and the House of Lords.

In the first instance legal aid can only be granted by the court before which the proceedings are to be heard. In addition, magistrates' courts have power to grant legal aid for proceedings before the Crown Court where the defendant has been committed for trial or for sentence, or is appealing against a decision of the magistrates' court.

2.6.2.1 When legal aid must be granted

Under the Legal Aid Act 1988, s. 21(3) legal aid *must* be granted (subject to the defendant's means):

(a) Where the defendant is committed for trial on a charge of murder.

(b) Where the prosecution is seeking to appeal to the House of Lords.

(c) To enable a bail application to be made where the defendant is:

 (i) unrepresented and wishes to be represented; and

 (ii) appears before a magistrates' court in pursuance of a remand in custody when he was not represented; and

 (iii) may be again remanded or committed in custody.

(d) Where the defendant is remanded in custody (by a magistrates' court or by the Crown Court) for the preparation of reports prior to sentencing.

Further, there are certain situations where a court may not pass sentence on a person who is not legally represented unless application for legal aid has been turned down on the ground of means, or the defendant has failed or refused to apply for legal aid. If neither of these two situations apply, then the defendant must be granted legal aid before any of the following sentences or orders may be passed:

(a) A sentence of imprisonment on a person who has not received such a sentence before (PCC(S)A 2000, s. 83).

(b) A sentence of detention in a young offender institution or a detention and training order (PCC(S)A 2000, s. 83).

(c) A sentence of custody for life, under PCC(S)A 2000, s. 94 (PCC(S)A 2000, s. 83).

(d) A sentence of detention under PCC(S)A 2000, s. 91 (PCC(S)A 2000, s. 83).

2.6.2.2 When legal aid may be granted

In all other situations, legal aid may be granted if it is in the interests of justice and the defendant's resources are such that he or she requires assistance in meeting the costs which he or she may incur. Factors that the court should take into account are set out in the Legal Aid Act 1988, s. 22(2), and include the following:

(a) the offence is such that if proved the accused is likely to lose his or her liberty, livelihood or suffer serious damage to his or her reputation; or

(b) the case may involve consideration of a substantial question of law; or

(c) the accused may be unable to understand the proceedings or state his or her own case because of inadequate knowledge of English, mental illness or mental or physical disability; or

(d) the defence involves the tracing and interviewing of witnesses or expert cross-examination of prosecution witnesses; or

(e) it is in the interests of someone other than the accused that the accused be represented.

By s. 21(7) any doubts as to eligibility must be resolved in favour of the defendant.

The list set out in s. 22(2) is not exhaustive. There may be other factors according to the circumstances of a particular case which have to be taken into consideration in deciding whether or not the justice of the case requires that legal aid should be granted: *R* v *Liverpool City Magistrates, ex parte McGhee* [1993] Crim LR 609.

None of these provisions refer to appeals to the Divisional Court either by way of case stated or on an application for judicial review. Such matters are treated as civil matters (albeit arising out of criminal cases) and are governed by Part IV of the Legal Aid Act 1988. The applicant must establish 'reasonable grounds' for taking the action. In general, a convicted defendant who wishes to take a case to the Divisional Court is less likely to recieve legal aid than in other parts of the criminal justice system.

2.6.3 MAKING THE APPLICATION

An application for legal aid will usually have been made by the instructing solicitor, but where this has not been done counsel may:

(a) make a simple oral request to the magistrates. This should be accompanied by a statement of means (i.e. details of the defendant's financial resources and commitments — on Form 5). If no such statement has yet been made, legal aid may be granted, subject to means; or

(b) help the defendant to complete Form 5 (statement of means) and Form 1 (application).

These forms are available from the court clerk or usher and the completed forms must be handed in to the bench or court clerk. Form 1 is reproduced at the end of this Chapter.

Legal aid may be granted or refused by the justice(s) or the clerk.

If the applicant is in receipt of social security benefits (e.g. job-seeker's allowance), the applicant must produce evidence of receipt of the benefit. This evidence will take the form of the address of the relevant benefit office and the applicant's reference number (shown on the letter noting the award of the benefit or the payment book).

2.6.4 CHALLENGING REFUSAL OF LEGAL AID BY A MAGISTRATES' COURT

A justices' clerk may only refuse an application, other than on the grounds of means, where the refusal is reviewable by a criminal legal aid committee (see (d) below). In other circumstances, the decision must be referred to a magistrate or a bench of magistrates.

If legal aid is refused by the magistrate(s) otherwise than on the grounds of means the defendant may:

(a) Renew the application on every occasion on which the applicant appears before the court. In many cases, however, the number of appearances is small, and thus the opportunity for repeated applications is likewise small.

(b) If the case is to be committed to the Crown Court, make a fresh application on Form 5 and Form 1 to the Crown Court. Note that the Crown Court has no power to grant legal aid in respect of summary trial or committal proceedings.

(c) Apply for judicial review of the refusal. This applies only where the grant of legal aid is obligatory under s. 21(3) (see **2.6.2.1**), or where the magistrates have acted unreasonably in exercising their discretion to grant legal aid under s. 21(2). However, the general rule where an inferior tribunal refuses to exercise its discretionary power in favour of a party to the proceedings is that the Divisional Court will intervene only if the decision was arrived at by taking into account irrelevant considerations, or ignoring relevant ones, or was manifestly unreasonable.

(d) Apply to the Area Committee of the Legal Aid Board. The decision may be reviewed if the following criteria are satisfied:

   (i) the refusal was by a magistrates' court, magistrate or clerk; and

   (ii) the defendant has been charged with an indictable offence or an offence triable either way; and

   (iii) the application was refused on the grounds that it was not in the interests of justice (see **2.6.2.2**); and

   (iv) the application for review was lodged within 14 days of the refusal; and

   (v) the application was made not later than 21 days before the trial date, if that had been set.

2.6.5 CONTRIBUTION ORDER

The defendant (or an 'appropriate contributor', i.e. parent or guardian, where the defendant is under 16) may be required to pay a contribution towards the cost of representation. If the defendant receives income support, family credit or disability working allowance there can be no contribution order. For other defendants the granting of legal aid may be conditional upon the payment of such a contribution. If a contribution from income is ordered this sum must be paid on a weekly, fortnightly or monthly basis at the discretion of the court. If the contribution is from capital the defendant must pay it immediately unless the court orders payment within a time it considers reasonable. Where sums due under the contribution order have not been paid before the conclusion of the case, the court can:

(a) require payment within seven days; and

(b) if that is not complied with, invite representations as to the reasons for non-compliance.

If satisfied that the assisted person is able to pay the contribution but has failed to do so, the court can revoke the grant of legal aid. In addition, unpaid contributions can be recovered in the same way as fines where the non-payment results from a wilful refusal to comply with the contribution order.

If a legally-aided defendant is acquitted, any contributions he or she has paid towards to the cost of his or her defence will be repaid to him or her and any unpaid contributions will be remitted, unless the court decides the defendant brought the prosecution on himself or herself.

If a legally-aided defendant is convicted, on the other hand, the court may remit any payments which have not yet fallen due, but has no power to return any contributions already made or to remit any payments which have fallen due but which have not yet been paid.

2.6.6 PAYMENT OF COUNSEL

Counsel has to fill in a claim form showing the work done and the time expended in the case. This must be submitted within three months of the conclusion of the case.

2.6.6.1 Crown Court

In respect of Crown Court fees, the amount to be paid by the Legal Aid Board to solicitors and counsel is initially fixed by a determining officer at the Crown Court. This figure will be a standard figure set out in the Legal Aid in Criminal and Care Proceedings (Costs) Regulations (which are amended yearly) unless it appears to the determining officer that the standard fee would be inappropriate taking into account all the relevant circumstances of the case. If counsel is not satisfied with the fees awarded, an application for reassessment can be made to the Crown Court, with further appeals to the taxing master and the High Court.

2.6.6.2 Magistrates' court

The Legal Aid Board pays counsel for work done in the magistrates' court. Most cases will be paid on the basis of standard fees. If a solicitor intends to instruct unassigned counsel the solicitor will negotiate counsel's fees with counsel's clerk. The Legal Aid Board will pay the agreed figure to counsel and the balance of the standard fee to the solicitor. Non-standard fees will be paid when counsel is assigned by the legal aid order.

If counsel is assigned he or she will be paid at an enhanced rate. An appeal against the level of fees can be made by counsel to the Legal Aid Area Committee. An application for review must be made within 21 days of notification of assessment.

2.7 Costs

Under the Prosecution of Offences Act 1985, ss. 16–21, the court finally disposing of a case has the power to make various orders as to costs, of which the most important are set out below.

2.7.1 DEFENDANT'S COSTS ORDER

Under s. 16, a defendant who has been acquitted may have an order made in his or her favour for the payment of sums out of central funds (i.e. the Government) for expenses properly incurred by him or her in the proceedings. This may, but need not, be the full amount which the defendant claims.

The same applies where the prosecution decide not to proceed with an information, offer no evidence at the Crown Court, or ask that counts remain on the file marked not to be proceeded with without leave of the court; or where the defendant is discharged at committal or successfully appeals against conviction or sentence.

Where the defendant is legally aided and acquitted, a defendant's costs order will not be made in his or her favour, except insofar as the defendant has incurred costs which are not covered by the legal aid order. Such costs do not include any contribution he or she has made under the order.

The defendant's costs order cannot be rescinded under the MCA 1980, s. 142, as the power under that section only applies where the defendant has been found guilty (*Coles* v *DPP, The Independent*, 22 June 1998).

2.7.2 PROSECUTION COSTS

Where the offence is indictable, under s. 17, a private prosecutor (but not the CPS or other prosecuting authority) may be awarded, out of central funds, an amount which the court thinks reasonably sufficient to compensate him or her for expenses properly incurred. The prosecution does not have to be successful for such an order to be made. Again, this need not be the full amount.

2.7.3 COSTS AGAINST THE DEFENDANT

Under s. 18, if the defendant is convicted, he or she may be ordered to pay to the prosecution such a sum as is just and reasonable. Proper account should be taken of the defendant's means.

2.7.4 MAKING THE ORDER

The making of an order for costs is discretionary, but the court will normally make an order for costs in the defendant's favour, unless there are positive reasons for not doing so, as where, for example, the defendant's own conduct has brought suspicion on himself or herself and has mislead the prosecution into thinking the case against him or her was stronger than it was (*Practice Direction* [1999] 1 WLR 1832).

The order may be made where a person:

(a) is not tried on an indictment for which he or she has been indicted or committed for trial; or

(b) has been acquitted on any count on the indictment.

Few guidelines have been issued on the making of an order for costs against a convicted defendant. However, it has been said that, while the costs of a trial on indictment are greater than those of a summary trial, the defendant should not be 'punished' for electing trial on indictment by an excessive order for costs (*R* v *Bushell* (1980) 2 Cr App R (S) 77). Where an order for costs is likely, the prosecution should be in a position to provide an estimate of costs, which should not be an overestimate (*R* v *Maher* (1983) 76 Cr App R 309).

Further, in *R* v *Nottingham Justices, ex parte Fohmann* (1986) 84 Cr App R 316, it was said that justices should not make an order for costs against a convicted person in such a sum that, through lack of means, he or she would be unable to pay that sum within a reasonable period of about a year. However, it has been held, in relation to the payment of fines, that a period of two years would seldom be too long, and that three years may be acceptable in appropriate cases (*R* v *Olliver and Olliver* (1989) 11 Cr App R (S) 10). However, in *R* v *Stockport Justices, ex parte Conlon, The Times*, 3 January 1997, the court held that where fines were imposed on those of limited means, they should be lesser in amount so that they could be paid '*in a matter of weeks*'. See also **18.7.4** for a full discussion.

Further guidelines for the court in making an order for costs, derived from the authorities, was set out in *R* v *Northallerton Magistrates' Court, ex parte Dove, The Times*, 17 June 1999:

(a) The defendant's means and any other financial order should be ascertained so that the costs order does not exceed a reasonable sum that the defendant is able to pay.

(b) The sum should never be more than the costs actually incurred.

(c) It is clear from the fact that there is no right of appeal from the making of a costs order that the policy is to compensate the prosecutor and not to further penalise the defendant.

(d) A costs order should be proportionate to the level of the fine and where the total of fine and costs are excessive, the costs should be reduced accordingly. (On the facts, the defendant had been fined £1,000, where the maximum was £5,000, but ordered to pay over £4,600 in costs. It was held that the amount of costs was grossly disproportionate.)

(e) The onus is on the defendant to provide details of his or her means and in default, magistrates are entitled to deduce his or her financial circumstances from the available evidence.

(f) The defendant must be allowed the opportunity to produce information as to his or her means and should be given notice of any unusual application for costs that is to be made.

For a further example, see *Mooney* v *Cardiff Magistrates' Court*, *The Times*, 17 November 1999.

2.7.5 REDUCING DELAY IN THE CRIMINAL PROCESS

The Crime and Disorder Act 1998 (CDA 1998) contains a number of provisions designed to reduce delay in the criminal process. Two measures will be dealt with here.

2.7.5.1 Powers of magistrates' courts exercisable by a single justice

Section 49 of the CDA 1998 empowers a single justice of the peace for a particular area to exercise the powers of a magistrates' court, such as extending bail or imposing or varying conditions of bail, and dismissing an information where no evidence has been adduced by the prosecution. Further, under s. 49(2), rules of court are to be developed to enable a justices' clerk to make a number of administrative (as opposed to judicial) decisions. Students should consult s. 49 for a full list of these powers and the restrictions placed upon the decisions of a justices' clerk. The purpose of this section is to reduce the delays inherent in a system which requires the decision of three people, and to attempt to achieve continuity in the handling of a case, particularly prior to trial.

2.7.5.2 Early administrative hearings

The Early Administrative Hearing (EAH) is designed to take place very early in the proceedings with the purpose of dealing with the issue of legal aid. Indeed, in some areas, such a practice has developed on a non-statutory basis. It is now placed on a statutory footing by the CDA 1998, s. 50.

Under s. 50, the first appearance after charge (other than indictable only and related offences (see **6.5.1**)) shall be before a court consisting of a single justice. At this hearing, under s. 50(2):

(a) the accused shall be asked if he or she wishes to receive legal aid; and

(b) if he or she does, his or her eligibility for it shall be determined; and

(c) if it is determined that he or she is eligible for it, the necessary arrangements or grant to him or her shall be made.

In addition, the single justice may exercise any of the powers of the single justice contained in s. 49(1) as he or she thinks fit (s. 50(3)(a)). Section 50(3)(b) specifically provides that the single justice may remand the accused in custody or on bail.

The powers of the single justice under s. 50(1) may be exercised by a justices' clerk, except that the justices' clerk has no power to remand the accused in custody or remand the accused on bail on conditions other than any previously imposed.

Application for Legal Aid in Criminal Proceedings Magistrates' or Crown Court

Form 1
Regulations 11 and 18
(also known as
Crown Court Form 5131)

I apply for Legal Aid –

For the purpose of proceedings before the ______ Crown / Magistrates' / Youth Court*

1. Personal Details *(Please use BLOCK letters and BLACK ink)*

(a) Surname ______ *(e)* Date of birth ______

(b) Forenames ______

(c) Permanent address ______

(d) Present address *(if different from above)* ______

2. Case Details

(a) Describe briefly what it is you are accused of doing, *e.g.*, "stealing £50 from my employer", "kicking a door causing £50 damage". ______

(b) The following other person(s) is/are charged in this case. ______

(c) Give reasons why you and the other persons charged in this case, if any, should not be represented by the same solicitor. ______

3. Court Proceedings *(Complete section (a) or (b) whichever applies)*

(a) I am due to appear before

the ______ Magistrates' / Youth Court*

on ______ 19 ______ at ______ a.m./p.m.

or

(b) I appeared before

the ______ Magistrates' / Youth Court*

on ______ 19 ______ at ______ a.m./p.m.

and *(tick whichever applies)*

☐ my case has been transferred to the Crown Court for trial

☐ I was convicted and committed for sentence to the Crown Court

☐ I was convicted and/or sentenced and I wish to appeal against the conviction and / or sentence*

*Cross out whichever does not apply.

1

4. Outstanding Matters

(a) If there are any other outstanding criminal charges or cases against you, give details including the court where you are due to appear (only those cases that are not yet concluded)

5. Your Financial Position *(Tick the box which applies)*

(a) ☐ I receive Income Support, Family Credit or Disability Working Allowance, and I authorise the court to make such enquiries of the Benefits Agency as it considers necessary. I consent to the disclosure of information to confirm that I am in receipt of benefit.

(You may also tick this box if your spouse or partner receives any of these benefits and you are living together)

Give:

(i) the address of the Social Security office dealing with the benefit

(ii) National Insurance number of person receiving benefit

(iii) Type of benefit

You should produce documentary evidence that you are receiving the benefit (*e.g.*, order book). If you cannot produce evidence you should give your reasons below

(b) ☐ I have already given a statement of my means to the ______ Court and there has been no change in my financial position. *(A new statement is required if there has been any change)*

(c) ☐ I attach a statement of my means in these proceedings *(details of your income and expenditure)*

(d) ☐ I am under 16 and I attach a statement of my parents' means. If you are unable to provide a statement of their means, give their name and address

6. Legal Representation

Note

(a) **If you do not have the name and address of a solicitor the court will select a solicitor for you.**

(b) **You must tell the solicitor that you have named him, unless he has helped you to complete this form.**

(c) **If you have been charged together with another person or persons, the court may assign a solicitor other than the solicitor of your choice.**

(a) The solicitor I wish to act for me is

(b) Give the firm's name and address (if known)

2

7. Reasons for wanting Legal Aid

- To avoid the possibility of your application being delayed or legal aid being refused because the court does not have enough information about the case, you must complete the rest of this form.
- When deciding whether to grant legal aid, the court will need to know the reasons why it is in the interests of justice for you to be represented.
- If you need help in completing this form, and especially if you have previous convictions, you should see a solicitor. He may be able to advise you free of charge or at a reduced fee.

Note: If you plead **NOT GUILTY** neither the information in this form nor that in your statement of means will be made available to the members of the court trying your case unless you are convicted or you consent. If you are acquitted, only the financial information you have given in your statement of means will be given to the court.

Tick any boxes which apply and give brief details or reasons in the space provided

	Details	Reasons for grant or refusal *(for court use only)*
(a) It is likely that I will lose my liberty *(You should consider seeing a solicitor before answering this question)* ☐		
(b) I am subject to a: suspended or partly suspended prison sentence ☐ conditional discharge ☐ probation order ☐ supervision order ☐ deferment of sentence ☐ community service order ☐ care order ☐ combination order ☐ *Give details as far as you are able, including the nature of the offence and when the order was made*		
(c) It is likely that I will lose my livelihood ☐		
(d) It is likely that I will suffer serious damage to my reputation ☐		
(e) A substantial question of law is involved *(You will need the help of a solicitor to answer this question)* ☐		

(Please give authorities to be quoted with law reports references)

3

		Details	Reasons for grant or refusal *(for court use only)*
(f) I shall be unable to understand the court proceedings or state my own case because: (i) My understanding of English is inadequate (ii) I suffer from a disability *(Give full details)*	☐ ☐		
(g) Witnesses have to be traced and/or interviewed on my behalf *(State circumstances)*	☐		
(h) The case involves expert cross examination of a prosecution witness *(Give brief details)*	☐		
(i) It is in someone else's interests that I am represented	☐		
(j) Any other reasons: *(give full particulars)*	☐		

8. Declaration

If you knowingly make a statement which is false, or knowingly withhold information, you may be prosecuted. If convicted, you may be sent to prison for up to three months, or be fined, or both *(section 39(1) Legal Aid Act 1988)*.

After your application has been considered by the court, you may be asked to give further information or to clarify information or to provide further proof of the information you have given.

If you stop receiving Income Support, Family Credit, Disability Working Allowance or if your financial position changes in any way after you have submitted this form, you must tell the court. This is a requirement of the Legal Aid regulations.

I understand that the court may order me to make a contribution to the costs of Legal Aid, or to pay the whole costs if it considers that I can afford to do so and, if I am under 16, may make a similar order with respect to my parents.

Signed | **Dated**

4

THREE

REMANDS AND BAIL

3.1 Introduction

The efficient working of the criminal justice system can be impeded in various ways. One of the most significant, certainly in terms of cost, is the number of times that a case has to appear in court. It can be seen in **Figure 3.2** that the percentage of defendants whose case is dealt with on their first appearance at court varies, thus:

- indictable offences — 20%
- summary non-motoring offences — 75%
- summary motoring offences — 54%.

Each time a case is not disposed of on its first appearance at court, it has to be adjourned. In a similar pattern, the average number of times that a case is listed to appear in the magistrates' court varies between these three categories of offence:

- indictable offences — 3.6 times listed in court
- summary non-motoring offences — 1.6 times listed
- summary motoring offences — 2.0 times listed.

Over the ten years up to 1995, there was a significant reduction in the number of indictable offences appearing in our criminal courts (for all indictable offences, including those triable in either the magistrates' court or Crown Court, the fall exceeded 10%). This reduction did not produce a corresponding increase in efficiency for the remaining cases. In fact, the opposite occurred, with the average time between first listing of a case in the magistrates' court and its completion there increasing from 41 days (1985) to 60 days (1995). The number of summary non-motoring offences has increased over the decade, by some 12%, and the average time taken to complete such cases has worsened by nearly 30%. According to a Report on the Joint Administration of Justice (published by the Lord Chancellor's Department, 1 December 1999), nearly 750,000 hearings have to be adjourned in magistrates' courts every year because of errors or omissions by one or more of the participants. Half of the adjournments arose because of failures within (or liaison between) the police, the CPS and the courts or other public bodies. A quarter of ineffective hearings resulted from the failure of the defendant to surrender to custody. The remaining 25% of adjournments arose from errors or omissions by defendants or defence lawyers.

Concern over delays in the system was the catalyst for a review, which reported in 1997 (*Review of Delay in the Criminal Justice System*, also known as the *Narey Report*). One of the main issues for the Narey Report was how to reduce the number of times each case appeared in court (whether as the result of an adjournment or remand). The incoming Labour government in May 1997 adopted many of the recommendations made in the Narey Report. Several proposals reached the statute book as part of the Crime and Disorder Act 1998. Although these changes affect various aspects of the working of the criminal justice system, it is appropriate to summarise them here since they share a common aim. The changes are as follows:

(a) 'Straightforward guilty pleas' should be disposed of within 24 hours. CPS staff are to work closely with the police (often in the local police station), and the local magistrates' court to ensure that the files in such cases are 'prepared, reviewed and disclosed to the defence in time for the case to be heard at the next available court hearing after charge'. Such cases should usually be prosecuted at court the day after charge. See CDA 1998, ss. 46 and 50. These provisions were initially introduced in pilot areas but came fully into force on 1 November 1999.

(b) A defendant in a 'straightforward guilty plea' case, who intends to plead guilty but requires legal advice, should normally obtain such advice from a duty solicitor at court in the morning (after being charged the day before). The defendant would then normally appear in court that afternoon. The government accepts, in principle, that an accused person may prefer to consult a solicitor of his or her choice and should be allowed to do so, where this does not cause delay in the proceedings. Where problems arise, 'choice must come second to speed'. See CDA 1998, ss. 49 and 50.

(c) The court before which a defendant appears, the day after being charged, may consist of a single justice of the peace. That JP has extensive powers and may, for example, order a pre-sentence report following a guilty plea, request a medical report, and give directions for the conduct of a trial where necessary. See CDA 1998, s. 50.

(d) One of the most common causes of delay is the failure of defendants, when released on bail, to obtain legal advice or representation (according to the Home Office). This results in 'ineffective first hearings and routine adjournments'. The courts therefore now have the power to make it a condition of bail that the defendant attends an interview with a legal representative. According to Home Office Circular 34/1998, this power is intended for use when a defendant is being 'particularly obstructive or indolent in this regard', so it will only be used where a defendant has expressed a wish to get such advice or representation. It is not intended to remove a defendant's right to represent himself or herself, if he or she so chooses. Breach of this condition may result in arrest without a warrant but it is not expected that a defendant's solicitor should inform the police if he or she fails to attend for an interview. The matter will probably come to the attention of the court at the next hearing. It might be dealt with by obliging the defendant to consult the duty solicitor there and then, if he or she still wishes to have advice and/or representation. See BA 1976, s. 3(6)(e), inserted by CDA 1998, s. 54(2).

(e) Crimes which must be dealt with by the Crown Court (e.g. homicide offences, robbery, rape) may be sent 'forthwith' in the course of their one and only appearance in a magistrates' court. Separate proceedings to commit such crimes for trial will be unnecessary and the magistrates' court will then be free to tackle other work. It has been said that such cases 'spend about half their life' in the magistrates' court (government consultation paper) so there may be significant time savings. See CDA 1998, s. 51. This procedure was introduced in pilot areas in 1999. The pilots officially ended in December 1999, although the procedures are still in use in the pilot courts. A decision on the nationwide implementation of this procedure is expected in April 2000.

(f) When a defendant is remanded in custody, the case may be delayed by his or her late (or even non-) appearance from prison. Where a pre-trial hearing is likely to be very short, and does not require the defendant to be present (e.g. a straightforward adjournment in the case), it may be conducted using a live television link between the court and the prison. See CDA 1998, s. 57, which is the subject of introduction in a number of pilot areas.

(g) If a defendant does not surrender to custody at court on the appointed day, then the hearing may be ineffectual and the case delayed. Insofar as one reason for this may be that the defendant has insufficient personal incentive to attend court, this is addressed by CDA 1998, s. 54(1) (in force from 30 September 1998). Hitherto, the power to demand a security from a defendant (or on his or her behalf) has been limited to cases where it appeared unlikely that the defendant would remain in the UK. Thus, it gave a defendant an incentive not to leave the jurisdiction. That limitation has been removed, so that security can be demanded with a view to securing attendance at court. As Home Office Circular 34/1998 puts it, 'there may be cases where the court takes the view that an up-front payment, in the form of a security, of a relatively small amount would be more effective in securing the defendant's attendance than the availability of a surety with the means to enter into a recognizance for a more substantial sum'.

(h) Statutory time limits can be set for specified stages of proceedings. Different time limits may apply to different types of cases. For example, one aim of the government is to reduce the time taken to process cases involving juveniles — now tight time limits may be set for such cases. Conversely, there may be longer deadlines in more complex cases, such as those involving serious fraud. These new statutory time limits were introduced in pilot areas in November 1999 and will probably be applied nationally in 2002. See Prosecution of Offences Act 1985, s. 22, as amended by CDA 1998, s. 43. Also, time limits in cases where the accused is held in custody have been 'toughened up'; for example, the criteria for granting extensions are now stricter.

The effect of some of these pilot schemes has been considered by the firm Ernst & Young. In a Report produced for the Home Office, published in August 1999, the firm reported the basically successful introduction of:

- Early First Hearings (see (a) above; CDA 1998, s. 46)
- Early Administrative Hearings (see (b) above; CDA 1998, s. 49)
- enhanced powers of case management for justices' clerks and single justices (see (c) above; CDA 1998, s. 50)
- the use of Designated Case Workers (i.e. non-lawyer staff) by the CPS to review files and present cases in court
- direct placing of CPS staff in police stations (necessary to speed up the throughput of case files and reviews in time for a court appearance the next day)
- making CPS staff available to provide legal advice to the police outside normal office hours (also thought to be necessary to assist in speeding up decisions, e.g. on whether to charge and which offence).

The Report (available on the Home Office website at http://www.homeoffice.gov.uk/cpd/pvu/delay1.htm) was largely positive in its recommendations. One exception was in the provision of out-of-hours advice by the CPS; this proved to be unnecessary. The police were able to anticipate the need for legal advice and seek it during normal hours.

Useful articles — Neil Corre, '3 Frequent Questions on the Bail Act' [1989] Crim LR 493; Brink and Stone, 'Defendants Who Do Not Ask for Bail' [1988] Crim LR 152 and Morgan, 'Remands in Custody: Problems and Prospects' [1989] Crim LR 481; editorial on Bail Decisions [1992] Crim LR 321; Brown and Hullin, 'Contested Bail Applications: the treatment of ethnic minority and white offenders' [1993] Crim LR 107.

3.2 What is a Remand?

Put in very simple terms, a remand is another name for an adjournment of a case — the postponement of its final resolution. However, the criminal justice system knows the remand as having a particular meaning. When a case is adjourned, the court may have the power or duty to remand the accused, rather than simply adjourn the case to another day. It would be accurate to say that, while all remands are adjournments, not all adjournments are remands.

The main Acts of Parliament referred to in this Chapter are:

(a) The Magistrates' Courts Act 1980 (MCA 1980).

(b) The Bail Act 1976 (BA 1976).

(c) The Criminal Justice Act 1988 (CJA 1988).

3.2.1 REMANDS IN THE CRIMINAL JUSTICE SYSTEM

If a criminal case before a court in England and Wales is not disposed of conclusively on one day, it will have to carry over into another day. For an analysis of how many cases are concluded on first appearance in court, see **Figure 3.1**.

Examples of such 'carry over' are:

(a) A trial which is too long to finish in a single day.

(b) A trial which has finished in a single day but the court wants more information on the offender before passing sentence (e.g. getting a pre-sentence report). See **14.6**.

(c) A case which has been listed for a preliminary matter only to be determined (e.g. which court will try a defendant charged with an offence triable either way).

(d) A case which has been listed for trial but either party (or perhaps the court, if it has insufficient time that day) is unable to proceed with the case there and then.

(e) A case which has finished in one court but is going to another — on appeal or committal.

Note that, with regard to (a) above, a part-heard trial in the Crown Court continues on the next day. A part-heard case in the magistrates' court may continue the next day or may resume in several weeks' time.

3.2.2 REMAND — BAIL OR CUSTODY?

In all of these examples, the case will be adjourned to another day. Whether this adjournment is a remand depends upon whether it falls within any one of several statutory situations. Essentially, the difference between 'remanding' a defendant and simply 'adjourning' the case is that when the court remands a defendant, it is under a duty to decide whether he or she should be released on bail or kept locked up in custody. If a case is simply 'adjourned', then the defendant is put on trust to return to court at the place, date and time that he or she is told to.

3.2.3 SURRENDERING TO CUSTODY

If the defendant is remanded, he or she will either:

(a) be kept in custody — i.e. stay locked up until produced by the (police, prison or other) authorities for the next court appearance; or

(b) be freed on bail. Being released on bail imposes a duty on a defendant to return to court at the appointed date, place and time (sometimes called 'surrendering to custody'). Failure to attend the next hearing is itself a crime (BA 1976, s. 6; see also **3.15** below).

It appears that a defendant surrenders to custody by:

(i) turning up at the court where he or she was due to appear;

(ii) on the due date;

(iii) at the appointed time (usually 10 am); and

(iv) reporting to the appropriate person.

See *DPP* v *Richards* [1988] QB 701.

Even though the defendant is then allowed to remain *apparently* at liberty, by staying in the public areas of the court building, nevertheless he or she is in custody until the case comes up in court. It follows that the defendant is under an implied obligation not to leave the building without first obtaining permission to do so. (Permission should be sought from the court or someone acting on its behalf.) If the defendant leaves without consent, the court may issue a warrant for his or her arrest. See BA 1976, s. 7(2); *DPP* v *Richards* above; confirmed in *R* v *Central Criminal Court, ex parte Guney* [1995] 1 WLR 376.

Remember that some defendants are released on police bail subject to a duty to surrender to custody at a police station. This occurs, typically, where enquiries are being pursued and the individual has not been charged with an offence.

3.3 When will a Case be Remanded?

Whenever magistrates adjourn a case, they may remand the defendant. The MCA 1980 provides several situations where, on an adjournment, a magistrates' court must remand a defendant and then consider the alternatives of bail and custody. See **Figure 3.1**, which is based upon MCA 1980, s. 10.

Figure 3.1 Will the adjournment be a remand?

1. When D first appeared in the court, was he on bail or in custody?
   If YES — he must now be remanded (on bail or in custody).
   If NO —
2. Has D been remanded at any time during the proceedings for this offence?
   If YES — he must now be remanded (on bail or in custody).
   If NO —
3. The magistrates have a choice to remand or simply adjourn the case.

3.3.1 SITUATIONS WHERE REMAND IS REQUIRED

(a) *Magistrates dealing with an offence triable either way.* If, before or during the summary trial of such an offence, an adjournment is needed, then usually the defendant must be remanded on bail or in custody. See **Figure 3.1**.

(b) *Magistrates determining which court will try an 'either way' offence.* If the magistrates adjourn a case while determining whether the defendant will be tried by the magistrates or a jury (MCA 1980, ss. 19–23), usually they must remand the defendant on bail or in custody (see MCA 1980, s. 18(4)). See **Figure 3.1**.

(c) *Magistrates committing an accused to the Crown Court for trial.* Following a decision to send the accused to the Crown Court for trial, if the accused is currently remanded in custody the magistrates may either order that he be kept in custody pending his trial or release him on bail with a direction that he appear before the Crown Court for trial (MCA 1980, s. 8(1); CDA 1998, ss. 51 and 52).

Figure 3.2 Defendants proceeded against at magistrates' courts — average time for criminal cases by offence type and stage of proceedings, percentage dealt with on first appearance, average number of times case listed and average length of adjournments[1]

England and Wales

Offence type	Average number of days: from offence to completion	from offence to charge or summons	from charge or summons to first listing	from first listing to completion	Percentage of defendants dealt with on first court appearance	Average number of times case listed in court	Average length of adjournments in days	Percentage of defendants pleading: Guilty[2]	Not guilty[2]	Number of defendants in sample (thousands)
Indictable offences (including triable either way)										
1987	114	41	22	51	26	3.3	22	59	14	26.7
1988	117	40	21	55	24	3.4	23	57	14	26.4
1989	122	40	22	61	22	3.5	24	54	16	24.4
1990	127	40	22	64	22	3.5	26	53	17	25.5
1991	128	42	22	65	21	3.6	25	51	17	26.3
1992	129	43	22	64	20	3.4	27	48	19	26.3
1993[3]	120	39	25	56	21	3.3	24	48	19	24.1
1994[3]	128	43	25	60	20	3.5	24	50	19	22.0
1995[3]	130	43	26	61	20	3.6	24	50	19	22.2
1996[3]	132	45	28	60	19	3.6	23	50	17	21.6
1997[3]	135	46	29	60	20	3.6	23	50	17	22.7
Summary non-motoring offences										
1987	123	71	35	17	74	1.5	36	71	10	7.6
1988	127	73	35	20	73	1.5	40	69	10	8.0
1989	125	66	37	22	70	1.6	39	65	12	9.2
1990	134	69	40	25	69	1.6	43	63	13	9.0
1991	135	71	39	26	66	1.6	40	56	11	9.7
1992	137	79	37	21	70	1.5	42	52	10	11.0
1993[3]	132	75	38	19	67	1.6	32	52	10	9.4
1994[3]	137	81	37	20	68	1.6	32	47	10	9.2
1995[3]	138	80	40	18	75	1.6	30	46	9	10.4
1996[3]	133	79	39	15	76	1.5	28	49	8	10.4
1997[3]	128	70	36	21	68	1.8	27	47	12	7.2
Summary motoring offences										
1987	148	75	42	31	59	1.8	39	73	7	17.8
1988	146	73	42	31	61	1.8	39	73	9	18.7
1989	155	75	42	38	57	1.9	41	73	11	17.9
1990	156	77	41	38	55	2.0	39	71	12	17.3
1991	162	76	43	43	55	2.0	41	67	11	18.7
1992	163	79	42	41	53	2.0	41	61	12	18.8
1993[3]	152	80	38	33	52	2.0	33	59	11	17.0
1994[3]	158	84	40	34	53	2.0	32	59	11	16.2
1995[3]	153	82	39	32	54	2.0	31	55	10	16.8
1996[3]	146	76	40	30	54	2.0	29	57	9	15.3
1997[3]	152	83	40	29	57	2.0	29	57	9	15.3

Source: Time Intervals Surveys for Criminal Proceedings in magistrates' courts – conducted by Lord Chancellor's Department.

(1) Based on proceedings in 1 sample week in each of February, June and October for indictable offences, and June only for summary offences (see paragraph 39 of Appendix 2).

(2) Defendants pleading guilty (/not guilty) at a summary trial, as a proportion of those proceeded against in the sample weeks.

(3) Changes in recording procedures have led to small discrepancies with earlier years. From 1993, cases adjourned sine die are not counted until finally disposed of. In addition, cases are excluded which took more than one year to complete (either charge to first listing, or first listing to completion) for reasons which appear to be beyond the control of the court, for example, where the defendant absconded. It is estimated that this change reduced the average interval from first listing to completion by 2 days for indictable offences. Furthermore from the February 1994 survey onwards, cases where the defendant was charged or summonsed over 10 years after the offence occurred have been excluded.

There are two other situations to be aware of:

(d) *Magistrates dealing with a summary offence.* Prior to deciding whether a defendant is guilty or innocent in such a case, the magistrates may have to adjourn the proceedings. If they do so, they have a choice — either to remand the defendant or simply to adjourn (MCA 1980, s. 10(4)). If the defendant fails to appear at court on the next appointed date, the magistrates may proceed to try the case in the absence of the defendant or, in some circumstances, issue a warrant for arrest (MCA 1980, ss. 11 and 13). See **Chapter 5**.

(e) *Magistrates deferring sentence.* Where a magistrates' court defers sentence on a convicted defendant (for up to six months) under PCC(S)A 2000, s. 1, this is not a remand, and the defendant, although released subject to a duty to return to court, is not on bail. (See *R* v *Ross* (1988) 86 Cr App R 337.)

3.3.2 THE USE OF REMANDS OR ADJOURNMENTS BY MAGISTRATES

For an analysis of the use of remands or adjournments by magistrates, see **Figure 3.3**.

3.4 Who Can Remand a Case?

3.4.1 REMANDS IN THE MAGISTRATES' COURT

It might seem, from what you have just read, that only magistrates can remand a criminal case. This is not the whole story. The vast majority of remands occur in the magistrates' court simply because that is where the bulk of criminal litigation takes place, particularly when you realise that almost all hearings in a case prior to trial occur in the magistrates' court.

3.4.2 REMANDS IN THE CROWN COURT

The question of a simple adjournment never seems to arise in the Crown Court. A defendant who is committed to the Crown Court (whether for trial or sentence) will be remanded either on bail or in custody. Once there, the Crown Court judge has the power to grant bail for the period before the matter is dealt with (see Supreme Court Act 1981, s. 81, as amended). In 1987 (the last year for which figures are available), about 35% of those tried at the Crown Court had been remanded to a future sitting of the court (either on bail or in custody) at some stage of their case.

Once a Crown Court trial has started, the judge will remand the accused either in custody or on bail during any lunch or overnight breaks in the trial. Whether or not to release on bail is usually regarded as a matter solely within the power and discretion of the trial judge; see the observation by Peter Gibson LJ in *R* v *Central Criminal Court, ex parte Guney* [1995] 1 WLR 376 that from 'the commencement of a [Crown Court] trial it is for the court conducting the trial to decide whether the defendant should be in custody or on bail'.

Figure 3.3 Persons proceeded against at magistrates' courts by type of court remand and outcome of proceedings

England and Wales 1997 — **Thousands and percentages**

Outcome	All persons charged or summoned: Not remanded by magistrates	Bailed by magistrates	Remanded in custody by magistrates(2)	Total: 1997	1996	1995
			Number of persons (thousands)			
Acquitted or not proceeded with etc.	293.9	142.9	18.4	455.2	464.1	468.2
Convicted:						
Discharge(3)	69.5	52.0	3.7	125.1	121.3	121.6
Fine(3)	880.4	109.3	5.6	995.3	1,058.2	982.2
Community Sentence(4)	16.2	90.7	10.9	117.8	112.8	107.5
Fully suspended sentence	0.2	1.0	0.1	1.2	1.3	1.3
Immediate custody(5)	7.7	23.5	15.3	46.5	41.2	38.7
Total number sentenced(6)	984.5	283.3	37.4	1,305.2	1,351.8	1,268.7
Committed for sentence:						
on bail	0.3	2.4	0.4	3.1	2.2	2.0
in custody	0.4	0.4	3.4	4.2	2.7	2.2
Committed for trial:						
on bail	5.4	54.7	5.2	65.2(2)	60.9(2)	60.7(2)
in custody	1.3	1.5	19.6	22.4(2)	20.3(2)	18.3(2)
Failed to appear to a summons	111.3	*	*	111.3	120.7	102.4
Failed to appear to bail(7)	*	60.7	4.0	64.6	62.2	61.3
proceeded against for failing to surrender to bail(8)	*	*	*	44.2	41.2	39.2
Total	1,397.1	545.9	88.3	2,031.3	2,084.8	1,983.7

England and Wales 1997 — **Thousands and percentages**

Outcome	All persons charged or summoned(1): Not remanded by magistrates	Bailed by magistrates	Remanded in custody by magistrates(2)	Total: 1997	1996	1995
			Percentage of persons			
Acquitted or not proceeded with etc.	21	26	21	22	22	24
Convicted:						
Discharge(3)	5	10	4	6	6	6
Fine(3)	63	20	6	49	51	50
Community Sentence(4)	1	17	12	6	5	5
Fully suspended sentence	0	0	0	0	0	0
Immediate custody(5)	1	4	17	2	2	2
Total number sentenced(6)	70	52	42	64	65	64
Committed for sentence:						
on bail	0	0	0	0	0	0
in custody	0	0	4	0	0	0
Committed for trial:						
on bail	0	10	6	3	3	3
in custody	0	0	22	1	1	1
Failed to appear to a summons	8	0	0	5	6	5
Failed to appear to bail(7)	*	11	4	3	3	3
Proceeded against for failing to surrender to bail(8)	*	*	*	2	2	2
Total	100	100	100	100	100	100

(1) Includes those remanded for part of the time in custody and part on bail.
(2) Differ from figures in Table . . . which shows cases completed at the Crown Court in 1997.
(3) Includes estimates from those summoned for summary offences and omitted from 1995 data (see paragraph 27, Appendix 2).
(4) Includes Probation Orders, Supervision Orders, Community Service Orders, Attendance Centre Orders and Combination Orders.
(5) Includes detention in a young offender institution and unsuspended imprisonment.
(6) Includes offences otherwise dealt with.
(7) It is not known whether the persons prosecuted were remanded partly in custody as well as on bail.
(8) Prosecutions arise from failure to surrender to bail at both magistrates' and Crown Courts; they may not be completed in the same year in which the bail was breached.

3.5 Duration of Remands

3.5.1 GENERAL EXAMPLES

There are various maximum periods for a remand by magistrates in different circumstances.

Before conviction

(a) Three clear days in police custody.

(b) Eight clear days in prison custody. (Exception: if an 'either way' offence is to be tried by the magistrates but they cannot convene in time, remand to whenever they can convene the court.)

(c) Twenty-eight clear days in prison custody if the defendant is legally represented in court, aged 17 or over and consents to being remanded for this length of time. (But see **3.5.2**.)

(d) Twenty-eight clear days in prison custody if the defendant has at least that long still to serve on a current custodial sentence.

(e) Any period to which both the prosecution and defence agree on bail.

After conviction

(f) Three weeks in custody for inquiries or reports for sentencing.

(g) Four weeks on bail for inquiries, etc.

Each of these periods is the maximum duration for a *single* remand. At its conclusion, the defendant will be produced before the magistrates once more. At that time, and subject to the custody time limits (see **3.7.4** below), the magistrates may again remand him or her either on bail or in custody for a further period. Once a defendant is sent to the Crown Court, either for trial or sentence to be passed, he or she is remanded on bail or in custody until such time as the case is listed for hearing (again, subject to the custody time limits).

3.5.2 EXTENSION OF THE MAXIMUM PERIOD FOR REMANDS

The proportion of the prison population which is on remand is quite large. It is a tremendous administrative and logistical burden to produce defendants from custody once a week, every week. It was to save on time, energy and costs that MCA 1980, s. 128 was amended by the CJA 1982 to allow the usual remand period of one week to be extended effectively to four weeks, if the defendant had a lawyer and consented to this extended period (see now MCA 1980, s. 128(3A)).

Clearly, this meant that if there was no defence lawyer in the case or the defendant did not consent, the defendant still had to be produced in court every week. Even if MCA 1980, s. 128(3A) could be used in a case so that the defendant did not appear at court each week, strictly speaking he or she was still being remanded every eight days in his or her absence. His or her case still had to be listed at court once a week and the magistrates had formally to announce that it (and he or she) would be remanded to the following week.

This situation was altered by CJA 1988, s. 155. This introduced an additional element to the MCA 1980, namely s. 128A. This allows magistrates to remand an accused person for up to 28 clear days. This time no consent is required from the defendant, nor need there be a defence lawyer at court. Basically, all that is necessary is that:

(a) the accused has been remanded in custody already in the case; and

(b) the accused is present in court when the extended remand is ordered; and

(c) the court has fixed a date when the next stage in the proceedings will take place.

3.6 What are the Alternatives to Remanding a Case?

These have been mentioned already but, in brief, the court may:

(a) *Try the case anyway*. If a case is ready for summary trial and the accused does not appear, the magistrates may go ahead and try the case in his or her absence, having entered a formal plea of not guilty. This power to try absent defendants does not exist in the Crown Court — the accused must be present at the start of a jury trial to enter a plea to the indictment personally. (See **5.1.1** and MCA 1980, s. 11(1).) The power to hold a summary trial in the absence of the accused is used sparingly. One reason for reluctance is the 'statutory declaration': see MCA 1980, s. 14. This refers to the ability of a convicted person to declare that he or she did not know of the proceedings or summons which resulted in his or her conviction. Once the declaration is made, and served on the clerk to the justices, then the summons and all subsequent proceedings (such as a summary trial and guilty verdict) are void: see MCA 1980, s. 14(1)(b).

(b) *Adjourn to another date*. A case may be simply adjourned to another date and the prosecution and accused told to be at court on that date. No penal sanction exists in this situation to compel attendance on the adjourned hearing. The defence may seek an adjournment in order, for example, to instruct an expert witness to appear as a witness for the defendant. (See *R* v *Sunderland Justices, ex parte Dryden*, *The Times*, 18 May 1994.)

(c) *Adjourn indefinitely and issue a warrant for arrest*. If the accused does not appear at court, the result will often be the issue of a warrant for his or her arrest (sometimes called a 'bench' warrant) (see MCA 1980, s. 13). When the defendant is arrested on a bench warrant, he or she will usually stay in custody until a court hearing can be arranged. Sometimes, if the magistrates suspected there might be a reasonable excuse for the defendant's non-attendance, they could decide to issue the warrant *and* release the defendant on bail without requiring a court hearing upon arrest. The effect of this combination is that the defendant will be arrested and taken to a police station (this constitutes execution of the warrant); at the police station, he or she is then released on bail to attend the magistrates' court at a later date. Crown Court judges can also issue such warrants if a defendant is absent from court without permission. (See also **2.4** and **3.15**.) The warrant may be issued once the court is satisfied that the information against the accused has been supported on oath, that the accused is aware of the hearing and the offence is imprisonable. Warrants may be issued for non-imprisonable offences if the first two criteria are satisfied *and* the court proposes to impose a disqualification on the defendant.

(d) *Dismiss the case*. If the prosecution is not ready to proceed with a summary trial, it is possible that the magistrates will dismiss the charge if there has been a long delay between the commission of the alleged offence and the court hearing. See, for example, *R* v *Oxford City Justices, ex parte Smith* (1982) 75 Cr App R 200; cf. *R* v *Barnet Magistrates' Court, ex parte DPP, The Times*, 8 April 1994. See also **2.3.1**.

3.7 Bail — Practice and Procedure

3.7.1 'UNCONDITIONAL' BAIL

The question of whether to release a defendant on bail or keep him or her in custody arises whenever a case is remanded (see **3.2** above). If a defendant is granted bail, this means that he or she is released from court subject to a primary duty to attend the next court hearing in the case. This is known as the duty to surrender to custody. (See BA 1976, s. 3(1).) Failure to do so at the appointed place, time and date is itself a criminal offence leading to a fine or imprisonment (BA 1976, s. 6 — see **3.15** below).

The primary duty may be accompanied by secondary duties imposed on the defendant — for example, to keep a curfew within certain hours; to report to the local police station once a week; to surrender one's passport. These secondary duties are often described as 'conditions of bail' (see **3.13** below). A defendant who is released on bail, subject only to the primary duty to surrender to bail at the next court hearing, is often referred to by lawyers and magistrates as being released on 'unconditional' bail.

The text of the BA 1976, s. 3(1), is as follows:

Incidents of bail in criminal proceedings

3.—(1) A person granted bail in criminal proceedings shall be under a duty to surrender to custody, and that duty is enforceable in accordance with section 6 of this Act.

3.7.2 THE RIGHT TO BAIL

The Bail Act 1976, s. 4 gives a 'general right to bail' (sic) for defendants in criminal litigation. However, s. 4 does not apply to all defendants in the criminal justice system nor at all stages of the system (see **3.7.3** below). Furthermore, even those defendants to whom BA 1976, s. 4 applies cannot demand to be released on bail automatically. There is a presumption, but no more, that such a defendant will be released on bail if a case is remanded. Section 4(1) says that a person to whom s. 4 applies shall be granted bail (this is the 'right'), *except* as provided in BA 1976, sch. 1. When sch. 1 applies, bail will be denied, and he or she will be remanded in custody (see **3.10** below). For the views of one experienced practitioner on how the right to bail works in practice and how it might be reformed, see Michael Mansfield QC, *Presumed Guilty*, Mandarin, 1993, Chapter 12.

When considering bail issues, pay attention to the Human Rights Act 1998 (HRA 1998) and the European Convention on Human Rights (ECHR). The combination of these provisions may lead to either different considerations applying to bail applications, or a different set of procedures. ECHR, Article 5 — the right to liberty and security — is clearly relevant to bail matters. Its effect has been seen already, with the amendment of CJPOA 1994, s. 25, following several cases in which the European Commission found this provision (which required courts to deny bail to all potential repeat 'serious' offenders) to violate Article 5. The amendment, effected by CDA 1998, s. 56, provides that courts may now release defendants accused of their second serious offence if there are 'exceptional circumstances which justify it'. See *Cabellero* v *UK*, 8 February 2000, unreported); and **3.7.3**.

Relevant provisions in Article 5 include:

(1) Everyone has the right to liberty and security of person. No one shall be deprived of his liberty save in the following cases and in accordance with a procedure prescribed by law:

. . .

(c) the lawful arrest or detention of a person effected for the purpose of bringing him before the competent legal authority on reasonable suspicion of having committed an offence or when it is reasonably considered necessary to prevent his committing an offence or fleeing after having done so;

(d) the [lawful] detention of a minor . . . for the purpose of bringing him before the competent legal authority;

. . .

(3) Everyone arrested or detained in accordance with the provisions of paragraph 1(c) of this article shall be brought promptly before a judge or other officer authorised by law to exercise judicial power and shall be entitled to trial within a reasonable time

or to release pending trial. Release may be conditioned by guarantees to appear for trial.

. . .

(5) *Everyone who has been the victim of arrest or detention in contravention of the provisions of this article shall have an enforceable right to compensation.*

The relevance of these provisions is perhaps best shown by the publication, in November 1999, of a Consultation Paper by the Law Commission of England and Wales. Consultation Paper No. 157, *Bail and the Human Rights Act 1998*, is an extremely thorough review of the bail laws and procedures in England and Wales and examines them critically against the provisions of the ECHR. The consultation period expired in March 2000. Where provisional suggestions are made in the Consultation Paper, for amendment or repeal, those suggestions are noted where relevant in this Chapter.

Figure 3.4 Persons directed to appear at magistrates' courts[(1)] by type of offence, how directed to appear and outcome

England and Wales 1997 — Number of persons (thousands)

How directed to appear	Total	Outcome		
		Dealt with by magistrates[(2)]	Committed for trial	Failed to appear[(3)]
Indictable offences				
Summoned	47	35	4	8
Arrested and bailed	438	312	59	67
Arrested and held in custody	84	53	25	7
Total	569	399	88	83
Summary offences (other than motoring)				
Summoned	333	328	*(4)	5
Arrested and bailed	204	181	*(4)	22
Arrested and held in custody	23	21	*(4)	2
Total	560	530	*(4)	29
Summary motoring offences				
Summoned	743	693	*(4)	50
Arrested and bailed	144	131	*(4)	13
Arrested and held in custody	15	14	*(4)	1
Total	902	838	*(4)	64
All offences				
Summoned	1,124	1,056	4	63
Arrested and bailed	786	625	59	103
Arrested and held in custody	122	87	25	10
Total	2,031	1,768	88	176

(1) The number of persons directed to appear includes those who failed to appear to a summons or to bail . . .
(2) Including those committed to the Crown Court for sentence.
(3) At any stage before final disposal by magistrates' court.
(4) Not applicable, because summary offences committed for trial will not be counted as principal offences as they must accompany an indictable only or triable-either-way offence.

3.7.3 WHERE THERE IS NO RIGHT TO BAIL

It is important to realise that the 'right' to bail under BA 1976 *usually* applies only prior to conviction. It also only applies when a defendant appears in court (see BA 1976, s. 4). So there is no right to bail in the following situations:

(a) When being arrested.

(b) When being charged with an offence.

(c) When a warrant for the arrest of an accused person is issued.

(d) After conviction for an offence **unless:**

(i) the case is adjourned so that inquiries or reports can be made to assist the court when passing sentence (BA 1976, s. 4(4)); or

(ii) the defendant is subsequently brought before a magistrates' court to be dealt with for breach of a requirement of a probation, community service, combination or curfew order (BA 1976, s. 4(3)).

In situations where there is no right to bail, it should not generally be thought that the defendant cannot be released on bail. The court, if it remands such a case, usually has a *discretion* to grant bail. This discretion is unfettered by the need to satisfy BA 1976, sch. 1, if bail is to be refused — in other words, the court has more freedom to refuse bail in such circumstances. On the grant of bail at the police station following charge, see PACE 1984, s. 38 (see **2.2.9**).

There are two further exceptions to the general right to bail that we must note; they are created by the Criminal Justice and Public Order Act 1994 (CJPOA 1994). First, if a defendant is charged with murder, manslaughter or rape (or an attempt, where appropriate) and he has a previous conviction for one of those offences, then he shall only be granted bail if there are 'wholly exceptional circumstances which justify it' (see CJPOA 1994, s. 25, as amended). In a case where the previous conviction was for manslaughter, the restriction only applies if the defendant received a custodial sentence for that offence. Secondly, where a defendant appears in court charged with an offence triable either way and it appears to the court that he was already on bail at the time of the present offence, he need not be granted bail; that is, bail is simply a matter for the discretion of the court (see CJPOA 1994, s. 26, inserting paragraph 2A into BA 1976, sch. 1, part I).

Both of these provisions may need amendment in the light of the HRA 1998. As noted above (**3.7.2**), CJPOA 1994, s. 25, has been amended already by allowing bail to be granted in exceptional circumstances. However, the Law Commission has taken the view (see its Consultation Paper No. 157, 1999) that these provisions in their present form either cannot be applied in a manner which is compatible with the ECHR, or are highly likely to be applied in an incompatible manner.

3.7.4 CUSTODY TIME LIMITS

There are certain limits on the length of time that a defendant can be kept on remand in custody, under the Prosecution of Offences Act 1985. These limits do not apply to summary offences or treason. See the Prosecution of Offences (Custody Time Limits) Regulations 1987 (SI 1987 No. 299), as amended. That there should be limits on the time to be spent in custody awaiting trial cannot be doubted. As Lord Bingham CJ declared in *R* v *Manchester Crown Court, ex parte McDonald* [1999] 1 WLR 841, to proceed without time limits:

> . . . would manifestly afford inadequate protection to unconvicted defendants, since a person could, if the Bail Act conditions were satisfied, be held in prison awaiting trial indefinitely, and there would be no obligation on the prosecuting authority to bring him to trial as soon as reasonably possible.

The regulations impose deadlines within which the proceedings must reach a specified stage. For example, a defendant who is kept in custody must be sent for trial within 70 days of his first appearance in court. If the deadline is not met, the defendant *must* be released on bail. There are also deadlines which apply generally, regardless of whether or not the defendant is in custody. These are sometimes referred to as *statutory time limits*. They were introduced in the Prosecution of Offences Act 1985, s. 22. In their original form, the result of non-compliance was that the defendant was acquitted of the charge. This provision has now been amended so that non-compliance results in the proceedings merely being stayed. In certain circumstances, the case may be re-started later. See also CDA 1998, ss. 43 and 45, on statutory time limits; these provisions came into effect on 1 June 1999 and were introduced in pilot courts in Autumn 1999 with a view to national implementation in January 2001. The prosecution can apply for a deadline to be extended. It must show (on a balance of probabilities) that there is good and sufficient cause for the extension and that it has acted with all due expedition.

When a defendant is freed on bail due to the expiry of a custody time limit, his bail should only have conditions attached to it that the defendant can comply with *after* his release (e.g. reporting to a police station or a condition to reside at a specified address). Conditions which must be complied with *prior* to release (e.g. providing a financial surety) cannot be imposed. The significance of this can be seen in *Re Ofili* [1995] Crim LR 880, where O was originally granted bail, subject to providing a surety of £4,000. O could find no one to stand surety in that sum, so he remained in custody. When O challenged this, the Divisional Court held that on the expiry of the custody time limit, he was entitled to be freed on bail, subject only to reporting or residence conditions.

In a magistrates' court the maximum length of time that a defendant should spend in custody is 70 days. This period should be calculated as follows:

(a) 70 days from first court appearance to the start of summary trial (for either way offences);

(b) 70 days from first court appearance to a decision on committal for trial (for either way offences and offences which must be tried on indictment).

Note that, in (a) above, if the magistrates take a decision to proceed to summary trial within 56 days of the defendant's first court appearance, the custody time limit becomes 56 (not 70) days. Note further that, in (b) above, if the committal proceedings are held pursuant to MCA 1980, s. 6(1) (i.e. with consideration of the evidence), then the 70-day limit is satisfied if the magistrates start to hear the prosecution's evidence within that period: they need not reach a decision on whether to commit the accused for trial within that period.

Once the case goes to the Crown Court, the maximum length of time that a defendant should spend in custody prior to his or her trial is 112 days, beginning with the date that he or she was sent for trial by the magistrates and expiring with the date of his or her arraignment (i.e. being asked in Crown Court to plead either guilty or not guilty). This period can be extended, but any use of a 'sham' arraignment simply to defeat the purpose of the custody time limit will be struck down. See, for example, *R* v *Maidstone Crown Court, ex parte Hollstein, The Times*, 4 November 1994 — H was sent for trial on 24 March 1994, his custody time limit should have expired on 14 July 1994 but was extended to 22 July 1994. He should then have been released on bail but was kept in custody and produced in court on 27 July 1994 when he was arraigned on the indictment and further remanded in custody. He was still remanded in custody on 13 October 1994 (some three months after the expiry of the original time limit) when the Queen's Bench Divisional Court granted his application to quash the decision of 27 July 1994 to remand him in custody — no date for his trial had been fixed and the arraignment was an artificially created situation.

If the 112-day period expires, the CPS should either apply for an extension or bring the defendant back to court to be released on bail. The prison governor has no power to release the defendant without an order from the court. If the defendant continues to be detained in the absence of a court order for release, the appropriate remedies are either to apply to the Crown Court for bail or to seek *habeas corpus* or judicial review. No action will lie against the Home Office for false imprisonment, nor will the CPS be liable for breach of statutory duty if it fails to return the defendant to court after expiry of a custody time limit. See *Olotu* v *Home Office and another* [1997] 1 WLR 328.

The precise length of the custody time limits may need to be reviewed in the light of the HRA 1998 and Article 5(3) of the ECHR (which provides that everyone detained 'shall be entitled to trial within a reasonable time or to release pending trial'). However, the matter has been considered already by Lord Bingham CJ in *R* v *Manchester Crown Court, ex parte McDonald* [1999] 1 WLR 841. After reviewing the ECHR case law on the subject, he felt that:

> We do not . . . find anything in these European cases which in any way throws doubt on the English law . . . It would indeed appear that the term of 112 days prescribed by the regulations imposes what is, by international standards, an exacting standard.

Finally, one should note that the 112-day limit does not apply to defendants who are awaiting trial for offences of homicide and rape (see BA 1976, s. 4(8) (as amended).

One should note that, where an indictable-only case is sent straight to the Crown Court (under CDA 1998, s. 51), the maximum length of the custody time limit is 182 days. Time runs from the date the case is sent up by the magistrates, less any time already spent in custody.

See *Archbold*, 2000 edn, paras. 1–270, 3–56; *Blackstone's Criminal Practice*, 2000, D5.20 and D10.4.

3.7.5 BAIL ACT 1976, s. 4

4.—(1) A person to whom this section applies shall be granted bail except as provided in Schedule 1 to this Act.
(2) This section applies to a person who is accused of an offence when—
(a) he appears or is brought before a magistrates' court or the Crown Court in the course of or in connection with proceedings for the offence, or
(b) he applies to a court for bail in connection with the proceedings.
This subsection does not apply as respects proceedings on or against a person's conviction of the offence or proceedings against a fugitive offender for the offence.
(3) This section also applies to a person who, having been convicted of an offence, appears or is brought before a magistrates' court to be dealt with under Part II of Schedule 3 to the Powers of Criminal Courts (Sentencing) Act 2000 (breach of certain community orders).
(4) This section also applies to a person who has been convicted of an offence and whose case is adjourned by the court for the purpose of enabling inquiries or a report to be made to assist the court in dealing with him for the offence.

3.8 Taking a Decision on Bail — When and How

3.8.1 WHEN IS THE DECISION TAKEN?

Usually, the question of bail or custody is decided at the end of each day's proceedings in the case, immediately prior to remanding it to another day. If a case is being heard in court in the morning, and will continue in the afternoon, the court should determine whether the accused will take lunch in the cells (custody) or in the restaurant of his or her choice (bail), immediately before breaking for lunch. Another example of this is in committal proceedings in the magistrates' court — the court will determine whether the defendant is to be sent for trial to the Crown Court first, then consider the twin issues of bail and legal aid. Sometimes, though, the question of bail is the sole reason for a case appearing in court. Examples are:

(a) The defendant, committed in custody to the Crown Court for trial or sentence, who applies to the Crown Court for bail pending the anticipated appearance in the Crown Court (see **3.17.1** below).

(b) The defendant who has been refused bail by magistrates and appeals to a Crown Court judge (see **3.17.1** below).

(c) The defendant who has been refused bail by magistrates and/or a Crown Court judge and appeals to a High Court judge (see **3.17.2** below).

3.8.2 HOW IS THE DECISION TAKEN?

The court must decide for itself whether or not to grant bail. It may be addressed by representatives of both prosecution and defence if the grant of bail is opposed, but the decision is one for the court. Lay magistrates will often retire briefly to consider whether to grant bail if release on bail is opposed by the prosecution. Stipendiary magistrates and Crown Court judges will normally decide in court, straight after counsel have finished their submissions. If the release of the defendant on bail is unopposed by the prosecution (and especially if the defendant is already on bail in the current proceedings), the decision to grant bail is usually a formality.

3.8.3 RECORDS, REASONS, CERTIFICATES AND RIGHTS

3.8.3.1 Records

There are two common situations when a record must be kept of a decision on bail. Pursuant to BA 1976, s. 5(1), these are:

(a) whenever bail is granted (either by the police or a court);

(b) whenever a defendant with the right to bail under BA 1976, s. 4 is remanded in custody by a court.

Also, if an application is made to a court either:

(i) to attach conditions to a grant of bail which was hitherto unconditional; or

(ii) to vary any extant conditions of bail,

the court must make a record of its decision. Examples of such records can be seen in *Stone's Justices' Manual*, vol. 3, part IX, Forms 149–153.

If the defendant asks for a copy of the record, he or she must be given one (BA 1976, s. 5). In some of the situations set out below, the defendant must be given a copy of the record even if one is not requested.

3.8.3.2 Reasons

Reasons for refusing to grant bail, etc. If a defendant has a right to bail under BA 1976, s. 4, then if a court:

(a) refuses to grant bail; or

(b) grants bail subject to conditions; or

(c) on application for the purpose, imposes or varies conditions in respect of bail,

the court shall give reasons for its decision (BA 1976, s. 5(3)).

These reasons shall be entered on the s. 5 record and a copy must be given to the defendant (s. 5(4)). However, if the decision is taken by the Crown Court, the defendant is legally represented in court, and the representative does not request a copy, a copy need not be given (BA 1976, s. 5(5)). The purpose of giving reasons in these situations is to enable the defendant to make an informed decision about applying to another court about bail.

As well as the specific obligations imposed by BA 1976, s. 5(3), there is a more general obligation to provide reasons when refusing bail. Case law decided under the ECHR establishes that a court must:

> . . . examine all the facts arguing for or against the existence of a genuine requirement of public interest justifying, with due regard to the principle of the presumption of innocence, a departure from the rule of respect for individual liberty and set them out in their decisions on applications for release.

See, for example, *Letellier* v *France* (1992) 14 EHRR 83.

In its Consultation Paper on Bail and the HRA 1998 (No. 157, 1999), the Law Commission proposed that:

> . . . magistrates and judges should be provided with appropriate guidance and training on making bail decisions in a way which is compliant with Article 5, and recording those decisions in such a way as to indicate clearly how they have been reached; and that magistrates' courts should be required to use forms which encourage compliant decision-making and the recording of decisions in a compliant way.

Reasons for granting bail If a defendant is charged with any one of five specific offences, then, if a court grants bail notwithstanding that the prosecution have made certain representations, the court must state its reasons for granting bail, and these should be entered on the s. 5 record. The offences are: murder (including attempts); manslaughter; and rape (including attempts).

The prosecution must have made representations that, if the defendant was granted bail, he or she would either fail to surrender to custody, or commit an offence whilst on bail; or interfere with witnesses or otherwise obstruct the course of justice.

The requirement to state reasons in this situation is imposed on the court by BA 1976, sch. 1, part I, para. 9A (inserted by CJA 1988, s. 153).

3.8.3.3 Certificates

Under BA 1976, s. 5(6A), if magistrates withhold bail after hearing a fully argued application for bail, they must issue a certificate stating that they heard full argument. After two unsuccessful bail applications in a case, if the magistrates allow the defendant a third application (which is unsuccessful), they should issue a certificate indicating the change in circumstances or new consideration that persuaded them to hear the third application. See BA 1976, s. 5(6A) and (6B); also BA 1976, sch. 1, part IIA (inserted by CJA 1988, s. 154). See further **3.16** and **3.17** below.

3.8.3.4 Rights

If a magistrates' court withholds bail from an unrepresented defendant, it must inform the defendant of his or her right to apply to a judge of the High Court to be granted bail. In addition, if the magistrates are committing the defendant to the Crown Court for trial, or have issued a certificate of 'full argument', they must also tell the defendant that he or she may apply to a Crown Court judge for bail. (See BA 1976, s. 5(6).)

3.9 Applying for Bail— What Happens in Court?

The procedure for determining whether a defendant is to be released on bail does not really vary from court to court, either between courts on the same level of the court system or between courts on different levels. Although some defendants have a right to bail under BA 1976, s. 4, while others can only seek the exercise of the court's discretion in their favour, in practice it is incumbent on the defendant to apply for bail. See [1988] Crim LR 397 for a contrary view.

3.9.1 THE BAIL APPLICATION WHICH IS OPPOSED

When a court hearing is adjourned and the defendant is to be remanded, the defendant (or defence counsel) is asked whether he or she seeks release on bail. If the answer is yes, the prosecution will be asked if there are any objections to bail (see **3.10** below). If there are, these will now be given to the court, usually by the prosecutor (note that the strict rules of evidence do not apply to bail applications).

If no agreement can be reached between defence and prosecution prior to coming into court (see **3.9.3**), after the objections have been set before the court, defence counsel makes oral submissions dealing with the objections to bail. Counsel may suggest that the objections are groundless and/or propose any conditions which might be attached to bail to overcome the objections (see further **3.12** and **3.13.4** below). The defence may call potential sureties into the witness box in an attempt to persuade the court that the defendant is unlikely to abscond. Finally, the court takes its decision to remand either on bail or in custody.

(See further **Chapter 34** in the ***Advocacy Manual*** for a checklist and flow chart on bail applications.)

3.9.2 THE UNOPPOSED APPLICATION FOR BAIL

In this situation, the defence having indicated that bail is sought, the prosecution offer no objection. Although the court could try to investigate whether there are reasons why it should withhold bail from the accused, it is unlikely to do so — largely because the prosecution is its normal source of information critical of the accused. If prosecuting counsel sees no reason to object, the court is unlikely to discover such a reason from that source for itself.

3.9.3 DEALING WITH THE OPPOSITION

Usually, defence counsel will seek out the prosecution before the case is called into court and ask whether there are any objections to bail. If not, the application will be unopposed and is likely to succeed (see **3.9.2**). If there are objections, defence counsel may ask what these are and then think about what bail conditions might overcome them. If defence counsel can get the defendant's agreement to such conditions, the approval of the prosecution may then be sought. If this is obtained, the defence can apply to the court for bail and offer the 'agreed' terms. As the application is now unopposed in effect, success (with the agreed conditions) is likely.

3.10 Objections to a Release on Bail

As mentioned above, the prosecution may object to the defendant being freed on bail. In practice, any objections will correspond to one or more of the reasons for refusing bail to a 's. 4' defendant, found in BA 1976, sch. 1. These will be substantiated with information, provided to the court by the prosecutor. Examples are:

(a) 'The accused is likely to fail to surrender to bail': he failed to turn up last time and we had to get a warrant; he has three convictions for this sort of thing already and faces a long spell in prison; he has no permanent address.

(b) 'The accused is likely to commit offences if freed': he was already on bail for an offence when he was arrested for this lot; he's done it in the past; he makes his living from crime.

(c) 'The accused must be remanded in custody for his own protection': he is on 12 charges of burglary, all from houses on the estate where he lives. Some of the residents have told the police that he's a dead man if he shows his face round there.

3.11 Refusing to Release a Defendant on Bail

3.11.1 CIRCUMSTANCES WHEN THIS CAN HAPPEN

If a defendant has the right to bail under BA 1976, s. 4, and asks to be released, then the court can only withhold bail where the offence is imprisonable if one (or more) of the following criteria is present in the case:

(a) The court is satisfied that there are substantial grounds to believe that the defendant would:

(i) fail to surrender to custody;

(ii) commit an offence whilst on bail;

(iii) interfere with witnesses or otherwise obstruct the course of justice.

(b) The defendant is charged with an offence triable either way and it appears to the court that he or she was already on bail at the time of the present offence.

(c) The court is satisfied that the accused must be kept in custody for his or her own protection (or welfare, if the accused is a child or young person — see **Chapter 7** for definitions of these terms).

(d) The accused is currently serving a custodial sentence imposed for a previous offence.

(e) If this is the first time that the case has been in the court and the court is satisfied it has not been practicable to obtain all the information necessary for a proper decision on bail to be made.

(f) If the accused has already failed to surrender to bail in the current case (or has broken the conditions attached to the grant of bail) and has been arrested for this.

(g) If, after conviction, the case is adjourned for inquiries or reports and it appears to the court that it would be impracticable to complete the inquiries or report without keeping the accused in custody.

(See BA 1976, sch. 1, part 1.)

It remains to be seen exactly how the list set out in BA 1976, sch. 1, is compatible with the HRA 1998 and ECHR. The ECHR does not explicitly identify the grounds on which bail may be refused prior to trial but the matter has been considered by the European Court and the ECHR Commission. Four grounds have been recognised:

- fear of absconding (reflected in sch. 1; see (a)(i) above)
- prevention of crime (see (a)(ii) above)
- interference with the course of justice (see (a)(iii) above)
- preservation of public order (not explicitly within sch. 1; debatable which of grounds (b)–(g) would be covered).

The Law Commission of England and Wales has suggested (in its Consultation Paper No. 157, 1999) that grounds (a)(ii) and (c) above are compatible with the ECHR but may require further guidance on their application. Ground (b), the Paper suggests, is highly likely to be applied in a manner that is incompatible with the ECHR; the Paper proposes its repeal and that the point be subsumed into sch. 1, Part I, para. 9 (see **3.11.2**) simply as a consideration to be taken into account. Ground (f) above is described as an automatic inference of a kind ('that a person who has done a given thing in the past is likely, given the chance, to do it again') which the ECHR does not permit. The Law Commission proposes that ground (f) be repealed. If the circumstances which it describes occur, they should simply be a factor which is relevant to a possible refusal of bail on ground (a).

3.11.2 CONSIDERATIONS FOR THE COURT

Schedule 1 to BA 1976 (at part I, para. 9) says that when a court is considering whether one of the reasons for refusing bail referred to in (a) (in **3.11.1**) exists, it should take account of:

(a) The nature and seriousness of the offence (and probable sentence).

(b) The character, antecedents, associations and community ties of the accused.

(c) His or her record of fulfilling bail requirements in the past.

(d) The strength of the case against the accused (unless adjourning for reports or inquiries before passing sentence).

(e) Any other considerations as appear relevant.

With regard to (b), the disclosure of D's *antecedents* means that the magistrates learn of his or her criminal record, if any. There are several points to note about this:

(i) evidence of any criminal record should be tendered in writing, not orally (*R* v *Dyson* (1944) 29 Cr App R104);

(ii) the press *should not* report any convictions which are publicised, at that time (*R* v *Fletcher* (1949) 113 JP 365) (note that there is no direct power to coerce the media, although note Contempt of Court Act 1981, s. 4(2));

(iii) any magistrate who sits on a bail application hearing and learns of previous convictions is disqualified from subsequently trying D's guilt/ innocence in that case (MCA 1980, s. 42).

Also on 'associations and community ties', see the suggestions in *Stones' Justices' Manual* (1999) at 1–433. The phrase covers:

(i) name, age, nationality and (if applicable) length of residence in the UK;

(ii) family circumstances (married? dependent children? does he live with wife/parents/other relatives?);

(iii) residence (type of accommodation; recent addresses and length of stay);

(iv) employment (recent record; present job — location and income);

(v) possible sureties, any relative, friend, employer in court . . .;

(vi) anything else that the defendant wants to put forward, e.g. medical problems, difficulties with job or home if remanded in custody.

Remember, if a court withholds bail from a 's. 4' defendant, it must give its *reasons* in open court and on the record (BA 1976, s. 5(3); see **3.8.3** above).

3.11.3 BAIL FOR NON-IMPRISONABLE CRIMES

The grounds for refusing bail set out in **3.10.1** are applied only to defendants charged with crimes for which they can be sent to prison, if convicted. The Bail Act 1976, sch. 1 also covers bail for non-imprisonable offences and is more liberal in allowing bail. The grounds for withholding bail now are:

(a) For the protection of the defendant.

(b) Where the defendant is already serving a custodial sentence.

(c) Where the defendant has been arrested for a bail offence in connection with this case (see **3.15** below).

(d) Where the defendant has previously failed to surrender to bail and, in the light of that failure, the court is satisfied he or she would not surrender to bail if released now.

There is no power to remand a defendant in custody for the purpose of preparing medical/psychiatric reports if the offence is non-imprisonable.

The detailed provisions which govern the imposition of bail conditions are to be found in BA 1976, sch. 1, part I, para. 8. Part I applies to defendants 'accused or convicted of *imprisonable* offences' (emphasis added). There is no corresponding text in sch. 1, part II, which deals with *non-imprisonable* offences. It might be thought, then, that the BA 1976 makes no provision for attaching conditions to a grant of bail where a defendant is accused or convicted of a non-imprisonable offence. In fact, it has been decided that the basic power to attach conditions to a grant of bail (BA 1976, s. 3) applies to both imprisonable and non-imprisonable offences (see *R* v *Bournemouth Magistrates' Court, ex parte Cross* (1989) 89 Cr App R 90).

This decision can produce a rather odd result by virtue of the different criteria which now apply to non-imprisonable offences when (i) refusing bail and (ii) imposing conditions. BA 1976, s. 3(6) and sch. 1, part I, para. 8 both allow a court to attach conditions to a grant of bail if it appears necessary to do so in order to ensure that the defendant surrenders to custody; but sch. 1, part II, does not allow a court to withhold bail on the grounds that it believes the defendant will not surrender to custody. So if the court fears that a defendant will abscond, it may attach conditions to his bail but if there are no conditions that will allay such fears, they must release on bail anyway.

3.12 Overcoming Objections to Bail — The Power of Imagination

It was mentioned earlier (in **3.9.1** above) that if the prosecution is objecting to the release of the defendant on bail, defence counsel can suggest that certain conditions be attached to the grant of bail. These suggestions can be made to the prosecutor before going into court or once the prosecutor states the objections in court. Additionally, defence counsel can make (or repeat) these suggestions in his or her final submissions to the court. Apart from some qualifications on the power of the courts to attach conditions to a grant of bail, the conditions which can be used to overcome the fears of the prosecution or court are almost limitless.

3.12.1 KEEPING ONE'S IMAGINATION WITHIN REASONABLE BOUNDS

There are some very common conditions (see **3.13** below) which will be suggested by the defence almost as an automatic reaction to certain objections. Nevertheless, one should not be afraid to put forward novel solutions to allay any objections, subject only to two observations. First, that one should always get the defendant's consent before putting a suggestion forward. Apart from the ethical problem of arguing a case with no instructions from the lay client to do so, there is a practical problem — to get your client released on bail, subject to conditions which he or she will not or cannot accept, is effectively not getting bail. Secondly, remember that the everyday bail conditions are used so often because they are workable and answer a particular objection sensibly. Do not invent new ones which fail to satisfy those criteria. One should seek only to improve the commonplace conditions to deal with novel situations when they arise.

3.13 Attaching Conditions to Release on Bail

In **3.7.1** above it was said that any grant of bail was subject to a primary duty — to surrender to bail at the appointed time, date and place — but also that secondary duties (known as 'conditions of bail') could sometimes be imposed on a defendant. The BA 1976 specifies two forms of condition and the circumstances in which they may be used — the surety and security (see BA 1976, s. 3(3) and (4)). Originally, the police were limited to just these two conditions when releasing a defendant on bail from a police station. Conversely, courts could impose any conditions that they thought necessary to secure certain objectives — e.g. that the defendant would surrender to custody, not offend whilst on bail and not interfere with witnesses (see BA 1976, s. 3(6) below).

The 1993 Royal Commission on Criminal Justice, chaired by Lord Runciman, recommended that the police should have the power to release a suspect on bail subject to conditions (see para. 5.22 and recommendation 94 of the report). There was concern that people who could properly have been released on bail, if conditions were attached to their bail, were instead being kept in custody. This often led to defendants being brought from custody to a magistrates' court where they would apply for bail and have it granted subject, perhaps, to those conditions that the police were prepared to impose but lacked the power to do so. The Runciman Commission's recommendation was taken up by the Government, and the police now have far greater powers to attach conditions to a grant of bail. Section 47 of PACE 1984 has been amended so that now the 'normal powers to impose conditions of bail' shall be available to a custody officer (PACE 1984, s. 47(1A)). Section 3(6) of the BA 1976 has also been amended so that the police are now almost as free as the courts to impose conditions on a grant of bail (see CJPOA 1994, s. 27).

The main restrictions that the police are subject to now are that the condition(s) must appear to be necessary to ensure that a defendant surrenders to custody, or does not offend whilst on bail, or does not interfere with witnesses or otherwise obstruct the course of justice (see BA 1976, s. 3A(5)). In addition, police cannot make it a condition of bail that the accused resides in a bail hostel (BA 1976, s. 3A(2)), nor do the special provisions on obtaining medical reports relating to defendants facing a charge of murder apply to police bail (BA 1976, s. 3A(3)).

As regards a person granted bail, BA 1976, s. 3, provides that:

(2) No recognizance for his surrender to custody shall be taken from him.
(3) Except as provided by this section—
(a) no security for his surrender to custody shall be taken from him,
(b) he shall not be required to provide a surety or sureties for his surrender to custody, and
(c) no other requirement shall be imposed on him as a condition of bail.
(4) He may be required, before release on bail, to provide a surety or sureties to secure his surrender to custody.
(5) He may be required, before release on bail, to give security for his surrender to custody.
The security may be given by him or on his behalf.
(6) He may be required to comply, before release on bail or later, with such requirements as appear to the court to be necessary to secure that—
(a) he surrenders to custody,
(b) he does not commit an offence while on bail,
(c) he does not interfere with witnesses or otherwise obstruct the course of justice whether in relation to himself or any other person,
(d) he makes himself available for the purpose of enabling inquiries or a report to be made to assist the court in dealing with him for the offence, and, in any Act, 'the normal powers to impose conditions of bail' means the powers to impose conditions under paragraph (a), (b) or (c) above,
(e) before the time appointed for him to surrender to custody, he attends an interview with an authorised advocate or authorised litigator, as defined by section 119(1) of the Courts and Legal Services Act 1990.

3.13.1 THE SURETY

If the court (or police, following an arrest or charge) considers it is necessary to ensure that the defendant surrenders to custody, the defendant may be required to provide sureties to guarantee his or her surrender (BA 1976, s. 8). If no sureties are forthcoming, the defendant stays in custody, although technically bail has been granted. A surety is a person — usually a friend, relative or employer — who agrees to ensure that the defendant attends court at the next hearing. The surety acknowledges that, should the defendant fail to surrender, the surety is liable to forfeit a specified sum of money to the court. See also **3.15.3** below on forfeiture. A person may stand as a surety either in the courtroom or in any of the situations covered by BA 1976, s. 8(4) (for example, at the police station after the accused is charged; by the gaoler at court if the surety arrived too late to appear in court; at the prison holding the defendant).

3.13.2 THE SURETY IN COURT

Before starting the final submissions to the court, defence counsel should call any proposed sureties into the witness box. The 'surety' will take an oath and defence counsel should then explain the obligation to ensure the defendant's surrender to bail and the possibility of the surety losing money should this not happen. He or she should then be asked if he or she is still willing to be a surety. If so, counsel will enquire what sum of money he or she is prepared to run the risk of forfeiting and how this will be paid if required by the court to do so. The court will examine the surety's financial resources, character and any criminal record, and relationship to the defendant (kinship, geographical, etc.).

If the procedure outlined above is followed, there should be no problems about lack of resources if the surety is subsequently called on to forfeit his or her recognisance. The issue of the surety's ability to pay was considered by the Divisional Court in *R* v *Birmingham Crown Court, ex parte Ali and another* [1999] Crim LR 504. The Court declared that a qualified lawyer, or legal executive, should not put someone forward as a possible surety unless they have reasonable grounds for believing that the surety would, if necessary, be able to meet the financial undertaking. Failure to observe this requirement is irresponsible and possibly a matter for consideration by a professional disciplinary body. Furthermore, a court should conduct appropriate enquiries with an individual before accepting them as a surety. It might be necessary to require evidence of the assets that the would-be surety claims to have. How far that enquiry would go depends upon all of the circumstances, the most important of which is the amount of money at stake. (See **3.1.5.3**; also ***Advocacy Manual*, Chapter 36**.)

3.13.3 SECURITY

The defendant may be required to provide security for his or her surrender (BA 1976, s. 3(5) as amended by CDA 1998, s. 54(1)). This may take the form of money or other valuables (BA 1976, s. 5(9)) and may be demanded from the defendant personally, unlike a surety. It will be deposited with the court and, if the defendant fails to surrender to custody, it may be forfeited by court order, either totally or in part. (See (g) in **3.1**.)

The obligation to pay a security, if it is held forfeit, is that of the defendant alone. If a third party actually supplies the funds to deposit with the court, he or she should note that the court is under no obligation to ascertain his or her ability to pay the money. Further, the third party's position need not be considered by the court when it imposes (or varies) bail conditions. Such a third party has far less protection here than when standing as a surety for a defendant: see *R* v *Maidstone Crown Court, ex parte Jodka, The Times*, 13 June 1997.

3.13.4 OTHER BAIL CONDITIONS

A court can impose any conditions it (or defence counsel) can think of, but they must be considered to be necessary to ensure that the defendant either:

(a) surrenders to custody; or

(b) does not commit offences while on bail; or

(c) does not interfere with witnesses; or

(d) does not obstruct the course of justice; or

(e) is available for inquiries or reports to be completed; or

(f) attends an interview with a legal representative.

(See BA 1976, s. 3(6).)

See *Stone's Justices' Manual* (1999) at 1–435. Remember also that the police have considerable flexibility now in attaching conditions to a grant of bail (BA 1976, s. 3(6), as amended), but are unlikely to be influenced by representations from defence counsel since counsel will not be in attendance at the police station. The ability of a defendant's solicitor to suggest or influence bail conditions remains to be explored.

3.13.5 COMMON CONDITIONS

3.13.5.1 Reporting to a police station

A defendant may be ordered to do this in order to ensure that he or she stays within the vicinity. This may be strictly enforced — for example, 'daily at 7 am and 7 pm' — or be a quite loose check — for example, 'every Thursday'. The purpose of this is to ensure the defendant is around to surrender to custody on the appointed date.

Now that the police are able to be more creative in attaching conditions to bail, there is room for confusion here. The police could always release a suspect on bail, subject to a requirement that he attend subsequently at the police station for further inquiries — that was not conditional bail as the attendance was a primary obligation on the accused. Nowadays, the police may also require a suspect to report to the police station if they are concerned that he may abscond — this would be a secondary obligation (he is not being required to surrender to custody) and if the suspect failed to report as required he would only be in breach of a bail condition; he would not have committed an offence under BA 1976, s. 6 (see **3.15.1** below).

3.13.5.2 Keeping curfew

Originally a medieval rule requiring fires to be extinguished at a certain hour at night, this now means the obligation to stay indoors between certain hours (usually at night). This condition is often used where a number of crimes have allegedly occurred at roughly the same time of day — for example, five houses have been burgled in the early hours of the morning: curfew to be kept between 11 pm and 6 am. It is commonly used for juvenile defendants.

3.13.5.3 Staying out of/in a certain area

These are separate conditions. The first aims to separate the accused from temptation — the woman who has been charged with shoplifting from four West End stores in London may be ordered not to go within a two mile radius of Oxford Circus. (As precise measurement of this is virtually impossible for the average citizen, it is wiser not to tempt fate!) The second condition is intended to prevent the defendant either absconding or, occasionally, from contacting prosecution witnesses. Compliance with both conditions may be very difficult to check but, if a breach does come to the attention of a police officer, the defendant may be re-arrested. In a novel twist on this common condition, it was reported in the press in May 1994 that the Marquis of Blandford had a bail condition that he must not use taxi-cabs unless accompanied by his solicitor; at the time, he was charged with, *inter alia*, using taxis and dishonestly not paying the fares.

3.14 Changing Bail Conditions

If circumstances change, so that the original conditions are no longer appropriate, the defence can apply to the court to alter or remove them. In exceptional situations, the prosecution can apply for existing conditions to be altered (presumably to strengthen them), or for conditions to be attached to an unconditional grant of bail.

Such application is made under BA 1976, s. 3(8), either to the magistrates' court which is dealing with the case or, if the case has been sent to the Crown Court, to a Crown Court judge. Where a defendant has been sent to Crown Court for trial but has not yet been required to surrender to custody at the Crown Court, then the magistrates' court which sent him for trial has concurrent jurisdiction with the Crown Court to hear any application for variation of bail conditions (see *R* v *Lincoln Magistrates' Court, ex parte Mawer* [1995] Crim LR 878). Once the defendant has surrendered to custody at the Crown Court, the magistrates cease to have any jurisdiction over the matter. See also BA 1976, s. 3(8A) — this extends the Crown Court's jurisdiction to cover applications made in serious fraud cases which go to Crown Court on a notice of transfer. (For notices of transfer, see **6.5**.) See *Blackstone's Criminal Practice*, 2000, Appendix 1 and D5.42 for the relevant Crown Court Rules (rr. 19 and 20) and the procedure for Crown Court applications.

It should be noted that if a defendant is released by the police on conditional bail, he or she may apply to a custody officer to vary those conditions (see BA 1976, s. 3A(4)). The custody officer may impose different conditions and may even make them more onerous than before. Counsel is very unlikely to be involved in such an application. However the defendant may choose to apply to the magistrates' court and counsel may then be briefed (see MCA 1980, s. 43B).

3.15 What Happens if the Defendant Disobeys?

3.15.1 THE PENALTY FOR FAILURE TO SURRENDER TO CUSTODY

Under BA 1976, s. 6, it is an offence for a defendant to fail to surrender to custody at the appointed time and place. The crime is usually referred to by the court (and by counsel when in court) as 'absconding'. It is otherwise commonly referred to, particularly by defendants, as 'doing a runner'. It is punishable, following summary conviction or as a contempt of court, by a fine and/or imprisonment. Any securities or sureties will be liable to forfeiture by court order.

The absconder should always be given the chance to explain such absence, and his or her counsel should be invited to address the court, if appropriate (see *R* v *Davis (Seaton Roy)* (1986) 8 Cr App R (S) 64); *R* v *Boyle* [1993] Crim LR 40; *R* v *How* [1993] Crim LR 201). The punishment may be severe if it is thought necessary to deter others. See, e.g., *R* v *Neve* (1986) 8 Cr App R (S) 270, where a defendant (who had been acquitted at a trial) was nevertheless sentenced to six months' imprisonment and ordered to forfeit £10,000 for going to Spain in an attempt to avoid his trial.

The court will usually issue a warrant for the arrest of the accused unless, perhaps, defence counsel is able to offer an explanation for the absence. These are known as *bench warrants*.When the warrant is executed and the accused is brought before the court, the court is very likely to remand the accused in custody; if the accused originally had the right to bail (BA 1976, s. 4), he or she has not got it now (BA 1976, sch. 1). No offence is committed if the accused can show he or she had reasonable cause for failing to surrender to custody as required. See also *Murphy* v *DPP* [1990] 1 WLR 601. Bench warrants may be *backed for bail*. This means that the warrant is executed by taking the defendant to a police station. He or she will then be re-released, upon whatever conditions have been endorsed on the warrant, and will not be produced in court, but will be under a duty to surrender to custody on a date to be notified by the court. It is unusual for magistrates to issue a warrant backed for bail; some *prima facie* good reason will normally need to be put before the court.

It seems that around 5–7% of all defendants who are remanded on bail by magistrates subsequently fail to surrender to custody. The proportion does not vary much whether one looks at indictable offences or summary offences; see **Figure 3.4**.

As well as incurring any penalty under BA 1976, s. 6, for the failure to surrender to custody, the defendant who absconds may find that his or her sentence for the original offence has effectively been increased. Normally, a defendant who pleads guilty to the charge is entitled to a reduced sentence (see **20.3.1** and *R* v *Buffrey* [1993] 14 Cr App R (S) 411). It has been held that a defendant who absconds, is later returned to court and pleads guilty to the original offence, has cancelled out the discount that would otherwise have accrued for the plea of guilty. See *R* v *Byrne* [1997] 1 Cr App R (S) 165.

3.15.2 NON-COMPLIANCE WITH OTHER CONDITIONS

No separate offence is committed in this situation but the accused is at risk of arrest (without warrant) by a police officer who has reasonable grounds to believe that a bail condition has been broken. Indeed, a police officer can arrest a defendant when he or she has reasonable grounds to believe that the defendant is likely to break a bail condition (see BA 1976, s. 7(3)). Once arrested, the accused must be produced in court within 24 hours, when the question of remand on bail or in custody will be considered afresh.

When the defendant is produced in court, a magistrate (*not* a Crown Court judge — see *Re Marshall* (1995) 159 JP 688) has to form an opinion whether the defendant is unlikely to surrender to custody or has broken (or is likely to break) any condition of his bail (BA 1976, s. 7(5)). This hearing is quite informal — usually a police officer will attend the court to state the grounds for his belief that a bail condition either has been or is likely to be broken. This may involve hearsay evidence being tendered to the court. The defendant should be given an opportunity to respond. If the magistrate forms the requisite opinion, then the defendant may be remanded in custody or released on conditional bail (the conditions may be the same as the original ones). See *R* v *Liverpool City Magistrates' Court, ex parte Director of Public Prosecutions* (1992) 95 Cr App R 222.

3.15.3 FORFEITURE OF A SURETY

If a defendant was granted bail subject to providing a surety, then a failure by the defendant to surrender to custody puts the surety in jeopardy of losing the sum which he or she guaranteed by his or her oath to the court.

In the past, forfeiture was likely to occur, usually for the whole sum. The test was that the whole sum would fall to be paid, unless it was fair and just to forfeit a lesser amount or nothing at all. Forfeiture provisions have now been tightened, as a result of CDA 1998, s. 55, which came into effect on 30 September 1998. When a defendant fails to surrender, the court is required to declare any surety to be forfeit *automatically*. It shall then require the surety (if present in court) to explain why he or she should not have to pay the whole sum. The court retains its discretion to demand payment of a lesser sum. If the surety is absent from court, or the court allows him or her time to produce evidence of his or her lack of culpability, it will issue a summons requiring his or her appearance at a later date.

There is a heavy onus on the surety to prove why he or she should not forfeit the full amount. This should be done either by showing a lack of means to meet the forfeiture or by establishing that he or she acted responsibly. The surety has a duty to maintain contact with the defendant and to keep him- or herself informed as to the conditions of bail in order to ensure the defendant's surrender to custody. It has recently been pointed out by the Court of Appeal that any reduction in the amount ordered to be forfeit, following a defendant absconding, 'must be the exception not the rule and be granted only in really deserving cases'. Hoffmann LJ observed that 'in one sense the system has unfairness built into it. It may result in persons entirely innocent having to suffer on account of the wrongdoing of another'. Lack of culpability by a surety is a factor to consider but in *R* v *Maidstone Crown Court, ex parte Lever* [1995] 1 WLR 928, two sureties who were found to be blameless for the absconding nevertheless were ordered to forfeit 85% of their total surety of £59,000.

If the initial enquiry into the surety's means was conducted properly (see **3.13.2**), the surety should have no problem finding the money to pay the forfeit. However, where the enquiry was inadequate, or the surety's means have changed, the sum which the surety is ordered to forfeit should be such as is within his or her or actual means. So, in a case where a surety of £25,000 was forfeited but the surety had originally provided an extremely exaggerated account of his assets, the magistrates' court ordered him to pay the forfeit at £12 per fortnight. The matter was then considered by the Divisional Court who observed that it would be correct in any normal case for the court to think of a sum which the surety could be reasonably expected to pay in full within two or three years (not 80 years as here). The matter was remitted to the magistrates for a rehearing. See *R* v *Bristol Magistrates' Court, ex parte Davies* [1999] Crim LR 504.

Usually, the obligation of a surety will end when the defendant is arraigned on the charges as this is when trial normally commences. At this moment, the defendant is understood to have surrendered to the custody of the court and the surety has done all that the court required of him or her. This is subject to exceptions, though, and a surety should remain well-informed as to the exact status of the defendant and the view of the court as to whether the surety's obligation is at an end or continues. The penalty for being ill-informed is seen in *R* v *Central Criminal Court, ex parte Guney* [1994] 1 WLR 438, where a surety for Asil Nadir was ordered to forfeit £650,000 following Mr Nadir's departure to Northern Cyprus. It could have been worse, as originally he stood surety for £1 million; in fact, it got even better for Mr Guney, as the Court of Appeal later quashed the forfeiture completely (see [1995] 1 WLR 376 and [1996] AC 616).

See also MCA 1980, s. 120; *Archbold,* 2000 edn, para. 3–143/185; *Blackstone's Criminal Practice,* 2000, D5.48.

3.15.4 PROCEDURE FOR BAIL ACT 1976, s. 6

BA 1976, s. 6(1), creates a single offence — failure to surrender to custody. The following distinctions may be made.

Police bail: must be dealt with (by magistrates) as a summary offence in such circumstances. It is irrelevant whether the duty to surrender is to a police station or magistrates' court. The prosecution must either charge the defendant or lay an information. A six-month time limit (MCA 1980, s. 127) applies. There is a maximum penalty of three months' imprisonment and/or a £5,000 fine for absconding while on police bail.

Magistrates' bail: if bail was granted by the magistrates and the duty is to surrender to the *magistrates' court,* it is not necessary or desirable to lay an information. There is no time limit. Magistrates should initiate proceedings of their own motion *but* only on the express invitation of the prosecutor (compare *France* v *Dewsbury Magistrates' Court,* below).

It seems that the magistrates are then dealing with the offence as if it were a contempt of court. The result is that the maximum punishment is 12 months' imprisonment and/or an unlimited fine under s. 6(7), although in practice this is restricted by PCC(S)A 2000, s. 78, i.e. to six months' imprisonment rather than 12 months. It seems unnecessary to conclude whether magistrates have the power to treat a failure to surrender to custody at the magistrates' court as a contempt of court or must regard it as a summary offence: *Schiavo* v *Anderton* [1987] QB 20 and the *Practice Direction (Bail: Failure to Surrender)* [1987] 1 WLR 79 favour contempt; *R* v *Harbax Singh* [1979] QB 319 and BA 1976, s. 6(7) favour a summary offence (according to Parker LJ in *Murphy* v *DPP* [1990] 1 WLR 601). The matter was expressly left by the Court of Appeal in *Murphy* for decision in a more relevant case.

Crown Court bail: when bailed to attend Crown Court either by magistrates or by the Crown Court itself. Failure here will usually be dealt with as if it were a contempt of court. No time limit applies. The Crown Court's powers are to imprison for up to 12 months and/or an unlimited fine. BA 1976, s. 6(5), allows an offence of absconding to be punishable as if it were a contempt of court but this simply indicates a method of dealing with the matter; it does not convert an offence under BA 1976, s. 6, into an actual contempt of court. See *R* v *Lubega, The Times,* 10 February 1999.

Note: In *France* v *Dewsbury Magistrates' Court* [1988] Crim LR 295 the Divisional Court warned justices against tying the hands of the prosecution over an absconding charge — magistrates should not fetter the Crown Prosecution Service by expressing a view (of leniency) at an interim hearing in the case. It is for the accused to show that he or she had reasonable cause for not surrendering (BA 1976, s. 6(3)). The standard of proof is on a balance of probabilities.

3.16 Renewing an Application for Bail

(or 'If at first you don't succeed, try again — but only once!')

See BA 1976, sch. 1, part IIA:

> 1. *If the court decides not to grant the defendant bail, it is the court's duty to consider, at each subsequent hearing while the defendant is a person to whom s. 4 above applies and remains in custody, whether he ought to be granted bail.*
> 2. *At the first hearing after that at which the court decided not to grant the defendant bail, he may support an application for bail with any argument as to fact or law that he desires (whether or not advanced previously).*
> 3. *At subsequent hearings the court need not hear arguments as to fact or law which it has heard previously.*

3.16.1 OBLIGATION TO CONSIDER BAIL

According to BA 1976, sch. 1, part IIA (inserted by CJA 1988, s. 154), at every hearing of a case (when the defendant is in custody) the magistrates' court is obliged to consider whether he or she should be released on bail. The defence is allowed to make up to two applications for bail at which the same arguments may be used. If the accused is still in custody after this, the court may consider the matter of bail no longer open to argument from the defence.

Although the court is under a duty (CJA 1988, s. 154) to consider bail at subsequent hearings in the case, these will be formalities. The defence may only reopen the issue of bail by raising fresh circumstances or arguments. Section 154 represents the statutory embodiment of a common law rule which was first reported in *R* v *Nottingham Justices, ex parte Davies* [1981] QB 38.

There have been several cases involving decisions as to what constitutes a 'change in circumstances'. It seems to be a question of fact in each case, although the Queen's Bench Divisional Court has stated that the change need not be major. *R* v *Blyth Juvenile Court, ex parte G* [1991] Crim LR 693 offers an illustration. Where there has been no application for bail by a defendant on the first appearance of a case at court and he has been remanded in custody, it seems that he has a right to apply for bail at a later hearing of the case (see *R* v *Dover and East Kent Justices, ex parte Dean* [1992] Crim LR 33).

It seems possible that, with the advent of the HRA 1998 and the need to comply with decisions already made under the ECHR, a slight amendment to English law may be needed. It has usually been the position that simple effluxion of time does not give rise to a change in circumstances. However, in *Neumeister* v *Austria (No. 1)* (1979–80) 1 EHRR 91, the European Court declared that a person should be released at the point when it is no longer reasonable to continue his or her detention. So, as time passes, the prisoner who is held in custody on remand should be able to seek review by the court of the decision to detain.

The matter has been considered by the Law Commission of England and Wales (in its Consultation Paper No. 157, 1999). The Law Commission felt that it was adequate that bail should be reconsidered by magistrates at least every 28 days (see **3.5.2**) but was concerned that the possibility of a renewed application for bail might be denied by operation of sch. 1, Part IIA. It pointed out that para. 3 only says the court '*need not* hear arguments as to fact or law which it has heard previously' and thus has a discretion to hear such arguments. However, in practice courts seem to be reluctant to do so and also rarely accept that there has been a change in circumstances. The Law Commission noted reports asserting that if the accused got a job, found sureties or a fixed address, these were seldom sufficient to show a change in circumstances. The Law Commission suggest that sch. 1, Part IIA, can be interpreted and applied consistently with the ECHR, Article 5(4), but that guidance should be given to courts to the effect that 'the lapse of 28 days since the last fully-argued bail application should itself be treated as an argument which the court has not previously heard'.

3.16.2 THE MAGISTRATES' CERTIFICATE

Under BA 1976, s. 5(6A), if magistrates withhold bail after hearing a fully argued application for bail, they must issue a certificate stating that they heard full argument. After two unsuccessful bail applications in a case, if the magistrates allow the defendant a third application (which is unsuccessful), they should issue a certificate indicating the change in circumstances or new consideration that persuaded them to hear that third application. See BA 1976, s. 5(6A) and (6B); also BA 1976, sch. 1, part IIA (inserted by CJA 1988, s. 154); Form 151A, *Stone's Justices' Manual*, vol. 3.

3.17 Appealing Against a Refusal to Release a Defendant on Bail

3.17.1 APPLY TO A CROWN COURT JUDGE

A defendant can apply to a Crown Court judge for bail in the following situations (contained in the Supreme Court Act 1981, s. 81, as amended by CJA 1982).

(a) Where a magistrates' court has committed the defendant to the Crown Court in custody (either for trial or sentence).

(b) Where the case is proceeding in the magistrates' court but magistrates have heard a fully argued application for bail and refused bail (proved by producing a BA 1976, s. 5(6A) certificate — see **3.16.2** and **3.8.3** above).

(c) Where the defendant has been convicted by magistrates, given a custodial sentence, and refused bail pending an appeal to the Crown Court.

The appeal is heard either by the Crown Court to which the case has been committed or by the nearest Crown Court dealing with Class 4 (low-grade) crime. The appeal is usually heard by a judge sitting 'in chambers' — this means that counsel need not wear a wig and gown, even though the appeal often takes place in a court room. Unless the appeal is made by the prosecution (rare), the accused will not be present at the appeal unless the Crown Court grants permission for this (also rare).

3.17.2 APPLY TO A HIGH COURT JUDGE

Under RSC, O. 79, r. 9, a High Court judge may grant bail in the following situations:

(a) Where a magistrates' court has refused to grant bail.

(b) Where a defendant who is in custody applies to the Divisional Court (QBD) for *certiorari* to quash a decision of the magistrates.

(c) Where a defendant in custody appeals by way of case stated to the High Court against a decision of the Crown Court (or applies for *certiorari* to quash a Crown Court decision).

(d) Where bail has been granted and variations in the conditions are proposed.

The application is made by summons, supported by an affidavit. The summons is served on one's opponent at least 24 hours before the hearing. The summons will be heard by a High Court judge, sitting in chambers. In the Royal Courts of Justice, the judge in chambers (as he is known) sits in Room 92. One should also note the possibility of seeking the issue of a writ of *habeas corpus* under RSC, O. 54. This application is made to the Divisonal Court (QBD). See also SCA 1981, s. 81. An illustration of the application of RSC O. 79, r. 9, may be found in *R* v *Croydon Crown Court, ex parte Cox* [1997] 1 Cr App R 20. On application by the prosecution, a Circuit Judge had made it a condition of bail that the defendant submit to examination for a medical report. Subsequently, another Circuit Judge refused the defendant's application to remove the condition. The Queen's Bench Divisional Court declared that the appropriate means of challenging the condition was not to seek judicial review, but was to apply to the High Court judge in chambers under O. 79, r. 9.

3.17.3 DEFENDANT'S CHOICE

A defendant may apply to either a Crown Court judge or a High Court judge, assuming they both have jurisdiction to hear the application. The defendant may try first one, and, if unsuccessful, the other. In such circumstances the second judge should be told of the earlier, unsuccessful attempt.

What a defendant should *not* do is apply for judicial review under RSC, O. 53. This method of challenging bail decisions was criticised by the Queen's Bench Divisional Court in *R* v *Blyth Juvenile Court, ex parte G* [1991] Crim LR 693. The case involved a decision by magistrates not to hear an application for bail on the grounds that the defendant could not demonstrate a change in circumstances. She was advised that she could demonstrate this and sought to challenge the decision by judicial review. The Divisional Court allowed the application (and directed the justices to hear the application for bail) but stated that the appropriate means to challenge an improper refusal to grant bail was through an application to the judge in chambers under RSC, O. 79, r. 9. It is not thought that this judgment affects the choice between High Court or Crown Court judge, where it is available. See also *R* v *Croydon Crown Court, ex parte Cox* [1997] 1 Cr App R 20.

3.17.4 APPEALS BY THE CROWN PROSECUTION SERVICE

A limited right of appeal *against* the grant of bail has been conferred on the prosecution by the Bail (Amendment) Act 1993. It is confined to cases where the magistrates grant bail to a person who has been charged with (or convicted of) either:

(a) an offence punishable with imprisonment for five or more years; or

(b) an offence of taking a conveyance without authority; or

(c) an offence of aggravated vehicle taking.

If such a person was granted bail despite objections from the prosecution, and the prosecution is being conducted by the Crown Prosecution Service, an appeal may be made. If the Crown Prosecution Service decides to appeal, it must say so (give oral notice of appeal) before the defendant is released from custody. Written notice of appeal must follow, within two hours, and be served on the court and the defendant. The defendant will be kept in custody until the appeal is determined by the Crown Court — the appeal must be heard within 48 hours (excluding bank holidays and weekends). The Crown Court judge will decide the application on its merits and may remand the defendant in custody or release him or her on bail. The judge may attach conditions to a grant of bail if it is thought appropriate to do so.

The prosecution now has a limited ability to ask for 'reconsideration' of a decision to release a defendant on bail. The BA 1976, s. 5B, enables a prosecutor to apply to a magistrates' court to reconsider such a decision, whether it was originally taken by the court or by a custody officer. Having reconsidered, the magistrates may attach conditions to unconditional bail, vary the current conditions, or withhold bail (BA 1976, s. 5B(1)) or, presumably, preserve the status quo. Reconsiderations may only be sought where the defendant is on bail for an offence which must or may be tried on indictment; the application must be based upon information which was not available to the magistrates (or custody officer) when the original decision was taken.

Useful article: David Tucker, 'The Prosecutor on the Starting Block: The Mechanics of the Bail (Amendment) Act 1993' [1998] Crim LR 728.

3.18 Legal Aid for Bail Applications

3.18.1 APPLICATIONS IN THE MAGISTRATES' COURT

A defendant who has legal aid in the magistrates' court will find that this covers all applications for bail to magistrates and to the Crown Court on appeal. Even if a defendant is not in receipt of legal aid for a case in the magistrates' court, he or she must be given legal aid to apply for bail in the following situation: if the defendant has been remanded in custody by the court on an earlier occasion; was not legally represented then; is in danger of being remanded in custody again (or committed to the Crown Court in custody) now; and wishes to be legally represented; then (subject to his or her financial resources), the defendant must be granted legal aid for representation on the question of bail. See Legal Aid Act 1988, s. 21(3)(c).

3.18.2 CASES IN THE CROWN COURT AND APPEALS TO THE HIGH COURT

Once a case has been committed to the Crown Court (or has gone there on appeal against conviction/sentence), if the accused is legally aided then bail applications are covered by his or her legal aid order. No criminal legal aid is available for appeals to a High Court judge. If a defendant cannot afford to appeal to a High Court judge on his or her own resources, he or she can ask that the Official Solicitor be appointed to represent him or her for the appeal. If this is done, the Official Solicitor prepares the papers but does not attend the hearing, so this is not a popular method of appeal with defendants, and is rarely successful. It appears to be the case that a defendant may be granted legal aid to be represented on an application to the High Court, on an *ad hoc* basis, by applying for emergency legal aid in **civil** proceedings.

3.19 Juvenile Bail

Present government policy is that juveniles should spend as little time as possible awaiting final disposal of their cases. Overall time limits for specified stages of preliminary proceedings are being introduced for all cases but they will be 'tougher' for juvenile cases, and even more strict in cases involving persistent young offenders (see Prosecution of Offences Act 1985, ss. 22 and 22A and **3.1** above).

While awaiting disposal of their cases, most juveniles will be on bail. There is concern that, in this period, juveniles may commit further offences. Steps are being taken to discourage such re-offending or 'spree' activity. In particular, the government is encouraging the involvement of the voluntary sector in bail support schemes, e.g. the 'Youth Bail Support Scheme' in Manchester, run by Manchester Children's Society. Youngsters on the Manchester scheme have an individual programme of activities; this is designed to create constructive leisure time, to institute weekly meetings with volunteers, and to provide accompaniment on court appearances. The scheme can also provide support in tackling difficulties at home, at school or in the workplace.

Fast-track procedures are being introduced nationally, to cope with persistent young offenders. By this, the Home Office means young offenders who have been dealt with by a court on three or more occasions and who re-offend within three years of their previous court appearance (see e.g. Home Office Research Findings, No. 74, 1998). A variety of reasons exist for the fast-track procedures which were devised by different courts around the country but the government has set a target that all courts should aim to complete at least 50 per cent of their persistent young offender cases within 71 days. Fast-track procedures may also be used for other categories of offender, such as those engaged on 'spree' offending. The procedures work by, for example, being tough on adjournments. There will be resistance to granting an adjournment and the first hearing at court should deal with substantive business. Pre-sentence reports may be required within 15 working days; courts may keep copies of these reports and simply have them updated orally if necessary. In addition to these steps, the government has set guidelines for the length of time which each stage in the youth court should take, in a case involving a persistent young offender. So, no more than two days from arrest to charge; seven days from charge to first appearance in court. From first appearance in a youth court to commencement of a trial there, no more than 28 days. Thereafter, no more than 14 days to reach the stage of verdict and sentence.

The provisions of BA 1976 apply to juveniles in basically the same manner as they do to adult defendants. That is, juveniles may be remanded on bail or into custody, when proceedings in court are adjourned. If a young person is not released on bail, he or she may be remanded to local authority accommodation. Such accommodation is not secure, however, and the only ways for a juvenile to be placed in secure accommodation are:

(a) if the local authority applies to the court for an order to hold the juvenile in secure accommodation; or

(b) directly, on order of the court, if the juvenile is male and aged 15 or 16, he may be detained in Prison Service accommodation.

There are provisions in the CJA 1991 and CJPOA 1994 which allow courts to remand juveniles into secure local authority accommodation but they have not been brought into force. In any event, there is a shortage of such secure accommodation. The previous government began a building programme to supply 170 extra places in local authority secure accommodation; the programme is due for completion in 1998. It is not thought that these places will be sufficient to cope with the likely demand for places to hold remand prisoners aged 12–16.

Notwithstanding the anticipated shortfall, the present government has enabled courts to remand juveniles direct to secure local authority accommodation. See CDA 1998, ss. 97–98, which came into effect on 1 June 1999. These provisions apply to all children aged 12–14 and girls aged 15 or 16. Boys aged 15 or 16 will continue to be remanded to Prison Service accommodation (either a remand centre or a prison) unless they are considered to be 'vulnerable'. A youth is vulnerable if the court forms the opinion that a remand to Prison Service accommodation would be undesirable due to his 'physical or emotional immaturity or a propensity of his to harm himself' (see CYPA 1969, s. 23(5A)).

3.20 Final Note

Any question of bail being granted which is not governed by s. 4 of BA 1976 or some other statutory provision is at the discretion of the court.

FOUR

MODE OF TRIAL

4.1 Classification of Offences

All offences fall into one of the following categories:

(a) Summary offences, i.e. those which must be tried in the magistrates' court.

(b) Offences triable only on indictment, i.e. those which must be tried in the Crown Court.

(c) Offences which are triable either way, i.e. those which may be tried in either the magistrates' court or the Crown Court.

4.1.1 SUMMARY OFFENCES

Summary trial, i.e. trial by magistrates, is a creature of statute, and all summary offences, similarly, are created by statute. The statute usually does this by providing a maximum penalty for summary conviction, with no alternative penalty for conviction on indictment. A huge number of offences are summary. See **Figure 4.1** for examples.

4.1.2 OFFENCES TRIABLE ONLY ON INDICTMENT

All common law offences are triable only on indictment, i.e. by a judge and jury in the Crown Court, such as murder and manslaughter. Other offences in this category are created by statute which provides for a maximum penalty for conviction on indictment, with no alternative penalty on summary conviction. See **Figure 4.1** for examples.

4.1.3 OFFENCES WHICH ARE TRIABLE EITHER WAY

Offences which are triable either way are technically indictable but may be tried in the magistrates' court if both the magistrates and the defendant agree. See **4.2** below for details. Offences are shown to be triable either way by either:

(a) the statute which created them providing for alternative penalties on summary conviction or conviction on indictment; or

(b) re-classification by statute, in particular the MCA 1980, s. 17, which downgrades to triable either way many offences which were formerly triable only on indictment: see the list in sch. 1 to the Act.

4.2 Procedure for Determining the Mode of Trial

Where the offence is triable either way, and may be tried in *either* the magistrates' court or the Crown Court, it must first be determined which court should try the case.

The procedure is governed by the MCA 1980, as amended by the CPIA 1996. The amendments were intended to reduce the workload of the Crown Court, by ensuring that cases in which the defendant intends to plead guilty are dealt with summarily unless the case is serious. To achieve this, the defendant is asked, before a mode of trial decision is made, to indicate his or her plea.

Figure 4.1 Classification of Offences

Type of Offence	Triable only on Indictment	Triable Either Way	Triable only Summarily
1. Offences against the person	Murder Manslaughter Attempt to procure an abortion Causing grievous bodily harm with intent	Inflicting grievous bodily harm Unlawful wounding Assault occasioning actual bodily harm Assault with intent to resist arrest	Common assault Assault on a police constable in the execution of his duty
2. Sexual offences	Rape: Intercourse with a girl under 13 Buggery Incest	Unlawful sexual intercourse with a girl under 16 Indecent assault Living on the earnings of a prostitute	Soliciting
3. Theft Act offences	Robbery Aggravated burglary Blackmail Assault with intent to rob Burglary comprising commision of, or intention to commit, an offence only triable on indictment Burglary of a dwelling with threats to occupants	All Theft Act offences not being in the other two categories	Taking a motor vehicle without consent Taking a pedal cycle without consent
4. Criminal damage	Damage or arson with intent to endanger life	Damage where the value involved is over £5,000	Damage where the value involved is £5,000 or less
5. Road traffic	Causing death by dangerous driving	Dangerous driving	Most other traffic offences, e.g.: Speeding Failing to report an accident Driving while disqualified Driving without insurance Drunk in charge of a motor vehicle Failing to stop at a red traffic light Aggravated TWOC where only damage is caused and of value less than £5,000
6. Miscellaneous	Perjury Attempt to pervert the course of justice Possessing a firearm with intent to endanger life Using a firearm to resist arrest Carrying a firearm to commit an indictable offence Collecting, communicating, etc. information intended to be useful to an enemy Riot	Making false statements on oath not being in judical proceedings Carrying a loaded firearm in a public place Shortening a shot gun Having an offensive weapon in a public place Using, communicating, etc. information entrusted in confidence to a person holding office under the Crown Violent disorder Affray Stirring up racial hatred All offences under the Forgery & Counterfeiting Act 1981 Offences under the Misuse of Drugs Act 1971	Interference with vehicles Being drunk and disorderly Obstructing police Using threatening words or behaviour Dropping litter Failure to pay TV licence All offences under the Factories Act 1961

4.2.1 ABSENCE OF THE DEFENDANT

MCA 1980, s. 17A(2) provides that the defendant must be present during the proceedings in which he or she is asked to indicate his or her plea. There are two exceptions to this:

(a) Section 17B provides for the proceedings to continue in the defendant's absence due to his or her unruly behaviour. In order for the proceedings to continue in the defendant's absence, the following conditions must be satisfied:

  (i) the defendant is legally represented; and

  (ii) the court considers that by reason of the defendant's disorderly conduct before the court it is not practicable for proceedings under s. 17A above to be conducted in his or her presence; and

  (iii) the court considers that it should proceed in the absence of the defendant.

  In these circumstances, the procedure contained in s. 17A and described in **4.2.1** is followed, except that all the indications as to plea are provided by the defendant's legal representative on the defendant's behalf, rather than by the defendant.

(b) Where the defendant is legally represented and consents to the case continuing in his or her absence (such consent being indicated by the representative), and the court is satisfied that there is a good reason (such as illness) for that absence (MCA 1980, s. 23(1)(a) and (b)).

4.2.2 THE STANDARD PROCEDURE

MCA 1980, s. 17A, applies where a defendant who has attained the age of 18 is charged with a triable either-way offence whether or not he or she is legally represented. The defendant must be present in court for this stage of the proceedings, unless one of the exceptions set out in **4.2.1** above applies.

The procedure may be followed by a lay justice sitting alone, under MCA 1980, s. 18(5), though it is more usual to have two or more lay justices.

The procedure is as follows:

(a) The charge is written down, if it has not been written down already, and read to the defendant.

(b) The court explains to the defendant in ordinary language that he or she may indicate whether he or she would plead guilty should the case proceed to trial. The court should further explain to the defendant that if he or she indicates a plea of guilty, the court will:

  (i) proceed as if the proceedings had constituted a summary trial from the outset;

  (ii) proceed as if the defendant had in fact pleaded guilty to the charge;

  (iii) warn the defendant of the possibility of a committal for sentence under PCC(S)A 2000, s. 3, should the court consider their powers to be inadequate.

  The court will then ask the defendant whether, if the case were to proceed to trial, he or she would plead guilty or not guilty.

  The form of words set out below are included in Home Office Circular 45/1997 for magistrates to use when inviting the defendant to indicate a plea:

  This offence(s) may be tried either by this court or by the Crown Court before a judge and jury.

Whether or not this court can deal with your case today will depend upon your answers to the questions which I am going to put to you. Do you understand?

You will shortly be asked to tell the court whether you intend to plead guilty or not guilty to (certain of) the offence(s) with which you are charged. Do you understand?

If you tell us that you intend to plead guilty, you will be convicted of the offence. We may then be able to deal with (part of) your case at this hearing. The prosecutor will tell us about the facts of the case, you (your representative) will have the opportunity to respond (on your behalf), and we shall then go on to consider how to sentence you. Do you understand?

We may be able to sentence you today, or we may need to adjourn the proceedings until a later date for the preparation of a pre-sentence report by the Probation Service. If we believe that you deserve a greater sentence than we have the power to give you in this court, we may decide to send you to the Crown Court, either on bail or in custody, and you will be sentenced by that court which has greater sentencing powers. Do you understand?

[*In cases where* [*s. 4 of the Powers of Criminal Courts (Sentencing) Act 2000*] [power to commit adult offenders for trial in the Crown Court where he or she has already been committed or will be committed for trial on a related either-way offence(s)] *applies:*

If you indicate a guilty plea for this/these offence(s), even if we believe that our own sentencing powers are great enough to deal with you here, we may still send you to the Crown Court to be sentenced for this/these offence(s) because you have also been charged with a related offence(s) [for which you have already been committed for trial in that court] [for which you will be committed for trial to that court]. Do you understand?]

If on the other hand, you tell us that you intend to plead not guilty, or if you do not tell us what you intend to do, we shall go on to consider whether you should be tried by this court or by the Crown Court on some future date. If we decide that it would be appropriate to deal with your case in this court, we shall ask whether you are content for us to do so or whether you wish your case to be tried in the Crown Court.

Before I ask you how you intend to plead, do you understand everything I have said or is there any part of what I have said which you would like me to repeat or explain?

(c) The defendant indicates a plea of guilty, a plea of not guilty or fails to indicate a plea:

  (i) *Indication of a plea of guilty*: it should be noted that this is not the plea itself, but an indication of what the plea would be in the event of a trial. However, by virtue of s. 17A(6), the court proceeds as if the proceedings had constituted a summary trial from the beginning, and treats the indication of plea as if it were, in fact, a plea of guilty. No further pleas are taken. The court proceeds on to the sentencing stage.

  (ii) *Indication of a plea of not guilty*: where the defendant indicates that he or she will plead not guilty, the court proceeds to determine the mode of trial, set out in (d) to (h) below.

  (iii) *No indication of plea*: where the defendant fails to indicate a plea, he or she is taken to have indicated a plea of not guilty (MCA 1980, as amended by CPIA 1996).

(d) The prosecution and defence (in that order) have the opportunity of making representations to the court as to the more appropriate forum. The preference of the prosecution is not conclusive unless the prosecution is being carried on by the Attorney General, Solicitor General or Director of Public Prosecutions. If one of these applies for trial on indictment, the court must comply.

(e) The court decides which mode of trial is suitable, taking into account:

(i) the nature of the case;

(ii) whether the circumstances make the case one of a serious character;

(iii) whether the penalties available in the magistrates' court are likely to be adequate;

(iv) any other circumstances which indicate that one mode of trial could be more suitable than the other;

(v) any representations made by the prosecution or defence.

Where magistrates consider their sentencing powers inadequate, they should take this into account at this stage and commit for trial, rather than for sentencing at a later stage (*R* v *Manchester Magistrates' Court, ex parte Kaymanesh* (1994) 158 JP 401, DC).

Guidance has been given to magistrates in making an appropriate mode of trial decision in the National Mode of Trial Guidelines. These were first produced in October 1990 and revised and updated in March 1995 by the Secretariat of the Criminal Justice Consultative Council.

The guidelines are intended to assist magistrates in making an appropriate mode of trial decision, and are not intended as directions. They begin by making a number of general observations about mode of trial, and then set out features which would render trial on indictment appropriate for the following offences: burglary, criminal damage, dangerous driving, drugs offences, fraud, handling, indecent assault, Public Order Act offences, social security frauds, theft, unlawful sexual intercourse, violence (including domestic violence) and violence to and neglect of children. See **4.7** below for details of the general observations and features of some offences by way of example.

(f) If the court decides on summary trial, the court must explain to the defendant in ordinary language that:

(i) summary trial is more appropriate, but that the final choice belongs to the defendant, who can consent to summary trial, or elect trial on indictment; and

(ii) if he or she is tried summarily, he or she may still be committed to the Crown Court for sentence under MCA 1980, s. 38. See **5.3**.

(g) The defendant is then asked if he or she consents to summary trial, or wishes to be tried by jury. The choice is only that of the defendant, who should respond personally. He or she may either:

(i) consent to summary trial. If he or she consents, the court will proceed to trial, though an adjournment may be necessary, for example, if there is insufficient court time; or

(ii) elect trial on indictment, in which case the court will commence committal proceedings. Again, an adjournment may be necessary.

(h) If, as an alternative to (e) above, the court decides that *the case is more suitable for trial on indictment*, nothing is explained to, or asked of, the defendant as in (e) and (f) above. The court will simply tell the defendant of its decision. His or her consent is not required. The court will commence committal proceedings, after an adjournment if necessary,

Note: The fact that the prosecution prefers an additional charge in order to secure a trial on indictment is not an abuse of process as long as such a course is appropriate on the facts (*R* v *Redbridge Justices, ex parte Whitehouse* (1992) 94 Cr App R 332); but the facts may be such as to make it an abuse of process: *R* v *Brooks* [1985] Crim LR 385 and *R* v *Horseferry Road Magistrates' Court, ex parte DPP*, 1996, unreported.

Similarly, should the defendant elect trial on indictment, there is nothing to prevent the prosecution adding a further charge which is triable only summarily, and offering no evidence on the triable either way charge (*R* v *Canterbury and St Augustine Justices, ex parte Klisiak* [1982] QB 398; and see *R* v *Barking Magistrates, ex parte DPP* [1993] COD 108). The CPS must however be careful to act within the Code for Crown Prosecution (see para. 7.3 of the Code).

Under provisions under consideration at the time of writing, the right of the defendant to elect trial on indictment will be abolished, subject to safeguards to ensure that he or she is not prejudiced. Magistrates will be required to consider the defendant's representations, the gravity of the offence and the possible effect of a conviction on the defendant's livelihood and reputation. In addition, the defendant will have a right of appeal.

4.2.3 FAILURE TO COMPLY WITH THE PROCEDURE

The procedure outlined in **4.2.2** is obligatory. Any deviation from it is likely to render the whole proceedings null and void. The defendant then has the option of applying for judicial review to quash any eventual conviction. For example, in *R* v *Kent Justices, ex parte Machin* [1952] 2 QB 355, the magistrates failed to tell the defendant of the possibility of a committal for sentence, and the conviction and subsequent committal were quashed.

It is open to the prosecution to seek judicial review of the magistrates' decision, although such proceedings are rare, and are unlikely to be successful. However, for a case where the Divisional Court did overrule the magistrates, see *R* v *Northampton Magistrates' Court, ex parte CCE* [1994] Crim LR 598.

4.2.4 CHANGING THE MODE OF TRIAL

Either the defendant or the magistrates may alter their decision as to the mode of trial in the following circumstances:

4.2.4.1 The defendant

The defendant may change his or her election from summary trial to trial on indictment, or vice versa, if the magistrates consent. The typical situation is that the defendant has elected summary trial without taking proper advice and then sought legal representation for the purposes of trial or sentence. In these circumstances the magistrates are likely to allow the change, but it is a matter within their discretion. The test is whether the defendant understood the nature and significance of the choice which he or she was being asked to make (*R* v *Birmingham Justices, ex parte Hodgson* [1985] QB 1131).

According to *R* v *Bourne Justices, ex parte Cope, The Times*, 12 November 1988, the essential issue is whether the defendant realised that by his or her election he or she was depriving himself or herself of the right to a jury. The fact that the prosecution witnesses were present and ready to give evidence, and that it would not be desirable to delay the case further was not relevant to the defendant's understanding. However, once it was established that he or she did understand the decision he or she was being asked to make, these matters were ones which the justices could take into account in exercising their discretion to allow a change of election.

If the magistrates allow a change of election, they should also allow a change of plea, if one has been given, as the plea is a major influence on where the defendant should be tried (*R* v *Birmingham Justices, ex parte Hodgson* [1985] QB 1131).

The principles outlined above pre-date the CPIA 1996, but do not appear to be affected by the passing of that Act.

4.2.4.2 The magistrates

The magistrates may themselves change their decision from summary trial and vice versa:

(a) *From summary trial to trial on indictment.* Under MCA 1980, s. 25(2), the magistrates may make the change at any stage before the close of the prosecution case. Thus they will have the opportunity of examining the prosecution evidence and, if it appears that the case is more serious than they first thought, may proceed with a view to committal for trial. If the defendant elects summary trial and pleads guilty, then the court cannot change from summary trial because there has been no trial as such, and no prosecution evidence within the meaning of s. 25(2) (*Re Gillard* [1986] AC 442). On a similar point see *R* v *Telford Justices, ex parte Darlington* (1988) 87 Cr App R 194 and *R* v *Birmingham Stipendiary Magistrates, ex parte Webb* (1992) 95 Cr App R 75.

The power of the magistrate does not arise under s. 25(2) until he has 'begun to try the information summarily'. These words should be given a narrow interpretation (*R* v *Birmingham Stipendiary Magistrates, ex parte Webb* (1992) 95 Cr App R 75). The entering of a not guilty plea initiates the trial process, but is not sufficient of itself to begin a trial within the meaning of s. 25(2) so as to permit the magistrates to redetermine the mode of trial. However, the trial process not only begins with the giving of evidence, but there are a number of other circumstances where the court could begin a trial, for example where the court makes a preliminary ruling on a point of law. See generally *R* v *Horseferry Road Magistrates' Court ex parte, K, The Times*, 22 February 1996.

Where the magistrates decide to change from summary trial to committal proceedings, they must adjourn (MCA 1980, s. 25(2), as amended by CPIA 1996, sch. 1, para. 5). An adjournment is necessary because much of the evidence at summary trial is oral, and committal proceedings are in written form only. The adjournment therefore provides the prosecution with the opportunity to put all its evidence into the proper form.

(b) *From trial on indictment to summary trial.* Under MCA 1980, s. 25(3) magistrates may change from committal proceedings to summary trial after the court has begun to enquire into the information as examining justices. See *R* v *Liverpool Justices, ex parte CPS* [1990] Cr App R 261 for a discussion of the meaning of '*begun to enquire as examining justices*'. In making the change:

(i) both prosecution and defendant must be asked if they have any representations to make; and

(ii) the possibility of a committal for sentence must be explained to the defendant; and

(iii) the defendant must consent.

If the magistrates decide to change, and the prosecution wish to rely on the evidence given at committal, an adjournment is again necessary. The evidence at committal will be in written form and the prosecution will need to call the maker of the statement, unless the evidence is admissible in written form by virtue of some other enactment, such as CJA 1988, ss. 23 and 24.

Further reading: Paul Tain, 'Pleas before venue' (1998) 142(7) SJ 156.

4.3 Criminal Damage

Under MCA 1980, s. 22, where the defendant is charged with criminal damage (other than where the damage was caused by fire) the magistrates must proceed as if the offence were summary only, when the value of the damage is less than £5,000. The court is only proceeding *as if* the offence is summary, but it is not summary for all purposes (*R* v *Considine* (1980) 70 Cr App R 239).

4.3.1 SPECIAL PROCEDURE IN CRIMINAL DAMAGE CASES

Under s. 22, before embarking on the normal procedure for determining the mode of trial as set out in **4.2** above, the procedure set out below must be followed:

(a) The court shall, having regard to any representations made by the prosecution or defence, consider the value of the thing involved. There is no appeal on the basis that the value was mistaken (s. 22(8)).

(b) If the value is:

   (i) £5,000 or less, the court proceeds to summary trial. The defendant has no right to trial on indictment, nor may he or she be committed for sentence under PCC(S)A 2000, s. 3. The maximum penalty is three months' imprisonment or a £2,500 fine;

   (ii) more than £5,000, the offence is triable either way, and the court follows the procedure to determine the mode of trial set out in **4.2** above. If the offence is tried summarily the maximum penalty is six months' imprisonment and a £5,000 fine;

   (iii) uncertain, the court will ask the defendant if he or she consents to summary trial, after the lower penalty and absence of any power to commit for sentence have been explained. If consent is given then the court proceeds to summary trial. If not, the court will follow the procedure for determining the mode of trial set out in **4.2** above. See s. 22(4)–(6).

4.3.2 A SERIES OF OFFENCES

If the defendant is charged with two or more offences which appear to the court to be a series of offences of the same or a similar character, then the court has regard to the aggregate value in determining the mode of trial. Thus, if the value of all items damaged totals £5,000 or less, then the magistrates proceed as if the offences are all summary, regardless of the number of offences. See s. 22(11), inserted by CJA 1988, s. 38. For an example of the operation of s. 22(11) see *R* v *Braden* (1988) 87 Cr App R 289.

You are referred to Home Office Research Study No. 125, entitled *Magistrates' Courts or the Crown Court? Mode of Trial Decisions and Sentencing*, London: HMSO, 1992.

4.4 Linked Summary and Indictable Offences

The CJA 1988, ss. 40 and 41, introduced two exceptions to the otherwise inflexible rule that summary offences are only triable summarily. The two sections are similar, but contain important distinctions, and should be analysed with care.

Note: If the defendant is dealt with by the Crown Court under either section, the powers of the Crown Court with regard to sentence are limited to those of the magistrates.

4.4.1 TRIAL OF A SUMMARY OFFENCE ON INDICTMENT: s. 40

If the defendant has been committed for trial in respect of an indictable offence, then the prosecution may include in the indictment a count for a summary offence if:

(a) the summary offence is common assault, taking a motor vehicle without consent, driving whilst disqualified, criminal damage within MCA 1980, s. 22, assaulting a prison custody officer or secure training officer, or is punishable by imprisonment or disqualification and is specified by the Home Secretary as being suitable for inclusion; and

(b) the summary offence is either founded on the same facts as the indictable offence or is, or forms part of, a series of offences of the same or similar character; and

(c) the evidence before the committing court discloses a summary offence.

The magistrates simply commit for trial on the indictable offence. The initiative for including the summary offence must come from the prosecution. Once the summary offence is included in the indictment, then, if the defendant pleads not guilty to both the indictable and summary offences, or even just the summary offence, the defendant will be tried by jury, following the procedure set out in **Chapter 11**. If he or she is convicted the Crown Court powers of sentence in respect of the summary offence are limited to those of the magistrates.

The effect of s. 40, taken together with CLA 1967, s. 6(3), is that if a person is indicted on a count charging assault occasioning actual bodily harm, he or she can only be found guilty of common assault if that offence is specifically included in the indictment. This also applies to other offences included in s. 40 (*R* v *Mearns* (1990) 91 Cr App R 312). See also **Chapter 11** for CLA 1967, s. 6(3).

In *R* v *Lewis* (1991) 95 Cr App R 31, the Court of Appeal decided that if a count was incorrectly joined under s. 40, then, following *R* v *Newland* [1988] QB 402 (see **9.6**), the whole indictment was defective, as was everything that flowed from it. *R* v *Callaghan* (1991) 94 Cr App R 226 held that, since summary offences are essentially parasitic, the misjoinder of a summary offence does not render the counts alleging indictable offences invalid. The latest case on this point, *R* v *Simon* [1992] Crim LR 444 preferred *Callaghan*, but did not finally decide the point.

4.4.2 COMMITTAL FOR PLEA: s. 41

Where magistrates commit for trial on an either way offence, they may also commit the defendant for any summary offence, punishable with imprisonment or disqualification, that arises out of circumstances which are the same as, or connected with, the either way matter.

The summary offence need not be disclosed by the evidence. The prosecution merely indicates that, in the course of committing the either way offence, he or she also committed the summary offence. The offence itself is not included in the indictment, and the magistrates do not commit for trial, but only for a plea to be taken.

Under s. 41, the offence for which the defendant is committed to the Crown Court *must* be an offence which is triable either way. If the committed offence is triable only on indictment, the committal under s. 41 is null and void (*R* v *Miall* [1992] QB 836).

Where a summary offence is committed to the Crown Court under s. 41, it is *not* committed for a not guilty plea to be taken followed by a trial, as would be appropriate under s. 40. Under s. 41, assuming the defendant has been convicted of the triable either way offence, he or she will plead guilty to the summary offence, and the court will proceed to sentence. If he or she does not wish to plead guilty to the summary offence, or is acquitted of the triable either way offence, the case is remitted to the magistrates' court to be dealt with summarily.

The correct approach when dealing with committals under s. 41 was described in *R* v *Foote* (1992) 94 Cr App R 82, CA:

(a) The court must first deal with the indictable offence or offences.

(b) Only if the court convicts on one indictable offence does it then go on to consider whether s. 41 applies to the summary offence.

(c) If s. 41 does apply, a plea may be taken.

(d) Only if the accused pleads guilty to the summary offence can the Crown Court deal with it, and then only with the powers of the magistrates.

(e) If the accused is acquitted of the indictable offence, the Crown Court powers cease. The case goes back to the magistrates who are deemed merely to have adjourned it unless the Crown Court dismisses it.

In *R* v *Bird* [1995] Crim LR 745, the defendant was tried in the Crown Court on a charge of possessing an offensive weapon, and was acquitted. He was also charged with driving while disqualified, which was added to the indictment by virtue of s. 40. He was convicted of this charge. The question was whether, in these circumstances, the Crown Court could deal with him for driving without insurance, on which charge he had been committed under s. 41. The Court of Appeal held that it could, on the basis that he had been convicted on indictment of driving while disqualified, which meant that that offence was to be treated as an indictable offence for the purposes of s. 41.

4.4.3 DIFFERENCES BETWEEN s. 40 and s. 41

Sections 40 and 41 are easy to confuse. The following table, containing the points described above, is intended to highlight the differences between the two sections.

	Committal for trial: s. 40	Committal for plea: s. 41
1.	The summary offence must be common assault, taking a motor vehicle without consent, driving whilst disqualified, criminal damage or assaulting a prison custody officer or secure training centre officer.	The summary offence must be one which is punishable by imprisonment or disqualification, but is not otherwise specified.
2.	The magistrates play no part in including the summary offence in the indictment. It is a matter for the prosecution.	The magistrates must commit for a plea to be taken.
3.	The offence must be disclosed by the evidence.	The offence need not be disclosed by the evidence. The prosecution merely indicates that a summary offence has been committed.
4.	The summary offence must be founded on the same facts or form or be part of a series of offences of the same or a similar character as the main offence.	The summary offence must arise out of the same or connected circumstances as the main offence.
5.	The main offence may be triable either way or triable only on indictment.	The main offence must be triable either way.
6.	The defendant is *tried* in the Crown Court for the summary offence, following a plea of not guilty.	The defendant is *sentenced* in the Crown Court, following a plea of guilty, and assuming that a conviction on the either way offence has been recorded.

4.5 Advantages and Disadvantages of Each Mode of Trial

There are many matters to be taken into account in advising on the most appropriate forum:

(a) *Speed* Whether a case in the magistrates' court is likely to be heard more quickly than if it had been listed for hearing in the Crown Court depends on local waiting lists. However, the case itself is likely to take less time in the magistrates' court.

(b) *Expense* Proceedings in the magistrates' court are much less expensive than in the Crown Court — a very important consideration if the defendant is not legally aided.

(c) *Informality* Proceedings in the magistrates' court are much more informal than in the Crown Court, as fewer people are involved, and counsel do not wear wig and gown. The Crown Court can be daunting to someone who has little experience of criminal courts.

(d) *Sentence* The magistrates' powers of sentence are very much less than those of the Crown Court, though they do have the power to commit to the Crown Court for sentence. However, if the defendant intends to plead guilty, he or she is likely to opt for a hearing in the magistrates' court in the hope that they do not commit him or her to Crown Court for sentence. See **Chapters 15–24** for details of the magistrates' powers of sentence.

(e) *Division between the tribunals of fact and law* In the magistrates' court, the tribunals of fact and law are the same, so that they will first have to hear evidence before deciding on any question of admissibility, and then, if inadmissible, endeavour to forget it. In the Crown Court this problem simply does not arise. The judge alone will decide on admissibility, and evidence will only go before the jury if it is admissible.

(f) *Legal submissions* Despite the fact that lay magistrates are advised by a clerk, nevertheless any submissions on the law are made to laymen. (The case may be heard by a stipendiary magistrate, but this would not be known when determining the mode of trial.) In the Crown Court, the same submission would be made to a professional lawyer.

(g) *Appeals* Appeals from magistrates may be made without leave, see **Chapter 8**. Appeals from the Crown Court always require leave, and the procedure generally is much more complicated. See **Chapter 12**.

(h) *The benefit of the doubt* It is generally assumed that a jury is more likely to give the defendant the benefit of the doubt than magistrates. In any event, if the case involves a substantial attack on the police evidence, the defendant is likely to find a jury more sympathetic than magistrates.

4.6 Advance Information

The prosecution has a duty to provide the defence with the evidence upon which it will rely at trial on indictment, and with undisclosed material in certain circumstances. See **Chapter 10** for a full discussion of the rules relating to disclosure.

The Magistrates' Courts (Advance Information) Rules 1985 provide that where the accused is charged with a triable either way offence, the prosecution must provide the defence with copies of its witness statements, *or* a summary of the evidence upon which they propose to rely, on receiving a request for such information. The purpose of obtaining advance information is to facilitate a mode of trial decision.

The prosecution is entitled to refuse a request, but, under r. 5, only where it thinks that compliance would lead to the intimidation of witnesses or some other interference with the course of justice. Failure to comply for any other reason will lead to an adjournment, unless the court considers that the defendant has not been prejudiced. See generally r. 7.

The request for information should be made *before* mode of trial proceedings have been held, and the information should be provided as soon as practicable. Thus, the defendant is able to make his or her decision as to the mode of trial with full knowledge of all the circumstances. It is the duty of the court, under r. 6, to satisfy itself that the defendant is aware of his or her right to advance information.

Obtaining advance information is now very common, but the defence may decide against a request if clearly one mode of trial is preferable. However, it is the duty of the court under r. 6 to satisfy itself that the defendant is aware of his or her rights.

Note that the magistrates have no power to *order* disclosure under these rules (*R* v *Dunmow Justices, ex parte Nash* (1993) 157 JP 1153, DC).

Further reading: David Sunman, 'Advancing disclosure. Can the rules for advance information in the magistrates' courts be improved?' [1998] Crim LR 798.

4.7 National Mode of Trial Guidelines

The guidelines are intended as assistance and not as directions, and are not intended to impinge on the magistrates' duty to consider each case individually and on its own special facts. They begin by making the following general observations about the mode of trial decision:

(a) The court should never make its decision on the grounds of convenience or expedition.

(b) The court should assume for the purpose of deciding mode of trial that the prosecution version is correct.

(c) The fact that the offences are alleged to be specimens is a relevant consideration; the fact that the defendant will be asking for other offences to be taken into consideration, if convicted, is not.

(d) Where cases involve complex questions of fact or difficult questions of law, including difficult issues of disclosure of sensitive material, the court should consider committal for trial.

(e) Where two or more defendants are jointly charged with an offence, each has an individual right to elect his mode of trial.

Note that the original guidelines stated that where two or more defendants were jointly charged, and the court decided that the case was more suitable for summary trial, and one defendant elects trial on indictment, then the court *must* proceed as examining justices. However, in *R* v *Brentwood Justices, ex parte Nicholls* [1992] 1 AC 1 applied in *R* v *Ipswich Justices, ex parte Callaghan, The Times*, 3 April 1995, it was held that where only one of a number of defendants elects trial on indictment, and the rest do not, the magistrates are *not* bound to commit all the defendants for trial on indictment. The right of election in MCA 1980, s. 20 is given to each defendant individually, and is unaffected by any different decision made by a co-defendant. The new guideline follows their decision.

The prosecution should not attempt to persuade the magistrates to exercise their discretion under MCA 1980, s. 25(2) (discontinuing the summary trial and proceeding with committal proceedings, see **4.2.4** above) in order to get round the decision in *ex parte Nicholls*, even if they thought it was unfortunate that the defendants should not be tried together. See *R* v *West Norfolk Justices, ex parte McMullen* [1993] COD 25.]

(f) In general, except where otherwise stated, either way offences should be tried summarily unless the court considers that the particular case has one or more of the features set out as follows *and* that its sentencing powers are insufficient. (It should be noted that this observation is repeated in relation to almost all the offences dealt with by the guidelines.)

(g) The court should also consider its powers to commit an offender for sentence, under PCC(S)A 2000, s. 3, if information emerges during the course of the hearing which leads it to conclude that the offence is so serious, or that the offender is such a risk to the public, that its powers to sentence him or her are inadequate. This amendment means that the committal for sentence is no longer determined by reference to the character and antecedents of the defendant.

Case law prior to the guidelines decided that the magistrates should not take into account any previous convictions that may be recorded against the defendant and should proceed on the basis that he was a man of good character. See *R* v *Colchester Justices, ex parte North East Essex Building Co. Ltd* [1977] 1 WLR 1109. Further, the original Mode of Trial Guidelines provided that the antecedents and personal mitigating circumstances of the defendant were irrelevant in determining the mode of trial. However, this guideline has now been removed, reflecting the provisions of PCC(S)A 2000, s. 151. Under s. 151, the defendant's antecedents may aggravate the matter, and his or her personal mitigating circumstances may be such as to reduce the seriousness of the offence, so that the matter may properly be dealt with by the magistrates.

Where reference is made to property or damage of 'high value' it means a figure equal to at least twice the amount of the limit (currently £5,000) imposed by statute on a magistrates' court when making a compensation order.

The following offences included in the guidelines are included here by way of illustration.

4.7.1 OFFENCES UNDER THE GUIDELINES

4.7.1.1 Burglary

Dwelling house

(a) Entry in the daytime when the occupier (or another) is present.

(b) Entry at night of a house which is normally occupied, whether or not the occupier (or another) is present.

(c) The offence is alleged to be one of a series of similar offences.

(d) The offence has professional hallmarks.

(e) The unrecovered property is of high value (see **4.7** for definition of high value).

Note: Attention is drawn to para. 28(c) of sch. 1 to the Magistrates' Courts Act 1980, by which offences of burglary in a dwelling *cannot* be tried summarily if any person in the dwelling was subjected to violence or the threat of violence.

Non-dwellings

(a) Entry of a pharmacy or doctor's surgery.

(b) Fear caused or violence done to anyone lawfully on the premises (e.g. night-watchman, security guard).

(c) The offence has professional hallmarks.

(d) Vandalism on a substantial scale.

(e) The unrecovered property is of high value (see **4.7** for definition of high value).

4.7.1.2 Theft and fraud

(a) Breach of trust by a person in a position of substantial authority, or in whom a high degree of trust is placed.

(b) Theft or fraud which has been committed or disguised in a sophisticated manner.

(c) Theft or fraud committed by an organised gang.

(d) The victim is particularly vulnerable to theft or fraud, e.g. the elderly or infirm.

(e) The unrecovered property is of high value (see **4.7** for definition of high value).

4.7.1.3 Handling

(a) Dishonest handling of stolen property by a receiver who has commissioned the theft.

(b) The offence has professional hallmarks.

(c) The property is of high value (see **4.7** for definition of high value).

4.7.1.4 Dangerous driving

(a) Alcohol or drugs contributing to dangerousness.

(b) Grossly excessive speed.

(c) Racing.

(d) Prolonged course of dangerous driving.

(e) Degree of injury or damage sustained.

(f) Other related offences.

4.7.1.5 Indecent assault

(a) Substantial disparity in age between victim and defendant, and the assault is more than trivial.

(b) Violence or threats of violence.

(c) Relationship of trust or responsibility between defendant and victim.

(d) Several similar offences, and the assaults are more than trivial.

(e) The victim is particularly vulnerable.

(f) Serious nature of the assault.

FIVE

SUMMARY TRIAL

5.1 Procedure at Trial

Some 96% of all criminal cases are tried in magistrates' courts. The procedure is the same, whether the offence is triable only summarily, or triable either way, though if the offence is triable either way, the magistrates must first determine the mode of trial (see **Chapter 4**).

See generally *Stone's Justices' Manual* (1999) at 1–410 *et seq* and *Blackstone's Criminal Practice*, 2000, at D18 and D19.

5.1.1 THE ABSENCE OF THE DEFENDANT

Although the defendant will in fact often be present in court for the hearing, the magistrates have the power to proceed in his absence. There are three situations in which this may arise:

5.1.1.1 Where the defendant fails to attend

Under MCA 1980, s. 11(1), the magistrates have a discretion to hear the case in the defendant's absence if he or she fails to attend court in answer to a summons. If the offence is triable either way, the prosecution must first establish that the defendant actually knew of the summons, for example, through attending an earlier hearing.

If the offence is triable only summarily, then the prosecution may prove that the summons was served simply by establishing that, for example, it was sent by registered post to the defendant's last known address, but the prosecution does not have to prove that the defendant received it.

Once service of the summons has been proved, a plea of not guilty will be entered on the defendant's behalf and the prosecution evidence will be called. Such hearings often end in the conviction of the defendant, as none of the prosecution evidence will have been tested by cross-examination, and the magistrates will not have heard the defence case.

If the defendant did not, in fact, know of the proceedings, he or she may make a 'statutory declaration' of this under MCA 1980, s. 14, within 21 days of finding out about them. If the declaration is made, the summons, trial and conviction are rendered void. However, the information remains valid, so that the prosecution can start again.

The discretion to proceed in the absence of the defendant should be exercised judicially. This includes giving the defendant a fair opportunity to be present, and to give or call evidence. See *R* v *Bolton Magistrates' Court, ex parte Merna* [1991] Crim LR 848, where the court proceeded in the absence of the defendant, despite a letter from his doctor saying that he was unfit to attend court.

Whether the defendant's absence should lead to a rehearing of the case was a matter within the justices' discretion, and as long as this was based on facts the justices were entitled to find, the divisional court would not overturn it (*R* v *North Shields Justices, ex parte Darroll* [1991] COD 317).

The s. 11 procedure tends to be used only for the less serious offences. In any event, if the defendant is charged with a triable either way offence, the defendant normally has to be present during mode of trial proceedings.

5.1.1.2 Pleading guilty by post

Under MCA 1980, s. 12 as substituted by sch. 5 to the CJPOA Act 1994, a defendant may plead guilty by sending a letter to court. This can be done if:

(a) the offence is summary;

(b) the maximum penalty is not more than three months' imprisonment; and

(c) proceedings have been started by the service of a summons.

In such circumstances the procedure is as follows:

(a) The prosecution serves on the defendant:

  (i) the summons;

  (ii) a brief statement of the facts upon which the prosecution proposes to rely or a copy of such written statements as comply with CJA 1967, s. 9(2)(a) and (b);

  (iii) any information relating to the accused which will or may be placed before the court; and

  (iv) a notice explaining the procedure.

(b) If he or she wishes to plead guilty, the defendant notifies the court and may enclose a statement of his or her mitigation. Subsequently, the defendant may withdraw this plea, and the case then proceeds as if it were a not guilty plea.

(c) Neither the prosecution nor the defence is represented or appears at court, and the court proceeds on the basis of the statements which are read out in court. Failure to do so will lead to the conviction being quashed, as in *R* v *Epping and Ongar Justices, ex parte Breach* [1987] RTR 233 where the defendant's statement in mitigation was not read out. The magistrates may refuse to accept the plea of guilty if the statement in mitigation discloses information which amounts to a defence.

(d) The magistrates, if content to accept the plea, may sentence, or adjourn for the accused to be present. The magistrates may only sentence the defendant in his or her absence if he or she is to be fined, absolutely discharged, or have his or her driving licence endorsed.

Note that the court ought to be reluctant to try, in his absence, an offender who is young, has not been placed on bail and/or has no record of failing to appear (*R* v *Dewsbury Magistrates' Court, ex parte K, The Times*, 16 March 1994).

Section 12A of the MCA 1980 deals with the situation where the defendant actually appears in court. Two situations may occur:

(a) The defendant has informed the court that he or she wishes the case to proceed under s. 12, but he nevertheless appears in court at the appointed time. The court may proceed to deal with the matter as if he or she were absent, if he or she consents to such a course: s. 12A(1).

(b) The defendant has not notified the court that he or she wishes the case to proceed under s. 12, and appears at the appointed time. If he or she indicates that he or she wishes to plead guilty, and consents, the court may proceed to deal with the matter as if he or she were absent (s. 12A(2)).

In either case, the court must afford the defendant an opportunity to make oral submissions with a view to mitigation of sentence (s. 12(5)(c)).

5.1.1.3 The disorderly defendant

If the defendant's behaviour is so disruptive that the proceedings cannot continue, he or she may be removed, and the court may proceed in his or her absence under MCA 1980, s. 11.

Note: If the defendant is represented, he or she is deemed to be present unless his or her presence is expressly required by statute (MCA 1980, s. 122(2)).

5.1.2 ABSENCE OF THE PROSECUTION

Under MCA 1980, s. 15, if the prosecution fails to appear at the time and place fixed for the summary trial, the magistrates may adjourn the case or dismiss the information. Where the magistrates act unreasonably in dismissing a case, their decision is a nullity, and the mandamus would issue (*R* v *Hendon Justices, ex parte DPP* [1994] QB 167, DC).

If the case is adjourned part-heard, then the magistrates may proceed in the absence of the prosecution, the evidence given on the earlier occasion being treated as the entirety of the prosecution case. In these circumstances, the defendant will not face cross-examination of his or her evidence by the prosecution.

5.1.3 REPRESENTATIONS IN PRIVATE

A decision to hear representations in private is within the magistrates' discretion, but careful consideration should always be given to whether such a step is appropriate, given the magistrates' role as fact-finder. In order to guard against injustice, steps must be taken to ensure that all parties are notified of the hearing and are represented, with a contemporaneous note being taken, normally by the clerk (see *R* v *Nottingham Justices, ex parte Furnell*, *The Times*, 18 December 1995).

5.1.4 TAKING THE PLEA

The defendant must plead unequivocally guilty or not guilty. In practice, this often throws up two separate problems:

(a) *The defendant who wishes to change his plea* The court may consider an application made by a defendant who has unequivocally pleaded guilty to change his or her plea, at any time before sentence (see *S (an infant)* v *Recorder of Manchester* [1971] AC 481). Whether he or she will be allowed to change the plea is entirely within the discretion of the magistrates. If they take the view that the defendant understood the charge, the consequence of his or her plea, and had intended to make it, they will be unlikely to allow a change. See generally *R* v *McNally* [1954] 1 WLR 933.

Where the magistrates have allowed the defendant to change his plea from guilty to not guilty, they should also allow him to reconsider his consent to summary trial (*R* v *Bow Street Magistrates' Court, ex parte Welcome* (1992) 156 JP 609).

Where the defendant has pleaded not guilty, and wishes to change his or her plea to guilty, he or she may do so with leave of the court (which for obvious reasons is likely to be granted) any time before the court retires to consider the verdict.

(b) *The defendant's plea is equivocal* This covers three situations:

(i) The defendant, when pleading guilty, explains his or her plea in words amounting to a defence. See *R* v *Emery* (1943) 29 Cr App R 47, where the defendant said 'Plead guilty in self-defence'. The magistrates should then explain the law and the defendant is asked to plead again. If the plea is still equivocal, the magistrates must record a plea of not guilty and proceed to trial. If they make no enquiry into the plea, the defendant may later challenge the validity of the plea on appeal.

(ii) The defendant unequivocally pleads guilty, but the plea is rendered equivocal by information given to the magistrates before sentence (see *R* v *Durham Justices, ex parte Virgo* [1952] 2 QB 1 contrasted with *R* v *Birmingham Crown Court, ex parte Sharma* [1988] Crim LR 741). In *P. Foster (Haulage) Ltd* v *Roberts* [1978] 2 All ER 751, it was said that this should not be termed an equivocal plea, and is merely a situation in which the magistrates have a discretion to allow a change of plea.

(iii) The defendant unequivocally pleads guilty and no further information is given to the court casting doubt on the correctness of the plea. However, if the defendant argues that the plea was made under duress, the Crown Court may treat it as an equivocal plea. See *R* v *Huntingdon Crown Court, ex parte Jordan* [1981] QB 857.

In any event, the magistrates should always ensure that the defendant, particularly an unrepresented defendant, understands the offence, the consequences of the plea, and intends to make that plea. The proper forum for any dispute is the Crown Court, which may review the case, and, if it decides that the plea was equivocal, it should remit it to the magistrates with an order that they enter a plea of not guilty and proceed to trial. Before making any such order, the Crown Court should read affidavits from the magistrates and the clerk as to what happened, and magistrates and clerks should cooperate by swearing such affidavits. See *R* v *Plymouth Justices, ex parte Hart* [1986] QB 950.

5.1.5 THE PROSECUTION OPENING SPEECH

Magistrates will be familiar with the cases that frequently come before them, so that, although the prosecution has the right to an opening speech, it is usually brief and is often not made.

In *L and B* v *DPP* [1998] 2 Cr App R 69, the case was adjourned for a month after hearing the prosecution witnesses. The defendants appealed against their convictions as the prosecution had made a second speech on the resumed hearing, at the magistrates' request, to remind them of the evidence given at the earlier hearing. It was held that there was nothing unfair in that, subject to the safeguard that the defence should always be asked to address the court in reply to correct any errors or draw attention in differences of recollection.

5.1.6 THE PROSECUTION EVIDENCE

The prosecution calls the evidence upon which it relies. This will take the form of witnesses and written statements, if admissible and appropriate. See **11.5.2** and ***Evidence Manual***.

As to the defence knowledge of the prosecution case, see **4.6** and **Chapter 10**.

5.1.7 THE SUBMISSION OF NO CASE TO ANSWER

At the end of the prosecution evidence, the defence may make a submission of no case to answer. According to Lord Parker CJ, in *Practice Direction (Submission of No Case)* [1962] 1 WLR 227, a submission that there is no case to answer may properly be made and upheld:

(a) when there has been no evidence to prove an essential element in the alleged offence; or

(b) when the evidence adduced by the prosecution has been so discredited as a result of cross-examination or is so manifestly unreliable that no reasonable tribunal could safely convict on it.

The magistrates have to decide, not whether they would convict, but whether a reasonable tribunal might convict on the evidence of the prosecution witnesses, and if not, they should dismiss the case. (See further **Chapter 21** of ***Advocacy Manual*** for how to make, or respond to, a submission of no case to answer.)

5.1.8 THE DEFENCE CASE

Assuming no submission of no case to answer is made, or is made and fails, the defence may present its case. The right of the defence to make an opening speech is rarely exercised (see **5.1.9**) and the defence usually begins to call its evidence straight away. The defendant should give evidence before any other witnesses he intends to call (PACE 1984, s. 79).

5.1.9 CLOSING SPEECHES

The defence has the right to either an opening or a closing speech, and invariably elects a closing speech, thus having the benefit of the last word.

If either party wishes to make a second speech, it may do so with the leave of the court; but if the court is going to allow one party to make a second speech, it must allow the other party a second speech also. If both parties are allowed a second speech, the prosecution must go first, thus allowing the defence the benefit of the last word.

5.1.10 THE VERDICT

Lay magistrates usually retire to consider their verdict, and no one must retire with them as this may create the impression that they have somehow influenced the decision. As to the position of the clerk to the justices, see **5.2** below. The verdict is a majority decision, and the chairman has no casting vote. Therefore, if an evenly numbered court is equally divided, it must adjourn for a fresh hearing before a new bench (*R* v *Redbridge Justices, ex parte Ram* [1992] QB 384).

Stipendiary magistrates rarely retire, and usually announce their decision immediately after the defence's closing speech.

In reaching their decision, the magistrates may rely on any local knowledge that they may have, but both prosecution and defence should have been informed of this during the trial so that they might be afforded an opportunity to comment upon that knowledge (*Norbrook Laboratories (GB) Ltd* v *Health and Safety Executive, The Times*, 23 February 1998).

Magistrates should not, and do not, give reasons for their decisions.

It should be noted that the provisions of CLA 1967, s. 6(3), do not apply in magistrates' courts. Thus the magistrates have no power to find the defendant guilty of a lesser offence not specifically charged (except under s. 24(3) and (4) of the Road Traffic Offenders Act 1988, under which a defendant charged with dangerous driving may be found guilty of careless driving). See generally *Lawrence* v *Same* [1968] 2 QB 93. However, it would be open to the magistrates to ask for a summons for the lesser offence to be preferred immediately and proceed to deal with it at once. As to where the magistrates convict on a more serious charge and dismiss others because further convictions would be oppressive, see *DPP* v *Gane* [1991] Crim LR 711, DC.

For a discussion of CLA 1967, s. 6(3), see **Chapter 11**.

5.1.11 SENTENCE

If the magistrates find the case proved, they will proceed to sentence, after an adjournment if necessary. A detailed analysis of the procedure prior to sentence is found in **Chapter 14**, but in brief is as follows:

(a) The prosecution gives details of the defendant's character and antecedents.

(b) Any pre-sentence or other reports are placed before the court.

(c) The defence enters a plea in mitigation.

(d) The court passes sentence.

The magistrates' sentencing powers are discussed in full in **Chapters 15** to **24**. However, in brief, the magistrates may sentence a person over the age of 21 to a maximum period of six months' imprisonment on each offence, or the statutory maximum, whichever is the less. Where the person is convicted of two or more offences, triable either way, the sentences may be made to run consecutively to a maximum of 12 months. The jurisdiction to exceed a total of six months' imprisonment only arises where the defendant is convicted of two or more offences which are triable either way. If the defendant is convicted of, say, theft (a triable either way offence carrying a maximum sentence on summary conviction of six months) and assaulting a police officer (a summary offence carrying a maximum sentence of three months), the magistrates cannot exceed an aggregate sentence of six months. The same rules apply where the court is sentencing a person between the ages of 17–20 inclusive to detention in a young offender institution. In addition to any period of imprisonment the magistrates may fine an offender up to £5,000 per offence. See generally PCC(S)A 2000, s. 78 and MCA 1980, ss. 32 and 133.

5.1.12 POWER TO RECTIFY MISTAKES

Under MCA 1980, s. 142 as amended by the Criminal Appeal Act 1995, a magistrates' court may vary or rescind a sentence or other order imposed or made by it, if it appears to the court to be in the interests of justice to do so. The purpose of this provision is to prevent the judicial review of proceedings which clearly should be re-heard.

The following points should be noted:

(a) The magistrates may reopen the case regardless of whether the defendant pleaded guilty or not guilty.

(b) There is no time limit to the re-opening of the case. The original 28-day time limit (abolished in 1995) is still a useful guideline, but delay is not the only factor to be taken into account by the magistrates in exercising their discretion under s. 142 (*R* v *Ealing Magistrates' Court, ex parte Sahota*, *The Times*, 9 December 1997).

(c) The magistrates reopening the case need not be the same magistrates who dealt with the case originally.

These three points were introduced by the Criminal Appeal Act 1995, and considerably widen the magistrates powers under s. 142. It may be that many matters which could previously only have been dealt with by way of appeal may now be dealt with under s. 142. For this reason, students should always consider s. 142 when dealing with any error made by the magistrates.

In exercising their discretion, the magistrates were entitled to consider the inconvenience to witnesses if defendants did not appear for their trial through their own fault. They were also able to take into account the apparent strength of the prosecution case, though they should attach little weight to that factor (*R* v *Newport Justices, ex parte Carey*, *The Times*, 16 July 1996).

Two further points should be made:

(a) The power to rescind under s. 142 only applies where the defendant has been found guilty. See, for example, *Coles* v *DPP, The Independent*, 22 June 1998.

(b) When a person is convicted by a magistrates' court, and it appears in the interest of justice that the case should be re-heard by a different bench, the court may so direct (s. 142(2), as amended). In this situation the case is treated as if it had simply been adjourned.

(c) The court's right to exercise its powers under s. 142 are lost after the case has been appealed to the Crown Court or the High Court by way of case stated, and the court has determined the appeal (s. 142(1A) and (2A) inserted by the Criminal Appeal Act 1995, s. 2B(3) and (5)).

The amendments to s. 142 came into force on 1 January 1996.

5.2 The Clerk to the Justices

The clerk to the justices is a barrister or solicitor of at least five years' standing. He or she is usually supported by assistant clerks who often are, but need not be, legally qualified.

The clerk has a wide administrative function. This derives from the magistrates' jurisdiction over both domestic and licensing matters in addition to their criminal jurisdiction. Here the clerk is involved in a number of areas, such as the taking of informations, the issue of summonses, and the grant of legal aid.

During a trial, the clerk has several duties. The most important are:

(a) To speak on behalf of the court, if required to do so. This includes reading the charge to the defendant, putting the election as to the mode of trial to him or her, and taking the plea.

(b) To advise the justices on any question of law and procedure. This advice should be given in open court, so that all parties know the advice given, and the basis upon which the magistrates made their decision.

Where the justices wish their clerk to advise them on matters of law, it is essential that the clerk is present in court during the submissions of the parties (*R* v *Chichester Magistrates' Court, ex parte DPP* (1993) 157 JP 1049). The clerk should give his or her advice in open court, so that all parties know the advice given, and the basis on which the magistrates made their decision. For example, where the clerk wishes to refer the justices to an authority not previously cited, the advocates in the case should be informed and given the opportunity to comment (*W* v *W*, *The Times*, 4 June 1993).

The clerk plays no part in deciding either the facts or the defendant's guilt, but may advise the justices on the law, after they have retired to consider their verdict, and should accompany them only if specifically requested to do so. As soon as he or she has given the advice the clerk should withdraw, unless the case is so complex that his or her advice is required throughout the decision-making process. (See *R* v *Consett Justices, ex parte Postal Bingo Ltd* [1967] 2 QB 9.) For recent examples of where the decision-making process was interfered with, see *R* v *Eccles Justices, ex parte Farrelly* (1992) 157 JP 77 and *R* v *Birmingham Justices Court, ex parte Ahmed* [1994] COD 461.

(c) To take a note of the evidence. The clerk may refresh the magistrates' memories, and draw their attention to any issues involved in the matters before the court.

(d) To intervene in the case to assist the course of justice when the court is dealing with an unrepresented defendant. But it should be noted that the clerk is there to assist the court by ensuring that the parties present their case clearly and unambiguously, and that he or she is not there to assist one party as against the other.

(e) To advise the magistrates on the range of sentences available. As reaching a decision on sentence can be a very involved process, it is rarely done in open court, to avoid an unseemly debate as to the appropriate sentence taking place in front of the defendant.

5.3 Committal to the Crown Court for Sentence

In certain circumstances, the magistrates, having found the defendant guilty of an offence or if the defendant pleads guilty may commit him or her to the Crown Court for sentence. The most important powers of committal are as follows:

5.3.1 COMMITTAL UNDER POWERS OF CRIMINAL COURTS (SENTENCING) ACT 2000, s. 3

When magistrates accept the summary trial of an offence triable either way, they do so on the basis that the defendant is a person of good character, and that they have sufficient powers to deal with him or her. However, having heard all the evidence in the case, the court may form the opinion that it does not, in fact, have sufficient powers. In these circumstances, the magistrates may wish to commit the defendant to the Crown Court, so that the Crown Court, using its greater powers, may impose an appropriate sentence. Under PCC(S)A 2000, s. 3, the magistrates may commit for sentence *only* in view of either the seriousness of the offence or the nature of the offence, as explained below.

(a) *The seriousness of the offence* Under PCC(S)A 2000, s. 3(2)(a), in order to commit for sentence, the court must be of the opinion that the offence, or the combination of the offence and other associated offences, is so serious that greater punishment should be inflicted than the court has power to impose. The associated offences are those offences of which the defendant has been convicted or sentenced at the same time as the main offence, or is an offence which he or she is asking the court to take into consideration on sentencing (PCC(S)A 2000, s. 161(1)). In order to commit under PCC(S)A 2000, s. 3(2)(a), the court must be dealing with a person of not less than 18 years old (s. 3(1)).

The following matters may also render the offence 'serious' and justify a committal under s. 3:

(i) Where the defendant has previous convictions (PCC(S)A 2000, s. 151).

(ii) Where new information has come to light since the decision to try summarily was made. However, there is nothing in PCC(S)A 2000, s. 3, as amended, to suggest that a magistrates' court which accepted jurisdiction initially could not change its mind at a later stage in the proceedings. To that extent, the discretion of the magistrates is unfettered (*R* v *Sheffield Crown Court, ex parte DPP* (1994) 15 Cr App R (S) 768; *R* v *Dover Justices, ex parte Pamment* (1994) 15 Cr App R (S) 778; *R* v *North Sefton Magistrates' Court, ex parte Marsh* (1994) 159 JP 1).

It should be said, however, that in most cases where the magistrates commit for sentence on this basis, they do so because new information arises during the trial (see, for example, *R* v *King's Lynn Justices, ex parte Carter* [1969] 1 QB 488; *R* v *Lymm Justices, ex parte Brown* [1973] 1 WLR 1039; and *R* v *Tower Bridge Magistrates, ex parte Osman* [1971] 1 WLR

1109). Further, in *R* v *Manchester Magistrates' Court, ex parte Kaymanesh* [1994] COD 380, it was stressed that the new sentencing policy of the CJA 1991 did not entitle the magistrates to ignore the principles established by earlier cases, which still remain applicable. These principles make it clear that if magistrates consider their sentencing powers inadequate, this should be dealt with at the time of deciding the mode of trial. See also *R* v *Flaxburton Justices, ex parte CCE* (1996) 160 JP 481 on this point. Further, both *ex parte Pamment* and *ex parte Marsh* stressed the importance of the magistrates' initial decision, on the basis that the defendant is entitled to expect that he would not be committed for sentence on the same facts upon which the magistrates accepted jurisdiction.

(iii) Where the defendant asks for other offences to be taken into consideration (see **12.9**).

(b) *The protection of the public* Under s. 3(2)(b), in order to commit for sentence, the court must be of the opinion, in the case of a violent or sexual offence, that a sentence of imprisonment for a term longer than the court has power to impose is necessary to protect the public from serious harm from the offender.

Students should refer to PCC(S)A 2000, s. 161, for a full definition of the terms 'sexual offence' and 'violent offence', and should consult the sentencing section of this Manual. The reference to protecting the public from harm means protecting them from death or serious injury, whether physical or psychological, occasioned by further such offences committed by the defendant.

Guidelines for magistrates considering a committal for sentence were set out in *R* v *Warley Magistrates' Court, ex parte DPP* [1998] 2 Cr App R 308:

(a) The magistrates must have regard to the discount to be given to a plea of guilty in deciding whether their powers of sentence are adequate.

(b) Where, even when allowing for that discount and for mitigation, it was obvious their powers of sentence were inadequate, they should commit to the Crown Court without obtaining a pre-sentence report or hearing mitigation.

(c) The defendant should be allowed to make a brief submission in opposition to that decision, but if he or she does so, the prosecution must also be allowed to address the court.

(d) The magistrates should hold a *Newton* hearing if there is a dispute as to the facts, if they consider that whatever the outcome, they have adequate powers of sentence. See **14.4** for a discussion of the *Newton* hearing.

(e) If, on the other hand, they consider that, whatever the outcome, they do not have adequate powers, it was preferable to leave the *Newton* hearing to the Crown Court.

(f) If the decision to commit depended on the outcome of the *Newton* hearing, the magistrates should proceed to conduct it.

The committal may be in custody or on bail (s. 3). The traditional view has been that, as the defendant is likely to be sentenced to a reasonably long period of imprisonment, the committal should be in custody. In *R* v *Rafferty* [1998] 2 Cr App R (S) 449, however, the Court of Appeal suggested that if the defendant had been on bail prior to the committal, he or she should remain on bail until his or her appearance at the Crown Court, even if a long period of imprisonment were anticipated, unless there were good reasons for revoking bail. If, on the other hand, he or she were already in custody, then it would be unusual to change that, if the reasons for the remand in custody remained unchanged.

At the Crown Court, the case is heard by a judge, usually a circuit judge or recorder. The defendant is asked if he or she admits the conviction and committal, which in most cases he or she does. If the defendant does not admit them, then they must be formally proved against him or her. The court will then sentence, the procedure being similar to that on a plea of guilty, detailed in **Chapter 14**, and in brief is as follows:

(a) The prosecution outlines the brief facts of the offence.

(b) The prosecution supplies the court with the defendant's character and antecedents.

(c) Any pre-sentence or other reports are placed before the court.

(d) The defence enters a plea of mitigation.

(e) The court proceeds to sentence.

The Crown Court may sentence the defendant, under the PCC(S)A 2000, s. 5, as if he or she had just been convicted on indictment before it. Thus, the court can exercise any of its usual sentencing powers and impose any sentence, including a sentence which had been available to the magistrates, if it takes a less serious view of the matter than did the magistrates. However, in many cases the Crown Court takes an equally serious view of the matter and usually imposes a fairly heavy sentence.

The Crown Court may remit the case to the magistrates, but only where the committal order was bad on its face (*R* v *Sheffield Crown Court, ex parte DPP* (1994) 15 Cr App R (S) 768).

5.3.2 COMMITTAL UNDER POWERS OF CRIMINAL COURTS (SENTENCING) ACT 2000, s. 4

PCC(S)A 2000, s. 4, is intended to deal with the situation where a defendant indicates a plea of guilty to a triable either way offence, and is also committed for trial in respect of a related offence. Where this happens, the magistrates are given the power to commit the defendant to the Crown Court for sentence in respect of the either way offence to which he or she has indicated a plea of guilty. The power can only be exercised where the offences are related, i.e., they could be included in the same indictment (see **9.2.1**). Unlike s. 3, however, s. 4 is not subject to the magistrates deciding that their powers of punishment are inadequate.

When the Crown Court deals with the defendant, its powers of sentence depend on whether:

(a) it convicts the defendant of one or more related offences; or

(b) the magistrates' court on committal for sentence under s. 4 stated that it also had power to do so under s. 3.

If either (a) or (b) applies, then the Crown Court will have the power to impose any sentence which it could have imposed after conviction on indictment. If not, then its powers are limited to those of the magistrates.

5.3.3 BREACH OF CROWN COURT ORDER

Where the defendant is convicted of an offence which constitutes a breach of a Crown Court order, the magistrates may commit the offender to the Crown Court (see **19.10** for further details). The most important orders are:

(a) A suspended sentence. If the defendant is convicted of an imprisonable offence committed while subject to a suspended sentence, the magistrates may either commit for sentence or simply notify the Crown Court of the breach (PCC(S)A 2000, s. 120).

(b) A probation order or conditional discharge. If the defendant is in breach of either order the magistrates may commit him or her in custody or on bail or deal with him or her themselves. If it is a breach of a conditional discharge, the committal is likely to be on bail.

5.3.4 COMMITTAL UNDER POWERS OF CRIMINAL COURTS (SENTENCING) ACT 2000, s. 6

Section 6 provides that where the magistrates are committing a defendant to the Crown Court in any of the circumstances outlined in **5.3.1** or **5.3.3**, they may also commit for any other offences of which the defendant has been convicted.

The effect is that the magistrates may commit to the Crown Court summary offences which could not otherwise be committed. Thus, a single court can deal with the defendant for all outstanding offences, and this avoids the otherwise inconvenient result of the magistrates' court dealing with the summary offences and the Crown Court dealing with everything else.

The purpose of the section is convenience, and to ensure consistency of sentencing. In these circumstances it would be unfair to the defendant if he or she incurred any greater penalty as regards the summary offences, and therefore the powers of the Crown Court when dealing with a defendant on a committal under s. 6 are limited to those of the magistrates. For a recent example, see *R* v *Whitlock* (1992) 13 Cr App R (S) 157, CA.

5.3.5 APPEALS

If the defendant wishes to appeal against committal, he or she must apply for judicial review (see **8.3**). He or she cannot appeal to the Crown Court as a committal is neither a conviction nor a sentence (see **8.1**). Nor can he or she appeal by way of case stated as the case has not yet finished (see **8.2.1**).

SIX

COMMITTAL PROCEEDINGS

The vast majority of cases which are dealt with by the Crown Court, are dealt with initially by the magistrates. This being so, a mechanism is required to remove the matter from the magistrates' court and place it before the Crown Court. This mechanism is in the form of committal proceedings.

Committal proceedings are not used in every case which is transferred to the Crown Court. The exceptional situations are serious fraud cases, cases involving children, and voluntary bills of indictment. They are dealt with after committal is considered.

6.1 Background

Committal proceedings have come under considerable scrutiny in recent years. In the CJPOA 1994 provision was made for the abolition of committal proceedings and their replacement with transfer proceedings, similar to cases involving children and serious fraud. Transfer proceedings were themselves considered unsatisfactory and the proposed changes were never brought into effect. Instead, by virtue of the CPIA 1996 the existing system of committal proceedings has been retained and refined.

There are two types of committal proceedings: the full committal proceedings with consideration of the evidence, under MCA 1980, s. 6(1); and the short form of committal, without consideration of the evidence under MCA 1980, s. 6(2). The CPIA 1996 maintains this distinction but has amended the procedure.

Prior to the CPIA 1996, full committal proceedings, that is committal with consideration of the evidence, involved the consideration of at least some oral evidence and were similar to preliminary trials. It was usually the defence which decided to adopt full committal proceedings, although in exceptional cases the prosecution opted for them in order to test the strength of their own case.

The change made by the CPIA 1996 retains the principle of committal with consideration of the evidence, but removes the element of live witnesses. The court still decides whether there is a case to answer, but only on the basis of the written evidence.

It remains an option for the defence to elect full committal proceedings. It seems, however, that they are little used. It is unlikely that the prosecution witness statements will not disclose a case to answer, and without the opportunity to cross-examine witnesses, it is impossible for the defence to investigate any weakness in the prosecution case. Further, the court is precluded from considering the admissibility of a confession, or the possible unfairness of any evidence at committal (CPIA 1996, sch. 1, paras 25 and 26).

In the event that full committal proceedings are chosen, the defence have the opportunity of making a submission of no case to answer, as a result of which the accused is discharged, saving the trouble, expense and distress of a trial. It should be noted, however, that the standard of proof at committal is very low, and in the past such discharges have not been common. Without the chance to cross-examine and discredit the witnesses, it is likely that they will become even more uncommon. In any event, a discharge does not rank as an acquittal, and the prosecution may seek to commit the accused for trial a second time, or apply for a voluntary bill of indictment. See **6.5.3**.

The CPIA 1996 has made few changes to the short form of committal, which remains essentially the same.

6.1.1 THE EXAMINING JUSTICES

Where magistrates sit on committal proceedings they are known as 'examining justices'. A single examining justice, sitting in open court, may conduct committal proceedings (MCA 1980, s. 4(1) and (2)). In certain circumstances a justices' clerk, or a member of his or her staff, may conduct committal proceedings under s. 6(2) (Justices' Clerks Rules 1970, rr. 3 and 4 and sch. 1).

Committal proceedings are open to the public, although the justices have a discretion to sit *in camera* (MCA 1980, s. 4(2)). The press may also attend, but reporting is restricted.

6.1.2 PRESENCE OF THE ACCUSED

Under MCA 1980, s. 4(3), the accused must be present throughout committal proceedings. However, the proceedings may continue in his or her absence, under s. 4(4) if:

(a) conduct before the justices is so disorderly that it is not practicable for the evidence to be given in his or her presence; or

(b) the accused cannot be present for reasons of health, but is legally represented and consents to proceedings taking place in his or her absence.

6.2 Committal Proceedings with Consideration of the Evidence

MCA 1980, s. 6(1), as substituted by CPIA 1996, sch. 1, para. 4, provides that a magistrates' court enquiring into an offence as examining justices shall, on consideration of the evidence, either:

> *(a) commit the accused for trial if it is of the opinion that there is sufficient evidence to put him on trial by jury for any indictable offence;*
> *(b) discharge him if it is not of that opinion and he is in custody for no other cause than the offence under enquiry.*

In deciding whether to discharge or commit the accused for trial, the examining justices must consider the evidence against the accused. The procedure which they follow is set out in **6.2.1** below. Committal proceedings under s. 6(1) will also be held where the defendant is unrepresented.

6.2.1 PROCEDURE

The following procedure for committal proceedings is obligatory:

(a) The charge is written down by the clerk of the court (if it has not been written down already) and is read to the accused. The accused is not asked to plead.

(b) The prosecution make an opening speech.

(c) The prosecution then deals with the written evidence provided by the prosecution witnesses. The evidence must be in the form dictated by MCA 1980, s. 5(A), discussed in full in **6.3** below. The prosecution reads out all the statements or, with leave of the court, summarises them. See ss. 5B(4), 5C(4) and 5D(5), which all provide that, at committals with consideration of the evidence, each statement:

> *shall, unless . . . the court otherwise directs, be read aloud at the hearing, and where the court so directs, an account shall be given orally of so much of any statement as is not read aloud.*

No witnesses are called, and no oral evidence is adduced.

By virtue of CPIA 1996, sch. 1, paras 25 and 26, the court, at committal proceedings with consideration of the evidence, shall not consider the admissibility of any confession under PACE 1984, s. 76, nor any issue as to the exclusion of evidence because it is unfair under PACE 1984, s. 78.

(d) At the end of the prosecution case, the defence may submit that there is '*insufficient*' evidence to justify committing the accused for trial (MCA 1980, s. 6(1)(a)). The prosecution has the right to reply to the submission, and address the examining justices as to the strength of the evidence.

(e) The examining justices make their decision. Note that no evidence is tendered on behalf of the defence. If the examining justices decide that there is sufficient evidence, and the submission of no case has therefore failed, the accused is committed for trial at the Crown Court. If the examining justices decide that there is not sufficient evidence, and the submission of no case has therefore succeeded, the accused is discharged. A discharge does not rank as an acquittal, and the prosecution may bring further committal proceedings (*R* v *Manchester City Stipendiary Magistrate, ex parte Snelson* [1977] 1 WLR 911) though such a course of action has been criticised. Alternatively, the prosecution may apply for a voluntary bill of indictment (see **6.5.4**). These alternatives precede the CPIA 1996 but appear to remain the law.

Note that neither the MCA 1980 nor the rules define what is meant by 'sufficient evidence to put the accused on trial by jury'. The *Practice Direction* in relation to submissions at summary trial has traditionally been relied on (see **5.1.7**), but this has less relevance without witnesses whose evidence may be discredited. However, it is still possible that the prosecution case may fail to contain evidence on an essential element, or may be manifestly unreliable. The magistrates, however, are likely to consider only evidential sufficiency and leave matters of credibility to the Crown Court. The test set out in *R* v *Galbraith* [1981] 1 WLR 1039 (see **11.6**) that the court should accept a submission if the evidence, taken at its highest, is such that a properly directed jury could not convict is likely to be used more frequently.

In appropriate circumstances, the submission of no case to answer may succeed in part. In these circumstances, the examining justices decide that there is insufficient evidence to commit the accused to the Crown Court on the charges on which he or she was originally brought to court, but that other indictable offences are made out. The accused is then committed on the other offences. A typical example is where the accused is charged with burglary, but the examining justices do not find sufficient evidence of entry as a trespasser to justify committing the accused for trial on that charge. If, however, they consider that there is sufficient evidence of the theft element of the offence, they may commit the accused to the Crown Court on the charge of theft.

6.3 Committals without Consideration of the Evidence

The procedure in relation to committals without consideration of the evidence under MCA 1980, s. 6(2) remains essentially unchanged by the CPIA 1996. It is a swift and simple procedure to send cases to the Crown Court.

In order for committals without consideration of the evidence to be held, the following conditions must be satisfied:

(a) All the evidence must be contained in documents which, under MCA 1980, s. 5A, must be one of the following:

(i) Written statements complying with MCA 1980, s. 5B. To comply with s. 5B the statement must be:

(a) signed by the person who made it;

(b) contain a declaration as to its truth;

(c) served on each of the other parties to the proceedings before it is tendered in evidence.

(ii) Depositions which comply with MCA 1980, s. 5C. A deposition is similar to a statement, except that it is sworn before a magistrate, rather than simply containing a declaration as to the truth. Such a deposition may be taken, for example, if the witness is seriously ill and unlikely to recover.

(iii) Copies of any documents referred to in the statements or depositions under s. 5B or 5C.

(iv) Statements which the prosecution reasonably believe would be admissible by virtue of CJA 1988, s. 23 or 24 (statements in certain documents) (s. 5D).

(b) Each accused must be legally represented (MCA 1980, s. 6(2)(a)) though the representative need not be present in court. In most cases, however, the representative will be present in order to deal with ancillary matters such as bail and legal aid.

(c) The accused must not have requested the examining justices to consider a submission of no case to answer.

6.3.1 PROCEDURE

If these conditions are satisfied, the examining justices formally commit the accused to the Crown Court following the procedure set out below:

(a) The charge is read to the accused by the clerk of the court. No plea is taken.

(b) The examining justices will ask the accused whether he or she wishes to make a submission of no case to answer. The accused, usually through his or her legal representative, declines to do so.

(c) The prosecution hands to the examining justices all the statements and other documents complying with MCA 1980, s. 5(A) (see above) upon which the case is brought. Note that all the documents have been served on the accused prior to the hearing.

(d) The examining justices formally commit the accused for trial. Note that the witness statements and other documents are not read to them or summarised, nor do they read them themselves.

(e) Decisions as to bail, legal aid and other ancillary matters are dealt with if appropriate.

6.4 Common Considerations

The following matters are common to both types of committal.

6.4.1 REPORTING RESTRICTIONS

At committal proceedings, the reporting restrictions are explained to the accused, and any application to lift them is made. Under MCA 1980, s. 8, only the technical details of the case, as opposed to the evidence, may be reported. This is to prevent any potential jury forming a view as to the accused's guilt before the case comes to trial.

Under s. 8(4) the media may report:

(a) the identity of the court; and

(b) the names of the examining justices, counsel and solicitors; and

(c) the names, ages and occupations of the parties and the witnesses; and

(d) the charges against the accused, and those on which he or she is committed for trial; and

(e) decisions as to bail and legal aid.

Note: Magistrates should be slow to impose restrictions on reporting over and above those contained in MCA 1980 (*R* v *Beaconsfield Magistrates' Court, ex parte Westminster Press* (1994) 158 JP 1055).

By s. 8A it is an offence to publish material other than that permitted. A person is liable to a fine not exceeding level 5 on the standard scale, upon summary conviction.

Reporting restrictions will be lifted in committal proceedings if the accused charged alone applies. An accused may wish restrictions to be lifted in the hope, for example, that publicity will attract the attention of potentially helpful witnesses who may then come forward.

If one of several defendants applies for the restrictions to be lifted, and the others object, restrictions will be lifted only if the justices consider it necessary in the interests of justice (see MCA 1980, s. 8(2A)). The onus is on the accused who wishes the restrictions to be lifted to show that his or her chances of a fair trial will be prejudiced in the absence of publicity (*R* v *Leeds Justices, ex parte Sykes* [1983] 1 WLR 132), but the court must give all the accused a chance to make representations (*R* v *Wirral District Magistrates' Court, ex parte Meikle* (1990) 154 JP 1035).

Once restrictions have been lifted, MCA 1980, s. 8 will not operate to re-impose them. However, if it is appropriate to do so, the justices may make an order under s. 4(2) of the Contempt of Court Act 1981. Such an order postpones the reporting of all or part of a case if contemporaneous reporting would involve a 'substantial risk of prejudice to the administration of justice'. In deciding whether to make such an order, the magistrates have a discretionary power to hear representations from the press (*R* v *Clerkenwell Metropolitan Stipendiary Magistrate, ex parte The Telegraph plc* [1993] QB 462).

6.4.2 BAIL

Committal proceedings are often an appropriate time to review bail, although such review is not automatic.

6.4.3 LEGAL AID

At committal proceedings, the court has power to extend legal aid to cover the Crown Court proceedings. This is likely to be granted if the accused's resources are unchanged from the time the legal aid was originally granted.

6.4.4 WITNESS SUMMONSES

Prior to the coming into force of the CPIA 1996, the examining justices at committal proceedings made orders under the Criminal Procedure (Attendance of Witnesses) Act 1965, s. 1, requiring the witnesses to attend at the trial. This section has been repealed by the CPIA 1996, s. 65. Section 66 of the 1996 Act substitutes a new s. 2 into the 1965 Act, allowing the Crown Court to issue a summons requiring a witness to attend.

The summons will be issued if the following conditions are satisfied:

(a) The Crown Court must be satisfied that the witness will give material evidence, or produce something which is likely to be material.

(b) The Crown Court must be satisfied that the witness will not attend voluntarily.

(c) An application must be made for the issue of the summons by the party requiring the witness. However, the issue of a summons is not automatic and the Crown Court may refuse to issue a summons if the provisions relating to the application for a summons are not met.

The application for a summons must be made as soon as practicable after committal proceedings (or transfer), or after a voluntary bill of indictment has been preferred.

6.4.5 USE OF STATEMENTS AT TRIAL

By virtue of CPIA 1996, sch. 2, para. 1(2), a statement tendered at committal under s. 5B 'may without further proof be read as evidence on the trial of the accused', provided (para. 1(3)(c)) that the accused does not object. Any objection should be given in writing to the prosecutor and the Crown Court within 14 days of committal (Magistrates' Courts Rules 1981, r. 8). The purpose of this provision is to ensure that only those witnesses whom the defence wish to cross-examine are called before the Crown Court.

However, even if the accused does object, the court may order that the objection has no effect, if it is 'in the interests of justice so to order'. It seems that such an order, depriving the defendant of the right to cross-examine those who have given evidence against him, is likely to be used rarely and it has been suggested that it should only be used if the same conditions as apply to the admissibility of hearsay statements under CJA 1988, ss. 23 and 24 apply. You should consult the ***Evidence Manual*** for a full discussion of these sections.

6.4.6 APPEALS AGAINST THE DECISION TO COMMIT

The prosecution may, in effect, appeal against a refusal to commit, by applying for a voluntary bill of indictment (see **6.5.4**). It is somewhat more difficult for a defendant, however, who cannot appeal to the Crown Court against the decision, as it is neither a conviction nor a sentence (see **8.1**). Nor can he or she appeal by way of case stated, as the case has not yet finished (see **8.2.1**). The only way in which a defendant may appeal is therefore to apply for judicial review (see **8.3**). The Divisional Court has, however, been reluctant to interfere on the basis that the examining justices admitted inadmissible evidence and it is only in the case of a really substantial error leading to demonstrable injustice that they will do so (*R* v *Bedwelty Justices, ex parte Williams* [1997] AC 225).

If the error at committal is so significant that the committal must be regarded as null, the consequent trial, indictment and conviction are similarly null, and will be quashed by the Court of Appeal (*R* v *Gee* [1936] 2 KB 442 and *R* v *Phillips* [1939] 1 KB 63).

6.5 Avoiding Committal Proceedings

In certain circumstances, cases may reach the Crown Court without first going through committal proceedings.

6.5.1 INDICTABLE-ONLY OFFENCES

Since January 1999, a number of areas are piloting a scheme contained in CDA 1998, s. 51, whereby indictable-only offences, and related offences, are sent straight to the Crown Court for trial, without spending any time in the magistrates' court, other than the first hearing. This is a measure designed to reduce delay in the criminal justice process, and is consistent with the close management of the case, through the Plea and Directions Hearings, which the Crown Court now has.

Section 51 provides as follows:

> *(1) Where an adult appears or is brought before a magistrates' court ('the court') charged with an offence triable only on indictment ('the indictable-only offence'), the court shall send him forthwith to the Crown Court for trial—*
> *(a) for that offence, and*
> *(b) for any either-way or summary offence with which he is charged which fulfils the requisite conditions (as set out in subsection (11) below).*

Under s. 51(11), an offence fulfils the '*requisite conditions*' if:

(a) it appears to the court to be related to the indictable-only offence; and

(b) in the case of a summary offence, it is punishable with imprisonment or disqualification.

Under s. 51(12):

(a) An either-way offence is '*related*' to an indictable-only offence if it could be '*joined in the same indictment*' as the indictable-only offence. Students should consult r. 9 of the Indictment Rules 1971 and **9.2.1** below for the meaning of the words '*joined in the same indictment*'.

(b) A summary offence is '*related*' to an indictable-only offence if it '*arises out of circumstances which are the same as or connected with those*' giving rise to the indictable-only offence. Students should consult CJA 1988, s .41 and **4.4.2** for the meaning of the words '*same or connected circumstances*'.

The CDA 1998 deals with three further specific situations:

(a) Where the accused is jointly charged on the same occasion, with another adult with a related either-way offence, the second adult must be sent to the Crown Court for trial with the first accused, if it fulfils the '*requisite conditions*' (s. 51(3)).

(b) Section 51(1) provides for the situation where a single accused appears before the court charged with an indictable-only offence and related offence(s). Section 51(2) and (3) deal with the situation where the accused is *subsequently* charged with related offences, or a second accused is *subsequently* charged with related offences. In either of these situations, the court may send the accused to the Crown Court for the related offences, if they fulfil '*the requisite conditions*' In other words, in these situations the court has a discretion to send the related offences to the Crown Court instead of an obligation to do so.

(c) Where a child or young person is jointly charged with an indictable-only offence with an adult whom the court has sent to the Crown Court under s. 51(1), the court shall send the child or young person to the Crown Court forthwith if '*it considers it necessary in the interests of justice to do so*' (s. 51(5)). If the court decides to do so, then it may also send any either-way or summary only offences which fulfil the '*requisite conditions*'.

CDA 1998, sch. 3, contains detailed provisions relating to the procedure to be adopted when a person is sent for trial under s. 51, and in particular, the opportunity to have the case dismissed in advance of the trial.

6.5.2 SERIOUS FRAUD CASES

Under CJA 1987, s. 4, the prosecution may serve notice transferring a case of serious fraud to the Crown Court if the following conditions are satisfied:

(a) a person has been charged with an indictable offence; and

(b) in the opinion of the prosecuting authority:

  (i) there is sufficient evidence for the person charged to be committed for trial; and

  (ii) the charge reveals a case of fraud of such seriousness or complexity that it is appropriate that the management of the case should, without delay, be taken over by the Crown Court; and

(c) the magistrates' court has not yet begun to inquire into the case as examining justices.

The prosecuting authorities in serious fraud cases are the Director of Public Prosecutions, the Director of the Serious Fraud Office, the Commissioners of Inland Revenue and Customs and Excise, and the Secretary of State.

The notice of transfer must specify the charges against the accused, and the appropriate Crown Court, and must be accompanied by written statements of the evidence. Once the case has been transferred to the Crown Court, a preparatory hearing will normally take place at which the judge may rule that the written statements do not reveal a case to answer. Note that this matter is dealt with by a judge, and not by a magistrates' court. See generally CJA 1987, ss. 3 to 10.

6.5.3 CASES INVOLVING CHILDREN

Under CJA 1991, s. 53, if a person is charged with one of the offences listed below, the Director of Public Prosecutions (or someone acting on his or her behalf) may serve notice transferring the case to the Crown Court, if he or she is of the opinion:

(a) that the evidence is sufficient for the person charged to be committed for trial;

(b) that a child will be called as a witness who is alleged:

  (i) to be a person against whom the offence was committed; or

  (ii) to have witnessed the commission of the offence; and

(c) that for the purpose of avoiding any prejudice to the welfare of the child, the case should be taken over, and proceeded with by the Crown Court without delay.

Such a notice should be served before the magistrates begin to sit as examining justices (s. 53(2)).

The decision to transfer the proceedings is not appealable in any court (s. 53(4)). However, the accused can apply to a judge of the Crown Court for the case to be dismissed (sch. 6, para. 5) but the child in question may not be called as a witness on that application (sch. 6, para. 5(5)).

Notices of transfer in this situation apply:

(a) to an offence which involves an assault on, or injury or threat of injury to, a person;

(b) to an offence under CYPA 1933, s. 1 (cruelty to persons under 16);

(c) to an offence under the Sexual Offences Act 1956, Indecency with Children Act 1960, Sexual Offences Act 1967, Criminal Law Act 1977, s. 54, and the Protection of Children Act 1978; and

(d) to an offence which consists of attempting or conspiring to commit, or aiding and abetting, counselling, procuring or inciting the commission of an offence.

For the purpose of notices of transfer, a child is a person under the age of 14, in relation to the offences mentioned in (a) and (b) above and 17 in relation to the offences in (c) above. Note that if the child's evidence is given by way of a video recording, made while the child was under 14 or under 17 respectively, then the relevant ages of the child are 15 and 18 respectively.

The purpose of transferring the proceedings by notice is to protect child victims and child witnesses, by sparing them the stress of court appearances (e.g. at committal proceedings) and by getting the case tried expeditiously.

For the detailed provisions of the procedure, students should consult CJA 1991, sch. 6.

6.5.4 VOLUNTARY BILLS OF INDICTMENT

Under the Administration of Justice (Miscellaneous Provisions) Act 1933, s. 2, a High Court judge has the power to prefer a voluntary bill of indictment, that is, he or she may order that the accused be tried on indictment. In making such an order, committal proceedings or transfer for trial proceedings are avoided.

The preferment of a voluntary bill is exceptional, and consent to the preferment should only be given where a good reason to depart from the normal procedure is clearly shown, and 'only where the interests of justice rather than administrative convenience require it' (*Practice Direction* [1999] 1 WLR 1613, para. 3).

Traditionally, voluntary bills have been sought in two situations:

(a) where committal proceedings have resulted in the discharge of an accused, and the prosecution does not wish to hold a second set of committal proceedings — although the prosecution should be slow to reject the views of the magistrates; or

(b) where the prosecution case is that an offence was committed jointly by two or more persons, and at least one of them has already been committed for trial, and an indictment signed against him or her. In these circumstances, the prosecution will wish to try all the accused together, but may only do so if a second indictment is signed against all the accused. A voluntary bill of indictment will achieve the desired result.

Under para. 2 of the *Practice Direction*, applications for a voluntary bill must be accompanied by:

(a) a copy of any charges on which the defendant has been committed for trial;

(b) a copy of any charges on which his committal for trial was refused by the magistrates' court;

(c) a copy of any existing indictment which has been preferred in consequence of his committal;

(d) a summary of the evidence or other document which:

   (i) identifies the counts in the proposed indictment on which he has been committed for trial (or which are substantially the same as charges on which he has been so committed); and

   (ii) in relation to each other count in the proposed indictment, identifies the pages in the accompanying statements and exhibits where the essential evidence said to support that count is to be found;

(e) marginal markings of the relevant passages on the pages of the statements and exhibits identified under (d) (ii) above.

The judge will consider the application and any written submission from the defendant, and may seek amplification if necessary. He or she may invite oral submissions from either party or accede to a request for the opportunity to make such oral submissions if he or she considers it necessary or desirable in order to make a sound and fair decision. Any such oral submission should be made on notice to the other party (*Practice Direction* [1999] 1 WLR 1613, para. 6).

Guidance to prosecutors on the procedures to be adopted in seeking judicial consent to the preferment to voluntary bills has also been given, directing prosecutors:

(a) on the making of the application, to notify the defendant;

(b) at about the same time, serve on him or her a copy of all the documents delivered to the judge;

(c) inform the defendant of his or her right to make written submissions to the judge within nine working days of giving the notice.

These procedures should be followed unless there are good reasons for not doing so, in which case the prosecutor must inform the judge, and ask for leave to dispense with all or any of them. The judge will only give leave if good grounds are shown.

A High Court judge's decision to issue a voluntary bill is subject to review, according to *R* v *IRC, ex parte Dhesi, The Independent*, 14 August 1995, despite other authority to the contrary (*R* v *Manchester Crown Court, ex parte Williams* (1990) 154 JP 589). However, given the nature of the voluntary bill, where the application is made *ex parte* and therefore against the rules of natural justice, the courts' jurisdiction in respect of judicial review is limited and could only be exercised in the case of alleged malice on the part of the prosecutor.

Once the bill of indictment has been preferred, it is an indictment like any other, and capable of amendment under the Indictments Act 1915, s. 5 (*R* v *Wells* (1995) 159 JP 243).

SEVEN

JUVENILES AND THE COURTS

7.1 Introduction

The youth justice system of England and Wales has been subjected to considerable scrutiny over recent years. The system is in the process of going through major changes. It may be helpful to review, briefly, some of the history and objectives that lay behind the root and branch changes that began in 1998 and which were continuing at the time of writing.

Since Parliament passed the Children and Young Persons Act 1933 (CYPA 1933), courts have been under a statutory duty to have regard to the welfare of juveniles when dealing with them. In a 1996 report, *Misspent Youth*, the Audit Commission said that:

> The current system for dealing with youth crime is inefficient and expensive, while little is done to deal effectively with juvenile nuisance. The present arrangements are failing the young people who are not being guided away from offending to constructive activities. They are also failing victims . . . and they lead to waste in a variety of forms, including lost time, as public servants process the same young offenders through the courts time and again . . .

In November 1997, the Home Office published a White Paper, *No More Excuses — A New Approach to Tackling Youth Crime in England and Wales*. The White Paper set out proposals for change in the short term, but also considered that a longer term review of the work of the youth court was needed. The White Paper agreed with the suggestion that 'much of the effort put into the [youth justice] system is "processing", with . . . very little indeed on "preventing crime" or "service" [to victims, offenders and witnesses]'. The government believed that:

> the efforts of the youth justice system are currently weighted too heavily towards dealing with young offenders whose behaviour has been allowed to escalate out of control, rather than intervening early and effectively to prevent and reduce crime and anti-social behaviour. [There has to] be a new focus on nipping crime in the bud — stopping children at risk from getting involved in crime and preventing early criminal behaviour from escalating into persistent or serious offending.

With those considerations in mind, the White Paper stated that:

> the purpose of the youth court must change from simply determining guilt or innocence and then issuing a sentence. In most cases, an offence should trigger a wider enquiry into the circumstances and nature of the offending behaviour, leading to action to change that behaviour. This requires in turn a fundamental change of approach within the youth court system.

Whilst the courts are still under their statutory duty to have regard to the welfare of juveniles when dealing with them, the White Paper pointed out that concerns for the welfare of the offender have in the past 'too often been seen as in conflict with the aims of protecting the public, punishing offences and preventing offending. This confusion ... has contributed to the loss of public confidence in the youth justice system'. One keynote change has been to assert that:

(a) It shall be the principal aim of the youth justice system to prevent offending by children and young persons.

(b) In addition to any other duty to which they are subject, it shall be the duty of all persons and bodies carrying out functions in relation to the youth justice system to have regard to that aim.

(See CDA 1998, s. 37.)

Recent, and proposed, changes to the youth court (such as new sentences, speedier procedures, revised layout of the courtroom) should be seen as part of a much larger plan to tackle youth criminality. In the White Paper, research was quoted as showing that the key factors related to youth criminality are:

- being male;
- being brought up by a criminal parent or parents;
- living in a family with multiple problems;
- experiencing poor parenting and lack of supervision;
- poor discipline in the family and at school;
- playing truant or being excluded from school;
- associating with delinquent friends; and
- having siblings who offend.

The 'single most important factor in explaining criminality is the quality of a young person's home life, including parental supervision' (White Paper, chapter 1). So, youth courts will have the power to refer first-time offenders, who show contrition, to youth offender panels who will draw up a contract, regulating the juvenile's future behaviour. The police will have the power to give a warning to a juvenile (i.e. rather than prosecute) and to refer the juvenile to rehabilitation programmes, run by youth offending teams. Youth offending teams are multi-agency bodies, created by local authorities, in co-operation with the local chief officer of police, probation service and health authority, under powers given by CDA 1998, s. 39. The Home Office has asserted that these teams will be at the cutting edge of the government's reforms for youth justice. Amongst their tasks, they will:

> tackle the issues — from poor parental supervision and domestic violence or abuse to peer group pressure, from truancy and school exclusion to substance misuse or mental health problems — which can place young people at risk of becoming involved in crime.

New sentences include reparation orders and parenting orders. Juvenile offenders may be confronted by the victims of their crimes and required to make a direct apology; children and parents may have to attend family counselling sessions. To try to stop offending before it starts, new powers are given to make child safety orders (for individual children who are at risk of being drawn into crime), and local child curfews (to minimise the risk that peer pressure and the absence of responsible adult role models will foster anti-social behaviour). Many of these reforms are contained in CDA 1998. Several reforms are the subject of pilots around the country. Those pilots began in September 1998 and ran for 18 months, to the end of March 2000. A Home Office press release, 22 February 2000, stated that on 1 June 2000 there would be a nationwide roll-out of reparation orders, action plan orders, child safety orders and parenting orders, while detention and training orders were to be implemented on 1 April 2000. In March 1999, the government made £50 million available over the next three years to pay for youth justice services and intervention programmes which are designed to change offending behaviour. In a keynote address to the first national conference of the Youth Justice Board, the Home Secretary stated that:

> The priorities for funding will be programmes aimed at providing effective supervision; developing cognitive thinking and basic literacy and numeracy skills; making reparation to victims; improving the parenting of young offenders; and providing mentoring to keep young offenders out of further trouble and get them back into education or training.

Although only some of these changes will apply directly to the work of the youth courts, and thus to practitioners in those courts, nevertheless it is important that everyone working within the youth justice system is aware of the overall picture.

7.2 Why Distinguish the Juvenile from Other Defendants?

7.2.1 DIFFERENT COURT, DIFFERENT SYSTEM

For most people charged with a criminal offence, there are only two courts to worry about. These are the magistrates' court and Crown Court. (Although remember that cases can go *on appeal* to the Divisional Court or Court of Appeal and then to the House of Lords.)

For juveniles there is another, separate court — the youth court. This court is a special type of magistrates' court (see **7.5** below). For the avoidance of confusion, the ordinary magistrates' court will be referred to in this chapter as the *adult* magistrates' court.

The usual method of classifying offences (i.e. in terms of which court can or must try the offence; see **4.1**) does not apply to juveniles. Apart from homicide offences, there are no offences for which a juvenile *must* be tried on indictment. The concept of offences triable either way is inapplicable to juveniles — the mode of trial procedure (set out in MCA 1980, ss. 17A–21) is not used and juveniles cannot elect trial by jury. (See further **7.6.1** below.) The general principle is that juveniles should be tried summarily and that such trials will usually be in the youth court.

7.2.2 WHAT DO WE MEAN BY 'JUVENILE'?

A juvenile is basically anyone under the age of 18 (CJA 1991, s. 68). Once an individual has reached his or her eighteenth birthday, he or she must be treated like any other adult defendant. This could lead to problems if the defendant's eighteenth birthday occurs while a case is pending at court (see **7.7** below). Thus, while for the layman the term 'juvenile' generally means a youth or young person, for the criminal justice system one's youth ends on the eighteenth birthday.

As part of its long-term review of the youth court, the government is currently considering a proposal to return 17-year-olds to the jurisdiction of the adult courts. This was originally put forward by the Narey Report in 1997 (published by the Home Office).

(For sentencing purposes, it is also necessary to divide those 'adult' defendants aged 18–20 inclusive from defendants aged 21 and over. See **Sentencing** at **Chapter 13** et seq.)

7.2.3 TWO SUBCATEGORIES: 'CHILDREN' AND 'YOUNG PERSONS'

Juveniles between the ages of 10 and 13 inclusive are often described in criminal law statutes as 'children', but this is not a universal usage. Those aged between 14 and 17 years inclusive are usually described as 'young persons'. See CJA 1991, s. 68 and sch. 8. Historically, these two groups have been distinguished for two reasons — sentencing powers, and the presumption of innocence.

7.2.3.1 Sentencing powers for 'children' and 'young persons'

Sentencing powers for young offenders are dealt with at length in **Chapter 24**. In summary, the range of sentences available to courts when dealing with juveniles has differed significantly from those available for adult offenders. Again, different types of sentence (or different maxima) apply to juveniles of different ages. However, the trend in recent years has been to toughen the sentences available, even when dealing with the youngest offenders. One example is the power to sentence defendants as young as 10 to long-term detention for various grave offences (e.g. burglary of a house, certain types of arson and criminal damage, and robbery). Another example is the power to make *detention and training orders* (DTOs). These were made available to courts from the 1 April 1999. A DTO may be used for 15–17 year olds who are convicted of any imprisonable offence which is sufficiently serious to cross the custody threshold in CJA 1991. Twelve to 14 year olds would be at risk of a DTO when convicted of an imprisonable offence, if they have a record of persistent offending. Even 10 and 11 year olds may be sentenced to a DTO, if they are persistent offenders. One of the new community penalties — *the action plan order* — will be available for use with offenders ranging in age from 10 – 17 years (nationwide from June 2000). Finally on sentencing, an existing community penalty for older offenders — *the curfew order* — was extended to offenders aged 10–15 years in 1998, with electronic tagging being available from December 1999.

7.2.3.2 The presumption of innocence

A second reason to distinguish between 'children' and other juvenile defendants was the presumption of innocence, or incapacity, which has been applied to juveniles aged 10–13 inclusive. The presumption (also known as the presumption of *doli incapax*) was rebuttable in cases involving these children. To rebut it, prosecutors had to establish beyond a reasonable doubt, in addition to the elements of the crime, that the child defendant knew that he or she was doing something *seriously wrong*, rather than simply naughty, when committing the offence. In 1997, a government White Paper, *No More Excuses*, proposed the abolition of this common law presumption and abolition was effected by CDA 1998, s. 34, which came into effect on 30 September 1998. The rationale behind the abolition was the concern that the need to produce evidence to rebut the presumption 'could lead to real practical difficulties, delaying cases or even making it impossible for the prosecution to proceed' (*No More Excuses*, chapter 4). One might have argued that the presumption existed precisely in order to cause difficulties for prosecutors and ensure that, in some cases, a prosecution would not succeed (cp. a report by the Howard League for Penal Reform, *Protecting the Rights of Children*, March 1999). One might have pointed out that many other European countries do not consider youngsters to bear criminal responsibility for their actions until their fourteenth birthday. However, those arguments would have fallen on deaf ears.

The age of criminal responsibility was considered by the European Court of Human Rights in the case of *T* v *UK*; *V* v *UK*, 16 December 1999, unreported. The Court considered whether the attribution of criminal responsibility to the applicants in respect of acts committed at the age of ten could in itself amount to inhuman or degrading treatment, contrary to ECHR, Article 3. In its judgment:

> it did not find that there was any clear common standard amongst the member States of the Council of Europe as to the minimum age of criminal responsibility. While most had adopted an age-limit which was higher than that in force in England and Wales, other States, such as Cyprus, Ireland, Liechtenstein and Switzerland, attributed criminal responsibility from a younger age, and no clear tendency could be ascertained from examination of the relevant international texts and instruments, for example, the United Nations Convention on the Rights of the Child. Even if England and Wales was among the few European jurisdictions to retain a low age of criminal responsibility, the age of ten could not be said to be so young as to differ disproportionately to the age limit followed by other European States. The attribution of criminal responsibility to the applicants did not, therefore, in itself give rise to a breach of Article 3.

7.2.3.3 The under-tens

For the time being, at least, children aged under ten years are irrebuttably presumed to be incapable of committing any crime. Therefore, they do not fall within the criminal jurisdiction of any court (CYPA 1933, s. 50). However, the move to make it easier to convict 10–14 year olds (see **7.2.3.2**) comes at the same time as two new statutory provisions are introduced, both aimed at the under tens. The first is the *local child curfew*. This is a power given to local authorities to enable them to bar all children under the age of ten from being in a specified public area after a specific time (not earlier than 9 pm). The second new measure is the *child safety order*. This is aimed at individual children, unlike the local child curfew. The child safety order will enable courts to require a child to be at home at specific times or to keep away from specific places or people. Certain conduct can be forbidden; the example given in the White Paper, *No More Excuses*, is truanting from school. See CDA 1998, ss. 11–15.

The use of children aged under ten by older criminals, to commit crimes on their behalf, is not new (cp. the relationship of Fagin and Oliver Twist, described by Charles Dickens). It may result in the conviction of the 'manipulator', usually as the principal offender, with the child being regarded as an innocent agent, or tool, of the other. See *Archbold*, 2000, paras 1–91 and 18–2; *Blackstone's Criminal Practice*, 2000, A5.6.

7.3 Juveniles Who Could be Prosecuted But are Not

7.3.1 THE OLD SYSTEM: THE CAUTION

The current version of the Code for Crown Prosecutors states:

> 6.8 Crown Prosecutors must consider the interests of a youth when deciding whether it is in the public interest to prosecute. The stigma of a conviction can cause very serious harm to the prospects of a youth offender or a young adult. Young offenders can sometimes be dealt with without going to court. But Crown Prosecutors should not avoid prosecuting simply because of the defendant's age. The seriousness of the offence or the offender's past behaviour may make prosecution necessary.

It has sometimes been felt that juveniles may be damaged by contact with the criminal justice system. Consequently, an alternative method developed whereby the juvenile was given a *caution*, instead of prosecuting him or her. The effect was less traumatic because no court appearance was involved. The caution was given by a senior police officer, usually in uniform. He or she would emphasise the likelihood of a court appearance should the juvenile reoffend, how fortunate the juvenile was to escape with a caution, and the shame which must have been suffered by his or her parents, together with a reminder of any damage caused by the juvenile. Cautions could only be given in certain circumstances (i.e., if there was sufficient evidence to prosecute, the juvenile admitted the offence and the parents consented to the offence being disposed of by use of a caution).

It might be thought that cautions were an effective tool for nipping a criminal career in the bud. Between 70–80% of offenders who were cautioned did not re-offend in the following two years. However, there was also a small core of persistent juvenile offenders to whom a caution meant nothing. It was seen as a 'let-off', they were not deterred and even found themselves being cautioned several times (3% of young offenders are said to be responsible for 25% of crimes: *Aspects of Crime Young Offenders 1995*, Home Office, 1997). There was a clear need for a thorough reform of the cautioning system, despite attempts to impose consistency and rigour through Home Office Circulars (see e.g. Home Office Circular 18/1994; Evans, 'Cautioning: Counting the Cost of Retrenchment' [1994] Crim LR 566).

7.3.2 THE INTERMEDIATE SYSTEM: CAUTION-PLUS

In early 1997, the Conservative government proposed a new system — caution-plus — which would be administered by the courts. This system did not simply administer a warning to the juvenile but provided schemes to support him or her in not re-offending. In Milton Keynes, for example, the Retail Theft Initiative educated young thieves that shoplifting was not a victimless crime, to appreciate the consequences of their actions for themselves, the shops and others, and how to resist the temptation to re-offend. Home Office research showed a recidivism rate of just 3%, compared to 35% for first-time offenders in other forms of disposal. There was also a 500% reduction in the time spent by police officers dealing with shop thieves. Nevertheless, in May 1997 the new Labour government decided not to adopt this idea of court-cautions (see its White Paper, *No More Excuses*, 1997). Instead, there was a proposal to scrap the existing system of cautions in its entirety and replace it with a formal system of reprimands and warnings, issued by the police.

7.3.3 THE NEW SYSTEM: THE FINAL WARNING SCHEME

Repeat cautioning has gone. The Crime and Disorder Act 1998, ss. 65–66, introduced a *final warning scheme* under which each offence committed by a young offender will be met with a progressive response, which is designed to prevent further offending. The scheme came into effect on 30 September 1998 and is initially operative by way of pilots in the following areas:

- the London boroughs of Kensington and Chelsea, Hammersmith and Fulham and the City of Westminster (jointly)
- Hampshire, Southampton, Portsmouth and the Isle of Wight (again, jointly)
- Wolverhampton
- Sheffield
- Blackburn.

It is anticipated that the final warning scheme will apply nationally during 2000–2001. Thereafter, no caution will be given to a child or young person (CDA 1998, s. 65(8)).

In summary, the final warning scheme sets up three levels of response to a first-time offender. He or she may receive a reprimand, or a final warning, or be charged with the offence and appear in court. A juvenile who receives a final warning will be referred to a *youth offending team* (created under CDA 1998, s. 39). The youth offending team will assess the juvenile to see whether it is appropriate to use a rehabilitation programme, aimed at preventing re-offending.

In a related move, the Youth Justice and Criminal Evidence Act 1999 (YJCEA) introduced a new sentencing power for magistrates. In the case of first-time offenders, the magistrates may make a *referral order*. This will dispatch the juvenile to a *youth offender panel*. A panel will contain magistrates, members of the local youth offending team, members of the public and, possibly, police officers. A referral order is intended to become the normal method of disposal for young offenders with no previous convictions. A referral order should last no longer than 12 months and will involve the juvenile agreeing to comply with a programme of behaviour, or contract. The contract should involve an element of reparation, possibly financial or a direct apology to the victim. Examples of other requirements that might be included are: undertaking unpaid work in the community, attending school, participating in family counselling sessions, refraining from visiting particular places.

7.3.4 DECIDING UPON THE APPROPRIATE ACTION

Unlike the caution-plus scheme, where decisions were taken by courts, the responsibility for taking decisions under the final warning scheme rests with the police (as it did under the old cautioning system). In exceptional circumstances, it will still be possible for the police to take informal action but otherwise the police must choose between a reprimand, a warning or a charge.

In order to impose a reprimand or a warning, the following four criteria must be satisfied:

- there is sufficient admissible, reliable evidence to provide a realistic prospect of conviction, if the juvenile was prosecuted
- the juvenile admits committing the offence
- the juvenile has no previous convictions
- a prosecution is not in the public interest.

Once those criteria are satisfied, the juvenile may be given a *reprimand* if:

(a) he or she has not previously been reprimanded or warned; *and*

(b) the offence is not so serious as to require a warning.

The juvenile may receive a *warning* if:

(a) he or she has not been warned before; or

(b) there has been one previous warning but it was given more than two years before the date of the present offence; *and*

(c) the offence is not so serious as to require a charge against the juvenile.

Any caution which a juvenile receives before the final warning scheme comes into force will thereafter count as a reprimand for the purposes of the scheme. However, any second or subsequent caution that the juvenile has received will be treated as a warning (CDA 1998, sch. 9 para. 5).

Reprimands are thought to be appropriate for most first-time offenders. There can be no repeat reprimands, so a second-time offender should normally expect a warning, unless he or she was previously warned in which case the police officer will normally decide to charge the juvenile. The usual decision for third-time offenders will be to charge them with the offence. Fourth-time (and subsequent) offenders cannot be reprimanded or given a warning in any circumstances; the only decision can be to charge the juvenile with the offence. It must be emphasised that if a juvenile does not make a clear and reliable admission to all elements of the offence, the only choice facing the police officer is whether or not to charge the juvenile with the offence.

It is most unlikely that reprimands and warnings will be used for very serious, indictable-only offences (e.g. murder, rape). Other offences may be too serious to be dealt with by a reprimand or warning, depending on their circumstances. It can be seen that the key factors in making a decision under the final warning scheme are therefore:

(a) the seriousness of the offence; and

(b) the offending history of the juvenile.

Important factors, when determining the seriousness of an offence, include its impact on the victim. Victims will normally be asked for their views on the offence, information on any loss or harm suffered and the impact of the offence in the light of their circumstances. An important aggravating factor will be if an offence was racially motivated. A general list of aggravating and mitigating factors has been devised by the Association of Chief Police Officers and this is likely to be relied on by police officers when assessing the seriousness of an offence (and whether a prosecution is in the public interest). This list, known as the ACPO Gravity Factors, endeavours to attach a numerical value to many offences. That numerical value may change, depending on the presence of aggravating or mitigating factors. Essentially, what the Gravity Factors do is to rank crimes in an abstract hierarchy of seriousness, and then allow aggravating or mitigating factors to 'fine tune' that ranking to accord with the circumstances of the actual offence which the juvenile committed. This exercise should produce a 'Final Gravity Score' which will work like this:

FINAL SCORE	ACTION
4	Always charge.
3	Normally warn for a first offence. If offender does not qualify for a warning then charge. Only in exceptional circumstances should a reprimand be given. Decision maker needs to justify reprimand.
2	Normally reprimand for first offence. If offender does not qualify for a reprimand but qualifies for a warning then give warning. If offender does not qualify for a warning then charge.
1	Always the minimum response applicable to the individual offender, i.e. reprimand, warning or charge.

7.3.5 WHAT WILL HAPPEN WHEN A JUVENILE OFFENDER IS REPRIMANDED OR WARNED?

A reprimand or warning must be given orally by a police officer in a police station. The officer should normally be in uniform, and should be of inspector rank, although specially-trained sergeants and constables may be used. Unless the juvenile is aged 17, an appropriate adult must be present when the reprimand or warning is given (defined in PACE Code of Practice, Code C). The oral action will be supported by written advice, usually in a standard form.

The officer should always specify the offence or offences which have resulted in the reprimand or warning. When giving a reprimand, the officer should also explain that:

- the reprimand is a serious matter
- any further offences will result in a final warning or prosecution in all but the most exceptional circumstances
- (if one or more of the offences is recordable) the reprimand constitutes a criminal record and will be cited in any future criminal proceedings.

When giving a warning, the officer should explain that:

- the warning is a serious matter
- any further offences will result in charges being brought in all but the most exceptional circumstances
- (if one or more of the offences is recordable) the warning constitutes a criminal record
- the warning may be cited in any future criminal proceedings
- in the event of a conviction within the next two years, the sentence of a conditional discharge will only be used in exceptional circumstances; in most cases, the juvenile should expect a more severe sentence (CDA 1998,s. 66(4))
- the juvenile will be referred to a local youth offending team
- the referral will result in contact by the youth offending team within two working days and, in general terms, what will happen thereafter.

A member of the youth offending team may be present to help explain to the juvenile what are the implications of the warning and the nature of the rehabilitation programme that he or she is likely to be put into.

All reprimands and warnings will be recorded. The record will be kept, in the case of 10 and 11 year olds, until they are 18; in the case of other juveniles, records will be kept for at least five years. Reprimands and warnings may be cited in court, in the same circumstances as convictions.

7.4 Who Will Be in Court?

7.4.1 WHO WILL TRY THE CASE?

In a youth court, the court will usually consist of three lay magistrates (or 'justices of the peace'). They will have been selected from a 'youth court panel' of magistrates who are thought to be specially qualified to deal with juveniles and who have also had some additional training for this purpose. Normally, there should be at least one male and one female magistrate present for a hearing in the youth court. If all the magistrates in court are of the same sex, they may only hear cases if:

(a) this situation could not have been foreseen; and

(b) having heard representations from the parties in open court, the magistrates do not consider it is expedient to adjourn proceedings, to see if a mixed gender bench might be formed.

7.4.2 STIPENDIARY MAGISTRATES

These professional magistrates usually sit in the adult magistrates' court, but may also deal with cases in the youth court. They are members of the youth court panel by virtue of their office. Until recently, stipendiary magistrates had to be accompanied by a lay magistrate, of the opposite gender, unless the two criteria set out in **7.4.1** were met. In 1997, the Narey Report (*Review of Delay in the Criminal Justice System*, a report commissioned by the Home Office to examine the causes of delays in the criminal justice system) recommended that stipendiaries should be able to sit, unaccompanied, in the youth court as a matter of course. This change was intended to keep delays in the youth courts to the minimum period possible (for example, previously, a trial lasting more than a day might have been adjourned over a long period if the three lay magistrates had difficulties in finding a mutually-convenient date for the next hearing). The Narey Report also suggested that stipendiaries should specialise in the management of particularly complex cases which, when they involve children and young persons, 'can be particularly difficult'. The CDA 1998, s. 48, amends CYPA 1933 so that metropolitan stipendiary magistrates can discharge their duties unaccompanied (s. 48 came into effect on 30 September 1998). For stipendiary magistrates in non-metropolitan areas, the necessary amendments have been made to the Youth Courts (Constitution) Rules 1954.

7.4.3 THE PARENTS OF THE JUVENILE

When a juvenile appears in court, accused of a crime, it is understandable that his or her parents may want to be present to support their child. This is not always the attitude of parents, however, and the trial courts possess the power to compel parents to attend court. If a juvenile is aged 15 or under, the court must order a parent to attend, unless it would be unreasonable to do so. If the juvenile is aged 16 or 17, the court *may* make such an order (see CYPA 1933, s. 34A, inserted by CJA 1991, s. 56). When parents attend court, they usually sit next to their child.

Part of the reason for requiring a juvenile's parents to be present in court may be that although '[p]arents of young offenders may not directly be to blame for the crimes of their children, [they] have to be responsible for providing their children with proper care and control' ((*No More Excuses*, 1997). Home Office research has shown that inadequate parental supervision is strongly associated with offending; also that the quality of the parent-child relationship is crucial. Bringing the parents to court may bring home to them the need to modify their behaviour as well as that of their child. However, *No More Excuses* also reported that parental firmness was not necessarily the answer: 'We know that parents who are harsh or erratic in disciplining their children are twice as likely to have children who offend.'

For many years, one of the sentences at the disposal of the youth courts has been the parental bind-over. The parents will forfeit a pre-determined sum of money if their child re-offends and is convicted. A more constructive approach is now being piloted in certain areas of the country. The CDA 1998, s. 8, introduced the *parenting order*. This will oblige the parents to attend counselling or guidance sessions for a maximum three month period and to comply with additional requirements for up to one year. Examples of additional requirements might be ensuring full school attendance by their child; or making sure that their child is at home by a certain time each night. If a parent fails, without reasonable excuse, to comply with any requirement of the parenting order, he or she will face a summary conviction and a fine of up to £1,000. In these circumstances, there is now arguably a greater need for parents to be present in court.

7.4.4 PUBLIC ACCESS TO THE COURTS

This can arise in two ways. First, through actual attendance at court. Secondly, through access to media reports of proceedings in court. These need to be considered separately.

7.4.4.1 Public attendance at court

A distinction must be drawn between public attendance at youth courts and at the two other trial courts — adult magistrates' courts and the Crown Court.

Youth courts

Youth courts operate rather differently from the other courts, in that there is no general right to enter a youth courtroom. Attendance is governed by CYPA 1933, s. 47(2) (as amended), so that no person shall be present at any sitting of a youth court except:

- the juvenile, his or her parents, the parties' legal representatives and the magistrate(s)
- court officers (the clerk, ushers)
- bona fide media reporters (but not to take photographs or to film)
- witnesses (both during and after giving their evidence)
- anyone else directly concerned in that case (probation officers, social workers etc.)
- such other persons as the court may specially authorise to be present.

In the past, these restrictions on access have usually been enforced strictly. The reason for this limited access was, in part, a desire to protect the juvenile from being (or feeling) stigmatised as a criminal. The effect was to exclude the general public and, not infrequently, the victim of the offence. The victim would enter the courtroom only when and if needed as a witness, where the juvenile pleaded not guilty. Recently, this has led to criticism of the youth court system as a 'secret garden', where proceedings take place in private and young offenders are not encouraged to face the consequences of their actions and take steps to change their behaviour. It has been suggested that the present practice placed too great an emphasis on protecting the identity of young offenders at the expense of victims and the community. In 1998, the former Home Office Minister Alun Michael observed that youth courts:

> . . . have wide discretion about who can attend [their] proceedings . . . We believe that justice is best served in an open court where the criminal process can be scrutinised and the offender cannot hide behind a cloak of anonymity.

Thus, in June 1998, the Home Office and Lord Chancellor's Department issued a joint circular which included the following recommendations:

- all victims of juvenile crime should have the opportunity to attend the youth court (for the trial or preceding hearings) unless to do so would not be in the interests of justice
- greater access should be allowed for the public to attend proceedings in the youth court (an example being a case where the offender's conduct has had an impact on the local community generally).

Adult magistrates' courts and the Crown Court
Both these trial courts operate their usual policy of being open to the general public when hearing a case, whether or not the case involves a juvenile (either as a witness or defendant). These courts have the power to order the public to be cleared from the courtroom if a juvenile witness is to testify in a trial involving offences of indecency or immorality. The possibility also exists for the court to order that a vulnerable witness may, in certain circumstances, give their evidence from behind a screen, or through a live television link, or in the form of a pre-recorded video (see further **7.4.5**).

7.4.4.2 Media reporting of juvenile proceedings

Youth court
Currently there is a ban on the media reporting any details which may identify any child or young person involved in a case in the youth court (whether as a defendant or as a witness; see CYPA 1933, s. 49 as substituted by CJPOA 1994, s. 49). Thus,

> no report shall be published which reveals the name, address or school of any child or young person concerned in the proceedings or includes any particulars likely to lead to the identification of [such a person]; [further] no picture shall be published [of any such person].

This ban may be lifted in three situations. First, it may be lifted on application by the defence. Here, publicity must be appropriate for the avoidance of injustice to the juvenile accused (for example, where the defence needs to publicise details of the incident to attract the attention of potential defence witnesses). Secondly, the prosecution may apply to lift the ban. The prosecution may seek publicity where the juvenile defendant is 'unlawfully at large' and the offence is:

- serious (in that it carries a maximum punishment of 14 or more years' imprisonment for an adult offender); or
- violent or sexual (defined in CJA 1991; see **21.5.3**).

The motive here is that publicity may assist in the recapture of the juvenile.

The third situation arises only after the juvenile has been convicted. If the youth court now considers it to be in the public interest to do so, the reporting restrictions may be lifted. Before doing so, the court should give the parties to the proceedings an opportunity to make representations on the matter. In this situation, the aims are to disclose the outcome of the case, to show that justice has been done and, perhaps, to shame the individual offender. See further CYPA 1933, s. 49(4A) and (4B), inserted by the Crime (Sentences) Act 1997, s. 45. The rationale is consistent with the recent moves to encourage greater access to proceedings in the youth court. In 1997, the government White Paper, *No More Excuses*, stated the belief that:

> . . . the youth court should make full use of its discretion to lift reporting restrictions in the public interest following conviction. This is particularly important where the

offence is a serious one; where the offending is persistent or where it has affected a number of people or the local community; and at the upper range of the youth court. Occasions where it would not be in the best interests of the public, and others concerned with the case, to lift reporting restrictions might include cases where an early guilty plea was entered or where naming the young offender would result in revealing the identity of a vulnerable victim.

Adult magistrates' court and the Crown Court
The general principle here is that the media can report proceedings unless ordered not to. Under CYPA 1933, s. 39 any court may direct that no newspaper report of its proceedings shall reveal the name, address, school or any particular calculated to lead to the identification of a child or young person in the proceedings, whether involved as accused, witness or victim. Similar powers exist to censor broadcasts in the sound, television and cable media.

One example of the Crown Court using s. 39 was at the murder trial at Preston Crown Court of Robert Thompson and Jon Venables in November 1993. The victim was a toddler, James Bulger, who had been abducted and the case had attracted nationwide publicity. The trial judge ordered that the two accused be known simply as 'child A' and 'child B'. The fact that the identities of these children were published subsequently illustrates the fact that such a ban may be temporary. Typically, it will last until the end of the trial. If the verdict is not guilty, the juvenile is acquitted and the ban will continue in force. If the juvenile is convicted, the ban may be removed. It is thought that the public interest served by naming the juvenile offender may outweigh the consequences of publicity for him or her. However, the court should consider the age of the juvenile and the potential damage that he or she may suffer by being publicly identified as a criminal, before lifting the ban. See further *R* v *Lee (Anthony William) (A Minor)* [1993] 1 WLR 103; *R* v *Inner London Crown Court, ex parte Barnes (Anthony)*, *The Times*, 7 August 1995.

7.4.4.3 Future developments in public access

In March 1999, the European Commission of Human Rights held that, in certain circumstances, conducting the trial of a child defendant in public, with attendant publicity, could have a serious effect on the child's ability to participate in the trial. The case under consideration by the European Commission was a complaint by Robert Thompson and Jon Venables, the defendants in the trial for the murder of James Bulger (see **7.4.4.2**). The European Commission concluded that the defendants had not received a fair trial, as they had been subjected to a 'severely intimidating procedure'. The Commission is described as saying that if the trial of a child is not to present the appearance of an exercise in the vindication of public outrage, the procedures which the trial court adopts must be conducive to active participation on the part of the accused. See further *T* v *UK*; *V* v *UK* [1999] Crim LR 579. *The Times* (23 March 1999) reported the Home Secretary as saying that the British government would be arguing matters fully in the hearing before the European Court of Human Rights.

The European Court reached its decision on 16 December 1999. Among a number of matters which the Court dealt with in its judgment, the Court held (by 16:1) that both youths' right to a fair trial (under ECHR, Article 6) had been violated. The formality and ritual in the Crown Court trial were described as incomprehensible and intimidating. Even modifications to the courtroom, which had been taken to help the youths, were found to have increased their levels of intimidation (for example, the dock in which they sat had been raised to enable them to see what was going on; in fact, it increased their sense of discomfort because they felt more exposed). The defendants were incapable of consulting with their lawyers both in court and outside. Reference was made to the youths' immaturity and disturbed emotional state, characteristics which may not be uncommon in juvenile defendants when such trials take place.

The Court indicated factors that could be taken into account when considering possible reforms to the working of the youth court. It was thought to be essential that:

> a child charged with an offence should be dealt with in a manner which took full account of his age, level of maturity and intellectual and emotional capacities, and that steps were taken to promote his ability to understand and participate in the proceedings. In respect of a young child charged with a grave offence attracting high levels of media and public interest, this could mean that it would be necessary to conduct the hearing in private, so as to reduce as far as possible the child's feelings of intimidation and inhibition, or, where appropriate, to provide for only selected attendance rights and judicious reporting.

It followed that the applicants had been denied a fair hearing in breach of ECHR, Article 6(1). See further ECHR Press Release 719,16 December 1999.

At the same time that it was arguing its' corner in front of the European Court in 1999, the British government was putting what is now the YJCEA 1999 through Parliament. The Act provides for *special measures* to be taken at trials to assist vulnerable witnesses. Vulnerable witnesses are those who might have difficulty in giving evidence in criminal proceedings, or who might be reluctant to do so (Venables and Thompson had made a complaint to the European Commission to this effect regarding their own participation). Amongst the categories of witness who will be eligible for assistance are those aged under 17. These measures exclude assistance for the accused, even if he or she is a juvenile, since the accused 'already has the benefit of a number of procedural safeguards' (according to the Explanatory Notes which accompanied the Bill).

The YJCEA 1999 changed the rules on reporting restrictions. The YJCEA 1999 amends CYPA 1933, s. 49(1), so that it now reads:

> No matter relating to any child or young person concerned in proceedings to which this section applies shall while he is under the age of 18 be included in any publication if it is likely to lead members of the public to identify him as someone concerned in the proceedings.

CYPA 1933, s. 49, applies mainly to proceedings in the youth court. The YJCEA 1999 introduces a complementary power to impose a prohibition on reporting information which may lead to the identification of a defendant, victim or witness under the age of 18. This is a discretionary power which will apply to court proceedings other than those covered by CYPA 1933, s. 49. It replaces CYPA 1933, s. 39, for criminal proceedings but s. 39 will continue to govern non-criminal proceedings. A court may decide to not use the new provision at all (in which case there will be no restrictions on reporting), or the court may order a partial ban on reporting (i.e. the ban will be subject to specific exceptions); otherwise, if the ban is imposed, it will work in a similar way to that imposed automatically by CYPA 1933, s. 49. Any restriction will last until the minor reaches the age of 18, unless lifted earlier either by the court which imposed the ban or by an appellate court.

A more far-reaching change also appears in the YJCEA 1999. Whenever an allegation is made that a crime has been committed, the media may not report any information which would enable anyone under the age of 18 who is involved in the offence to be identified. This restriction will start when the police commence a criminal investigation and will last until the minor's eighteenth birthday, or a court removes the restriction in the interests of justice, or criminal proceedings commence in court. In the latter situation, reporting restrictions may continue to apply, under either CYPA 1933, s. 49, or the YJCEA 1999. The ban on publication (in all these situations) will be extended to cover the media in Scotland and Northern Ireland, although this is likely to be significant only in exceptional cases which the media see as having a national profile (either because of the nature of the crime or because of the person(s) involved).

7.4.5 PROTECTING YOUNG WITNESSES

7.4.5.1 Provisions under the Criminal Justice Act 1988

Since 1989, if a child aged 14 or under was called to give evidence, he or she could do so via a live television link if the court gave permission. That facility was *not* accorded to an accused juvenile if he or she testified in their own defence. Under CJA 1988, s. 32, the use of live TV links was limited to trials where the accused was charged with an offence involving an assault, or injury or threat of injury to any person, or one of various specified offences involving cruelty to, or sexual misconduct with, a juvenile. In such trials, since 1991, courts have also been able to receive children's evidence in the form of a pre-recorded interview on video. The interview would be between an adult and the child witness. Permission from the court was necessary. Video evidence could be used in the same circumstances as the live TV link. See CJA 1988, s. 32A, inserted by CJA 1991, s. 54.

The video effectively stood as the child's evidence-in-chief but the child would be available at the trial for cross-examination. That would usually occur via a live TV link. A code of practice was created to govern the production of video evidence — the Memorandum of Good Practice on Video Recorded Interviews with Child Witnesses for Criminal Proceedings. The code of practice had no statutory basis but indicated, for example, that the interviewer should avoid using leading questions, should not encourage references to earlier statements and should not discuss the character of the accused.

7.4.5.2 Special measures under the YJCEA 1999

The YJCEA 1999 established a coherent set of provisions which deal with all of the so-called 'special measures' which may be used by courts to protect vulnerable (or intimidated) witnesses. In summary, these are:

- the power to clear the public from the courtroom while the witness gives evidence (in trials involving sexual offences or when it appears that someone is trying to intimidate the witness)
- that the lawyers and the judge may remove their wigs and gowns
- that a screen may be used in court, to shield the witness from the accused
- that a pre-recorded video may serve as part or all of the evidence of the witness
- that the witness may give evidence at the trial from a separate room via a live link.

Some of these provisions existed already, either in statute or more informally. The intention of the YJCEA 1999 appears to be to clarify and strengthen the facilities which are available to aid children (and other vulnerable witnesses). Also, the process of making decisions on which special measures to adopt is put onto a rational basis. In principle, the special measures are available for proceedings in all criminal trial courts. In practice, a specific court will need notice from the Home Secretary that appropriate facilities are available to it, either permanently or temporarily, before it can consider making a special measures order.

7.4.5.3 Three categories of child witness

Special measures are not available for defendants of any age. Any other witness will be eligible for help if they are found to be vulnerable or intimidated. Children under the age of 17 at the time of the trial are presumed to be in need of such help. The procedure for determining which special measure to use for a child witness will depend upon which of three categories the witness falls into:

(a) children testifying in a case involving a sexual offence;

(b) children testifying in a case involving an offence of violence, abduction or neglect;

(c) children giving evidence in all other cases.

For most child witnesses, YJCEA 1999, s. 21, creates a presumption that their evidence will be given by pre-recorded video (for evidence-in-chief) and live link (for all other evidence). The appropriate orders for special measures should be made unless the court decides that the measures would not be likely to maximise the quality of the witness's evidence as far as practicable.

A child testifying in a trial for a sexual offence will give evidence-in-chief through a pre-recorded video. Any cross-examination should also take place at a pre-trial hearing and be recorded for playback at the trial unless the witness tells the court that he or she does not want that protection. Video evidence may be excluded in certain circumstances (see YJCEA 1999, s. 27). Sexual offences are specified in YJCEA 1999, s. 35.

A child witness in a trial for an offence involving violence, abduction or neglect will have his or her examination-in-chief recorded on video for playback at the trial. Any further evidence (including cross-examination and re-examination) will normally be via a live link. The court is not required to take a decision on whether the special measures are likely to maximise the quality of the evidence.

It should also be noted that a child witness must not be cross-examined by an unrepresented defendant, where the trial involves sexual offences. In such cases, the defendant will be given an opportunity to appoint a lawyer specifically to cross-examine the witness. If he or she does not take that opportunity, the court must decide whether it should appoint a cross-examiner in the interests of justice (YJCEA 1999, s. 38).

See also, Jenny McEwan, 'In the Box or on the Box? The Pigot Report and Child Witnesses' [1990] Crim LR 363; Glaser and Spencer, 'Sentencing, Children's Evidence and Children's Trauma' [1990] Crim LR 371; Birch, 'Children's Evidence' [1992] Crim LR 262.

7.5 How Will the Youth Court Work?

7.5.1 WHERE WILL THE YOUTH COURT BE?

Youth courts often sit in the same buildings and rooms that are used by the local adult magistrates' court. In the past, there was a requirement that at least one hour should elapse between a courtroom being used to hear adult cases and its subsequent use as a youth courtroom (or vice versa; see CYPA 1933, s. 47(2)). The aim was to minimise casual contact between juvenile defendants and adult criminals. Typically, the one hour lunch adjournment would provide the necessary break between sittings. The Narey Report (Home Office, 1997, see **7.4.2**) described this temporal cordon as an 'inefficient arrangement [which] seems generally to be regarded as out of date and unnecessary'. It recommended the abolition of the requirement and this was effected by CDA 1998, s. 47(7). However, as the Explanatory Notes which accompanied the Crime and Disorder Bill recognised, courts will still be required to make arrangements so 'that young defendants do not associate with adult defendants whilst awaiting hearing' (see CYPA 1933, s. 31). A draft Home Office Circular indicates that 'if the hour's interval is no longer set, courts will need to provide separate waiting areas when youth courts are in session'.

In some places, mainly inner city areas where the scale of juvenile proceedings justifies the cost, special youth courts have been built to deal with the workload. Adult defendants never appear in these courtrooms.

7.5.2 WHERE DOES EVERYONE SIT?

There will not usually be seating provided for members of the public in dedicated youth courtrooms (see also **7.4.4.1**). These courtrooms usually provide seating only for those people who are specifically allowed to be present during the proceedings (see CYPA 1933, s. 47(2)). The magistrates do not sit up on a raised platform, but often are on ordinary chairs behind plain tables. Since the court clerk, lawyers, probation officers and social workers also sit on ordinary chairs behind desks, it is not as obvious as in other courtrooms where one should sit.

As a rule of thumb, the chairs in the centre of the room will be reserved for the juvenile defendant(s) and parents. These chairs will face the desk where the magistrates sit (and the Royal Coat of Arms may be on the wall behind the magistrates). The clerk's desk will be at the side of the one used by the magistrates and, usually, the lawyers' seats and desks will be on the same side of the room as the clerk. These dedicated youth courtrooms do not contain docks to hold a prisoner.

In adult magistrates' courts and the Crown Court, public seating is always provided. When an adult courtroom is used as a youth court, typically the public seating will be left empty. Everyone will sit where they normally would, except that no dock will be used even if there is one. In such cases, the juvenile defendant will sit in front of the dock.

The government has indicated a wish to promote proceedings which involve the juvenile more directly than at present and which are less adversarial. Youth courts are being encouraged to think about changing the physical environment of the courtroom. One result might be to have everyone involved in a case sitting around a single table (subject to security constraints). How this will work, given that another wish of the government is to open up the youth courts more to the general public and particularly to victims of crime, remains to be seen.

7.5.3 PROCEDURE AT THE HEARING

As the youth court is a special type of magistrates' court, most of what happens in a hearing is the same as for adults in the adult magistrates' court. In particular, a juvenile can be tried summarily, sentenced if found guilty and remanded if a case is adjourned for any reason by the youth court. The youth court can issue a warrant for the arrest of a juvenile defendant who fails to attend the hearing (see BA 1976, s. 7; MCA 1980, s. 13). There are some differences, however, which are largely semantic. See **Figure 7.1**.

Figure 7.1

Name
Juveniles (both defendants and witnesses) are addressed by their first names.

Oath
Juveniles promise to tell the truth. The usual form of oath requires a witness to swear to do so. (Those aged under 14 give evidence *unsworn*: YJCEA 1999, s. 55.)

Guilt
A juvenile is never 'convicted' of an offence, the court will simply record a finding of guilt.
The difference is largely cosmetic, presumably to avoid the trauma of conviction.

Sentence
A juvenile is not sentenced to a punishment after the case has been proved, rather the court makes an order upon a finding of guilt. Again, the distinction is semantic.

7.6 Which Courts Can a Juvenile Defendant Appear in?

7.6.1 THE USUAL SYSTEM FOR CLASSIFICATION OF OFFENCES DOES NOT APPLY TO JUVENILES

A juvenile *never* has the right to elect trial in the Crown Court, and the usual distinction between offences which must be tried summarily, those which must be tried on indictment, and those which are triable either way has no relevance when determining where a juvenile will be tried.

7.6.2 THE USUAL FORUM — YOUTH COURT

By a combination of statutory provisions, the court in which the juvenile makes his or her first appearance when being prosecuted for any offence is normally the youth court (CYPA 1933, s. 46; CYPA 1963, s. 18). The juvenile may be the sole defendant or may be charged with others. If the juvenile is charged alone or with other juveniles, then he or she will appear in the youth court. This court will hear all the proceedings in the case, from the first occasion when the juvenile comes before a court up to the final disposal of the case. There is only one exception to this — if the youth court decides that the juvenile should be sent to the Crown Court. This can happen for three different reasons and is considered below at **7.6.6**.

7.6.3 WHEN WILL A JUVENILE APPEAR IN AN ADULT MAGISTRATES' COURT?

Exceptionally, a juvenile defendant may make his or her first court appearance, after being charged, in an adult magistrates' court. This will occur in any of the following four situations:

(a) the juvenile is on a joint charge with an adult defendant;

(b) the court mistakenly believes the juvenile to be aged 18 or over;

(c) the juvenile is charged with aiding and abetting an adult to commit a crime (or vice versa);

(d) the juvenile is charged with a crime which arises out of circumstances which are the same as, connected with, those which resulted in a charge against an adult defendant.

It should be noted that in three of these situations the appearance of the juvenile in an adult magistrates' court is the consequence of being allegedly involved with an adult defendant. (See **Figure 7.2**.)

7.6.4 A JUVENILE CHARGED JOINTLY WITH AN ADULT DEFENDANT

Here, the juvenile and the adult will appear together as defendants in an adult magistrates' court. What will happen next is governed by the classification of the offence (see **4.1**):

(a) If the offence is *summary*, the procedure is governed by MCA 1980, s. 29 (see **7.6.4.2**).

(b) If the offence *must be tried on indictment* (e.g. robbery), then CDA 1998, s. 51, applies (see **7.6.4.1**).

(c) If the offence is *triable either way* (e.g. theft), then MCA 1980, s. 24(1)(b) applies. It then becomes necessary first to determine whether the adult defendant will be tried in the magistrates' court or Crown Court. The adult magistrates' court must follow the mode of trial procedure in MCA 1980, ss. 19–21, for the adult. This will result in a decision either to hold proceedings for committal for trial (see **7.6.4.1**) or summary trial. If the decision is for summary trial, the procedure thereafter is the same as that for a summary offence (see **7.6.4.2**).

7.6.4.1 Adult defendant to be tried in the Crown Court

Whether the adult must be committed to the Crown Court for trial (under the CDA 1998, s. 51) or is committed there after a mode of trial determination (under MCA 1980, s. 24(1)(b)), the magistrates must then consider what to do with the juvenile on the joint charge. The test in both situations is the same — the court shall commit the juvenile for trial to the Crown Court if it considers it necessary in the interests of justice to do so.

What happens if the prosecution case is weak?

(a) In the case of an offence triable either way, both the adult and juvenile defendants are entitled to apply to the magistrates to dismiss the charge against them on the ground that there is no case to answer. If the juvenile makes this application and succeeds, clearly he or she will not be committed for trial on the charge. If the juvenile fails in the application, or does not make one, but the charge against the adult is dismissed, MCA 1980, s. 24(1)(b) ceases to apply. In that case, the magistrates must consider MCA 1980, s. 24(1)(a). Is the case one where the juvenile is charged with a grave offence (see **7.6.7** and **Figure 7.3**) which could result in an order of long-term detention? If it is, then the magistrates should commit the juvenile to Crown Court for trial. If the charge is one to which MCA 1980, s. 24(1)(a), does not apply, the magistrates should proceed with a summary trial of the juvenile. The juvenile will enter a plea to the charge. If the plea is guilty, the adult magistrates' court could pass a limited range of sentences on the juvenile but they are far more likely to use their discretionary power to send the juvenile to the youth court for sentence to be passed. If the plea is not guilty, the juvenile may (and usually would) be sent to the youth court for summary trial there. See further *R* v *Tottenham Youth Court, ex parte Fawzy* [1999] 1 WLR 1350.

(b) If the offence is one which must be tried on indictment only, any application to dismiss the charge on the ground of insufficient evidence must be made to a judge in the Crown Court, after the defendants are committed for trial (see CDA 1998, s. 51, sch. 3).

What if the juvenile faces other charges, in addition to the joint charge?

In principle, charges against the juvenile which are connected to the joint charge may also be committed to the Crown Court for trial.

(a) Where a juvenile is committed for trial for an indictable offence under MCA 1980, s. 24(1)(b), the magistrates may also commit the juvenile for trial for any other indictable offence with which he or she is then charged (whether jointly with the adult or not). See MCA 1980, s. 24(2). The additional charges must satisfy the rules for a joint trial of the offences (see Indictment Rules 1971, r. 9; **9.2**).

(b) Under CDA 1998, s. 51(5), where the juvenile is committed for trial for an indictment-only offence, the magistrates may also send him or her for trial for any either way or summary offence with which he or she is charged and which fulfils certain criteria. The criteria require that:

   (i) The additional charge is *related* to the indictment-only offence. It will be related if, in the case of an offence triable either way, it satisfies the rules for a joint trial of both offences (see Indictment Rules 1971, r. 9; **9.2**). A summary offence will be related if it arises out of circumstances which are the same as or connected with those giving rise to the indictment-only offence.

   (ii) If the additional charge is for a summary offence, it must be punishable by imprisonment or involve obligatory or discretionary disqualification from driving.

Finally, it should be noted that hitherto MCA 1980, s. 24(1)(b), applied both to offences which are triable either way *and* to offences which had to be tried in the Crown Court. The introduction of what is in effect a 'fast track' procedure for indictment-only offences under CDA 1998, s. 51, probably should have led to appropriate amendments being made to MCA 1980, s. 24(1)(b), to limit it to offences triable either way. This appears not to have happened but the text in **7.6.4** *assumes* that an overlap between the two statutory provisions is unintended and that, once s. 51 comes into force, s. 24(1)(b) will thereafter apply only to offences which are triable either way.

Figure 7.2 Juvenile Appears with an Adult Defendant in the Adult Magistrates' Court

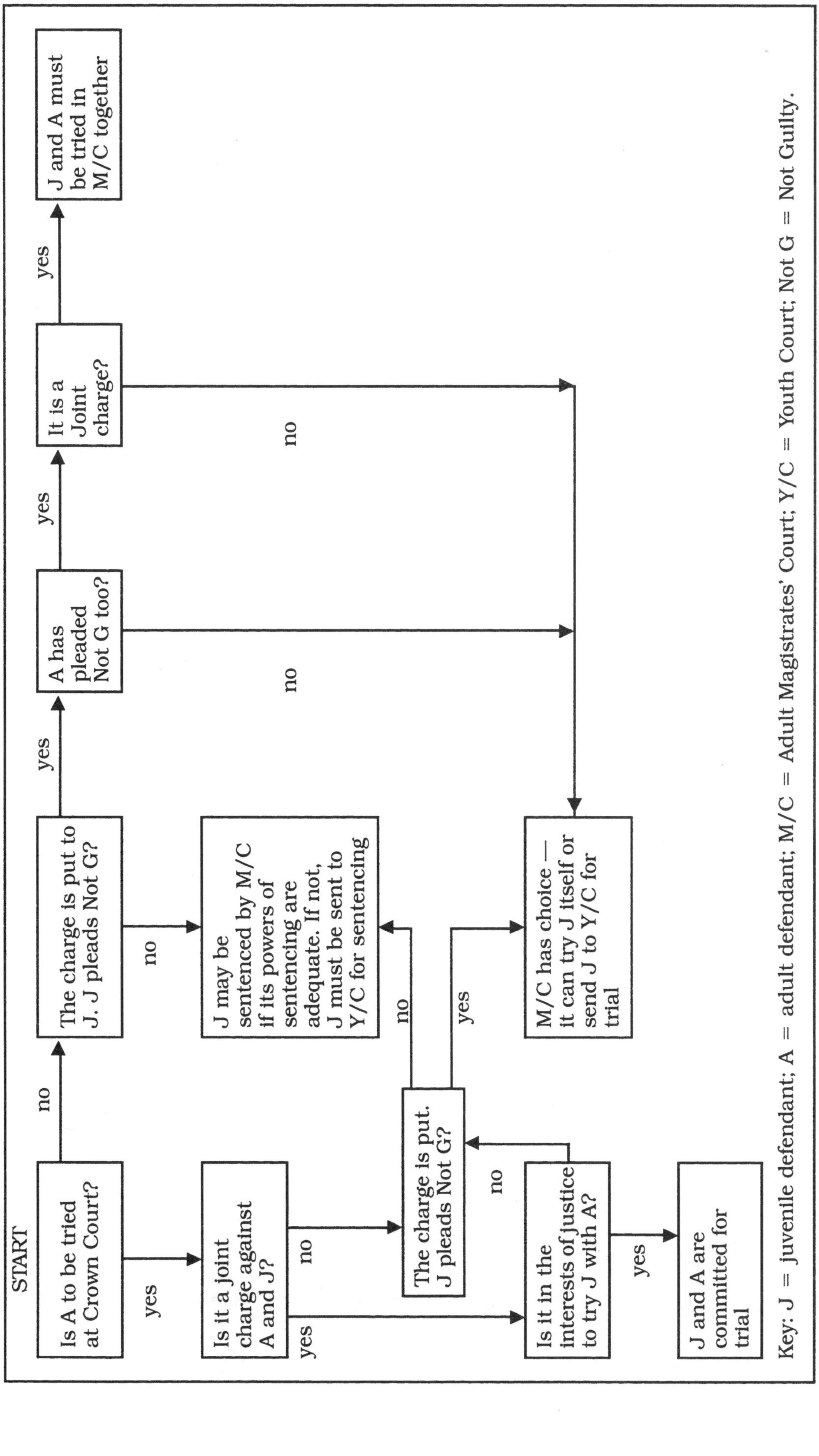

7.6.4.2 Adult defendant to be tried in the magistrates' court

If the adult is not to be committed to the Crown Court for trial (*either* after mode of trial procedure or because the joint charge alleges a *summary offence*), the procedure will differ according to whether they plead guilty or not guilty to the charge.

(a) *Juvenile pleads not guilty* If juvenile and adult both plead not guilty, they *must* be tried together in the adult magistrates' court. If the juvenile pleads not guilty but the adult pleads guilty, the magistrates may try the juvenile but have a discretion (which would almost certainly be used) to send the juvenile to the youth court for the trial. (See MCA 1980, s. 29(2)(a).)

(b) *Juvenile pleads guilty* If the juvenile pleads guilty, the adult's plea is irrelevant in determining what will happen to the juvenile. The adult magistrates' court can now proceed to pass sentence on the juvenile, but their sentencing powers are limited. They may only impose a fine or a conditional/absolute discharge or require a recognisance from his or her parents to ensure future good behaviour (and make ancillary orders, e.g. disqualification from driving). If none of these sentences is suitable, they must send the juvenile to the youth court for sentence (PCC(S)A 2000, s. 8(6)).

Note: The adult magistrates' court cannot pass a custodial sentence on a juvenile; nor can it commit a juvenile to the Crown Court for sentence under PCC(S)A 2000, s. 3 (the juvenile is too young for this section to be used).

7.6.5 THE JUVENILE WHO DOES NOT FACE A JOINT CHARGE

If one of the other situations in **7.6.3** occurs where the juvenile appears with an adult defendant, the adult magistrates' court has a discretion to try both juvenile and adult together or send the juvenile to the youth court for trial. As above, if the adult pleads guilty and the juvenile not guilty, it is very likely that the juvenile will be sent to the youth court for trial.

An adult magistrates' court may start to deal with a single defendant, *mistakenly* thinking him or her to be an adult. Once the mistake is discovered it can continue to hear the case or remit it to the youth court for further proceedings, whichever seems to be more appropriate. See CYPA 1933, s. 46(1).

7.6.6 WHEN WILL A YOUTH COURT SEND A JUVENILE TO THE CROWN COURT?

The general principle for juveniles is that they should be tried, and sentenced if necessary, summarily (i.e. by magistrates), and that such trial should normally be in a youth court. Only in exceptional circumstances will a juvenile be sent for trial to the Crown Court:

(a) Committal for trial by an adult magistrates' court. As we saw in **7.6.4.1**, if the juvenile is jointly charged with committing an offence with an adult, then the adult magistrates' court may commit the juvenile to the Crown Court for trial if the adult is to be tried in the Crown Court (see **Figure 7.2**).

(b) Committal for trial by a youth court. A youth court must deal with any case where a juvenile appears in that court, except as set out below. A youth court can only send a juvenile to the adult magistrates' court if he or she reaches the age of 18, whilst proceedings are continuing in the youth court (and see **7.7.2**). The youth court can send a juvenile to the Crown Court only in two situations. The first is when the juvenile is charged with homicide; the second is when the juvenile is charged with a serious, or grave, offence. Both situations are dealt with in more detail in **7.6.7**.

7.6.7 COMMITTING A JUVENILE FROM YOUTH COURT TO CROWN COURT FOR TRIAL

The youth court is empowered to commit a juvenile defendant to the Crown Court for trial where either:

(a) he or she is charged with homicide (in which case the defendant *must be* sent to Crown Court for trial); or

(b) he or she is charged with a grave offence, for which the sentence may be one of long-term detention pursuant to PCC(S)A 2000, s. 91 (in which case the defendant *may be* sent to Crown Court for trial).

The power to commit a juvenile to Crown Court for trial in the latter situation is given by MCA 1980, s. 24(1)(a). Its purpose is to enable the Crown Court to deal with those offenders whose crimes are sufficiently serious to warrant long-term detention in a young offender's institution. MCA 1980, s. 24(1)(a) is necessary because the Crown Court can only pass a sentence pursuant to PCC(S)A 2000, s. 91, when the juvenile has been tried on an indictment in the Crown Court and convicted there. So, if a juvenile defendant appears in the youth court on a charge alleging a grave offence, the magistrates should consider carefully whether a sentence of long-term detention under PCC(S)A 2000, s. 91 might be appropriate. If it might be appropriate, then they should commit the juvenile to Crown Court for trial. The offences (and age ranges) which fall within the ambit of PCC(S)A 2000, s. 91 are set out in **Figure 7.3** at point 2.

When should a youth court use its power under MCA 1980, s. 24(1)(a)? The maximum period for long-term detention is easy to determine — a sentence passed by the Crown Court for a grave offence pursuant to PCC(S)A 2000, s. 91, has the same maximum as would apply to imprisonment by the Crown Court in the case of an adult offender. It is necessary to determine what is the maximum term of detention which may be imposed on the juvenile normally, and then see if a term of detention longer than that is called for. The answer to this problem will differ according to the age of the juvenile.

(a) *Juveniles aged 10–14* Such defendants cannot receive a custodial sentence unless certain criteria are satisfied. First, of course, the offence must cross the custody threshold (see PCC(S)A 2000, s. 79). Secondly, the normal form of custodial sentence for offenders in this age range will be the *detention and training order* which comes into force in April 2000. For the court to use a DTO on an offender in this age range, the juvenile must be a persistent offender. For those aged 10–11, the court must also be of the opinion that only a custodial sentence would be adequate to protect the public from further offending by him or her. If a youth court felt that a defendant in this age range, being charged with a grave offence, should receive a term of detention in excess of one year (which is the maximum duration of the detention component in a detention and training order), it should commit for trial to the Crown Court. Further, if the youth court felt that the criteria for a detention and training order might not be satisfied (e.g. the juvenile was not a 'persistent offender'), but that detention (of any duration) was an appropriate sentence as the offence was a grave one, it could commit the juvenile to Crown Court for trial.

(b) *Juveniles aged 15–17* Juveniles in this age range will also be subject to detention and training orders when that sentence comes into force (see (a) above). The criteria mentioned there (persistent offending and the need to protect the public from further offences) are not requirements for this age range. The maximum duration of detention under a detention and training order is usually 12 months (CDA 1998, s. 75(2) and (5)). If a youth court was dealing with a 15–17 year old defendant charged with a grave offence, and it considered that he or she should be detained for a period in excess of a year if guilty of the offence, the youth court should commit for trial to the Crown Court.

The magistrates have a supplementary power to commit the juvenile for trial on other, related, charges. Under CDA 1998, s. 47(6), where magistrates commit a juvenile to Crown Court for trial on a homicide charge or a grave offence (under MCA 1980, s. 24(1)(a)) they are further able to commit him or her for trial on any other indictable offence with which the juvenile is charged at the same time and which could be the subject of a joint trial with the original offence. (On joint trials, see the Indictment Rules 1971, r. 9; **9.2.1**). This power is created by adding a new subsection — s. 24(1A) — to the MCA 1980. It came into effect on 30 September 1998. The purpose of this new power is to reduce delays in dealing with 'lesser' charges. Previously, such related charges would have had to stay in the youth court, usually adjourned without a fixed date, to await the outcome of the proceedings in the Crown Court.

The CDA 1998 makes two other changes to try to reduce delays in youth court proceedings. First, the Act provides that, where the youth court commits a young person to the Crown Court for trial, the youth court need not delay passing sentence on any other, less serious, offences until after the more serious offence has been dealt with. Secondly, the Act provides that where a defendant faces several, unrelated, charges, the youth court can proceed to pass sentence for any one of those charges as soon as it is appropriate to do so; the court is not required to delay passing sentence in order to tie up all of the outstanding charges against the defendant. See CDA 1998, s. 47(5), amending MCA 1980, s. 10.

Figure 7.3 When can a youth court send a juvenile to the Crown Court

1. **Homicide** The youth court has no power to deal with such crimes and the case against the juvenile must be committed to the Crown Court for trial.

2. **Serious offences** If the youth court considers that, if he or she is found guilty of an offence, a juvenile should be sentenced to a long period of detention due to the exceptional seriousness of the offence, it may transfer him or her to the Crown Court for trial. See MCA 1980, s. 24(1)(a). This applies only to certain serious offences as follows:

(a) any offence which is punishable with 14 or more years' imprisonment for adult offenders (not being an offence which has a sentence fixed by law);

(b) indecent assault (max. 10 years' imprisonment for adult offenders);

(c) causing death by dangerous driving (max. 10 years' imprisonment for adult offenders);

(d) causing death by careless driving while under the influence of drink or drugs (max. 10 years' imprisonment for adult offenders).

Items (a) and (b) apply to all juvenile defendants, from age 10 to 17; items (c) and (d) apply only to young persons, aged 14–17. Following committal for trial, the case will be tried by a judge and jury (as usual in the Crown Court) and if the juvenile is found guilty (or pleads guilty), he or she may be ordered to be detained 'in such place and on such conditions... as the Secretary of State may direct... or arrange . . .'. See PCC(S)A 2000, s. 91.

When considering the possible application of s. 24(1)(a), magistrates should hear representations from both prosecution and defence lawyers about the seriousness of the offence but should not consider any evidence (*R* v *South Hackney Juvenile Court, ex parte R. B. and C. B.* (1983) 77 Cr App R 294). Further, the magistrates should not be told about the accused's previous criminal record (*R* v *Hammersmith Juvenile Court, ex parte O* (1988) 86 Cr App R 343). It seems that it is only the gravity of the offence then charged which is decisive of the operation of s. 24(1)(a). A decision by the youth court not to use its powers under MCA 1980, s. 24(1)(a), is reviewable by the Divisional Court on application by the Crown Prosecution Service. See, for example, *R* v *Fareham Youth Court, ex parte M; ex parte Director of Public Prosecutions* [1999] Crim LR 325. Here, the decision of the magistrates to retain jurisdiction over two charges of indecent assault and one of attempted rape was so plainly wrong that the Divisional Court quashed it. The case also establishes that, once magistrates have accepted jurisdiction to try a grave offence, they can only be asked to reconsider in the circumstances provided in MCA 1980, s. 25. Where the accused juvenile has pleaded guilty to the charge, MCA 1980, s. 25, will not apply.

7.7 Can the Youth Court Deal with an Adult Defendant?

7.7.1 DEFENDANTS AGED 18 OR OVER AT THE START OF PROCEEDINGS

The youth court has no jurisdiction over such defendants. If a defendant was aged under 18 when charged with an offence, but is 18 when the case first comes to court, he or she should appear in the adult magistrates' court. Parents may be charged with offences such as not sending their child to school. This will be a matter for an adult magistrates' court to hear and to determine the appropriate steps to take to ensure the well-being of the juvenile.

7.7.2 DEFENDANTS WHO REACH THEIR EIGHTEENTH BIRTHDAY AFTER THEIR CASE HAS BEGUN IN THE YOUTH COURT

This situation is governed by CDA 1998, s. 47(1)–(4). This provides a youth court with the discretionary power to remit a defendant to an adult magistrates' court either for trial or for sentence. The power is exercisable if the defendant, having appeared initially before the youth court as a juvenile, subsequently has his or her eighteenth birthday. In that situation, the youth court may remit the defendant either:

(a) before the start of the trial, or

(b) after conviction and before sentence.

The defendant has no right of appeal against a decision to remit. The adult magistrates' court may proceed as if all previous proceedings relating to the offence had taken place in that court. The intention behind s. 47(1) appears to be to enable the courts to deal with young people in the most appropriate way, taking into account their maturity, attitude and offending history.

The youth court has no power to remit a defendant to the Crown Court for trial or sentence, simply because he or she is now aged 18. Some of the defendants who are remitted to the adult magistrates' court will have been awaiting trial for an offence which, for adults, is triable either way (see **4.1**). It is possible that when such defendants appear in the adult magistrates' court, they will now have the opportunity to opt for trial in the Crown Court; case-law on the subject prior to s. 47 is unhelpful. It is also possible that a remitted defendant will have only a brief stay in the adult magistrates' court. He or she may be charged with an offence which must be tried on indictment, in the case of an adult. That classification was inapplicable only whilst the case was in the youth court. Now that the defendant is appearing in the adult magistrates' court, the magistrates should send the defendant to Crown Court for trial (and see CDA 1998, s. 51).

If a defendant reaches the age of 18 before sentence is passed, he or she may be remitted to the adult magistrates' court for sentence (PCC(S)A 2000, s. 9). One effect might be to take the offender out of the detention and training order scheme, and make him or her eligible for detention in a young offender institution. Also, if the offence is triable either way, the offender may be remitted from the youth court into the adult magistrates' court and may then even be committed to the Crown Court for sentence (pursuant to PCC(S)A 2000, s. 3). Alternatively, it appears that the youth court can decide to retain jurisdiction over the 18 year old and sentence him or her as if still a juvenile (CYPA 1963, s. 29).

EIGHT

APPEALS FROM DECISIONS OF MAGISTRATES

There are three ways of appealing against the decision of the magistrates:

(a) Appeal to the Crown Court.

(b) Appeal to the High Court by way of case stated.

(c) Application for judicial review.

Students should also be aware of the power of the magistrates to rectify mistakes under MCA 1980, s. 142, discussed at **5.1.12**. This may often prove to be a quick and simple way to correct an error.

8.1 Appeal to the Crown Court

The defendant may appeal against conviction and/or sentence to the Crown Court, except that, if he or she has pleaded guilty, he or she may only appeal against sentence (MCA 1980, s. 108). If the defendant has pleaded guilty, in order to appeal against the conviction he or she must argue that the plea is equivocal (see **5.1.2**).

Note that if the Criminal Cases Review Commission refers a conviction in the magistrates' court to the Crown Court, such a reference is treated as if it had been made by the person under s. 108, whether or not he or she pleaded guilty.

8.1.1 PROCEDURE FOR APPEALING

(a) Notice of appeal is given in writing to the clerk of the magistrates' court and to the prosecution within 21 days of sentence. The 21 days run from the date of sentence, even if the appeal is against conviction and the appellant was convicted and sentenced on different days.

(b) The notice of appeal must state whether the appeal is against conviction, sentence or both, but the grounds of appeal need not be given.

(c) All documents are forwarded to the Crown Court, where the listing officer will place the appeal on the list, and send notice of the time and place to the appellant, the prosecution and the magistrates' court.

(d) The appellant may appeal out of time by applying for leave in writing from the Crown Court. Leave is not otherwise required.

8.1.2 BAIL

If the appellant is in custody and gives notice of appeal, the magistrates may grant him or her bail, with a duty to appear at the hearing of the appeal (MCA 1980, s. 113). If bail is refused, or unacceptable conditions are imposed, the appellant may appeal against the decision to the Crown Court under the SCA 1981, s. 81, or to a judge of the High Court in chambers under the CJA 1967, s. 22. (See further **3.17**.)

The appellant does not have the right to bail, but bail may well be granted if the sentence is likely to have been served before the appeal is heard.

8.1.3 THE HEARING

At the hearing, the judge (usually a circuit judge or recorder) sits usually with two lay magistrates who have not been concerned with the case in the magistrates' court.

Where the appeal is an appeal against conviction, the hearing itself is a complete re-hearing of the whole case. It is not a review of what happened before the magistrates. Thus, either party may call evidence not called before the magistrates, or omit evidence that was called before the magistrates.

The lay magistrates must accept the law from the judge, but the decision on the appeal itself is a majority decision. Thus, the lay magistrates may outvote the judge. However, if an evenly numbered court is equally divided, the judge has a casting vote.

A Crown Court judge giving the decision of the court must give reasons for its decision, and a refusal to do so might amount to a breach of natural justice. The reasoning required would depend on the circumstances of each case, but should be enough to demonstrate that the court had identified the main contentious issues, and how it had resolved them. An appellant is entitled to know the basis upon which the prosecution case had been accepted by the court. See *R* v *Harrow Crown Court, ex parte Dave* [1994] 1 WLR 98, DC.

8.1.4 POWERS OF THE CROWN COURT

Under the SCA 1981, s. 48, as amended by the CJA 1988, s. 156, the Crown Court may:

(a) Confirm, reverse or vary any part of the decision appealed against. Thus, if the defendant has appealed against only part of the magistrates' decision, the Crown Court is not restricted to reviewing just that part, but may review the whole decision.

(b) Remit the case to the magistrates with its opinion. This will usually be a direction to enter a plea of not guilty and hear the case, if it thinks the plea was equivocal.

(c) Make any such order as it thinks just. This includes a power to increase sentence up to the maximum sentence which was available to the magistrates. This power is rarely exercised, but its existence is a means of discouraging frivolous appeals, bearing in mind that no leave to appeal is required.

8.1.5 APPEAL AGAINST SENTENCE

The appropriate court to deal with an appeal against sentence is normally the Crown Court, where the case may be appealed by way of re-hearing (see **8.2.1(d)**).

8.1.6 APPEALS AGAINST ORDERS MADE UNDER THE CRIME AND DISORDER ACT 1998

The Crown Court has additional powers when dealing with an appeal against the making of an anti-social behaviour order or a sex offender order, created by ss. 1 and 2 of the CDA 1998 respectively. In determining the appeal, the Crown Court may, under s. 4(2):

(a) make such orders as may be necessary to give effect to its determination of the appeal; and

(b) also make such incidental or consequential orders as appear to it to be just.

Any order so made is treated as if it were an order of the magistrates' court from which the appeal was brought and not an order of the Crown Court.

Note that there is no appeal to the Crown Court against the refusal of the magistrates to make either sort of order.

8.2 Appeals to the High Court by Way of Case Stated

Under MCA 1980, s. 111, either party to the proceedings, or any person aggrieved by the decision of the magistrates, may question that decision on the ground that it was wrong in law or in excess of jurisdiction by asking the magistrates to state a case for the opinion of the High Court.

8.2.1 SUBSIDIARY POINTS ON APPEALS BY WAY OF CASE STATED

(a) The magistrates have no power to state a case until they have reached a final determination on the matter. Thus, they have no power to state a case during the hearing and must wait until the end. Similarly, it is not an appropriate method of challenging a committal for trial or sentence (see **5.3.6**).

(b) Both the defence and the prosecution have the right to apply for a case to be stated, and so may a third party whose legal rights have been affected. This means that effectively the prosecution can appeal against the defendant's acquittal, and if it is successful the acquittal will be reversed.

(c) The appellant must show that the decision of the magistrates was either wrong in law or in excess of jurisdiction. Questions raised will therefore be questions of jurisdiction, admissibility of evidence and so on. If the appeal is based on the facts of the case, then generally speaking it will be refused, unless the magistrates have made a finding of fact which is totally unsupported by the evidence, or is one which no reasonable tribunal, properly directing itself, could have reached, in which case the High Court may treat it as an error of law. As to where the magistrates are entitled to draw inferences from facts, see *Plowden* v *DPP* [1991] Crim LR 850.

(d) An appeal against sentence by way of case stated should only proceed in the most exceptional of circumstances (*R* v *St Albans Crown Court, ex parte Cinnamond* [1981] QB 480 applied in *Tucker* v *DPP* [1992] 4 All ER 901 and *R* v *Ealing Justices, ex parte Scrafield, The Times*, 29 March 1993, DC). The Divisional Court can only interfere where the magistrates have passed a sentence they have no power to pass, or where the sentence they have passed is so harsh as to be in excess of jurisdiction.

(e) Once an application to state a case to the High Court is made, the right to appeal to the Crown Court is lost (MCA 1980, s. 111(4)).

(f) If the same point arises in several cases on the same day, the appellants may apply for a collective case to be stated.

8.2.2 PROCEDURE

(a) The application must be made in writing within 21 days of the sentence, and should state the point of law upon which the opinion of the High Court is sought.

(b) The application is sent to the clerk of the convicting magistrates' court.

(c) The magistrates may refuse to state a case, but this decision is reviewable by the High Court on an application for judicial review. For an example of such an application see *R* v *Huntingdon Magistrates' Court, ex parte Percy* [1994] COD 323. Magistrates may legitimately refuse to state a case in two situations:

(i) If they consider that the application is frivolous. The test is whether the application raises an arguable point of law (*R* v *City of London Justices, ex parte Ocansey*, 1995, unreported, and *R* v *East Cambridgeshire Justices, ex parte Stephenson*, 1995, unreported. The magistrates must give the appellant a certificate to that effect, enabling him or her to seek judicial review of the decision not to state a case.

(ii) They may refuse to state the case unless the appellant enters into a recognisance to prosecute the appeal without delay, and to pay such costs as the High Court may award. Such a condition would be imposed if the magistrates think the appellant is likely to abandon the appeal halfway through, having incurred expense and wasted time.

(d) The statement itself is usually drafted by the clerk of the magistrates' court, though exceptionally it may be drafted by either the appellant or the magistrates. The draft must be prepared within 21 days.

Note: It is a part of the procedure for stating a case that if a properly drafted question was to be altered, the party which framed the original question must be allowed to comment on the changes (*Waldie* v *DPP, The Times*, 18 April 1995).

(e) The draft statement is submitted to the parties for their comments, which must be lodged with the court within 21 days. The statement may be adjusted in response. Where it is adjusted, the court will consider only the final statement, and not any earlier variations.

(f) The contents of the statement are:

(i) The names of the parties and of the court.

(ii) The charges.

(iii) The findings of fact, but not the evidence upon which those findings were made, unless the appellant's argument is that, on that evidence, the magistrates could not have come to the conclusion that they did (see *Crompton and Crompton* v *North Tyneside Metropolitan Borough Council* [1991] COD 52).

(iv) The points of law involved, and the authorities relied on. This should include the arguments heard by the justices (*DPP* v *Kirk, The Times*, 4 December 1992).

(v) The decision of the magistrates.

(vi) A request for the opinion of the High Court, posing the question which the appellant wishes the High Court to answer.

(g) Once the final draft is completed, the magistrates sign it and send it to the appellant.

(h) The appellant then has ten days in which to lodge the statement at the Crown Office of the High Court, and a further four days to serve notice on the respondent.

Note: All the time limits set out above may be extended except the first limit of 21 days, which is statutory and cannot be varied (see s. 111(2) and *Michael* v *Gowland* [1977] 1 WLR 296. And see *Reid* v *DPP* [1993] COD 111, DC, where 'pressure of work' on the part of the solicitor was insufficient reason for extending time).

8.2.3 BAIL

Under MCA 1980, s. 113, the appellant may be granted bail pending the outcome of the hearing in the High Court. Bail will be granted on the basis that the appellant returns to the magistrates' court within ten days of the High Court hearing, unless the conviction is quashed.

8.2.4 THE HEARING

Under the SCA 1981, s. 66(3), the court must consist of at least two judges, though there are usually three. The court acts entirely on the basis of the facts as set out in the case, and no new evidence is adduced. The hearing therefore consists solely of legal argument by counsel.

If only two judges are sitting, and cannot agree, the decision of the judge who agrees with the court below prevails, and thus the appeal will fail.

Note: In considering the matter, the judge should not act as prosecutor in the absence of the prosecution advocate. This amounts to a procedural irregularity, as the judge is not sufficiently removed from the proceedings to meet the requirement of justice (*R* v *Wood Green Crown Court, ex parte Taylor, The Times*, 25 May 1995).

8.2.5 POWERS OF THE HIGH COURT

Under the Summary Jurisdiction Act 1857, s. 6, the High Court may affirm, reverse or vary the decision of the court below, make any other order it thinks fit, or remit it back to the original court with its opinion. The High Court decision is enforced as if it were the decision of the court below. Thus, if the High Court thinks that the acquittal is incorrect, it can remit it back to the magistrates with a direction to convict and sentence. Generally speaking, the High Court does not deal with sentence itself, taking the view that it is not the appropriate forum. However, it may deal with sentence if it is obvious what the sentence should be.

The power of the High Court under s. 6 includes a power to order a rehearing of the case before the same or a different bench of justices whenever such a course is appropriate (see *Griffith* v *Jenkins* [1992] AC 76; *R* v *Farrand and Galland* [1989] Crim LR 573).

8.2.6 CASE STATED FROM THE CROWN COURT

Appeal lies to the High Court from the Crown Court on matters not related to a trial on indictment, by way of case stated. Thus, if the defendant has appealed to the Crown Court against conviction or has been committed to the Crown Court for sentence, either party may appeal to the High Court by way of case stated, under the SCA 1981, s. 28, on the basis that the final decision was wrong in law or in excess of jurisdiction.

The procedure is much the same as for applications from the magistrates' court, except that it is usually the appellant who drafts the statement. The respondent also has the right to submit a draft. The judge, who was the judge at the hearing of the appeal or the committal, will read the drafts submitted to him and state a case on that basis.

For a recent example, see *R* v *Crown Court at Portsmouth, ex parte Thomas* [1994] COD 373.

A useful article is, 'Rights of appeal by way of case stated — should it be satisfied?', J Backhouse, 156 JPN 310.

8.3 Application for Judicial Review

Judicial review is the method by which the High Court controls the activities of inferior tribunals, that is, magistrates' courts and the Crown Court, in matters not relating to trial on indictment. The existence of a right of appeal to the Crown Court does not preclude a person convicted by magistrates from seeking relief by way of judicial review where the complaint was of procedural impropriety, unfairness or bias. Leave, however, should only be granted where the applicant has an apparently plausible complaint, and immaterial and minor deviations from the rules would not have this effect (*R* v *Hereford Magistrates' Court, ex parte Rowlands, The Times*, 2 February 1997). In reaching this decision, the Divisional Court considered *R* v *Peterborough Justices, ex parte Dowler* [1996] 2 Cr App R 561, which held that it was unnecessary to grant the defendant judicial review because, on the facts of the case, the procedural irregularity complained of could be rectified on appeal to the Crown Court. The court in *ex parte Rowlands* did not doubt the correctness of the decision in *ex parte Dowler* on the facts, but held that it was not authority for the proposition that parties complaining of procedural irregularity or unfairness in the magistrates' court should be denied leave to apply for judicial review. To hold otherwise would be to deprive a defendant of the right to a proper trial before the magistrates with a right of appeal to the Crown Court, and would emasculate the supervisory jurisdiction of the Divisional Court over the decisions of the magistrates.

Note that the right to apply to the Divisional Court from the Crown Court on matters not relating to a trial on indictment includes the right to apply for reviews of the decision of the Crown Court after an appeal to it from a decision of the magistrates. See, for example, *R* v *Aylesbury Crown Court, ex parte Lait* [1998] Crim LR 264.

8.3.1 PREROGATIVE ORDERS

The High Court exercises its control by the use of prerogative orders, namely *certiorari, mandamus* and prohibition.

(1) *Certiorari. Certiorari* has the effect of quashing the decision appealed against. In addition, the High Court may:

(a) Remit the case to the court concerned with a direction to reconsider it and reach a decision in accordance with the finding of the High Court (SCA 1981, s. 31(5)).

(b) Substitute for an unlawful sentence one which the court had the power to pass (SCA 1981, s. 43(1)).

It is usually said that *certiorari* 'will go' (i.e. be issued) in three situations:

(a) Where there is an error on the face of the record. However in a magistrates' court, the record is brief, and in any event magistrates rarely give reasons for their decisions. If the magistrates in fact give reasons, or include them in any affidavit that they are swearing for consideration of the High Court, the High Court will treat them as part of the record.

(b) Where the court acts in excess of jurisdiction. See, for example, *R* v *Tunbridge Wells Justices, ex parte Tunbridge Wells Borough Council*, 1 May 1994, unreported, where the justices adjourned the case, part heard, after a submission of no case to answer was made. The High Court set aside the decision to accept the submission, which was subsequently pronounced in open court by a different bench of magistrates, as being *ultra vires*. See also *R* v *Parker and the Barnet Magistrates' Court, ex parte DPP* (1994) 158 JP 1061. The High Court may also set aside a sentence if it is one which the magistrates have no power to pass, but such an error is rare. However, in very limited circumstances, the High Court will treat a sentence which is so harsh and oppressive that no reasonable tribunal could have passed it, as being in excess of jurisdiction, and quash it accordingly, even though it was in fact within the court's powers (see *R* v *St Albans Crown Court, ex parte Cinnamond* [1981] QB 480). But such a course is exceptional, and should only be followed when an appeal against sentence to the Crown Court has failed (*R* v *Battle Justices, ex parte Shepherd* (1983) 5 Cr

App R (S) 124). But see also on this point *R* v *Bradford Justices, ex parte Wilkinson* [1990] 1 WLR 692 and *R* v *Truro Crown Court, ex parte Adair* [1997] COD 296.

(c) Where the court acts in breach of the rules of natural justice. The court is under a duty to act fairly, there being two aspects of this duty:

(i) No person may be a judge in his or her own cause. See, for example, *Dimes* v *Grand Junction Canal* (1852) 3 HLC 759 and *R* v *Altrincham Justices, ex parte Pennington* [1975] 1 QB 549.

(ii) The court must hear both sides of the case. This rule will be relied on where there has been some procedural irregularity which has prejudiced the appellant, and the court must now employ the test laid down by the House of Lords in *R* v *Gough* [1993] AC 646, and ask: Was there a real danger that the appellant did not receive a fair trial? There are many and varied examples of the application of this principle to be found in the law reports and the following are included merely by way of example:

— *R* v *Thames Magistrates' Court, ex parte Polemis* [1974] 1 WLR 1371 (where the defendant was not given sufficient time to prepare his case);

— *R* v *Marylebone Justices, ex parte Farrag* [1981] Crim LR 182 (where a verdict of guilty was announced before defence counsel's closing speech);

— *R* v *Romsey Justices, ex parte Gale* [1992] Crim LR 451 (where one of the magistrates, during the prosecution case, prepared a note of what he proposed the bench should say if it were to convict);

— *R* v *Ely Justices, ex parte Burgess* [1992] Crim LR 888 (where the justices travelled to view the *locus in quo* with the prosecutor, and did not allow the defendant to be present — either or both of these factors would allow the conviction to be quashed);

— *R* v *Hendon Justices, ex parte DPP* [1994] QB 167 (where the magistrates announced an acquittal without hearing prosecution evidence and without having a good reason to refuse to hear witnesses);

— *Vincent* v *The Queen* [1993] 1 WLR 862, PC (where the fact that the defendant, following normal practice, was not given detailed notice of the evidence against him was not sufficient to establish that he had been denied a fair hearing);

— *R* v *Newbury Justices, ex parte Drake* [1993] COD 24 (where the allegedly partisan demeanour of the clerk was held not to have affected the magistrates' decision);

— *R* v *Nottingham Justices, ex parte Fraser, The Times*, 13 May 1995 (where the magistrates took into account the adequacy of the defendant's representation);

— *R* v *Worcester Justices, ex parte Daniels, The Times*, 31 December 1996 (where a member of the bench failed to give full attention to the defendant's evidence, and had been reading material unconnected with the trial);

— *Johnson* v *Leicestershire Constabulary, The Times*, 7 October 1998 (where a magistrate recognised the defendant from his role as a prison visitor, thereby apprising the bench that the defendant had spent some time in prison).

The Divisional Court has on occasion issued *certiorari* even though the failure to provide the defence with the necessary information lay with the prosecuting authority and not with the court itself. Consider the following examples:

- *R* v *Leyland Justices, ex parte Hawthorn* [1979] QB 283 (where the defence were not informed of witnesses who could assist their case);
- *R* v *Knightsbridge Crown Court, ex parte Goonatilleke* [1986] QB 1 (where the store detective failed to tell the police that he had a conviction for wasting police time);
- *R* v *Liverpool Crown Court, ex parte Roberts* [1986] Crim LR 622 (where the police did not inform the defence of an additional statement made by the victim which was inconsistent with another statement and with his testimony);
- *R* v *Bolton Justices, ex parte Scally* [1991] 1 QB 537 (where a want of care in the provision of medical kits used for testing the level of alcohol in the blood were themselves contaminated with alcohol).

Note: An order of *certiorari* to quash an acquittal on the ground that it had been procured by fraud or perjury should seldom if ever be made (*R* v *Portsmouth Crown Court, ex parte DPP* [1994] COD 13, DC).

(2) *Mandamus.* An order of *mandamus* compels an inferior tribunal to carry out its duties. It will be ordered when the court refuses to act when it should; not when it has acted and made a mistake. The appropriate remedy in the latter case would be *certiorari.* See, for example *R* v *Hendon Justices, ex parte DPP* [1994] QB 167, CA.

(3) *Prohibition.* Prohibition will be ordered to stop the court acting in excess of its powers. Parties do not have to wait for the final outcome of the hearing, and if there is genuine doubt as to the court's powers, the court will adjourn, so that the opinion of the High Court can be sought.

8.3.2 DISCRETION

The power to award any of the prerogative orders is entirely discretionary, and even though the appellant has established a prima facie case, the order may still be refused. See, again, *R* v *Battle Justices, ex parte Shepherd* (1983) 5 Cr App R (S) 124.

8.3.3 PROCEDURE

Under the SCA 1981, s. 31, and the Rules of the Supreme Court, O. 53, the procedure is as follows:

(a) Within three months of the decision, the applicant must file an application for leave to apply for judicial review, setting out his or her name and address and that of his or her solicitor, the relief sought and the grounds. This application must be supported by affidavit evidence.

(b) The application for leave is heard *ex parte* (i.e. in the absence of the other side), usually without a hearing. If there is no hearing, the judge will simply read the papers in chambers. If the applicant specifically applies for a hearing, one may be held, and this may be in court.

(c) If leave is refused, the applicant has ten days in which to renew his or her application before the Divisional Court.

(d) If leave is granted, the application is made by originating motion. Notice of motion must be served on the other side, and on the court below.

(e) The hearing itself consists of affidavit evidence and argument from counsel. Evidence is not usually called, though it may be necessary to establish the error of the court below.

(f) The court will reach a decision, and make any appropriate orders.

8.3.4 BAIL

Magistrates have no power to grant bail for an application for judicial review. The application for bail must be made to the High Court judge in chambers under the CJA 1967, s. 22. However, if the application is from the Crown Court on a matter not relating to trial on indictment, the Crown Court may grant bail.

Further reading: Inigo Bing, 'Curing bias in criminal trials — the consequences of *R* v *Gough*' [1998] Crim LR 148.

8.3.5 CASE STATED AND JUDICIAL REVIEW COMPARED

In many situations, the appellant could apply for either a case to be stated or judicial review, and in some respects the two are similar. However, by appealing by way of case stated, the appellant is challenging the actual decision of the court, alleging, for example, that a statute has been misapplied. In some circumstances this may be said of judicial review, but judicial review tends to be directed, not at the decision itself, but more at the decision-making process. It is the legality of the process which is under review, not whether the decision is right or wrong.

If both remedies do apply, the appellant should appeal by way of case stated, as all the facts can then be placed before the High Court (*R* v *Ipswich Crown Court, ex parte Baldwin* [1981] 1 All ER 596 and *R* v *Oldbury Justices, ex parte Smith* (1995) 7 Admin LR 315). See also *R* v *Ipswich Justices, ex parte D*, 5 December 1994, unreported, and *R* v *Gloucester Crown Court, ex parte Chester*, *The Independent*, 6 July 1998.

8.4 Appeal to the House of Lords

A decision of the High Court in a criminal cause or matter is appealed directly to the House of Lords, and there is no right of appeal to the Court of Appeal (Administration of Justice Act 1960, s. 1). The appeal will lie if the following conditions are satisfied:

(a) the High Court certifies that the case involves a point of law of general public importance; and

(b) leave is granted by either the High Court or the House of Lords.

NINE

INDICTMENT AND PLEAS

9.1 What is an Indictment?

The indictment is the factual document on which a Crown Court trial is based. It contains a list of the counts (i.e. offences) to which the defendant must plead before the trial begins.

9.1.1 WHAT DOES AN INDICTMENT CONTAIN?

(a) The heading or commencement contains the word 'Indictment', the venue of the trial and the name of the case. After the names(s) of the defendant(s) come the words 'charged as follows'.

(b) Then there follows the count or counts with which the defendant is charged.

See **Figure 9.1**.

9.1.2 WHAT DOES A COUNT CONTAIN?

There may be only one count in the indictment (as in **Figure 9.1**) or there may be several. Each count must contain:

(a) The statement of the offence. This will consist of the name of the offence (e.g. 'attempted burglary') and, where appropriate, the statute and the section contravened (e.g. 'contrary to Section 1(1) of the Criminal Attempts Act 1981').
(b) The particulars of the offence. This will give reasonable information about the nature of the charge, usually including the essential elements of the offence.

9.1.3 EXAMPLES

Examples of counts for some of the more common indictable offences follow. Note that you need only say where the offence occurred if it is material, e.g. 'a building' for burglary — see Specimen Count (3).

The drafting of indictments is dealt with in more detail, with further examples, in the chapter entitled 'Indictments' in the ***Drafting Manual***.

Figure 9.1 Example indictment

INDICTMENT No. 000316

The Crown Court at Greenbridge

The Queen v PAUL MARTIN

PAUL MARTIN is charged as follows

Statement of Offence

ATTEMPTED BURGLARY contrary to Section 1(1) of the Criminal Attempts Act 1981

Particulars of Offence

PAUL MARTIN on the 1st day of January 2000, attempted to enter as a trespasser a building known as 12 Coleridge Crescent, Greenbridge, with intent to steal therein.

Date: 10th April 2000 D Thomas

An Officer of the Crown Court

Example Counts

(1) **Theft**

Statement of Offence

Theft, contrary to Section 1(1) of the Theft Act 1968.

Particulars of Offence

Alan Adamson, on the 2nd day of February 2000, stole a wallet belonging to Arthur Archer.

(2) **Robbery**

Statement of Offence

Robbery, contrary to Section 8(1) of the Theft Act 1968.

Particulars of Offence

Bronwen Beale, on the 3rd day of March 2000, robbed Basil Brush of a gold chain and £56 in money.

(3) **Burglary**

Statement of Offence

Burglary, contrary to Section 9(1)(a) of the Theft Act 1968.

Particulars of Offence

Charles Craddock, on the 4th day of April 2000, entered as a trespasser a building known as 83 Lower Marsh Avenue, Ambridge, with intent to steal therein.

Statement of Offence

Burglary, contrary to Section 9(1)(b) of the Theft Act 1968.

Particulars of Offence

Charles Craddock, on the 4th day of April 2000, having entered as a trespasser a building known as 83 Lower Marsh Avenue, stole therein a television set and a video recorder.

(4) **Deception**

Statement of Offence

Obtaining property by deception, contrary to Section 15(1) of the Theft Act 1968.

Particulars of Offence

Desmond Deacon, on the 5th day of May 2000, dishonestly obtained from David Dawson the sum of £500 with the intention of permanently depriving David Dawson thereof by deception, namely, by falsely representing that he, Desmond Deacon, was entitled to the sum of £500 in payment for goods delivered to the employee of David Dawson.

(5) **Handling**

Statement of Offence

Handling stolen goods, contrary to Section 22(1) of the Theft Act 1968.

Particulars of Offence

Eleanor Etheridge, on the 6th day of June 2000, dishonestly received certain stolen goods, namely a cheque card and cheque book belonging to Ethel Elden, knowing or believing the same to be stolen goods.

or

Statement of Offence

Handling stolen goods, contrary to Section 22(1) of the Theft Act 1968.

Particulars of Offence

Eleanor Etheridge, on the 6th day of June 2000, dishonestly undertook or assisted in the retention, removal, disposal or realisation of certain stolen goods, namely a cheque card and cheque book belonging to Ethel Elden, by or for the benefit of another, or dishonestly arranged so to do, knowing or believing the same to be stolen goods.

(6) **Criminal Damage**

Statement of Offence

Damaging property, contrary to Section 1(1) of the Criminal Damage Act 1971.

Particulars of Offence

Frederick Fraser, on the 7th day of July 2000, without lawful excuse, damaged a motor car belonging to Felicity Falstaff, intending to damage such property or being reckless as to whether such property would be damaged.

(7) **Arson**

Statement of Offence

Arson, contrary to Section 1(1) and (3) of the Criminal Damage Act 1971.

Particulars of Offence

Gerald Goodman, on the 8th day of August 2000, without lawful excuse damaged by fire a boat belonging to George Gladstone, intending to damage such property or being reckless as to whether such property would be damaged.

(8) **Assault ABH**

Statement of Offence

Assault occasioning actual bodily harm, contrary to Section 47 of the Offences Against the Person Act 1861.

Particulars of Offence

Harold Hewitt, on the 9th day of September 2000, assaulted Henry Howard, thereby occasioning him actual bodily harm.

(9) **Wounding**

Statement of Offence

Unlawful wounding, contrary to Section 20 of the Offences Against the Person Act 1861.

Particulars of Offence

Ian Inglis, on the 10th day of October 2000, unlawfully and maliciously wounded Ingrid Inman.

(10) **Wounding with Intent**

Statement of Offence

Wounding with intent, contrary to Section 18 of the Offences Against the Person Act 1861.

Particulars of Offence

James Jarvis, on the 11th day of November 2000, unlawfully wounded John Jameson with intent to do him grievous bodily harm.

(11) **GBH with Intent**

Statement of Offence

Causing grievous bodily harm with intent, contrary to Section 18 of the Offences Against the Person Act 1861.

Particulars of Offence

Kevin Killick, on the 12th day of December 2000, unlawfully caused grievous bodily harm to Keith Kitson, with intent to do him grievous bodily harm.

(12) **Possession of Drugs**

Statement of Offence

Possessing a controlled drug, contrary to Section 5(2) of the Misuse of Drugs Act 1971.

Particulars of Offence

Laura Lyle, on the 13th day of January 2000, had in her possession a controlled drug, namely cannabis resin.

9.1.4 WHO DRAWS UP THE INDICTMENT?

Usually, an employee of the Crown Prosecution Service drafts the indictment and sends it to the Crown Court with the committal papers. Where the case is sufficiently complex, counsel may be instructed to advise on the indictment. In any event, it is checked by an officer of the Crown Court to ensure that there has been a committal for trial, a notice of transfer or a voluntary bill of indictment. Provided that the defendant is properly in the charge of the Crown Court by one of these routes, the appropriate officer is obliged to sign. Until he or she does so, the document is, strictly speaking, a 'bill of indictment'. After signature by the Crown Court officer, it is an indictment.

Once counsel is instructed in the case (either to draft the indictment or, in due course, for trial), it is his or her responsibility to ensure that the indictment is correct (*R* v *Moss* [1995] Crim LR 828).

The bill of indictment should be preferred (i.e. delivered to an appropriate officer of the Crown Court) within 28 days of committal. The period may be extended by an appropriate officer for 28 days, or by a Crown Court judge for any period.

9.1.5 WHAT COUNTS CAN BE INCLUDED?

The person drafting the bill of indictment will read the evidence from the committal proceedings, decide what indictable offences are disclosed, and draft the indictment on that basis. Crucially, the indictment is *not* limited to the offences upon which the defendant was committed. Even if the magistrates dismissed a particular charge, it can be included in the indictment. Of course, that will only be done rarely, and must be based on the facts or evidence contained in the committal papers.

By proviso (i) to s. 2(2) of the Administration of Justice (Miscellaneous Provisions) Act 1933, any charge upon which the accused was not committed can only form part of the indictment if it is 'in substitution for or in addition to' a count upon which he was committed. Further, any such extra counts must be of a kind that can lawfully be joined in that indictment, e.g. such joinder must be in accordance with r. 9 of the Indictment Rules (see **9.2.1**).

In *R* v *Lombardi* [1989] 1 WLR 73, L was committed for trial by the magistrates on a number of charges of counterfeiting. The prosecution later drew up two indictments, the first in relation to those charges of counterfeiting, and the second in relation to bankruptcy offences, in respect of which there had been ample evidence before the magistrates, but no charge and no committal. These bankruptcy offences were unconnected to the counterfeiting offences, and did not fulfil the conditions laid down in r. 9 of the Indictment Rules (see **9.2.1**). The defendant was tried and found guilty on the first indictment. His counsel then moved to quash the second indictment, on the basis that it did not comply with s. 2(2) of the Administration of Justice (Miscellaneous Provisions) Act 1933. The trial judge rejected that application and L pleaded guilty to the bankruptcy offences. In due course he appealed on the basis that the ruling was wrong, the indictment was bad, and the conviction on the bankruptcy charges should be quashed. The Court of Appeal agreed. The magistrates could have committed on both sets of charges, but they did not. The prosecution could not then add the bankruptcy charges because of the terms of r. 9 (see **9.2.1**). Nor could they prefer a second, different indictment because s. 2 of the 1933 Act only permits addition or substitution to the existing indictment, and makes no provision for the preferring of an altogether fresh indictment. The only solution from the prosecution's point of view was to obtain a voluntary bill of indictment, or else to charge the defendant with the bankruptcy offences, and apply to have him committed for trial by the justices on the fresh charges. In *R* v *Lockley* [1997] Crim LR 455, however, the Court of Appeal said that technical points should not generally nullify the whole indictment where there was misjoinder, provided there was no possible prejudice to the accused. This appears to run counter to the decision in *R* v *Lombardi* (see also *R* v *Bell* (1984) 78 Cr App R 305, *R* v *Callaghan* (1992) 94 Cr App R 226 and *R* v *Simon* [1992] Crim LR 444).

9.1.6 CHECKLISTS

In order to identify the offences disclosed by a particular set of facts, it is vital to know the elements of the common offences. A series of checklists of the elements necessary for some of the more common indictable offences follows:

Checklists of Elements

(**Note:** These are a rough guide only, and should be compared with the precise wording of the statute.)

(1) **Theft** The elements (see Theft Act 1968, s. 1):

- (a) dishonestly
- (b) appropriates
- (c) property
- (d) belonging to another
- (e) with intention of permanently depriving.

(2) **Robbery** The elements (see Theft Act 1968, s. 8):

- (a) theft (see '**Theft**' above) and
- (b) immediately before or at the time of the theft
- (c) uses or threatens force in order to commit the theft
- (d) on any person.

(3) **Burglary** The elements (see Theft Act 1968, s. 9), **either** (s. 9(1)(a)):

- (a) entry
- (b) to any (part of a) building
- (c) as a trespasser
- (d) with intent to
  - (i) steal (see '**Theft**' above) or
  - (ii) inflict grievous bodily harm (see below) or
  - (iii) rape or
  - (iv) do unlawful damage to the building or its contents.

or (s. 9(1)(b))

(a) having entered

(b) any (part of a) building

(c) as a trespasser

(d) (i) (attempts to) steal any contents (see **'Theft'** above) or

(ii) (attempts to) inflict grevious bodily harm (see below).

(4) **Deception** The elements (see Theft Act 1968, s. 15):

(a) by

(b) deception

(c) dishonestly

(d) obtains

(e) property

(f) belonging to another

(g) with intention of permanently depriving.

(5) **Handling** The elements (Theft Act 1968, s. 22), **either** Receiving

(a) otherwise than in the course of stealing

(b) dishonestly

(c) receives

(d) stolen goods

(e) (i) knowing or

(ii) believing them to be stolen.

or Handling

(a) otherwise than in the course of stealing

(b) dishonestly

(c) (i) undertakes or arranges to undertake or

(ii) assists or arranges to assist in

(d) (i) retention

(ii) removal

(iii) disposal or

(iv) realisation

(e) of stolen goods

(f) (i) knowing or

(ii) believing them to be stolen

(g) by or for the benefit of another.

(6) **Criminal damage** The elements (see Criminal Damage Act 1971, s. 1):

(a) without lawful excuse

(b) (i) destroys or

(ii) damages

(c) property

(d) belonging to another

(e) (i) intentionally or

(ii) recklessly.

(7) **Offensive weapon** The elements (see Prevention of Crime Act 1953, s. 1):

(a) without

(i) lawful authority or

(ii) reasonable excuse

(b) has with him

(c) in any public place

(d) any article

(i) made or

(ii) adapted or

(iii) intended by him to cause injury to the person.

(**Note**: In (a) the legal burden of proof is on the accused.)

(8) **Assault occasioning actual bodily harm** The elements (see Offences against the Person Act 1861, s. 47):

(a) does an act

(b) (i) intentionally or

(ii) recklessly

(c) which applies to another

(d) unlawful force

(e) thereby

(f) occasioning

(g) that other

(h) actual bodily harm.

(9) **Wounding, etc.** The elements (see Offences against the Person Act 1861, s. 20):

(a) unlawfully and maliciously

(b) (i) wounds or

(ii) inflicts grievous bodily harm

(c) (on) any other person

(10) **Section 18 wounding, etc. with intent** The elements (see Offences against the Person Act 1861, s. 18):

(a) unlawfully and maliciously

(b) (i) wounds or

(ii) causes grievous bodily harm

(c) (to) any other person

(d) with intent to

(i) cause GBH or

(ii) resist arrest/detention or

(iii) prevent arrest/detention of anyone.

9.2 Joinder of Offences and Defendants

An indictment may contain one count only (as in our examples so far) or it may contain several. Where a defendant is alleged to have committed more than one offence, it may be very important to decide whether the offences are tried together on one indictment, or separately, by different juries, on different indictments. Frequently, the defence is anxious to avoid a joint trial so that the jury does not know about the other matters alleged against the defendant. On the other hand, a single trial of several offences can save a lot of court time and minimise inconvenience to witnesses.

There are two separate but related issues:

(a) When can different offences be joined in one indictment?

(b) When can two or more defendants be joined in one indictment?

9.2.1 WHEN CAN OFFENCES BE JOINED IN A SINGLE INDICTMENT?

Under the Indictment Rules 1971, r. 9, the rule is that separate counts can be included in an indictment if:

EITHER (a) They are founded on the same facts (e.g. the defendant is alleged to have taken someone's car without permission, driven it dangerously, and stolen the radio-cassette on leaving the car. The indictment would usually include counts of theft, dangerous driving, and taking a motor vehicle without consent — the last count being added by virtue of s. 40 of the Criminal Justice Act 1988).

OR (b) They are part of a series of offences of the same or similar character (e.g. the defendant is alleged to have been involved in a 'shoplifting expedition' from a number of shops on the same afternoon).

As far as (b) is concerned, the courts have given a wide interpretation to the phrase 'series of offences of the same or similar character'. In *Ludlow* v *MPC* (1970) 54 Cr App R 233, HL, L was charged with attempted theft from a public house in Acton and robbery at a different public house in Acton. The second offence occurred 16 days after the first. The House of Lords held:

(i) that two offences can constitute a 'series' for the purposes of r. 9 of the Indictment Rules;

(ii) that in deciding whether the offences are similar in character, both the law and the facts should be taken into account. For the offences to be similar, there must be a nexus between them;

(iii) that in this case, the offences were similar in law and fact. Both had the same ingredient of actual or attempted theft. They involved public houses in the same neighbourhood. The time interval was only 16 days.

Although r. 9 is widely interpreted, its requirements must be carried out. For example in *R* v *Hudson* (1952) 36 Cr App R 94, the indictment contained counts for:

(a) breaking and entering (now burglary);

(b) receiving; and

(c) criminal damage.

It was held wrong to include the count for criminal damage, which was unconnected, on the facts, with any breaking and entering.

Even if the counts all fit one or other of these two rules for joinder, the judge has a discretion to 'sever' (under Indictments Act 1915, s. 5) and order separate trials if the defendant would be embarrassed or prejudiced by a joint trial. If the counts are tried together, the judge will in any event explain to the jury that it must come to a separate decision on each count, and exclude from its mind evidence relevant only to another count.

9.2.2 JOINDER OF DEFENDANTS

When can two or more defendants be indicted jointly? There are two different situations:

(a) A single count in the indictment charges two or more defendants with committing a single offence. This can be done when they were parties to the offence in question. It does not matter whether each was a principal offender. A defendant who aided, abetted, counselled or procured the commission of the offence can be charged in the same count with the principal offender(s). In fact, by s. 8 of the Accessories and Abettors Act 1861, a secondary party is liable to be 'tried, indicted and punished as a principal offender'. Hence, if A acted as lookout while B and C burgled the premises, all three can be jointly charged in a single count alleging that 'A, B and C, having entered a building . . . as trespassers, stole therein'. Whilst A did not actually enter the building, the prosecution case is that he or she is guilty on the basis of joint enterprise.

(b) The defendants may be charged in separate counts, but in the same indictment, provided that there is a linking factor between the counts. Assume, for example, in the burglary dealt with above, D handles the proceeds of the burglary. He or she must be charged in a separate count, since the offence is different. But the offence is linked to the burglary, so A, B, C, and D may be charged in the same indictment.

Again, the trial judge has a discretion to sever the trials. This is more likely to happen in situation (b) above than in situation (a).

9.2.3 ALTERNATIVE COUNTS

Sometimes the facts alleged by the prosecution will be open to two or more conclusions, each of which would be consistent with finding the defendant guilty, but of an offence which is more serious or less serious, e.g. D assaults P, injuring her. The extent of the injury, and D's intention, is in dispute. He or she can be charged in a single indictment with counts alleging:

(a) Causing grievous bodily harm with intent to cause grievous bodily harm (Offences against the Person Act 1861, s. 18).

(b) Inflicting grievous bodily harm (s. 20).

(c) Assault occasioning actual bodily harm (s. 47).

These offences are in decreasing order of gravity. When summing up, the judge will direct the jury to consider count (a). If that is proved to the necessary standard, the jury can disregard counts (b) and (c). If it is not, it should then consider (b). Again, if the jury is satisfied so that it is sure about (b) that ends the matter. If not, it must consider (c).

It is also possible that the indictment may contain alternative counts of roughly equal gravity. A common example is the pairing of theft and handling, e.g. where D is found in possession of stolen goods and may or may not be the original thief. The jury should then be asked to convict on one or the other. It may not convict on both, since theft and handling are mutually contradictory (s. 22 of the Theft Act 1968 lays down that handling must be otherwise than in the course of theft). The two alternative forms of handling are also commonly paired in an indictment (see Specimen Count (5) in **9.1.3** above).

9.2.4 DUPLICITY

Each count must, on its face, allege one offence only. If two or more offences are wrapped up in a single count, then that count is 'duplicitous' or 'bad for duplicity'. The defence can bring a motion to quash that count, which should not be put to the defendant in that form. For example, a count alleging that 'Oliver Oakland assaulted Oswald Oxley on the 16th day of April 2000, and Otis Osprey on the 17th day of April 2000, thereby occasioning them actual bodity harm' is bad for duplicity and should be quashed. The reason is simple. How should Oliver plead if he committed one assault but not the other? Even if Oliver denies both assaults, what verdict should the jury return if it is sure he committed one but not the other? To proceed with a count such as this would be a recipe for confusion.

But note that several different acts can together constitute one offence, in certain circumstances. For example, in *R* v *Wilson* (1979) 69 Cr App R 83, the indictment contained two counts for theft. The first alleged that W stole from Debenhams, on 10 August 1977, three jumpers, a pair of shorts, two pairs of trousers, four dimmer switches and a cassette tape. The second alleged that on the same day he stole from Boots eight records and a bottle of aftershave lotion. At the close of the prosecution case, the defence submitted that the evidence called showed that the stolen goods had come from different departments of the stores in question. The counts were, it was argued, bad for duplicity, and there should be a separate count in relation to the goods stolen from each department. The submission was rejected by the trial judge, W appealed, and his appeal failed. He had 'entirely failed to satisfy' the court that either of the counts complained of disclosed more than one offence. Browne LJ concluded that 'Whether there is one or more offence disclosed is really a question of fact and degree'.

9.2.5 OVERLOADING THE INDICTMENT

There are two main situations in which the prosecution may be said to be 'overloading the indictment':

(a) A number of different defendants and/or offences may be included so that an unnecessarily long and complicated trial ensues. In *R* v *Novac and Others* (1977) 65 Cr App R 107 the Court of Appeal said that it was convinced that nothing short of the criterion of absolute necessity could justify the imposition of a very long trial upon the court. It considered that the trial should have been split into five separate trials.

(b) What the defendant did may make him or her guilty of a number of different offences, as a matter of strict law. The prosecution should nevertheless consider carefully what the 'real' offence(s) were, and confine the counts in the indictment accordingly. Only if there is uncertainty should alternative counts be included (*R* v *Staton* [1983] Crim LR 190).

The Court of Appeal has perceived a particular problem in relation to counts of conspiracy, where the indictment charges conspiracy in addition to the substantive offence. This offends against the principles outlined in both (a) and (b) above, since it may lead to an inordinately long trial (as it did in *Novac*), and may also mean that the defendant is charged with two offences where one would be appropriate to deal with the wrongdoing. As a result, the following Practice Direction was issued:

Practice Direction (Crime: Conspiracy) [1977] 1 WLR 537

1. In any case where an indictment contains substantive counts and a related conspiracy count, the judge should require the prosecution to justify the joinder, or, failing justification, to elect whether to proceed on the substantive or on the conspiracy counts.
2. A joinder is justified for this purpose if the judge considers that the interests of justice demand it.

It follows that the prosecution will have to justify the inclusion of a substantive count and a related conspiracy count. If they are not justified, then the prosecution must elect one on which to proceed (see *R* v *Watts*, *The Times*, 14 April 1995).

9.3 Voluntary Bills of Indictment

So far, we have been dealing with an indictment drafted on the basis of committal proceedings. There are two other routes by which indictable offences can come to the Crown Court for trial. One is by preferment of a voluntary bill of indictment (see **6.5.3**). The other is by notice of transfer (see **6.5**). The rules about duplicity, joinder, etc., apply equally to indictments which arise in either of these ways.

9.4 Amending the Indictment

The court's power to amend the indictment is governed by s. 5 of the Indictments Act 1915, which reads in part:

5.—(1) Where, before trial, or at any stage of a trial, it appears to the court that the indictment is defective, the court shall make such order for the amendment of the indictment as the court thinks necessary to meet the circumstances of the case, unless, having regard to the merits of the case, the required amendments cannot be made without injustice . . .

Prior to amendment, it is usual for the judge to invite the views of counsel on the proposed amendment.

The power to amend is a wide-ranging one, subject to the court being satisfied that there is no injustice occasioned thereby. It includes, for example, the substitution of a different offence for that originally charged in the indictment, or even the inclusion of an additional count for an offence not previously charged. Amendment can be made at any stage of the trial, although the longer the interval between arraignment and amendment the less likely it is that the amendment can be made without injustice (*R* v *Johal and Ram* (1972) 56 Cr App R 346).

The crucial point is whether the amendment might result in injustice. Contrast:

(a) *R* v *Harris* (1976) 62 Cr App R 28, CA. After the Crown had closed its case and a submission of no case had been rejected, the trial judge directed amendment of the indictment. The count in question alleged an express false representation ('. . . he had sufficient funds to pay the debt. . .'). It was amended to allege a false representation by conduct ('. . . he intended to pay the said sum . . .'). The Court of Appeal held that no injustice could have resulted.

(b) *R* v *Thomas* [1983] Crim LR 619, CA. At the end of the prosecution case, a count of receiving was added to an indictment alleging theft. The facts disclosed recent possession of stolen property. The Court of Appeal quashed the conviction. It was not possible to say that the conduct of the defence up to the close of the prosecution case could not have been hampered in some way by the fact that the indictment did not include the second count. Injustice may have been caused.

One way in which injustice may be caused by late amendment of the indictment is that defence counsel's cross-examination may have been made on the wrong basis.

9.5 Quashing the Indictment

The indictment (or a count in it) can be quashed if, for example, the bill has been preferred without authority, or if the count is bad on its face for duplicity. Where the indictment includes a count on which the justices did not commit for trial, that is not in itself objectionable (see **9.1.5**). But if the evidence upon which the prosecution applied for committal does not disclose a case to answer on that count, the defendant may apply for the count to be quashed. The judge will read the papers in order to decide whether there is a case to answer. If there is not, then that count will be quashed.

This is an exception to the general rule that the trial judge at the Crown Court may not go behind the result of the committal proceedings to decide whether the indictment is correct.

As far as the defence is concerned, a motion to quash is unlikely to be of much practical use. The prosecution is often able to prevent the indictment from being quashed by amending it, e.g., splitting in two a count which appears to be bad for duplicity. In any event, a successful motion will result, not in acquittal, but merely in the accused being discharged. Nevertheless, a successful motion to quash at least has the merit of ensuring that the issues to be decided are clear.

9.6 Effect of Invalid Indictment

Assume that the indictment is invalid because it joins two sets of counts contrary to r. 9 of the Indictment Rules. One way of proceeding is for the court to amend the indictment by exercise of its power under s. 5(1) of the Indictments Act 1915 to delete the counts which have no nexus. There can then be a trial on the remaining counts. A separate trial of the deleted counts will not be possible, however, without a voluntary bill of indictment. This cannot be ordered by the trial judge unless he or she is a High Court judge and acts under the appropriate procedure. (See *R* v *Newland* [1988] QB 402.)

Provided that the original indictment is stayed rather than quashed, however, the trial judge (whether a High Court judge or not) may give leave to the Crown to prefer two or more fresh indictments out of time, provided that each complies with r. 9 of the Indictment Rules, and is based upon the depositions and statements at committal proceedings (*R* v *Follett* [1989] QB 338).

9.7 The Arraignment

At the start of a trial on indictment, the defendant is arraigned. The indictment is read over to the defendant by the clerk. After each count, the clerk will ask the defendant whether the plea is 'guilty' or 'not guilty'. (See **11.2**.)

The defendant must be present for the arraignment, and a bench warrant for arrest will be issued by the judge if he or she has failed to surrender to bail.

9.8 Fitness to Plead

Occasionally the question arises whether the defendant is fit to plead. A defendant is not unfit merely because he or she is mentally disturbed, or suffering from amnesia and hence unable to remember the incident. The question is: Can the defendant comprehend the proceedings of the trial so as to be able to make a defence against the charge? Crucial in determining this will be a decision as to whether the defendant is able to understand the evidence and instruct legal representatives. If the issue is raised, a jury will be specially empanelled to make this decision. The court is permitted to postpone the consideration of whether the defendant is fit to plead until any time up to the opening of the defence case, if it is in the defendant's interests to do so (Criminal Procedure (Insanity) Act 1964, s. 4(2)).

Where the jury has determined that the defendant is unfit to plead, then the question that must be decided is whether he or she committed the *actus reus* ('did the act or made the omission charged against him'). If the jury is satisfied that the defendant did commit the *actus reus*, it must find accordingly. If it is not, it must acquit (Criminal Procedure (Insanity) Act 1964, s. 4, as inserted in 1991).

Under s. 5 of the 1964 Act (as amended in 1991), if the accused is found unfit to plead, and the jury determines that he or she did the act or made the omission as charged, then the court may make:

(a) an admission order to a hospital approved by the Secretary of State;

(b) a guardianship order under the Mental Health Act 1983;

(c) a supervision and treatment order; or

(d) an order for the accused's absolute discharge.

(See **Chapter 23**.)

See also D. Carson, 'Prosecuting People with Mental Handicaps' [1989] Crim LR 87 and R. D. Mackay, 'The Decline of Disability in Relation to the Trial' [1991] Crim LR 87.

9.9 Plea of Guilty

If the defendant pleads guilty to all the charges, then the sentencing procedure begins. If he or she pleads guilty to some charges and not guilty to others, then sentencing on the guilty plea(s) is postponed until the trial on the not guilty pleas(s) has ended.

What if one defendant pleads guilty and another pleads not guilty? The usual course is for sentencing to take place at the end of the trial of the defendant who has pleaded not guilty. The judge is then in a better position to sentence the defendant who has pleaded guilty, in the light of evidence which has been heard. (See **11.2.5** for details.)

9.10 Plea of Not Guilty

If the defendant pleads not guilty to some or all of the charges, a trial will normally commence. But sometimes the prosecution will not proceed further. There are two main possibilities:

(a) The prosecution offers no evidence. The defendant is then entitled to a verdict of not guilty. This course would be taken where, for example, evidence has come to light since committal which suggests the defendant is not guilty.

(b) The prosecution asks that the count(s) to which the defendant has pleaded not guilty remain on file, marked 'not to be proceeded with without leave of this court or of the Court of Appeal'. The prosecution usually adopts this course when the defendant has pleaded guilty to some counts, but not all, and when proving the case would be a waste of court time in view of the guilty pleas entered. In practice, the counts left on the file are not reactivated unless, for example, the Court of Appeal sets aside the convictions on the other counts because the defendant's guilty pleas were involuntary (see **9.16** and **11.2.3**).

9.11 Ambiguous Pleas

The defendant may give an ambiguous answer when asked how he or she pleads, e.g. to a count of assault occasioning actual bodily harm: 'Guilty, but I didn't mean to hit him.' If so, the judge should explain the elements of the offence and try to ensure that the defendant pleads unambiguously. If the plea remains ambiguous, a plea of 'not guilty' should be entered (compare **5.1.4** and see **11.2.6**).

9.12 Guilty to an Alternative Offence

9.12.1 ALTERNATIVE OFFENCE INCLUDED IN OFFENCE CHARGED

Under the Criminal Law Act 1967, s. 6, if the defendant is charged with one offence, he or she may plead guilty to, or be found guilty of, any offence included in the offence charged. This can happen where the alternative offence is included (either expressly or by implication) in the offence charged.

For example, the offence of robbery is committed when a person commits theft together with actual or threatened violence. Therefore, if a person is charged with robbery, he or she may be found guilty of theft by the jury or plead 'guilty to theft, but not guilty to robbery'.

9.12.2 PROSECUTION PROCEDURE

If the defendant wishes, for example, to plead guilty to theft, but not guilty to robbery as charged, the prosecution can either:

(a) Accept the plea. The defendant is acquitted on the offence charged, and has pleaded guilty (and hence falls to be sentenced) on the alternative offence.

(b) Reject the plea. A plea of not guilty is entered, and a trial will be held. The guilty plea to the lesser offence must in these circumstances be treated as a nullity (*R* v *Hazeltine* [1967] 2 QB 857).

Note that if prosecuting counsel is minded to accept the plea, he or she will usually ask the judge whether it is proper to do so. The judge's decision on this point must then be accepted. A defendant often offers a plea to an offence he or she sees as less important than the one charged and which is thus likely to attract a lighter sentence.

9.12.3 WHERE DEFENDANT DISPUTES PART OF PARTICULARS

What if the defendant wishes to plead guilty to the offence charged, but disputes some part of the particulars? For example, Tommy Tucker is charged with the theft of £500 from Terence Thompson. He says he stole only £150. The position is that he should plead guilty, but counsel on his behalf should put forward Tommy's version in mitigation. The judge *may* then wish to hold a '*Newton*-style' hearing on the facts before sentencing. (See **14.4.**)

9.13 Pleas to Alternative Counts

Look again at the section above on 'Alternative Counts' (**9.2.3**). Where the defendant offers a guilty plea to the charge under s. 18, it would clearly be a waste of time to put the counts under s. 20 and s. 47. So this is not done, and the alternatives are not proceeded with. But if the defendant pleads guilty to, say, the s. 47 offence, the prosecution may well wish to proceed to trial on the s. 18 and s. 20 offences. A trial on those disputed counts will then follow. Such counts should therefore appear in the indictment in *decreasing* order of gravity, *viz*, s. 18, then s. 20, then s. 47.

9.14 Other Pleas

There are other pleas which occur very rarely in practice:

(a) *Autrefois acquit* and *autrefois convict* (see below).

(b) Pardon, i.e. the defendant has been pardoned for the offence.

(c) Demurrer (a written version of the motion to quash the indictment).

(d) Plea to the jurisdiction, i.e. the court has no power to try the case.

9.14.1 THE MEANING OF *AUTREFOIS ACQUIT* AND *AUTREFOIS CONVICT*

In essence, these pleas aver that the defendant has, on a previous occasion, been acquitted or convicted of the offence charged. The plea is made in writing by defence counsel on behalf of the defendant, normally before arraignment. If the prosecution does not accept the plea, it joins issue through a written replication, signed by an officer of the Crown Court.

The question of whether *autrefois* applied was formerly decided by a jury. Now, by CJA 1988, s. 122: 'Where an accused pleads *autrefois acquit* or *autrefois convict* it shall be for the judge, without the presence of a jury, to decide the issue.'

If the judge decides that *autrefois* does not apply, then the indictment is put in the usual manner, and the defendant pleads guilty or not guilty.

The principle behind a plea of *autrefois* is the rule against double jeopardy — nobody shall be tried to acquittal or conviction for the same offence twice. That principle applies also to summary proceedings in the magistrates' court. There, however, there is no special plea or procedure — the issues are canvassed on a not guilty plea.

9.14.2 WHEN DOES *AUTREFOIS* APPLY?

The principles relating to *autrefois* were set out in the leading case of *Connelly* v *DPP* [1946] AC 1254, and were recently applied by the Court of Appeal in *R* v *Beedie* [1997] 3 WLR 758. Beedie was landlord of a bedsit whose occupant died of carbon monoxide poisoning caused by a defective gas fire. He was prosecuted by the Health and Safety Executive for failing to maintain the fire and flue properly, pleaded guilty and was fined. He was later charged with manslaughter. At his trial, an application was made on his behalf to stay the indictment, relying upon *autrefois convict*. The judge refused the application, whereupon Beedie pleaded guilty and appealed. The Court of Appeal held that the case did not fall within the *autrefois* principle. That applied only in a case where the *same* offence, in fact and law, was alleged in the second indictment. Importantly, however, judicial discretion should be exercised where the offence in the second indictment arose out of the same or substantially the same set of facts as that in the first indictment. As to the way in which the trial judge ought to exercise his or her discretion, the Court of Appeal emphasised that it was for the prosecution to show that there were special circumstances before the judge should allow the trial to proceed. In addition, there should not be sequential trials for offences on an ascending scale of gravity (relying on the principle in *R* v *Elrington* (1861) 1 B & S 688). As it was put in *R* v *Forest of Dean Justices, ex parte Farley* [1990] RTR 228 at 239, 'there is an almost invariable rule that when a person is tried on a lesser offence he is not to be tried again on the same facts for a more serious offence'. In the case of *Beedie*, the Court of Appeal held that a stay should have been ordered, because the manslaughter allegation was based on substantially the same facts as the earlier summary prosecution, and it was a prosecution for an offence of greater gravity (no new facts having emerged). It was therefore in breach of the *Elrington* principle. There were in any event no special circumstances such as to allow the prosecution to proceed, and the appeal was allowed.

A major statutory exception to the availability of *autrefois acquit* was introduced by ss. 54 to 57 of the Criminal Procedure and Investigations Act 1996, which relate to 'tainted acquittals'. They enable the prosecution of a defendant for a second time for an offence of which he or she has already been acquitted, if certain conditions are met. The conditions are:

(a) the defendant was acquitted of an offence;

(b) a person has been convicted on an administration of justice offence involving interference with or intimidation of a juror or a witness or potential witness;

(c) the court convicting on the administration of justice offence certifies that there is a real possibility that, but for the interference or intimidation, the acquitted person would not have been acquitted;

(d) that court certifies that it would not be contrary to the interests of justice to proceed against the acquitted person; and

(e) the High Court grants an order quashing the acquittal after satisfying itself that:

   (i) it is likely that, but for the interference or intimidation, the acquitted person would not have been acquitted;

   (ii) it would not be contrary to the interests of justice (e.g. because of lapse of time) to take proceedings against the acquitted person;

   (iii) the acquitted person has had a reasonable opportunity to make written representations to the High Court; and

   (iv) the conviction for the administration of justice offence will stand.

9.14.3 THE JUDGE'S DISCRETION

Even where a prosecution does not strictly fall within the three categories above, there are circumstances in which the judge may exercise a discretion to halt the prosecution as oppressive in view of previous proceedings against the defendant.

This might happen, for example, where the offence charged is *substantially or in effect* the same as one of which the defendant has previously been acquitted or convicted. In *Connelly*, the court was divided as to whether such cases fell within the ambit of *autrefois*. In any event, as Lords Devlin and Pearce pointed out, there is a judicial discretion to stop a prosecution which offends the principles underlying *autrefois*. For example, in *R* v *Moxon-Tritsch* [1988] Crim LR 46, the defendant was the driver in an accident in which her passengers were killed. She was fined and disqualified for careless driving. A private prosecution was then brought for causing death by reckless driving. The trial judge held that the proceedings were oppressive, and ordered that the count lie on the file marked 'not to be proceeded with'.

9.14.4 ISSUE ESTOPPEL

Assume that a plea of *autrefois* is not available to the defendant on the above principles. Is the prosecution estopped from raising an issue of fact which has been decided in the defendant's favour at an earlier trial?

In *DPP* v *Humphreys* (1976) 73 Cr App R 95, the facts were that H had been charged with driving while disqualified. The only issue at trial was whether a police officer had correctly identified H as the driver on that particular day. H was acquitted and then charged with perjury for swearing that he had not driven during the year in question. The officer was allowed to give the same evidence. He was supported by other witnesses (not reasonably available at the first trial) who testified that H had driven on other occasions during that year. The House of Lords upheld H's conviction for perjury (reversing the Court of Appeal). It held:

(a) it was not a case of 'double jeopardy';

(b) nor was it an abuse of the court's process; and

(c) the doctrine of issue estoppel has no application to the criminal law.

9.15 Plea Bargaining

Frequently, defence and prosecution counsel will have discussions as to the charges, which may result in agreement being reached. The usual basis of such agreement is either:

(a) If the defendant pleads guilty to one or more counts in the indictment, the prosecution will not proceed with the remainder (see **9.9** above).

(b) If the defendant pleads guilty to a lesser offence, the prosecution will accept the plea, and not press for trial on the more serious offence (see **9.12** above).

This form of plea bargaining is widely accepted by the courts. It saves time and money, and avoids what can be the agonising experience of a trial for the defendant and witnesses. (Such discussions usually occur before a trial starts but can happen at any time before the jury retires to consider its verdict.)

For a case where the Court of Appeal said that the Crown was clearly wrong on the facts to accept a plea to a lesser offence, see *R* v *Stubbs* (1989) 88 Cr App R 53. See also the ***Professional Conduct Manual***, *R* v *Turner* [1970] 2 QB 321 and para. 11.6 of Annexe F in the Code of Conduct.

Sometimes there is discussion between prosecution and defence not only as to the counts in the indictment to which the defendant will plead guilty, but as to the facts which form the basis of the plea. On occasion this may result in an agreement as to the facts on which the plea of guilty is entered. In *R* v *Beswick*, *The Times*, 10 October 1995, the Court of Appeal dealt with the situation where agreement had been reached between prosecution and defence counsel as to the facts upon which a plea of guilty was to be based, and the judge declined to give effect to that agreement. Their Lordships set out five principles for the guidance of the court in such cases:

(1) Whenever the court has to sentence an offender it should seek to do so on a basis which is true. The prosecution should not, therefore, lend itself to any agreement with the defence which was founded on an unreal and untrue set of facts.

(2) When that had happened, the judge was entitled to direct the trial of an issue (i.e. a *Newton* hearing (see **14.4.2**)) in order to determine the true factual basis for sentence.

(3) Such a decision did not create a ground upon which a defendant should be allowed to vacate his or her plea of guilty, provided he or she does admit his or her guilt of the offence to which he or she has pleaded guilty.

(4) The decision that there should be a trial of an issue meant that the judge was entitled to expect the assistance of prosecuting counsel in presenting evidence, and in testing any evidence called by the defence. The agreement which the prosecution had previously entered into with the defence must be viewed as conditional on the approval of the judge. If the judge's approval is not forthcoming, the defence cannot seek to hold the prosecution to the agreement.

(5) Before the trial of an issue was embarked on, the judge might consider whether there was any part of the agreement by which the prosecution should be bound. Counsel should also consider which issues are to be tried, and which of the prosecution statements were relevant to them.

9.16 Involuntary Pleas

If the defendant is subjected to pressure, so that he or she pleads guilty involuntarily, then the plea is a nullity. On appeal, the Court of Appeal will quash the conviction and order a retrial.

Such pressure may allegedly have come from defence counsel, e.g. defence counsel says to the defendant 'You have no chance of being acquitted. Whether you are guilty or not, you should plead guilty. That way you will get a more lenient sentence'. That would make any subsequent plea of guilty a nullity. Of course, counsel should advise on the strength of the prosecution case and the credit which the defendant will get for a plea of guilty. But the defendant should be left in no doubt that it is his or her decision. It is safest to say 'Only plead guilty if you are guilty'.

The pressure to plead guilty may be alleged to have come from the judge. The classic case is where counsel goes to see the judge in his or her private room, and the defendant then decides to plead guilty as a result of what counsel says took place (see **9.17** and **14.1**). See also para. 12.3 of Annexe F in the Code of Conduct.

9.17 Seeing the Judge about a Plea

Sometimes counsel will ask to see the judge in his or her private room in order to get an indication on sentence. Many judges will not agree to this, and the Court of Appeal has expressed reservations about the practice. If the judge agrees to see counsel for this purpose:

(a) Counsel for both the prosecution and the defence should be present.

(b) A shorthand writer should be present, so there can be no dispute about what was said.

(c) Any indication by the judge will usually be in the broadest terms, e.g. 'On what I have read and heard from you, I do not think an immediate custodial sentence will be imposed'.

(d) There should be no indication of a more severe sentence in the event of not guilty plea or a more lenient one for a guilty plea.

The most obvious situation in which such a course is adopted is where the defendant really knows that he or she is guilty, but is afraid to plead guilty because of the fear of a custodial sentence. Once the air has been cleared by the judge indicating to counsel that prison is not in prospect, the defendant can decide on a plea with clearer judgment. The process can lead to misunderstanding, however, and the Court of Appeal has emphasised point (d) above. It has also stressed that such discussions should take place only where necessary. (See *R* v *Smith* [1990] Crim LR 354 and, generally, *R* v *Turner* [1970] 2 QB 321. See also **14.1** and the ***Professional Conduct Manual***.)

9.18 Changing the Plea

At any stage of the trial, the defendant may change his or her plea from not guilty to guilty. Defence counsel asks for the indictment to be put again, it is put, and the defendant pleads guilty to the count in question. The jury then returns a formal verdict of guilty on the judge's direction. The defendant will get some credit for a guilty plea, but not as much as if the plea had been guilty from the start.

At any time before sentence is passed, the defendant can also change a guilty plea to not guilty with the judge's consent. One reason for consenting might be that the defendant was not represented at the time of the original plea.

9.19 Exercises

(**Note:** These are intended for self-assessment. Suggested solutions may be found in **Appendix 2** of this Manual.)

(1) Michael Masters is seen on 14 February 2000 trying to take something from Mary Martin's handbag. When interviewed by the police, he tells them that he wanted to take hold of her wallet, but withdrew his hand when he saw he was being watched. Draft an indictment for trial at the Bluebridge Crown Court containing one count only.

(2) Would it make any difference to your answer if the Bluebridge magistrates had dismissed the charge in relation to the handbag, but committed Michael for trial on a charge of receiving stolen credit cards found on him at arrest?

(3) Noreen Naylor is lawfully searched by the police on 15 March 2000. They find in her jeans pocket 18.6 grams of cocaine. Draft an indictment containing a single count, for trial in the Newtown Crown Court.

(4) Peter Parsley is charged in an indictment containing a single count alleging that 'on the 18th day of May 2000 he raped or indecently assaulted Polly Pepper'. What should the defence do?

(5) Robert Rawlings is arrested as he runs from the scene of a burglary of a house. On him he has a set of skeleton keys which the police say were used to effect entry

to the house in question. Robert has already been charged with robbery as a result of a street mugging which took place two months previously. Should the offences of burglary, going equipped and robbery be charged in the same indictment?

(6) Would it make any difference to your answer to (5) if Richard Rendell is also charged with robbery arising from the street mugging, the allegation being that he acted as look-out for Robert?

(7) Assume that you act for Richard, in the situation outlined in (5) and (6) above. Assume also that Robert has, in an interview with the police, stated that the robbery was all Richard's idea. What application can you make on Richard's behalf at the trial of both on an indictment for the various offences?

(8) Simon Schofield is found, two hours after the burglary of a jeweller's shop on 19 June 2000, with some of the proceeds of the burglary. A man similar in appearance to Simon was seen running away from the jeweller's just after the alarm went off. Draw up an indictment for Simon's trial in the Blackbridge Crown Court. The goods taken from the jeweller's shop consist of six necklaces and four bracelets. When found, Simon had one necklace and all the bracelets. The jeweller's shop is at 108 High Road, Blackbridge, and is owned by Stanley Sutton.

TEN

CROWN COURT: PRE-TRIAL ISSUES

This chapter covers a series of issues relating to preparation for trial in the Crown Court, which are dealt with mainly in the Criminal Procedure and Investigation Act 1996 (CPIA).

10.1 Criminal Procedure and Investigations Act 1996

The effect of the CPIA 1996 upon criminal procedure was radical, particularly since for the first time it introduced the principle that the defence is expected to disclose its case in advance of trial. In this chapter, the central provisions of the Act are summarised. These deal with the duties of the prosecution and the defence in relation to disclosure, and the powers of the court in relation to preparatory hearings and pre-trial hearings.

In addition to the Act itself, the Home Office produced a Code of Practice which is intended to govern the duties of police officers in the conduct of investigations, and which fills in a lot of the detail necessary to understand the way in which the new scheme of disclosure is to work. This Code is intended to be the equivalent to the Codes of Practice under the Police and Criminal Evidence Act 1984 (see **2.2**).

For further reading, see: Leng, R., and Taylor, R., *Blackstone's Guide to the Criminal Procedure and Investigations Act 1996* (Blackstone Press, 1996); Sprack, J., 'The Criminal Procedure and Investigations Act: (1) The Duty of Disclosure' [1997] Crim LR 308; and Edwards, A., 'The Criminal Procedure and Investigations Act: (2) The Procedural Aspects' [1997] Crim LR 321.

10.2 Disclosure

An important issue in criminal procedure is the extent to which the prosecution and the defence must before trial disclose to each other the information pertaining to the case. Concentrating for the moment upon the prosecution, there is a central distinction between:

(a) the disclosure by the prosecution of its case, i.e. the evidence upon which it will rely at trial; and

(b) the disclosure of other material pertaining to the case, which it does not intend to use — 'used material'.

As far as Crown Court trial is concerned, it is clear that the prosecution has an obligation to disclose its case to the defence, in the sense described in (a). In practice, the bulk of this evidence will be contained in the bundle of documents resulting from the accused's committal by the magistrates (see **Chapter 6**). Any gaps will then be filled in by notices of additional evidence.

At common law, the prosecution has also had a duty to disclose to the defence any unused material, i.e. the material described in (b) above. This duty was refined and extended in the wake of a series of high-profile miscarriage of justice cases, and reached its high-water mark in the case of *R* v *Ward* [1993] 1 WLR 619. There were protests from the police and the Crown Prosecution Service among others that the duty upon the prosecution had become too onerous, and that it resulted in the abandonment of cases where the court ordered the disclosure of sensitive or confidential material. On the other hand, there were those who were anxious to preserve the prosecution's obligation to disclose relevant material, so that the defence (which usually lacks investigative resources) could be aware of any potentially helpful information which the prosecution held, but had decided not to use.

The Royal Commission on Criminal Justice, chaired by Lord Runciman, recommended in 1994 that the prosecution duty of disclosure should be brought within a more restrictive framework, and that it should be tied to a measure of defence disclosure. The notion that the defence should be under an obligation to disclose its case was a novel one, and was argued by some to undermine the prosecution's burden of proof. Nonetheless, restrictions on prosecution disclosure more radical than those suggested by the Runciman Commission and accompanied by a proposal for defence disclosure, formed part of the Criminal Procedure and Investigation Bill when it was introduced in Parliament in November 1995.

The scheme of the legislation is that there is a statutory duty upon the police officer investigating an offence to record and retain information and material gathered or generated during the investigation. The prosecution must, in what the Act calls 'primary prosecution disclosure', inform the defence of certain categories of that material which it does not intend to use at trial (as stated, there is a separate obligation to inform the defence of material which it *does* intend to use). The defence then has a duty to inform the prosecution of the case which it intends to present at trial. The prosecution then has a duty to present further material to the defence — 'secondary prosecution disclosure'. The legislation makes provision for applications to be made to the court in certain circumstances where there is a dispute about whether the prosecution should disclose certain material; and there are sanctions laid down for defence failure to disclose or disclosure which is false or inconsistent.

10.2.1 THE INVESTIGATOR'S DUTY

Section 23 of the CPIA 1996 required the Secretary of State to prepare a Code of Practice which will govern investigations carried out by police officers. By s. 26, those other than police officers charged with the duty of conducting criminal investigations (e.g. customs officers) must have regard to the Code's provisions.

The resultant Code of Practice makes the investigator responsible for ensuring that any information relevant to the investigation is recorded and retained, whether it is gathered in the course of the investigation (e.g. documents seized in the course of searching premises) or generated by the investigation (e.g. interview records). Where there is any doubt about the relevance of material, the investigator should retain it. The duty to retain material includes, in particular, the following categories (the list is not exhaustive):

(a) crime reports, including crime report forms, relevant parts of incident report books and police officers' notebooks;

(b) custody records;

(c) records from tapes of telephone messages (e.g. 999 calls) containing descriptions of an alleged offence or offender;

(d) final versions of witness statements (and draft versions where they differ from the final versions) and any exhibits mentioned;

(e) interview records (written or taped) of interviews with actual or potential witnesses or suspects;

(f) expert reports and schedules of scientific material;

(g) any material casting doubt upon the reliability of a confession;

(h) any material casting doubt on the reliability of a witness;

(i) any other material which may fall within the test for primary prosecution disclosure (see **10.2.2**).

But the duty to retain material does not extend to draft statements of opinion prepared by expert witnesses, routine exchanges of material or material purely ancillary to that in the above categories.

The material must be retained at least until criminal proceedings are concluded.

Where the accused is convicted, the material must be retained until the accused has been released from custody or discharged from hospital (where the court imposes a custodial sentence or hospital order). In all other cases, it must be kept until six months from the date of conviction. If an appeal against conviction is in progress at the date of release, or the end of the six months, all material which may be relevant must be kept until the appeal is determined.

Where the investigator believes that the person charged with an offence is likely to plead not guilty at a summary trial, or that the offence will be tried in the Crown Court, he or she must prepare a schedule listing material which has been retained and which does not form part of the case against the accused. If the investigator has obtained any sensitive material, this should be listed in a separate schedule. Sensitive material is material which the investigator believes it is not in the public interest to disclose. The Code gives a number of examples, which range from material relating to national security to material given in confidence, and includes material relating to informants, undercover police officers, premises used for police surveillance, techniques used in the detection of crime, and material relating to a child witness generated, for example, by a local authority social services department.

The investigator should draw the prosecutor's attention to any material which might undermine the prosecution case. The disclosure officer (defined as 'the person responsible for handling the administration of a criminal investigation') must certify that to the best of his or her knowledge and belief the duties imposed under the Code have been complied with.

After the defence has complied with *its* duty of disclosure (see **10.2.3**), the investigator must look again at the material retained, and draw the prosecutor's attention to any material which might reasonably be expected to assist the defence disclosed. Again, the disclosure officer must certify compliance with the duties imposed by the Code. If the investigator comes into possession of any new material after complying with the duties described above, then this must be treated in the same way.

If the prosecutor so requests, the investigator must disclose to the accused:

(a) material which might undermine the prosecution case;

(b) where the accused has given the prosecutor a defence statement (see **10.2.3**), material which might reasonably be expected to assist the defence which the accused has disclosed;

(c) any material which the court orders be disclosed.

10.2.2 PRIMARY PROSECUTION DISCLOSURE

Section 3 of the CPIA 1996 requires the prosecutor to disclose previously undisclosed material to the accused if, in the prosecutor's opinion, it might undermine the case for the prosecution. If there is no such material, then the accused must be given a written statement to that effect. Prosecution material includes material which the prosecutor possesses or has been allowed to inspect under the provisions of the Code (see **10.2.1**). It may be disclosed either by giving it to the defence, or allowing the defence to inspect it at a reasonable time and place. This step is called 'primary prosecution disclosure', and it must be carried out within a time limit which is to be laid down by statutory instrument. Until a specific time limit is laid down, the prosecution must make primary disclosure 'as soon as is reasonably practicable' (s. 13). Material must not, however, be disclosed under this provision if a court has concluded that it is not in the public interest that it be disclosed (see **10.2.5**). By s. 4, if the prosecutor has been given a document indicating any non-sensitive material which has not been given to the accused, that document must be given to the accused at the same time as primary prosecution disclosure takes place.

The test for primary disclosure, therefore, is whether in the prosecutor's opinion the material might undermine the case for the prosecution. Being based upon the prosecutor's opinion, it is clearly a subjective test (and can be compared with that laid down in s. 7(2) for secondary disclosure (see **10.2.4**). It seems likely that it would cover cases such as *R* v *Rasheed, The Times*, 20 May 1994 (decided under the common law, prior to the CPIA 1996).

In *Rasheed* the fact that a prosecution witness had, before the trial, asked to be considered for a reward was a matter which might have a bearing on his motives for coming forward to give evidence. The Court of Appeal held that it should have been disclosed to the defence.

Less certain, however, would be the current position in a case such as in *R* v *Phillipson* (1989) 91 Cr App R 226 where the prosecution failed to disclose in advance the existence of material incriminating to the accused. P, who was charged with the importation of heroin, claimed that she had been subjected to duress by her boyfriend, I. She claimed that he had threatened to kill her and their young child if she failed to carry out his instructions. In evidence, she said that I had beaten her, and had shown no affection for her or the child. In cross-examination, prosecuting counsel put to her letters written to her by I which indicated some affection, a letter written by her to I while she was in custody suggesting that he should have the child rather than the social services, and a photograph of I and the child in an affectionate pose. None of this material had been disclosed to the defence before the trial, despite the fact that the defence of duress appeared from P's interviews. At trial, the defence argued that the prosecution should have disclosed the material either as part of their case, or as unused material. The prosecution had withheld the material in order to stop P from tailoring her testimony to fit the adverse evidence. P was convicted and appealed. The Court of Appeal upheld the appeal. The reasons given did not justify withholding the material until P gave evidence. It was more important that an accused should be encouraged to tell the truth, and know the case which has to be met, than be induced to lie by thinking it was safe to do so. The prosecution should have disclosed the letters. (In addition, the court noted that they presented hearsay problems.) Their Lordships did not, however, rule out in an appropriate case the 'time-hallowed practice' of introducing material for the first time in cross-examination of an accused.

10.2.3 DEFENCE DISCLOSURE

Once primary prosecution disclosure has taken place and the case is committed to the Crown Court, the accused must give a defence statement to the prosecutor (s. 5). This must be done within 14 days (Criminal Procedure and Investigations Act 1996 (Defence Disclosure Time Limits) Regulations 1997).

The defence statement is a written statement setting out in general terms the nature of the defence and the matters on which the accused takes issue with the prosecution, with reasons (s. 5(6)).

Note: There is no question of the defence having to disclose 'unused material'.

If the defence statement discloses an alibi, particulars of alibi must be given, including the name and address of any alibi witness, or information which might be of use in finding the witness, if his or her name or address is not known. This provision replaces s. 11 of the Criminal Justice Act 1967, although a similar definition of alibi evidence is adopted — 'evidence tending to show that by reason of the presence of the accused at a particular place or in a particular area at a particular time he was not, or was unlikely to have been, at the place where the offence is alleged to have been committed at the time of its alleged commission'.

The duty which the CPIA 1996 puts upon the defence to reveal its case is a novel one to English law, and places a difficult tactical decision on the defendant's lawyers. They must weigh up the advantages and drawbacks of a detailed defence statement. An appropriate degree of detail can trigger off the release of further prosecution material (see **10.2.4**) whereas non-disclosure can result in the drawing of inferences potentially unfavourable to the defendant (see **10.2.8**). On the other hand, if the defence is bound by a detailed defence which later proves to be inaccurate, there is the danger of adverse inferences being drawn for that reason.

10.2.4 SECONDARY PROSECUTION DISCLOSURE

Once the defence has served a statement, the prosecutor must disclose to the accused any previously undisclosed prosecution material 'which might be reasonably expected to assist the accused's defence as disclosed by the defence statement' (s. 7). If there is no such material, the prosecutor must give to the accused a statement to that effect. This process is termed 'secondary prosecution disclosure', and must be carried out within a time-limit to be laid down by statutory instrument (again, until such a time limit is specified, the prosecution must act 'as soon as reasonably practicable'). The methods of disclosure are identical to those set out in respect of primary prosecution disclosure, and the process is subject to the same exception in respect of material which the court orders should not be disclosed because it would not be in the public interest to do so.

10.2.5 REVIEW BY THE COURT

The prosecutor may make application to the court that material should not be disclosed, either at the primary or the secondary stage, on the basis that it is not in the public interest to disclose it (ss. 3(6) and 7(5)). For its part, the defence can, under s. 8, apply to the court for an order that the prosecutor should disclose any material which might be reasonably expected to assist the accused's defence. Such application may only be made, however, after the defence has served a defence statement.

10.2.6 PUBLIC INTEREST IMMUNITY

The review by the court described in **10.2.5** will usually be focused on the issue of whether it is in the public interest to disclose material which is in the possession of the prosecution. For its part, the prosecution may allege that the material in question is subject to public interest immunity. Although the CPIA 1996 abolished the common law in relation to disclosure (s. 21(1)), it preserved the common law on the question of whether disclosure is in the public interest (s. 21(2)). As a result, the case law in relation to public interest immunity is preserved, and reference should be made to **14.3** in the ***Evidence Manual***. It should be emphasised that the fact that material is included in a 'sensitive schedule' (see **10.2.1**), e.g. because it is 'confidential', is not conclusive of the question whether it is in the public interest to disclose it.

Even if the Crown believes that the unused material should be immune from disclosure, that does not end the matter. The case of *R* v *Ward* [1993] 1 WLR 619 makes it clear that it is for the court, and not the prosecution, to make the final decision as to whether immunity from disclosure should be granted. Judith Ward had been convicted of multiple murder and explosives offences. The prosecution failed to disclose material relevant to her alleged confessions and certain scientific evidence. The Court of Appeal held that, if the prosecution claimed that they were entitled to withhold material documents on the basis of public interest immunity, the court must be asked to rule on the legitimacy of their claim. If the prosecution was not prepared to have the issue determined by a court, they would have to abandon the case.

In *R* v *Davis* [1993] 1 WLR 613 the Court of Appeal set out further guidance as to the procedure which should be adopted where the prosecution claim immunity from disclosure. After reiterating that it is for the court, not the prosecution, to decide whether disclosure must be made, Lord Taylor CJ put forward certain principles as to the proper approach to disclosure.

(a) In general it is the prosecution's duty to make disclosure voluntarily.

(b) If the prosecution wish to rely on public interest immunity or sensitivity to justify non-disclosure, then, whenever possible, which will be in most cases, they must notify the defence that they are applying for a ruling by the court, and indicate to the defence at least the category of the material which they hold. The defence must then have the opportunity of making representations to the court.

(c) Where, however, the disclosure of the category of material would be to reveal that which the prosecution contend it would not be in the public interest to reveal, a different procedure will apply. The prosecution should still notify the defence of the application, but need not specify the category of material, and the application will be *ex parte*. If the court, on hearing the application, considers that the normal procedure under (b) ought to have been followed, it will so order. If not, It will rule on the *ex parte* application.

(d) In a highly exceptional case, the prosecution might take the view that to reveal even the fact that an *ex parte* application is to be made could 'let the cat out of the bag' so as to stultify the application. Such a case would be rare indeed, but if it did occur then the prosecution should apply to the court *ex parte* without notice. Again, if the court on hearing the application considered that notice should have been given to the defence, or even that the normal *inter partes* hearing should have been adopted, it will so order.

After setting out these principles, Lord Taylor went on to say:

> We should add that where the court, on application by the Crown, rules in favour of non-disclosure before the hearing of a case begins, that ruling is not necessarily final. In the course of the hearing, the situation may change. Issues may emerge so that the public interest in non-disclosure may be eclipsed by the need to disclose in the interests of securing fairness to the defendant. If that were to occur, the court would have to indicate to the Crown its change of view. The Crown would then have to decide whether to disclose or offer no further evidence.
>
> It will therefore be necessary for the court to continue to monitor the issue. For that reason, it is desirable that the same judge or constitution of the court which decides the application should conduct the hearing. If that is not possible, the judge or constitution which does conduct the hearing should be apprised at the outset of the material upon which non-disclosure was upheld on the Crown's earlier application.

The principles set out in (a) to (d) have now been incorporated in the Crown Court (Criminal Procedure and Investigations Act 1996) (Disclosure) Rules 1997; and the Magistrates' Courts (Criminal Procedure and Investigations Act 1996) (Disclosure) Rules 1997. It is submitted that Lord Taylor's remarks about the necessity for the court to continue to monitor the position remain good law.

In an *ex parte* hearing there is, of course, no opportunity for the defence to argue in favour of disclosure. The court will hear arguments only from the prosecution against disclosure. As a result, the *ex parte* procedure has been challenged in the European Court of Human Rights in Strasbourg, on the grounds that it violates the rights of the defence under ECHR, Article 6 (*Rowe and Davis* v *United Kingdom* (Application No. 28901/95)). This is the sequel to the case reported under the title *R* v *Davis* and dealt with earlier in this section. The applicants, Rowe and Davis, were tried (together with Johnson) in February 1990 for murder, assault occasioning grievous bodily harm and three counts of robbery. Their appeal came before the Court of Appeal in October 1992. At the first hearing, counsel for the prosecution handed a document to the court, which was not shown to defence counsel, seeking a ruling on disclosure. He informed the court that the contents were sensitive, and that he should either be heard *ex parte*, or if *inter partes*, only on an undertaking by defence counsel not to disclose what took place to their solicitors or clients. At that hearing, defence counsel indicated that they could not conscientiously give such an undertaking, and the prosecution in effect argued *ex parte* for non-disclosure. The Court of Appeal in its judgment:

(a) stated that the procedure relating to material in the prosecution's possession which they sought to avoid disclosing had been changed by *R* v *Ward* [1993] 1 WLR 619. It was now for the court, not the prosecution, to decide whether disclosure should be made;

(b) set out the series of procedural guidelines to be followed in such cases, which are detailed earlier in this section, and are now incorporated in the Crown Court (Criminal Procedure and Investigations Act 1996) (Disclosure) Rules 1997; and

(c) refused to order disclosure.

At the hearing of the substantive appeal, the convictions of Rowe and Davis, and their co-defendant Johnson, were upheld.

In due course, the case was referred to the Criminal Cases Review Commission (CCRC), which investigated the case in the period 1997–1999. The investigation revealed that one of the leading prosecution witnesses was a long-standing police informant, who had approached the police and told them that the applicants Rowe and Davis were responsible for the crimes in question. He had received a reward of £10,300 and immunity from prosecution in relation to his admitted participation in the offences. He had never identified Johnson as one of the offenders. These facts had not previously been disclosed to the defence on grounds of public interest immunity. The CCRC commented that 'if the jury had been aware of this then the credibility of [the prosecution witnesses] might have been assessed in a more critical manner'. The case of the applicants and Johnson was referred back to the Court of Appeal, and is currently awaiting a hearing there.

Meanwhile, the applicants sought a ruling from the European Court of Human Rights that their trial violated ECHR, Article 6(1) and (3)(a) and (b). Their application was declared admissible by the Commission (see the report and commentary [1999] Crim LR 410).

At the hearing before the full court, the applicants argued that the procedure at their trial, whereby the prosecution withheld evidence from the defence without consulting the judge, violated Article 6. This defect was not rectified by the *ex parte* procedure before the Court of Appeal, which gave the defence no opportunity to put forward arguments on disclosure. It was argued on behalf of the applicants that the exclusion of the accused from this procedure should have been counter-balanced by the introduction of a special independent counsel who could argue the relevance of the undisclosed evidence, test the strength of the prosecution claim to public interest immunity, and safeguard against the risk of judicial error or bias. A special counsel procedure has now been introduced in this country in respect of fair employment cases in Northern Ireland, certain immigration appeals, complaints relating to the interception of electronic communications, and cases where the trial judge prohibits an accused from cross-examining in person the complainant in a sexual offence.

The following points emerge from the decision of the full European Court of Human Rights:

(a) The right to a fair trial means that the prosecution authorities should disclose to the defence all material evidence in their possession for and against the accused.

(b) That duty of disclosure is not absolute, and 'in any criminal proceedings there may be competing interests, such as national security or the need to protect witnesses at risk of reprisals or keep secret police methods of investigation which must be weighed against the rights of the accused'.

(c) But only such measures restricting the rights of the defence to disclosure as are strictly necessary are permissible under Article 6(1).

(d) Any difficulties caused to the defence by a limitation on its rights must be sufficiently counter-balanced by the procedure followed by the court.

(e) The pre-*Ward* procedure, whereby the prosecution could decide to withhold relevant evidence without notifying the judge, was in violation of Article 6(1).

(f) The procedure adopted by the Court of Appeal in relation to disclosure did not remedy the unfair procedure adopted at trial. It was *ex parte* and the Court of Appeal was therefore reliant upon prosecution counsel and transcripts of the trial for an understanding of the possible relevance of the undisclosed material. In any event, if the trial judge had received the material, he could have monitored the importance of the undisclosed evidence at a stage when it could have affected the course of the trial. Further, the Court of Appeal, in considering the evidence *ex post facto* may have been unconsciously influenced by the jury's verdict of guilty into under-estimating the significance of the undisclosed evidence.

The applicants did not therefore get a fair trial. The case could be contrasted with that of *Edwards* v *UK* (1992) 15 EHRR 417. In *Edwards*, appeal proceedings were able to remedy defects in the trial because, by the time of the appeal the defence had received most of the missing information, and was able to argue in detail about the impact of the new material upon the tests for disclosure laid down in the CPIA 1996, since the trial took place at a time when the (pre-*Ward*) common law rules were in place.

10.2.7 CONTINUOUS REVIEW

The prosecutor remains under a continuing duty to review questions of disclosure (s. 9). If he or she, at any time before the accused is acquitted or convicted, forms the opinion that there is material which might undermine the prosecution case, or be reasonably expected to assist the accused's defence, then it must be disclosed to the accused as soon as reasonably practicable (provided that the court has not ruled against disclosure in respect of that material).

For its part, the court must keep under review the question of whether it is still not in the public interest to disclose material affected by its order (s. 15).

10.2.8 SANCTIONS FOR DEFENCE DISCLOSURE

Integral to the scheme of the disclosure provisions is the notion that, if the defence fails to make disclosure, it will not trigger off the prosecution's obligation to make secondary disclosure (which is of material which may reasonably be expected to assist the defence advanced in the defence statement).

Section 11 lays down additional sanctions to which the defence will be liable if it is deficient in its duty of disclosure. They apply if the defence:

(a) fails to give a defence statement under s. 5;

(b) does so after the deadline laid down by statutory instrument;

(c) sets out inconsistent defences in its statement;

(d) puts forward a defence at trial which is different from the defence statement;

(e) at trial adduces evidence of alibi without having given particulars of alibi in the statement;

(f) at trial calls an alibi witness without having given details of that witness in the statement.

If any of these conditions apply then, under s. 11(3):

> *(a) the court or, with the leave of the court, any other party may make such comment as appears appropriate;*
> *(b) the court or jury may draw such inferences as appear proper in deciding whether the accused is guilty . . .*

In deciding what to do where the accused has put forward different defences, however, the court is to have regard to the extent of the difference and whether there is any justification for it.

10.2.9 SUMMARY TRIAL

The prosecution's duty of primary disclosure will apply wherever there is to be a summary trial in respect of which the accused pleads not guilty (s. 1(1)(a)). In addition, the defence may make voluntary disclosure (s. 6) which will trigger off the prosecution obligation to make secondary disclosure. In the event that the accused discloses inconsistent defences or a defence inconsistent with that later advanced at trial, however, similar consequences will follow to those which result in the Crown Court (see **10.2.8**).

10.3 Preparatory Hearings

By CPIA 1996, s. 29, a Crown Court judge may, on application or otherwise, order a preparatory hearing if a case is likely to be so long or complex that substantial benefits are likely to result. (This procedure does not, however, apply to serious or complex fraud, in which case s. 7(1) of the Criminal Justice Act 1987 would apply.)

The preparatory hearing takes place before the jury is sworn, but it marks the start of the trial. It may be held for any of the following purposes:

(a) identifying issues likely to be material to the jury's verdict;

(b) assisting its comprehension of any of the issues;

(c) expediting proceedings;

(d) assisting the judge's management of the trial.

10.3.1 POWERS OF THE JUDGE AT A PREPARATORY HEARING

The judge has the power at the preparatory hearing (s. 31) to order the prosecutor to give the court and the accused a written statement of its case, including the principal facts, the witnesses, any relevant exhibits, any proposition of law relied on, and any consequences which appear to flow from any of these matters. Where the judge has ordered the prosecution to give such a statement, he or she may also order the accused to give the court and the prosecutor a written statement in general terms of the nature of the defence, and the principal matters disputed, as well as any points of law and relevant authorities. Where the judge has decided to hold a preparatory hearing, he or she may require the prosecution or defence to supply such case statements in advance of the hearing (s. 32).

At the preparatory hearing itself, the judge may also make a ruling as to the admissibility of evidence and rule on any other question of law relating to the case (s. 31(3)). Any such ruling or order made by the judge shall have effect throughout the trial, unless there is an application to vary or discharge it, in which case the application must be decided in accordance with the interests of justice (s. 31(11)).

Although a party may depart from a case disclosed as a result of the judge's order at a preparatory ruling, comment may be made by the court (or by a party with the leave of the court) at trial, and 'the jury may draw such inference as appears proper'. A similar sanction attaches to a failure to comply with any requirement imposed under s. 31.

10.3.2 APPEALS FROM PREPARATORY HEARINGS

An appeal lies to the Court of Appeal from any ruling by the judge on the admissibility of evidence or other question of law, but only with the leave of the judge or of the Court of Appeal (s. 35). There is a similar possibility of appeal to the House of Lords, with the usual conditions (s. 36). The preparatory hearing may continue notwithstanding that an appeal is in progress, but no jury may be sworn until the appeal has been determined or abandoned. The policy is clearly to ensure that points of law are comprehensively dealt with before the court embarks upon a long and complex trial which may prove abortive due to a wrong decision on a point of law made at the preparatory hearing.

10.3.3 REPORTING RESTRICTIONS

By virtue of s. 37, any preparatory hearing (or appeal from it) may not be reported except in so far as the trial judge or the appellate court permits, until the trial is concluded. The court may order that these restrictions shall not apply if it decides that it is in the interests of justice to do so. Contravention of the reporting restrictions is an offence (s. 38).

10.4 Pre-Trial Hearings

Preparatory hearings apply to cases which are long and/or complex. A more limited set of provisions applies to run-of-the-mill cases, and these are contained in CPIA 1996, ss. 39 and 40. At any time after proceedings for trial have been committed to the Crown Court and before the start of the trial, the judge makes, at a pre-trial hearing, a ruling as to the admissibility of evidence or any other question of law, either on application by a party or of the judge's own motion. The ruling remains binding until the end of the trial, unless a judge decides to vary or discharge it (which may be on the application of a party). The judge who varies or discharges need not necessarily be the judge who made the original ruling. No application to vary or discharge may be made unless there has been a material change of circumstances since the ruling (or the last application) was made. It is apparent that these provisions envisage that the judge who conducts the pre-trial hearing may not be the trial judge, and that the extent to which the original rulings should be binding must be limited accordingly. There is, however, no right of appeal from the judge's ruling other than at the conclusion of the case in the usual way. There are reporting restrictions similar to those in respect of preparatory hearings (s. 41).

ELEVEN

JURY TRIAL

11.1 Preliminary Hearings

As we have seen in **10.3** and **10.4**, a preliminary hearing takes place before a Crown Court trial commences. In the case of complex or lengthy trials, the preliminary hearing is called a 'preparatory hearing'; in other cases, it is called a 'pre-trial hearing'. The requirement to have pre-trial hearings gives statutory effect to the system of 'plea and directions hearings' which was instituted by a *Practice Direction* in 1995 (see [1995] 1 WLR 1318).

The Direction stipulates that at the plea and directions hearing ('PDH'), pleas will be taken. If the defendant pleads guilty, the judge should proceed to sentencing whenever possible (although it may be necessary to adjourn in order for a pre-sentence report to be prepared).

In cases where the defendant pleads not guilty, the prosecution and defence will be expected to inform the court of:

(a) the issues in the case;

(b) whether the defendant or any witness is suffering from a mental or medical condition, and whether the prosecution will agree to defence witnesses who are ill giving written evidence;

(c) the number of witnesses who will be giving evidence orally or in writing;

(d) any additional witnesses likely to be called by the prosecution and the evidence they are expected to give;

(e) any formal admissions under s. 10 of the Criminal Justice Act 1967;

(f) any alibi which the defendant will rely on (which should already have been disclosed in accordance with s. 11 of the Criminal Justice Act 1967);

(g) any point of law or question of admissibility which is likely to arise in the trial;

(h) any applications for leave to give evidence via live television links or pre-recorded interviews or for the use of screens so that the identity of the witness remains secret;

(i) estimated length of trial;

(j) availability of witnesses and advocates.

The Direction envisages that this hearing will normally be conducted by the trial judge.

The hearing is normally held in open court and all defendants should be present unless the court otherwise directs.

The hearing should normally take place within six weeks of the committal of the case to the Crown Court if the defendant is on bail, and within four weeks if he is in custody. When the magistrates commit the case to the Crown Court, they should (after consultation with the Crown Court listing officer) specify the date on which the hearing should take place.

The defence should inform the prosecution, the court, and the probation service as soon as it is known that the defendant intends to plead guilty to all or part of the indictment.

Finally, the *Practice Direction* requires the defence solicitors to apply to the court for the case to be listed for mention if they are unable to obtain instructions from the defendant. If the defendant fails to attend this hearing, the judge is likely to issue a warrant for his arrest.

11.2 The Arraignment

At the arraignment (which should take place at the preliminary hearing), the indictment is 'put' to the defendant, in that he or she is asked to plead guilty or not guilty. The proceedings will go something like this:

Clerk of the Court: 'Are you Michael Smith?'
Smith: 'Yes.'
Clerk: 'Michael Smith, you are charged in an indictment containing one count of robbery contrary to s. 8 of the Theft Act 1968. The particulars of the offence are that on 8 May 2000 you robbed Alice Jones of £45 in cash. Michael Smith, to this indictment do you plead guilty or not guilty?'

If the indictment contains more than one count, each count will be put to the defendant separately, so that a plea is entered on each. The defendant must enter his or her plea personally (not through counsel or solicitor).

The defendant must he present to enter his or her plea. If the defendant fails to attend, the judge will issue a bench warrant for the defendant's arrest. If (having been present at the start of the trial) the defendant subsequently misbehaves or absconds, the judge has a discretion to continue with the trial in the absence of the defendant. However, if the defendant is absent through illness (again having been present to enter a plea of guilty or not guilty) the trial can only continue in the absence of the defendant if the defendant consents to this.

11.2.1 PROCEDURE ON A PLEA OF GUILTY

If the defendant pleads guilty to all the counts on the indictment, the prosecution will summarise the facts of the offence(s) and tell the court about the defendant's antecedents, that is basic details about his or her life (education, employment, income, etc.) based on what the defendant has told the police, together with details of any relevant previous convictions. The court will in fact have a complete list of this defendant's previous convictions, but will invite the prosecution to read out only those that are relevant, which will usually mean fairly recent ones. See *Practice Note (Crime: Antecedents)* [1997] 4 All ER 350.

11.2.2 THE *NEWTON* HEARING

In *R* v *Newton* (1982) 77 Cr App R 13, the defendant was charged with buggery of his wife. He claimed that she consented to this (not a defence, but relevant to sentence) but the prosecution alleged that she had not consented. The judge wrongly accepted the prosecution version without hearing evidence of the issue of consent. The Court of Appeal held that where there is a substantial divergence between the two stories (that is, a divergence which will have a material effect on the sentence imposed) the judge can reject the defence version only after hearing evidence of what happened.

Therefore, where the defendant has pleaded guilty, if there is a substantial conflict between the prosecution and the defence (i.e., there is sharp divergence between the prosecution version of the facts and the defence version of the facts), the judge must either accept the defence version and sentence accordingly or hear evidence of what happened and then make a finding of fact as to what happened, and sentence accordingly.

If the judge decides to hear evidence, then the evidence is heard without a jury. The parties are given the opportunity to call such evidence as they wish and to cross-examine witnesses called by the other side (for further details on *Newton* hearings, see **13.1**).

11.2.3 PROSECUTION OFFERING NO EVIDENCE; LEAVING COUNTS ON THE FILE

If the defendant pleads not guilty to some or all of the counts on the indictment, the next stage (which will take place some time after the hearing) is to empanel a jury. However, it may be that new evidence has come to light showing that the wrong person has been charged or considerably weakening the case against this defendant, or it may be that a vital witness has refused to testify (and although a person can be compelled to give evidence, a reluctant witness nearly always does more harm than good). In that case the prosecution will offer no evidence against the defendant, in which case a finding of not guilty is entered under CJA 1967, s. 17. An alternative to offering no evidence is for the prosecution to ask the judge to direct that one or more counts be left on the file marked not to be proceeded with without the leave of the Crown Court or the Court of Appeal. The advantage of this is that if the prosecution obtain a conviction on another count but the defendant successfully appeals against that conviction, the prosecution could (with leave) proceed on the other counts. Leaving a count on the file is not an acquittal, whereas if the prosecution offers no evidence this does result in an acquittal.

11.2.4 'PLEA BARGAINING' WITH THE PROSECUTION

If there are several counts on the indictment, the defendant might be willing to plead guilty to some but not to others. If that is acceptable to the prosecution, the counts to which the defendant pleads not guilty are either 'left on the file' or else the prosecution offers no evidence in respect of those counts. Furthermore, CLA 1967, s. 6(1)(b) provides that the defendant may plead not guilty to the offence on the indictment but guilty to a lesser offence of which the jury would be able to convict him or her under CLA 1967, s. 6(3). See **9.12**.

11.2.5 DIFFERENT PLEAS FROM DIFFERENT DEFENDANTS

If there is more than one defendant and one pleads guilty and the others not guilty, it is a matter for the judge whether to sentence the one who has pleaded guilty immediately or at the end of the trial of the others. The argument in favour of postponing sentence is that at the end of the trial, the judge will have a much better idea of who did what. However, it is a little more difficult if the defendant who pleads guilty also indicates that he or she is willing to 'turn Queen's evidence', giving evidence against his or her co-defendants. This will attract a very substantial discount in sentence, well beyond the one third normally credited to those who simply plead guilty. Such a person becomes a competent witness for the Crown after pleading guilty. However, if sentence is postponed, it may seem that the sentence imposed after the defendant has given evidence depends more on the quality of the evidence given than on the defendant's guilt; on the other hand if the defendant is sentenced before giving evidence, then he or she may have a change of mind and the lenient sentence given on the basis of the promised testimony cannot be altered (see *R* v *Stone* [1970] 1 WLR 1112). The Court of Appeal in *R* v *Weekes* (1980) 74 Cr App R 161 said that sentence should normally be postponed until after the trial of the other defendant. However, in *R* v *Clement, The Times*, 12 December 1991 the court observed that it is a matter for the judge whether the defendant is sentenced sooner or later.

If one defendant pleads guilty but another pleads not guilty, the jury should not be told about the guilty plea of the other defendant (unless, of course, that defendant gives evidence for the prosecution). For example, in *R* v *Manzur and Mahmood, The Times*, 6 December 1996, three people had been charged with rape. One defendant pleaded guilty, the other two pleaded not guilty, saying that the victim had consented to sexual intercourse. The judge allowed the jury to be told of the third defendant's plea of guilty. The Court of Appeal accepted the argument that the jury might have taken the view, on the basis of the third defendant's guilty plea, that the two appellants must have known that the victim was not consenting and so might not have given proper consideration to the evidence of the two appellants that they believed the woman to be consenting to intercourse. The admission of the evidence of the plea of the third defendant was therefore unduly prejudicial to the appellants and so a re-trial was ordered.

11.2.6 THE AMBIGUOUS PLEA

If the defendant pleads guilty but then advances mitigation which amounts to a defence, then the plea is ambiguous (e.g. guilty of theft but thought that the property was his or her own). In those circumstances, the law will be explained to the defendant, who will then be asked to plead again. If the plea remains ambiguous, a plea of not guilty will be entered on behalf of the defendant and a trial will take place in the usual way.

Sometimes a defendant will say to counsel, 'I didn't do it but I want to plead guilty to get things over and done with quickly'. In such a case, counsel should try to dissuade the client from pleading guilty to an offence which he or she denies. In particular, it should be pointed out that nothing can be said in mitigation which suggests innocence (since that would render the plea ambiguous) or even remorse (one cannot be remorseful for something one denies doing).

11.3 The Jury

11.3.1 WHO CAN SERVE?

The pool of potential jurors (the 'jury panel') is drawn by an officer of the Crown Court on a random basis from the register of electors aged between 18 and 70. The Juries Act 1974 (see s. 1 and sch. 1) sets out those people who may not serve on a jury. Anyone concerned with the administration of justice (lawyers, magistrates, police officers, probation officers, prison officers, etc.) is ineligible for jury service, as are the clergy and the mentally disordered. Others are disqualified from jury service. Anyone who has been sentenced to life imprisonment is disqualified for life; a custodial sentence (including a suspended sentence) disqualifies for ten years, as does a community service order; a probation order disqualifies for five years. Similarly, a person who is on bail at the time is disqualified. Of those who are eligible to serve, some have a right to be excused from jury service. This list includes members of parliament, medical personnel, full-time service personnel and those aged 65–70. The rest have the right (and duty) to serve when called to do so and will only be excused from jury service if they can show a good reason. The trial judge also has power to excuse from jury service a person who is not capable of acting as a juror because of physical disability. Furthermore, a person may be excused from jury service on the ground that he or she is practising member of a religious society or order, the tenets or beliefs of which are incompatible with jury service.

11.3.2 EMPANELLING THE JURY

A number of potential jurors come into the courtroom. The clerk reads out the names of 12 of them, selected randomly from the list of those present. The 12 go into the jury box. The clerk will also explain to the defendant that the list of names about to be called out will form the jury which will try the defendant but that he or she has the right to challenge jurors before they are sworn.

11.3.3 CHALLENGING POTENTIAL JURORS

There are two main types of challenge.

11.3.3.1 Stand by

The first type of challenge is the right of the prosecution to stand a juror by. Just as the juror starts to take the oath, the prosecuting counsel says 'Stand by'. The judge will then explain to that juror that he or she cannot sit on this jury but may be required to sit on another one. This challenge is confined to the prosecution, and prosecuting counsel does not have to give any reasons for the challenge. The fact that the prosecution would seem to have an advantage over the defence (who no longer has any right of peremptory challenge) led the Attorney-General to issue guidelines on the related issues of use of the stand by and jury vetting (see Appendix 4 to *Blackstone's Criminal Practice* for the full text). In many cases there will be no check at all on potential jurors. However, in ordinary cases the names of the potential jurors may be put through the Police National Computer to see if any have previous convictions which mean that they are disqualified from jury service or are unsuitable to serve on this particular jury. In cases involving national security and terrorism, however, a more thorough check is carried out, with use being made of Special Branch files. Unsuitable jurors can then simply be stood by. The other cases where use of the stand by is appropriate, according to the guidelines, is where the person is manifestly unsuitable to sit on this jury, and the defence agrees that he or she should not sit. An example might be the person who is clearly unable to read the words on the card which contains the jury oath and so is unsuitable for a case which involves perusal of documentary evidence.

It should be noted that the judge also has power to stand a juror by, but this power is exercised only very rarely. Some judges had used it (at the request of the defence) to try to secure a racially balanced jury so that some members shared the defendant's ethnic origin. However, in *R* v *Ford* [1989] QB 868 the Court of Appeal ruled that this practice was unlawful. Similarly, in *R* v *Tarrant* [1998] Crim LR 342, it was held that the judge cannot use his discretion to discharge individual jurors so as to interfere with the composition of the jury panel to select jurors from outside the court's catchment area, in order to minimise the risk of intimidation.

11.3.3.2 Challenge for cause

The other important form of challenge (and the only one open to the defence) is the challenge for cause. This challenge is used in cases where it is suspected that a potential juror might be biased. It should be remembered that although the names of potential jurors are available for inspection by the prosecution and defence, it is unlikely that any checks will have been carried out apart from the check for previous convictions carried out by the prosecution. The defence is unlikely to have information to show that a particular juror is biased (unless the defendant happens to recognise the person in question). Further (and this is different from the position in the United States) no questions may be asked of a potential juror unless the challenging party has already established a *prima facie* case that the person is likely to be biased (see *R* v *Chandler* [1964] 2 QB 322). An example of how this operates may be seen in the trial of the Kray brothers, presided over by Lawton J. A national newspaper had published a colourful account of the allegations against the Krays. The judge was persuaded that anyone who had read this material might well be biased against the defendants. He therefore allowed the defence to ask each juror whether he or she had read the material in question. If the juror said yes, that person was then successfully challenged. However, a more restrictive view was taken by the Court of Appeal in *R* v *Andrews* [1999] Crim LR 156. The appellant claimed that her conviction for murder was unsafe because of adverse pre-trial publicity. It was argued on her behalf that potential jurors should have been asked whether they had read or heard the reports in question. It was held that such questioning of jurors (whether done orally or by means of a questionnaire) is of doubtful efficacy and may even be counter-productive (by reminding the jurors of the publicity); it should therefore only be done in the most exceptional circumstances.

To challenge for cause, counsel merely says 'challenge' before the juror takes the oath. If it is a straightforward case (e.g. the juror knows the defendant) counsel will simply state that this is the case and the judge will ask that person to leave the jury box. If it is more complicated, the jurors who have already been sworn and the rest of the potential jurors (the 'jury in waiting') will be asked to leave court and counsel will have to explain the basis of the challenge and (if the judge so directs) question the challenged juror.

In *R* v *Gough* [1993] AC 646 the House of Lords held that the test where bias is alleged is whether there is a 'real danger' that the juror is biased. See also *R* v *Wilson*, *The Times*, 24 February 1995, where convictions were quashed (and retrials ordered) because one of the jurors was the wife of a prison officer serving at the prison where the appellants had been held on remand. The Court of Appeal said that the test is one of *possibility* of bias rather than *probability* of bias and so it was not necessary to inquire into the juror's actual state of mind. There was a real danger that, consciously or not, she may have been biased against the appellants.

11.3.3.3 Replacement of juror

When a juror has been stood by or successfully challenged, he or she is replaced by another member of the jury in waiting.

11.3.4 DISCHARGE OF JURORS

11.3.4.1 Discharge of individual jurors during the trial

A jury always starts off with 12 jurors. However, under the Juries Act 1974, s. 16, up to three jurors may be discharged during the course of the trial in case of illness or other necessity (e.g. bereavement).

What constitutes necessity is a matter for the trial judge. In *R* v *Hanberry* [1977] QB 924 a juror was discharged because the trial went on longer than expected and she would otherwise have had to cancel a holiday.

If more than three jurors can no longer serve the trial has to be abandoned; a fresh trial will take place later.

11.3.4.2 Discharge of entire jury

The entire jury may be discharged if, for example:

(a) The jury hears evidence that is inadmissible and prejudicial to the defendant: where evidence that is prejudicial to the defendant has inadvertently been adduced, it is not automatically the case that the jury should be discharged, since in some instances a direction to the jury to ignore the inadmissible evidence might be sufficient (*R* v *Weaver* [1968] 1 QB 353). Whether or not the jury should be discharged is a matter for the discretion of the trial judge. The test to be applied is the test for bias, namely whether there is real danger of injustice occurring because the jury, having heard the prejudicial matter, may be biased (*R* v *Docherty* [1999] 1 Cr App R 274).

(b) The jury cannot agree on a verdict (see **11.12.5** below).

(c) An individual juror has to be discharged and there is a risk that he or she may have contaminated the rest of the jury (e.g., because of knowing that the defendant has previous convictions or is facing further trials for other offences) (e.g., *R* v *Hutton* (1990) Crim LR 875). Where a juror has specialised knowledge of something relevant to the case against the defendant, and has communicated that knowledge to the rest of the jury, who have then come to a verdict, the judge is obliged to discharge the jury, as the defendant has had no opportunity to challenge what amounts to new evidence or to put forward his or her own explanation (*R* v *Fricker*, *The Times*, 13 July 1999).

If members of the jury misbehave during the course of the trial, the jury should be discharged if there is a 'real danger of prejudice' to the accused (*R* v *Spencer* [1987] AC

128). In *R* v *Sawyer* (1980) 71 Cr App R 283, for example, some jurors were seen in conversation with prosecution witnesses during an adjournment. The trial judge questioned them and it transpired that the conversation had been on subjects unconnected with the trial. The decision of the judge not to discharge the jury was upheld by the Court of Appeal.

Where the jury is discharged from giving a verdict, the defendant can be re-tried, as he is not regarded as having been acquitted.

11.3.5 START OF THE TRIAL

Once the jury has been empanelled, the trial begins with the clerk reading out the indictment and telling the jury that the defendant has pleaded not guilty. The jury is then told, 'It is your charge to say, having heard the evidence, whether he [or she] be guilty or not'.

11.4 Change of Plea

The defendant may change his or her plea from not guilty to guilty at any stage of the trial before the jury has returned a verdict. The defence simply asks for the indictment to be put again and the defendant pleads guilty. The jury must then return a formal verdict of guilty.

The defendant can change his or her plea from guilty to not guilty at any stage of the trial prior to the passing of sentence, but only at the discretion of the judge. The judge will want some explanation for the change of heart and may take into account matters such as the legal advice the accused has received, his or her age and level of intellect, and experience of criminal proceedings. See *R* v *Dodd* (1981) 74 Cr App R 50; *S* v *Recorder of Manchester* [1971] AC 481.

11.5 The Prosecution Case

After the indictment has been read to the jury, counsel for the prosecution opens the Crown's case:

> May it please your Honour [or your Lordship, if a High Court judge or sitting at the Old Bailey], members of the jury, I appear to prosecute and my learned friend Miss Green appears for the accused.

11.5.1 THE OPENING SPEECH

The purpose of the prosecution opening speech is to give the jury an overview of the prosecution case. The jury will be reminded of the charge(s) which the defendant faces, which should be explained to it in everyday language. Counsel will probably tell the jury what witnesses will be called by the prosecution and what it is hoped they will establish. Counsel will also mention the burden of proof and the standard of proof, and make it clear that anything said about the law is subject to what the judge will say in the summing up.

If counsel for the defence takes the view that an objection should be taken to the admissibility of some of the evidence which the prosecution will be calling (as disclosed to the defence in the bundle of committal statements, together with any notice of additional evidence), but no ruling on admissibility was sought at the preliminary hearing, then he or she should inform counsel for the prosecution. The prosecutor will then omit any reference to the disputed material from the opening speech. The judge will then be asked to rule on the admissibility of the evidence at the appropriate moment (see **11.5.2.4**). It may be, however, that the disputed evidence is such an important part of the prosecution case that an opening speech would make no sense if no reference were to be made to that evidence; for example, the only evidence against the defendant is a confession, the admissibility of which is disputed. In that case, once the jury has been empanelled, the judge will be informed (either by the prosecution or the defence) that a ruling on a matter of law is needed at the outset. The jury will be sent out of the court and counsel will then seek the judge's ruling on the admissibility of the evidence. If the judge rules the evidence inadmissible, the prosecution will almost certainly have little option but to offer no evidence (see **11.2.3** above), in which case the jury will be called back into court and directed to acquit the defendant.

11.5.2 THE PROSECUTION EVIDENCE

At the conclusion of the opening speech, prosecuting counsel calls the evidence. It is the rule that the prosecution must call all the witnesses whose evidence was included in the bundle of statements sent to the magistrates' court in the committal proceedings. If one witness is expected to duplicate the evidence of another (e.g. the second police officer present at an interview with the accused), the prosecution may 'tender' that second witness for cross-examination. This means that the witness is called into the witness box by counsel for the prosecution and having been identified and his or her relevance to the case established, he or she will be told to stay there in case the defence have any questions. The only exceptions to the rule that the prosecution must call (or tender for cross-examination) all the witnesses whose evidence was used in the committal proceedings are those set out in *R* v *Armstrong* [1995] 3 All ER 831:

(a) the defence has consented to the written statement of that witness being read to the court; or

(b) counsel for the prosecution takes the view that the evidence of that witness is no longer credible; or

(c) counsel for the prosecution takes the view that the witness would so fundamentally contradict the prosecution case that it would make more sense for that person to be called as a witness by the defence.

The other side of the coin is that the prosecution can *only* call as witnesses people whose evidence was used at committal proceedings or whose statements have been disclosed to the defence by way of notice of additional evidence. The notice of additional evidence procedure is used wherever the prosecution wants to use evidence which was not before the examining justices. A copy of the witness statement is served on the defence along with a notice saying that the prosecution will be adducing the evidence of this witness. The statement can be tendered in evidence (i.e. read to the court) unless the defence objects within seven days of the service of the notice, in which case the prosecution must either abandon that evidence or call the maker of the statement as a witness at the trial. There is no time limit within which a notice of additional evidence must be served, but if it is served just before the trial, so that the defence has had insufficient time to adjust its preparation in the light of the new evidence, then the judge should grant an adjournment. (For the position on disclosure of *unused* material, see **Chapter 10**.)

11.5.2.1 Taking evidence from the witnesses

Each witness called by the prosecution, having taken the oath (or affirmed) to 'tell the truth, the whole truth and nothing but the truth', is examined in chief by counsel for the prosecution (unless that witness is only being tendered for cross-examination) and may produce (i.e. identify) items of real evidence which then become exhibits in the case. Counsel must take great care not to lead the witness on matters which are contentious — if in doubt, ask your opponent if he or she will let you lead on specified matters.

Each witness is then subject to cross-examination by the defence. Cross-examination is not limited to matters arising from the examination-in-chief, but must be relevant to the issues arising in the case. The cross-examination is followed by re-examination by the prosecution; the rule against leading questions applies to re-examination and the questions must arise out of the cross-examination.

For the position on memory-refreshing documents, see the ***Evidence Manual*** (**5.1.2**).

11.5.2.2 Formal admissions

If the defendant pleads not guilty then that puts the prosecution to proof of each and every element of the offence(s) on the indictment to which a plea of not guilty has been entered. The only exception to this is where the defence has made a formal admission under CJA 1967, s. 10. This provides that either party in a criminal case (though it is usually the defence) may admit any fact which would otherwise be in issue and this admission is conclusive evidence of the fact admitted. This admission may be made orally in court (by counsel) or in writing signed by the person making it, in which case the document will be read to the jury (but note that in the magistrates' court the formal admission must be in writing).

11.5.2.3 Reading witness statements

Formal admissions are not in fact very common. Usually, where evidence is not disputed by the defence, it will consent to the prosecution reading out the written statement of the witness who deals with the uncontroversial evidence (e.g. the loser of the stolen property where the defence case is not that the property was not stolen but rather that the defendant is not the thief). If a witness says some things which are not disputed by the defence but others which are, that witness will have to give oral evidence (since it would not be appropriate for the written statement to be read to the court) and it will no doubt become apparent from the cross-examination by the defence which parts of that witness's evidence are disputed by the defence.

When the written statement of a witness is read to the court with the consent of the defence, the judge should explain to the jury that the contents of the witness statement are not in dispute and so the defence has consented to the statement being read to the jury without the maker having to attend court, thus saving time and money. The jury should be told that the evidence is just as good as evidence given 'live'. Counsel, in reading the statement, must read out the declaration signed by the maker of the statement, that it is true to the best of that person's knowledge and belief and is made knowing that a prosecution may be brought if the statement contains anything which the maker knows or believes to be false.

The main instances where a statement may be read to the jury without the consent of the defence are those set out in CJA 1988, s. 23 (see the ***Evidence Manual*** (**9.2.2.1**)). In summary, this applies where a witness does not testify because of fear. In order to satisfy the requirements of s. 23 of the CJA 1988, the court must hear oral evidence (for example, from a police officer) as to the fear of the witness (*R* v *Belmarsh Magistrates' Court, ex parte Gilligan* [1998] 1 Cr App R 14, following *Neill* v *North Antrim Magistrates' Court* [1992] 4 All ER 846).

Where a statement has been read to the jury without the consent of the defence, the jury must be warned to use particular care when considering that witness statement, since the maker of the statement was not in court to be cross-examined as to its contents; where the witness statement is vital to the prosecution case, failure to give such a direction will render any subsequent conviction unsafe (*R* v *Curry*, *The Times*, 23 March 1998).

11.5.2.4 Defence objections to prosecution evidence

If counsel for the prosecution agrees with the defence suggestion made before the start of the trial that certain evidence is inadmissible, the prosecutor should (via the Crown Prosecution Service representative or the police officer in charge of the case) warn the relevant witness not to give that particular evidence. If this involves evidence which will come into the possession of the jury (e.g. interview notes which count as real evidence and may be exhibited and so handed to the jury) this evidence may well have to be edited. In accordance with the *Practice Direction (Crime: Evidence by Written Statements)* [1986] 1 WLR 805, this should be done after consultation between both counsel and the judge.

If, however, the prosecution do not accept that the evidence in question is inadmissible, the question of admissibility may be dealt with at the pre-trial hearing, at which (as we saw in **10.4**) the judge is empowered to give binding rulings on the admissibility of evidence. Otherwise, the objection is made (in the absence of the jury) during the course of the trial. If the objection is made during the course of the trial, the prosecution evidence is called in the usual way until the part of the evidence to which there is objection is reached. At that point the jury is invited to retire to the jury room.

Although s. 82 of PACE expressly preserves the common law rules on the admissibility of evidence, objections to prosecution evidence are usually made under s. 76 (which applies only to confessions) or s. 78 (which applies to all prosecution evidence) of PACE 1984.

Where the defence invoke s. 76 and allege that a confession has been obtained by oppression or in circumstances likely to render it unreliable, the prosecution must prove beyond reasonable doubt that the confession was not so obtained. The requirement for the prosecution to prove this means that they must call evidence on the point and so a *voir dire* ('trial within a trial') takes place.

Unless the witness is in the middle of giving (or has already given) evidence in the course of the trial, a witness giving evidence on a *voir dire* takes a special form of oath: 'I swear by almighty God that I will answer truthfully all such questions as the court may ask'.

Each prosecution witness called in the *voir dire* may be cross-examined by the defence. When the relevant prosecution witnesses have given evidence, the defence may call evidence (including the evidence of the defendant himself); each defence witness may be cross-examined by the prosecution.

After the evidence has been called, both counsel may address the judge and the judge then rules on the admissibility of the confession. In *Mitchell* v *The Queen* [1998] 2 WLR 839, it was held by the Privy Council that where a judge conducts a *voir dire* and holds that a confession is admissible, the judge should not tell the jury of the ruling (the trial should simply continue with the prosecution leading evidence of the confession). If the judge indicates that he has ruled against the accused, this might lead the jury to think that the judge does not believe the accused.

The only question to be determined under s. 76 is *how* the confession was obtained. It is wholly irrelevant whether the confession was true or not.

If the defence case is simply that the police have fabricated the confession, that is a matter for the jury to decide and not a question of admissibility. However, there are cases where the defence allege that the confession has been fabricated but also argue that, even if that was not so, the confession is inadmissible anyway. In *Thongjai* v *The Queen* [1997] 3 WLR 667, the Privy Council (following *Ajodha* v *The State* [1982] AC 204) said that if the defendant denies making an oral admission and also alleges that he was ill-treated by the police before or at the time of the alleged admission, the two issues are not mutually exclusive. The judge has to assume that the admission was made and decide whether it is admissible, if (and only if) the judge decides that the evidence is admissible, it is then for the jury to decide whether the admission was in fact made.

If the objection to the prosecution evidence is brought *solely* on the basis of s. 78, that it would be unfair to the defence for the evidence to be admitted, the judge may hold a *voir dire* but is not obliged to: such applications can be dealt with on the basis of submissions by counsel if the factual basis for the submissions is agreed between prosecution and defence; for example, the custody record discloses breaches of the Codes of Practice under PACE and the only question to be determined is whether the evidence thereby obtained should be excluded under s. 78. These submissions will, of course, be heard in the absence of the jury. The judge gives a ruling and the trial then proceeds, either with or without the disputed evidence.

It should be noted that if inadmissible evidence is heard by the jury the judge has to consider whether the prejudicial effect can be cured by an appropriate direction in the summing up or whether the entire jury should be discharged and a new trial take place.

11.6 Submission of No Case to Answer

When the prosecution has called all its witnesses, counsel will say 'That is the case for the prosecution'. At the close of the prosecution case the defence may, if it wishes, make a submission that there is no case to answer (colloquially called 'a half-time submission').

This submission is made in the absence of the jury. Counsel for the defence makes the submission and counsel for the prosecution has the right to reply.

The submission is governed by the principles laid down in *R* v *Galbraith* [1981] 1 WLR 1039 (see p. 1042, per Lord Lane CJ):

(a) The submission should succeed if the judge comes to the conclusion that the prosecution evidence, taken at its highest, is such that a jury, properly directed, could not properly convict on it. In this case the judge should direct the jury to acquit on the count(s) in respect of which the submission has succeeded. If there are other counts on the indictment and either no submission was made in respect of them or a submission was made but failed, the trial proceeds on those counts.

(b) The submission should fail if the strength or weakness of the prosecution case depends on the view to be taken of the reliability of a witness and, on one possible view, there is evidence on which a reasonable jury, properly directed, could convict. In this case, the matter should be left to the jury and the trial should be allowed to take its course with the jury being left in ignorance about what has happened.

The basis for this distinction is that questions of the credibility of witnesses are matters of fact which are within the exclusive province of the jury. However, the words of Lord Lane must not be taken too literally. Regard should be had to the ruling of Turner J in *R* v *Shippey* [1988] Crim LR 767. His Lordship found no case to answer because of 'really significant inherent inconsistencies' in the complainant's evidence, which he found to be 'frankly incredible'. In other words, the judge can have regard to the sheer improbability of what the witness says and to internal inconsistencies in the evidence. If no reasonable jury could believe the witness, then the submission of no case to answer should succeed.

Note that where the only evidence against the accused is identification evidence, the special considerations highlighted in *R* v *Turnbull* [1977] QB 224 should be borne in mind and the case withdrawn from the jury if the evidence is weak.

If the judge wrongly refuses to uphold a submission of no case to answer this constitutes an error of law. Any evidence called afterwards (that is by the defence) is irrelevant on appeal as no evidence would have been called by the defence if the submission had been upheld. So if in the course of giving evidence the accused makes damaging admissions, those admissions will have to be ignored by the Court of Appeal. See *R* v *Smith* [2000] 1 All ER 263.

If, at the conclusion of all the evidence (that is, both the prosecution case and the defence case), the judge is of the view that no reasonable jury could convict, he should raise that view for discussion with counsel (in the absence of the jury), whether or not a submission of no case to answer was made at the close of the prosecution case. If, having heard submissions, the judge remains of the view that there is no case to answer, he should withdraw the case from the jury (*R* v *Brown* [1998] Crim LR 196).

11.7 The Defence Case

The defence is under no obligation to call any evidence and so it would be possible for counsel for the defence to address the jury on the basis that the prosecution evidence has failed to show beyond reasonable doubt that the defendant is guilty. This may be appropriate where there is only just a case to answer. However, the Criminal Justice and Public Order Act 1994, s. 35, enables adverse inferences to be drawn by the jury if the accused either fails to give evidence or fails without good cause to answer which is put to him or her; it follows that the accused should, in the vast majority of cases, be advised to give evidence. If a defendant decides not to give evidence, despite the advice to the contrary of counsel, that defendant should be asked to endorse a note on counsel's brief confirming that he or she has chosen not to give evidence (see *R* v *Bevan* (1993) 98 Cr App R 354). *Practice Direction (Crown Court: Defendant's Evidence)* [1995] 1 WLR 657 requires the judge to ensure that the defendant is aware of the possible consequences of not testifying.

The defence case may start with an opening speech outlining the evidence the defence will be calling and showing how it will rebut the evidence called by the prosecution. In fact, opening speeches are rarely made by the defence (unless the case is a complex one). In any event, the defence is not allowed to make an opening speech unless it will be calling at least one witness as to the facts of the case, in addition to the evidence of the defendant. So if the only defence evidence is from the accused and/or character witnesses, there can be no opening speech.

11.7.1 THE DEFENCE EVIDENCE

If the defendant does give evidence, then he or she must be called as the first defence witness (unless the judge gives leave to the contrary) (PACE 1984, s. 79).

Each defence witness (including the defendant, if he or she gives evidence) takes the oath (or affirms) and is then examined in chief on behalf of the defendant, cross-examined by the prosecution and (if necessary) re-examined on behalf of the defence.

For the position in relation to the loss of shield by the defendant, see the ***Evidence Manual*** (**7.3**).

11.7.1.1 Alibi evidence

If the defendant wishes to adduce evidence in support of an alibi, he or she must give particulars of that alibi to the prosecution (CPIA 1996, s. 5). Subsection 5(8) defines alibi evidence as:

> *evidence tending to show that by reason of the presence of the defendant at a particular place or in a particular area at a particular time he was not, or was unlikely to have been, at the place where the offence is alleged to have been committed at the time of its alleged commission.*

Thus, alibi evidence must show where the defendant was at the time of the offence: evidence which merely shows that the defendant was not present at the scene of the crime does not amount to alibi evidence (*R* v *Johnson* [1994] Crim LR 949).

Section 5(7) requires the defence to supply the prosecution with the name and address of any witness the accused believes is able to give evidence in support of the alibi or (where the defendant does not know the name or address) information which may help the prosecution to find the witness. The defence must give notice of the intention to adduce alibi evidence even if evidence in support of that alibi will come only from the defendant himself or herself.

If the defendant fails to give particulars of the alibi in the defence statement, or calls a witness without having giving particulars of that witness to the prosecution, the jury may draw 'adverse inferences' against the defendant (see **10.2.8**).

11.7.1.2 Expert evidence

The defence may not call any expert witness without leave of the judge if it has not disclosed the expert's written report to the prosecution before the trial. See the Crown

Court (Advance Notice of Expert Evidence) Rules 1997 (SI 1987 No. 716). When the Criminal Procedure and Investigation Bill becomes law, these two requirements of pre-trial disclosure by the defence will be subsumed within the general disclosure provisions applicable to the defence (see **Chapter 10**).

11.8 Closing Speeches

At the close of the defence case the prosecution may make a closing speech. However, the prosecution has no right to make a closing speech if the defendant is unrepresented and has called no witnesses as to the facts of the case apart from his or her own testimony. In a fairly straightforward case the prosecution will usually forgo a closing speech.

The defence always has the right to make a closing speech and this right should never be waived. It is a vital speech, giving counsel the chance to show how reasonable doubt has been cast on the prosecution case.

11.9 Two or More Defendants

Where two or more defendants are charged in the same indictment (and remember that joinder must satisfy the requirements of r. 9 of the Indictment Rules), and those defendants are separately represented, their cases will be presented in the order in which their names appear on the indictment. So if the indictment is against D1, D2 and D3, the order is:

D1 opening speech
D1's witnesses (including D1 if he or she wants to give evidence)
  Examination-in-chief by D1's counsel
  Cross-examination on behalf of D2
  Cross-examination on behalf of D3
  Cross-examination by prosecution
  Re-examination by D1's counsel (if necessary)
D2 opening speech
D2's witnesses (including D2 if he or she wants to give evidence)
  Examination-in-chief by D2's counsel
  Cross-examination on behalf of D1
  Cross-examination on behalf of D3
  Cross-examination by prosecution
  Re-examination by D2's counsel (if necessary)
and so on.
Closing speeches are in the order: prosecution, D1, D2, D3.

If the defendants are jointly represented, then they are regarded as putting forward a joint defence. Their counsel may make an opening speech. Then D1 may give evidence, followed by D2, then D3, then any other witnesses the defence wish to call.

11.10 The Summing Up

The judge's summing up follows the defence closing speech. It should contain the following matters:

(a) *The respective functions of judge and jury:* Questions of law are for the judge and questions of fact are for the jury. The judge is entitled to express a view on the facts but should always make it very clear that if he or she should seem to be expressing a view on the facts then the jury must regard itself as free to disregard what the judge has said about the facts. In *R* v *Jackson* [1992] Crim LR 214, the Court of Appeal approved a direction in these terms:

> It is my job to tell you what the law is and how to apply it to the issues of fact that you have to decide and to remind you of the important evidence on these issues. As to the law, you must accept what I tell you. As to the facts, you alone are the judges. It is for you to decide what evidence you accept and what evidence you reject or of which you are unsure. If I appear to have a view of the evidence or of the facts with which you do not agree, reject my view. If I mention or emphasise evidence that you regard as unimportant, disregard that evidence. If I do not mention what you regard as important, follow your own view and take that evidence into account.

(b) *Burden and standard of proof:* The prosecution has brought the case and it is for the prosecution to prove it, not for the accused to prove his or her innocence. Before convicting, the jury must be satisfied so that they are sure (a preferred formulation to the time-honoured 'beyond reasonable doubt'). The judge should not expand on what is meant by 'sure', as this is likely to generate confusion. However, if the jury later seeks further guidance, the judge can tell the jurors that they need to be as sure as they would be to make a decision which is very important in their own lives. If the case (exceptionally) involves a burden on the defendant (e.g. to show lawful authority or reasonable excuse for possession of an offensive weapon: Prevention of Crime Act 1957, s. 1) then the jury must be told that the standard is to the balance of probabilities, more likely than not. See *Ferguson* v *The Queen* [1979] 1 WLR 94 and *R* v *McVey* [1988] Crim LR 127.

(c) *The law and the evidence:* There should be an explanation of the law involved and how it relates to the facts of the case. The judge should remind the jury of the main features of the prosecution and defence evidence, even if the case is a straightforward one (see *R* v *McVey* [1988] Crim LR 127 and *R* v *Gregory* [1993] Crim LR 623). This involves fitting the evidence that has been heard into the legal framework of the charge(s) so that the jury knows what the prosecution must prove and what (if anything) the defence has said in response. In going through the evidence which has been heard, the judge must be careful to present both the prosecution and defence stories even-handedly (*R* v *Marr* (1989) 90 Cr App R 154). If there is an appeal, the Court of Appeal will look at the overall effect of the summing up (*R* v *Berrada* (1989) 91 Cr App R 131). In *R* v *Spencer*, *The Times*, 14 July 1994, the defendant's conviction was held to be unsafe as a result of excessive and largely one-sided comments made by the judge when directing the jury. It was said by Henry LJ that some comment is permissible, but not to the extent that the rehearsal of the evidence is interrupted and the jury's task made more difficult. See also *R* v *Farr* (1999) 163 JP 193 where a conviction was quashed, and a retrial ordered, because the summing up failed to refer to a number of the key features of the defence case and, instead of being fair and balanced, resembled a speech for the prosecution. Indeed, where the case against the defendant is strong, and his or her defence correspondingly weak, the judge has to be scrupulous to ensure that the defendant's defence is presented to the jury in an even-handed and impartial manner (*R* v *Reid*, *The Times*, 17 August 1999).

(d) *Identification evidence:* If the case against the accused depends on identification evidence, there should be a warning about the special need for care when examining identification evidence as a witness may appear convincing yet also be mistaken. The factors which should be taken into account in assessing the quality of the evidence should be set out. See *R* v *Turnbull* [1977] QB 224.

(e) *More than one count or defendant:* If there is more than one count or more than one defendant, a warning must be given that each count and each defendant must be considered separately. Where evidence is admissible against one defendant but not the other (e.g. a police interview in which a defendant implicates himself or herself and a co-accused), the judge must instruct the jury to disregard the evidence in so far as it relates to the other defendant.

(f) *Previous convictions:* If the defendant's previous convictions have been revealed, the judge must tell the jury that they are relevant only to the defendant's credibility as a witness and are not evidence that he or she has committed the present offence(s) (*R* v *McLeod* [1994] 3 All ER 254).

Where the defendant has no previous convictions, the jury should be directed that this is relevant both to the credibility of the defendant as a witness and to the likelihood that he or she committed the offence (*R* v *Vye* [1993] 1 WLR 471 and *R* v *Teasdale* [1993] 4 All ER 290) although it should be noted that in *Barrow* v *The Queen* [1998] 2 WLR 957, it was held by the Privy Council that the judge ought only to direct the jury on the relevance of the good character of the accused if the matter is raised by the defence either calling evidence or questioning prosecution witnesses with a view to establishing the defendant's good character.

(g) *Failure by accused to testify*: In *R* v *Cowan and others* [1995] 4 All ER 939 the Court of Appeal considered what should be said in the summing up if the defendant decides not to testify. The judge must remind the jury that the burden of proof remains on the prosecution. The jury must also be directed that:

(i) (as provided by s. 38(3) of the Criminal Justice and Public Order Act 1994) an inference from failure to give evidence could not on its own prove guilty;

(ii) it had to be satisfied (on the basis of the evidence called by the prosecution) that the prosecution had established a case to answer before inferences could be drawn from the accused's silence; and

(iii) it could only draw an adverse inference from the accused's silence if it concluded that the silence could only sensibly be attributed to the accused having no answer to the charge or none that would stand up to cross-examination.

In *R* v *Birchall* [1999] Crim LR 311, the Court of Appeal emphasised that where the defendant fails to testify, the trial judge must tell the jury that they should not start to consider whether to draw adverse inferences from the failure to testify until they have concluded that there is a case to answer, i.e. that the Crown's case against the defendant is sufficiently compelling to call for an answer by him or her. This is so even if there is plainly sufficient evidence to amount to a prima facie case against the defendant.

(h) In *R* v *Condron* [1997] 1 WLR 827, the Court of Appeal said that the guidelines set out in *R* v *Cowan* [1996] QB 373 regarding the drawing of adverse inferences where the accused fails to testify are equally applicable where the accused fails to answer questions when being interviewed by the police. More detailed guidance was given in *R* v *Argent* [1997] 2 Cr App R 27, where the Court of Appeal set out the conditions which have to be satisfied before adverse inferences can be drawn from a person's failure to answer police questions (CJPOA 1994, s. 34). The conditions include:

(i) the alleged failure must take place before the person has been charged;

(ii) the alleged failure must occur during questioning under caution;

(iii) the questioning must be directed at trying to discover whether and by whom the alleged offence has been committed;

(iv) the alleged failure must be a failure to mention a fact relied on by the defendant in his or her defence;

(v) the fact must be one which this particular defendant (not some hypothetical reasonable accused) could reasonably be expected to have mentioned when being questioned, taking account of all the circumstances existing at that time (for example, the time of day, the defendant's age, experience, mental capacity, state of health, sobriety, personality and access to legal advice).

It should be borne in mind that a defendant may rely on a fact even if that defendant does not give evidence of that fact: for example, a witness called on behalf of the defendant may testify to that fact, or a prosecution witness may be cross-examined on that basis of that fact. It follows that adverse inferences can be drawn under s. 34 even if the defendant does not give evidence at trial (*R* v *Bowers* (1999) 163 JP 33). Where the judge decides that it is not appropriate for the jury to draw adverse inferences from the defendant's silence, the jury should be specifically directed not to draw adverse inferences (*R* v *McGarry* [1999] 1 Cr App R 377).

(i) Where the defendant fails to provide a defence statement setting out the defence case (CPIA 1996, s. 5), or does so late, or sets out inconsistent defences in the defence statement, or presents to the court a defence which is inconsistent with the defence statement, or presents alibi evidence without having given details of the alibi to the prosecution, adverse inferences may be drawn by the jury. The judge must therefore give an appropriate direction to the jury.

(j) Where the defendant has relied on an alibi and the prosecution have sought to prove that the alibi was false, the judge should direct the jury to the effect that 'even if you conclude that the alibi was false, that does not entitle you to convict the defendant. The Crown must still make you sure of his guilt. An alibi is sometimes invented to bolster a genuine defence'. A failure to give such a direction does not, however, automatically render a conviction unsafe. The Court of Appeal will consider whether the jury might have come to a different conclusion had the direction been given (*R* v *Harron* [1996] Crim LR 581 and *R* v *Lesley* [1996] 1 Cr App R 39).

(k) Where there has been evidence from an expert witness, the jury should be directed that they are not bound by the opinion of the expert witness (*R* v *Stockwell* (1993) 97 Cr App R 260).

(l) *Reaching a verdict:* Finally the judge will tell the jury that at this stage at least he or she can only accept a unanimous verdict (and that they should not at this stage concern themselves with the possibility of a majority verdict) and the judge will suggest that the jury elect a foreman to chair its discussions.

11.11 Bail

In *R* v *Central Criminal Court, ex parte Guney* [1996] 2 All ER 705 the House of Lords held that when a defendant who has not previously surrendered to the custody of the court is arraigned, he or she thereby surrenders to the custody of the court at that moment. The result is that the Crown Court judge then has to decide whether or not to grant him or her bail; unless the judge grants bail, the defendant will remain in custody pending and during the trial.

In *R* v *Maidstone Crown Court, ex parte Jodka, The Times*, 13 June 1997, the Divisional Court went further and held that bail granted by magistrates ceases when the defendant surrenders to the custody of the Crown Court, whether or not the defendant is arraigned at the hearing at which he or she surrenders. Where the magistrates grant bail subject to a surety, the responsibility of that surety under the magistrates' court order ceases once the defendant surrenders to the custody of the Crown Court. If the Crown Court wishes to grant bail subject to the same surety, the court must consider the position of that surety before imposing such a condition.

It follows from this that the question of bail will have to be considered at the pre-trial hearing. In any event, if the defendant is on bail before the trial, his or her bail effectively expires at the start of the trial. Therefore, once a defendant who was on bail before the trial has surrendered to the custody of the court at the start of the trial, he or she will only be released from custody if the judge grants bail. So a very brief bail application has to be made at the lunchtime adjournment and the end of each day.

Such application should be made in the absence of the jury (as refusal might prejudice them against the accused). Some judges will withhold bail at lunchtime (e.g. where there is a risk that the defendant might come into contact with jurors); others grant bail but forbid the defendant to leave the court building or require the defendant to remain in the company of his or her solicitor. Once the judge has begun summing up the case to the jury, the defendant's chances of bail are, for some judges, slim; it is said that the prospect of imminent conviction is a good incentive to abscond. See *Practice Direction (Crime: Bail during Trial)* [1974] 1 WLR 770.

11.12 The Verdict

11.12.1 THE JURY'S RETIREMENT

The jury is put in the charge of a jury bailiff, who takes an oath to take it to a private place and not to allow anyone to speak to it. The jurors then go off to the retiring room to consider their verdict.

Section 13 of the Juries Act 1974 (amended by s. 43 of the CJPOA 1994) enables the court to allow the jury to separate after (as well as before) it has been sent out to consider its verdict. Formerly, separation was only permitted before the jury had been sent out to consider its verdict.

In *R* v *Oliver* [1996] 2 Cr App R 514, the Court of Appeal gave guidance on the directions which should be given to a jury which is allowed to separate before delivering its verdict. The jury must be warned that:

(a) it may only decide the case on the basis of the evidence it has heard in court; and

(b) jurors must not talk to anyone about the case except other jurors and even discussions with other jurors may only take place while they are deliberating in the retiring room.

Where a jury is sent to an hotel overnight, it must be told not to continue its deliberations in the hotel but only to discuss the case when it has returned to court the following day (otherwise, discussions might take place without all jurors being present) (*R* v *Tharakan* [1995] 2 Cr App R 368).

When deliberating, the jury is allowed to have with them it exhibit in the case. In *R* v *Tonge* (1993) 157 JP 1137 the Court of Appeal considered what should be done if the jury (after it has retired) asks to hear the tape recording of the defendant's interview at the police station. It was said that if the tape recording has not been played in open court during the trial and the jury asks to hear the tape, it should usually be played in open court. However, if the tape has already been played in court, the jury may be allowed to hear it again in the jury room.

Once the jury has retired, any communication between the judge and jury has to take place in open court in the presence of the entire jury, both counsel and the defendant (*R* v *McCluskey* (1993) 98 Cr App R 216). Where the judge receives a note from the jury he or she should follow the procedure laid down in *R* v *Gorman* [1987] 1 WLR 545: unless the note has nothing to do with the trial, the judge should, in open court (but in the absence of the jury), state the contents of the note and seek submissions from both counsel. The judge should then send for the jury and deal with the query in open court.

Once the jury has retired to consider its verdict, no further evidence can be adduced before them. This is an absolute rule, with no exceptions (*R* v *Owen* [1952] 2 QB 362). In that case, the jury came out of retirement to ask whether the premises where an indecent assault was alleged to have taken place would have been occupied or not at the relevant time. The Court of Appeal held that no further evidence can be called after the jury has retired to consider its verdict.

Each time the jury comes into court, it is asked by the clerk 'Have you reached a verdict upon which you are all agreed?' If it has come back with a query, the answer will of course be no. If it has come back with a verdict the answer should be yes. A verdict must be taken on each count of the indictment separately. However, if two counts were in the alternative, if the jury convicts on the first count, it will be discharged from giving a verdict on the second.

11.12.2 ALTERNATIVE VERDICTS

It is possible for the jury to acquit the defendant of the count on the indicment but convict of another offence, a 'lesser included offence'. This is only possible if CLA 1967, s. 6 applies. This provides that where allegations in an indictment amount to or include, whether expressly or by implication, an allegation of another offence which may be tried on indictment, then the jury may acquit of the offence charged and convict of that other offence.

'Express inclusion' means that if certain words are deleted, you are left with the allegation of another offence: e.g. the indictment alleges that 'AB on 1st January 2000 entered 4 Gray's Inn Place as a trespasser and stole therein a television set, the property of the Inns of Court School of Law'. If the words 'entered 4 Gray's Inn Place as a trespasser and' are deleted, that leaves a valid count alleging theft. So if the jury feels that the prosecution has failed to prove trespass, an essential ingredient of burglary, but none the less find that the defendant stole the goods in question, it can convict of theft.

'Implied inclusion' means that the lesser offence is either a necessary step towards committing the offence charged on the indictment or else is an offence which, in the vast majority of cases, is a step on the road to committing the offence charged. See *Metropolitan Police Commission* v *Wilson* [1984] AC 242. So, for example, theft is a valid alternative verdict to a charge of robbery (where the jury decides there was no assault); indecent assault is a valid alternative to rape. Section 47 of the Offences Against the Person Act 1861 is a valid alternative to s. 20 of that Act (*R* v *Savage* [1992] 1 AC 714); s. 20 is a valid alternative to s. 18 of the Act (*R* v *Mandair* [1995] 1 AC 208).

In *R* v *Mearns* [1991] 1 QB 82 the Court of Appeal held that common assault, a summary offence under CJA 1988, s. 40, cannot be a valid lesser included offence as the jury can only convict of a s. 40 offence if it appears on the indictment. Similarly, in *R* v *Burt* (1997) 161 JP 77 it was held that a jury cannot return a verdict of not guilty of criminal damage with intent to endanger life/recklessness as to endangerment of life but guilty of ordinary criminal damage, if the value of the damage is £5,000 or less, since such criminal damage is a summary offence. The simple answer, of course, is to invoke CJA 1988, s. 40 and add a count alleging the ordinary criminal damage to the indictment.

There are, in any event, some specific statutory provisions which enable the jury to convict the defendant of a summary offence if they acquit him or her of an indictable offence. The Theft Act 1968, s. 12(4) provides that taking a conveyance without the owner's consent is a valid alternative verdict to a charge of theft and the Road Traffic Offenders Act 1988, s. 24 provides that careless driving is a valid alternative verdict to a charge of dangerous driving or causing death by dangerous driving.

Of course a jury will only be aware of its power to convict of a lesser included offence if it is told that it can do so; and even if the possibility is raised by counsel, the judge can decide to direct the jury not to consider that possibility. So what attitude should the judge take? In *R* v *Fairbanks* [1986] 1 WLR 1202 the Court of Appeal said that if there was an alternative and less serious offence to that charged, the judge should put the alternative offence to the jury if it was necessary in the interests of justice to do so. The court seemed to create a presumption in favour of leaving the lesser offence to the jury. The defence might argue that the jury might think that the defendant was innocent of the offence charged but guilty of something and so convict as charged to prevent the defendant getting off scot-free; the prosecution might argue that if the jury took the view that the defendant was guilty of something, albeit not the offence on the indictment, it would be wrong for him or her to be acquitted altogether.

In any event, in *R* v *Maxwell* [1990] 1 WLR 401 the House of Lords took a more restrictive view. In that case, the defendant was charged with robbery but would have been willing to plead guilty to burglary. The prosecution declined to add a plea of burglary to the indictment and to accept the defendant's plea to that rather than to robbery. Defence counsel asked the judge to leave theft to the jury as an alternative to robbery. The judge refused and his refusal was ultimately upheld by the House of Lords. It was said that, in view of the way the prosecution has presented the case, the essential issue was whether or not violence had been used; the theft was trivial in comparison. To have left theft to the jury would have been to distract it from the main issue in the case. As such it represented an unnecessary and undesirable complication. This decision appears to say that the judge should give great weight to the view of the prosecution before letting the jury consider a lesser offence.

It will only be in the interests of justice as far as the accused is concerned if he or she has had the opportunity of fully meeting the alternative charge in the course of presenting the defence case. Would the cross-examination of prosecution witnesses have been different? Would the defence have called different witnesses or presented its case differently? In other words, it is the same test as that applied if the court is asked to add a count to an indictment during the course of the trial. See *R* v *Wilson* (1979) (supra).

Where a judge refuses to leave an alternative offence to the jury, the Court of Appeal will only quash a conviction for the offence charged on the indictment if satisfied that the jury convicted the defendant only because it was reluctant to allow him to get away completely with his misconduct (see *R* v *O'hAdhmaill*, *The Times*, 13 February 1996 and *R* v *Bergman and Collins* [1996] 2 Cr App R 399).

It would of course be inappropriate to leave a lesser offence to the jury if it is inappropriate to the way in which the defence has been conducted; e.g. if the defence is one of alibi.

In *R* v *Salter* [1993] Crim LR 891 a jury sent out to consider an allegation of rape asked if it could convict of attempted rape. The judge allowed them to return a verdict of guilty to attempted rape. It was held by the Court of Appeal that where a jury is directed after it has retired that it may bring in a verdict on an alternative offence, this should only be done if the judge has first discussed with counsel the precise formulation of the direction to the jury and canvassed the possible need to remind it of any relevant evidence.

Note that a verdict on a lesser offence is only possible if the jury acquits of the offence actually on the indictment. In *R* v *Collison* (1980) 71 Cr App R 249, for example, the jury was unable to agree on an acquittal. To enable it to convict of a lesser offence, that offence had to be added to the indictment as a new count (and the decision to do this even though the jury had been considering its verdict for some time was upheld as the defence would not have been conducted any differently).

11.12.3 MAJORITY VERDICTS

The Juries Act 1974, s. 17 provides that a majority verdict may be accepted after the jury has been out for two hours or such longer time as the judge thinks appropriate given the nature and complexity of the case. A *Practice Direction (Crime: Majority Verdict)* [1970] 1 WLR 916 adds a further 10 minutes to the two hours to give the jury a chance to settle down and elect a foreman.

In the summing up (as we have seen) the judge tells the jury that he or she can only accept a unanimous verdict. And for the first two hours (and ten minutes) of the jury's deliberations the judge has no choice. However, after at least two hours ten minutes have elapsed, the judge may (if he or she thinks it appropriate) give the jury the majority verdict direction. That direction asks the jury to make a further attempt to reach a unanimous verdict, but says that if it is unable to do so, then a majority verdict can be accepted.

The only permissible majorities are:

12 jurors: 11–1 or 10–2
11 jurors: 10–1
10 jurors: 9–1

The latter two cases are where one or two individual jurors have been discharged due to illness or other necessity. If the jury is down to nine people, then the only permissible verdict is a unanimous one.

Before the majority verdict direction has been given, whenever the jury returns to court the clerk asks 'Have you reached a verdict upon which you are all agreed?' Once the majority verdict direction has been given the question becomes (assuming there are 12 jurors): 'Have you reached a verdict upon which at least ten of you are agreed?' If the answer is 'Yes', the foreman is asked (for each count on the indictment) whether they find the defendant guilty or not guilty. If the jury finds the defendant not guilty, nothing further is said (so it is never known whether the acquittal was 12-0, 11–1 or 10–2); if it finds the defendant guilty the foreman will ask how many jurors find the defendant guilty (to make sure that the verdict is a lawful one and not, say, 9–3 and to provide a piece of information which may be relevant in the event of an appeal, as the Court of Appeal may be slightly more willing to overturn a majority conviction).

If the response to the question is that it has not reached a verdict upon which at least ten are agreed, the judge will ask it if there is any possibility of it reaching a verdict, whether it be unanimous or by majority. If the answer is 'yes' (or 'maybe'), the judge will probably give the jury more time (though of course he or she should never say how long — that would be to exert undue pressure). If the answer is 'no', the judge will almost certainly discharge that jury from giving a verdict.

11.12.4 REACHING A VERDICT

No pressure should be put on the jury to reach a verdict. An example of the attitude of the Court of Appeal is to be found in *R* v *Duggan* [1992] Crim LR 513. The judge said to the jury that it was important that the jury should not feel under pressure, and that if necessary hotel accommodation would be provided for the jurors. The appeal against the conviction which followed soon after the judge's words was allowed because some of the jury had expressed anxiety about commitments at home and the thought of not being able to go home might have exerted undue pressure on them. Presumably, the judge should simply have sent the jurors to a hotel without giving them advance warning of this possibility.

Another form of pressure was considered in *R* v *Watson* [1988] QB 690. In that case the Court of Appeal provided a model direction to be given to a jury which is having trouble in reaching a verdict. Essentially, the judge may encourage the jurors to listen to each other's views, pooling their wisdom and experience, and engaging in give and take provided that each remained within the scope of his or her oath. However, if the judge gives such a direction, there must be no reference to the cost and inconvenience that would be caused by the need for a re-trial if it could not reach a verdict. See also *R* v *Boyes* [1991] Crim LR 717.

The *Watson* direction was considered in *R* v *Buono* (1992) 95 Cr App R 338. It was held that there should rarely be any need for a *Watson* direction, but if one had to be given it should be given either during the summing up [which the present writer thinks unlikely ever to be justified] or after the jury has been given a reasonable time to consider a majority verdict direction: the *Watson* direction should never be given at the same time as a majority verdict direction. Further, the judge should not add to the words of the model direction given by the Court of Appeal in *Watson*.

Where the defendant is charged with a number of offences and the jury indicates that it has agreed on verdicts on some, but not all, of the offences, it is good practice to take the verdicts on those counts upon which the jury is agreed before it carries on considering the other counts (*R* v *F* [1994] Crim LR 377).

11.12.5 DISCHARGE OF THE JURY

If the jury cannot reach a verdict within what the judge holds to be a reasonable time, the jury will be discharged. This does not count as an acquittal and there is every chance that there will be a re-trial. There is no need for fresh committal proceedings. In the event of the second jury being 'hung', the prosecution is likely to let the matter rest there.

11.13 Sentence

If the defendant is convicted of some or all of the counts on the indictment, the judge will proceed to hear the defendant's antecedents (including any relevant previous convictions) from prosecuting counsel, just as on a plea of guilty (see **11.2.1** above). Obviously, there is no need for the prosecution to summarise the facts as the judge has just presided over the trial.

It is possible that a pre-sentence report will have been prepared already, but this is very unlikely. Normally, the case will have to be adjourned (with the presumption in favour of bail created by BA 1976, s. 4 still applying to the defendant) for the preparation of a report, although the court may dispense with a report if it takes the view that a report is unnecessary. If the case is adjourned in this way, prosecuting counsel may ask to be excused from attendance at the subsequent hearing. Once a report is available, counsel for the defence makes a plea in mitigation in the usual way.

TWELVE

APPEALS TO THE COURT OF APPEAL

12.1 The Criminal Division of the Court of Appeal

The Criminal Division of the Court of Appeal entertains appeals from the Crown Court on all matters relating to a trial on indictment, and appeals against any sentence imposed by the Crown Court following a committal for sentence. Appeals on matters not relating to a trial on indictment, such as when the Crown Court hears an appeal from a decision of the magistrates, are heard in the High Court, either on appeal by way of case stated, or on an application for judicial review.

The following have all been held to be matters relating to a trial on indictment, and hence not susceptible to appeal in the High Court:

(a) A ruling given at a pre-trial hearing (*R* v *Southwark Crown Court, ex parte Johnson* [1992] COD 364, DC).

(b) An order staying the whole or part of an indictment (*R* v *Manchester Crown Court, ex parte DPP* [1993] 2 WLR 846, HL).

(c) A decision, after argument, as to the date of the trial (*R* v *Southwark Crown Court ex parte Ward, The Times*, 19 August 1994).

12.1.1 COMPOSITION OF THE COURT

If the Court of Appeal is hearing an appeal against conviction, the court must comprise at least three judges. Very occasionally, if the court is dealing with a case of exceptional difficulty, the court will consist of five judges. If the court is dealing with an appeal against sentence, it is usual for two judges only to sit. However, it is rare to have more than one judgment delivered, in order to make for certainty of the law.

The Court of Appeal itself consists of 32 Lords Justices of Appeal, and a number of ex-officio judges including the Lord Chief Justice. In addition, the Lord Chief Justice may ask either of the following to sit in the Criminal Division:

(a) any High Court judge, who may deal with any case that comes before the Court of Appeal, except a case in which he was either the trial judge or passed sentence; or

(b) in certain circumstances, circuit judges, who may sit in appeals specified as suitable by the Lord Chancellor, except that they may not sit on any appeal from the decision of a High Court judge (s. 9(1) of the Supreme Court Act 1981, as amended by s. 52 of the CJPOA 1994).

12.1.2 THE COURT'S REGISTRAR

The administrative work of the Criminal Division is carried out by the Registrar of Criminal Appeals, who receives all notices and applications, and in turn serves all relevant notices on the parties to the appeal. In addition, the Registrar will obtain necessary transcripts, exhibits or other material. Certain additional powers have been conferred on him by virtue of the Criminal Appeal Act 1995. See **12.6.1** below.

12.1.3 THE RIGHT OF APPEAL

The statute governing the right to appeal is the Criminal Appeal Act 1968, as amended by the Criminal Appeal Act 1995 referred to in this chapter as the CAA 1968 and the CAA 1995 respectively. The changes effected by the CAA 1995 came into effect on 1 January 1996, unless otherwise indicated.

12.2 The Appeal Against Conviction

By virtue of CAA 1968, s. 2, as substituted by CAA 1995, s. 2, a person convicted on indictment may appeal on the single ground that the conviction is 'unsafe' (see **12.2.2**). Leave to appeal is always required (see **12.2.3**).

12.2.1 GROUND OF APPEAL: THE 1968 ACT

Prior to 1996, the Court of Appeal would allow an appeal if one of the three grounds of appeal, discussed in paragraphs (a) to (c) below, were made out. The proviso to this was that the Court of Appeal could dismiss the appeal if no miscarriage of justice had actually occurred. This was known as 'exercising the proviso'. In this situation, the Court of Appeal in effect agreed that a ground of appeal had been made out, but that the ground was so trivial that the jury would inevitably have come to the same conclusion.

(a) *That the conviction was unsafe or unsatisfactory:* In deciding whether the conviction was unsafe or unsatisfactory, the court considered the case as a whole and asked itself the subjective question, 'whether we are content to let the matter stand as it is, or whether there is not some lurking doubt in our minds which makes us wonder whether an injustice has been done'. See *R* v *Cooper* [1969] 1 QB 267, per Widgery LJ, applied in *R* v *O'Leary* (1988) 87 Cr App R 387.

(b) *That the trial judge had made a wrong decision on a question of law:* If the appeal was on the basis of a wrong decision by the trial judge on a question of law, even if this could be demonstrated, the Court of Appeal still had to consider whether the judgment of the trial court should be set aside on that account. In effect it considered the proviso. See *R* v *Moghal* (1977) 65 Cr App R 56.

The following are typical examples of appeals on a question of law, which were decided before 1996:

(i) The wrongful admission or exclusion of evidence. If the jury would inevitably have come to the same conclusion, though the point of law was established, the proviso was applied.

(ii) Defects in the indictment. Where the indictment, for example, was bad for duplicity, or fell foul of the Indictment Rules 1971, r. 9, (SI 1971 No. 1253), the court quashed the conviction only if the defect was serious.

(iii) Absence of corroboration. If there was no corroboration when it was required, the conviction was usually quashed, and the court only rarely applied the proviso.

(iv) A wrong direction as to the burden and standard of proof. If the trial judge failed to direct the jury on the burden or standard of proof, or directed it incorrectly, the conviction was usually quashed, and the court only rarely applied the proviso.

(v) A wrong rejection of a submission of no case to answer. If the trial judge wrongly rejected a submission of no case to answer, the appeal succeeded and the proviso was not applied. Had the judge not erred in law, the defendant would have been acquitted, and no matter what evidence was adduced in the trial subsequently, the acquittal would not have been affected. See *R* v *Cockley* (1984) 79 Cr App R 181.

(vi) A failure to deal with the essential thrust of the defence case in the summing-up. See, for example, *R* v *Jones* [1987] Crim LR 1701.

Note that the aim of a summing up is essentially practical. The fact that it contains something questionable from an academic point of view has been held not to give grounds for appeal (see *R* v *Ferrier; R* v *Barr, The Times*, 3 May 1995).

(c) *That there had been a material irregularity in the course of the trial*: An appeal on the basis that there has been a material irregularity succeeded if there had been a procedural error during the trial. But the irregularity must be major and material, i.e. serious enough to have affected the outcome of the trial.

The following are examples of irregularities which arose prior to 1996:

(i) Where the prosecution was wrongly allowed to make a speech. This was unlikely to be sufficiently material for the conviction to be quashed and the proviso was usually applied.

(ii) The constitution of the jury. Any suggestion that the jury was not properly constituted will be rebutted by the Juries Act 1974, s. 18, which says that no conviction will be quashed for this reason. But where, for example, a jury, having convicted one defendant, then sat on the trial of a former co-defendant who was being tried separately, the conviction was likely to be quashed. See *R* v *Gash* [1967] 1 WLR 454.

(iii) Interventions by the judge. If there was a large number of interventions by the judge, which effectively prevented the proper development of the defence case, then conviction was likely to be quashed. See *R* v *Matthews & Matthews* (1984) 78 Cr App R 23; *R* v *Gunning* (1994) 98 Cr App R 303; and *R* v *Ahmed, The Times*, 9 March 1995.

(iv) Improper basis for decision. In *R* v *Blackford* (1989) 89 Cr App R 239, the judge made a decision on a false basis of fact, and the resultant conviction was quashed.

(v) A failure by the prosecution to disclose to the defence material documents or information which should have been disclosed may be a material 'procedural' irregularity (see *R* v *Maguire* [1992] QB 936, CA).

(vi) A refusal by the judge to exercise a discretion in favour of the defence. The Court of Appeal was generally reluctant to interfere with the exercise of the judge's discretion, and would usually only do so if the discretion was exercised on the wrong basis (e.g. *R* v *Morris* [1991] Crim LR 385) or if the discretion was not exercised at all (e.g. *R* v *Dubarry* (1976) 64 Cr App R 7).

(vii) Errors on the part of defence counsel. The Court of Appeal will rarely allow an appeal on the basis that the defence counsel's actions had been mistaken or unwise (see e.g. *R* v *Satpal Ram, The Times*, 7 December 1995) but where it was shown that a decision not to call evidence was made without proper discussion and against all the promptings of reason and good sense, the court quashed the conviction (*R* v *Clinton* [1993] 1 WLR 1181, CA). See also *R* v *Swain* [1988] Crim LR 109; *R* v *Ensor* [1989] 1 WLR 497; *Sankar* v *State of Trinidad and Tobago, The Times*, 28 December 1994, PC; *R* v *Doherty and McGregor* [1997] 2 Cr App R 218; and *R* v *Nasser, The Times*, 19 February 1998.

12.2.2 GROUND OF APPEAL: THE 1995 ACT

The CAA 1995 abolishes the three grounds of appeal and the proviso, replacing them with the single test of the safety of the conviction.

The CAA 1995, s. 2 provides as follows:

> *2.—(1) In section 2 of the 1968 Act (disposal of appeal against conviction), for subsection (1) (grounds on which Court of Appeal are to allow to or dismiss appeal), including the proviso, substitute—*
> *'(1) Subject to the provisions of this Act, the Court of Appeal—*
> *(a) shall allow an appeal against conviction if they think that the conviction is unsafe; and*
> *(b) shall dismiss such an appeal in any other case'.*

The Act does not contain any definition of the word 'unsafe'. The meaning of that word has, however, been considered by the Court of Appeal in the following cases.

In *R* v *Chalkey* [1998] 3 WLR 146, it was described as 'in essence much the same as the intertwined and overlapping provisions of the old test, as was intended by the Royal Commission in recommending it, the Government in promoting it, the senior judiciary in supporting its parliamentary passage and Parliament in enacting it'.

It seems that the 'lurking doubt' test is still of assistance to the Court, but its use was disapproved of in *R* v *Farrow*, 20 October 1998, unreported, where the Court of Appeal described it as a brief, simple and clear test and one upon which it was undesirable to place any gloss, in particular that of the 'lurking doubt'. All appeals against conviction are different, but in deciding whether a conviction is safe, the Court would take account of the considerations relevant to the particular case.

The definition is wide enough to encompass an abuse of process prior to trial. However, every case should be approached on its own facts, and the court could properly allow a conviction to stand where the seriousness of the offence outweighed any abuse of process by the prosecution (*R* v *Mullen (No. 2), The Times*, 15 February 1999).

The following cases are illustrations of the approach of the Court of Appeal:

(a) *R* v *Diedrich and Aldrich* [1997] 1 Cr App R 361, where the verdicts returned by the jury were so inconsistent as to demand interference by the Court of Appeal, and where the judge introduced the questionnaire from the plea and directions hearing without warning and under a misapprehension as to the facts.

(b) *R* v *Ramzan, The Times*, 19 March 1999, where the judge raised an issue before the jury in summing up which was not part of the prosecution case, which he had not previously discussed with counsel and which the parties were given no time to consider and possibly argue the issues raised.

(c) *R* v *A, The Times*, 13 April 1998, where the judge made findings of fact concerning a father in care proceedings and subsequently presided over the trial relating to the father's alleged conduct towards his children.

(d) *R* v *Smith, The Times*, 31 May 1999, where the submission of no case to answer was wrongly rejected at the end of the prosecution case. On appeal, the defendants contended that the only test for allowing the appeal was the safety of the conviction and that any evidence adduced at the trial after the ejection of the submission was inadmissible for the purposes of the appeal. The Court of Appeal held that continuing with the trial after the wrongful rejection of the submission amounted to an abuse of process, rendering the conviction unsafe.

(e) In *R* v *Chatterjee* [1996] Crim LR 801, where the Court used the same approach as in *R* v *Clinton* [1993] 1 WLR 1181 (**12.2.1(c)(vii)**) and quashed the conviction as unsafe because impressive expert medical evidence available to defence counsel was not properly put before the jury. In *R* v *Doherty* [1997] 2 Cr App R 218, the Court set out the procedure to be followed where an appeal involved criticism of former counsel and in which the guidance issued in December 1995 by the Bar Council was quoted with the approval of the Lord Chief Justice. The Court further stated that such criticism should not be made unless it could be shown that, in the light of information then available, 'no reasonable competent counsel would sensibly have adopted' the course taken. See also *R* v *Hobson* [1998] 1 Cr App R 31 and *R* v *Nasser*, *The Times*, 19 February 1998.

12.2.3 LEAVE TO APPEAL

By virtue of the CAA 1968, as amended, leave to appeal against conviction is always required. This leave may be given by the trial judge or the Court of Appeal itself.

The CAA 1968, s. 1 provides as follows:

> *(2) An appeal under this section lies only—*
> *(a) with the leave of the Court of Appeal; or*
> *(b) if the judge of the court of trial grants a certificate that the case is fit for appeal.*

This provision removes a distinction drawn under the 1968 Act between questions of law and questions of fact or mixed law and fact. This was often difficult to determine, and this difficulty is now removed.

The power of the trial judge to certify that the case was fit for appeal should only be exercised if there were exceptional reasons. There would be very few circumstances which would justify a trial judge's assumption of powers normally exercised by judges of the Court of Appeal (*R* v *Bansal*, *The Times*, 29 December 1998).

12.2.4 APPEALS AFTER A PLEA OF GUILTY

The defendant may appeal against conviction after a plea of guilty, but only in the following circumstances:

(a) where the defendant did not appreciate the nature of the charge; or

(b) where the defendant did not intend to admit that he or she was guilty of the charge. This would include cases where the defendant was pressured into pleading guilty by either counsel or the judge; or

(c) where on the admitted facts he or she could not in law have been convicted of the offence charged;

(d) where the plea was founded upon an erroneous ruling on a point of law. This should be interpreted narrowly (*R* v *Chalkley and Jeffries*, *The Times*, 19 January 1998).

12.2.5 SINGLE RIGHT OF APPEAL

Under CAA 1968, the appellant has the right to bring an appeal before the Court of Appeal. If that appeal is dismissed, he or she has no right to bring a second appeal on the same matter (see *R* v *Pinfold* [1988] QB 462). Two apparent exceptions to this rule were recognised in *Pinfold:*

(a) where an appellant seeks to revive an abandoned appeal;

(b) where, owing to some defect in the procedure, the appellant has, on the first appeal being dismissed, suffered an injustice such as where he or she was not notified of a hearing date.

It appears that the appellant has a separate right of appeal on the basis that the proceedings were a nullity, as the powers of the Court of Appeal to issue a *venire de novo* exist independently of CAA 1968. See also *R* v *Larning* (1989) 90 Cr App R 450.

12.2.6 APPEALS IN THE CASE OF DEATH

Prior to CAA 1995, there was no procedure whereby the conviction of a deceased person could be challenged on appeal. CAA 1995, s. 7 inserts an entirely new provision into CAA 1968. Section 44A now gives a person approved by the Court of Appeal the right to begin or continue an appeal after the death of the deceased.

The persons approved by the Court of Appeal under s. 44A(3) must be one of the following:

(a) the widow or widower of the deceased;

(b) his personal representatives;

(c) any other person who, by family or other similar relationship with the deceased, has a substantial financial or other interest in the determining of the appeal.

The application for approval must be made within one year of death (s. 44A(4)).

R v *W, The Times*, 8 January 1997, is believed to be the first application under this section. A widow was held to be entitled to continue her deceased husband's appeal against conviction for assault on his daughter, where only death had prevented him from pursuing the appeal himself.

12.3 Evidence

Under CAA 1968 as amended by CAA 1995, s. 4, the Court of Appeal may receive any evidence if it considers that it is necessary or expedient in the interest of justice.

CAA 1968, s. 23 as amended provides as follows:

(1) For purposes of an appeal under this part of this Act [appeals against conviction and/or sentence and references to the Court of Appeal By the Home Secretary] the Court of Appeal may, if they think it necessary or expedient in the interests of justice—
(a) order the production of any document, exhibit or other thing connected with the proceedings, the production of which appears to them necessary for the determination of the case;
(b) order any witness who would have been a compellable witness in the proceedings from which the appeal lies to attend for examination and be examined before the court, whether or not he was called in those proceedings; and
(c) receive any evidence which was not adduced in the proceedings from which the appeal lies.
(2) The Court of Appeal shall, in considering whether to receive any evidence, have regard in particular to—
(a) whether the evidence appears to the Court to be capable of belief;
(b) whether it appears to the Court that the evidence may afford any ground for allowing the appeal;
(c) whether the evidence would have been admissible in the proceedings from which the appeal lies on an issue which is the subject of the appeal; and
(d) whether there is a reasonable explanation for the failure to adduce the evidence in those proceedings.
(3) Subsection (1)(c) above applies to any evidence of a witness (including the appellant) who is competent but not compellable.
(4) For purposes of an appeal under this Part of this Act, the Court of Appeal may, if they think it necessary or expedient in the interests of justice, order the examination of any witness whose attendance might be required under subsection (1)(b) above to

be conducted, in a manner provided by rules of court, before any judge or officer of the Court or other person appointed by the Court for the purpose, and allow the admission of any depositions so taken as evidence before the Court.

The following points may be noted about this section:

(a) The test for receiving evidence is that of the interests of justice. See *R* v *Jones, The Times*, 23 July 1996, where the court received fresh medical evidence, even though there was no strong argument to do so, holding that it was expedient in the interests of justice.

(b) The section permits any evidence to be called before the Court of Appeal, whether or not it was called at the trial.

(c) If evidence is to be received, the matters contained in s. 23(2) are important. These points, however, are merely matters to which the court should have regard and not conditions for the admissibility of the evidence namely:

  (i) whether the evidence appears to be capable of belief;

  (ii) whether the evidence affords any ground for allowing the appeal;

  (iii) whether the evidence would have been admissible;

  (iv) where there is a reasonable explanation for not calling the evidence at trial.

(d) Section 23(2)(a) provides that the evidence must be 'capable of belief', replacing the old test of 'Likely to be credible'. In *R* v *Parks* [1961] 1 WLR 1484, it was held that the test there was whether the witness's proof of evidence is intrinsically credible, and whether it fits in with at least some of the other evidence in the case.

(e) As to whether there is a 'reasonable explanation' for the failure to adduce evidence at the trial, the case of *R* v *Beresford* (1971) 56 Cr App R 143, on precisely similar words decided that the test was whether the evidence could have been obtained with 'reasonable diligence'.

(f) Rules on the receipt of fresh evidence have more relevance to factual evidence than to expert evidence, as experts are interchangeable to a certain extent, and if there is only one expert, and that expert is unavailable, the case may be postponed. See *R* v *Jones, The Times*, 23 July 1996. Fresh expert evidence will be received in appropriate circumstances, however. In *R* v *Latte*, 1996, unreported, fresh expert evidence was called and the Court of Appeal accepted that there was a reasonable explanation for not adducing the evidence at trial because the field of expertise (lighting and facial recognition) was highly specialised and not well known.

(g) The role of the Court of Appeal is not to make a finding of fact but to assess new evidence that had become available since the trial and make a decision on the safety of the earlier conviction (*R* v *Twitchell, The Times*, 10 November 1999).

(h) *R* v *Guppy, The Times*, 8 March 1994, a decision on the old law, held that on a true construction of ss. 11(3) and 23(1)(c), the Court of Appeal is empowered to receive fresh evidence of any witness, including the appellant, on an appeal against sentence. It would seem that this decision would be followed under the new formulation of s. 23(1)(c).

(i) In *R* v *Ahluwalia* [1992] 4 All ER 889, the fresh evidence which the appellant wished to adduce raised a defence which was not raised at the trial (psychiatric reports as to the appellant's diminished responsibility). The Court of Appeal admitted the reports as fresh evidence, concluding that there may have been an arguable defence which, for some unexplained reason, was not raised at the trial.

See also *R* v *Moringiello, The Times*, 25 July 1997, where the Court of Appeal did not allow fresh evidence to be called by the appellant's solicitor that the trial judge had fallen asleep during part of the evidence. Such an allegation had to be made at the time so that it could be known which parts of the evidence the judge was supposed to have missed.

12.4 Appeal against Sentence

The right of appeal against sentence after conviction on indictment is found in CAA 1968, s. 9. However, the Court of Appeal has always recognised that judges approach the question of sentencing in different ways, and must be allowed a measure of discretion in their approach. Thus, the court will not interfere merely because it would have passed a somewhat different sentence in a particular case.

The following are the most widely accepted grounds of appeal:

(a) The sentence is wrong in law. Where the judge passes a sentence which he has no jurisdiction to pass, such as a sentence of imprisonment on someone under the age of 21 years, the Court of Appeal will interfere. However, appeals on such grounds are rare.

(b) The sentence is wrong in principle. This contention covers two situations:

  (i) Where the appellant argues that entirely the wrong type of sentence was imposed, such as a sentence of custody when non-custodial measures were appropriate.

  (ii) Where the judge combines two sentences which are inconsistent with each other, such as a sentence of imprisonment and a probation order.

(c) The sentence is manifestly excessive. Here the appellant is arguing that the right type of sentence has been imposed, but that in the circumstances it is too severe.

(d) The judge took the wrong approach to sentencing. If the trial judge, in passing sentence, has taken into account an irrelevant consideration, such as the fact that the appellant has alleged that the police officers had fabricated their evidence, the sentence is likely to be reduced.

(e) The judge followed the wrong procedure prior to sentence. If, following a plea of guilty, there has been a dispute as to the facts of the case, and the judge accepts the prosecution version without any inquiry or investigation, then the Court of Appeal may feel obliged to reduce the sentence. See *R* v *Newton* (1982) 77 Cr App R 13 and, generally, **Chapter 14**.

(f) Disparity. Any disparity between the sentence imposed on co-defendants is probably best seen as merely a factor that the Court of Appeal will take into account when considering an appeal against sentence. It is unlikely, on its own, to support a successful appeal against sentence, but the view of the court has been inconsistent. On the one hand the court says that if the disparity is so marked that one of the former co-defendants is left with a burning sense of grievance, then it would be right to interfere (see *R* v *Dickinson* [1977] Crim LR 303). On the other hand, the court has also expressed the view that the mere fact that one sentence is wrong (the lighter sentence) is no reason for altering the right sentence and making two wrong sentences (see *R* v *Stroud* (1977) 65 Cr App R 150).

12.5 Procedure for Appeal

Preliminary note: The procedure is the same whether the appeal is against conviction or against sentence.

Within 28 days of the conviction (or sentence if the appeal is against sentence), notice of application for leave to appeal should be served on the Crown Court at which the proceedings took place. The notice should be served together with a document containing the grounds of appeal. Both documents are in standard form, with a space at the bottom for the appellant to fill in the grounds. If grounds are settled by counsel, they will be typed on to a separate sheet and attached.

Detailed guidance on the preparation of grounds of appeal may be found in 'A guide to Proceedings in the Court of Appeal Criminal Division' (1983) 77 Cr App R 138. See also the ***Drafting Manual*****, Chapter 25**.

It has recently been stated that practitioners should observe the 28-day time limit, notwithstanding that there may be practical difficulties if there has been a delay between conviction and sentence (*R* v *Long*, *The Times*, 24 October 1997). However, the 28-day time limit may be extended under CAA 1968, s. 18(3), if there are substantial grounds for so doing.

12.5.1 TRANSCRIPTS

The Crown Court sends the notice and grounds to the Registrar of the Court of Appeal. The Registrar may then order a transcript of any necessary part of the trial or summing-up, as specified by counsel in the grounds of appeal. It is rare to request a transcript of the entire case, and counsel should not do so unless it is essential.

12.5.2 GROUNDS OF APPEAL

Once counsel has received a copy of the transcript the grounds of appeal can then be set out in full, as counsel will now have, for example, the exact words with which the judge directed the jury.

No particular form of words is required when settling the grounds of appeal, but each point on which appeal is being made should be clearly identified. It is often convenient to make these points in chronological order. The grounds should refer to the transcript by page and paragraph number, and should cite any authorities upon which counsel proposes to rely. If counsel wishes to call a witness at the appeal, the reason why such a course is necessary should be explained fully.

The grounds of appeal should not include the judge's views on the verdict as revealed in his or her report to the Home Secretary containing his or her views on the minimum term to be served on a conviction for murder. The report should not be disclosed to defence counsel, and in any event is irrelevant to the court's determination of the appeal (*R* v *Jones* [1998] 2 Cr App R 53).

In complicated cases, counsel may send the court a document expanding the grounds of appeal, and outlining the arguments he or she intends to place before the court. This may save time, and therefore expense, at the hearing of the appeal itself.

The Lord Chief Justice has issued a *Practice Direction*, concerning the timetable for providing skeleton arguments. According to *Practice Direction (Court of Appeal (Criminal Division) Criminal Appeals: Skeleton Arguments)*, *The Times*, 31 December 1998, skeleton arguments should be lodged with the Registrar and served on the prosecuting authority within 14 days of the advocate receiving notification of leave to appeal, or such longer time as the Court or Registrar might direct. The prosecuting authority should lodge his or her skeleton arguments and serve it on the appellant within 14 days of receiving the appellant's skeleton argument or such other time as the Court or Registrar might direct.

Furthermore, where a skeleton argument relied on an unreported case, advocates should ensure that short head notes were included.

The Court of Appeal often reminds counsel not to make an appeal unless it is properly arguable. (See also section 6 of Annexe H to the Code of Conduct.)

12.5.3 THE SINGLE JUDGE

The application for leave to appeal, and any other applications (see **12.6** below), is placed before the single judge. No oral submission or arguments are heard by the single judge, who decides the matter on the basis of the papers before him or her.

If the single judge refuses to grant leave, the appellant has 14 days to renew the application before the full court, whose decision is final. When applying for leave to the single judge, or to the full court, the appellant should bear in mind the court's power to order 'loss of time' (see **12.7.1** below).

The court has power to extend the 14-day time limit, but very rarely does so. See *R* v *Dixon*, *The Times*, 19 May 1999.

If the single judge grants leave to appeal, the registrar ensures that all the matter is ready to be put before the Court of Appeal and prepares a summary of the case, to be read by the members of the Court of Appeal who will hear the case. Summaries of cases are now usually made available to counsel in the case (*Practice Direction (Criminal Appeals: Summaries)* [1992] 1 WLR 938). Where the appeal is against conviction, the court will consist of at least three judges; in the case of an appeal against sentence, it will consist of two judges.

Where the single judge grants leave in respect of certain grounds of appeal, but expressly refuses leave in respect of others, the latter grounds may only be argued on appeal with leave of the full court (*R* v *Jackson*, *The Times*, 20 May 1998). Further guidance on this issue was given in *R* v *Cox and Thomas*, *The Times*, 4 February 1999.

12.6 Powers of the Single Judge

Most of the powers of the Court of Appeal, short of deciding the appeal itself, are exercised by the single judge of the court under CAA 1968, s. 31. The single judge has power to:

(a) Grant leave to appeal.

(b) Allow the appellant to be present at the hearing of the appeal. Under CAA 1968, s. 22(1) the appellant is entitled to be present at the hearing of an appeal even if he or she is in custody. However, if he or she is in custody, he or she is not entitled to be present if the appeal is on the ground of law alone, nor on any preliminary application, without leave.

(c) Order a witness to attend for examination. The court may order a witness to appear before it, in pursuance of an appeal under CAA 1968, s. 23. This has the advantage of allowing both parties to the appeal to cross-examine.

(d) Allow bail pending the appeal hearing. Under CAA 1968, s. 19, the court has the power to grant bail to an appellant pending the hearing of the appeal. However, bail is granted only rarely, and only where it appears that the appeal is likely to be successful; or where the sentence is so short that it is likely to have been served before the appeal can be heard. In deciding whether to grant bail, the true test is, 'are there exceptional circumstances which would drive the court to the conclusion that justice can only be done by the granting of bail?' (*per* Geoffrey Lane LJ in *R* v *Watton* (1978) 68 Cr App R 293).

(e) Make, vary or discharge orders as regards, for example, whether the appellant is in custody or on bail pending re-trial.

(f) Make orders as to the costs of the appeal, including legal aid.

(g) Give directions for loss of time (see **12.7.1**).

12.6.1 POWERS OF THE REGISTRAR

By virtue of CAA 1968, s. 31A, inserted by CAA 1995, s. 6, certain of these powers may be exercised by the Registrar. These are:

(a) to extend the time within which notice of application for leave to appeal may be given;

(b) to order a witness to attend for examination;

(c) vary the conditions of bail granted by either the Court of Appeal or the Crown Court. However, he or she may not do so unless satisfied that the prosecution does not object to the variation (s. 31A(3)).

If the Registrar refuses any of these applications, the appellant may apply to the single judge.

12.7 Powers of the Court of Appeal

12.7.1 FOLLOWING APPEAL AGAINST CONVICTION

Having heard the appeal against conviction the Court of Appeal may do any of the following:

(a) Dismiss the appeal.

(b) Allow the appeal and quash the conviction.

(c) Allow part of the appeal and dismiss the other part. If it does this the court may pass a new sentence on the remaining conviction, but this must not be greater than the sentence as a whole passed by the convicting court (CAA 1968, s. 4(3)). For example, the defendant is convicted of two offences and sentenced to one year's imprisonment on each to run consecutively. On appeal, one conviction is quashed. The Court of Appeal may increase the sentence on the remaining conviction to up to two years, this being the total imposed by the convicting court.

(d) Find the appellant guilty of an alternative offence. Under CAA 1968, s. 3, if the appellant has been convicted of one offence, but the jury, under CLA 1967, s. 6, could have found him or her guilty of another offence, then the court may substitute a conviction for that other offence. Thus, if the jury has convicted of murder, the court may substitute a verdict of guilty of manslaughter. Further, if the defendant is charged with two counts in the alternative, and is convicted on one but the jury is discharged from giving a verdict on the other, the court may reverse the verdicts. The court must consider that the jury was satisfied of facts which proved him or her guilty of the other offence. See *R* v *Spratt* [1980] 1 WLR 554 and *R* v *Peterson, The Times*, 8 January 1997. Section 4(3) (above) applies. The power to find the appellant guilty of an alternative offence only applies where the appellant pleaded not guilty at the trial (*R* v *Horsman* [1998] QB 531).

(e) Determine the appeal summarily under CAA 1968, s. 20. If the Registrar considers that an appeal has no real merit, he or she may put it before the court for 'summary determination'. The court may, if it is of the same opinion, simply dismiss it without a full hearing and without hearing argument from either side. This process is to discourage vexatious or frivolous appeals, and applies to all appeals, whether on points of pure law, fact, or mixed fact and law.

(f) Order a re-trial. Under CAA 1968, s. 7, the court may order a re-trial if it considers that a re-trial is required in the interests of justice. The power to order a re-trial is generally available, whether the appeal is on the basis of fresh evidence, or because of some irregularity or misdirection in the trial.

(g) Make an order for loss of time. Under CAA 1968, s. 29(1), any time spent in custody pending the determination of the appeal is to be reckoned as part of the term of any custodial sentence which has been imposed, subject to any directions to the contrary that the court may give. In *Practice Direction (Crime: Sentence: Loss of Time)* [1980] 1 WLR 270, it was indicated that such directions would be made in the following circumstances:

(i) If leave to appeal is refused by the single judge, unless the grounds of appeal have been settled by counsel. It would be unfair to penalise the appellant for following the advice of counsel.

(ii) If leave to appeal is refused by the full court, even if the grounds of appeal have been settled by counsel. The appellant has renewed his or her application in the face of the single judge's opinion that leave should not be granted, and thus is not protected from a direction for loss of time even if the grounds are settled by counsel.

In addition, the Court of Appeal has inherent powers, independent of CAA 1968, to issue a writ of *venire de novo.* If there has been such an irregularity at the trial that the trial can be said to have been a nullity, and the appellant was never in danger of a valid conviction, then the court may order the writ of *venire de novo* to be issued and the appellant may be re-tried. The irregularity has to be so fundamental that there could not be said to have been a trial (*R* v *Rose* [1982] AC 822), followed in *R* v *Booth, Holland and Wood, The Times*, 26 November 1998.

See also Patrick O'Connor, 'The Court of Appeal Retrials and Tribulations' [1990] Crim LR 615.

12.7.2 FOLLOWING APPEAL AGAINST SENTENCE

Having heard the appeal against sentence the court may:

(a) Quash any sentence or order which is the subject of the appeal.

(b) Impose any sentence that was available to the Crown Court, except that it may not deal with the appellant, taking the sentence as a whole, more severely than he or she was originally dealt with.

12.7.3 FOLLOWING AN APPEAL AGAINST SENTENCE AFTER SUMMARY CONVICTION

Under CAA 1968, s. 10, the Court of Appeal also has the power to deal with an appeal against a sentence imposed by the Crown Court after the defendant has been convicted summarily. Section 10 covers two separate situations:

(a) After committal for sentence. A defendant who has been summarily convicted and committed to the Crown Court for sentence may appeal against that sentence if:

(i) the sentence was to imprisonment or detention in a young offender institution for a term of six months or more; or

(ii) the sentence was one which the magistrates did not have power to pass; or

(iii) the sentence included disqualification from driving, a recommendation for deportation, or activation of a suspended sentence.

(b) Breach of a probation order or conditional discharge. A defendant who has been summarily convicted of an offence which puts him or her in breach of a probation order or conditional discharge, and who is sentenced by the Crown Court for the original offence, may appeal against that sentence in the same circumstances as set out in (a) above.

12.8 Other Methods of Appeal

12.8.1 THE ATTORNEY-GENERAL'S REFERENCE

Under CJA 1972, s. 36(1), where a defendant has been acquitted following a trial on indictment, the Attorney-General may refer any point of law that arose in the case to the Court of Appeal for its opinion. The purpose is to prevent potentially false decisions becoming too widely accepted. Whatever conclusion the Court of Appeal reaches on the point of law, the acquittal is not affected.

In order to bring proceedings under s. 36, the Attorney-General serves a notice on the defendant within 28 days, containing the point of law to be argued, a summary of the argument, and the authorities the Attorney-General relies on. The Court of Appeal must hear the argument from the Attorney-General or his representative, and may hear submissions from the defence.

Under s. 36(3) the Court of Appeal may refer the point to the House of Lords, either on its own initiative or following an application from either party. The House of Lords then considers the matter and gives its opinion

12.8.2 REFERENCE BY THE ATTORNEY-GENERAL ON A MATTER OF SENTENCE

Under CJA 1988, ss. 35 and 36, the Attorney-General may refer a sentence, which includes any order made by a court when dealing with an offender, to the Court of Appeal for review if:

(a) he considers that the sentence was 'unduly lenient'. This may, but need not, be because the Attorney-General considers that the judge had erred in law as to his powers of sentence; and

(b) leave of the Court of Appeal is granted; and

(c) the offence was triable only on indictment, or was triable either way but specified as reviewable in an order made by the Home Secretary.

By the Criminal Justice Act 1988 (Reviews of Sentencing) Order 1994 (SI 1994 No. 119), indecent assault, threats to kill, cruelty to a person under 16, and attempts or incitement to commit any of these offences were specified as reviewable.

If an offender is sentenced for two separate matters, only one of which is triable only on indictment or specified as reviewable, they are to be treated as having been passed in the same proceeding if they are passed on the same day, or passed on different days but ordered to be treated as one sentence by the sentencing court. Thus, sentences may be reviewed by the Court of Appeal even though they do not fall within (c) above.

The procedure for bringing a sentencing reference is the same as for bringing an appeal against sentence (see **12.5** above). The Court of Appeal may quash any sentence, and impose such a sentence as it thinks appropriate, provided it is a sentence which the Crown Court had power to pass.

The correct approach to sentencing references was set out by the Court of Appeal in *Attorney-General's Reference (No. 4 of 1989)* [1990] 1 WLR 41:

(a) The sentence must be *unduly* lenient, that is it must fall out of the range of sentences which the judge could reasonably consider appropriate.

(b) Assuming that it is unduly lenient, the court still has a discretion as to whether to exercise its powers.

(c) The court's powers are not confined to increasing the sentence.

For recent examples, see *R* v *Shaw, Attorney-General's Reference (No. 28 of 1996)*, and *R* v *Harnett, Attorney-General's Reference (No. 60 of 1996)*, both reported in *The Times*, 27 January 1997.

Further reading: Ralph Henham, '*Attorney-General's Reference* Revisited' (1998) 62(5) JCL 468.

12.9 Appeal to the House of Lords

Under CAA 1968, s. 33, either the prosecution or defendant may appeal from any decision of the Court of Appeal to the House of Lords if:

(a) leave is granted by either the Court of Appeal or the House of Lords; and

(b) the Court of Appeal certifies that the case raises a point of law of general public importance which ought to be considered by the House of Lords. There is no appeal against the court's refusal to grant a certificate. See *R* v *Tang, The Times*, 23 May 1995.

One of the effects of s. 33 is that the prosecutor may appeal to the House of Lords against the order of the Court of Appeal quashing the appellant's conviction. If the prosecutor is successful in the House of Lords, the conviction will be restored.

12.10 Reference to the European Court of Justice

Under SI 1972 No. 1786, the Court of Appeal has power to refer a case to the European Court of Justice at any time before the determination of the appeal. (See *Archbold*, 2000 edn, paras. 7–315 to 7–317 or *Blackstone's Criminal Practice*, 2000, D26.3 for details.)

12.11 The Criminal Cases Review Commission

Prior to 1997, the Home Secretary had the power to refer a case, or any point arising in it, to the Court of Appeal: CAA 1968, s. 17. The reference was made in the exercise of the Home Secretary's discretion and could be made whether or not the defendant had made any application to the Home Secretary for the reference to be made. In any event the defendant could not be prejudiced by the reference as the Court of Appeal had no power to order loss of time in these circumstances.

If the whole case was referred, it was treated as if it were an appeal to the Court of Appeal by the defendant, who was then able to raise any questions of law, fact or mixed law and fact.

However, it became clear that the power was not satisfactory. In practice, the Home Secretary only referred cases to the Court of Appeal where there was fresh evidence, or some other significant matter arose which had not been investigated at the trial. In 1991, the then Home Secretary announced the creation of a Royal Commission on Criminal Justice to examine the ways in which alleged miscarriages of justice were dealt with. As a result of the recommendations of the Royal Commission, the Criminal Cases Review Commission (the Commission) was established by CAA 1995, replacing the Home Secretary's power to refer matters to the Court of Appeal. The Commission started work on 1 April 1997.

What follows is a general outline of the work of the Commission. A full discussion is beyond the scope of this Manual.

12.11.1 MEMBERSHIP OF THE COMMISSION

The Commission is a body corporate and is intended to be independent of government and the courts. It must consist of at least 11 members, appointed by Her Majesty on the recommendation of the Prime Minister. At least one-third must be legally qualified. At least two-thirds must be persons who have knowledge or experience of any aspect of the criminal justice system, and at least one of them should have such knowledge in relation to Northern Ireland. It may be noted that no specific requirement is made as to any representation from ethnic minorities, or of any technical or forensic expertise. Fourteen members have initially been appointed, under the chairmanship of Sir Frederick Crawford.

12.11.2 MAKING THE REFERENCE

The Commission may refer to the Court of Appeal any conviction or sentence following a trial on indictment, such a reference being treated as an appeal by the person concerned, under CAA 1968, s. 1 (CAA 1995, s. 9). Section 11 makes similar provisions in relation to a person convicted in a magistrates' court, referring the matter to the Crown Court.

Under CAA 1995, s. 13, three conditions must be fulfilled before any matter will be referred to the Court of Appeal:

(a) the Commission must consider that there is a 'real possibility that the conviction, verdict, finding or sentence would not be upheld were the reference to be made'; and

(b) the Commission must consider this:

  (i) in the case of a conviction, on the basis of an argument or evidence not raised in the trial *or* there must be exceptional circumstances which justify the reference;

  (ii) in the case of a sentence, on the basis of an argument on a point of law, or information not raised in the proceedings; and

(c) the appeal procedure has been followed without success or leave to appeal has been refused *or* there are exceptional circumstances which justify a reference.

The result of these conditions is that in general a reference will only be made if there is fresh evidence leading to a real possibility that the conviction will be quashed. It remains to be seen whether the Commission will exercise its power to refer a matter in exceptional circumstances in situations where there is no fresh evidence, but the existing evidence is weak and unsatisfactory.

In deciding whether to make a reference, the Commission should also have regard, under s. 14(2) and (3), to the following:

(a) Any application or representations made to the Commission by or on behalf of the person to whom it relates. Note that the reference may be made without any application being made to it by the person to whom it relates (s. 14(1)).

(b) Any other representations made to the Commission in relation to it.

(c) Any point on which it desires the assistance of the Court of Appeal.

(d) Any other matters which appear to the Commission to be relevant.

For an example of a reference by the Commission to the Court of Appeal, see *R* v *Bentley, The Times*, 31 July 1998.

12.11.3 INFORMATION TO THE PARTIES

Where the Commission decides to refer the matter to the court, it shall inform the court, and any likely party to the proceedings, of its reasons for making the reference (s. 14(4)). Further, where the Commission decides not to make a reference after an application has been made to it, the Commission must give the applicant the reasons for not so doing.

12.11.4 INVESTIGATIONS

The Commission has no power to carry out investigations itself into alleged miscarriages of justice. Instead, the police will be asked to carry out investigations for them, acting in a manner which is similar to the Police Complaints Authority. The Commission may require an appropriate person from the body which carried out the original investigation to appoint someone to make enquiries and report back to the Commission (CAA 1995, s. 19(1)). In the majority of cases this will be a police force, and the appropriate person will be the Chief Constable. The Chief Constable may be required to appoint someone from his own force or another force.

12.11.5 RELATIONSHIP WITH THE COURT OF APPEAL

For a discussion of the relationship between the Commission and the Court of Appeal, see *R* v *Criminal Cases Review Commission, ex parte Pearson* [1999] 3 All ER 498, where the appellant was convicted of murder and wished the Commission to refer her case to the Court of Appeal. The Commission refused to do so, on the basis that there was no likelihood that the Court of Appeal would receive the fresh evidence that the appellant wished to adduce, and there was therefore no real possibility that the conviction would be quashed. The appellant sought judicial review, in which the following principles were set out:

(a) The role of the Commission was to try to predict the response of the Court of Appeal, and it could only do this by making its own assessment based on the same process of reasoning that the Court of Appeal might follow. To do so was not to usurp the function of the Court of Appeal.

(b) The Commission's reasoning did not include any defects which would allow the court to interfere, and the conclusion of the Commission was not irrational and not legally misdirected. The issue was within the Commission's discretion and the only role for the court in such cases was to ensure that the Commission had acted lawfully.

Two final points may be made about the Commission:

(a) The Court of Appeal is not restricted to dealing with the matter on the point referred to, but may examine the case as a whole (s. 14(5)).

(b) The Court of Appeal has the discretionary power, if practical considerations so demand, to adjourn an appeal referred to it by the Commission. See *R* v *Smith*, *The Times*, 20 May 1999.

SENTENCING

THIRTEEN

INTRODUCTION

The Sentencing part of the Manual contains 12 chapters. This chapter includes an outline of the courts' sentencing powers, and **Chapter 14** describes the procedure between conviction and sentence. The remaining chapters do not purport to give complete coverage of the knowledge required for the sentencing part of the course. Rather, their purpose is to introduce the topics, to supply some basic information about the law and how it works in practice, and to provide a foundation for the lectures.

The material below goes beyond references to statutes and decided cases. It also directs attention to the statistics on how courts tend to use their sentencing powers, and how they approach sentencing for the different kinds of offences. (The latest statistics on the use of sentencing powers for offenders aged 21 and over convicted of indictable offences are to be found in **Figure 13.1** at the end of this introduction.) It also draws upon research into the factors which seem to weigh more or less heavily with courts when sentencing. Several of the Court of Appeal's guideline judgments on sentencing refer to the sentencing statistics and the aims of sentencing, as well as to the law itself. These chapters build upon that approach.

13.1 The Duties of Counsel

Most persons who are prosecuted plead guilty, which means that the criminal law and the laws of evidence hardly come into play in those cases. But in all cases of a plea of guilty or a conviction the court will pass sentence. In a small number of these it may be necessary to hold a *Newton* hearing in order to establish a factual basis for sentencing (*R* v *Newton* (1982) 77 Cr App R 13); the burgeoning case law may be found in D. A. Thomas (ed.), *Current Sentencing Practice;* in all cases, before sentence is passed, counsel may be called upon to make a plea in mitigation. This task places emphasis not only on advocacy skills but also on knowledge of the sentencing system and how it works. In addition to the detailed provisions of the Criminal Justice Act 1991 there has been further legislation on sentencing in 1993, 1994, 1997 and 1998. Courts may need the assistance of counsel in avoiding sentences which are unlawful or even unprincipled. Thus, there is a longstanding duty of counsel to prevent a court from passing an unlawful sentence:

> It was a matter for regret that in those three cases counsel had not considered, either in advance, or as soon as the sentence or order had been made, what power the court had to pass the sentence or make the order. It cannot be too clearly understood that there is a positive obligation on counsel, both for the prosecution and for the defence, to ensure that no order is made which the court has no power to make.

(*R* v *Komsta* (1990) 12 Cr App R (S) 63, in accord with such earlier decisions as *R* v *Clarke* (1974) 59 Cr App R 298.) Strong words on the same point were spoken by the Court of Appeal in *R* v *Hartrey* [1993] Crim LR 230 and *R* v *Bruley* [1996] Crim LR 913.

A similar duty has been recognised in respect of guideline judgments and major decisions of principle:

> It seems to all members of the court that the time has come when counsel for the prosecution should draw the court's attention to guideline cases, not to ask for any particular penalty, but because a court is entitled to have its attention drawn to any guidelines which the Court of Appeal has laid down.

(*R* v *Panayioutou* (1989) 11 Cr App R (S) 535; the decision concerned compensation orders, and the term 'guideline' was used by the Court in a broad way to refer to any decisions on major issues of sentencing principle.) Occasionally, the Court of Appeal has encouraged counsel to cite appropriate appellate decisions when mitigating at trial (*R* v *Ozair Ahmed* (1994) 15 Cr App R (S) 286).

There is also increasing recognition of the duty of the sentencer to give counsel an opportunity to make submissions for or against a particular type of sentence:

> The Court has repeatedly held that if a judge is contemplating passing a sentence which is within his power but which a defendant or his counsel may not be anticipating, the judge is under a duty in fairness to the defendant to give notice of what is in his mind, so that counsel may have the opportunity of making submissions to him on that issue.

(*R* v *Scott* (1989) 11 Cr App R (S) 249, at p. 253.)

These decisions underline the importance of an understanding of sentencing practice and a knowledge of the sources for checking matters of detail.

13.2 Finding the Details of Sentencing Law

What are the principal sources? The statutory provisions and the cases are organised according to subject-matter in the regularly updated encyclopaedia *Current Sentencing Practice*, and there are also substantial sections on sentencing in *Blackstone's Criminal Practice* and in *Archbold*. Reports of Court of Appeal decisions are published each month in the *Criminal Law Review* (Crim LR), and there is a series of reports consisting entirely of sentencing appeals — *Criminal Appeal Reports (Sentencing)* (Cr App R (S)). However, these official reports convey only one part of the picture. In order to grasp the practical issues, the good advocate will also be familiar with the statistical trends in the use of sentences, will be aware of the latest research findings on factors which appear to influence courts in deciding to impose one sentence rather than another, and will also have an awareness of developments in penal policy (for example, the prisons, and statements of Government policy) insofar as they may affect sentencing. Some extracts from the Criminal Statistics are provided below. The best way to keep abreast of developments is to look through the relevant journals, notably *Criminal Law Review*, *British Journal of Criminology* and *Howard Journal of Criminal Justice*.

Legislative provisions on sentencing are scattered throughout the statute book, in such places as the Road Traffic Acts, the Magistrates' Courts Act 1980 and the Drug Trafficking Act 1994. For many years the most important statute was the Powers of Criminal Courts Act 1973, which was intended as a consolidating statute. It included most of the courts' general powers to impose non-custodial sentences. However, during the 1980s the pace of change quickened, and significant sentencing reforms were introduced by the Criminal Justice Acts of 1982 and 1988. The CJA 1991 created a new sentencing framework, and also altered many of the details of particular forms of sentence, technically, by way of amendments of the Powers of Criminal Courts Act 1973. The 1991 Act was itself amended by the Criminal Justice Act 1993, and the Criminal Justice and Public Order Act 1994 contained further sentencing changes. The Crime (Sentences) Act 1997, the Crime and Disorder Act 1998 and the Youth Justice and Criminal Evidence Act 1999 also contained some fundamental changes. The Powers of Criminal Courts (Sentencing) Act 2000 (PCC(S)A) has consolidated the relevant provisions of these Acts. The purpose of the paragraphs below is to give an outline of the courts' sentencing powers, leaving the details to the chapters that follow.

13.3 Outline of Principal Sentences

Before considering the choice of sentence, counsel and the court must consider two preliminary issues. One is the maximum sentence for the offence: this will usually be found in the statute creating the offence, but the legislature does alter maximum penalties from time to time. For example, the CJA 1991 reduced the maximum for theft from ten to seven years' imprisonment, and the maximum for non-residential burglary from 14 to ten years. The other matter is the powers of the court: magistrates' courts are restricted by maximum fines and are limited to six months' custody (or 12 months on two or more convictions for offences triable either way). The Crown Court is subject to limits when hearing appeals from magistrates' courts.

The framework of sentencing established by the CJA 1991 may be seen as a pyramid, in the following form:

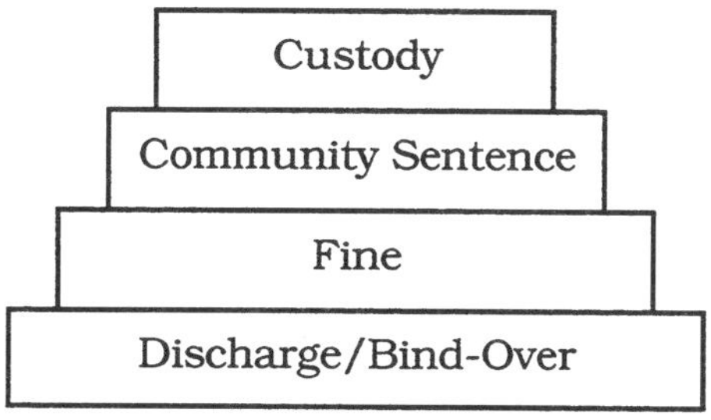

Starting at the base of the pyramid, the least that a court can do on conviction is to grant an absolute discharge (PCC(S)A 2000, s. 12). A stronger alternative is the conditional discharge, governed by the same statutory provisions, which discharges the offender on condition that he or she commits no further offence within a specified period of up to three years. If there is a further offence in that period, he or she is liable to be sentenced both for the new offence and for the original offence too. Some courts use, as an alternative, the power to bind over an offender to keep the peace, under one of several powers such as the Justices of the Peace Act 1361.

On the next level of the pyramid is the fine. The Crown Court may impose unlimited fines for indictable offences, unless the particular statute states otherwise. Whenever the Crown Court imposes a fine, it must also fix a term in default (PCC(S)A 2000, s. 139(2)). Magistrates' courts are limited to certain maxima, expressed in terms of five levels of fines. Most triable-either-way offences are on level 5, whereas offences triable summarily only are placed on different levels according to their relative seriousness (CJA 1982, s. 37(2), as amended by CJA 1991).

On the next higher level of the pyramid are community sentences, of which there are three main forms for adults — probation, community service and combination orders. A court may only make such an order if it is of the opinion that the offence is 'serious enough to warrant' a community sentence (PCC(S)A 2000, s. 35). Some offences may be at a level where the court feels that the choice lies between a high fine or a community sentence, but most of the offences for which community sentences are considered will be too serious for a fine. A *probation order* places the offender under the supervision of a probation officer for a specified period between six months and three years (PCC(S)A 2000, s. 41). Certain additional requirements may be included in a probation order (PCC(S)A 2000, s. 42). A *community service order* requires the offender to perform unpaid work for between 40 and 240 hours, as specified by the court (PCC(S)A 2000, s. 46). *A combination order* is a more restrictive order, part probation (from one to three years' supervision) and part community service (between 40 and 100 hours) (PCC(S)A 2000, s. 51). (A fourth form of community sentence, the *curfew order with electronic monitoring*, is available to courts in some areas: PCC(S)A 2000, ss. 37–38.) Before making a community order the court must usually obtain and consider a pre-sentence report (PCC(S)A 2000, s. 36). When choosing among community orders, the court is required to select the order 'most suitable for the offender' and to ensure that the restrictions on liberty imposed by the order are commensurate with the seriousness of the offence (PCC(S)A 2000, s. 35).

A custodial sentence may only be imposed if one of three justifications in PCC(S)A 2000, s. 79 applies. In most cases, the court will need to be satisifed that the offence was 'so serious that only [a custodial] sentence can be justified' (PCC(S)A 2000, s. 79(2)(a)). The Act goes on to provide that aggravating and mitigating factors that bear on the seriousness of the offence(s) must be taken into account (s. 81(4)). The court may then take account of any other mitigating factors (s. 158), and this may have the effect of reducing the sentence from custody to a community sentence. All these matters are discussed in **Chapters 21** and **22** below. They are equally relevant in determining length of sentence, because s. 80(2)(a) provides that the sentence shall be 'for such term . . . as is commensurate with the seriousness of the offence'. The power to suspend a sentence of imprisonment of up to two years (s. 118) is restricted to 'exceptional circumstances'.

The two other justifications for custody are invoked less frequently. Section 79(3) of the 2000 Act is now relevant chiefly where there has been 'wilful default' in breaching a community order. Section 79(2)(b) provides that custody may be imposed for a violent or sexual offence if 'only such a sentence would be adequate to protect the public from serious harm.' On this point, s. 80(2)(b) also provides that, for a violent or sexual offence, the sentence may be longer than commensurate if this is 'necessary to protect the public from serious harm from the offender.'

This pyramid of measures does not exhaust the court's powers and duties at the sentencing stage. In every case where there is death, injury, loss or damage, the court has a duty to consider ordering the offender to pay compensation to the victim (PCC(S)A 2000, s. 130). There are other forms of sentence not mentioned above, such as disqualification from driving, forfeiture of property connected with the commission of a crime (PCC(S)A 2000, s. 143), deprivation of profits of a drug trafficking offence (Drug Trafficking Act 1994, a mandatory procedure), and deprivation of profits of any other offence (CJA 1988 as amended by the Proceeds of Crime Act 1995).

Where the offender is aged under 21, the court's powers differ from those outlined above. The details are given in **Chapter 24**. Custody for young offenders is called 'detention in a young offender institution'. Where the offender is under 18 he or she will normally be dealt with in a youth court (CJA 1991, s. 70), and the powers are limited: the Crime and Disorder Act 1998 introduced the detention and training order, with various restrictions on availability and length. In exceptional circumstances custodial sentences are available for longer periods (PCC(S)A 2000, s. 91). The statutory framework for fines, community sentences and custody established by the CJA 1991 applies to all young offenders. Two additional forms of community order are available. The *attendance centre order* requires a young offender under 21 to attend for a certain number of hours (the absolute maximum is 36) at an attendance centre (PCC(S)A 2000, s. 60). The *supervision order* requires a young offender under 18 to undergo supervision by the local authority, and certain requirements may be included (PCC(S)A 2000 s. 63 and sch. 6). Both supervision orders and attendance centre orders are available from the age of 10, whereas probation, community service orders and combination orders are available only from the age of 16. When a court imposes a fine or a compensation order on an offender under 16, it must order the parents to pay in most circumstances. A new form of community order for young offenders, the *action plan order*, is available in some areas under the PCC(S)A 2000 which consolidated the relevant provisions in the CDA 1998.

There is also a different range of powers when the court is dealing with a mentally disordered offender. In addition to all the measures mentioned above, there are further possibilities such as a hospital order (Mental Health Act 1983, s. 37) and a hospital order with restrictions (Mental Health Act 1983, ss. 37 and 41). If a probation order is made, the court may add a requirement as to treatment for a mental condition. However, before imposing any custodial sentence on a mentally disordered offender, a court must obtain and consider a medical report and must take account of the likely effect of prison on the mental condition and on any treatment that may be available for it (PCC(S)A 2000, s. 82).

There is a separate set of penalties for road traffic offences, in addition to many of the general measures listed above, but they are outside the scope of the Manual.

Figure 13.1 Persons aged 21 and over sentenced for indictable offences by sex and type of sentence or order

England and Wales — Number of persons (thousands) and percentages

Sex and year	Total number of persons sentenced	Absolute or conditional discharge	Fine	Probation order	Community service order	Combination order	Curfew order	Imprisonment			Otherwise dealt with	Total immediate custody	Total community sentence
								Fully suspended	Partly suspended	Un-suspended			
	Number sentenced for indictable offence												
Males													
1987	198.3	19.5	81.0	15.4	14.4	*	*	23.2	2.4	39.6	2.8	42.0	29.8
1988	207.4	20.5	86.6	16.0	14.2	*	*	24.7	2.4	39.4	3.6	41.9	30.2
1989	186.6	21.8	79.5	14.4	10.9	*	*	20.2	1.9	34.0	4.0	35.9	25.3
1990	188.4	24.5	80.2	15.6	12.8	*	*	18.5	1.3	31.4	4.2	32.7	28.4
1991	190.0	28.4	73.6	15.8	14.7	*	*	18.7	1.0	33.3	4.6	34.3	30.5
1992[1]	190.1	32.5	70.3	16.2	17.1	0.5	*	15.1	0.5	32.8	5.0	33.3	33.8
1993[1]	183.1	33.0	69.3	17.5	20.7	3.5	*	2.3	*	32.1	4.7	32.1	41.7
1994	187.0	30.1	67.3	20.3	21.1	4.6	*	1.9	*	37.0	4.6	37.0	46.0
1995	178.4	26.0	60.7	19.1	19.2	5.1	0.0	1.9	*	42.0	4.3	42.0	43.3
1996	175.6	24.6	57.1	19.1	17.4	5.7	0.1	2.1	*	44.9	4.6	44.9	42.3
1997	186.6	26.0	59.1	20.4	17.6	6.4	0.2	2.2	*	49.4	5.4	49.4	44.5
Females													
1987	32.0	8.2	11.4	5.9	1.0	*	*	2.6	0.3	2.1	0.4	2.5	6.9
1988	31.4	8.4	11.0	5.8	1.0	*	*	2.6	0.3	1.9	0.5	2.2	6.8
1989	29.8	8.5	10.1	5.2	0.9	*	*	2.6	0.2	1.8	0.5	2.0	6.1
1990	30.5	9.7	9.7	5.4	1.2	*	*	2.3	0.1	1.5	0.6	1.7	6.6
1991	29.2	9.9	8.3	5.0	1.2	*	*	2.5	0.1	1.7	0.5	1.8	6.2
1992[1]	28.5	10.2	7.7	4.6	1.5	0.1	*	1.9	0.1	1.8	0.6	1.8	6.2
1993[1]	27.6	9.4	8.6	4.6	1.8	0.4	*	0.4	*	1.9	0.6	1.9	6.7
1994	28.5	9.2	8.0	5.5	1.9	0.6	*	0.4	*	2.3	0.5	2.3	8.1
1995	26.8	8.0	7.0	5.3	1.9	0.7	—	0.5	*	2.8	0.5	2.8	7.9
1996	27.2	7.7	6.8	5.7	1.8	0.9	0.0	0.6	*	3.2	0.6	3.2	8.4
1997	30.3	8.3	7.3	6.3	2.0	1.0	0.0	0.7	*	4.0	0.7	4.0	9.3

England and Wales — Number of persons (thousands) and percentages

Sex and year	Total number of persons sentenced	Absolute or conditional discharge	Fine	Probation order	Community service order	Combination order	Curfew order	Imprisonment: Fully suspended	Imprisonment: Partly suspended	Imprisonment: Un-suspended	Otherwise dealt with	Total immediate custody	Total community sentence
	Percentage sentenced for indictable offences												
Males													
1987	100	10	41	8	7	*	*	12	1	20	1	21	15
1988	100	10	42	8	7	*	*	12	1	19	2	20	15
1989	100	12	43	8	6	*	*	11	1	18	2	19	14
1990	100	13	43	8	7	*	*	10	1	17	2	17	15
1991	100	15	39	8	8	*	*	10	1	18	2	18	16
1992(1)	100	17	37	9	9	0	*	8	0	17	3	18	18
1993(1)	100	18	38	10	11	2	*	1	*	18	3	18	23
1994	100	16	36	11	11	2	*	1	*	20	2	20	25
1995	100	15	34	11	11	3	0	1	*	24	2	24	24
1996	100	14	33	11	10	3	0	1	*	26	3	26	24
1997	100	14	32	11	9	3	0	1	*	26	3	26	24
Females													
1987	100	26	36	18	3	*	*	8	1	7	1	8	22
1988	100	27	35	18	3	*	*	8	1	6	1	7	22
1989	100	28	34	17	3	*	*	9	1	6	2	7	20
1990	100	32	32	18	4	*	*	8	0	5	2	6	21
1991	100	34	28	17	4	*	*	8	0	6	2	6	21
1992(1)	100	36	27	16	5	0	*	7	0	6	2	6	22
1993(1)	100	34	31	17	6	1	*	2	*	7	2	7	24
1994	100	32	28	19	7	2	*	2	*	8	2	8	28
1995	100	30	26	20	7	3	—	2	*	10	2	10	30
1996	100	28	25	21	7	3	0	2	*	12	2	12	31
1997	100	27	24	21	7	3	0	2	*	13	2	13	31

(1) Improvements in the data collection methods used by the Metropolitan Police District have led to an increase in the number recorded as sentenced of about 2 per cent in 1993 and 1 per cent in 1992 for indictable offences.

FOURTEEN

PROCEDURE BETWEEN CONVICTION AND SENTENCE

14.1 Advance Indications of the Sentence

If he or she wishes, a Crown Court judge may — prior to the indictment being put to the accused — indicate that the sentence either will or will not take a particular form, regardless of how the accused pleads (see *R* v *Turner* [1970] 2 QB 321, at p. 327). Usually such indications are given to counsel privately in the judge's room, and are then transmitted to the accused.

It is vital that, if an indication of sentence is given, it is not made conditional on how the accused pleads. If the judge were to promise a non-custodial sentence in the event of a guilty plea, and either expressly say that the promise would not apply were the accused to be convicted by a jury, or simply not state what would happen in that event, then the accused would be placed under intolerable pressure to plead guilty. In fact, his or her plea of guilty would, on appeal, be treated as a nullity. The Court of Appeal would quash the conviction and order a re-trial at which, presumably, the accused would plead not guilty (see **9.15**, **9.16** and **11.2.3**).

Anything the judge says privately to counsel about sentence should be passed on to the accused. The court will then be bound by what the judge has indicated, even if there is an adjournment prior to sentence and a different judge actually deals with the accused (see *R* v *Moss* (1984) 5 Cr App R (S) 209).

Making pre-trial promises about sentence, made only in the minority of cases, restricts the court's freedom of action when the time to sentence arrives. It can do little to influence the plea because of the rule that the promises must not be conditional on how the accused pleads. Perhaps their greatest value is in a case where defence counsel suspects that the client really wants to plead guilty but is terrified that the result will be a custodial sentence. This saves a lot of court time, and is good for the accused as well, because the eventual sentence will reflect the credit he or she has earned by this plea.

No advance indications of sentence are given in the magistrates' courts because nothing is known of the accused or his or her offence prior to the hearing. A Crown Court judge, however, can familiarise himself or herself with the case by reading through the committal statements. He or she is also entitled to see the accused's written antecedents and list of previous convictions. Thus the papers in the case give the judge an adequate basis for such indications as to the sentence he or she considers proper to pass.

14.2 Advising on Sentence

Counsel has to rely upon knowledge of the tariff for the offence in question and on prior experience (if any) of the judge. There are suggestions (see *R* v *Cain* [1976] Crim LR

464) that, when completely unsure as to what the penalty is likely to be, counsel can ask the judge for a private *and confidential* indication of what the latter has in mind. In basing advice on such an indication, counsel would not reveal to the accused that he or she had seen the judge. In the light of *R* v *Turner*, however, it is highly unlikely that this procedure would now be approved by the Court of Appeal, and it is rarely, if at all, resorted to in practice. Either the judge gives a '*Turner*-type' indication which can be passed on openly to the accused, or he or she tells counsel nothing at all about the probable sentence.

An accused should always be told, assuming he or she does not know it already, that credit is given to an offender who pleads guilty. He or she receives a lighter sentence than he or she would have done had he or she pleaded not guilty and been found guilty by a jury. Strong advice, stressing the advantage of a guilty plea from the point of view of the eventual sentence, is permissible (*R* v *Peace* [1976] Crim LR 119), but it must not be so strong as effectively to deprive the accused of his or her free choice as to how he or she pleads (*R* v *Inns* (1975) 60 Cr App R 231). See also *R* v *Keily* [1990] Crim LR 204, *R* v *Smith* [1990] 1 WLR 1311, *R* v *Pitman* [1991] 1 All ER 468, CA and *R* v *Thompson* (1995) 159 JP 568.

14.3 Adjournments

The court does not necessarily sentence the offender on the day on which he or she pleads guilty or is found guilty. It has power to adjourn prior to passing sentence. The Crown Court's power to adjourn is one which it possesses at common law; a magistrates' court's power to do so is governed by MCA 1980. During the period of an adjournment before sentence, the offender is remanded in custody or on bail. He or she has a prima facie right to bail by reason of BA 1976, s. 4, but bail may be refused, not only on the grounds which apply before conviction as well, but also on the ground that the adjournment is for the purpose of preparing a report and it would be impracticable to do that if the offender were at liberty (see BA 1976, sch. 1, part I, para. 7). Where an offender remanded for reports is granted bail the court may, at its discretion, include a condition that he or she must be available for interview, etc. so that the report can be compiled (BA 1976, s. 3(6)(d)).

14.3.1 ADJOURNMENTS FOR REPORTS

Independent reports on offenders are often a vital factor in the sentencing decision, coming from sources such as probation officers and social workers producing pre-sentence reports, or from doctors and psychiatrists producing medical reports. Where an accused intimates an intention to plead guilty and it seems likely that the court will need reports before sentencing, they are prepared before the hearing if that is at all possible. If, however, the accused is pleading not guilty it is unlikely that reports will be prepared. Even if pleading guilty, reports are not prepared automatically. Sometimes the court can properly proceed without reports, but in many cases the sentencer's provisional view of the proper sentence will be such that to pass it without consulting a report would either be positively unlawful or at least bad sentencing practice. The court must then adjourn for reports. Two or three weeks will probably be sufficient, although the Crown Court could in theory adjourn for any period. Section 10(3) of MCA 1980 provides that when magistrates adjourn for reports it must be for not more than four weeks if the offender is remanded on bail, and not more than three weeks if he or she is in custody.

Section 10(3) of the MCA 1980, which applies to adjournments for any type of report, is supplemented by PCC(S)A 2000, s. 11, which applies only to medical reports. The main difference between the two sections is that under s. 11 the magistrates can adjourn for a medical report even before convicting the accused, provided they are satisfied that he or she committed the *actus reus* of the offence charged. This may enable them to make a *hospital* order without finding the accused guilty. Adjournments under s. 10(3) of the 1980 Act, on the other hand, presuppose that the magistrates have convicted the accused. In addition, provisions under ss. 35 and 36 of the Mental

Health Act (MHA) 1983, allow both the Crown Court and magistrates' courts to remand offenders to a hospital for the preparation of reports.

14.3.2 ADJOURNMENTS WHERE THERE ARE SEVERAL ACCUSED

Sentencing joint offenders together should ensure consistent treatment for them all, with any disparity in sentence being justified by the differing degrees to which they were involved in the criminal conduct or by differences in their records.

If there are consistent pleas between the accused there should be no problem. But, if one accused (A1) pleads guilty and another accused (A2) pleads not guilty, then difficulties arise. A2 obviously cannot be sentenced unless and until he or she is convicted by a jury. The desirability of dealing with A1 and (if convicted) A2 together has led to a general rule that sentence on A1 should be postponed until after the trial of A2. This has the additional advantage of allowing the judge to hear the evidence called at A2's trial, and proportion his or her sentence according to which, if either, of the accused apparently played the leading role in the offence(s) (see *R* v *Payne* [1950] 1 All ER 102).

However, a special problem arises if A1 is going to be called by the prosecution at the trial of A2, since he or she might be tempted to give false evidence minimising his or her own part in the crime. For this reason, it used to be the practice in such cases to depart from the general rule and sentence A1 before A2's trial (*R* v *Payne, supra*). More recently, the Court of Appeal has indicated strongly that the general rule should always be followed, notwithstanding that Al will be a prosecution witness (see *R* v *Weekes* (1982) 74 Cr App R 161). Perhaps, though, the matter should be left to the discretion of the trial judge, who is in the best position to balance the interests of the co-accused (that the accomplice, when he or she testifies, should have no motive for giving false evidence) against the wider interests of justice (that confederates in crime should be sentenced together so as to avoid unjustified differences in sentence).

If the accomplice is sentenced before testifying for the prosecution, defence counsel in mitigation may outline the evidence his or her client proposes to give. This will no doubt secure a significant reduction in sentence. Should the accomplice fail to give the evidence thus foreshadowed, his or her sentence may *not* be increased (*R* v *Stone* [1970] 1 WLR 1112).

The desirability of sentencing confederates in crime together applies when they are to be dealt with in the magistrates' court just as much as when they are to be dealt with in the Crown Court.

14.3.3 ADJOURNMENTS WHERE THERE ARE OUTSTANDING CHARGES

It is desirable that an accused with several charges outstanding against him or her should be sentenced on one occasion for all matters in respect of which he or she is ultimately convicted. If he or she is sentenced piecemeal by different judges (or even by the same judge on different occasions) there is a danger that the aggregate sentence will be out of proportion to the overall gravity of his or her conduct. There is also a danger that the first judge, dealing perhaps with the less serious offences, will pass a non-custodial sentence and thus create a dilemma for the second judge. The latter may feel that a custodial sentence is necessary for the offences with which he or she is dealing, but to pass such a sentence might prevent the earlier non-custodial sentence running its natural course. To avoid such difficulties, it is better that one sentencer should deal with everything on one occasion, even if this means adjournments and some extra administrative work behind the scenes.

Much will depend on whether or not the offences have been joined in the indictment, under r. 9 of the Indictment Rules 1971. A court and jury can try only one indictment at a time, so sentence on one indictment where the accused is found guilty may have to be postponed until trial of a second indictment. Furthermore, where an accused has indictments outstanding against him or her at different locations of the Crown Court, it will be necessary for one location to transfer its indictment to the second location (see *R* v *Bennett* (1980) 2 Cr App R (S) 96).

14.4 The Facts of the Offences

If the accused pleads guilty, the first stage in the procedure (before sentence is passed) is for the prosecution to present the brief facts of the offence. In the Crown Court this is always the task of counsel, or solicitor with rights of audience in the Crown Court, for the prosecution must be legally represented for proceedings on indictment (*R* v *George Maxwell Developments Ltd* [1980] 2 All ER 99).

In the magistrates' court, the prosecution case will be presented by a Crown Prosecutor (or by an agent instructed by the CPS). The procedure before sentence is passed is essentially the same in both the Crown Court and magistrates' courts, but it is less formal in the latter.

14.4.1 PRESENTING THE FACTS

The prosecuting advocate in the Crown Court has the benefit of the statements from the committal proceedings. Counsel summarises the prosecution case based on these statements. He or she will probably describe in sequence: (i) the circumstances, method and gravity of the offence; (ii) the manner in which the offender was arrested; and (iii) his or her questioning at the police station.

Concerning the advocate's account of the offence itself, details which should be included will obviously vary according to the nature of the offence. The degree of planning which apparently preceded the commission of the offence is always a relevant factor, as is any other aggravating factor, e.g. breach of trust in an offence involving dishonesty committed by an employee against his or her employer.

As to the arrest and questioning of the offender, the judge will want to know whether the offender was frank and cooperative with the police. If he or she was, that is useful mitigation. Also, what the offender said to the police may foreshadow what defence counsel will say in his or her speech in mitigation about the way the offence was committed, the motive for it, and the offender's degree of involvement in it if it was a joint offence. Where the offender followed up verbal admissions by making a written statement under caution, the advocate can either read it out in full or give the gist of it, whichever seems more convenient.

When presenting the facts, the prosecuting advocate should not try to make the offence seem as serious as possible so as to obtain a heavy sentence. Traditionally, the prosecution has taken a neutral attitude to the sentence which ought to be passed, not asking for any particular sentence. So, the advocate must present the facts fairly in the light of the prosecution evidence contained in the committal statements, conceding to the defence those points in mitigation which are apparent from the statements, but equally giving full weight to any aggravating factors which make the offence a serious one of its type. In particular, if the offender (in his or her statements to the police) or defence advocate (in mitigation) puts forward a version of the facts of the offence which does not accord with the evidence the prosecution has available, the advocate should indicate that he or she cannot accept what the defence is saying about the offence.

Two further points should be made:

(a) Prosecuting advocate should apply for compensation, confiscation or forfeiture if appropriate.

(b) Both prosecuting and defence advocates should draw the court's attention to any limits on its sentencing powers (*R* v *Komsta* [1990] 12 Cr App R (S) 63). In addition, prosecuting advocate should also mention guideline cases (*R* v *Panayioutou* [1989] 11 Cr App R (S) 535. See also *R* v *Hartrey* (1993) 14 Cr App R (S) 507.

It is appropriate for the judge to receive factual information (not expressed in colourful or emotive language) as to the effect of the offence on the victim. Such information should be in proper form, e.g. a witness statement which can then be served on the defence and form part of the judge's papers relating to the case (*Attorney-General's Reference (No. 2 of 1995)* [1996] 1 Cr App R (S) 274).

14.4.2 DISPUTES ABOUT THE FACTS AFTER A GUILTY PLEA

By pleading guilty an offender does not necessarily concede that the prosecution case against him or her is correct in its entirety. He or she admits, of course, that he or she committed the offence described in each of the counts of the indictment to which he or she enters a guilty plea, and if the defence advocate says anything in mitigation which is inconsistent with the pleas the judge will ignore that part of the mitigation or invite the defence to consider a change of plea. But the particulars about an offence given in a count of an indictment are so basic that they only partially reveal whether the offence is a serious or trivial one of its type. Thus, it occasionally happens that an offender quite properly pleads guilty and then, after the facts have been presented by the prosecuting advocate, denies that his or her crime was as grave as has been alleged. However, the sentence can be significantly affected by whether the judge accepts the prosecution statement of facts or the defence mitigation.

Guidance in these circumstances is given by *R* v *Newton* (1982) 77 Cr App R 13, followed in *R* v *Costley* (1989) 11 Cr App R (S) 357. After the guilty plea, the judge may either:

(a) hear whatever evidence the parties wish to call on the disputed issue, and come down on one side or the other (this is usually referred to as a '*Newton* hearing'); or

(b) act merely on the basis of counsels' respective submissions, in which case he or she must accept the defence version as far as possible; or

(c) empanel a jury to decide the issue. In such a case a count will be added to the indictment by way of amendment and a trial on that count will ensue.

There have been a considerable number of cases on this area since the case of *R* v *Newton*, and the cases considered below are merely an example of the issues which have arisen. Students are referred to *Blackstone's Criminal Practice*, 2000, from D17.5 for a full discussion.

Defence solicitor and counsel have a duty to notify the Crown that a guilty plea will be put forward, but that the prosecution version of the facts would be contested, so that the prosecution could ensure the presence of any necessary witnesses, to enable a *Newton* hearing to proceed (*R* v *Mohun* [1992] Crim LR 598, CA; *R* v *Gardener* [1994] Crim LR 301).

When the judge conducts a *Newton* hearing, the rules of evidence should be strictly followed, and the judge should give himself or herself the same directions which he or she would give to a jury, for example, in accordance with the guidelines in *Turnbull* (*R* v *Gandy* (1989) 11 Cr App R (S) 564). Further he or she should openly direct himself or herself that the facts have to be proved to the criminal standard, though failure to do so will not necessarily be fatal (*R* v *Kerrigan* (1992) 156 JP 889, CA).

It is not right, on a *Newton* hearing, to sentence the defendant on the basis of a more serious offence than charged. In *R* v *Druce* (1993) 14 Cr App R (S) 691, CA, the prosecution alleged rape although the charges were unlawful sexual intercourse and indecent assault. The Court of Appeal held that if that was the prosecution case, he should have been so charged. The judge had no alternative but to deal with the case by giving the defendant the benefit of the doubt, and proceed on the basis that the complainant had consented (cf. *R* v *Nottingham Crown Court, ex parte DPP* [1995] Crim LR 902).

It should be noted that the defence cannot frustrate the *Newton* inquiry procedure by declining to give evidence. In these circumstances, where the basic facts are not in dispute, the judge is entitled to draw inferences from these undisputed facts (*R* v *Mirza* (1992) 14 Cr App R (S) 64, CA).

Where the alleged facts relied upon by the offender to reduce the gravity of the offence are exclusively within his or her knowledge, so that the prosecution cannot reasonably be expected to call evidence in rebuttal, the judge is entitled to reject the offender's evidence of what happened as unbelievable, notwithstanding that it is the only evidence there is (*R* v *Kerr* (1980) 2 Cr App R (S) 54); and see *R* v *Hawkins* (1985) 7 Cr App R (S) 351 where it was said that the judge is entitled to reject the defence version without hearing evidence if the story is 'incredible'.

Occasionally, a defendant will decide to change his or her plea halfway through the trial, after at least some evidence has been given for the prosecution. In these circumstances, the judge should hear evidence from the defendant and then decide upon the version of facts upon which he or she is going to sentence, forming his or her view on the whole of the evidence which was given. See *R* v *Mottram* [1981] 3 Cr App R (S) 123 and *R* v *Archer* [1994] Crim LR 80.

Section 80(2)(b) of the PCC(S)A 2000 provides for the imposition of longer than normal sentences where the offence is of a violent or sexual nature and the court is of the opinion that it is necessary in order to protect the public from harm from the offender. In such a situation, the court must hold a *Newton* hearing to resolve any important issue relevant to sentence. See *R* v *Oudkerk* [1994] Crim LR 700.

Credit should be given for a plea of guilty, since court time has been saved, even if the judge rejects the version of the facts put forward by the defendant, taking the view that the plea was put forward on a false basis: *R* v *Williams* (1990) 12 Cr App R (S) 415.

If the judge wrongly fails to hold a *Newton* hearing, the Court of Appeal, may vary the sentence to one which is appropriate on the basis that the defendant's version of events is correct (*R* v *Mohun* (1993) 14 Cr App R (S) 5).

See *R* v *Cranston* (1993) 14 Cr App R (S) 103, CA, for a recent example and note that further guidance has been provided by the Court of Appeal in *R* v *Beswick* (1996) 160 JP 33. See **9.15** and *R* v *Tolera* [1999] 1 Cr App R (S) 25 where the Court of Appeal clarified the practice to be followed where the defendant pleaded guilty but sought to be sentenced on a factual basis other than that which was advanced by the prosecution.

14.4.3 DISPUTES ABOUT THE FACTS AFTER A VERDICT OF NOT GUILTY

Post-conviction disputes about the circumstances of the offence are not limited to cases where the offender pleaded guilty, for a jury's verdict of guilty after a not guilty plea is not necessarily a total vindication of the prosecution's case. In such cases it is for the judge to form a personal view of the evidence adduced before the jury, and decide what the facts of the offence were. He or she should not ask the jury the reasons for its verdict or what facts it found proved (*per* Humphreys J in *R* v *Larkin* [1943] KB 174, although that case recognised an exception to the rule where the jury finds the accused not guilty of murder but guilty of manslaughter, and may be asked whether the verdict was on the basis of provocation, diminished responsibility or something else). The judge is not obliged to adopt as a basis for sentencing the least serious version of events consistent with the jury's verdict (*R* v *Solomon* (1984) 6 Cr App R (S) 120), but should be 'extremely astute' to give the benefit of any doubt to the offender (*per* Watkins LJ in *R* v *Stosiek* (1982) 4 Cr App R (S) 205). In *R* v *Wood* (1991) 13 Cr App R (S) 207, the Court of Appeal said that it would only interfere with the finding of fact by a judge after hearing evidence in exceptional circumstances.

The view the judge takes of the facts must naturally be consistent with the jury's verdict. Thus, if the jury refuses to find the accused guilty as charged but only convicts him or her of a lesser offence, the sentence must be appropriate to the lesser offence, notwithstanding that the judge is convinced there should have been a conviction for the more serious offence (*R* v *Hazelwood* (1984) 6 Cr App R (S) 52 and *R* v *Dowdall* (1992) 13 Cr App R (S) 441, CA).

14.5 Character and Antecedents Evidence

After the prosecution summary of the facts or (in the case of a not guilty plea) immediately after the guilty verdict, the Crown Prosecutor in the magistrates' court or prosecuting counsel in the Crown Court provides the court with information about the character and antecedents of the offender. Information about the character of the offender will be wholly or principally concerned with the matter of his or her previous convictions, if any. Information about antecedents deals with his or her general background and circumstances.

14.5.1 THE ANTECEDENTS

The *Practice Direction (Crime: Antecedents) (No. 2)* [1997] 1 WLR 1482 sets out the procedure for the provision of antecedents in magistrates' and Crown Courts.

Antecedent evidence is usually provided by prosecution counsel, provided that defence counsel has agreed that they are not in dispute.

Should the defence challenge anything in the antecedents, the antecedents officer and any other witnesses may have to be called, as the prosecution is expected to provide proper proof of what it has alleged, i.e. evidence of a type which would be admissible in a trial of a not guilty plea. If it fails to provide such proof, the judge should ignore the challenged allegation, and state that he or she is ignoring it (*R* v *Campbell* (1911) 6 Cr App R 131). It follows that where the prosecution does not have proper proof of an allegation prejudicial to the offender, it should not make the allegation in the first place (see *R* v *Van Pelz* [1943] KB 157 and *R* v *Wilkins* (1977) 66 Cr App R 49). Where the prosecution does propose to adduce first-hand antecedents evidence of a factual nature, but it realises that the facts may well be challenged by the defence, it should give notice of the proposed evidence (*R* v *Robinson* (1969) 53 Cr App R 314). It is not entirely clear whether the prosecution is ever entitled to refer to the offender as having criminal associates. In *R* v *Bibby* [1972] Crim LR 513 it was held that it was unfair of the antecedents officer to say that B mixed with criminals, but in *R* v *Crabtree* [1952] 2 All ER 974 Lord Goddard CJ held such evidence to be acceptable provided the officer could speak from his personal knowledge. In the light of these cases the safest rule for a police officer giving antecedents evidence must be to restrict himself or herself to what is on the antecedents form, and not start making additional allegations likely to be disputed by the defence.

14.5.2 PREVIOUS CONVICTIONS

Section 151(1) of the PCC(S)A 2000 provides that when considering the seriousness of any offence, the court may take into account any previous convictions or any failure of the offender to respond to previous sentences. Prosecutors therefore make available to the court a list of any previous convictions of the offender in accordance with the 1997 Practice Direction on the provision of antecedents.

14.5.3 SPENT CONVICTIONS

The Rehabilitation of Offenders Act 1974 (ROA) was passed with the aim of helping criminals who had decided to 'go straight' to live down their past. Its main effect is that, once a certain time (the 'rehabilitation period') has elapsed from the date of an offender's conviction, the conviction becomes spent and the offender, in respect of that conviction, is a rehabilitated person. As a rehabilitated person he or she is, for most purposes, treated as if he or she had never committed or been convicted of the offence.

Whether a conviction is capable of becoming spent depends upon the length of the sentence imposed for the offence. The length of the sentence, assuming that it is within the limit, also governs the length of the rehabilitation period.

Section 7 of ROA 1974 provides that the ban on revealing or asking questions about spent convictions does *not* apply in criminal proceedings. But Lord Widgery CJ, in *Practice Direction (Crime: Spent Convictions)* [1975] 1 WLR 1065, stated that neither judge nor counsel should refer to a spent conviction where 'such reference can be reasonably avoided'. Mention of a spent conviction always requires the judge's authority, that authority being given only where the interests of justice so require. At the sentencing stage, the list of previous convictions given to the court should mark those which are spent. When passing sentence the judge should say nothing about spent convictions unless it is vital to do so to explain the penalty he or she has decided upon.

14.5.4 DEFENCE QUESTIONS

If a police officer has testified about the offender's antecedents and previous convictions, defence counsel can ask him or her questions. The questioning is unlikely to be hostile in nature, but counsel might wish to confirm that his or her client was cooperative when questioned about the offence or that he or she showed signs of genuine remorse. If there has been a change in the offender's circumstances since the antecedents were prepared the officer can be asked if he or she knows anything about that. Upon the officer leaving the witness box the prosecution case is closed.

14.6 Reports

After information as to the character and antecedents has been presented to the court the judge — if he or she has not already done so before court — reads any reports which have been prepared about the offender. Sometimes sentence may properly be passed without the benefit of reports, but there are many occasions when the court must have them either because there is a statutory provision to that effect or because good sentencing practice demands it.

14.6.1 THE NECESSITY FOR PRE-SENTENCE REPORTS

A pre-sentence report is defined by s. 162 of the PCC(S)A 2000 as a report in writing which is made or submitted by a probation officer or social worker or member of a youth offending team with a view to assisting the court to reach the most suitable method of dealing with the offender, and contains such information as may be specified by the Secretary of State.

Under s. 81(1) of PCC(S)A 2000, when a court is forming any necessary opinion under s. 79(2) or s. 80(2) of that Act (whether a custodial sentence should be imposed and the length of that order) the court is under a duty to obtain and consider a pre-sentence report. Section 81(1) does not apply, however, if the offender is aged 18 or over, and in the circumstances of the case, the court is of the opinion that it is unnecessary to obtain a pre-sentence report (s. 81(2)). This would apply where the sentence was clear, and the report would, in practice, make no difference.

Failure to obtain a report does not invalidate a sentence, but any court sitting on appeal against sentence must obtain one and consider it, unless it is of the opinion that it is unnecessary (s. 81(5) and (6)).

Where the offender is aged under 18, by virtue of s. 81(3), the court must obtain and consider a report unless either:

(a) the offence is triable only on indictment, and the court is of the opinion that it is unnecessary to obtain one; or

(b) there already exists a report, and the court has considered the information. If more than one report exists, the court should consider the most recent.

When making any of the following orders, the court, under s. 36, is under a duty to obtain and consider a pre-sentence report, unless it considers it unnecessary (s. 36(5)):

(a) a probation order which includes additional requirements authorised by the PCC(S)A 2000, sch. 2;

(b) a community service order;

(c) a combination order;

(d) a drug treatment and testing order; and

(e) a supervision order which includes requirements authorised by sch. 6.

Section 36 contains provisions relating to failure to obtain a report, and offenders under 18 which are parallel to those in s. 81 above.

A probation officer writing a report will draw upon many sources. Of prime importance is the interview with the accused. He or she may also visit the accused's home and speak with members of the family. With permission, he or she might talk to the accused's employer, although great care would obviously have to be taken not to jeopardise continued employment. He or she will also have access to background sources of information such as police antecedents and any records the probation service has of previous contact with the accused. If the accused has recently been released from a custodial sentence, the probation officer could consult the authorities at the relevant establishment to see what effect the sentence apparently had on him or her. Where medical or psychiatric reasons seem to have contributed to the offence, assistance might be sought from the accused's doctor, and the report might suggest the preparation of full medical reports.

14.6.2 CONTENTS OF A PRE-SENTENCE REPORT

By s. 162(1) and (2) a pre-sentence report is defined as a report in writing which:

(a) with a view to assisting the court in determining the most suitable method of dealing with an offender, is made or submitted by a probation officer or by a social worker of a local authority social services department or a member of a youth offending team; and

(b) contains information as to such matters, presented in such manner, as may be prescribed by rules made by the Secretary of State.

In the White Paper (para. 3.10 and 11) the Government outlined the purpose of the pre-sentence report:

> The purpose of requiring the courts to consider a report by the probation service when a custodial sentence is contemplated will be to provide the court with detailed information about how the offender could be punished in the community, so that option can be fully considered. Its purpose will not be to make recommendations about sentencing or to be a plea in mitigation.

In addition, the Green Paper entitled 'Punishment and Supervision in the Community' described (at para. 9.6) what such a report should contain:

> The reports should include: information about the offence and the offender's attitude towards it, background information about the offender, an assessment of the offender's ability and willingness to stop committing crimes, and a detailed programme of supervision to achieve this. Preparing a report of this sort needs skill in assessing the likely outcome of various sentencing options; these assessments can be made only against a background of detailed knowledge about court practice, about the resources available for supervising offenders together with knowledge and

understanding of offending; judgements involving issues of public safety have to be made; and those preparing the reports exercise their discretion in ways which can have serious and lasting consequences for offenders under sentence.

The report does not contain a recommendation, made by the probation officer or social worker involved, as to the appropriate sentence. On the other hand, the contents of reports will need to reflect a clear understanding of sentencing principles and practice. Reports have to deal with the various factors in the commission of the crime that may or may not make it 'serious' for purposes of s. 79(2)(a).

Pre-sentence reports are discussed in detail in **Chapter 17**.

14.6.3 THE PRESENTATION OF PRE-SENTENCE REPORTS

A representative of the probation service should always be available at court to hand in reports and assist the court in any other way he or she can (e.g. by interviewing an offender so as to bring an old report up to date). Unless required to do so by the defence, the probation officer who prepared a report need not attend when its subject appears to be sentenced, although may choose to do so if, for instance, the offence was committed while on probation. Such a practice is confirmed by s. 162(1) which indicates that the report is 'made or submitted' by a probation officer, social worker or member of a youth offending team. The report would then be presented by a liaison officer. It is clear from s. 162(1) that the pre-sentence reports must be in writing. This ends the occasional practice of probation officers or social workers giving their report orally in court.

A copy of the report must be given to the offender or his or her legal representative, except that in cases of unrepresented juveniles it should be given to their parents (PCC(S)A 2000, s. 156(3)). It is considered bad practice to read out the whole of a pre-sentence report in open court since it may well contain matters which, in the offender's best interests, should not be publicly emphasised. The defence, in mitigation, may, however, refer the sentencer to passages in the report or perhaps read isolated sentences which are especially favourable. The defence can challenge allegations made in the report by requiring the probation officer concerned to attend for questioning in open court.

Particular care must be taken where the allegations in the report contain an admission of the full facts of the offence, not formally accepted in court. In *R* v *Cunnah* [1996] 1 Cr App R (S) 393, the report contained details of the defendant's admission to the full seriousness of the offences as alleged by the victims, but pleas of guilty had been accepted by the prosecution on a more limited basis. There was no discussion of the implications of this with counsel and, on appeal, the sentence was reduced to the level which was appropriate to the pleas given and accepted.

14.6.4 OTHER REPORTS

In addition to pre-sentence reports, the court may be assisted by the following types of report:

(a) *Medical reports* These may be on the offender's physical condition or on his or her mental condition or on both. If an offender is remanded on bail, it may be made a condition of bail that he or she attend a hospital, etc. for the preparation of medical reports (see BA 1976, s. 3(6)(d) and PCC(S)A 2000, s. 11(3)). If remanded in custody, he or she may be examined by the prison medical officers. Also, there is now the possibility under the Mental Health Act (MHA) 1983 of a remand to a mental hospital for reports in cases where the court is considering a hospital order under s. 37 of the MHA 1983. A hospital order can only be made on the basis of reports from two doctors, one of whom must be a psychiatrist.

A copy of a report on an offender's mental condition must be given to his or her counsel or solicitor, but the offender personally is not entitled to a copy. If unrepresented, he or she should be told the gist of what is in the report (MHA 1983, s. 54(3)). The psychiatrist who prepared the report may be required to attend court to give oral evidence.

(b) *Reports on juveniles* Having found a juvenile guilty, the youth court sometimes remands him or her to local authority accommodation for two or three weeks so that a detailed report can be prepared. Such a report will deal with intelligence, aptitudes, attitudes to those in authority, relationships with peers and many other matters. The school he or she attends (or fails to attend) may also submit a report, together with a record of attendance.

(c) *Remand centre reports* There is nothing to stop the court adjourning for a remand centre report on a young offender (under the age of 21), if it considers that that would be helpful. Generally, reports on the behaviour of offenders held at custodial institutions are more likely to be prepared for the assistance of the Court of Appeal than for sentencers at first instance. In determining an appeal against a custodial sentence, the Court of Appeal is quite often given information about the appellant's progress in prison, young offender institution, or whatever, during the period between the passing of the sentence and the hearing of the appeal.

14.7 Defence Mitigation

After the judge has read the reports the defence has the opportunity to present mitigation on behalf of the offender. If he or she wishes, defence counsel may call character witnesses. The offender personally will not be called unless either there is a dispute about the facts of the offence, or it is a road traffic case and he or she would be liable to mandatory disqualification unless he or she can show special reasons for not disqualifying. In most cases there will not be any character witnesses, and defence counsel will proceed immediately to make a plea in mitigation. (See ***Advocacy Manual.***)

There is no set pattern for mitigation, and what ought to be said will obviously vary from case to case. However, a plea in mitigation will usually include a discussion of the facts of the offence, the circumstances which led up to it, and the offender's personal circumstances. As regards the potential sentence, one possible approach is to discuss all the available sentences, explaining why they would not be appropriate in this case, concluding with the sentence that is thought appropriate. However, counsel should bear in mind the seriousness of the offence in deciding what is appropriate. If the offence is so serious that only a custodial sentence would be justified, the judge's patience should not be tried by discussing non-custodial sentences at length. Conversely, counsel will look foolish if he or she virtually concedes that the offender must go to prison, and then the judge imposes a community sentence.

The fact that the defendant has pleaded guilty has always been seen as an important point in mitigation, and has been said to reduce the sentence by as much as a third. Section 152 of the PCC(S)A 2000 provides as follows:

> *(1) In determining what sentence to pass on an offender who has pleaded guilty to an offence in proceedings before that or another court, a court shall take into account—*
>
> *(a) the stage in the proceedings for the offence at which the offender indicated his intention to plead guilty, and*
>
> *(b) the circumstances in which this indication was given.*
>
> *(2) If, as a result of taking into account any matter referred to in subsection (1) above, the court imposes a punishment on the offender which is less severe than the punishment it would otherwise have imposed, it shall state in open court that it has done so.*

It should be noted, however, that the section does not go on to provide that failure to comply invalidates the sentence.

Other matters which are generally accepted as being good mitigation include the youth of the offender or his or her age; previous good character; that the offender had assisted the police; that the offender has expressed genuine remorse or made attempts to compensate the victim; that the offender was under some sort of particular stress at the time of the offence; and the potential effect on the offender's family in the event, for example, of a custodial sentence. For a more detailed discussion on mitigation, see the later chapters of this Manual, and the ***Advocacy Manual***.

One important point to bear in mind is that counsel almost always has the most up-to-date information on the offender. The antecedents are taken at the time of the arrest, which may have been some considerable time before the trial, and in any event are only an outline of the offender's circumstances. There is not always a pre-sentence report, and even if there is, it may also be out of date, or not contain the information that is required. Consequently, courts are increasingly looking to counsel to provide accurate, detailed, up-to-date information concerning the offender.

The Code of Conduct of the Bar, para. 610(e), provides that defence counsel must not make statements or ask questions which are merely scandalous or intended or calculated only to vilify, insult or annoy. If defence asserts facts which the prosecution dispute, this should be drawn to the attention of the defence, and if necessary a *Newton* hearing will be held.

CPIA 1996, ss. 58–61, allow the judge to impose reporting restrictions where, under s. 58(4), there are substantial grounds for believing that:

(a) the assertion is derogatory to a person's character, and

(b) the assertion is false or irrelevant to sentence.

Any order made will not apply to an assertion previously made at trial or during any other proceedings relating to the offence (s. 58(5)).

The order may be revoked by the court and if not so revoked will cease to have effect after a period of a year (s. 58(8)).

It is an offence to publish material in breach of an order under s. 58, the sentence being a fine on summary conviction not exceeding level 5 on the standard scale.

Sometimes, when counsel has concluded his or her mitigation, the judge asks the offender whether he or she personally has anything to say. After that it is for the judge to pronounce sentence.

14.8 Pronouncing Sentence

A Crown Court judge sitting alone will normally pronounce sentence immediately after defence mitigation (or after giving the offender the opportunity to make a personal statement). If he or she is sitting with lay magistrates and the decision is a difficult one, they sometimes retire to consider it. Similarly, a lay bench of magistrates may wish to retire to consider sentence, and they may also ask their clerk to retire with them to advise on their sentencing powers. In the magistrates' court, the decision on sentence may be taken by a majority but it is pronounced by the chairman of the bench.

Crown Court judges are encouraged to give their reasons for deciding upon a particular sentence. They should certainly give reasons when the sentence prima facie seems a severe one in the circumstances of the case (see *R* v *Newman* (1979) 1 Cr App R (S) 252 and ss. 79(4) and 80(3) of the PCC(S)A 2000). The reasons will be brief and couched in language which the offender may be expected to understand. The judge might say why he or she could not follow a proposal in the pre-sentence report that the offender be given a non-custodial sentence; or, if he or she does pass a non-custodial sentence, the offender might be warned that this really is a last chance and if he or she offends again the penalty will be severe; or, where the offender is going to prison for the first time after a series of convictions which were dealt with by other means, he or she could be told that he or she still has time to reform but if he or she does not learn his or her lesson now he or she is in danger of becoming an habitual criminal who will spend half his or her life in prison. Occasionally the judge's comments on passing sentence get him or her into trouble. It may be evident that he or she has taken irrelevant matters into account, and for that reason passed a sentence which is more severe than would otherwise have been passed. The Court of Appeal is then likely to reduce the sentence, even if it was a proper sentence in itself.

In a few cases, statute obliges the court to give reasons for its decisions. For instance, both the magistrates and the Crown Court must explain a decision not to activate a suspended sentence if they are dealing with an offender who is in breach of such a sentence. In other cases (notably the making of a probation order with a requirement for treatment for mental disorder or for treatment for drug or alcohol dependency) the offender's willingness to comply with such requirement must be sought by the court. In yet other cases (e.g. suspended sentences) the effect of the sentence must be explained to him or her by the court. See the later chapters of this Manual for details.

The Crown Court may vary or rescind a sentence within 28 days of its being passed (if the offender was jointly indicted with other accused the period is 56 days from the passing of the sentence or 28 days from the conclusion of the joint trial, whichever expires sooner). The variation must be made by the Crown Court judge who originally passed the sentence, but if he or she was then sitting with lay justices they need not be present for the variation. It is clear that the power to vary may be used to correct technical errors in the original sentence or to alter it in the offender's favour. The extent to which a sentence may be fundamentally varied to the offender's detriment is unclear. The Crown Court's power to vary sentence is now contained in s. 155 of the PCC(S)A 2000.

Once the statutory period for variation has expired a court may *not* vary its sentence even if, through inadvertence, it failed to consider including in the sentence an order which really ought to have been included.

Magistrates' courts may also vary or rescind a sentence at any time if it is considered to be in the interest of justice to do so (MCA 1980, s. 142) (see **5.1.1**).

14.9 Taking Other Offences into Consideration

An offender is sentenced for the offences to which he or she pleads guilty or of which he or she is found guilty. In deciding on sentence, the judge or magistrates must not be influenced by any circumstances which lead them to think that the offender may also have committed other offences with which he or she has not been charged (e.g. *R* v *Courtie* [1984] AC 463). There is one major exception to this rule, namely the practice of taking other offences into consideration.

Other offences taken into consideration when sentence is passed (or 't.i.c.'s as they are colloquially known) are offences of which the offender is never convicted, but which are admitted by him or her in court and, at his or her request, are borne in mind by the judge when passing sentence for the offences in respect of which there is a conviction ('conviction offences'). The sequence of events leading up to offences being 't.i.c.'ed will vary from case to case. Typically it will involve a suspect who has been arrested on suspicion of one or more crimes, admitting at the police station that he or she committed those crimes, and making it obvious that he or she is going to plead guilty. The police may then ask him or her about other similar offences which they believe he or she may have committed, but which, in the absence of an admission from him or her, they will find it difficult to prove. Since he or she is resigned to having to plead guilty to the offences for which he or she was arrested, the suspect often decides to make a clean breast of everything on the understanding that some or all the offences he or she is now being asked about will not be the subject of separate charges but will merely be taken into consideration. A list is then drawn up of the offences to be 't.i.c.'ed and the suspect signs the list. The offences for which he or she was arrested and with which he or she was charged are then prosecuted in the normal way, and, if the matter is to be dealt with in the Crown Court, appear as counts on the indictment. He or she duly pleads guilty. Then at some convenient stage during the procedure before sentence is passed, prosecuting counsel mentions to the judge that the offender wants other matters considered. The judge is handed the list of offences signed by the offender at the police station, and he or she (or the court clerk) asks whether he or she admits committing them and whether he or she wants them taken into consideration. Assuming the offender answers 'yes' to both questions, the judge may, at his or her discretion, comply with the request. Prosecuting counsel should be in a position to give the judge brief details of the nature of the offences. The sentence the judge eventually passes for the conviction offences will no doubt be somewhat more severe than it would have been in the absence of 't.i.c.'s, but the addition to the sentence will almost certainly not be as great as the penalty for the offences would have been had they been prosecuted separately. Thus, the system of taking offences into consideration has advantages for offenders. It also has advantages for the police, because they clear up offences which might otherwise have remained unsolved. This is why the system flourishes even though it has no solid basis in law.

The following points about taking offences into consideration should be noted:

(a) The sentence the court may pass is restricted to the maximum permissible for the offence(s) of which the offender has been convicted. This does not in practice deter the courts from 't.i.c.'ing offences because maximum penalties are usually far higher than a sentencer would wish to impose even for a grave instance of the offence in question. It is thus possible to add something to the sentence to reflect the 't.i.c.'s without exceeding the maximum penalty.

(b) Which offences to charge and which to refrain from charging in anticipation of their eventually being taken into consideration is essentially a matter for the police and the prosecution. Sometimes the most serious offences are charged and later appear on the indictment, while other less grave but broadly similar crimes are taken into consideration. Or perhaps the most recent offences will be charged and the remainder 't.i.c.'ed. On occasions, the 't.i.c.'s vastly outnumber the conviction offences (see, e.g., *R* v *Sequeira* (1982) 4 Cr App R (S) 65).

(c) Offences should not be taken into consideration unless the offender clearly requests the sentencer to do so. The offender should also admit in open court that he or she committed the offences (R v *Griffiths* (1932) 23 Cr App R 153). It is not, however, necessary to put the particulars of each offence to him or her one by one. Usually the offender is asked whether he or she signed at the police station the list of other offences, whether he or she admits committing those offences, and whether he or she wants them considered.

(d) Since the taking of an offence into consideration does not, as a matter of strict law, amount to a conviction, the offender is unable to bar a subsequent prosecution for the offence by reliance on a plea of *autrefois convict* (*R* v *Nicholson* [1947] 2 All ER 535). However, the police do not in practice prosecute for matters which have already been 't.i.c.'ed because to do so would undermine a system which they themselves find very convenient. If a prosecution were to be brought, the court would almost certainly pass a nominal sentence such as an absolute discharge.

(e) Although the 't.i.c.' system is geared to offenders pleading guilty, there is nothing to stop the prosecution using a short adjournment after the accused has been found guilty on a not guilty plea to ask him or her whether, given the outcome of the trial, he or she would now like other offences considered.

(f) The court is not obliged to comply with a request to take offences into consideration. It is generally bad practice to 't.i.c.' offences of a different type from the conviction offences, and the court should never consider offences which carry endorsement of the driving licence and disqualification if the conviction offences are not so punishable (*R* v *Collins* [1947] KB 560). The reason for this is that taking endorsable offences into consideration will not entitle the court to endorse the licence/disqualify if the conviction offences are non-endorsable, whereas if the offences are prosecuted in the normal way endorsement would be virtually certain and disqualification a possibility.

(g) The practice of taking offences into consideration is as common in the magistrates' courts as it is in the Crown Court. However, magistrates should not 't.i.c.' offences which are triable only on indictment (see *R* v *Simons* [1953] 1 WLR 1014).

(h) The court should state when passing sentence how many other offences it has taken into consideration.

14.10 Sample Offences

From time to time, the prosecution may invite the judge to treat the offences on which he or she is now passing sentence as samples of a continuing course of conduct over a period of time. This is a convenient way of proceeding if the offences are numerous and were committed over a long period. It would be possible to include all the offences as t.i.c.'s but this may result in an over-long list, as in *R* v *Sequeira* (1982) 4 Cr App R (S) 65, where the defendant admitted 150 offences.

The problem for the court is how such sample offences should be sentenced. Recent authorities take the view that the defendant should not be sentenced for offences for which he or she has not pleaded guilty or been found guilty. Thus the fact that the offences are described as 'specimens' does not entitle the court to sentence him or her as if he or she had been found guilty of offences not included in the indictment (*R* v *Burfoot* (1990) 12 Cr App R (S) 252), unless the offender admitted them (*R* v *Clark* [1996] 2 Cr App R (S) 351 and *R* v *Canavan* [1998] 1 Cr App R 79). Previous authority to the contrary (*R* v *Mills* (1979) 68 Cr App R 154; *R* v *Singh* (1981) 3 Cr App R (S) 90 and *R* v *Bradshaw* [1997] 2 Cr App R (S) 128) was rejected.

Two further points should be made:

(a) Prosecutors should ensure that offenders are charged with sufficient offences to reflect the overall criminality involved.

(b) PCC(S)A 2000, s. 80(2)(a), provides that the sentence shall be 'commensurate with the seriousness of the offence, or the combination of the offence and one or more offences associated with it'. Included in the definition of an associated offence is where the offender has admitted the offence and 'requests the court to take it into consideration in sentencing him for that offence' (s. 161). It would seem that the court is therefore precluded from sentencing on any other offences.

14.11 Legal Representation

The offender can, of course, represent himself or herself if he or she so wishes, and present his or her own mitigation. If the offence is a trivial one, for which he or she is obviously only going to be fined, he or she would be well advised not to employ a lawyer because his or her solicitor's bill will exceed any slight reduction in the fine which might be achieved by eloquent mitigation. In more serious cases, especially where the offender's liberty is at stake, legal representation is desirable.

Legal representation not only assists the offender but it should assist the court, in that the lawyer can clarify the issues, highlight those matters which are in the offender's favour and remind the judge that although the offender might qualify for a custodial sentence, the court is still under a duty to consider whether such sentence is appropriate having regard to the mitigating factors available and relevant to the offender (see *R* v *Cox* [1993] 1 WLR 188). The court will not want to resort to the drastic expedient of prison unless there is really no alternative. The same applies whenever a custodial sentence of any description is contemplated for a young offender. So, in these types of cases the offender is not merely allowed to have legal representation, but is positively encouraged to have it by the grant of the right to funded representation as part of the Criminal Defence Service.

The general effect of the relevant legislation is that, when dealing with an offender who is not legally represented in court, the court *must* give him or her an opportunity to apply for funded representation before doing any of the following:

(a) Passing a sentence of imprisonment if the offender has never previously been sentenced to imprisonment (PCC(S)A 2000, s. 83(1)).

(b) Passing a sentence of detention in a young offender institution, custody for life, detention during Her Majesty's pleasure or making a detention and training order (PCC(S)A 2000, s. 83(2)).

(c) Making an order for detention under PCC(S)A 2000, s. 91.

Situation (a) above applies both to the passing of an immediate sentence of imprisonment and to the passing of a suspended sentence, but in deciding whether an offender has previously been sentenced to imprisonment a suspended sentence which has not been brought into effect must be ignored. Points (b) and (c) apply irrespective of whether the offender has previously received the sentence in question.

The court must not pass the relevant sentence on an unrepresented offender unless either:

(a) he or she was granted a right to funded representation as part of the Criminal Defence Service but the right was withdrawn because of his or her conduct; or

(b) having been informed of his or her right to apply for funded representation and having had the opportunity to do so, he or she refused or failed to apply (PCC(S)A 2000, s. 83(3)).

The effect of the legislation is that, if the court is considering a first sentence of imprisonment, etc. for an unrepresented offender, it must (if it has not been done already) tell him or her that he or she can apply for funded representation as part of the Criminal Defence Service and grant him or her an adjournment of sufficient length to make the application and instruct solicitors. If the offender fails to use the adjournment for the purpose for which it was granted, that is his or her fault, and the court at the resumed hearing can pass whatever sentence it considers appropriate even if the offender is still unrepresented.

If s. 83 of PCC(S)A 2000 is not complied with, but a sentence of imprisonment is nonetheless passed on an offender who has not previously been so sentenced, it would seem that the consequences of the error depend on which court makes it. If it was a magistrates' court which failed to comply with s. 83, the Crown Court (which hears appeals against sentences passed in the magistrates' courts) must replace the sentence of imprisonment with a sentence the magistrates could lawfully have passed on the occasion on which they dealt with the offender. So the replacement sentence cannot be a sentence of imprisonment (*R* v *Birmingham Justices, ex parte Wyatt* [1976] 1 WLR 260). If it was the Crown Court which forgot about s. 83, the Court of Appeal can uphold the lower court's sentence if, notwithstanding the procedural irregularity, it considers that the sentence was the appropriate one for the offender (*R* v *McGinlay* (1976) 52 Cr App R 156). Presumably the same consequences will flow from breach of any of the other sections requiring the court to allow time for an application for funded representation to be made.

14.12 Differences Between Sentencing Procedure in the Crown Court and in the Magistrates' Courts

The procedure before sentence is passed is essentially the same whatever the court. The practice of taking other offences into consideration and the power to defer sentence are equally applicable to both the Crown Court and the magistrates' courts. For minor driving matters, the court relies merely on the endorsements, if any, on the offender's licence.

FIFTEEN

PENAL POLICY AND SENTENCING POLICY

15.1 Introduction

The Criminal Justice Act 1991, most of which came into force on 1 October 1992, is currently the major legislation governing the aims and practice of sentencing. The Act was intended to be revolutionary — to change the basis on which all sentencers consider sentences. It set out, for the first time, a detailed set of prescriptions for the way in which sentencers should think about sentences for different kinds of offences and different offenders. Before the Act, sentencers could for the same offender, decide to give precedence in their consideration of sentencing to deterring others, or to reforming that offender, or to providing compensation for the victim, or to marking the seriousness of the offence (see **Chapter 16** for a discussion of these philosophies of sentencing). As a result, prior to the Act, different sentencers could, quite properly, give different sentences. The Criminal Justice Act 1991 attempted to produce greater uniformity in the sentencing process, through elevating one particular philosophy of sentencing (making the sentence proportionate to the seriousness of the offence) over others.

However, certain provisions in the Act attracted considerable criticism from magistrates and others and, as a result, two of the major provisions were abolished in 1993. These were the calculation of financial penalties by using a unit fine system, and the prohibition of sentencers being able to take into account previous convictions unrelated to that offence. Some would say that the major principle of the Act — to make all sentences proportionate to the seriousness of the offence — has been put into jeopardy (for example, because previous convictions may be taken into account, and so sentences will not relate solely to the present offence). It is certainly true that sentencers remain confused by the changes. On financial penalties, for example, there is no nationally prescribed way of calculating how the penalty should be related to the means of the offender to pay. The main provisions of the Act are consolidated in the PCC(S)A 2000.

Research findings on the operation of the CJA 1991 suggest that practice is varying considerably between different courts. Courts are interpreting the provisions of the Act and subsequent legislative changes in slightly different ways. The tougher mandatory sentencing for serious offenders, to protect the public (in the Crime (Sentences) Act 1997, the relevant provisions of which were also consolidated in the PCC(S)A 2000) and the resurgence of a rehabilitative approach for drugs offenders and young offenders, as well as reparation to victims, by the present Government, are likely further to increase the plurality of sentencing policy and practice. Counsel starting practice in 2001–02 will need to bear in mind that there are likely to be differences between the courts in which they practise. It makes it doubly important for counsel to go into court and listen to previous cases before they make a plea in mitigation in a court in which they have not previously appeared.

15.2 The Manual, Lectures and Tutorials in Sentencing

Sentences must be within the range specified in the statute defining the offence for which the defendant has been convicted. In England and Wales, however, the permitted maxima for offences reflect the worst possible case and hence give little guidance to sentencers for common instances of that offence. It is very rare for any other statutory guidance to be given in statutes setting out the offence. Guidance for sentencers comes from a wide range of sources, including the statutes setting up each sentence, the guideline decisions of the Court of Appeal, publications of the Magistrates' Association (such as their guidelines), research reports on the effectiveness and use of different sentences, the experience of probation officers, doctors and others set out in their reports to the courts, Home Office publications on the effect of gender and of race (required to be produced for sentencers by CJA 1991, s. 95), and, not least, the mitigation speeches of counsel or solicitors.

The Crime and Disorder Act 1998 contains provisions for the Court of Appeal to have a wider power to consider a whole category of cases in framing or reviewing sentencing guidelines. This provides an important new source of sentencing guidance. It is backed up by the creation of a Sentencing Advisory Panel, which seeks the views of relevant bodies (for example, the probation service) and advises the Court of Appeal. The Court is able to consider guidelines either if it has an appeal before it of a case which falls within the category it wishes to consider, or (and this is totally new) if the Panel proposes that new guidance should be produced. Guidance on sentencing practice will thus be informed on a continuing basis not only by judicial practice, but by the effects of sentencing. In producing guidelines, the Act requires the Court to have regard to the need to promote consistency in sentencing, the current sentences being imposed, the costs of different sentences and the effectiveness in preventing re-offending, the need to promote public confidence, and the views of the Panel.

The practice of sentencing is hence constantly changing. Textbooks almost immediately become out of date. The role of this Manual and of the lectures in sentencing cannot, therefore, be to give students a potted guide to sentencing. Instead, they aim to give an appreciation of the factors which are currently moulding sentencing, such that, as changes occur, they can be slotted in to counsel's framework of understanding. In particular, they aim to:

(a) Provide an appreciation of the more common statutory sources, decisions of the Court of Appeal and other factors affecting sentencers.

(b) Relate these to the actual pattern of sentencing in the courts.

(c) Relate the statutory possibilities to the facilities which are most commonly available in different parts of the country. Particularly in relation to community sentences and the mentally disordered, the actual sentences which are given are strongly affected by the availability of particular types of programmes or residential accommodation (hostels, attendance centres, treatment programmes, types of community service, etc.).

(d) Attune the student to the way sentencers are thinking and what they are trying to achieve by their sentences.

(e) Relate all these to what happens in court and the role of the different participants between conviction and sentence.

The aim of this chapter is to set out the way in which the sentencing structure has developed, current patterns of sentencing, and the major provisions of CJA 1991 consolidated in PCC(S)A 2000. Subsequent chapters deal in more detail with specific sentences (imprisonment, community sentences, etc.) and with kinds of offenders for whom special sentences have been developed (the young, the mentally disordered, the dangerous).

Tutorials in sentencing provide an opportunity to ask about any of these aspects, but also, more importantly, the opportunity to practise preparing and making speeches in mitigation on real-life examples.

Since sentencing provisions, sentencing policy and sentencing practice are constantly changing, these materials can only form a first building block in the materials that will be needed as you pursue your career at the Bar. Written materials of value include not only case reports but statistical studies. It is very much worth amassing such a collection, using these materials as a beginning for that. In particular, the booklet *The Sentence of the Court* (published by HMSO) is revised periodically to provide magistrates and others with official guidance on how sentences might be used. Case reports on sentencing can be found particularly in the *Criminal Appeal Reports (Sentencing)* and the *Criminal Law Review*. Articles on the effectiveness of different sentences and on sentencing practice may be found in journals such as the *British Journal of Criminology, the Criminal Law Review*, and the *Howard Journal of Criminal Justice*.

15.3 Changes Affecting Mitigation

Over this century, there has been a continuous *increase* in the number of different types of sentences made available to the courts. This has affected the role of counsel in three ways:

(a) sentencers require more *information* from professionals in the courtroom (including counsel) before passing sentence, and expect those professionals to be able to discuss, where appropriate, the merits of different kinds of sentence;

(b) more *professionals* are involved in the sentencing process, with whom counsel must interact, and must know their roles;

(c) mitigation has become, as a result, a more complicated and more important task, which requires considerable *preparation*.

The Criminal Justice Act 1991 and the Crime and Disorder Act 1998 continue these trends. The Acts have introduced more sentences. More pre-sentence reports are being prepared by probation officers, and these reports will contain, in certain instances, not only the opinion of the probation officer as to the appropriate sentence, but also a sentence plan for supervision. Defence counsel will need to be familiar with the local facilities for community sentences and with the appropriate forms of supervision (and so must make a practice of talking to the local probation liaison officer for the court before finalising mitigation). Counsel must be able to anticipate what kinds of sentences may be suggested by the probation service and what will be found realistic by the sentencer, and be prepared to put forward what is best for his or her client and to discuss this, as necessary, with the judge.

One of the major difficulties in this process is that the current existing sentences have been introduced at different times and that there has been no overall review of how they will fit into the schema proposed in the CJA 1991. To understand sentencing today, it is necessary to appreciate this history. This chapter hence first considers current sentencing practice in the courts and then gives a brief résumé of the major developments in sentencing which affect current practice, before turning to the CJA 1991 and subsequent legislation. Finally, we shall consider how this affects mitigation.

15.4 Parameters of Current Sentencing Practice

Since the decisions of the Court of Appeal largely focus on serious cases involving substantial terms of imprisonment, it might be thought that most defendants are sentenced to imprisonment. However, both at the magistrates' court and at the Crown Court, this is far from the case.

Considering only male defendants aged 21 and over, custodial sentences were given to only 11% of defendants in the magistrates' court and 63% of defendants at the Crown Court in 1996. Hence, even at the Crown Court, immediate custody is not inevitable, though there was a substantial increase in the proportions being given immediate custody between 1995 and 1996. Overall, taking both courts together and looking at indictable offences, the most common sentence in 1996, as it has been for many years, was a financial penalty (33%), with 26% getting immediate custody, 14% an absolute or conditional discharge, 10% a community service order, 11% a probation order, 3% a combination order and only 1% a suspended sentence. Women are more commonly given sentences at the lower end of the tariff, but the pattern of offences for women is different from that for men. The number of suspended sentences being given has fallen dramatically since the provision in the CJA 1991 that it can only be justified by 'exceptional circumstances' of the case, and the restricted interpretation of such circumstances in *R* v *Okinikan* (1993) 14 Cr App R (S) 453.

1993 was the first complete year during which the Criminal Justice Act 1991 was in force. The first few months of the Act showed a significant decrease in imprisonment, but since then there have been substantial rises in both the proportion of people sent to prison and the lengths of imprisonment given, in parallel with ministers' advocacy of the need for more severe punishment of serious and violent offending. The trend towards giving more people custodial sentences was particularly marked in 1995 and 1996. The last few years have shown that there can be substantial shifts in sentencing practice, according to public and judicial mood, in the space of a few months, and counsel should be aware that this may occur in the future. The total prison population on 21 January 2000 was 63,450 and Home Office estimates indicate that this is likely to rise to over 70,000 in 2001.

15.5 Major Developments in Sentencing Policy

The sentences available to the courts have been expanded greatly in number and type since the turn of the century. The ways in which the courts are supposed to use them reflect the philosophies of punishment dominant at the time of their introduction (see **Chapter 16** for a discussion of the different philosophies of punishment). The imposition by the CJA 1991 of one particular philosophy as pre-eminent (retribution) is a recent major development.

15.6 The Criminal Justice Act 1991

15.6.1 PRINCIPLES OF THE CJA 1991

The advent of CJA 1991 was intended to produce substantial changes in sentencing. For the first time, the Government decided to state relatively clearly and unambiguosly its sentencing philosophy. The White Paper introducing the Bill states:

> The Government's aim is to ensure that convicted criminals in England and Wales are punished justly and suitably according to the seriousness of their offences; in other words that they get their just desserts [sic]. No Government should try to influence the decisions of the courts in individual cases. The independence of the judiciary is rightly regarded as a cornerstone of our liberties. But sentencing principles and sentencing practice are matters of legitimate concern to Government, and Parliament provides the funds necessary to give effect to the courts' decisions.
>
> The sentence of the court prescribes the punishment for criminal behaviour. Punishment in proportion to the seriousness of the crime has long been accepted as one of many objectives in sentencing. It should be the principal focus for sentencing decisions. This is consistent with the Government's view that those who commit very serious crimes, particularly crimes of violence, should receive long custodial sentences; but that many other crimes can be punished in the community, with greater emphasis on bringing home to the criminal the consequences of his actions, compensation to the victim and reparation to the community. . . .

> The Government's proposals therefore emphasise the objectives which sentencing is most likely to meet successfully in whole or in part. The first objective for all sentences is denunciation of and retribution for the crime. Depending on the offence and the offender, the sentence may also aim to achieve public protection, reparation and reform of the offender, preferably in the community. This approach points to sentencing policies which are more firmly based on the seriousness of the offence, and just desserts [sic] for the offender. (From *Crime, Justice and Protecting the Public,* 1990, HMSO.)

The Government thus finally set out the relative priorities it wished the courts to give to the different philosophies of sentencing in dealing with offenders. Retribution or just deserts — concentrating on the seriousness of the offence — was the primary aim in sentencing. It was unlawful to pass a more severe sentence in the hope of achieving reform, or because of the prevalence of the offence. The sentence had to be proportionate to the seriousness of the crime.

15.6.2 THE PYRAMID OF THRESHOLDS OF SERIOUSNESS

The Act made a distinction between four different kinds of sentences graded according to the severity of their consequences to the offender. At the bottom of the pyramid were discharges, seen as the least severe sentences. Next came fines and other financial penalties. Then there were community orders or community sentences and finally, at the top of the pyramid of severity, custody. It was clear that the sentencer's choice between these four types should be governed by the seriousness of the offence. The Act and the associated documentation set out the 'custody threshold' of seriousness of offence which had to be passed before an offender was given a custodial sentence. Similarly there was a 'community sentence threshold'.

Was there then no place for rehabilitation? What about all the community sentences which were originally introduced for rehabilitative or reparative reasons, such as probation or community service? Within the custody band, and within the financial penalties band, the choice of sentence (number of months of custody, or levels of fine) was indeed only to be made according to the seriousness of the offence. But *within* the community sentence band, the choice of sentence was to depend not only on proportionality to the offence, but also on the individual problems of the offender and his or her rehabilitation. Hence the choice between probation, community service, combination order, or a probation order with restrictions (such as attendance at a probation centre) should reflect both the seriousness of the offence (and the severity of the consequences of the community sentence to the offender) and the best sentence to suit the individual offender.

These principles are set out in the following sections of the PCC(S)A 2000 which consolidates the relevant provisions of the CJA 1991:

The 'custody threshold'

> *. . . the court shall not pass a custodial sentence on the offender unless it is of the opinion—*
> *(a) that the offence, or the combination of the offence and one or more offences associated with it, was so serious that only such a sentence can be justified for the offence.* (s. 79(2))

Proportionality within the custody band

> *. . . the custodial sentence shall be—*
> *(a) for such term (not exceeding the permitted maximum) as in the opinion of the court is commensurate with the seriousness of the offence, or the combination of the offence and one or more offences associated with it.* (s. 80(2))

The 'community sentence threshold'

> *A court shall not pass a community sentence on an offender unless it is of the opinion that the offence, or the combination of the offence and one or more offences associated with it, was serious enough to warrant such a sentence.* (s. 35(1))

Proportionality and suitability within the community sentence band

> *. . . where a court passes a community sentence—*
> *(a) the particular order or orders comprising or forming part of the sentence shall be such as in the opinion of the court is, or taken together are, the most suitable for the offender; and*
> *(b) the restrictions on liberty imposed by the order or orders shall be such as in the opinion of the court are commensurate with the seriousness of the offence, or the combination of the offence and one or more offences associated with it.* (s. 35(3))

Proportionality within the band of fines

> *The amount of any fine fixed by a court shall be such as, in the opinion of the court, reflects the seriousness of the offence.* (s. 128(2))

However, the word 'seriousness' is not defined within the Acts and few clues are given in the Act as to how sentencers should interpret it, or which factors should be seen as mitigating or aggravating (see subsequent chapters for cases on mitigating and aggravating factors). In addition, *R* v *Cox* [1993] 1 WLR 188 sets out that even if the custodial threshold has been passed in relation to the seriousness of the *offence*, it is possible for a lesser sentence to be given if there are mitigating factors relevant to the *offender*.

15.6.3 THE MAGISTRATES' ASSOCIATION GUIDELINES

Sentencing guidelines for use by magistrates in the magistrates' court were introduced in June 1992 by the Magistrates' Association, the professional association for magistrates, and revised versions were produced in September 1993, April 1997 and June 2000. They apply only to offenders aged 18 and over. They are only a voluntary code and have no legal force, but previous versions have been shown in a survey to be used by 89% of magistrates in road traffic cases and 75% in other cases (see M. Wasik and A. Turner, 'Sentencing guidelines in the magistrates' courts' [1993] Crim LR 345–56). For each non-motoring offence, the guidelines set out a guide to sentencing, in relation to some 'seriousness indicators' which may be present.

The 1997 guidelines indicate consideration of certain types of sentence for each type of offence — types of sentence which should be considered first for that kind of offence. They relate to what would be seen as cases of average seriousness. So, for example, for 'theft from vehicle' (Theft Act 1968, s. 1), the guideline is a community penalty, whereas for criminal damage it is a fine. At the most serious end, the offences for which not only should a custodial sentence be considered, but magistrates should be *committing the offender for sentence* at the Crown Court, are production, supply possession with intent to supply of Class A drugs, and possession with intent to supply of Class B drugs (unless small scale). The offences for which guidelines are given as *custody* are: aggravated vehicle taking, assault on police, burglary of dwelling, driving whilst disqualified, violent disorder and wounding/GBH (Public Order Act 1986, s. 2). The offences for which guidelines are given as a *community penalty* are affray, actual bodily harm, burglary of non-dwelling, common assault, dangerous driving, possession of Class A drugs, causing fear (or provocation) of violence (Public Order Act 1986, s. 4), handling, obtaining by deception, false representation in relation to social security, taking a vehicle without consent, theft from vehicle and theft in which a breach of trust is involved. All other offences listed have a *financial penalty* as the guidelines. It should be noted that the guidelines are based on a first-time offender pleading not guilty and that 'a timely guilty plea may attract a sentencing discount of up to one third but the precise amount of discount will depend on the facts of each case and a last minute plea of guilty may attract only a minimal reduction'. Other mitigating and aggravating factors will also need to be taken into account for particular offences.

The sentencing guidelines also contain some suggested fines, which relate to offences of average seriousness committed by first offenders. The guidelines are set at three levels: low income — about £100 net per week, average income — about £250 net per week and high income — about £600 net per week from all sources. The guideline fine for shoplifting is low income £135, average income £340 and high income £810. For television licence evasion the relevant figures are low income £90, average income £225 and high income £540. For driving with no insurance the relevant figures are low income £215, average income £540 and high income £1,300.

The later sentencing guidelines appeared harsher than the earlier ones in respect of some offences and it was acknowledged that sentencing had moved 'up tariff', especially for offences of violence, house burglary, criminal deception or those involving hard drugs. Again, the lesson for counsel is that sentencing levels can change substantially over a 12-month period and that it is important to remain up to date with the penal mood and with any guidance being given to sentencers, whether by the courts or by bodies such as the Magistrates' Association. (See also **20.2.4** for further discussion.)

It must be stressed that these sentencing guidelines are only suggestions for magistrates. The Home Office *Information on the Criminal Justice System in England and Wales* indicates clearly that there is still substantial regional and local disparity in sentencing levels around the country and it is important that counsel attune themselves to local patterns of sentencing, particularly in courts at which they appear only rarely.

15.6.4 WHAT IS SERIOUSNESS?

In relation to probation, the national standards first issued in the spring of 1992 have set out some ideas of how probation officers should deal with ideas of seriousness in their reports (see **Chapter 19**). **Chapters 20–22** consider the current cases relating to seriousness for custody. In *R* v *Howells* [1999] 1 All ER 50 Lord Bingham CJ delivering the reserved judgment of the Court of Appeal gave some guidance on the determination of offence seriousness as follows:

> We do however think that in approaching cases which are on or near the custody threshold courts will usually find it helpful to begin by considering the nature and extent of the defendant's criminal intention and the nature and extent of any injury or damage caused to the victim. Other things being equal, an offence which is deliberate and premeditated will usually be more serious than one which is spontaneous and unpremeditated or which involves an excessive response to provocation; an offence which inflicts personal injury or mental trauma, particularly if permanent, will usually be more serious than one which inflicts financial loss only. In considering the seriousness of any offence the court may take into account any previous convictions of the offender or any failure to respond to previous sentences (s. 151(1) of the PCC(S)A 2000) and must treat it as an aggravating factor if the offence was committed while the offender was on bail (s. 151(2) of that Act).
>
> In deciding whether to impose a custodial sentence in borderline cases the sentencing court will ordinarily take account of matters relating to the offender.
>
> (a) The court will have regard to an offender's admission of responsibility for the offence, particularly if reflected in a plea of guilty tendered at the earliest opportunity and accompanied by hard evidence of genuine remorse, as shown (for example) by an expression of regret to the victim and an offer of compensation. Attention is drawn to s. 152 of the PCC(S)A 2000.
>
> (b) Where offending has been fuelled by addiction to drink or drugs, the court will be inclined to look more favourably on an offender who has already demonstrated (by taking practical steps to that end) a genuine, self-motivated determination to address his addiction.
>
> (c) Youth and immaturity, while affording no defence, will often justify a less rigorous penalty than would be appropriate for an adult.
>
> (d) Some measure of leniency will ordinarily be extended to offenders of previous good character, the more so if there is evidence of positive good character (such as a solid employment record or faithful discharge of family duties) as opposed to a mere absence of previous convictions. It will sometimes be appropriate to take account of family responsibilities, or physical or mental disability.

(e) While the court will never impose a custodial sentence unless satisfied that it is necessary to do so, there will be even greater reluctance to impose a custodial sentence on an offender who has never before served such a sentence.

Courts should always bear in mind that criminal sentences are in almost every case intended to protect the public, whether by punishing the offender or reforming him, or deterring him and others, or all of these things. Courts cannot and should not be unmindful of the important public dimension of criminal sentencing and the importance of maintaining public confidence in the sentencing system.

Where the court is of the opinion that an offence, or the combination of an offence and one or more offences associated with it, is so serious that only a custodial sentence can be justified and that such a sentence should be passed, the sentence imposed should be no longer than is necessary to meet the penal purpose which the court has in mind.

15.6.5 A DISTINCTION BETWEEN SERIOUS OFFENDERS AND THE REST

In addition to the focus on seriousness, the overall sentencing policy of the Government is now set more firmly than before on a course of bifurcation. This term, originally coined by Professor Bottoms, means that a distinction is drawn between sentencing for the serious, violent and dangerous — who should be given long periods of incarceration, and for whom a protective sentencing policy is envisaged — and sentencing for the majority of ordinary offenders. For ordinary offenders, prison will not be seen as a necessary, or even desirable, response, and a community alternative may be far better. Quoting the White Paper again:

> Most offenders can be punished by financial penalties — by paying compensation to their victims and by fines. When offences are too serious to be properly punished by financial penalties alone, the courts have a choice of community penalties, such as probation or community service, or of custody . . .
>
> For most offenders, imprisonment has to be justified in terms of public protection, denunciation and retribution. Otherwise it can be an expensive way of making bad people worse. The prospects of reforming offenders are usually much better if they stay in the community, provided the public is properly protected.

This has been embodied in the PCC(S)A 2000 in s. 79(2)(b) and s. 80(2)(b), which state:

> [*the court shall not pass a custodial sentence on the offender unless it is of the opinion—*]
> *where the offence is a violent or sexual offence, that only such a sentence would be adequate to protect the public from serious harm from him.* (s. 79(2)(b))
>
> [*the custodial sentence shall be—*]
> *where the offence is a violent or sexual offence, for such longer term (not exceeding the maximum) as in the opinion of the court is necessary to protect the public from serious harm from the offender.* (s. 80(2)(b))

In *R* v *Baverstock* [1993] 1 WLR 202 it was held that the judge should clearly state under which section the sentence he or she is passing falls and why that is so. The judge is also required to explain his or her reasoning to the offender in ordinary language (s. 79(4) — though the Court of Appeal will not be sympathetic to appeals based on 'fine linguistic analysis' of sentencing remarks). The judge must give an express indication to counsel if he or she is considering imposing a longer sentence than is commensurate with the seriousness of the offence under s. 80(2)(b). Sentences for the violent and dangerousness are discussed further in **Chapter 23**.

15.6.6 HELP FOR SENTENCERS

In order to help sentencers with CJA 1991, a major training and information programme took place in 1992. Previous experience with substantial new legislation on sentencing, however, has proved that it is very difficult to change sentencing practice quickly over the whole range of sentencers and courts in England and Wales. Within the Act, the Government is relying on procedural criteria and information to help sentencers.

The Act provides that courts should consider a pre-sentence report before passing a custodial sentence (s. 81 — though it will not invalidate such a sentence if they do not). They should give their reasons for giving a custodial sentence (s. 79(4)). Sentencers should consider the circumstances of the case and also consider information about it (including any aggravating or mitigating factors — s. 81(4)). This of course implies that counsel will have a major role in helping to provide this information. Sentencers should take into account any information before the court which is relevant to the offender's attitude to the offence and his or her physical and mental condition.

15.7 New Developments in Sentencing Policy and Practice

15.7.1 LONG SENTENCES FOR THE PERSISTENT AND DANGEROUS

There has been a significant recent shift by the judiciary towards sentencing a greater proportion of those sentenced to immediate custody. Average sentence lengths have also increased very substantially. During this time, there was no clear change in sentencing legislation which would have caused this shift. The judges were responding to a different mood in Parliament, in the media and amongst the public which stressed the need for public protection, particularly in relation to violent and sexual offences. This mood reached a peak in the White Paper, *Protecting the Public*, HMSO, Cm 3190, foreshadowing the Crime (Sentences) Act 1997. The Act was inspired by the knowledge that a small minority of offenders commit a considerable proportion of offences and was intended to deal with the fear that dangerous, violent and sexual offenders, as well as persistent burglars, would be released after only a short period, only to re-offend. Provisions relating to dangerous violent and sexual offenders and to repeat drugs offenders were brought into force in October 1997. The debate about the Act has also significantly affected judicial practice.

15.7.2 THE CRIME (SENTENCES) ACT 1997

The Crime (Sentences) Act 1997 (C(S)A) received Royal Assent in April 1997, immediately before the General Election. It has, for the first time, created mandatory minimum sentences for certain types of serious crime (as in the United States). Previously, the only mandatory sentence was for murder (life imprisonment) and the maxima prescribed in the statutes creating the offences are intended to indicate what would be suitable for the most heinous offence. There is judicial discretion to pass any sentence under the maximum.

The relevant provisions of the 1997 Act have been consolidated in the PCC(S)A 2000 and require judges to pass an automatic life sentence for offenders convicted of a second serious violent or sex offence; and mandatory minimum prison sentences of seven years for those with two or more similar previous convictions who are convicted of drug-trafficking offences involving Class A drugs. Judicial discretion to pass more lenient sentences is confined to 'exceptional circumstances' in the case of the automatic life sentence (s. 109), and 'unless the court considers this to be unjust in all the circumstances' for the drugs provision (s. 110).

There has been significant judicial disquiet at this reduction in discretion. The first cases have arisen under the C(S)A 1997 and the early appeals are establishing the parameters of what will be seen as 'exceptional circumstances' or 'unjust in all the circumstances'. See, for example, *R* v *Kelly* [1999] 2 WLR 1100 (discussed at **21.8**). In *R* v *Newman* [2000] Crim LR 309, the Court of Appeal held that the offender's paranoid psychotic illness was not an exceptional circumstance under what is now PCC(S)A 2000, s. 109. In *R* v *Buckland* [2000] Crim LR 307, the Court of Appeal held that the circumstances were exceptional where the offender had shown incompetence and lack of aggression in an attempted robbery where he had entered a bank, produced an envelope addressed to himself bearing a note demanding money and stating that he had a gun. No gun was produced, though a plastic imitation handgun was found on his arrest. Finally, in *R* v *Stephens* [2000] Crim LR 402, the Court of Appeal held that trial counsel's failure to advise the offender of the risk of an automatic life sentence under s. 109 amounted to exceptional circumstances.

15.7.3 SENTENCING DISCOUNTS FOR THOSE PLEADING GUILTY

The move towards longer sentences has been mitigated, however, by a much clearer appreciation of the mitigating effect of pleading guilty. The Court of Appeal has always allowed a sentence discount for those pleading guilty and this was formalised by PCC(S)A 2000, s. 152. The introduction of a new computer system at the Crown Court allows us for the first time to be able to quantify the current difference in sentencing for those pleading guilty and those pleading not guilty. For 1996, 72% of adult males convicted of indictable offences after a plea of not guilty were given an immediate custodial sentence, compared with 61% of those pleading guilty. The average sentence length for those pleading not guilty was 36 months, that for those pleading guilty 21 months – very near the proportion suggested by s. 152. However, the difference was particularly marked for drugs offences where average lengths of imprisonment were 52.3 for not guilty pleas and 27.0 for guilty pleas (though there may have been differences in previous convictions between those pleading guilty and not guilty).

15.7.4 A MOVE TOWARDS REHABILITATION AND REPARATION?

Preliminary indications of the new Government's penal policy suggest that sentencing policy will continue the trend towards bifurcation. Serious offences will continue to attract prison sentences, but there is likely to be far more emphasis on creating new rehabilitative and reparative possibilities in the community for the judiciary to use with young offenders and with those addicted to drugs. So, for example, the CDA 1998 gives the judiciary the power to create reparation orders, whereby offenders apologise to victims, pay compensation to victims, or do community service work, in order to bring home to offenders the nature and effects of their offending. There is likely to be an expansion of places for drugs treatment for offenders, coupled with powers to compel attendance for those whose offending is linked to drugs misuse. At the same time, if the use of cautions by the police is restricted, it is likely that minor offences will fall to be dealt with by the magistrates' courts and the youth courts, rather than the police. Hence we may see the number of offences before the magistrates' court rising, and, as a result, the average seriousness of offences before the court falling. The overall tone of proceedings is likely to start emphasising more rehabilitative, rather than punitive, sentencing.

Just as we have seen the passage of the C(S)A 1997 accompanied by a trend towards harsher sentencing for serious offences, so we are likely to see the beginnings of a greater emphasis on rehabilitation and reparation by courts for less serious offending. The courts already have powers which they can use for rehabilitation (probation, supervision and combination orders) and reparation (community service, compensation orders) and we may see a greater emphasis on these community sentences for offences which are not very serious.

Both rehabilitation (with its emphasis on the offender and his or her circumstances) and reparation (with a focus on both offender and victim) require rather different information to be presented to sentencers than the major thrust of the CJA 1991, which makes sentencing proportionate to the seriousness of the offence, and tends to ignore the circumstances of the offender and victim. Counsel need to be aware that recent developments are likely to lead to sentencers requiring information about a much wider range of factors. It is likely to be less clear initially what approach the bench may take in a particular case and so counsel will need to be prepared for a range of possibilities and alive to indications from the bench.

15.7.5 DEVELOPMENTS CONTAINED IN THE YOUTH JUSTICE AND CRIMINAL EVIDENCE ACT 1999

Further developments have occurred in relation to disposals for young offenders. Part I of the YJCEA 1999 provides that the youth court may refer an offender under the age of 18 to a youth offender panel where that offender has pleaded guilty to an offence, has no previous findings of guilt, nor has ever been bound over. The offender will be required to attend meetings of the panel established by the youth offending team responsible for implementing the order, and the order will specify a period from 3 to 12 months during which any youth offender contract between the offender and the panel is to have effect. The panel will seek to reach agreement with the offender on a programme of behaviour with the aim of preventing re-offending. The terms of the programme may include provision for financial or other reparation, mediation, unpaid work or service in the community, home curfew, educational or work attendance, participation in specified activities, attendance before specified persons, avoidance of specified places and/or persons, and enabling supervision and recording of the offender's compliance with the programme. In the absence of agreement, or in the event of a breach of the terms of the offender's contract with the panel, it may refer the offender to the court. These provisions have been consolidated in Part III of the PCC(S)A 2000.

15.8 The Role of Defence Counsel

The number of sentences available to the court has increased considerably over the last decade. A range of both custodial sentences and community sentences is provided in all courts. We have seen that as the numbers and aims of sentences have changed, so the need for information in the process between conviction and sentencing has grown and grown. The CJA 1991 and the CDA 1998 continue this trend. Even more work will need to be done by probation officers and by counsel and solicitors before the sentencing hearing.

This makes it essential that counsel should have full instructions from the defendant as to any mitigating or aggravating factors, and as to his or her financial and personal circumstances. Counsel should also liaise with the probation officer at court in relation to whether a pre-sentence report should be prepared, whether one exists and the availability of different community sentences in that particular local area. Possible sentences should be discussed with the client and all should be completed in sufficient time so that counsel can prepare the final mitigation, go into court and listen to previous cases, to see how that court views particular factors.

Mitigation plays a vital information-providing role for the judge. Currently, defence counsel is one of the major providers of information to the judiciary. The information-gathering and information-providing role of counsel is very important. Mitigation in particular is not just an exercise in rhetoric, but an exercise in persuasion. The best persuasion is based soundly on facts and moulded by an appreciation of how the sentencing and penal systems are put together.

SIXTEEN

THE AIMS OF SENTENCING

16.1 Introduction

What aims do the courts pursue when passing sentence? What aims should they pursue? These have often been regarded as academic questions, of no importance to the criminal practitioner. That view has always been an exaggeration: magistrates, trial judges and the Court of Appeal have from time to time proclaimed that the purpose behind a particular sentence is to rehabilitate the offender, or to deter others, or to protect the public, etc. But, as **Chapter 15** makes clear, the legislation requires sentencers to consider the aims of sentencing: the Criminal Justice Act 1991 promoted one aim of sentencing — 'just deserts' (proportionality) — as the leading criterion for the imposition and the length of custodial sentences. You will therefore need to have a grasp of what the proportionality principle includes and what it excludes. To begin with, there are two short sections on the varieties of crime and on the prevention of crime.

16.2 Varieties of Crime

Whilst it is true to say that the vast bulk of summary offences are road traffic crimes, and that the vast bulk of indictable offences are crimes contrary to the Theft Acts, the wide variety of crimes which comes before the courts for sentence should not be overlooked.

In the magistrates' courts there are the many road traffic offences and property offences, but also a range of offences from non-payment of television licences to unlawful wounding, from selling alcohol without a licence to the discharge of oil from an oil tanker, from offences against the Health and Safety at Work etc. Act 1974 to minor public order offences, from the sale of impure food to assault on a police officer.

The Crown Court is preoccupied chiefly with offences of theft, handling and deception, but it also has to deal with serious violence and sexual offences, public order offences, neglect and cruelty to children, possession of firearms, offences under the Official Secrets Acts, drug offences, pollution offences, and so forth.

Any sentencing system has to be able to adapt to and cope with this great variation in types of offence, as well as the differences among offenders and their previous records (considered further in **Chapters 20** and **21**).

16.3 Crime Prevention

'The ultimate objective of the Government is to reduce crime, particularly crimes committed by young people, before they embark on a career of criminality' (White Paper, *Crime, Justice and Protecting the Public*, para. 1.7). Most people would accept that it is preferable to prevent crimes from happening at all, rather than waiting until they do happen and then passing sentences for them. To this end a variety of crime prevention strategies has been adopted over the years — some of them well known, such as 'Neighbourhood Watch' schemes, others less well known. However, it is common for people to speak as if sentencing is the primary tool for the prevention of crime, and as if the sentences passed by the courts constitute the main hope for reducing the amount of crime in society. In its 1990 White Paper the Government sounded a cautionary note on this argument: 'Punishment has a major part to play in reducing crime, but its role must not be over-stated'.

In fact, the role of sentencing is limited by the small proportion of all crimes which result in conviction in the courts. The 1997 British Crime Survey made enquiries of some 15,000 citizens, to try to discover how many crimes are committed but never reported by their victims. This survey, which focused on offences of theft, burglary, robbery, wounding and sexual offences, found that only about 45% of crimes are reported. By no means all the incidents reported as crimes were recorded by the police as such, so that the proportion of these crimes actually reported and recorded was only 24%. Of these, the police 'cleared up' fewer than one-fifth, with the result that only 5.5% of all crimes are reported, recorded and cleared up. Some of these were not prosecuted, some resulted in a caution, and some resulted in an acquittal; eventually only 2% ended in a conviction. (*Digest of Information on the Criminal Justice System*, Home Office, 1999, p. 29.)

Thus, the fact that a relatively small proportion of offences may come before the courts for sentence places a severe limitation on the ability of the courts to influence patterns of behaviour in society as a whole. This is not to suggest that sentencing is unnecessary: far from it, since the existence of the police, prosecutors, courts, the probation service and the prison service has an underlying general deterrent effect on behaviour. But we must be wary of believing that increases and decreases in the levels of court sentences will necessarily, or even probably, have an effect on the crime rate. Crime prevention strategies may prove to be more effective for these purposes than changes in sentencing practice.

16.4 Deterrent Sentencing

It could be argued that, although only a small proportion of crimes result in the offender being sentenced in court, those few sentences have a considerable deterrent effect. At the outset a distinction must be drawn between *general deterrence*, i.e. sentences aimed at deterring potential lawbreakers from committing crimes, and *individual deterrence*, i.e. sentences aimed at deterring the particular offender from committing further crimes.

16.4.1 INDIVIDUAL DETERRENCE

A sentencing strategy based on individual deterrence would presumably require courts to pass increasingly severe sentences on offenders if they repeat their offending, in the hope that eventually the sentences persuade the offender to 'go straight'. In practice this seems rarely to happen, as Lawton LJ recognised in *R* v *Sargeant* (1974) 60 Cr App R 74, at p. 77:

> Experience has shown over the years that deterrence of the offender is not a very useful approach, because those who have their wits about them usually find the closing of the prison gates an experience which they do not want again. If they do not learn that lesson, there is likely to be a high degree of recidivism any way.

The statistics certainly tend to show that most first offenders (71%) are *not* reconvicted within six years, whereas the vast majority of those with five or more previous convictions (87%) are reconvicted within six years. (See Philpotts, G. and Lancucki, L., *Previous Convictions, Sentence and Reconviction*, Home Office Research Study No. 53 (HMSO, 1979), p. 16.)

16.4.2 GENERAL DETERRENCE

From time to time courts have expressly justified sentences on grounds of general deterrence. Two questions are raised by this practice. First, is it right to punish one person more severely in the hope that this sentence will deter others? Some would argue that this is justifiable for the protection of innocent victims, whereas others would vigorously assert that an offender does not lose all rights and should not be used as a mere pawn in social policy by increasing the sentence beyond what is proportionate.

Even for the protectionists, however, much may depend on the answer to the second question: Is it likely that the sentence will succeed in deterring some others? Here, the picture is much less clear than is sometimes supposed. One favourite anecdote is the 'exemplary' sentences handed down in the trials following the Notting Hill race riots of 1958: these were indeed followed by a lull, but increased policing and the removal of leading rioters from circulation may be stronger explanations. Moreover, one key factor is the risk of detection, or, to be more precise, offenders' beliefs about the risk of detection. If offenders think that the risk of detection is low, this may go a long way towards nullifying the effect of higher sentences imposed by the courts.

16.4.3 THE EFFECTIVENESS OF GENERAL DETERRENCE STRATEGIES

Does research cast any light on the effectiveness of general deterrence strategies? There are many difficulties in the way of conducting reliable research on general deterrence. Its effects are likely to vary according to type of offence, as recognised by Lawton LJ, in *R* v *Sargeant* (1974) 60 Cr App R 74, at p. 77:

> So far as deterrence of others is concerned, it is the experience of the courts that deterrent sentences are of little value in respect of offences which are committed on the spur of the moment, either in hot blood or in drink or both. Deterrent sentences may very well be of considerable value where crime is premeditated. Burglars, robbers and users of firearms or weapons may very well be put off by deterrent sentences.

A recent survey of the available research has demonstrated yet again how little we know about deterrence, and how shaky some common assumptions about deterrence are. Research does suggest that a greater certainty of being punished has a deterrent effect, but many offences have a low detection rate. Many people assume that increasing the severity of sentences will have a marginal deterrent effect on offenders and potential offenders: although there is some reason to believe that enormous and well-publicized increases may have an effect, research has found little consistent evidence that simply increasing sentences deters people (von Hirsch, A., Bottoms, A. E., Burney, E., and Wikstrom, P-O., *Criminal Deterrence and Sentence Severity* (Hart Publishing, 1999)). A number of conditions need to be favourable before increased penalties deter, particularly in respect of the influences on a person's decision-making and behaviour, and rarely do these conditions come together. Showing an awareness of these difficulties, the 1990 White Paper counselled caution on deterrent sentencing (para. 2.8):

> Much crime is committed on impulse, given the opportunity presented by an open window or unlocked door, and it is committed by offenders who live from moment to moment; their crimes as impulsive as the rest of their feckless, sad or pathetic lives. It is unrealistic to construct sentencing arrangements on the assumption that most offenders will weigh up the possibilities in advance and base their conduct on rational calculation. Often they do not.

The intention was that the CJA 1991, the main provisions of which have been consolidated in the PCC(S)A 2000, based as it was on proportionality to the seriousness of the offence, would reflect this caution. However, in *R* v *Cunningham* (1993) 14 Cr App R (S) 444 the Court of Appeal held that a trial judge had not been wrong to refer to the need for deterrent sentences for robbery. Lord Taylor, CJ, held that the phrase in s. 80(2)(a) of the 2000 Act — '*commensurate with the seriousness of the offence*' — does allow the sentencer to take account of deterrence: it means 'commensurate with the punishment and deterrence which the offence required'. This was an unexpected reading of the Act, made without support from the White Paper that preceded it. However, Lord Taylor went on to say that s. 80(2)(a) does prohibit the addition of any extra length to the sentence which by the above criteria is commensurate with the seriousness of the offence, 'simply to make a special example of the defendant'. It seems that general sentencing levels may be set by reference to deterrence, but that a court in a particular case may not pass an exemplary sentence that goes above the general level. (The Crime (Sentences) Act 1997, ss. 3 and 4, now consolidated in ss. 110 and 111 of the PCC(S)A 2000, provide for minimum sentences for repeat burglars and drug dealers which rely heavily on individual and general deterrence.)

16.5 Rehabilitative Sentencing

In the 1960s there was considerable enthusiasm for sentences which were reformative or rehabilitative. The 1970s, however, saw the publication of two surveys of the available research on rehabilitative sentencing, both of which reached somewhat negative conclusions (in the United States, Martinson, R., 'What Works? Questions and Answers about Prison Reform', (1974) *Public Interest*, Spring, p. 22; in England, Brody, S. R., *The Effectiveness of Sentencing*, Home Office Research Study No. 35 (HMSO, 1975)). These conclusions have often been summarised in the pithy comment, 'Nothing works'. The reality is somewhat more complicated and more hopeful, as Brody argues ('Research into the Aims and Effectiveness of Sentencing' (1978) 17 *Howard Journal* 133 at p. 134):

> . . . both these publications presented similar evidence which has encouraged a widespread conviction that no one type of sentence works any better — that is, is no more effective in preventing reconviction — than any other. It has to be emphasised that even if it is true, research results have actually provided little evidence for such a belief. This is because, with one or two exceptions, only a very limited range of sentencing alternatives have ever been studied (and consequently only a relatively small proportion of the offender population has ever been considered).

It would therefore be more accurate to say that no sentence has been *proved* to be more effective than others, than to say that no sentence is more effective than others, in view of the limitations of the research. Brody continues in a more optimistic vein (at p. 135):

> One good reason for not completely abandoning a faith in rehabilitation is that a number of studies have shown that improvements *can* be effected in failure rates. What is strikingly consistent about these studies is that in all of them the treatment (whatever form it took) was effective only when it was applied to certain types of offenders, or simply when it was adapted to the particular requirements of individuals, or when it was aimed at modifying such specific aspects of behaviour as addiction or aggressiveness . . . There is nothing very astonishing in these discoveries. What is more surprising is that researchers have so rarely allowed for individual variations or 'interaction effects' in their research designs, but have expected one particular programme to work equally for all offenders.

To expect imprisonment to reform an offender is now rather far-fetched in most cases, for reasons which will be elaborated in **Chapter 21**. But there are forms of community order which aim to rehabilitate (see Home Office Research Study 187, *Reducing Offending*, 1998), as well as the special measures for mentally disordered offenders. Success might be possible if forms of treatment programme can be matched to suitable offenders, and in this respect much depends on the helpfulness of the pre-sentence report (see **Chapter 17**).

16.6 Incapacitative Sentencing

The present sentencing system provides a degree of public protection by exerting a general deterrent effect on potential offenders and by keeping some offenders out of circulation, i.e. for any period when they are incarcerated. But it is sometimes argued that an incapacitative sentencing policy ought to be pursued in respect of certain groups of high-risk offenders. Such a policy has long been in existence in the shape of the sentence of life imprisonment, a sentence which may only be imposed on certain offenders who meet the criteria of dangerousness laid down by the Court of Appeal in *R* v *Hodgson* (1967) 52 Cr App R 113. It is difficult to test whether all the discretionary life sentences which are imposed are necessary for public protection; no one knows. But questions have been raised about whether it is possible to identify other offenders who are so dangerous to the public that they ought to be given incapacitative sentences, longer than is proportionate to their current offences. The findings of research on this are not encouraging:

> In practice, assessments of dangerousness are no more than subjective expectations about the likelihood of any offender causing serious personal injury in the future. As these expectations naturally rely very heavily on knowledge of past behaviour, it is obviously an advantage to have the fullest possible accounts of offenders' histories and circumstances before coming to any decisions about them, but even so, no-one has been able to predict accurately more than half the time, and seldom as often as that. Most 'expert' predictions seem to be right for only one out of three individuals . . . The infrequency of really serious crimes of violence, their apparently generally random quality and the rarity of anything like a genuinely 'dangerous type' offers little encouragement for a policy which aims to reduce serious assaults by selective incapacitation of those with violent records. (Brody, S. and Tarling, R., *Taking Offenders out of Circulation*, Home Office Research Study No. 64 (HMSO, 1980), p. 37.)

Notwithstanding these doubts, the PCC(S)A 2000 which consolidated the main provisions of the CJA 1991 includes two provisions for incapacitative sentencing. Section 79(2)(b) of the 2000 Act allows a court to impose a custodial sentence on a violent or sexual offender where only such a sentence would be adequate to protect the public from serious harm from the offender (even though the present offence is not serious enough); and s. 80(2)(b) allows a court to lengthen a term of imprisonment in such a case, if it appears necessary to protect the public from serious harm from the offender. Moreover, the C(S)A 1997, s. 2, now consolidated in the provisions of s. 109 of the PCC(S)A 2000, has introduced mandatory life imprisonment for certain repeat violent or sexual offences. These points are taken further in **Chapter 23**. For the present, it may be suggested that any policy of incapacitative sentencing for dangerous offenders must be based on hope rather than experience, and is likely to involve longer periods of incarceration unnecessarily for perhaps two-thirds of the offenders subjected to the policy.

16.7 Deserved Sentences and Proportionality

Recent years have seen a resurgence of the retributive justification for sentences, which proposes that an offender should be sentenced proportionately to the seriousness of the offence, because that is what he or she deserves. This approach does not dispute the underlying deterrent rationale for having a system of courts, law and sentencing. But it argues that sentencing offenders according to what they deserve for the offence committed conforms to fundamental principles of justice and fairness. Censuring wrongdoers is seen as an integral part of everyday judgments of praise and blame which, transferred to the administration of criminal justice, means that sentences should express disapprobation of the conduct and its perpetrators. This disapprobation should be proportionate to the seriousness of the offence (von Hirsch, A., *Censure and Sanctions* (1993)).

The CJA 1991 embodied an attempt to install proportionality as the leading aim of sentencing in most cases. In the 1990 White Paper, the Government announced its policy thus (para. 2.2):

> Punishment in proportion to the seriousness of the crime has long been accepted as one of many objectives in sentencing. It should be the principal focus for sentencing decisions. This is consistent with the Government's view that those who commit very serious crimes, particularly crimes of violence, should receive

long custodial sentences; but that many other crimes can be punished in the community, with greater emphasis on bringing home to the criminal the consequences of his actions, compensation to the victim and reparation to the community.

16.8 Sentencing and Victims' Rights

The last quotation makes it clear that the compensation of victims is to be regarded, in general, as a concurrent aim with proportionate sentencing. Consciousness of victims' needs and victims' rights has grown considerably in recent years. Victim support schemes have developed; greater efforts are being made to inform victims of the progress of 'their' case; facilities for victims at courts have seen some improvements; experimental schemes of mediation between victims and offender have been started; the State compensation scheme for the victims of violent crime, administered by the Criminal Injuries Compensation Board, has been brought to the attention of more victims; and courts are imposing compensation orders on offenders in favour of victims. These developments, and further targets, are set out in the *Victim's Charter* (Home Office, 1996).

At the sentencing stage, PCC(S)A 2000, s. 130, empowers courts to order an offender to pay compensation to a victim for any injury, loss or damage caused (to include compensation to the relatives of a deceased victim). PCC(S)A 2000, s. 130, empowers a court to make a compensation order as the sole order upon a convicted defendant, and also provides that courts should give priority to compensation when an offender has insufficient means to pay both a fine and compensation. Section 130 also imposes on courts the duty to give reasons for not making a compensation order in cases where there is a power to do so. These developments are discussed further in **Chapter 18**. In a few cases the courts have permitted the reception of a 'victim impact statement' in which the victim sets out details of the offence from his or her point of view, but the Court of Appeal has warned of the procedural difficulties of this practice (*R* v *Hobstaff* (1993) 14 Cr App R (S) 605).

16.9 Sentencing and the Avoidance of Discrimination

The CJA 1991 includes a provision which gives legislative recognition to the duty not to discriminate. Section 95(1) requires the Home Secretary to publish information annually which will facilitate the performance, by persons engaged in the administration of criminal justice 'of their duty to avoid discriminating against any persons on the ground of race or sex or any other improper ground'.

This is an important symbolic declaration. Its relevance to sentencing practice is established by the research of Professor Roger Hood, *Race and Sentencing* (1992). This large-scale study of sentencing in the West Midlands showed that there were significantly different patterns of sentencing blacks and whites at one of the court centres, where blacks were some 23% more likely to receive a custodial sentence than similarly situated white offenders. Taking account of the seriousness of offences and other variable factors, there were also significant differences in the lengths of the custodial sentences, with both Asians and blacks receiving longer sentences than their white counterparts. Similar differences were found in respect of non-custodial sentences, with blacks being given measures that were more severe than similarly situated white offenders.

It has sometimes been suggested that sentencers discriminate in favour of females, the so-called 'chivalry hypothesis'. **Figure 13.1** above shows that the rate of imprisonment for women is far lower than for men. whereas the proportionate use of discharges and probation orders is much higher. A recent study for the Home Office attempted to discover whether these statistics are evidence of lenient attitudes towards women offenders or stem from some other cause (Hedderman, D., and Gelsthorpe, L., *Understanding the Sentencing of Women*, Home Office Research Study 170 (1997)). They confirmed that, if account is taken of criminal record and other relevant factors, women are still less likely than men to receive a prison sentence for shoplifting, and women first offenders are less likely than men first offenders to receive a custodial sentence for a drug offence, but that for a first violent offence men and women were sent to prison at roughly similar rates. Discussing these trends with magistrates, the researchers found that magistrates were reluctant to fine women with children because they feared that the fine would penalise the children, and that magistrates more frequently viewed women offenders as 'troubled' than as 'troublesome' and therefore tended to opt for probation orders more frequently. The study also confirms that magistrates pay considerable attention to the appearance and behaviour of defendants in the courtroom.

SEVENTEEN

PRE-SENTENCE REPORTS AND DEFERMENT OF SENTENCE

17.1 Pre-sentence Reports

Probation officers have always assisted the court by preparing reports on offenders prior to sentencing. Prior to the Criminal Justice Act 1991 (CJA), probation officers prepared social inquiry reports (renamed in the 1991 Act, pre-sentence reports). However, the only legal requirement for adult offenders was that such a report should be prepared before a community service order was passed. There was no statutory requirement to consider reports for other community sentences, such as probation, although it was good practice.

The PCC(S)A 2000, which consolidated the main provisions of the CJA 1991, states that a court should obtain a pre-sentence report before making a probation order with additional requirements (see **Chapter 19**), a community service order, a combination order, or a supervision order with requirements unless this is considered to be unnecessary (s. 36). However, no community sentence will be invalidated if the court does not do so, but if there is an appeal, then the court hearing the appeal should obtain such a report and consider it. There are therefore very strong presumptions that a pre-sentence report should be obtained if such community sentences are being considered and obviously it would be good practice so to do.

The PCC(S)A 2000 also states that courts should obtain and consider a pre-sentence report before passing a custodial sentence (s. 81(1)), but this will not apply if 'the court is of the opinion that it is unnecessary to obtain a pre-sentence report' (s. 81(2)). In the case of an offender aged under 18, this will not apply if the offence or any associated offence is triable only on indictment and the court considers it to be unnecessary to obtain a report or if there already exists a report, of which the information has been considered by the court (s. 81(3)).

The probation service will have guidelines as to whether such a report should be prepared, but it is of course only counsel who will know whether he or she should suggest one of these community sentences in mitigation. Hence, defence counsel may need to suggest that such a report should be prepared — and should one of the requirements such as a hostel be seen as a likely and useful opportunity, then it may be necessary for counsel to raise this in discussion with the probation liaison officer present in court. Essentially, the probation officer is an extremely useful resource, both to the court in sentencing, and to counsel.

Probation officers stand as the gateway to many community sentences and provisions for mentally disordered offenders — in particular, the facilities that may be available locally as part of a probation order, and as providing information on the local provisions suitable for a client. They will also of course have information on bail hostels and whether places are available there, so that offenders without ties in the community who are remanded for reports can live at the bail hostel rather than being remanded in custody.

It is highly recommended that defence counsel should always go and talk to the probation officer for the court as to whether he or she has had any dealings with counsel's client and whether he or she has prepared a report or can help, and that this discussion should take place before the final talk to the client at court before a guilty plea. If the client is pleading not guilty, then the probation service, if the client agrees, may still be able to prepare a more limited pre-sentence report which does not in any way discuss the offence, and this may be useful where there is a clear possibility of their services being needed, or there is a suggestion of mental disorder.

The PCC(S)A 2000, s. 156 provides for disclosure of a pre-sentence report both to the defence and to prescribed prosecutors (i.e. the CPS, Customs and Excise, DSS, Inland Revenue or the SFO).

17.1.1 NATIONAL STANDARDS FOR PRE-SENTENCE REPORTS

There are National Standards for pre-sentence reports (*National Standards for the Supervision of Offenders in the Community*, London: Home Office, 1995). The Standards define a pre-sentence report as a report in writing with a 'view to assisting the court in determining the most suitable method of dealing with an offender which imposes a restriction on liberty commensurate with the seriousness of the offence'. The probation officer should summarise the offence factually and objectively and then draw on his or her professional experience to analyse the offender's behaviour and attitude to the offence. If applicable he or she should also describe the community sentence under which the offender could most appropriately be supervised and the risk of future offending reduced.

The pre-sentence report will start with a front sheet, which will give basic information about the offender, the offence and the court hearing. Following that will be the introduction, an analysis of the offence, focusing upon seriousness, relevant information about the offender, an analysis of the risk to the public of re-offending, and a conclusion.

The introduction should contain a summary of the sources drawn upon to prepare the report (documents seen, people interviewed, agencies consulted). It will say whether the offender is known to the probation or social services.

The analysis of the offence is designed primarily to assist the court's understanding of the nature and seriousness of the offence, and why the offender committed the offence at this time. It will bring out any factors which, in the opinion of the report writer, the court might see as aggravating or mitigating, but it will not necessarily highlight them as such. Hence, counsel will need to read the report carefully and may be able to build upon some of the factors mentioned briefly in the report. Again, although the report writer is required to form a judgment about the seriousness of the offence (and many probation areas use numerical seriousness scales for this purpose), the report will not express a firm judgment about seriousness, since this is seen as the task of the court. The analysis of the offence is very likely to contain not only an assessment of the context in which the offence occurred, but also an assessment of its consequences, including the impact upon the victim, and an assessment of the offender's attitude to the victim and the consequences of the offence.

Information about the offender will look at his or her personal and social circumstances to help the court decide on relevant sentences. The section on the risk of re-offending is designed to distil the previous information into a concise statement of the risk of re-offending and the risk of harm to the public. It should be followed by a conclusion which is normally intended to contain only one sentencing disposal, unless the court has specifically asked for a range or number of options. Hence, counsel should be aware of this and, in the hearing which asks for a pre-sentence report, rehearse the need for the report to consider a variety of options where this is appropriate (for example, where local resources for mentally disordered offenders are scarce). Where the suggested disposal is a community sentence, it is likely that a specific programme will be proposed. Any requirements which might be attached to a probation order should be set out in the report in the precise terms proposed. A supervision plan for a probation order may be attached.

It is anticipated that at the Crown Court, pre-sentence reports may be prepared on the day to avoid adjournments, in particular to avoid a remand in custody.

17.1.2 TO WHAT EXTENT DO SENTENCERS FOLLOW PRE-SENTENCE REPORTS?

Research studies indicate that magistrates are more likely to adopt suggested sentencing disposals than Crown Court judges. In the Crown Court, and with more serious offences in the magistrates' court, it is necessary for counsel to be realistic in their sentencing suggestions, and it may not always be possible to follow the disposal stated in any pre-sentence report. However, even with a long record of previous convictions, and a moderately serious offence, such as burglary, custody is not an automatic sentence, and reports can still be very useful. Guidance to the probation service indicates that pre-sentence reports in the Crown Court may start to reflect current Crown Court sentencing practice more closely, in which case such reports are likely to become more important.

17.2 Deferment of Sentence

A court may defer sentence for up to six months, i.e. may require the offender to come back to the court (not necessarily before the same bench or judge, though efforts are made to ensure this) before he or she has been sentenced. The power is set out in PCC(S)A 2000, s. 1:

> *(1) The Crown Court or a magistrates' court may defer passing sentence on an offender for the purpose of enabling the court, or any court to which it falls to deal with him, to have regard in dealing with him to—*
> *(a) his conduct after conviction (including, where appropriate, the making by him of reparation for his offence); or*
> *(b) any change in his circumstances . . .*

The reasons can be various, but common ones include whether the offender will do what he or she and his or her counsel say in mitigation that they will do. This might be to get a job, or take voluntary treatment (though a straight probation order without conditions is more usual here), or to pay reparation to the victim or just to 'go straight' — another form of the 'last chance'. It is not possible to put a definite condition of paying compensation into deferment of sentence (the only definite way for the court to order compensation is via a compensation order made in conjunction with or instead of a sentence — and of course deferment happens *before* sentencing). However, defendants would be well advised to get ready to pay reparation if they say they are going to and that is taken up by the judge in deferment. Note that the offender has to consent to the deferment. If the offender successfully completes the period of deferment, he or she can certainly expect not to be sent to prison (a conditional discharge or a probation order is a more usual result).

But there are problems with the very vagueness of the order, and these are well set out in the case of *R* v *George* (1983) 6 Cr App R (S) 211 (judgment of Lord Lane CJ). A defendant definitely 'fails' if he or she commits another offence during the period of deferment. But the other expectations have often been less than clear. Following *George*, it can be stated that:

> The purpose of deferment is therefore to enable the court to take into account the defendant's conduct after conviction or any change in circumstances and then only if it is in the interest of justice to exercise the power. It will, one imagines, seldom be in the interests of justice to stipulate that the conduct required is reparation by the defendant.
>
> The court should make it clear to the defendant what the particular purposes are which the court has in mind under PCC(S)A 2000, s. 1, and what conduct is expected of him or her during deferment.

The failure to do so, or more often the failure on the part of the defendant or his or her representatives to appreciate what those purposes are or that conduct is, has been a fruitful source of appeals . . . It is essential that the deferring court should make a careful note of the purposes for which the sentence is being deferred and what steps, if any, it expects the defendant to take during the period of deferment. Ideally the defendant himself or herself should be given notice in writing of what he or she is expected to do or refrain from doing, so that there can be no doubt in his or her mind what is expected of him or her.

Thus the task of the court which comes to deal with the offender at the expiration of the period of deferment is as follows:

First, the purpose of the deferment and any requirement imposed by the deferring court must be ascertained. Secondly, the court must determine if the defendant has substantially conformed or attempted to conform with the proper expectations of the deferring court, whether with regard to finding a job or as the case may be. If he or she has, then the defendant may legitimately expect that an immediate custodial sentence will not be imposed. If he has not, then the court should be careful to state with precision in what respect he or she has failed.

. . . In many cases a short probation order may be preferable to a deferment of sentence. Such an order enables the defendant's behaviour to be monitored by the probation officer, and it ensures that formal notice of the requirements of the court are given to the defendant.

On the other hand, a deferment of sentence will be more appropriate where the conduct required of the defendant is not sufficiently specific to be made the subject of a condition imposed as part of a probation order without creating uncertainty in the mind of the probation officer and the defendant as to whether there has been a breach of the order; for example, where the defendant is to make a real effort to find work, or where the sentencer wishes to see whether a change in the defendant's attitude and circumstances, which appears to be a possibility at the time of deferment, does in fact come about. Again, deferment may be the appropriate course where the steps to be taken by the defendant could not of their nature be the subject of a condition, for example where he or she is to make reparation, or at least demonstrate a real intention and capacity to do so.

EIGHTEEN

DISCHARGES, COMPENSATION ORDERS AND FINES

18.1 Introduction

Most indictable offences (either-way offences and those triable only on indictment) result in either a fine or a discharge, often combined with a compensation order. This is because most either-way offences are tried in the magistrates' courts, which tend to use the fine most frequently. The Magistrates' Association guidelines (see **20.2.4**) tend to focus on fines, but they indicate that where aggravating features predominate in certain crimes, the guideline should be a community sentence or, as the case may be, a custodial sentence. On the other hand, where mitigating features predominate in certain crimes, the guideline should be a discharge or fine.

In this chapter we first consider discharges and bind-overs, and then move on to compensation orders and fines. It is important to bear in mind throughout that in any case involving death, injury, loss or damage, the court is obliged to consider making a compensation order. The order may be added to any other form of sentence, or may be the sole order in the case.

18.2 Absolute Discharge

The absolute discharge is exactly that: the offender is discharged absolutely from punishment for the offence. The law is now contained in s. 12 of the PCC(S)A 2000. The absolute discharge might be appropriate in response to 'the triviality of the offence, the circumstances in which it came to be prosecuted, or factors relating to the offender'. In practice, absolute discharges are granted rarely (1% of cases in magistrates' courts, even less in the Crown Court). They seem to be reserved for cases where the court takes the view that the offender had little or no moral guilt, or is in dire circumstances (e.g. suffering from a terminal disease).

Cases in which an absolute discharge is appropriate should come before the courts only rarely, because they should usually be eliminated at the stage of deciding whether to prosecute. The initial decision is usually that of the police, and the Home Office circulars to police forces on the use of police cautions (No. 59/1990 and No. 18/1994) recommend the use of a caution instead of prosecution in cases where the likely penalty in court will be nominal, and in cases where there are factors personal to the defendant (old age, infirmity, mental illness or stress) which would make a prosecution particularly traumatic. In these cases the police are urged to caution the defendant formally, usually involving the attendance of the defendant at a police station to be cautioned by a uniformed senior officer. The police have been encouraged to use cautions more widely for adult offenders, and in consequence the 'cautioning rate' rose from a mere 3% during the 1980s to 26% of male defendants aged 21 or over in 1997 (*Criminal Statistics 1997*, Table 5.4), even though a Home Office Circular (No. 18/1994) aimed to reduce the cautioning rate by restricting second and subsequent cautions.

There is a further filter in cases where the police decide upon prosecution and pass the papers to the CPS. According to the *Code for Crown Prosecutors*, issued under s. 10 of the Prosecution of Offences Act 1985, the CPS should consider 'whether the public interest requires a prosecution' in each case. The factors to be considered are similar to those enumerated in the police cautioning circular: a prosecution might properly be discontinued if the court 'would be likely to impose a purely nominal penalty' (such as an absolute discharge), and if the defendant is old, infirm, mentally ill or under great stress. If these filters work effectively, it will be rare that the courts will find a case in which an absolute discharge is the appropriate disposal.

18.3 Conditional Discharge

A conditional discharge, like an absolute discharge, now counts as a conviction for some purposes (PCC(S)A 2000, s. 151). The difference is that the court may discharge the offender 'subject to the condition that he commits no offence during such period, not exceeding three years', as the court may specify; and, if the offender does commit another offence during the specified period, the court which convicts him or her of that offence has the power to impose a sentence for the original offence as well (s. 12 of the PCC(S)A 2000). In that sense the conditional discharge carries the threat of a more severe sentence if the offender fails to conform to the law during the specified period.

Discharges were given to some 14% of male indictable offenders aged 21 and over in 1997, and to some 27% of female indictable offenders aged 21 and over. It is an appropriate measure for a non-serious offence by someone with no previous convictions, or with a substantial gap since the last conviction. It sounds a warning, and reserves to the courts the power to re-sentence if a further offence is committed within the specified period. Conditional discharges have also been used in cases where the offender is thought to lack the means to pay an adequate fine. The point is illustrated by *R* v *McGowan* [1975] Crim LR 113. The defendant was convicted of handling seven stolen crabs. The judge was informed that the defendant was impecunious and that a fine would be difficult to pay. He therefore imposed a suspended sentence of 12 months' imprisonment. The Court of Appeal held that this was wrong in principle: the offence was not serious enough for imprisonment of any kind and, if a fine was not thought to be practical, the proper course was to move down to a conditional discharge.

18.4 Binding Over

This option may be seen as an alternative to a conditional discharge. Some courts seem to have a tradition of using the power to bind over instead of the power to grant a conditional discharge. One of the principal modern restatements of the power is in s. 1(7) of the Justices of the Peace Act 1968, which declares 'the power to bind over to keep the peace, and the power to bind over to be of good behaviour, a person who or whose case is before the court, by requiring him to enter into his own recognisances or to find sureties or both, and committing him to prison if he does not comply'. The power to bind a person over to be of good behaviour, and not to act *contra bonos mores*, has been held by the European Court of Human Rights to amount to an unjustifiable interference with the right to freedom of expression under ECHR, Article 10 (*Hashman and Harrup* v *UK* [2000] Crim LR 185. The Court held that the order is not sufficiently certain in its terms, and this means that under the HRA 1998 it would be wrong for a court to impose such an order.

The chief practical differences between the bind-over and the conditional discharge are twofold. First, the bind-over specifies a sum of money to be forfeited, and thus takes the form of a suspended fine. Secondly, a bind-over can be breached without the commission of a subsequent offence, if it is proved that the person has failed to keep the peace or to be of good behaviour.

18.5 Deferment of Sentence

Section 1 of the PCC(S)A 2000 empowers a court to defer sentence on an offender for up to six months (see **17.2** above).

18.6 Compensation Orders

18.6.1 INTRODUCTION

The *Victim's Charter: a Statement of the Rights of Victims of Crime* (Home Office, 1996) includes a detailed description of rights and facilities for victims, and sets out standards which should be attained in dealing with victims by the police, the CPS, Victim Support, the probation service, and the courts.

In respect of compensation, there are two important features of the English system. First, there is the Criminal Injuries Compensation Scheme: the Criminal Injuries Compensation Board (CICB) is open to claims from anyone who suffers personal injury as a result of an offence of violence or as a result of an act of law enforcement. The Board does not deal with any claim in respect of an injury valued at less than £1,000. The Compensation for Criminal Injuries Act 1995 establishes the statutory framework.

This leads on to a discussion of the second aspect of the English system, the compensation order. From the victim's point of view there are major differences between the two. A claim may be made to the CICB even though the offender is never traced, whereas a court can only make a compensation order if the perpetrator is convicted (and has the means to pay). On the other hand, claims to the CICB for State compensation are limited to crimes of violence, whereas courts are empowered to make compensation orders in respect of injury, loss or damage.

The key features of the law on compensation orders are now as follows:

(a) In every case involving injury, death, loss or damage, a court must consider making a compensation order and must give reasons for not doing so if it decides not to exercise its power.

(b) In deciding whether to make a compensation order, and the amount of the order, a court must take account of the offender's means.

(c) If the court wishes to impose a fine as well as a compensation order, preference should be given to the compensation order if it appears that the offender has insufficient means to pay both.

(d) A compensation order may be made both for the offence of which the offender is convicted and for any offence or offences taken into consideration.

(e) A court may make a compensation order as the sole order on conviction.

18.6.2 THE IMPORTANCE OF COMPENSATION ORDERS

The importance of making compensation orders has been urged on the courts more and more, largely in response to the legitimate expectations of victims of crime. Research into the opinions of victims of crime in the early 1980s showed that victims in general are far more concerned to receive some compensation (not necessarily full compensation) from the offender, than to see severe sentences meted out. As Shapland reported, on the basis of research which involved the interviewing of victims (Shapland, J., 'Victims, the Criminal Justice System and Compensation' (1984) 24 BJ Crim 131, at pp. 144–5):

> Victims were, again, not particularly punitive either in the sentence that they would wish their offender to get or in their reactions to the sentence that those offenders who were convicted finally received. Their suggested sentences seemed to be very much within those of current English sentencing practice. They did, however, feel that compensation for the offender should have played a much larger part than in fact it did (only 20% of victims whose offenders were sentenced received compensation orders and many of these were for small amounts). These

> reactions on sentencing are not just confined to the victims of violent crime, as in our study. The recent British Crime Survey . . . has also suggested that: 'victims' recommendations are broadly in line with present practice', and that compensation is important.

It was quite clear from the research that victims tend to attribute great significance to compensation:

> How, then, did victims view state compensation and compensation by offenders? They regarded compensation not as mainly a matter of money or of financial assistance (charitable or otherwise), but rather as making a statement about the offence, the victim and the position that the criminal justice system was prepared to give to the victim. Even the element of payment in proportion to suffering and loss was subordinated to this symbolic function. This was most obvious in victims' enthusiasm for compensation from offenders as part of the sentence of the court.

18.6.3 AWARDING COMPENSATION

It is not for the victim to apply to the court for compensation: the duty is upon the court to make an order unless it gives reasons for not doing so. Section 130(4) of the PCC(S)A 2000 states that the compensation order 'shall be of such amount as the court considers appropriate, having regard to any evidence and to any representations that are made by or on behalf of the accused or the prosecutor'. The Victim's Charter declares that it is the prosecutor's responsibility to inform the court about the victim's loss: among the questions it poses to prosecutors are, '(1) Do case papers routinely include information on the victim's injury or loss? . . . (6) Is the prosecutor invariably put in a position to assist the court in considering a compensation order?' (p. 24).

It is wrong in principle for a court to allow an offender to 'buy his way out of prison' by paying a substantial sum by way of compensation (*R* v *Copley* (1979) 1 Cr App R (S) 55). The voluntary payment of compensation is sometimes regarded as evidence of remorse and therefore treated as mitigation, but it would be wrong to allow an offender's inability to pay compensation to the victim to increase the severity of the sentence (*R* v *Barney* (1989) 11 Cr App R (S) 448). The court has a duty to enquire into the offender's means, and should not impose a compensation order which is beyond those means (*R* v *Stanley* (1989) 11 Cr App R (S) 446). Where two or more persons are convicted of an offence, the compensation orders made against them should reflect the means of each individual, so that if one co-defendant is less wealthy than the others a lower compensation order should be imposed (*R* v *Bagga* (1989) 11 Cr App R (S) 497). Indeed, liability is joint and several, and if only one of the co-defendants has financial resources, it is quite proper to make a compensation order for the whole sum against that one (*R* v *Beddow* (1987) 9 Cr App R (S) 235).

Two further points about the use of the compensation order may be illustrated by reference to the decision in *R* v *Martin* (1989) 11 Cr App R (S) 424. The offender had attacked another woman, and was convicted of assault occasioning actual bodily harm and assault with intent to rob. The court sentenced her to 12 months' detention in a young offender institution (she was aged 20) and ordered her to pay £200 compensation to the victim. The propriety of the compensation order was attacked on two grounds. First, it was argued that it is wrong to make a compensation order which made it necessary for the offender to sell an asset (here, her car) which had no connection with the crime. The Court of Appeal held that the order was quite proper, although there are other decisions which emphasise the need for a court to be satisfied that the asset is sufficient to cover the amount of the compensation order (*R* v *Chambers* (1981) 3 Cr App R (S) 318, *R* v *Stewart* (1983) 5 Cr App R (S) 320). Secondly, it was argued that it is wrong to combine a compensation order with a substantial custodial sentence. The Court of Appeal held that this is not wrong, so long as the sentencer is satisfied that the offender has the means to pay the order (cf. *R* v *Jonge* [1999] 2 Cr App R (S) 1). Indeed, in *R* v *Love and Tomkins* [1999] Crim LR 171 the Court held that it may be appropriate to make an order if it appears that the offender will have sufficient earning capacity on release from prison.

18.6.4 THE LAWFULNESS OF COMPENSATION ORDERS

Section 130(1) of the PCC(S)A 2000, empowers a court to make a compensation order *'for any personal injury, loss or damage resulting from that offence or any other offence which is taken into consideration by the court in determining sentence'*. Two restrictions are embodied in this provision. First, a compensation order should be made only if the loss or damage results from the offence: thus in a case of handling where the stolen goods are returned to the owner, there is unlikely to be any loss (*R* v *Tyce* [1994] Crim LR 71). Secondly, where a person is convicted on one or more specimen counts, it is unlawful to make a compensation order in respect of losses alleged to result from other offences that were neither charged nor taken into consideration (*R* v *Crutchley* [1994] Crim LR 309 (applying the same principle also to confiscation orders, see **18.8**)).

18.7 Fines

The fine is the penalty imposed for the vast majority of summary offences, and also remains the most frequently imposed penalty for indictable offences. Its use has, however, declined, from some 60% of adult males sentenced for indictable offences in the mid–1970s to 32% in 1997. The maximum fine for most offences tried in the Crown Court is unlimited, but magistrates' courts are limited to a maximum fine of £5,000 (with a few exceptions), and the maxima for summary offences are ranged on five standard levels (levels 1 to 5) according to the relative seriousness of the offence.

18.7.1 TO FINE OR NOT TO FINE?

How should a court decide whether to fine an offender or not? If the case is not thought suitable for a conditional or absolute discharge (see **18.3** and **18.2**), then the court might presume that a fine is the appropriate measure unless the case is serious enough to warrant a community sentence (s. 35(1), discussed in **19.2**).

There are two dangers to be avoided at this stage. One is that it is wrong to impose a fine on an offender simply because he or she has the means to pay, when a less wealthy offender would receive a custodial or community sentence. This is the principle of equality before the law, that an offender should not be able to buy his or her way out of prison (*R* v *Markwick* (1953) 37 Cr App R 125). The second danger is perhaps less noticeable: it is wrong to impose a more severe penalty on an offender simply because he or she appears to lack the means to pay a substantial fine. Research has shown that courts tend to fine unemployed offenders less frequently than employed offenders: in magistrates' courts the difference is between 43% for unemployed offenders and 54% for employed offenders (Home Office Statistical Bulletin 20/94, para. 12). Such a decision may be acceptable if the court then selects a less severe sentence than a fine, such as a conditional discharge. But it is wrong in principle for a court to move up to a more severe sentence simply because the offender lacks the means to pay a sizeable fine (see *R* v *McGowan* at **18.3**).

This issue is revisited below: for the present, the point is that the decision whether or not to impose a fine should be taken by reference to the seriousness of the offence, not by reference to wealth or poverty.

18.7.2 THE EFFECT OF THE POWERS OF CRIMINAL COURTS (SENTENCING) ACT 2000

Sections 126 to 129 of the PCC(S)A 2000 contain provisions relating to the system of fines. The court must make a financial circumstances inquiry before fixing a fine.

18.7.3 CALCULATING THE AMOUNT OF THE FINE

Section 126 of the PCC(S)A 2000 contains provisions for the making of financial circumstances orders. Section 128 of the Act provides as follows:

> (1) *Before fixing the amount of any fine to be imposed on an offender who is an individual, a court shall inquire into his financial circumstances.*
> (2) *The amount of any fine fixed by a court shall be such as, in the opinion of the court, reflects the seriousness of the offence.*
> (3) *In fixing the amount of any fine to be imposed on an offender (whether an individual or other person), a court shall take into account the circumstances of the case including, among other things, the financial circumstances of the offender so far as they are known, or appear, to the court.*

It is possible to read subsections (1), (2) and (3) as being inconsistent with one another, but they are better interpreted as successive steps to be taken by the court. First, the court should decide what fine would reflect the seriousness of the offence. Second, the court should adjust that to reflect the means of the offender — s. 128(4) adds that this may have the effect of increasing or decreasing the amount of the fine. In order to determine an offender's means, s. 128(1) requires the court to inquire into the offender's financial circumstances, and s. 126 empowers a court to make a financial circumstances order requiring the defendant to disclose such details as are requested. Section 136 of the 2000 Act empowers the court to make such an order in respect of a parent or guardian of a young offender.

In taking the first step, magistrates' courts may consult the guideline fines' recommended in the Magistrates' Association Sentencing Guidelines (2000 revision). These guidelines are represented as three levels of starting point, A, B and C, and the actual fine at each level varies according to the court's calculation of the offender's net income.

In considering these guidelines, magistrates are encouraged to take account of factors that make the offence more or less serious, and then to take account of personal mitigating factors.

18.7.4 MAXIMUM REPAYMENT PERIOD

A number of decisions in the 1980s seemed to have settled the proposition that fines should normally be calculated so that they could be paid within 12 months (e.g. *R* v *Knight* (1980) 2 Cr App R (S) 82; *R* v *Nunn* (1983) 5 Cr App R (S) 203). However, in *R* v *Olliver and Olliver* (1989) 11 Cr App R (S) 10, the Court of Appeal held that there was nothing wrong in principle with the payment period being longer than 12 months, provided that it was not an undue burden and too severe a punishment, having regard to the nature of the offence and the offender. A period of two years would seldom be too long, and three years might be acceptable in an appropriate case. The court added (*per* Lord Lane CJ, at p. 15) that this was 'particularly important in the present climate, where every effort is required in the face of growing crime figures, to find alternatives to custodial sentences . . . it may well be that fines, where fines are possible, are the most effective and the most desirable alternatives to custody'.

The longer possible payment periods apply also to compensation orders.

18.7.5 IMPRISONMENT IN DEFAULT

One of the greatest practical problems with financial penalties is that if they are not properly calculated according to the offender's means, the offender may be unable to pay. The outcome is that an offence for which a fine was thought appropriate by the court may result in a short prison term. Research suggests that, among those who do not pay fines, there are some who genuinely cannot pay because their means are inadequate and some who can pay but refuse to do so. It is often said that it is necessary to retain the sanction of imprisonment in order to put pressure on those who can pay but wish to avoid their obligations, but it has proved difficult to separate these people from cases of genuine hardship.

The PCC(S)A 2000 which consolidated the relevant provisions of the C(S)A 1997 contains provisions to reduce the use of imprisonment for fine default. Section 59 introduces powers to make a curfew order or to make a community service order in lieu of the fine, for a person who has defaulted on a financial penalty, and these powers have been introduced experimentally in some areas. In addition, the Lord Chancellor's Working Group on the Enforcement of Financial Penalties issued a package of guidance to all magistrates' courts in July 1996, urging the use of enforcement measures other than custody in accordance with the Divisional Court's decision in *R* v *Oldham Justices, ex parte Cawley* [1996] 1 All ER 464. The use of imprisonment in default has already declined substantially.

18.8 Forfeiture and Confiscation

It is important to note that there are now some mandatory provisions for forfeiture. These provisions apply in offences concerned with drugs, and they are aimed at depriving offenders of their profits. (In fact the provisions strike at gross receipts rather than profits: see *R* v *Smith* [1989] Crim LR 752.)

The principal statute is the Drug Trafficking Act 1994, and this imposes on the court a duty, in the case of every person convicted of one of the listed offences, to proceed through a series of decisions designed to result in the making of a confiscation order under the Act where the offender has assets. Although details of the legislation are not pursued here, it must be complied with in all drug trafficking and some other drugs cases. For a summary of the law, see D. A. Thomas, 'Confiscation Orders and Drug Trafficking' [1994] Crim LR 93.

The Proceeds of Crime Act 1995 consolidated and reformed the procedures for confiscating the profits of non-drug offenders.

NINETEEN

COMMUNITY SENTENCES

19.1 The Basis of the Law

Since the mid-1960s several new forms of sentence have been introduced in order to provide courts with a wider range of options and thereby to reduce their use of custody. The suspended sentence, introduced in 1967, is discussed at **21.10**. In 1972 the community service order and day training centres were introduced. In 1982 the compensation order became a sentence in its own right, and 'Schedule 11' probation orders were introduced. Courts were frequently urged to use community service orders and probation orders as 'alternatives to custody', but overall the use of custody did not decline. Sentences such as the community service order became widely used, but often in the place of other non-custodial measures, and the imprisonment rate remained fairly constant.

Under the PCC(S)A 2000 which consolidated the relevant provisions of the CJA 1991 the emphasis is upon community sentences as tough and demanding measures in their own right, and as restrictions in liberty which should be enforced rigorously. To this end there is a set of National Standards for the Supervision of Offenders in the Community (latest edition, 2000), intended to set standards for the probation service and others. The PCC(S)A 2000 provides a threshold test before a community sentence may be passed, and then provides further criteria for determining the type and quantum of the sentence — requirements which are analogous to those which ss. 79 and 80 of the PCC(S)A 2000 apply to custody.

19.2 The Threshold Test for a Community Sentence

If a court is considering a community sentence, its attention must be drawn to s. 35(1) of the PCC(S)A 2000:

> *A court shall not pass a community sentence on an offender unless it is of the opinion that the offence, or the combination of the offence and one or more offences associated with it, was serious enough to warrant such a sentence.*

The definition of a community sentence is discussed at **19.3**. The reference to 'the combination of the offence and one or more . . .' incorporates the principles discussed at **20.5**.

The main thrust of s. 35(1) is that a court should satisfy itself that the offence was 'serious enough to warrant' a community sentence. This wording differs from that of the threshold test for custody in s. 79(2)(a), i.e. 'so serious that only a custodial sentence can be justified'. The difference suggests that there might be cases in which a court may have to choose between a heavy fine and a community sentence, and that the two are not mutually exclusive. Although para. 4.3 of the 1990 White Paper stated, 'punishment in the community should be an effective way of dealing with many offenders . . . when financial penalties are insufficient', the wording of s. 35(1) leaves open the possibility of imposing a community sentence where a heavy fine is a possible option.

19.3 The Definition of 'Community Sentence'

From the wording of PCC(S)A 2000, s. 33(1), it will have been observed that a community sentence 'consists of one or includes one or more community orders'. There are now eight forms of community order:

(a) a curfew order;

(b) a probation order;

(c) a community service order;

(d) a combination order;

(e) a drug treatment and testing order;

(f) an attendance centre order;

(g) a supervision order;

(h) an action plan order.

The last three orders are available only for offenders under 21, and they are therefore discussed only in **Chapter 24**.

As for the community orders available for adults, it is clear that any of them may be combined with a fine or compensation order or both. However, orders (b), (c) and (d) may not be combined with one another (s. 35(2)), since the whole purpose of the combination order (discussed at **19.7**) is to make provision for a combined probation and community service order. It should be noted that the curfew order is not yet available to all courts.

Although the 'cocktail sentences' that add fines to community orders may be lawful themselves, a court may only impose them if the conditions in s. 35(3) are also satisfied.

19.4 Proportionality and Suitability

The type and quantum of community order or orders are governed by the two requirements in PCC(S)A 2000, s. 35(3):

> *. . . where a court passes a community sentence—*
> *(a) the particular order or orders comprising or forming part of the sentence shall be such as in the opinion of the court is, or taken together are, the most suitable for the offender; and*
> *(b) the restrictions on liberty imposed by the order or orders shall be such as in the opinion of the court are commensurate with the seriousness of the offence, or the combination of the offence and one or more offences associated with it.*

These requirements are consistent with the general policy of CJA 1991 as consolidated in the PCC(S)A 2000. Section 35(3)(b) ensures that the proportionality principle applies to decisions on community sentences. Section 35(3)(a) aims to ensure that, within the framework of the proportionality principle, the selection of community orders(s) maximises the preventative and rehabilitative potential of the sentence. The 1990 White Paper commended the prevention of re-offending as an aim of the probation service (para. 1.9), and added that 'reforming offenders is always best if it can be achieved' (para. 2.6). Before pursuing this question of selecting the appropriate community order(s), each of the three orders available to adults must be described.

19.5 Probation Orders

The probation order has been used in courts for over a century, but the 1991 Act altered the statutory framework. In the past, a probation order was made 'instead of sentencing the offender'. Since 1992, probation has been a sentence of the court, and is to be found in s. 41 of the PCC(S)A 2000. The principal provision is:

> *Where a person aged 16 years or over is convicted of an offence and the court by or before which he is convicted is of the opinion that his supervision is desirable in the interests of—*
> *(a) securing his rehabilitation, or*
> *(b) protecting the public from harm from him or preventing the commission by him of further offences,*
> *the court may . . . make an order requiring him to be under supervision for a period specified in the order . . .*

A probation order may be for a period of six months to three years, as specified by the court. The CJA 1991 made it available for 16-year-olds in the youth courts.

Any award of compensation or restitution to the victim must be made using a separate compensation order and may not be a requirement attached to the probation order.

The sentencer may sentence the offender for one offence to both a probation order and a fine, or a suspended sentence, but may not make a probation order together with a community service order. Instead, the sentencer should then make a combination order (which combines community service with supervision).

19.5.1 WHAT HAPPENS IN A PROBATION ORDER?

The main idea of probation was not changed by the CJA 1991 or by subsequent legislation. Probation officers are under a duty to 'advise, assist and befriend' offenders under their supervision, i.e. it is a helping role, but, because it is supervision, it is also a controlling role, since the offender must report to them as they order, and receive visits from them as required in his or her home. The two elements of care and control have always been present in probation and in the work of probation officers, and they have always produced a dichotomy in which there is tension between the need to respond to the offender's problems and the need to control and supervise the offender. The provisions of the CJA 1991 have not been universally popular with probation officers, as some see it as reflecting a move towards the controlling, rather than caring, end of probation. Since the CDA 1998 introduced youth offending teams, members of those teams may be assigned to supervise offenders aged under 18 who are on probation (PCC(S)A 2000, s. 41(5)).

There are National Standards (*National Standards for the Supervision of Offenders in the Community*, London, Home Office, 1995) for the supervision of probation orders. These include the requirements that:

(a) supervision should commence promptly;

(b) there should be a supervision plan, regularly reviewed;

(c) there should be frequent appointments with the offender in the first three months;

(d) records should be kept of all appointments;

(e) there should be prompt and effective action to enforce orders, including the taking of breach proceedings.

The objectives of a probation order are:

(a) confronting offending behaviour, challenging the offender to accept responsibility for his or her crime and its consequences;

(b) making offenders aware of the impact of the crimes they have committed on their victims, the community and themselves;

(c) motivating and assisting the offender towards a greater sense of personal responsibility and discipline, and to aid his or her reintegration as a law abiding member of the community;

(d) intervening to remedy practical obstacles preventing rehabilitation (e.g., education, training, skills needed for employment and action to counter drug or alcohol misuse, illiteracy or homelessness) and to help the offender acquire relevant new skills; and

(e) ensuring that the supervision programme for the offender is demanding and effective. (National Standards 1995.)

Probation officers, like counsel, also have two duties — in their case to the offender and also to the court as they are officers of the court.

19.5.2 NUMBERS OF PROBATION ORDERS

The proportion of offenders placed on probation stood at 11% for males for indictable offences in 1996. The proposals in the CJA 1991 envisaged probation becoming more important and being used for more serious offences. The Act forecast there being around 2,200 to 3,300 additional orders involving supervision, 11,250 additional pre-sentence reports, and the likelihood of more supervision after release, leading to a need for 550 additional probation officers/staff nationally.

19.5.3 PROBATION'S PLACE IN THE TARIFF

19.5.3.1 Use of probation in the Crown Court

Moxon's research is the first to explore what is actually happening in the Crown Court — as opposed to the tables in the *Criminal Statistics*, which merely delineate the kinds of offenders who get fines, probation, etc. He looked at a very large sample of Crown Court cases and at the factors which seemed to be related to getting different sentences. In relation to probation he states:

> Probation is very much an individualised disposal, intended for those who do not pose a sufficient threat to society to require custody but who are seen as in need of an element of supervision while at liberty to help in guiding them towards a more law-abiding way of life. It is accordingly seen as particularly appropriate for offenders with personal problems who might benefit from professional help. For the most part probation was not strongly associated with particular offences except that it was used disproportionately for sex offenders. (Moxon, *Sentencing Practice in the Crown Courts*, 1989).

Figure 19.1 shows the factors associated with the use of probation by the Crown Court.

> A clear pattern discernible from the table is that those most likely to be given probation were offenders who had been involved in a fair amount of criminal activity — as indicated by the number of charges involved, offences taken into consideration, previous convictions and previous supervision.
>
> This is consistent with efforts to promote the use of probation as a fairly high tariff disposal — efforts which have contributed to an increase in the proportion of defendants who have previously served custodial sentences from 24% in 1981 to 32% in 1985. Defendants who had secured treatment for an addiction had often done so with probation help, and were clearly likely to need continuing support and

supervision. The low use of probation for those who pleaded not guilty was almost certainly influenced by the fact that social inquiry reports (now termed pre-sentence reports) were much less likely to have been available in those cases: a social inquiry report was available in 82% of cases involving a guilty plea but in only 51% of contested cases.

Figure 19.1 Use of probation as a proportion of all non-custodial disposals by factors related to the offence and the offender

Factors associated with higher use of probation	*Probation* % %	*Factors associated with with lower use of probation*	*Probation* % %
Treatment for addiction	59	Not mentioned	23
Good response to supervision	34	Poor response	0
Convicted on 4 counts or more	46	3 offences or less	22
Severe stress	44	Not mentioned	21
Female	42	Male	21
Unemployed	33	Employed	17
1 or more t.i.c.'s	38	No t.i.c.'s	23
Pleaded guilty	27	Pleaded not guilty	13
Property not recovered	27	Property recovered	13
3 or more previous convictions	31	2 or less previous convictions	20
Premeditated	25	Spontaneous	16

Such a pattern will of course cause problems if the 'just deserts' principle of the CJA 1991 is adopted as strictly the only philosophy of sentencing to be used. However, when discussing non-custodial sentences, the White Paper refers to the need that: 'Each order should be tailored both to the seriousness of the offence and the characteristics of the offender. A comparatively short order may make more severe demands on some offenders than more severe orders would on others'. It remains to be seen how this may work out in practice — it will certainly require a more sophisticated approach by sentencers, counsel and probation officers to reflect both factors in the discussion between conviction and sentence — and considerable preparation for the sentencing hearing by counsel.

19.5.3.2 Probation where there is mental disorder, drug or alcohol misuse

The position with regard to mental disorder or drug or alcohol misuse is rather more complicated and varies locally. Courts are ready to give probation orders in such cases, but local clinics may not be willing to take offenders under such a court order, because they feel that treatment has to be truly voluntary to be of benefit. Sometimes they will take the person if the treatment is not a condition of the order — i.e. a straight probation order is specified. Sometimes, the sentencer and the clinic and the offender will agree on voluntary treatment, with the actual disposal being a fine or conditional discharge or suspended sentence, etc. Local knowledge is essential.

The CDA 1998 contains a provision which has been consolidated in the PCC(S)A 2000 to try to cope with this: the drug treatment and testing order. The drug treatment and testing order is an entirely separate community sentence, not part of a probation order. However, it contains two elements: treatment and a limited element of supervision by a probation officer. The order will only be passed if the offender is dependent on or has a propensity to misuse drugs and that this dependency requires and may be susceptible to treatment. The order will last for a period between six months and three years and the treatment should reduce or eliminate the offender's dependency on or propensity to misuse drugs, either by being resident in a treatment facility or being treated as a non-resident. Local arrangements for treatment need to be in place.

19.5.3.3 The effect of the Criminal Justice Act 1991

There has been a definite attempt to move probation up the tariff in recent years and this is now very much encouraged by the Government. The National Statement of the

Home Office on the priorities for the probation service in 1983–84 said that pre-sentence reports should concentrate on those at imminent risk of going into custody — and probation practice is following. It is, therefore, possible to suggest probation even for an offender with quite a high number of previous convictions. However, it should be stressed to clients that not cooperating with the probation officer preparing the pre-sentence report is likely to be disastrous for the client's chances of obtaining a community sentence.

The PCC(S)A 2000 which consolidated the relevant provisions of the CJA 1991 also envisages requirements being attached to probation orders in relation to treatment for drug or alcohol abuse as well as for treatment for mental disorders (see **Chapter 23**). It must be said, however, that clinics offering such treatment can be very reluctant to admit offenders subject to an order of the court. They feel that such an order represents compulsion and that offenders need to prove to the clinic that they themselves wish to have such treatment. In such instances, counsel should consider suggesting to the court that a probation order without requirements, or another penalty, might be more appropriate, with the offender attending the clinic voluntarily. The advice of the probation service should be sought.

19.5.4 REVOCATION AND AMENDMENT

A probation order can be revoked either by the probation officer supervising the order or by the offender on application to the court which made the order (PCC(S)A 2000, sch. 3, part III). The order should be revoked if the probation officer feels that all the purpose of the order has been fulfilled, or if he or she finds the offender cannot comply with the terms of the order. If revoked, then any other order which could originally have been made by that court may be made. Overall more than 80% of orders are completed satisfactorily. Some of the relevant provisions are in paras 10(1)–(3), 12(1)–(4) and 13(1)–(3) of sch. 3 of the PCC(S)A 2000 which provide as follows:

10.—(1) This paragraph applies where a relevant order made by a magistrates' court is in force in respect of any offender and on the application of the offender or the responsible officer it appears to the appropriate magistrates' court that, having regard to circumstances which have arisen since the order was made, it would be in the interests of justice—

(a) for the order to be revoked; or

(b) for the offender to be dealt with in some other way for the offence in respect of which the order was made.

(2) In this paragraph 'the appropriate magistrates' court' means—

(a) in the case of a drug treatment and testing order, the magistrates' court responsible for the order;

(b) in the case of any other relevant order, a magistrates' court acting for the petty sessions area concerned.

(3) The appropriate magistrates' court may—

(a) revoke the order; or

(b) both—

(i) revoke the order; and

(ii) deal with the offender, for the offence in respect of which the order was made, in any way in which it could deal with him if he had just been convicted by the court of the offence.

12.—(1) This paragraph applies where a probation order or combination order is in force in respect of any offender and on the application of the offender or the responsible officer to the appropriate court it appears to the court that, having regard to circumstances which have arisen since the order was made, it would be in the interests of justice—

(a) for the order to be revoked; and

(b) for an order to be made under section 12(1)(b) of this Act discharging the offender conditionally for the offence for which the probation or combination order was made.

(2) In this paragraph 'the appropriate court' means—

> *(a) where the probation or combination order was made by a magistrates' court, a magistrates' court acting for the petty sessions area concerned;*
>
> *(b) where the probation or combination order was made by the Crown Court, the Crown Court.*
>
> *(3) No application may be made under paragraph 10 or 11 above for a probation order or combination order to be revoked and replaced with an order for conditional discharge under section 12(1)(b); but otherwise nothing in this paragraph shall affect the operation of paragraphs 10 and 11 above.*
>
> *(4) Where this paragraph applies—*
>
> *(a) the appropriate court may revoke the probation or combination order and make an order under section 12(1)(b) of this Act discharging the offender in respect of the offence for which the probation or combination order was made, subject to the condition that he commits no offence during the period specified in the order under section 12(1)(b); and*
>
> *(b) the period specified in the order under section 12(1)(b) shall be the period beginning with the making of that order and ending with the date when the probation period specified in the probation or combination order would have ended.*
>
> *13.—(1) This paragraph applies where—*
>
> *(a) an offender in respect of whom a relevant order is in force is convicted of an offence by a magistrates' court unconnected with the order;*
>
> *(b) the court imposes a custodial sentence on the offender; and*
>
> *(c) it appears to the court, on the application of the offender or the responsible officer, that it would be in the interests of justice to exercise its powers under this paragraph, having regard to circumstances which have arisen since the order was made.*
>
> *(2) In sub-paragraph (1) above 'a magistrates' court unconnected with the order' means—*
>
> *(a) in the case of a drug treatment and testing order, a magistrates' court which is not responsible for the order;*
>
> *(b) in the case of any other relevant order, a magistrates' court not acting for the petty sessions area concerned.*
>
> *(3) The court may—*
>
> *(a) if the order was made by a magistrates' court, revoke it;*
>
> *(b) if the order was made by the Crown Court, commit the offender in custody or release him on bail until he can be brought or appear before the Crown Court.*

An order may also be amended (sch. 3, part IV). Again there needs to be an application to the court by the probation officer or the offender. Amendment may be used to cancel some requirements or to add new ones if the offender consents (except that a condition of mental treatment or treatment for drug abuse may not be added if the application occurs more than three months from the commencement of the order). The length of the order cannot be changed in this way; orders can only be lengthened if breached, shortened if discharged.

19.5.5 BREACH

The National Standards' provisions on enforcement (breach) of orders state that breach proceedings should be taken at any stage and without prior warning if the failure to comply is serious, such as an attempt to prevent its completion or serious misconduct. Where breach action is not being taken, on the first occasion of failure to comply with an order the offender should be given a formal warning in writing of the likely consequences of further failure. At most, two warnings within any 12-month period of the order may be given before breach proceedings are instituted.

The provisions for breach of a probation order have, under the CJA 1991, been brought into line with those for other community sentences and are dealt with in **19.10**. In *R* v *Oliver* (1992) 14 Cr App R (S) 457, the Court of Appeal's guidance shows that if an offender breaches a probation order and the breach is dealt with at the Crown Court, then the penalty which is given then may well be a custodial sentence. Obviously, when the original probation order was given, the court must either have decided that the offence was not sufficiently serious to merit a custodial sentence or the mitigating factors related to the defendant were sufficient to bring the sentence back below the custodial threshold. However, in breaching the probation order, the defendant is likely to have deprived himself or herself of much of that mitigation (contrition, etc.) and so may on breach be in danger of a custodial sentence.

19.5.6 REQUIREMENTS ATTACHED TO A PROBATION ORDER

A probation order can have various requirements (formerly termed conditions) attached to it: a requirement to receive mental treatment; a requirement of attendance at a probation centre (formerly termed a day centre or day training centre) for up to 60 days; a requirement of residence at a hostel; and indeed any other requirement which is written in the order. Conditions vary according to the facilities available locally, which will be run by the probation service or by local voluntary groups. In some areas there is group therapy available, in others drop-in centres for the long-term unemployed and socially inadequate, or for those with drink problems. In some areas there is specific alcohol abuse or drug counselling, and related programmes, and in others social skills training. It varies enormously around the country and it is essential that you should begin to build up a knowledge of the facilities available in the various areas in which you normally practise. None the less you are likely to have to rely on the advice of the probation service as to what is currently available and whether your particular client fits the rules for acceptance onto the programme. All these requirements are those for which a pre-sentence report should be obtained and considered by the court (see **Chapter 17**).

19.5.6.1 Hostels

Probation hostels are run by the probation service or by voluntary agencies but approved by the probation committee. They have three purposes: to provide residence for those of no fixed abode, to apply group therapy in modern group home techniques, and to have a fairly strict rule basis which the offender is supposed to learn to accept and thus learn to regulate his or her life, and not commit offences.

There is a shortage of hostels, though the Home Office is now trying to open more. It is important to suggest a hostel as a possible solution open to the solicitor for him or her to talk to the probation officer — or if there is a remand for a report, for you to talk to the liaison officer in appropriate cases. Before making a requirement that an offender must reside in a particular place on an order, the court *must* consider his or her home surroundings — and the name of the hostel must be specified in the order — so a place must be available. Someone can be remanded on bail to a hostel for three or four weeks to assess his or her likely response — then there should be a report from the hostel. The period of residence can be for any period not exceeding the term of the order but it may be helpful to have the supervision to extend for a time such as one year after the offender has left the hostel for the person to be helped to move into the outside world.

19.5.6.2 Probation centres

Until now, there have been two forms of day training centre (renamed probation centre in the CJA 1991). One is the informal drop-in centre or other non-residential place often catering for particular groups and this may be mentioned in a pre-sentence report but may not be a legal requirement of an order. The other is a legal requirement to attend for up to 60 days at a centre approved by the local probation committee (sch. 2, para. 3 to the PCC(S)A 2000). This requirement is supposed to be for offences relatively high up the tariff, i.e. for those in imminent danger of a custodial sentence (like all other requirements attached to a probation order it requires the consent of the offender). It has been criticised by Vanstone and others as being an extension of custody into the community without the cost and the overt position of making a custodial sentence. It is definitely an infringement on someone's liberty, so it should not be suggested for 'down tariff' offences or people who are inadequate, even if they have a long record of nuisance offences.

Few of these approved centres currently exist, though the numbers are growing. Again, the gateway to such a requirement is via the probation service and the pre-sentence report. For a requirement to attend a probation centre to be made, the court must consult a probation officer, it must be shown that arrangements can be made and the person in charge of the centre must consent to having that particular offender.

19.5.6.3 Requirements as to activities, etc.

Schedule 2 to the PCC(S)A 2000, inserted by CJA 1991, contains the provision that a probation order may require the offender to 'present himself to a person or persons specified in the order at a place or places so specified' (sch. 2, para. 2(1)(a)) or 'participate or refrain from participating in activities specified in the order (i) on a day or days so specified; or (ii) during the probation period or such portion of it as may be so specified' (sch. 2, para. 2(1)(b)). It is this provision which allows the court to specify that certain offenders should attend group work sessions on controlling anger, treating sexual offences, etc.

19.5.6.4 Requirements as to treatment for mental disorder

This is dealt with in **Chapter 23**. It is governed by the CJA 1991.

19.5.6.5 Requirements as to treatment for drug or alcohol dependence

Paragraph 6 of sch. 2 to the PCC(S)A 2000, provides a power for the court to impose a requirement on an offender 'dependent on drugs or alcohol' to attend a treatment facility if the 'dependency is such as requires and may be susceptible to treatment'. One doctor's report recommending such a course of action is required. The treatment must be by a doctor (not a psychologist or other professional) and must be with a view to the reduction or elimination of the dependency. The offender must express his or her willingness to comply with the requirement. Some doubt was expressed as to whether this power would often be used, given that offenders need to express their willingness to comply with requirements and that clinics are reluctant to take clients on court orders. It is likely that the response will vary between different areas of the country.

19.5.7 PROPOSALS FOR REFORM

There are currently over 185,000 offenders on probation in England and Wales supervised by 55 local probation services. The government proposes to reduce the number of local probation services to 42, and to reorganise the service which will be headed by a National Director and chief probation officers, who will be paid by and appointed by the Home Office. It is also proposed that the probation order will be renamed the community supervision order.

19.6 Community Service Orders

The community service order (CSO) is an order by which an offender is ordered to perform between 40 and 240 hours' work (as specified) in the community. Community service is organised by the probation service, although much of the work is usually carried out under the supervision of voluntary workers and others involved in community projects. Section 46 of the PCC(S)A 2000 states that a court must not make a CSO unless it is satisfied:

> *(4) . . . after hearing (if the court thinks it necessary) an appropriate officer, the court is satisfied that the offender is a suitable person to perform work under such an order.*
>
> *(6) . . . that provision . . . can be made under the arrangements for persons to perform work under such orders which exist in the petty sessions area in which he resides or will reside.*

The CSO was introduced in 1973 on an experimental basis, and made available to all courts in 1975. Since then, it has been widely used, accounting for 19% of all sentences on adult males for indictable offences in 1997. In the 18–20 age group, it accounted for 12% of male offenders and 8% of female offenders.

19.6.1 THE ORGANISATION OF COMMUNITY SERVICE

This is now governed by the National Standards. Offenders placed on a CSO must have their first work session within 10 days of sentencing. They are placed on one of the schemes currently being run — which may involve such activities as working in a Salvation Army hostel, working in a hospital or with mentally handicapped children, making wooden toys for playgroups, painting community centres, etc. Work under a community service order is done in the offender's spare time, usually at weekends and in the evenings, and should be completed within 12 months of the court order. Where the offender is unemployed it may be possible for him or her to do community service during weekdays, but some areas do not permit unemployed offenders to complete their orders in this way.

It is the job of the probation service to ensure that each offender's attendance for work is monitored, although reliance may be placed on volunteer supervisors to report this. Over the years sentencers have complained, from time to time, about lax attitudes towards work attendance on CSO, some probation officers being more willing to accept excuses from offenders than others, and some officers rarely bringing offenders back to court for breach of the order. The 2000 National Standards for the Supervision of Offenders in the Community, para. D16, require the CSO work to be 'physically, emotionally or mentally demanding'; they also require an offender to be brought back to court after one or two unexplained failures to attend work appointments.

19.6.2 THE PHILOSOPHY

What is the CSO designed to achieve, and what aims of sentencing does it fulfil? In proposing the CSO as a new measure, the Advisory Council on the Penal System put it this way (*Non-Custodial and Semi-Custodial Penalties* (1970)):

> . . . the proposition that some offenders should be required to undertake community service should appeal to adherents of different varieties of penal philosophy. To some, it would be simply a more constructive and cheaper alternative to short sentences of imprisonment; by others it would be seen as introducing into the penal system a new dimension with an emphasis on reparation to the community; others again would regard it as a means of giving effect to the old adage that the punishment should fit the crime; while still others would stress the value of bringing offenders into close touch with those members of the community who are most in need of help and support.

This passage may help to explain why the CSO has been welcomed and used relatively widely by the courts.

19.6.3 USING COMMUNITY SERVICE AS A SENTENCE

Formerly, the Court of Appeal held that a court should consider making a CSO in all cases where it is minded to impose a short custodial sentence. In *R* v *Clarke* (1982) 4 Cr App R (S) 197, Lord Lane CJ held that even when a court has formed the opinion that the case is so serious that a custodial sentence is necessary, the court should ask itself this: 'can we make a community service order as an equivalent to imprisonment, or can we suspend the whole of the sentence? That problem requires very careful consideration'. Under CJA 1991 the CSO is no longer an 'alternative to custody', but courts should still consider a CSO when the offence is serious enough for custody and there is substantial personal mitigation. The cases in which it might be appropriate to make a CSO may involve relatively serious offences which are either committed by a person of good character or committed in circumstances of strong mitigation. One example of this might be a house burglary committed by a young first offender (see *R* v *Brown* (1981) 3 Cr App R (S) 294 and *R* v *Mole* (1990) 12 Cr App R (S) 371); another example might be a burglary committed by an offender with a criminal record but who appears to have 'gone straight' for a number of years prior to the latest conviction (*R* v *Lawrence* (1982) 4 Cr App 2 (S) 69). Research shows that CSOs are used in the Crown Court for offenders who are slightly older than those placed on probation, less likely to have problems with alcohol, less likely to be suffering from stress or mental disorder, and more likely to be employed (Flood-Page and Mackie, *Sentencing Practice in the mid-1990s* (Home Office Research Study, No. 180, 1998), p. 102). As the authors comment, 'this is not surprising as community service on its own is generally seen as unsuitable for people with an unsettled lifestyle, who would be highly likely to breach the order'.

A court is required to consider a pre-sentence report before making a CSO, and this should assist in ensuring that a CSO satisfies the requirement of being 'the most suitable' order for the offender. As to the length of the order, the court should calculate the number of hours on the scale from 40 to 240 hours according to the seriousness of the offence(s).

19.6.4 BREACH OF COMMUNITY SERVICE

Most CSOs are completed satisfactorily. Some 75% run their course without the offender being returned to court either for breach or for a further offence. Since many of the offenders placed on CSOs are relatively young and do have previous convictions, and are therefore at high risk of re-offending, this suggests that the order is sufficiently demanding to keep most of them out of trouble for around 12 months. The powers of the courts on breach are dealt with at **19.10**.

19.7 Combination Orders

Although courts do not have the power to make both a probation order and a CSO on an offender as the sentence for an offence, the CJA 1991 introduced an entirely new order which consists partly of probation and partly of community service. In other words, the law permits probation and community service to be combined, but only under the restricted conditions of a combination order. The White Paper explained (1990, para. 4.16):

> Under this new order, an offender could be required to carry out a period of community service work while under the supervision of a probation officer and subject to any of the requirements which could be attached to a probation order. It would enable the courts to introduce an element of reparation but, at the same time, to provide the probation service with an opportunity to work with offenders, to reduce the likelihood of future offending . . .

Section 51 of the PCC(S)A 2000 provides that the probation component of the order may be one to three years, whereas the community service component may only be 40 to 100 hours. The probation element is therefore uppermost, and indeed s. 51 provides that the court must consider that a combination order is desirable in order to secure the rehabilitation of the offender or to protect the public from harm from him or her or to prevent the commission by him or her of further offences — the same justifications as for a probation order. The probation component of a combination order may also include any of the additional requirements set out in sch. 2 to the PCC(S)A 2000.

By s. 36(3) and (4) of the PCC(S)A 2000, a court is obliged to obtain and consider a pre-sentence report before forming an opinion on the suitability of a combination order for a particular offender.

The combination order was conceived as the most demanding form of community sentence, and it was not expected that most combination orders would be made in the magistrates' courts, as the statistics show. The 2000 National Standards make it clear that combination orders should be demanding in their content and enforced rigorously. A written supervision plan for the probation component of the order must be completed within 15 days of the court sentence, and this must include strategies for addressing offence-related and offender-related issues (National Standards, para. C10).

19.8 Curfew Orders

Section 37(1) of the PCC(S)A 2000 empowers a court to make a curfew order, 'that is to say, an order requiring him to remain, for periods specified in the order, at a place so specified'. Section 38 of the PCC(S)A 2000 makes provision for the possibility of electronic monitoring of curfew orders. These provisions have been brought into force in seven areas so far.

19.8.1 REQUIREMENTS OF A CURFEW ORDER

What times and places may be specified in a curfew order? Section 37(3) outlines the limits on the power:

> *A curfew order may specify different places or different periods for different days, but shall not specify—*
> *(a) periods which fall outside the period of six months beginning with the day on which it is made; or*
> *(b) periods which amount to less than two hours or more than twelve hours in any one day.*

Curfew of periods of less than two hours would hardly be sensible, and for more than 12 hours might impede too many ordinary obligations. Section 37(5) further provides that the requirements should avoid conflict with religious beliefs, work and attendance for education. Section 37(10) requires a court to explain the effect of the order, and the consequences of failure to comply with it, to the offender in court in ordinary language. There is no statutory requirement for a pre-sentence report before making a curfew order, although it may be added to another community order for which a pre-sentence report is obligatory.

19.8.2 PROBABLE USE OF A CURFEW ORDER

A kind of curfew order has been available to courts dealing with juvenile offenders since 1982, but it has been little used. The White Paper put forward the view that, for adults and young adults, 'curfews could be helpful in reducing some forms of crime, thefts of or from cars, pub brawls and other types of disorder. A curfew order could be used to keep offenders away from particular places, such as shopping centres or pubs, or to keep them at home in the evenings or at weekends' (1990, para. 4.20). A curfew order might well be added to another community sentence (e.g., probation), so long as s. 35(3)(b) on proportionality is complied with.

19.8.3 ELECTRONIC MONITORING

Section 37(6) requires that any curfew order should include provision for making a person responsible for monitoring the offender's whereabouts during the curfew periods. Section 38 further provides that a curfew order may include requirements for securing the electronic monitoring of the offender's whereabouts during curfew periods, but only if the court has been notified by the Home Secretary that arrangements are available. Electronic monitoring is currently available in some areas of the country, but not in others.

19.9 Selecting Community Orders

Having considered the types of community order available to courts when dealing with adult offenders, we must now return to the statutory criteria in s. 35(3), i.e. proportionality and suitability (see **19.4**).

There is little guidance on the question of proportionality. The PCC(S)A 2000 says that the restrictions on liberty must be 'commensurate with the seriousness of the offence' and that seems to require both an estimate of the relative seriousness of the offence and an assessment of the relative severity of the community order(s). On seriousness of the offence, the court is required by s. 36(1) to take account of 'all such information as is available to it about the circumstances of the offence or (as the case may be) of the offence and the offence or offences associated with it, including any aggravating or mitigating factors'. The discussion in **Chapter 20** is therefore relevant to this point. Equally, s. 158 allows the court to take account of any other mitigating factors. But what about the relative severity of community orders? Is a 120-hour CSO more severe or restrictive of liberty than a one year probation order with a requirement of attendance at a probation centre? Is a 240-hour CSO with an added fine more severe than a combination order? Guidance on these points is scanty, but the Act seems to envisage that courts might find that two or more community orders may be 'commensurate' in a given case, and that they should then decide between them on grounds of suitability for the offender. For example, both a certain length of probation order and a number of hours CSO might be considered proportionate, but the court might regard the former as more suitable for this offender.

The PCC(S)A 2000 is somewhat clearer on the question of suitability. Section 36(2) permits a court to take account of any information about the offender which is before it. In many cases that will include a pre-sentence report. In all cases there should be details of any previous convictions, and they are relevant on suitability (although less so when assessing the seriousness of the offence).

19.10 Breach or Re-offending

Any one of the four community orders may be breached by an offender, e.g. by failing to attend when and where required, or by failing to notify the probation officer of a change of circumstances etc. The 2000 National Standards provide that 'breach action may be taken after one unacceptable failure, where appropriate' (para. D20). Where breach action is not taken on the first unacceptable failure, a formal warning must be given to the offender, and only one formal warning is permissible within any 12-month period. Breach action involves returning the offender to court, and the court's decision is regulated by sch. 3 to the PCC(S)A 2000.

If a breach is established, the court may fine the offender up to £1,000, or make a community service order of up to 60 hours, or (where the offender is under 21) make an attendance centre order. If one of these courses is taken, the original order remains in force. Paragraph 4(1)(d) and (3) of sch. 3 also provides that the court may decide to revoke the original order and deal with the offender again for the offence.

The above powers apply when the offender is brought back to the magistrates' court responsible for enforcing the order. If the original community order was made by the Crown Court, a magistrates' court can deal with the breach in any way other than revocation of the original order. If it regards this as the proper course, it must commit the offender to the Crown Court, which then may choose between the various powers set out in the previous paragraph.

The commission of a further offence during the currency of a community sentence does not constitute a breach of that sentence. However, the court may, in certain circumstances, revoke the order(s) and deal with the original offence as well as the new offence when passing sentence on the second occasion. The Crown Court has wide powers in this respect, varying according to whether the further offence results in conviction at the Crown Court, or in committal for sentence to the Crown Court. The powers of magistrates' courts outlined in para. 10 of sch. 3 are limited to cases in which the original community order was made by a magistrates' court: essentially, the magistrates may impose any sentence which they could have imposed for the original offence (see **19.5.4**). If the community sentence was imposed by the Crown Court, the magistrates must commit the offender to appear before the Crown Court for revocation of the order but the Crown Court may revoke the community order and deal with the offender only if the order is still in force at the time of the proceedings (*R* v *Bennett* (1993) 15 Cr App R (S) 213 and para. 11 of sch. 3). If the original order made by a magistrates' court is revoked by a magistrates' court, it apparently has no power then to commit the offender to the Crown Court to be sentenced (*R* v *Jordan* [1998] Crim LR 353 (where the Court of Appeal described the revocation provisions as Byzantine in their intricacy)).

When a court is dealing with an offender for the original offence, following revocation, it may have regard to the circumstances leading to the revocation. In *R* v *Oliver* (1992) 14 Cr App R (S) 457 it was argued that the imposition of a community sentence originally for the offence showed that it could not be considered to be sufficiently serious to justify a custodial sentence. This argument was rejected by the Court of Appeal which said (per Lord Taylor of Gosforth CJ):

> . . . there may well be cases where, notwithstanding that the offence itself passes the custody threshold, there is sufficient mitigation to lead the court to impose a community sentence. Nevertheless if a further offence was or offences were committed while the community sentence was in force . . . the defendant . . . would have deprived himself of much of the mitigation, such as good character, genuine remorse, isolated lapse and similar considerations, which had led the original court to pass a community rather than a custodial sentence.

Since then, the court has made it clear that it may be proper to impose a consecutive custodial sentence for the original offence (*R* v *Newton* [1999] Crim LR 338, reviewing earlier decisions). In all cases in which the court re-sentences the offender, either for breach or for a further offence, it is required to take account of the extent to which the offender complied with the original order, i.e. giving credit for substantial part performance where that has happened (a principle established since *R* v *Paisley* (1979) 1 Cr App R (S) 196).

TWENTY

GENERAL PRINCIPLES AND THE POWERS OF CRIMINAL COURTS (SENTENCING) ACT 2000

20.1 Introduction

The general principles of sentencing are those which apply to most types of offence and most types of sentence. In this chapter we shall deal with the principles relating to aggravation and mitigation, previous record and multiple offences. These principles apply not only to custodial sentences, but also to non-custodial sentences. The CJA 1991 made some alterations, with the result that the relevant principles now consist of a mixture of statute and common law. Within the provisions of the CJA 1991 there is an important distinction between cases in which 'the seriousness of the offence' is the key issue, and others such as 'public protection' cases. However, this distinction will be explained more fully at the end of the chapter, after the various principles have been outlined. The provisions have been consolidated in the PCC(S)A 2000.

20.2 Aggravation, Mitigation and the Powers of Criminal Courts (Sentencing) Act 2000

20.2.1 THE RESTRICTED SENSE OF AGGRAVATION AND MITIGATION

It has already been noted, in **Chapters 18** and **19**, that 'the seriousness of the offence' is a key issue in deciding questions relating to fines and community sentences. **Chapter 21** will show that 'the seriousness of the offence' is also central to decisions on custodial sentences. The common law approach was that, in assessing the seriousness of a case, a court would naturally consider factors which aggravate and factors which mitigate. However, this is a matter which must be approached carefully under the 2000 Act. In relation to custodial sentences, s. 81(4)(a) states that, in forming an opinion about the seriousness of an offence, a court:

> *. . . shall take into account all such information as is available to it about the circumstances of the offence or (as the case may be) of the offence or offences associated with it, including any aggravating or mitigating factors.*

Section 36(1) states the same principle with respect to community sentences. Do these provisions do anything other than confirm the common law approach?

The answer is that they achieve something different. What they say is that in determining the seriousness of *the offence(s)* a court should take account of aggravating and mitigating factors which bear on the circumstances of *the offence(s)*. This means that factors which bear on the offender are irrelevant for this purpose (e.g. the offender's bad criminal record), as are matters which have arisen since the offence(s) (e.g. assistance to the police, a plea of guilty, reparation to the victim). Sections 81(4)(a) and 36(1) require the court to focus on the circumstances of the offence(s) when assessing its (their) seriousness.

Later in this chapter the relevance of such factors as previous convictions and a plea of guilty will be considered. For the present, we must look in greater detail at those aggravating factors and those mitigating factors which bear on the seriousness of an offence.

20.2.2 AGGRAVATING CIRCUMSTANCES OF THE OFFENCE

To a large extent these vary with the type of offence under consideration. In offences of violence, the more violence that is used, the more serious the offence. In property offences, the more property that is taken the more serious the offence. The Court of Appeal precedents give plenty of examples of aggravating factors when discussing the various types of offence, and they can be consulted, by offence, in *Current Sentencing Practice.* One of the advantages of guideline judgments is that they usually contain a list of the major aggravating factors. For example, in the cases of *R* v *Mussell* (1990) and *R* v *Brewster* (1998), see **22.1.9**, the Court of Appeal identified certain aggravating features of burglary. When dealing with social security frauds in *R* v *Stewart* (1987) 9 Cr App R (S) 135, the Court of Appeal stated that the offence would be more serious where (i) the fraud was committed over a lengthy period, (ii) the fraud began by deliberate deception rather than by omission, (iii) the money was taken to finance lavish spending rather than the purchase of necessities, and (iv) the fraud was carefully organised. Further aggravating factors recognised in the various guideline decisions will be discussed in **Chapter 22** below.

The last factor mentioned in *R* v *Stewart,* i.e. careful organisation, is a more general aggravating factor, and one well supported by authority. A central element in seriousness is the culpability of the offender, and carefully planned offences are generally much more serious than sudden, momentary actions. Unprovoked offences are generally treated as more serious than provoked crimes. Moxon's survey of 2,000 Crown Court cases showed that four factors were strongly associated, in practice, with a high use of immediate custodial sentences (*Sentencing Practice in the Crown Court,* 1988, p. 9):

Where the victim was elderly	97% immediate custody
Where offender was ringleader	77%
Where offence planned/premeditated	71%
Where weapon used	71%

The effect of the first factor is confirmed by *R* v *Allen* (1988) 10 Cr App R (S) 466, where two young men had entered a house at night and, on finding a woman aged 82 in the house, had held her down on the floor until she told them where she kept her money. The Court of Appeal upheld sentences of six years for robbery, stressing the significance of the fact that the victim was elderly:

> Cowardice and brutality seem to know no bounds in this connection. It was said in this case that these two appellants did not know that this house was occupied or that they would encounter an old lady when they went inside. But having found her, they did not desist . . .

In some cases of crimes against the elderly, the aggravating element seems greater than the offence itself (e.g. *R* v *Hanrahan* [1999] 1 Cr App R (S) 308, upholding four years' imprisonment on a boy of 18 for 'distraction' burglary of a watch from a woman aged 90).

Turning to cases in which the offender was the ringleader, it must first be stated that offences committed by groups are often treated as more serious than offences committed by individuals, because of the fear which groups of people can cause. This factor often comes to the fore in public order cases, and an example is *R* v *Rogers-Hinks* (1989) 11 Cr App R (S) 234. The appellant was one of seven men convicted of affray following a large-scale disturbance involving football supporters on a North Sea ferry, resulting in extensive damage to the ship and fear among other passengers. The general level of the sentences passed at the trial was approved by the Court of Appeal, on account of the fear caused by the disturbance and the difficulty of controlling the disorder. The Court further made it clear that the trial judge was right to differentiate among the offenders according to the degree of their involvement. A sentence of eight years' imprisonment was upheld on the offender who was identified as the ringleader, who had not only joined in the fighting but had also seized a microphone and incited further disorder. Lesser sentences were imposed on the others.

It is also well established that an offence will be aggravated if it is committed against a police officer (or other public servant), or by a police officer (or other public servant). The decision in *R* v *Nawrot* (1988) 10 Cr App R (S) 239 is one example of the former point, the Court of Appeal upholding a sentence of two years' imprisonment for punching a police officer on the jaw, knocking him unconscious. By the same token, police officers who commit offences of violence against suspects can expect to receive longer sentences. This may be seen as an aspect of the general proposition that people who offend whilst holding a position of trust deserve a more severe sentence for the breach of that trust. The guideline case of *R* v *Barrick* (1985) 7 Cr App R (S) 143 supports this, as does *R* v *Lowery* (1992) 14 Cr App R (S) 485 (see **21.10.2**).

There is statutory authority for the common law principle that an offence committed whilst on bail for another offence is to be treated as aggravated (see *Attorney-General's References (Nos. 3, 4 and 5 of 1992)* (1992) 14 Cr App R (S) 191). Section 151(2) of the PCC(S)A 2000 declares that the court 'shall' treat this as an aggravating factor.

Section 153 of the PCC(S)A 2000, gives statutory authority to the common law principle that a racially motivated offence should be treated as aggravated (see *Attorney-General's Reference (Nos 29, 30 and 31 of 1994)* (1995) 16 Cr App R (S) 698). Section 153 requires the court to treat this as an aggravating factor, and a definition of 'racial aggravation' for this purpose is found in s. 28 of the CDA 1998. Sections 29 to 32 of the 1998 Act create four new racially aggravated offences (assault, criminal damage, public order, and harassment) with higher maximum penalties. Section 153 of the 2000 Act is applicable to all other types of offence.

20.2.3 MITIGATING CIRCUMSTANCES OF THE OFFENCE

Once again, many mitigating factors are dependent on the type of offence committed. In this sense, 'mitigating' merely means 'reducing the seriousness of the offence' and includes such factors as the slightness of the injury caused, the smallness of the amount of money taken, etc. Most of the guideline judgments list such factors in relation to the offence concerned. For example, the judgment in *R* v *Stewart* (1987) 9 Cr App R (S) 135 states that a social security fraud will generally be less serious where the offence arose from an omission rather than a deliberate deception, or where the money was taken in order to buy necessaries.

Among the general mitigating factors which relate to the seriousness of the offence, the most important are those connected with culpability. An offence is usually less serious if it was committed impulsively rather than deliberately, recklessly rather than intentionally, and so on. Similarly, if the offender was close to having a defence to criminal liability, this will tend to reduce the seriousness of the offence. For example, in *R* v *Beaumont* (1987) 9 Cr App R (S) 342 the appellant's sentence was reduced by the Court of Appeal to reflect the fact that he had been entrapped into committing the offence: entrapment is no defence in English law, but it may constitute mitigation. However, 'entrapment' here does not include the placing of temptation in the way of a person 'pre-disposed' to commit the offence (*R* v *Mayeri* [1999] 1 Cr App R (S) 304). Elements of duress, mistake of law and mental disturbance might have a similar effect. For present purposes, however, it is important to bear in mind that only mitigating factors which affect the circumstances of the offence (including the offender's culpability) are relevant to 'seriousness'.

20.2.4 THE MAGISTRATES' ASSOCIATION GUIDELINES

The Magistrates' Association, a voluntary body to which most of the 30,000 magistrates belong, has issued to its members a set of sentencing guidelines covering many of the offences with which magistrates' courts frequently deal. Most road traffic offences and many non-motoring offences are listed. The most recent version is that issued in 2000. The main part of the guidelines consists of an offence-by-offence consideration of sentencing. Each page deals with an offence, states the maximum penalty, lists some seriousness factors, and then sets out some starting points for sentencing. Our interest here lies with the seriousness indicators. These do not deal with personal mitigation (see **20.3**): they list some aggravating and mitigating factors related to the seriousness of each offence. For example, the factors which may make theft offences more serious include 'high value', 'planned', 'sophisticated', 'vulnerable victim', and 'adult involving children'. The 'mitigating' factors for theft offences include 'low value' and 'impulsive action'. Turning to offences of violence, the table of factors for assault occasioning actual bodily harm is as follows:

Aggravating — for example	*Mitigating — for example*
Deliberate kicking or biting	Minor injury
Extensive injuries	Provocation
Group action	Single blow
Headbutting	
Offender in position of authority	
On hospital/medical premises	
Premeditated	
Victim particularly vulnerable	
Victim serving public	
Weapon	

These sentencing guidelines have no legal force, but they are widely used. A survey of fining practice in 1996 found that 55% of magistrates' benches were using the Magistrates' Association's Guidelines *in toto*, and a further 28% were using the guidelines with significant local variations: Charman et. al., 'Fine Impositions and Enforcement following the Criminal Justice Act 1993', *Home Office Research Findings No. 36* (1996). The document itself urges magistrates to treat them as starting points, not finishing points. The lists of factors are not intended to be exhaustive, and it remains for the court to take account of personal mitigating factors in each case. See **15.6.3**.

20.3 General Mitigating Factors

When the Criminal Justice Bill (which became the CJA 1991) was first presented to Parliament, there was no other provision on aggravation and mitigation apart from those already set out. It was protested that this would prevent the courts from taking account of long-established mitigating factors such as the plea of guilty, assistance to the authorities and other matters which had no bearing on the seriousness of the offence as such. Eventually various provisions were inserted, the most important of which is the first, which is now contained in s. 158 of the PCC(S)A 2000:

> *(1) Nothing . . . shall prevent a court from mitigating an offender's sentence by taking into account any such matters as, in the opinion of the court, are relevant in mitigation of sentence.*

This has two effects. First, it ensures that the common law principles of mitigating sentence survive the 1991 Act and subsequent legislation. Secondly, it is confined to mitigating factors. So far as aggravating factors are concerned, the court may only take account of those which arise from the circumstances of the offence, not any conduct or events before or after the crime.

In many cases the mitigation is personal to the offender, relying on such matters as stress, financial difficulties, and family or other personal problems. Brief mention can now be made of three further types of mitigating factor which may be taken into account by virtue of s. 158(1): those associated with contributions to the smooth running of the system; those associated with good social deeds; and those stemming from the expected impact of the sentence on the offender.

20.3.1 CONTRIBUTING TO THE SMOOTH RUNNING OF THE SYSTEM

It is well established that a person who reports the offences to the police before he or she has been discovered deserves a significant sentence discount (*R* v *Whybrew* (1979) 1 Cr App R (S) 121). It is also well established that an offender who co-operates with the police should receive a discount which reflects the degree of help given. This may range from helping the police to trace stolen goods to 'turning Queen's evidence' and testifying against other offenders. The principles on which enhanced discounts for co-operation should be given were re-stated by Lord Bingham CJ, in *R* v *A and B* [1999] 1 Cr App R (S) 52. Co-operation with the prosecution, and making statements against others, should be rewarded with a larger discount than a mere guilty plea. An enhanced discount would be proper, depending on the extent of assistance given, where the offender assists the prosecution in detecting and suppressing other crimes. Where the offender pleaded not guilty at the trial but gave significant assistance after being convicted, it is not the Court of Appeal's function to alter a sentence properly passed: if such an offender is to be rewarded, it should be the task of the Parole Board or Home Office.

The most frequent mitigating factor in this group is the plea of guilty. In general, a person who pleads guilty should receive a reduction in sentence which a person who is convicted after a trial should not receive. Section 152 of the PCC(S)A 2000 provides:

> *(1) In determining what sentence to pass on an offender who has pleaded guilty to an offence in proceedings before that or another court, a court shall take into account—*
>
> *(a) the stage in the proceedings for the offence at which the offender indicated his intention to plead guilty, and*
>
> *(b) the circumstances in which this indication was given.*
>
> *(2) If as a result of taking into account any matter referred to in subsection (1) above, the court imposes a punishment on the offender which is less severe than the punishment it would otherwise have imposed, it shall state in open court that it has done so.*

In broad terms this merely confirms the position at which the courts have arrived: Parliament's purpose in enacting the provision was apparently to give statutory authority to the notion that larger discounts should be given for earlier pleas. This had been recognised judicially in many cases, notably *R* v *Buffrey* (1993) 14 Cr App R (S) 411, where Lord Taylor CJ spelt out the 'general guidance' that 'something of the order of one-third would very often be an appropriate discount from the sentence which would otherwise be imposed on a contested trial'. The greatest discount should be reserved for pleas indicated at the earliest stage, e.g., 'plea before venue' (*R* v *Rafferty* [1998] 2 Cr App R (S) 449). Where the offender is given the maximum possible sentence despite having pleaded guilty, an appeal will usually succeed: see, for example, *R* v *Sharkey and Daniels* (1995) 16 Cr App R (S) 257, where the Court of Appeal held that 'it is an erroneous approach to sentencing to refuse to give a discount for a plea of guilty, unless the case falls within a limited, albeit not closed range of cases where this court had held the maximum sentence to be appropriate even on a guilty plea'.

One of those exceptions to the discount principle is where the circumstances of the case leave no real defence open to the offender. In *R* v *Landy* (1995) 16 Cr App R (S) 908, L, who was disqualified from driving, took a car and drove it at high speed before crashing. The trial judge took the view that on the facts this was one of the worst cases of aggravated vehicle-taking, and he imposed the maximum sentence of two years, refusing to give a discount for the guilty plea because in 'the circumstances in which [the offender was] arrested, namely, at the wheel of an upside down car, . . . conviction for this offence was inevitable'. The Court of Appeal upheld this approach, but in *R* v *Fearon* [1996] 2 Cr App R (S) 25 the Court stated that 'the law properly requires sentencing judges to give discounts for guilty pleas, however strong the case may be'. It is not clear on what basis the Court reached this view, but it added that 'the discount need only be a small one, because this appellant was caught red-handed'.

In practice it seems that substantial discounts are given, especially for early pleas. In their research, Flood-Page and Mackie found that in the Crown Court 'the average length of sentence where the offender had pleaded guilty from the start was 21.8 months compared to 24.6 months when they had initially pleaded not guilty but eventually pleaded guilty and 36.4 months where the offender pleaded not guilty and was convicted after a trial' (*Sentencing Practice* (Home Office Research Study 180, 1998), p. 92).

Subsection (3) to s. 152 of the PCC(S)A 2000 (above), allows courts to give credit for a guilty plea in cases where a prescribed sentence applies. This is discussed at **21.9**.

20.3.2 MITIGATION FOR GOOD SOCIAL DEEDS

Both the newspapers and the law reports yield several examples of sentences being reduced for 'good deeds' which have no connection at all with the offence committed. Thus in *R* v *Reid* (1982) 4 Cr App R (S) 280 the Court of Appeal reduced a sentence for burglary to reflect the fact that, whilst awaiting trial, the offender had rescued three children from a blazing house. The Court commented that this suggested that 'the appellant was a much better and more valuable member of society' than his criminal activities would lead one to believe. Likewise in *R* v *Ingham* (1980) 2 Cr App R (S) 184, the Court reduced a sentence for burglary on the ground that 'this man shows some indications of social responsibility because he has done quite a lot of good voluntary work'. These practices suggest that to some extent sentencing involves the drawing up of a social 'balance sheet', and that counsel should take advantage of that in advancing mitigating factors.

20.3.3 EXCEPTIONAL IMPACT OF SENTENCE ON OFFENDER

Where the sentence for the crime would have an unusually harsh impact on the particular offender, this is a ground for imposing a less severe sentence. Examples would be where the offender is pregnant (*R* v *Beaumont* (1987) 9 Cr App R (S) 342, the entrapment case mentioned in **20.2.3**, or where the offender has young children to care for (*R* v *Whitehead* [1996] 1 Cr App R (S) 1).

More controversial are those cases where the offender held a position of trust which has been lost, together with job prospects and pension rights, as a result of the conviction. The collateral effects of conviction for such a 'white collar' offender can be considerable: should they mitigate? In the guideline case of *R* v *Barrick* (1985) 7 Cr App R (S) 142 (see **22.1.8**) the Court of Appeal took the view that these collateral effects are insufficient to deflect courts from substantial sentences:

> Despite the great punishment that offenders of this sort bring upon themselves, the court should nevertheless pass a sufficiently substantial term of imprisonment to mark publicly the gravity of the offence.

The Court went on to say that 'it will not normally be appropriate in cases of serious breach of trust to suspend any part of the sentence'.

Since then, legislative restrictions have also been placed on the use of suspended sentence (see **21.10.2**). However, Flood-Page and Mackie found that 8% of thefts in breach of trust resulted in a suspended sentence compared with 3% of other cases (*Sentencing Practice* (1998), pp. 85–86), which suggests that some courts are less reluctant to suspend than the guideline case on breach of trust ordains.

It can be assumed that prison will have a particularly harsh effect on an elderly offender, but the Court of Appeal allows only modest concessions to this. Thus in *R* v *Anderson* [1999] 1 Cr App R (S) 273 a man aged 77 was sentenced to seven years' imprisonment for some 14 sexual offences against children committed as long as 20 years earlier. The Court held that the sentence properly reflected the scale and gravity of the criminality, and reduced the sentence only by one year (to six years) 'in mercy' in view of the offender's advanced age. The Court may in some circumstances allow an appeal based on a deterioration in an offender's health whilst in prison (*R* v *Bernard* [1997] 1 Cr App R (S) 135), but not where the basis is the offender's mistreatment by other prisoners (*R* v *Nall-Cain* [1998] 2 Cr App R (S) 145, threats and violence from other inmates regarded as a matter for the prison authorities and the Home Secretary).

20.4 Previous Convictions

The CJA 1991 included an apparently restrictive provision on previous convictions, which has since been repealed. We look first at the common law, then at the current statutory position.

20.4.1 THE PRINCIPLE OF PROGRESSIVE LOSS OF MITIGATION

The leading decision at common law is that of the Court of Appeal in *R* v *Queen* (1981) 3 Cr App R (S) 245. A man with a 25-year history of convictions had been sentenced to 18 months' imprisonment for, essentially, stealing a cheque for £50. On appeal, counsel submitted that the sentence should be quashed because Queen had been sentenced on his record, and the Court replied that counsel was:

> . . . right in the enunciation of that principle. Of course no prisoner is to be sentenced for the offences which he has committed in the past and for which he has already been punished. The proper way to look at the matter is to decide a sentence which is appropriate for the offence for which the prisoner is before the court. Then in deciding whether that sentence should be imposed or whether the court can extend properly some leniency to the prisoner, the court must have regard to those matters which tell in his favour, and equally to those matters which tell against him; in particular his record of previous convictions. The matters have to be balanced up to decide whether the appropriate sentence to pass is one at the upper end of the bracket or somewhere lower down.

This has been called the 'principle of progressive loss of mitigation' (see Ashworth, *Sentencing and Criminal Justice*, Ch. 6): the idea is that a first offender can usually expect a substantially reduced sentence, but that with each subsequent conviction an offender progressively loses the mitigation which he or she had as a first offender. The idea also incorporates an important limitation: no matter how bad the record of previous convictions, this 'will not justify the imposition of a term of imprisonment in excess of the permissible ceiling for the facts of the immediate offence' (Thomas, *Principles of Sentencing*, p. 41).

20.4.2 THE LAW ON PREVIOUS CONVICTIONS

Section 151(1) of the PCC(S)A 2000 which replaces s. 29(1) of the CJA 1991 provides as follows:

> *In considering the seriousness of any offence, the court may take into account any previous convictions of the offender or any failure of his to respond to previous sentences.*

The proper interpretation of this provision remains unclear. Whether it allows courts to treat a bad previous record as an aggravating factor is doubtful: Lord Taylor CJ stated extra-judicially that the common law principle of progressive loss of mitigation, beneath a 'ceiling' set by reference to the seriousness of the current offence, is preserved by s. 151. However, cases such as *Hollis* (see **22.1.9**) suggest otherwise.

A good example of progressive loss of mitigation is provided by *R* v *Cox* [1993] 1 WLR 188 (discussed at **21.5.2.1**): the reckless driving of the motorcycle was considered so serious that only a custodial sentence could be justified, but the Court of Appeal held that two mitigating factors took the case beneath the custody threshold. One was the appellant's youth (he was 18), and the other was his antecedent history (he had only one previous conviction). This decision shows the operation of the principle of progressive loss of mitigation, in that even an offender with one previous conviction can expect significant mitigation of sentence. It is not clear when all mitigation is lost and the offender reaches the 'ceiling', but presumably this is after three or four convictions.

The section also includes a further element, however. It allows courts to take account of any failure of the offender 'to respond to previous sentences'. What this means is also unclear. An offender who has re-offended during the currency of an existing sentence (e.g., community service, probation, suspended sentence) may be said to have failed to respond. But can the same be said of an offender who re-offends soon after *completing* a community service order, or paying a fine, or being released from prison? At least the provision refers to the plural, response to previous sentences (one failure to respond is insufficient), but in other respects an authoritative Court of Appeal decision is awaited. (For further discussion, see Wasik and von Hirsch, 'Section 29 Revised: Previous Convictions in Sentencing' [1994] Crim LR 409.)

20.4.3 THE IMPORTANCE OF THE 'QUALITY' OF A CRIMINAL RECORD

In general, the relevance of a criminal record relates not only to the quantity of previous convictions but also to what might be termed the 'quality' of the record. Thus courts might view a criminal record differently according to the type of previous offences (similar to the present?), the seriousness of previous offences, the nature of previous sentences received, the frequency of previous convictions, the existence of a conviction-free 'gap' prior to this offence (see, e.g. *R* v *Fox* (1980) 2 Cr App R (S) 188), and the age of the defendant when previously convicted. How can counsel make use of these factors when putting together a mitigation speech of behalf of an offender with previous convictions? (See Shapland, J., *Between Conviction and Sentence,* Routledge and Kegan Paul 1981, pp. 70–1.)

20.5 Multiple Offences

The problem here arises where a person is convicted of two or more offences at one court hearing, or where a person has been committed for sentence for two or more offences. How should a court approach the passing of sentence on one occasion for two or more offences? The problem might arise in a case where a defendant is convicted on an indictment charging, say, eight separate offences. Another possible example would be where a defendant is convicted of two offences and agrees that ten other offences should be 'taken into consideration', an informal procedure approved by the courts (*Anderson* v *Director of Public Prosecutions* [1978] AC 964). The numbers of convictions and of offences taken into consideration may vary, but the principles are the same.

20.5.1 THE CHANGE IN THE LAW

Originally, the CJA 1991 stated that a court could only treat offences as sufficiently serious for a community sentence or for custody, as the case may be, if any two of the offences were (taken together) so serious that only a community sentence or custody would be adequate. This 'two offence' rule was designed to prevent the courts from aggregating a whole series of minor offences and sending the offender to prison. However, this policy came under great strain when courts were confronted with offenders who had committed large numbers of relatively small offences, sometimes over 100. This led to the abolition of the 'two offence' rule. Courts may now aggregate all the 'associated' offences, whether convictions or offences taken into consideration, in deciding whether they are sufficiently serious for custody or for a community sentence. The approach in cases such as *R* v *Clugston* (1991) 13 Cr App R (S) 165 (three years' imprisonment upheld for 103 offences of obtaining £50 by deception with stolen cheques) therefore prevails over that in *R* v *Choudhary* (1991) 13 Cr App R (S) 290 (two months' detention quashed for 140 offences of theft of amounts between £20 and £30, because no individual offences were sufficiently serious).

It should be noted that a court can only take into account other offences 'associated with' that for which the offender now stands convicted. Section 161(1) of the PCC(S)A 2000 states that an offence is 'associated with' another if:

(a) the offender is convicted of it in the proceedings in which he is convicted of the other offence, or (although convicted of it in earlier proceedings) is sentenced for it at the same time as he is sentenced for that offence; or

(b) the offender admits the commission of it in proceedings in which he is sentenced for the other offence and requests the court to take it into consideration in sentencing him for that offence.

Paragraph (b) refers to offences taken into consideration. Paragraph (a) seems to exclude cases in which a suspended sentence is activated. Thus in *R* v *Crawford* (1993) 14 Cr App R (S) 782 it was held that the offence in respect of which the suspended sentence was originally passed does not become an 'associated offence' when the sentence is activated in subsequent proceedings. However, if the original sentence was a conditional discharge, and a court subsequently revokes it (because of a breach) and deals with the offender for the original offence, that does become an 'associated offence' because it is an offence for which sentence is passed in the same proceedings (*R* v *Godfrey* (1993) 14 Cr App R (S) 804).

20.5.2 MULTIPLE OFFENCES AND LENGTH OF SENTENCE

If a court decides that the offences for which it is passing sentence are, taken together, so serious that only custody can be justified, then the length of the custodial sentence must be determined. Section 80(2)(a) of the 2000 Act states that the sentence must be for such term as is 'commensurate with the seriousness of the offence, or the combination of the offence and one or more offences associated with it'. This means that a court can take account of all the offences, including t.i.c's, for which it is passing sentence. A similar provision in s. 35(3)(b) governs the extent of the restrictions on liberty imposed by means of a community sentence.

So far as custody is concerned, this seems to mean that the common law principles relating to whether the prison terms should be *concurrent* or *consecutive* remain in vigour. The extensive caselaw on this point can be reduced to three basic principles:

(a) Where it can be said that the offences formed part of the same transaction, the sentences should generally be concurrent; the main exceptions to this are firearms offences (*R* v *Faulkner* (1972) 56 Cr App R 594) and offences committed whilst resisting arrest (*R* v *Kastercum* (1972) 56 Cr App R 298), which should receive consecutive sentences even where they arise out of the 'same transaction'.

(b) In all cases where the offences did not form part of a single transaction, the sentences should generally be consecutive (the principle applies to other forms of sentence — e.g. fines and community service order — as well as to custody). This applies particularly to offences committed whilst on bail (see *R* v *Baverstock* [1993] 1 WLR 202, and s. 151(2) of the PCC(S)A 2000).

(c) Where the court imposes consecutive sentences, it must not content itself by doing the arithmetic and passing the sentence which the arithmetic produces. It must look at the totality of the criminal behaviour and ask itself what is the appropriate sentence for all the offences taken together, by comparison with sentencing levels for other crimes. This principle is preserved by s. 158(2) of the 2000 Act.

20.5.3 SPECIMEN COUNTS FOR MULTIPLE OFFENCES

In some cases the prosecution have chosen to charge a person with one specimen count, even though the substance of their case is that a whole sequence of offences was committed by the defendant. In *R* v *Clark* [1996] 2 Cr App R (S) 351 the Court of Appeal held that it is wrong in principle to sentence an offender for offences of which he has not been convicted, or to which he has not admitted by asking them to be taken into consideration. The fact that the count was charged as a specimen does not alter this. In many cases an offender will ask for other offences to be t.i.c., but prosecutors should not rely on this. After a period of uncertainty, this approach was confirmed in *R* v *Canavan and Kidd* [1998] 1 Cr App R (S) 243 (*sub nom. R* v *Kidd and Canavan* [1998] 1 WLR 604). Lord Bingham CJ added that 'prosecuting authorities will wish, in the light of this decision and *Clark*, to include more counts in some indictments', in order to give the court access to a sentencing range appropriate to the scale of the alleged lawbreaking. Thus where a defendant is convicted on seven counts of handling, said by the prosecution to be specimen charges, it is wrong in principle for the court to pass sentence on the basis that the defendant had been involved in a greater number of offences of handling if those offences have been neither proved nor admitted: *R* v *Pitt* [1998] Crim LR 137. The sentence should be commensurate with the seriousness of the offences of which the defendant has been convicted, or which he has admitted (*R* v *Rosenburg* [1999] Crim LR 94).

20.6 General Principles and the Powers of Criminal Courts (Sentencing) Act 2000

It will have been observed that many of the general principles discussed in this chapter relate to the seriousness of offences. It is important now to make the point that there are sentencing questions under the PCC(S)A 2000 which are not governed by the seriousness of the offence; and therefore where the more restrictive provisions above are not applicable. Two main classes of case stand out:

(a) *'Public protection' cases.* If a court is seeking to justify the use of a custodial sentence under s. 79(2)(b), or to impose a longer-than-proportionate sentence under s. 80(2)(b), by reference to the need to protect the public from serious harm from a particular sexual or violent offender, there are no apparent restrictions on what it may take into account when forming its opinion. It can take account of previous convictions — indeed, it may well use them as the basis for predicting future conduct; and it can consider any other offences for which it is now passing sentence. It will usually have a pre-sentence report in such cases, and that report may well discuss the previous convictions.

(b) *'Suitability' in relation to community sentences.* As we saw in **19.4**, a court which makes a community order must satisfy itself that the order is 'the most suitable for the offender' (s. 35(3)(a)). To reach such a conclusion the court may have to consider previous convictions and other wider matters, and it is likely that a pre-sentence report would discuss previous record and previous sentences.

However, apart from these decisions, the court will be focusing on the seriousness of the offence, and will therefore be bound by the narrow conception of aggravating factors (relating only to the circumstances of the offence) and the rules on taking account of other offences.

TWENTY-ONE

IMPRISONMENT

21.1 Introduction

Imprisonment is the most severe sanction which an English court can impose. Life imprisonment is the mandatory sentence for murder and under s. 109 of the PCC(S)A 2000 for a second serious sexual or violent offence (unless the court finds 'exceptional circumstances'). It is also the maximum sentence for several serious crimes, including manslaughter, attempted murder, causing grievous bodily harm or wounding with intent (Offences against the Person Act 1861, s. 18), robbery, rape, buggery, intercourse with a girl under 13, arson, and criminal damage endangering life. In practice life imprisonment is not used as the sentence for the most serious varieties of these offences, but is reserved for serious cases in which the offender is mentally unstable (see **Chapter 23**).

Apart from those crimes which carry the maximum of life imprisonment, each indictable offence has a maximum prison sentence assigned to it by statute. In theory these maxima should form a hierarchy, with the most serious offences carrying the longest sentences and the least serious carrying lower maxima. In practice there are several anomalies, although Parliament acts from time to time to raise or lower certain maxima. For example, the CJA 1988 raised the maxima for neglect of or cruelty to children to ten years; and for various corruption offences, to seven years. The 1988 Act also reduced to six months' imprisonment the maxima for common assault, driving whilst disqualified, and taking a motor vehicle without the owner's consent. The CJA 1991 reduced the maximum for theft from ten to seven years, and the maximum for non-residential burglary from 14 to ten years. The CJA 1993 doubled, from five to ten years, the maxima for causing death by dangerous driving and causing death by careless driving whilst intoxicated.

21.2 The English Prison System

What does imprisonment involve? In all cases it involves deprivation of liberty, but beyond that the 'pains of imprisonment' may vary considerably from institution to institution. The prison establishment in the English system may be divided broadly into three groups — local prisons, training prisons, and open prisons. The local prisons contain prisoners who are on remand awaiting trial, and also contain most sentenced prisoners who are serving terms of up to 18 months. Prisoners serving longer sentences will usually be sent to a training prison. Open prisons provide for those serving prison sentences who are thought not to be in need of security, and consequently the regimes in open prisons are considerably more flexible than in the closed prisons.

21.3 Some Problems of the Prison System

The prison system in England and Wales has been the subject of several major inquiries in recent years. Foremost among these is the Woolf Inquiry, set up after the acute problems of English prisons came to the notice of a wider audience in this country, and indeed in the world, as a result of the riots and disturbances at Strangeways prison, Manchester, and at several other prisons during 1990. The Woolf Inquiry recommended sweeping changes in the organisation of the prison service and in its approach to its tasks. However, the Government subsequently lost enthusiasm for the Woolf reforms, and the Learmont Inquiry into escapes from top security prisons (1996) ushered in a greater emphasis on security. The emphasis shifted to greater austerity in prisons, despite the experience of the 1990 riots, and despite the increased pressure on the prison system produced by the sharp rise in the prison population from 41,000 in early 1993 to 66,000 in 1999. However, at least two major recommendations from the Woolf Inquiry have been implemented. Integral sanitation has been put into cells, and 'slopping out' in English prisons ended in April 1996. A national Criminal Justice Consultative Committee has been established, with a view to promoting 'better understanding, cooperation and coordination in the criminal justice system'. This kind of development serves to underline the importance, for counsel as for others, of acquiring a basic knowledge of the prison system and the meaning of imprisonment.

21.4 Prison Policy and Sentencing Policy

It is sometimes said that, whatever the conditions in prison, 'prison works' because it keeps offenders out of circulation for a period of time and therefore protects society. This is true only to an extent. It is certainly true that escapes from prison are rare; indeed, escapes from local or training prisons are so rare that it may be concluded that the prisons provide almost 100% protection for society for the duration of the sentence. But in another sense the statistics are far less encouraging: over one half of male prisoners are reconvicted within two years of their release (at least 54%, according to Home Office Research Study No. 136, *Explaining Reconviction Rates* (1994)).

The previous government proclaimed that 'prison works', and presided over a four-year period (1993–7) in which the prison population rose by 50%. Some pronouncements of the present Government have placed greater emphasis on crime prevention by other, more effective methods than mere incarceration. The high reconviction rates of ex-prisoners may embolden them to reduce reliance on custody, but there have been few signs of a change of emphasis so far. However, some prisoners are now released early and subject to electronic monitoring.

21.5 The Powers of Criminal Courts (Sentencing) Act 2000 and the Custody Threshold

21.5.1 THE STATUTORY FRAMEWORK

The policy behind the CJA 1991 (which has been consolidated by the PCC(S)A 2000) was the twin-track approach:

> . . . that those who commit very serious crimes, particularly crimes of violence, should receive long custodial sentences; but that many other crimes can be punished in the community, with greater emphasis on bringing home to the criminal the consequences of his actions, compensation to the victim and reparation to the community (1990 White Paper, para. 2.2).

At the lower end of the proportionality scale, prison was to be replaced by community penalties (discussed in **Chapters 18** and **19**). At the higher end of the scale, the Government envisaged little change in the policy of long prison sentences for serious crimes.

The PCC(S)A 2000 seeks to establish a framework for custodial sentencing which reflects both the proportionality principle and the policy of reducing the use of prison for non-serious offences. To this end, s. 79 introduces a 'custody threshold' which has to be surmounted before any court can impose a custodial sentence, and s. 80 imposes limits on the length of any custodial sentence. These provisions apply to custodial sentences for all offences except murder, to all courts and to all ages of offender, including those under 21.

Section 79 sets out three lawful grounds for a custodial sentence: the seriousness of the offence; the protection of the public; and wilful breach of a community order. Each of them will be discussed in turn, but the first is likely to be much the most important in practice. The Act also imposes requirements on courts to give reasoned explanations for custodial sentences, and these are set out in **21.5.5**.

21.5.2 CUSTODY BECAUSE THE OFFENCE IS 'SO SERIOUS'

The first 'custody threshold' is that established by s. 79(2)(a) as follows:

> . . . *the court shall not pass a custodial sentence on the offender unless it is of the opinion—*
>
> *(a) that the offence, or the combination of the offence and one or more offences associated with it, was so serious that only such a sentence can be justified for the offence.*

The phrase, 'or the combination of the offence and one or more offences associated with it', refers to offenders who are being sentenced for more than one offence: such cases were discussed separately at **20.5**. The focus here is on an offender being sentenced for one offence.

21.5.2.1 How should the courts interpret s. 79(2)(a)?

The pre-1991 precedents provided a few clear markers. The possession of a small amount of cannabis for personal consumption is unlikely to be sufficiently serious for custody (*R* v *Robertson-Coupar and Baxendale* (1982) 4 Cr App R (S) 150), as are consensual homosexual acts in public lavatories (*R* v *Dighton* (1983) 5 Cr App R (S) 233) and social security frauds without aggravating features (*R* v *Stewart* (1987) 9 Cr App R (S) 135).

The first leading case under the 1991 Act (now consolidated by PCC(S)A 2000) was *R* v *Cox* [1993] 1 WLR 188, where the court held that a course of reckless driving involving flagrant breach of traffic regulations was so serious that only custody could be justified, although it subsequently found personal mitigating circumstances which took the case below the custody threshold. Lord Taylor of Gosforth CJ held that an offence was 'so serious' if it was 'the kind of offence which . . . would make right-thinking members of the public, knowing all the facts, feel that justice had not been done by the passing of any sentence other than a custodial one', following the words of Lawton LJ in *R* v *Bradbourn* (1985) 7 Cr App R (S) 180. The test of the 'right-thinking members of the public' was repeated in several Court of Appeal decisions, but in *R* v *Howells* [1999] 1 Cr App R 98 Lord Bingham CJ dismissed it as unhelpful. However, the judgment in *Howells* does not propose a new test: it recognises that 'there is no bright line' illuminating which cases fall below and which above the custody threshold, and encourages courts to consider all the aggravating and mitigating factors in each case. The only definite statement is that, where a case is held to lie above the custody threshold, the sentence should be as short as is possible (following the exhortation of Rose LJ in *R* v *Ollerenshaw* [1998] Crim LR 515).

There are some cases where the Court of Appeal has quashed custodial sentences under s. 79(2)(a). Although almost all sentences of custody for burglary have been upheld, there are two decisions, one case of residential burglary (*R* v *Bennett* (1993) 15 Cr App R (S) 213) and at least two cases of minor commercial burglary (*R* v *Tetteh* (1994) 15 Cr App R (S) 46 and *R* v *Carlton* (1994) 15 Cr App R(S) 335) in which the court has regarded custody as out of proportion to the crime. Overall, there is no clear pattern to the cases. Perhaps the most important point is that it is wrong to assume that the legal category of the offence is conclusive. This was the main implication of the pre-1991 case of *R* v *Hearne and Petty* (1989) 11 Cr App R (S) 316; even if the case is one of burglary of a dwelling, counsel should urge the court to look at the particular facts and should not assume that custody is 'automatic', especially for a young offender. There may often be room for counsel to mitigate on the particular facts.

The relevance of previous convictions, aggravating and mitigating factors to findings of 'seriousness' was discussed in **Chapter 20**.

21.5.3 CUSTODY FOR 'PUBLIC PROTECTION'

The second custody threshold established by the CJA 1991 and consolidated by the PCC(S)A 2000 is found in s. 79(2)(b):

> *. . . the court shall not pass a custodial sentence on the offender unless it is of the opinion—*
> *(b) where the offence is a violent or sexual offence, that only such a sentence would be adequate to protect the public from serious harm from him.*

This provision is unlikely to be invoked in many cases. On the face of the statute it is restricted to 'violent or sexual' offences, both of which are defined in s. 161(3):

> *. . . 'violent offence' means an offence which leads, or is intended or likely to lead, to a person's death or to physical injury to a person, and includes an offence which is required to be charged as arson (whether or not it would otherwise fall within this definition).*

It will be seen that the definition is artificially extended so as to include arson, and also that the opening phrases are wide enough to encompass all attempted offences against the person, aggravated criminal damage contrary to s. 1(2), Criminal Damage Act 1971, many cases of dangerous driving, and other offences which would not normally be classified as 'violent'. An issue which has come before the Court of Appeal on more than one occasion is whether robbery falls within the definition of a 'violent offence' — the Court of Appeal appears to have strained to ensure that robbery is included (see, e.g., *R* v *Bibby* [1994] Crim LR 610 and *R* v *Cochrane* (1994) 15 Cr App R (S) 708) but the point still gives rise to difficulty (*R* v *Robinson* [1997] Crim LR 365).

The definition of 'sexual offence' in the 1991 Act was soon revealed to be inadequate (see *R* v *Robinson* (1993) 14 Cr App R (S) 448), and the new definition is in s. 161(2) of the PCC(S)A 2000:

> *. . . 'sexual offence' means any of the following—*
> *(a) an offence under the Sexual Offences Act 1956, other than an offence under section 30, 31 or 33 to 36 of that Act;*
> *(b) an offence under section 128 of the Mental Health Act 1959;*
> *(c) an offence under the Indecency with Children Act 1960;*
> *(d) an offence under section 9 of the Theft Act 1968 of burglary with intent to commit rape;*
> *(e) an offence under section 54 of the Criminal Law Act 1977;*
> *(f) an offence under the Protection of Children Act 1978;*
> *(g) an offence under section 1 of the Criminal Law Act 1977 of conspiracy to commit any of the offences in paragraphs (a) to (f) above;*
> *(h) an offence under section 1 of the Criminal Attempts Act 1981 of attempting to commit any of those offences;*
> *(i) an offence of inciting another to commit any of those offences.*

However, once it has been established that the offence with which the court is dealing falls within one of the above definitions, the court must be satisfied that only a custodial sentence would be adequate to protect the public from serious harm from the offender. There is no legal requirement to obtain a medical report unless the offender appears to be mentally disordered, but we have seen in **Chapter 16** that a pre-sentence report will often be necessary. In deciding whether serious harm is likely to be caused by the offender, the court should be directed to the definition in s. 161(4):

> . . . *any reference, in relation to an offender convicted of a violent or sexual offence, to protecting the public from serious harm from him shall be construed as a reference to protecting members of the public from death or serious personal injury, whether physical or psychological, occasioned by further such offences committed by him.*

The nub of the definition therefore lies in 'serious physical or psychological injury', and it is clear that such offences must be likely to be committed by this offender, not by others — general deterrence is not a relevant consideration here.

Further discussion of factors which may or must be taken into account when applying s. 79(2)(b) will be found in **Chapter 23**. Few cases in which custody has been justified by reference to s. 79(2)(b) alone, i.e., where the offence was not also so serious as to qualify under s. 79(2)(a), have reached the Court of Appeal.

21.5.4 CUSTODY FOR REFUSAL OF CONSENT

Section 79(3) provides as follows:

> *Nothing in subsection (2) above shall prevent the court from passing a custodial sentence on the offender if he fails to express his willingness to comply with—*
> *(a) a requirement which is proposed by the court to be included in a probation order or supervision order and which requires an expression of such willingness . . .*

Although the general requirement of consent to community sentences has been removed, there remain two requirements (mental treatment, or treatment for drug or alcohol dependency) that may only be inserted into a probation or supervision order if the offender is willing (see **19.5**). This subsection allows a court to move up-tariff to a custodial sentence if the offender is unwilling to accept the requirement. In practice, the sub-section is more frequently invoked in cases where there is 'wilful default' in breaching a community order.

21.5.5 DUTY TO GIVE REASONS AND EXPLANATIONS

Section 79(4) imposes two duties on a court when it passes a custodial sentence. The first duty applies unless the custodial sentence is under s. 79(3) (refusal of consent): it must '*state in open court that it is of the opinion that either or both of paragraphs (a) and (b) of subsection (2) above apply and why it is of that opinion*'. The second duty is '*to explain to the offender in open court and in ordinary language why it is passing a custodial sentence on him.*' These were considered by the Court of Appeal in *R* v *Baverstock* [1993] 1 WLR 202, where Lord Taylor of Gosforth CJ held that:

> this should not normally be a two-stage process; in most cases the judge should be able at one and the same time to explain in ordinary language the reasons for his conclusions and tell the offender why he is passing a custodial sentence.

His Lordship added that the statutory provisions are not to be treated 'as a verbal tightrope', and the precise words used by the court are 'not critical'. These requirements apply equally to magistrates' courts, which are additionally required by s. 79(5) to record their reasons.

21.6 The Criminal Justice Act 1991 and the Length of Custodial Sentences

21.6.1 THE STATED LENGTH AND THE ACTUAL LENGTH

When the court states that a custodial sentence of so many months or years is imposed, it is important to know exactly what this means in terms of time to be served.

That is discussed in **21.6.2**. After that, the two provisions on length of sentence in the PCC(S)A 2000 are examined (s. 80(2)(a) and (b)), and finally there is reference to the suspended sentence of imprisonment.

21.6.2 EARLY RELEASE UNDER THE CRIMINAL JUSTICE ACT 1991

The general rule during the second half of this century was that prisoners were entitled to one-third remission on the sentence announced in court, which they would only forfeit if they committed disciplinary offences in prison. The effect of the CJA 1991 was to abolish remission.

Since 1968 it has been possible for prisoners serving medium and long-term sentences to be released on parole after one-third of their sentence. Parolees receive supervision from the probation service, and fewer than 10% are recalled for breach of the conditions or the commission of a further offence. The system was reshaped by the CJA 1991: the essence of the arrangements for early release is that all parts of the sentence announced in court should have some meaning and some effect. All offenders serving custodial sentences of less than four years are granted conditional release after serving one half (s. 33(1)). The condition is that they do not commit another offence before the expiry of the full term of their sentence. If they do so, then they are liable to be ordered to serve the unexpired balance of their sentence, in addition to any sentence for the new offence (s. 116(2) of the PCC(S)A 2000). The 'unexpired balance' is that portion between the date on which the new offence was committed and the date on which their sentence would expire. In addition, those serving at least one year and under four years are released subject to licence until the three-quarters point of their sentence: during that period they are under the supervision of the probation service, and breach of licence may lead to proceedings (s. 38(1)). Any disciplinary offences committed in prison may result in time being added on to the sentence.

The following provides an example of the operation of these provisions:

1. D is sentenced to 2 years' imprisonment.

2. 12 months later he is released on licence.

3. 15 months after sentence he breaches the conditions of his licence. He is then liable to serve up to 3 months' imprisonment until the expiry of his licence.

4. 18 months after sentence, his period of licence expires.

5. 21 months after sentence, D commits an imprisonable offence. He is liable to be recalled to serve the unexpired balance of 3 months of his sentence.

For offenders serving four years or longer, a discretionary system remains. Such prisoners must be released on licence after serving two-thirds, but they may be released on licence after serving one half if the Parole Board and the Home Secretary agree (ss. 33 and 39). In all cases the licence continues until the three-quarters point in the sentence, and the last quarter consists of conditional release, with a liability to serve the unexpired portion if convicted of a new offence. The Act also introduced new provisions on the release of prisoners serving discretionary life sentences (s. 34).

21.6.3 THE DUTY OF THE COURT

Lord Bingham CJ has laid down that it is the duty of the court to explain, to the offender, the victim and the general public, the practical meaning of the custodial sentence it is passing. Thus in *Practice Direction (Custodial Sentences: Explanations)* [1998] 1 WLR 278 Lord Bingham held that 'whenever a custodial sentence is imposed on an offender, the court should explain the practical effect of the sentence, in addition to complying with existing statutory requirements'. The *Practice Direction* includes statements which judges can use as models.

21.6.4 PROPORTIONALITY AND CUSTODIAL SENTENCING

Once a court is satisfied that an offence has overcome the 'custody threshold' established by s. 79 of the PCC(S)A 2000, the length of the sentence is governed by s. 80. The main provision is the proportionality principle (s. 80(2)(a)), but it is as well to bear in mind that courts are permitted to exceed the proportionate sentence in limited circumstances when sentencing violent or sexual offenders for public protection (see s. 80(2)(b) and **21.7**).

Most cases will be governed by the first part of s. 80, which states:

> (1) *This section applies where a court passes a custodial sentence other than one fixed by law or falling to be imposed under section 109(2) below.*
> (2) *Subject to sections 110(2) and 111(2) below, the custodial sentence shall be—*
> (a) *for such term (not exceeding the permitted maximum) as in the opinion of the court is commensurate with the seriousness of the offence, or the combination of the offence and one or more offences associated with it . . .*

The key phrase here is 'commensurate with the seriousness of the offence.' As noted in **16.4.3**, this has been interpreted by the Court of Appeal in *R* v *Cunningham* [1993] 1 WLR 183 to mean 'commensurate with the the punishment and deterrence which the offence requires.' This made it unlikely that, following the 1991 Act, there would be any significant reappraisal of sentence levels. Parliament has never undertaken such a task, preferring simply to alter a few maximum penalties from time to time. The courts, too, appear to have assumed that existing sentence levels, particularly for the more serious offences, do reflect proportionality. It will therefore continue to be important to understand the way in which the 'tariff' has been shaped in recent years and that is the subject of **Chapter 22**.

21.7 Public Protection: The Exception to Proportionality

As mentioned earlier, there is only one group of cases in which courts are permitted to sentence above the level which is commensurate with the seriousness of the offence(s) committed. Section 80(2)(b) of the PCC(S)A 2000 provides that the custodial sentence shall be:

> *where the offence is a violent or sexual offence, for such longer term (not exceeding that maximum) as in the opinion of the court is necessary to protect the public from serious harm from the offender.*

The definitions of 'violent' and 'sexual' offences, and of serious harm, were discussed in **21.5.3**. Section 80(4) provides that discretionary sentences of life imprisonment and detention for life must also be justified according to s. 80(2)(b).

This 'public protection' provision is the equivalent to the threshold provision in s. 79(2)(b), but it is not limited to cases which qualified for custody under s. 79(2)(b). So long as the criteria in s. 80(2)(b) are fulfilled, it would not matter if the case qualified for custody under s. 79(2)(a). These 'public protection' sentences are aimed at so-called 'dangerous' offenders: the difficulties of predicting dangerousness were mentioned in **16.6** and are examined in **Chapter 23**.

If a court imposes a disproportionate custodial sentence for public protection reasons, there are various procedural requirements. By s. 80(3), the court must state in open court that s. 80(2)(b) applies and why it is of that opinion, and it must explain to the offender in open court and in ordinary language why the sentence is for such a term. The leading cases on s. 80(2)(b) include *R* v *Bowler* (1993) 15 Cr App R (S) 78; *R* v *Mansell* (1994) 15 Cr App R (S) 771 and *R* v *Fawcett* (1995) 16 Cr App R (S) 55, and these are discussed below at **23.2.3**.

21.8 Mandatory Sentences of Life Imprisonment

Life imprisonment is the mandatory sentence for murder, but s. 109 of the PCC(S)A 2000 provides for a further mandatory life sentence. It applies to any offender convicted after 30 September 1997 of a second serious offence (as defined). This is a considerable departure for English sentencing law, and is to some extent modelled on the 'three strikes and you're out' statutes in certain US jurisdictions. Senior judges opposed the new law, on the ground that it restricts judicial discretion in a way that may lead to unjust sentences, but their objections were not heeded.

The mandatory sentence is required when a person aged 18 or over is convicted of one of a list of serious offences, having already been convicted of a listed serious offence previously (at any age). The list of serious offences includes attempt, conspiracy or incitement to murder; manslaughter; s. 18 wounding or grievous bodily harm with intent; rape or attempted rape; unlawful sexual intercourse with a girl under 13; firearms offences contrary to s. 16, s. 17 or s. 18 of the Firearms Act 1968; and robbery with a firearm or imitation firearm. In these circumstances the court must impose a sentence of life imprisonment unless it can find 'exceptional circumstances': this was intended to be a narrow exception and the Court of Appeal applied it narrowly in *R* v *Kelly* [1999] 2 WLR 1100. D had attacked a man who threw stones at him across a railway line, punching and kicking him in the face. He was convicted of causing grievous bodily harm with intent. He had previously been convicted of robberies with firearms in 1980, when he was 19. He had served the sentence, and then had gone 10 years without a conviction before the present incident. The case clearly fell within the mandatory life sentence, but the defence urged that there were exceptional circumstances — D's youth when he committed the earlier offences; the long trouble-free gap before the present offence; the different nature of the present offence; and, in consequence, the fact that D did not represent a danger to the public. Lord Bingham CJ, speaking for the Court, rejected this approach and held that to be 'exceptional' the circumstances relied upon must be unusual or out of the ordinary. A similar decision was reached in *Attorney-General's Reference (No. 53 of 1998) (Sandford)* [1999] 2 WLR 1100, where the trial judge had failed to impose the mandatory life sentence. D was convicted of wounding with intent by 'glassing' another man in a pub brawl. Eight years earlier he had been convicted of various offences including the possession of an imitation firearm with intent to commit an indictable offence. The trial judge had recognised that that was a qualifying offence for the mandatory life sentence, but had accepted the argument that there were 'exceptional circumstances', in that the earlier firearms offence had attracted a sentence of only one year's detention. The Court of Appeal held that the trial judge had not been entitled to reach that conclusion: the offence with the imitation firearm was far from trivial, and such crimes had often been under-sentenced in the past.

Once it has been decided that the mandatory life sentence must be passed in a particular case, the court must then fix the minimum period of detention to be specified under s. 28 of the C(S)A 1997. In *R* v *Errington* [1999] Crim LR 91 the Court of Appeal held, following the authority of *R* v *Marklew and Lambert* [1999] 1 Cr App R (S) 6 on discretionary life sentences, that the correct approach is to decide what the appropriate determinate sentence would have been if the mandatory sentence had not applied; to deduct half from that sentence, unless there were circumstances making it appropriate for the offender to serve more than a half; and then to deduct any time spent in custody awaiting trial; and then to fix the resulting period as the specified minimum period under s. 28.

21.9 Required Custodial Sentences

Sections 109 and 110 of the PCC(S)A 2000 provide for required custodial sentences, or minimum sentences (the Act uses both terms), of seven years for the third conviction of Class A drug trafficking and of three years for the third conviction of domestic burglary.

Section 109 applies to any person aged 18 or over who is convicted of a Class A drug trafficking offence, and who has previously been convicted on two separate occasions of such offences. Such an offender must be sentenced to a minimum of seven years' imprisonment, although the sentence may be (and usually would be) longer than seven years. However, this is not a mandatory minimum sentence, for there are two statutory grounds on which a court might go below the prescribed sentence.

First, the court need not impose the minimum if it is:

> . . . *of the opinion that there are particular circumstances which—*
> *(a) relate to any of the offences or to the offender; and*
> *(b) would make it unjust to do so in all the circumstances.*

This grants a much wider judicial discretion than 'exceptional circumstances', and should enable the courts to avoid injustice.

Secondly, the court may go below the minimum in order to grant a limited discount for pleading guilty. Section 152(3) of the PCC(S)A 2000 provides as follows:

> *In the case of an offence the sentence for which falls to be imposed under subsection (2) of section 110 or 111 above, nothing in that subsection shall prevent the court, after taking into account any matter referred to in subsection (1) above, from imposing any sentence which is not less than 80 per cent of that specified in that subsection.*

There is no equivalent provision for s. 109 cases (mandatory life sentence), but it was thought that the incentive to plead guilty should be retained for repeat drug trafficking and domestic burglary defendants. It will be noted, however, that the available discount is somewhat lower than that applicable in other cases (which may be up to one-third).

Section 111, on domestic burglary, is unlikely to have a practical impact for some months, since not only does it apply to the third domestic burglary conviction but it must also be established, according to s. 111(1)(c), that 'one of [the two previous] burglaries was committed after he had been convicted of the other, and both of them were committed after the commencement of the section'. Since the commencement date of the original provision was 1 December 1999, it will be some time before domestic burglars begin to accumulate the criminal record required to qualify them for the prescribed (minimum) sentence under s. 111, and those who qualify first will clearly have committed two relatively non-serious burglaries before — otherwise they would probably have received one or more significant custodial sentences.

21.10 Suspended Sentences of Imprisonment

The suspended sentence was introduced into English law in 1967 as the first of several measures designed to reduce the use of imprisonment by the courts. The legislative framework is to be found in the PCC(S)A 2000, ss. 118 and 119.

Essentially, a court is empowered to suspend, for a period of not less than one year nor more than two years, any sentence of imprisonment of two years or less. If the offender is convicted of an imprisonable offence committed within the operational period of the suspended sentence, the court which deals with the new offence must activate the suspended sentence and commit the offender to prison unless it would be 'unjust to do so'. The suspended sentence therefore operates as a definite threat to the particular offender. It should be noted that only a sentence of imprisonment can be suspended: this means that suspension is unavailable for custodial sentences for offenders under 21, which are termed 'detention in a young offender institution'.

21.10.1 THE DECISION SEQUENCE

Before imposing a suspended sentence of imprisonment, the court must go through the decision sequence indicated by PCC(S)A 2000, s. 118(4):

A court shall not deal with an offender by means of a suspended sentence unless it is of the opinion—

(a) that the case is one in which a sentence of imprisonment would have been appropriate even without the power to suspend the sentence; and

(b) that the exercise of that power can be justified by the exceptional circumstances of the case.

This means that the court must first ensure that the case passes over the custody threshold established by s. 79 of the PCC(S)A 2000, usually, that the offence was so serious that only a custodial sentence can be justified. The second step is to decide on the appropriate length of the custodial sentence, applying s. 80(2)(a). The third step, if the appropriate length is two years or less, should be to decide whether or not the sentence should be suspended. This depends on the requirement of 'exceptional circumstances'.

21.10.2 'THE EXCEPTIONAL CIRCUMSTANCES OF THE CASE'

Following the implementation of the CJA 1991, a court may only suspend a prison sentence if this can be justified by the exceptional circumstances of the case. The intention was that this would result in far fewer suspended sentences than in previous years, and the hope was that most of those who had formerly benefited from suspension would instead qualify for a community sentence. The Court of Appeal quickly established the extremely narrow ambit of 'exceptional circumstances'. In *R* v *Okinikan* (1993) 14 Cr App R (S) 453 the Court held that:

> . . . taken on their own, or in combination, good character, youth and an early plea are not exceptional circumstances justifying a suspended sentence. . . . They may amount to mitigation sufficient to persuade the court that a custodial sentence should not be passed or to reduce its length.

This makes it clear that frequently-invoked mitigating circumstances cannot be regarded as 'exceptional'. A similar conclusion was reached in *R* v *Sanderson* (1993) 14 Cr App R (S) 361, where the appellant's good record, the fact that his wife and mother-in-law were dependent on him and his remorse were not regarded as 'exceptional'. In *R* v *Lowery* (1993) 14 Cr App R (S) 485 the offender was a police officer who had stolen money collected as fines, in order to help finance alterations to his house when his wife became disabled. He subsequently attempted suicide and was placed under psychiatric care. However, the court held that these were not 'exceptional circumstances' sufficient to justify suspension of the prison sentence for theft. It appears that in both this case and *R* v *Sanderson* (a case of unlawful wounding), the seriousness of the offence led the court to conclude that only an immediate custodial sentence would be adequate. Later decisions of the Court of Appeal such as *R* v *Khan* (1993) 15 Cr App R (S) 320 (suspending a sentence of imprisonment on an elderly solicitor suffering from serious health problems), *R* v *French* (1993) 15 Cr App R (S) 194, and *R* v *Weston* [1995] Crim LR 900, are more flexible. Thus 'exceptional circumstances' were upheld in *R* v *Bellikli* [1997] Crim LR 612 (offender's son gravely ill) and in *Attorney-General's References (Nos 62, 63 and 65 of 1996)* [1998] 1 Cr App R (S) 9 (mother of young children with special needs).

The use of the suspended sentence declined from 10% in 1991 to 1% in 1997. Research into sentencing in the Crown Court shows that women are four times as likely as men to receive a suspended sentence (9% compared with 2%), and that the leading factors in cases where the sentence is suspended are the physical or mental illness of the offender, the need to care for a dependent relative, and previous good character (Flood-Page and Mackie, *Sentencing Practice* (1998), p. 96). Some sentencers resent the restrictions imposed by Parliament and believe that suspended sentences should be more widely available (see Campbell, J. Q., 'A Sentencer's Lament on the Imminent Death of the Suspended Sentence' [1995] Crim LR 293).

21.10.3 ADDING A FINANCIAL PENALTY

To insert an immediate punitive impact into cases where a suspended sentence is imposed, there is provision in s. 118(5) of the PCC(S)A 2000:

> *A court which passes a suspended sentence on any person for an offence shall consider whether the circumstances of the case are such as to warrant in addition the imposition of a fine or the making of a compensation order.*

This is merely a duty to consider, but its manifest intent is to ensure that a higher proportion of suspended sentences are combined with a financial penalty. (The principles relevant to fines and compensation orders were discussed in **Chapter 18**.)

21.10.4 BREACH OF SUSPENDED SENTENCE

If a person who is subject to a suspended sentence is convicted of an imprisonable offence committed during the operational period of the suspended sentence, the court which sentences him or her for the new offence must activate the suspended sentence unless it appears 'unjust to do so' (PCC(S)A 2000, s. 119(1) and (2)). Moreover, the suspended sentence should run consecutively to any custodial sentence imposed for the new offence (*R* v *Ithell* [1969] 2 All ER 449). This severely restricts the sentencing powers of the second court, especially since the Court of Appeal has laid down that the fact that the new offence is of a different kind from the original offence is not a ground for failing to activate the suspended sentence (*R* v *Moylan* [1970] 1 QB 143). If the new offence is minor in nature and would not itself warrant a custodial sentence, this is a 'strong circumstance' for not activating the suspended sentence (*R* v *McElhorne* (1983) 5 Cr App R (S) 53; *R* v *Dobson* (1989) 11 Cr App R (S) 332), although a court may properly decide to activate the sentence in these circumstances, e.g., because of the rapidity with which the offender returned to crime (*R* v *Calladine* (1993) 15 Cr App R (S) 345; *R* v *Stacey* [1994] Crim LR 303).

21.11 Suspended Sentence Supervision Orders

Where a court imposes a suspended sentence of more than six months' imprisonment, it is empowered to add to that a suspended sentence supervision order. Section 122 of the PCC(S)A 2000 states that the supervision should be for a period not exceeding the operational period of the suspended sentence; and, the restriction to sentences of more than six months means that this order is only available in the Crown Court.

TWENTY-TWO

ASPECTS OF THE TARIFF

The aim of this chapter is to give an outline of certain aspects of the 'tariff', or 'going rate', for offences. Within the present context it is not possible to attempt a complete survey of all offences or of all Court of Appeal decisions. What can be conveyed is the basis of the tariff, the structure of the upper echelons of the tariff for serious offences, the relevance of guideline judgments and judgments on Attorney-General's references, and some aspects of the lower reaches of the tariff.

22.1 Structuring the Tariff

The 'going rate' of prison sentences for serious offences has developed since the late nineteenth century, and can be inferred from some of the judgments of the Court of Criminal Appeal in the first half of the twentieth century. However, it was not until 1975 that the Court of Appeal delivered a judgment that surveyed the upper echelons of the tariff and attempted to impose some logic on the different levels of sentence there. The leading case is *R* v *Turner* (1975) 61 Cr App R 67, where the court had to decide on the appropriate length of sentences for grave armed robberies. The court stated that 'it is not in the public interest that even for grave crimes, sentences should be passed which do not correlate sensibly and fairly with the time in prison which is likely to be served by somebody who has committed murder in circumstances in which there were no mitigating circumstances' (at pp. 90–1). The court took 15 years' imprisonment as the period likely to be served by such a murderer. That was equivalent to a determinate sentence of some 22 years, which, less the one-third remission which applied before 1992, would work out at 15 years in prison. So the court started from the position that determinate sentences should not usually exceed 22 years for non-murder offences.

Beneath this notional ceiling of 22 years should come, first, what Lawton LJ referred to as 'wholly abnormal' crimes — 'bomb outrages, acts of political terrorism and possibly in the future acts of political kidnapping'. Then, beneath that group of crimes, should come offences which are very grave but not 'wholly abnormal'. The court therefore concluded (at p. 91):

> . . . that the normal sentence for anyone taking part in a bank robbery or in the hold-up of a security or Post Office van, should be 15 years if firearms were carried and no serious injury done.
>
> . . . something must be added to the basic sentence passed on those who committed more than one robbery, but the maximum total sentence should not normally be more than 18 years. That is about the maximum sentence which should be passed for crimes which do not come into the category of offences on which we have put the description 'wholly abnormal'.

This framework is still used by the Court of Appeal as a means of ordering sentences at the top end of the scale, particularly in cases of armed robbery (see, e.g., *R* v *Copeland and Hegarty* (1994) 15 Cr App R (S) 601) and also for explosives offences (see the guideline case of *R* v *Martin* [1997] Crim LR 97). It does not mean, however, that courts may never justifiably impose a determinate prison sentence longer than 22 years. In *R* v *Hindawi* (1988) 10 Cr App (S) 104 the offender had persuaded his girlfriend to carry on to an aircraft a bag, in which (unknown to her) he had placed an explosive device. The bomb was discovered before the aircraft took off, and he was convicted of attempting to place on an aircraft a device likely to destroy or damage the aircraft, contrary to the Criminal Attempts Act 1981 and the Aviation Security Act 1982. Upholding the sentence of 45 years' imprisonment, Lord Lane CJ, stated (at p. 105):

> Put briefly, this was about as foul and as horrible a crime as could possibly be imagined. It is no thanks to this applicant that his plot did not succeed in destroying 360 or 370 lives in the effort to promote one side of a political dispute by terrorism.
>
> In the judgment of this court the sentence of 45 years' imprisonment was not a day too long.

Both *Turner* and *Hindawi* were appeals in individual cases. During the 1980s the major developments came through guideline judgments, in which the Court of Appeal, usually with the Lord Chief Justice presiding, used the judgment in a particular case as a vehicle for laying down general guidance for dealing with offences of a certain kind. During the 1990s this approach has continued, bolstered by the use of judgments in Attorney-General's reference cases to give guidance. In the paragraphs that follow, special attention will be given to judgments of these two types.

22.1.1 ATTEMPTED MURDER

The penalty for murder is mandatory: life imprisonment. An offender who is convicted of attempted murder faces a maximum sentence of life imprisonment, but generally that sentence is reserved for offenders who are thought unstable and dangerous (see further **Chapter 23**). The range of sentences for attempted murder may be said to reflect the effective range for murder itself. Thus in *R* v *Al-Banna* (1984) 6 Cr App R (S) 426 the Court of Appeal upheld sentences of 35 and 30 years' imprisonment on men who had attempted to assassinate the Israeli ambassador in London, wounding him severely in the process. The Court took the view that minimum recommended terms of 35 and 30 years for murder would have been appropriate if the victim had died. At the other end of the scale, sentences in the 10–12 year range have been approved for attempted murders arising out of 'domestic' quarrels (*R* v *Haynes* (1983) 5 Cr App R (S) 58; *R* v *Green* (1986) 8 Cr App R (S) 246; *R* v *Bedford* (1992) 14 Cr App R (S) 336).

22.1.2 ROBBERY

The judgment in *R* v *Turner* (1975) 61 Cr App R 67 remains the principal authority for serious armed robberies. However, the legal elements in robbery (theft, use or threat of violence) may be satisfied by a wide range of conduct, and for a push combined with the snatch of a purse the sentence will clearly be at the bottom of the scale. Whilst *Turner* sets the tariff at 15–18 years for armed robberies of banks, security vehicles and so on, much of the attention in recent years has focused on the sentencing of robberies outside the so-called 'first division'.

In *Attorney-General's Reference (No. 2 of 1989) (Major)* (1989) 11 Cr App R (S) 481 the offender had acted as lookout at a betting-shop robbery in which a gun had been used to injure the manager's leg and some £200 was taken. The offender had been unaware that the gun was loaded and played a secondary role in the offence, but the Court of Appeal nevertheless increased the sentence from three to seven years. In *Attorney-General's Reference (No. 9 of 1989) (Lacey)* (1990) 12 Cr App R (S) 7 the offender had smashed protective glass and threatened a sub-postmistress with a baseball bat, escaping with a small amount of money. The Court of Appeal increased the sentence from 30 months to five years. In *Attorney-General's References (Nos. 3, 4, 8, 9, 10, 11 and 16 of 1990)* (1990) 12 Cr App R (S) 479 the Court seemed to establish a guideline range of four to seven years for cases of the following type:

> The small shop or off-licence often provides a valuable service to the local community. The shop is likely to have considerable sums of money upon the premises or upon the person of the proprietor. The premises are not likely to be able to afford the sort of protection in the shape of modern electronic devices which banks or building societies are able to install to protect their premises. Consequently . . . it is necessary for courts to make it clear that when this type of offender is apprehended he will be able to be subject to condign punishment.

In *Attorney-General's References (Nos. 5 and 6 of 1991)* (1992) 14 Cr App R (S) 425, two offenders who stole £10,000 from the safe at a service station, threatening the attendants with a loaded shotgun, had their sentences increased to seven and six years for the robbery (with 12 months consecutive for the shotgun offence). Robberies involving imitation firearms may attract similar sentences (*R* v *Curry and Taylor* [1997] 1 Cr App R (S) 417 (cucumber in plastic bag)). It will be recalled that a second robbery with a firearm or imitation firearm requires the court to impose an automatic life sentence (**21.8**).

22.1.3 RAPE

The Lord Chief Justice handed down a guideline judgment on sentencing for rape in *R* v *Billam* [1986] 1 WLR 349. The judgment begins with a discussion of the severe emotional and psychological trauma suffered by many victims of rape, and then moves to an examination of the sentencing statistics. Lord Lane concluded that rape was being under-sentenced in proportion to other crimes, and therefore set out guidelines designed to remedy that imbalance. Life imprisonment might be appropriate for mentally disturbed rapists, and a sentence of 15 years or more might be appropriate for an offender who has carried out a campaign of rapes (see *R* v *John Thomas W* [1998] 1 Cr App R (S) 24, sentence of 20 years for 11 rapes). Beneath that:

> For rape committed by an adult without any aggravating or mitigating features, a figure of five years should be taken as the starting-point in a contested case. Where a rape is committed by two or more men acting together, or by a man who has broken into or otherwise gained access to a place where the victim is living, or by a person who is in a position of responsibility towards the victim, or by a person who abducts the victim and holds her captive, the starting-point should be eight years. ([1986] 1 WLR 349 at p. 351.)

Lord Lane then went on to list some of the possible aggravating factors and mitigating factors, which courts should take into account when assessing a particular case in relation to the guidelines (at p. 351):

> The crime should in any event be treated as aggravated by any of the following factors: (1) violence is used over and above the force necessary to commit the rape; (2) a weapon is used to frighten or wound the victim; (3) the rape is repeated; (4) the rape has been carefully planned; (5) the defendant has previous convictions for rape or other serious offences of a violent or sexual kind; (6) the victim is subject to further sexual indignities or perversions; (7) the victim is either very old or very young; (8) the effect upon the victim, whether physical or mental, is of special seriousness. Where any one or more of these aggravating features are present, the sentence should be substantially higher than the figure suggested as the starting-point.
>
> The extra distress which giving evidence can cause to a victim means that a plea of guilty, perhaps more so than in other cases, should normally result in some reduction from what would otherwise be the appropriate sentence. The amount of such reduction will of course depend on all the circumstances, including the likelihood of a finding of not guilty had the matter been contested.

Another important feature of the *Billam* judgment on rape is its clear statement of two factors which judges should *not* take into account when determining sentence:

> The fact that the victim may be considered to have exposed herself to danger by acting imprudently (as for instance by accepting a lift in a car from a stranger) is not a mitigating factor; and the victim's previous sexual experience is equally irrelevant.

The judgment also states that 'The starting-point for attempted rape should normally be less than for the completed offence, especially if it is desisted at a comparatively early stage'.

Subsequently, the guidelines have been developed in other decisions. In *Attorney-General's Reference (No. 7 of 1989)* (1990) 12 Cr App R (S) 1, the offender had been convicted of raping his former fiancée and had been sentenced to two years. The Court of Appeal increased the sentence to four-and-a-half years, for two main reasons. First, the mere fact that the parties had previously lived together and had regular sexual intercourse did not license the man to have intercourse with the woman after cohabitation had ceased, although 'it is a factor to which some weight can be given'. Second, there had not been a guilty plea, and therefore no reduction of sentence was due on that account. In *R* v *W* (1992) 14 Cr App R (S) 256 Lord Taylor of Gosforth CJ said that 'it should not be thought that a different and lower scale of sentencing attaches automatically to rape by a husband', and upheld a sentence of five years in a case with aggravating features and no plea of guilty (see also *R* v *W* [1998] 1 Cr App R (S) 375). In two subsequent cases of rape of a cohabitant followed by forgiveness on the part of the victim, the Court of Appeal reduced the sentences (to five years in *R* v *Hutchinson* (1993) 15 Cr App R (S) 134, and to six years in a case with various aggravating features, *R* v *Hind* (1993) 15 Cr App R (S) 114), holding that the forgiveness meant that the trauma suffered by the victim was less than normal. It should be noted that a second conviction for rape or attempted rape now attracts a mandatory life sentence under the C(S)A 1997.

22.1.4 OTHER SERIOUS SEXUAL OFFENCES

Probably the oldest sentencing guideline case, *R* v *Willis* [1975] 1 WLR 292, gives some general guidance on the aggravating and mitigating features of buggery without the victim's consent. The general tendency has been to use similar starting points to those indicated by the *Billam* judgment on rape. Thus in *R* v *Mendez* (1991) 13 Cr App R (S) 94 the Court of Appeal upheld a sentence of five years, commenting that 'forcible buggery of a woman is equivalent to rape but worse than normal vaginal rape. . . . There is no mitigation here of a guilty plea. Indeed . . . one might well regard this as an aggravated rather than a standard rape'.

On incest the Court of Appeal laid down guidelines in *Attorney-General's Reference (No. 1 of 1989)* [1989] 1 WLR 1117. The judgment contains elaborate guidelines for the different forms of the offence, listing several aggravating and mitigating factors. A term of around six years was suggested where the girl is under 13 years; terms in the range from three to five years where the girl is aged 13 to 15; and terms of up to three years where the girl is aged at least 16. As with the *Billam* guidelines, a plea of guilty would reduce the sentence.

22.1.5 DRUG OFFENCES

The first major guideline judgment by Lord Lane CJ was *R* v *Aramah* (1982) 4 Cr App R (S) 407 on drugs. The judgment sets out sentencing levels for the importation, supply or possession of drugs in the various classes. An example of the style of the judgment is provided by the following extract, amended in the light of *R* v *Bilinski* (1987) 9 Cr App R (S) 360:

> I turn to the importation of heroin, morphine and so on. Large scale importation, that is where the street value of the consignment is in the order of £100,000 or more, sentences of [ten] years and upwards are appropriate. There will be cases where the values are of the order of £1 million or more, in which cases the offence should be visited by sentences of [14 years and upwards]. It will seldom be that an importer of any appreciable amount of the drug will deserve less than four years.

> This, however, is one area in which it is particularly important that offenders should be encouraged to give information to the police, and a confession of guilt, coupled with considerable assistance to the police, can properly be marked by a substantial reduction in what would otherwise be the proper sentence.
>
> ... Importation of cannabis: importation of very small amounts for personal use can be dealt with as if it were simple possession. ... Otherwise importation of amounts up to about 20 kilogrammes of herbal cannabis, or the equivalent in cannabis resin or cannabis oil, will, save in the most exceptional cases, attract sentences of between 18 months and three years, with the lowest ranges reserved for pleas of guilty in cases where there has been small profit to the offender. The good character of the courier (as he usually is) is of less importance than the good character of the defendant in other cases. The reason for this is, it is well known that the large-scale operator looks for couriers of good character and for people of a sort which is likely to exercise the sympathy of the court if they are detected and arrested. Consequently one will frequently find students and sick and elderly people are used as couriers. ... There are few, if any, occasions when anything other than an immediate custodial sentence is proper in this type of importation.

The basis of the sentencing guidelines was changed more firmly from 'street value' to weight by the Court of Appeal in *R* v *Aroyewumi* [1994] Crim LR 695 (sometimes referred to as *Aranguren*). The intention of Lord Taylor CJ was to make the change without significantly altering effective sentence lengths. He held that sentences for the importation of 500 grammes of heroin or cocaine should be around ten years, and for 5 kilogrammes around 14 years. Other examples are also included in the judgment, which goes on to make the important point that not all drugs are of 100% purity. An allowance must therefore be made in the sentence where the drugs are of a lesser purity.

The last few years have seen considerable refinement of sentencing guidelines to deal with the varying nature and form of different drugs. Thus the Court of Appeal formulated guidelines for 'ecstasy' in *R* v *Warren and Beeley* [1996] 1 Cr App R (S) 233, for LSD offences in *R* v *Hurley* [1998] 1 Cr App R (S) 299, for large-scale cannabis importation in *R* v *Ronchetti* [1998] 2 Cr App R (S) 100, and for amphetamine offences in *R* v *Wijs* [1998] Crim LR 587.

22.1.6 SERIOUS DRIVING OFFENCES CAUSING DEATH

Guidelines for the former offence of causing death by reckless driving were laid down in *R* v *Boswell* [1984] 1 WLR 1047. In 1991 the offence of causing death by reckless driving was replaced by the offence of causing death by dangerous driving, a somewhat wider statutory formula. In 1993 the maximum penalty for causing death by dangerous driving was increased from five to ten years, and in *Attorney-General's References (Nos 14 and 24 of 1993)* [1994] Crim LR 305 the Court of Appeal revised the *Boswell* guidelines upwards, so that they now read:

> The situation where there are no aggravating features present is that, so far as sentencing is concerned, a non-custodial penalty may well be appropriate, but where aggravating features, or an aggravating feature is present then a custodial sentence is generally necessary. At present, as already indicated, the statistics seem to show that the general maximum term is about 12 to 18 months as imposed by the courts. It is not easy to see why this should be so. Drivers who for example indulge in racing on the highways and/or driving with reckless disregard for the safety of others after taking alcohol, should understand that in bad cases they will lose their liberty for [upwards of five years]. It will seldom be that a community service order, or a suspended sentence will be appropriate in a serious case. By the same token that type of driver should be removed from the road by a long period of disqualification.

In 1993 the maximum penalty for the offence of causing death by careless driving while affected by alcohol, introduced in 1991, was also doubled to ten years. It is not clear whether this is the lesser offence of the two, and the decisions suggest that the effective sentence levels are similar: see the survey of decisions in *Archbold News* (1996), issue 8, p. 5.

One apparent anomaly is that the offence of causing death by aggravated vehicle taking remains subject to a maximum sentence of five years (although this offence has fairly low culpability requirements). In *R* v *Ore* [1994] Crim LR 304 the Court of Appeal upheld sentences of four years' detention in a young offender institution imposed on young men of 20, on facts that were close to the worst conceivable type of case. Earlier, in the case of *R* v *Bird* (1993) 14 Cr App R (S) 343 the Lord Chief Justice laid down sentencing guidelines for this offence under the Aggravated Vehicle-Taking Act 1992. The most important circumstance is the fact that the vehicle was driven dangerously, since that bears on the culpability of the driver. In assessing that, the driving should be assessed according to 'how bad it was and for how long'. Presumably some of the factors stated in the guideline judgment on reckless driving in *R* v *Boswell* (above) are relevant. In this context, however, Lord Taylor acknowledged that 'the incidence and severity of any injury or damage caused were to some extent a matter of chance', and were thus only 'to a lesser extent' aggravating. Where the offence is careless driving, and a person has been killed, the Court has recently held that it is right to take account of the unforeseen consequences. In *R* v *Simmonds* [1999] Crim LR 421 it held that, at a time when there is increased public and parliamentary concern about deaths on the roads, a sentencing court is entitled to take account of the fact that the careless driving led to death, even though that is not material to the definition of the offence of conviction.

22.1.7 SERIOUS WOUNDINGS

Serious woundings in which an intent to kill can be proved may well result in conviction for attempted murder and will be sentenced accordingly. Sentences for wounding with intent to cause grievous bodily harm, and other forms of the offence under the Offences against the Person Act 1861, s. 18, slot into the tariff just below attempted murder. In *R* v *Sullivan* (1987) 9 Cr App R (S) 196 the Court of Appeal upheld a sentence of 15 years for luring a man out of a house and then shooting him in both legs. This case, aggravated by the use of a firearm, is among the most serious. The normal range seems to be from six to ten years for stabbings and for attacks with blunt instruments. For example, the beating of an elderly man with a hammer was held to justify nine years in *Attorney-General's Reference (No. 13 of 1992)* (1992) 14 Cr App R (S) 756. Offences of 'glassing', in which a beer glass is used to wound the face, have tended to attract sentences in the three- to five-year range. A second s. 18 offence now attracts a mandatory life sentence under the C(S)A 1997.

22.1.8 THEFT IN BREACH OF TRUST

Here, the guideline judgment in *R* v *Barrick* (1985) 7 Cr App R (S) 142 has recently been revised upwards in *R* v *Clark* [1998] 2 Cr App R (S) 95. Pointing out that most of these offenders will be of good previous character, Lord Lane stated in *R* v *Barrick* that:

> In general a term of immediate imprisonment is inevitable, save in very exceptional circumstances or where the amount of money obtained is small. Despite the great punishment that offenders of this sort bring upon themselves, the court should nevertheless pass a sufficiently substantial term of imprisonment to mark publicly the gravity of the offence. The sum involved is obviously not the only factor to be considered, but it may in many cases provide a useful guide. Where the amounts involved cannot be described as small but are less than £17,500 or thereabouts, terms of imprisonment ranging from the very short up to about 21 months are appropriate. . . . Cases involving sums of between about £17,500 and £100,000 will merit a term of about two to three years' imprisonment; cases involving sums between £100,000 and £250,000 will merit three to four years; cases involving between £250,000 and £1 million will merit between five and nine years; cases involving £1 million and more will merit 10 years or more . . . In any case where a plea of guilty is entered, however, the court should give the appropriate discount.

The amounts and sentencing ranges in this passage have been amended in the light of *Clark*. The judgment in *Barrick* went on to list some of the aggravating and mitigating factors in this type of case. Many lesser forms of theft in breach of trust, committed by sales assistants and cashiers, might be dealt with summarily. The Magistrates' Association Sentencing Guidelines (2000 version) indicate a guideline sentence of custody for these offences, and list five factors that might reduce seriousness: impulsive action, unsupported junior, single item, low value, and previous inconsistent attitude by employer.

22.1.9 BURGLARY OF A DWELLING

Burglary of a dwelling still carries a maximum of 14 years, while the maximum for other forms of burglary was reduced to ten years by the CJA 1991. The decision in *R* v *Mussell* (1990) 12 Cr App R (S) 607 laid down general guidance for the sentencing of dwellinghouse burglaries. Lord Lane CJ held that the general level of sentences should reflect the anxiety and distress to householders commonly caused by the offence. He emphasised the aggravating effect of premeditation and planning, and also any ransacking or fouling of the house during the burglary. Particularly important was his concluding remark: that burglary of a dwelling is not always so serious that only a custodial sentence can be justified. 'An example would be that of a sneak thief walking past an open door, who puts his hand inside the door and steals a £5 note or some food from the kitchen table.' Indeed, some burglaries of dwellings are properly tried in magistrates' courts.

Lord Bingham CJ delivered a new guideline judgment on burglary in *R* v *Brewster* [1998] 1 Cr App R (S) 181. This confirms that domestic burglary is not in all cases so serious that only a custodial sentence can be justified. Where a custodial sentence is required, the criminal record of the offender will be significant for sentencing. The Lord Chief Justice was particularly insistent that burglaries of unoccupied houses are not necessarily less serious than burglaries of occupied premises: the targeting of unoccupied premises shows planning and premeditation. The Court concluded that to establish sentence ranges and brackets for burglary is neither possible nor desirable. An example of the current judicial approach is provided by *R* v *Hollis* [1998] 2 Cr App R (S) 359, where a man broke into a cottage whilst the owner was out and stole jewellery. The Court of Appeal upheld the sentence of four years' imprisonment for this single offence, citing *Brewster* and noting that the offender's record (29 previous burglaries) indicated that he should be treated as a professional burglar. However, there are still cases of domestic burglary that fall below the custody threshold, e.g., *R* v *Finney* [1998] 2 Cr App R (S) 239.

22.1.10 THEFT FROM A SHOP

A survey of sentencing in the mid-1990s shows that in the Crown Court some 36% of persons convicted of theft to a value under £100 (not involving breach of trust) received a custodial sentence, compared with 57% of those sentenced for theft of a greater amount (Flood-Page and Mackie, *Sentencing Practice in the 1990s* (1998), p. 85). In their survey of magistrates' courts some 10% of those convicted of theft from a shop received custody (p. 26). The Magistrates' Association's Sentencing Guidelines (2000 version) do not classify theft from a shop separately: they have a general category of theft (excluding theft in breach of trust), for which the guideline sentence is a community sentence. Among the aggravating factors are: 'high value, planned, sophisticated, adult involving children, organised team, related damage and vulnerable victim'; among the mitigating factors are 'impulsive action, low value'.

22.2 Counsel and the Tariff

It will be evident that this chapter has discussed in outline only a small number of offences for which sentence may be passed. Within the context of the course, however, this should be sufficient to give a general idea of the sentencing tariff. How should counsel ascertain the 'going rate' for a particular offence? The following checklist may be helpful:

(a) Is there a guideline judgment for this offence? (This may be found in an ordinary appeal judgment or an Attorney-General's reference case.)

(b) If not, do the decisions collated and classified in Dr Thomas's loose-leaf encyclopaedia, *Current Sentencing Practice*, disclose a pattern or a clear range of sentences?

(c) How do those decisions relate to the actual sentencing practice of the courts for this crime? Court of Appeal cases are often said to be untypical, and it is important to find out whether the going rate in practice is significantly lower than the appellate decisions suggest. One way of doing this is to consult the latest volume of *Criminal Statistics*, although it must be remembered that the sentencing statistics give only 'net' figures, reflecting sentences arrived at after taking account of any aggravating or mitigating factors in each case.

(d) If the case is in a magistrates' court, consult the latest version of the Magistrates' Association Sentencing Guidelines (now, the 2000 revision). It is, however, worth checking whether the guidelines are respected in the particular court, since they have not been adopted in some areas.

TWENTY-THREE

DANGEROUSNESS AND MENTAL DISORDER

23.1 Introduction

There are several good texts and research studies dealing with different aspects of this enormous subject, which will certainly need to be read if counsel's practice is to take in, for example, considerable work with Mental Health Review Tribunals. It is also an area with which most members of the Bar will have some acquaintance, but one which will only be commonplace for few. Mentally disordered offenders and offenders considered dangerous by the courts are only rarely encountered in criminal practice. Useful articles include: A. Ashworth 'Sentencing Mentally Disordered Offenders' [1996] Crim LR 457; M. Cunneen and S. Tarrant 'Detaining the untreatable' (1999) Legal Action, June, 8–9; N. Eastman and J. Peay 'Sentencing Psychopaths: Is the "Hospital and Limitation Direction" an Ill-Considered Hybrid?' [1998] Crim LR 93; R. Henham 'Dangerous Trends in the Sentencing of Mentally Abnormal Offenders' (1995) 34 Howard Journal 10–18; and J. Laing 'Mentally disordered offenders' (1997) 147 NLJ 1313.

This is the paradox. The rhetoric of dangerousness is very prevalent in sentencing decisions, and the volume of academic literature and of policy decisions concerning dangerousness is considerable. However, the numbers of people given disposals reflecting dangerousness or mental disorder specifically are extremely small. There are several specialist sentences, but compared to the non-custodial alternatives previously discussed and compared to imprisonment, the numbers are minute. The rule must be that if you are likely to have to deal with someone for whom the words 'mental disorder' or 'dangerousness' are likely to crop up, it is important to look up the relevant powers of the court beforehand. They are complicated, and even if you are guided to the right sentence by medical and pre-sentence reports when you arrive at court, you still need to know what they are talking about.

In mitigation you are promoting the best interests of your client according to the instructions you are given. You may feel that your client's wishes are not always the best thing to get him or her the non-custodial sentence he or she desires, but provided that you are not misleading the court you must follow them. With a mentally disordered client, it can be very difficult — you will feel that you need to do what will be in his or her best interests. But this may not entirely be as per instructions. Essentially there is no obvious fixed answer to this. Your twin duties remain, but it is specially important to listen to your client and to explain the options to him or her. Not all mentally disordered clients are incapable — if they have been found guilty, they must by definition be responsible for their actions. So they must be considered as being able to take some responsibility in considering what mitigation to put forward. It is now good psychiatric practice to include clients as far as possible in decisions affecting them. Decisions on mitigation are clearly important ones. But involving disordered people will take more time, which needs to be allowed for. It may be helpful to seek advice from the probation service, since they are likely to have more experience than counsel with certain kinds of disorder.

23.1.1 THE RELATION BETWEEN MENTAL DISORDER AND DANGEROUSNESS

It is very important to realise that there is no necessary connection between mental disorder and dangerousness. Violent offenders, terrorists and so forth, are clearly dangerous, but may well not be mentally disordered at all. Equally, most of the offences committed by the mentally disordered are property offences and such defendants should not be considered any more dangerous than any other offender committing the same kinds of offence. Though there may be a connection between the disorder and the commission of offences, there may well not be. For less serious offenders, the legislation on mentally disordered offenders has primarily been influenced by humanitarian considerations of the need to ensure treatment for such offenders.

At the most serious end of the spectrum of offences, however, the legislation has clearly been influenced by the problem of the continuing dangerousness of offenders who are mentally disordered. The protection of the public is seen as the priority, although treatment for the offender is also important, both to reduce the likelihood of re-offending and for humanitarian reasons.

It is important, therefore, to distinguish those sentencing provisions primarily intended to deal with the dangerous from those primarily intended for the mentally disordered. The new proposals in the C(S)A 1997 (see **15.7** and **23.3**) are clearly intended for dangerous and persistent offenders, but not specifically for mentally disordered offenders.

23.2 Dangerousness

There are several provisions specifically designed to deal with those considered dangerous by the courts, but they vary in the extent to which the defendants given these sentences might be mentally disordered. The major provisions are:

(a) determinate prison sentences which are longer than those commensurate with the seriousness of the offence, under PCC(S)A 2000, ss. 79(2)(b) and 80(2)(b) (no need to show any evidence of mental disorder) — see **23.2.3**;

(b) a sentence of life imprisonment (only available for offences which carry life as their maximum sentence), for which the courts normally require some evidence of mental disorder (though no specific disorder need be diagnosed) — see **23.8**;

(c) mandatory life sentences for specific violent offences where there are previous convictions under PCC(S)A 2000, s. 109 — see **23.3**;

(d) a restriction order under the Mental Health Act 1983 (MHA), for which the offender must be diagnosed as mentally disordered and falling within one of the four categories of mental disorder defined in s. 1 of the Act — see **23.7.2(d)**;

(e) the provision in the CDA 1998, for an extended period of licence on release from a custodial sentence for those convicted of sexual or violent offences — see **23.4**.

We shall deal first with the problems of defining and measuring dangerousness, before turning to the CJA 1991 provisions for those who are not mentally disordered.

23.2.1 THE DIFFICULTY OF DEFINING 'DANGEROUSNESS'

There has been considerable and unceasing controversy about dangerousness, with the most vexed questions centering on the problem of definition.

The statutes have taken one of two approaches. Some, such as the C(S)A 1997, have set out elaborate rules relating to previous convictions and the current offence in order to try to specify the kinds of defendants who would be eligible for what is usually considerable extra punishment. But these elaborate schemes have tended to pick up the persistent nuisance or property offender, rather than the violent offender at whom they were aimed, because violent offenders are only rarely reconvicted for violence on several occasions within a relatively short time span.

The other approach is the 'everybody knows' approach: that you cannot define dangerousness but you can recognise it when you see it. It is sad that the 1990 White Paper and the CJA 1991 adopt this approach (see **Chapter 21**). The White Paper advocates that dangerous and serious offenders should be given long sentences out of the range of the normal offences of the type (though still within the statutory maximum). The requirement on judges to remain within a range specified by 'just deserts' and the tariff will be lessened, though reasons will clearly be required. The difficulty with the 'everybody knows' approach is that it leaves almost total discretion to the judiciary and the medical profession on necessarily imprecise grounds. There is thus some potential for abuse, and difficulty in formulating guidelines so that counsel, probation officers and the public can understand what is happening.

The White Paper states that:

> The Government proposes to take this approach (of the Court of Appeal) further by giving the Crown Court power to give custodial sentences longer than would be justified by the seriousness of the offence to persistent violent and sexual offenders, if this is necessary to protect the public from serious harm. There are a small number of offenders who become progressively more dangerous and who are a real risk to public safety. Some will be mentally disordered and can be detained under mental health legislation. For those convicted of the most serious crimes, a sentence of life imprisonment may be justified. The proposed restrictions on the use of custody in the White Paper will not apply to the most serious crimes which are tried only in the Crown Court. Some offenders will be convicted of less serious offences but the Crown Court will recognise that they are a serious risk to the public. In these circumstances the Government considers that an exception should be made to the principle that the length of the individual sentence should be justified by the seriousness of the offence. The Crown Court would be able to give a longer sentence within the maximum penalty for the offences for which the offender has been convicted. . . . The Court would, of course have to state in open court why it was giving a longer sentence and it would be open to the defendant to appeal against his sentence.

A similar approach is currently used in the restriction order where all that is required is to show that it is necessary in order to protect the public from serious harm, the nature of such harm being left undefined.

Note, by the way, the problems of this approach in dealing with the dangerous. The difficulty with all determinate sentencing (the foundation of a 'just deserts' approach) in relation to the dangerous is that it does not deal with those you do not want to release at the end of their sentence. In essence, it is the prospect of release that always causes concern, rather than the problem of detention at the time of sentencing (where the concern is usually from the human rights angle). It is not possible by definition to solve the problem of release at the time of sentence. This is the reason given for adopting an indeterminate sentencing approach in the 1996 White Paper — though requiring a mandatory life sentence for any second conviction for a serious violent/sexual offence seems a drastic remedy.

23.2.2 POWERS OF CRIMINAL COURTS (SENTENCING) ACT 2000 PROVISIONS RELATING TO DANGEROUSNESS

Under PCC(S)A 2000, s. 79(2)(b), for a violent or sexual offence, a court may pass a custodial sentence if it is of the opinion that 'only such a sentence would be adequate to protect the public from serious harm' from the offender. Under s. 80(2)(b), again only for a violent or sexual offence, the court may pass a custodial sentence 'for such longer term (not exceeding the maximum) as in the opinion of the court is necessary to protect the public from serious harm from the offender'. Both of these powers permit courts to pass sentences which are longer (or more severe) than normal on the grounds of public protection, i.e., that the offender is considered potentially dangerous.

Both 'violent offence' and 'sexual offence' are defined in s. 161(2) of the Act. The definition of 'violent offence' is given in **21.5.3**.

Note here that there is no specific list of offences and so any offence which either causes injury or is likely to lead to injury may qualify. This might, for example, include dangerous driving.

The definition of 'sexual offence' is given in **21.5.3** and consists of a list of offences as defined by particular statutes.

'Serious harm' is defined in the PCC(S)A 2000, s. 161(4) and this is set out in **21.5.3**.

Before imposing a longer than normal sentence under s. 80(2)(b), the court should always give a warning to counsel (*R* v *Baverstock* [1993] 1 WLR 202). The court should also obtain and consider a pre-sentence report, and obtain and consider any information about the circumstances of the case.

There have been some indications of the Court of Appeal's view of these cases. They fall into two types: ones where the Court has been reviewing ordinary determinate sentences passed under s. 80(2)(a), but has considered them as justified under s. 80(2)(b); and a few which were originally given longer sentences for public protection under s. 80(2)(b). They have given us indications of the Court's view on the kinds of information seen as suitable for courts to consider when thinking of a longer than normal sentence, and of the kinds of offence in which such sentences have been used.

23.2.2.1 The information the court may consider for s. 80(2)(b) cases

If the offence is a 'violent' or a 'sexual' offence, then it has been held that it is the court's *mandatory* duty to consider whether a longer sentence is necessary to protect the public from serious harm (*R* v *Bowler* (1993) 15 Cr App R (S) 78). Counsel should, therefore, be prepared whenever a client is charged with such an offence.

How can the court see if serious harm might result, i.e., whether there is a predisposition to violence or sexual assault? Generally, the courts have looked to the defendant's previous convictions and to any psychiatric report that has been prepared, though any information before the judge may be used. There is no bar to the court considering previous convictions and a range of similar previous convictions (for violent or sexual offences) may be seen as such a predisposition. There does not have to be evidence that serious harm was actually caused in the past (*R* v *Bowler*).

Though most of the cases have related to physical injury ('serious personal injury'), the likelihood of future serious psychological injury being caused to members of the public would also be sufficient to found a longer sentence (*R* v *Bowler*). The potential serious harm need not be to the public in general or to average members of the public: those who are more vulnerable to this kind of psychological injury should also be considered if the defendant is likely to prey upon them (*R* v *Bowler*). The target of this future serious harm might even be just one particular person. *R* v *Nicholas* (1993) 15 Cr App R (S) 381 was a domestic violence case involving a charge of actual bodily harm and here it was said that the likelihood of serious harm to that victim in the future would be sufficient, though in the circumstances of that case it was held that there was little likelihood of a recurrence. The potential scope of the s. 80(2)(b) provision is hence wide.

All reports and all information available to the court will be considered and both pre-sentence reports and psychiatric reports have been seen as providing evidence in relation to the risk of reoffending. In *R* v *Oudkerk* (1995) 16 Cr App R (S) 172, the Court of Appeal stated that where the court contemplates the imposition of a longer than normal sentence under s. 80(2)(b), in addition to putting the defendant upon notice, it will be necessary for the sentencing court to resolve by a *Newton* hearing any important issue relevant to the application of the section (in that case, whether the defendant knew the victim and the assault was a 'lover's tiff', or whether he had attacked a stranger). The court should also have adequate information on the defendant's previous convictions. In *R* v *Fawcett* (1995) 16 Cr App R (S) 55, it was held that the court should obtain a medical report before passing a s. 80(2)(b) sentence if the danger was due to a medical or personality problem, in order to exclude the need to make a medical disposal.

23.2.2.2 The offences for which s. 80(2)(b) has been used

There has been a range of cases of indecent assault in which the Court of Appeal has approved the use of a s. 80(2)(b) sentence. In fact, David Thomas, in his commentary on *R* v *Lyons* [1994] Crim LR 145 considered this case of indecent assault as a 'classic case'. The offender admitted a relatively serious indecent assault on a woman on her own in a public place and had previous convictions for similar offences (thus indicating a predisposition). The pre-sentence report indicated some disorder, including a distorted attitude to women and a psychiatric report said the appellant was a great danger to women. The sentence of five years under s. 80(2)(b) was upheld. Although this case involved possible mental disorder (though not treatable or in need of treatment), other cases (for example, *R* v *Bowler* discussed in **23.2.2.1**) have involved no element of mental disorder. Quite often the previous convictions have been relatively minor offences (for example, *R* v *Apelt* (1993) 15 Cr App R (S) 420).

It must not be thought, however, that these provisions are reserved for indecent assault cases. Longer sentences have already been justified by the Court of Appeal for charges of unlawful wounding (*R* v *Coull* (1993) 15 Cr App R (S) 305), robbery (*R* v *Fowler* (1993) 15 Cr App R (S) 456), s. 18 wounding (*R* v *Utip* (1993) 14 Cr App R (S) 746, *R* v *Clarke* (1993) 15 Cr App R (S) 102), and even for s. 47 plus threatening to kill (*R* v *Etchells* [1996] 1 Cr App R (S) 163). Sometimes, the sentence upheld under s. 80(2)(b) is only slightly longer than that which the court would see as appropriate to the seriousness of the instant offence in any case.

In *R* v *Mansell* (1994) 15 Cr App R (S) 771, the Lord Chief Justice, sitting in the Court of Appeal, held that, in determining the period that needed to be added on, in a s. 80(2)(b) case, the sentencer had to perform a balancing act.

> In theory, someone who was addicted to conduct which could cause serious harm to members of the public might need to be prevented from doing so for a very long time. In the ultimate case, an indeterminate sentence might be necessary where the harm was likely to be very serious and the predilection for indulging in such conduct looked likely to continue for an indefinite time. The sentencer in each individual case had to try to balance the need to protect the public on the one hand with the need to look at the totality of the sentence and see that it was not out of all proportion with the nature of the offending.

This suggests that the extent of the risk of re-offending has to be balanced against the seriousness (and hence the potential harm) of the instant offence and of any future offences. Similarly, in *R* v *Crow and Pennington* (1995) 16 Cr App R (S) 409, it was indicated that the sentence should bear a reasonable relationship to the offence for which it is imposed. In *R* v *Johnson* [1998] 1 Cr App R (S) 126, the court said that in principle a s. 80(2)(b) sentence should not be consecutive to any existing sentence.

The 'balancing' act set out in *R* v *Mansell* has been commended again recently, with more recent cases trying to set out how the court should go about calculating the right balance between protection of the public and proportionality with the seriousness of the offence. *R* v *Gabbidon and Bramble* [1997] Crim LR 137 at p. 139 rejects complicated approaches to calculating this balance: 'It was better that the Court simply applied the principle of balance stated by Lord Taylor CJ in *Mansell*'. Hence the sentencer should start with a sentence which would be the appropriate or commensurate sentence if this was not to be a s. 80(2)(b) sentence (i.e. one which reflects the current guideline cases for determinate sentencing) and then add an 'enhancement for the protection of the public'. Unfortunately, the Court of Appeal took a rather different approach in *R* v *Campbell* [1997] 1 Cr App R (S) 119, where the sentencer was enjoined to try to find what would have been the right normal sentence, disregarding all questions of protecting the public (often included in ordinary proportionate sentencing), and then add on a pure element of protection. This is a very difficult, almost archaeological excavation approach to determining the balance and the approach adopted in *Gabbidon and Bramble* appears to be preferable.

23.3 Powers of Criminal Courts (Sentencing) Act 2000

Section 109 of the PCC(S)A 2000 requires courts to pass a mandatory life sentence if a person aged 18 or over is convicted of a second serious offence, 'unless the court is of the opinion that there are exceptional circumstances relating to either of the offences or to the offender which justify its not doing so' (s. 109(2)). The court will be required to state the exceptional circumstances.

A 'serious offence' is defined as an attempt to commit murder, a conspiracy to commit murder, or an incitement to murder; soliciting murder; manslaughter; s. 18 of the Offences Against the Person Act 1861 (wounding or causing grievous bodily harm with intent); rape or an attempt to commit rape; intercourse with a girl under 13 (s. 5 of the Sexual Offences Act 1956); possession of a firearm with intent to injure, use of a firearm to resist arrest, or carrying a firearm with criminal intent (Firearms Act 1968); or a robbery where at some time during the commission of the offence the offender had in his or her possession a firearm or imitation firearm.

This means that if a defendant aged 18 or over is convicted in England and Wales of any such serious offence committed after 30 September 1997, he or she would qualify for a mandatory sentence of life imprisonment (sometimes referred to as an automatic life sentence), if at the time of commission of that offence, he or she had been convicted in any part of the United Kingdom of another such serious offence.

The PCC(S)A 2000 does not define the meaning of 'exceptional circumstances', but in *R* v *Kelly* [1999] 2 WLR 1100, the Court of Appeal stated that for a circumstance to be exceptional it had to be out of the ordinary course, or unusual, special or uncommon. The circumstance need not be unique, or unprecedented, or very rare, but it could not be one that was regularly, or routinely, or normally encountered. The Court went on to say that in addition to being exceptional, the circumstances had to be such as justified the court in not imposing a life sentence. For examples of what would amount to exceptional circumstances, see *R* v *Buckland* [2000] Crim LR 307 and *R* v *Stephens* [2000] Crim LR 402, discussed at **15.7.2**, and *R* v *Newman* [2000] Crim LR 309 (paranoid psychotic illness not an exceptional circumstance).

23.4 Proposals in the Crime and Disorder Act 1998

23.4.1 EXTENDED SENTENCES

There has been considerable concern that, when offenders convicted of sexual or violent offences are released from prison, they are not subject to sufficient supervision if they are still dangerous. The CDA 1998 provides that a court should be able to pass a new sentence, called an extended sentence, which would embody a period after release during which the offender would be on licence. This would mean both that the offender would be supervised by a probation officer and that he or she could be recalled to prison. The custodial part of the sentence (the 'custodial term') would need to be at least four years for a violent offence. The licence period (the 'extension period') needs to be for the time the sentencing court thinks is necessary to prevent the offender committing further offences and to secure his or her rehabilitation and should not exceed ten years for a sexual offence and five years for a violent offence (with the total sentence not exceeding the maximum for the offence). The meanings of sexual and violent offences are the same as under the PCC(S)A 2000 (see **21.5.3**).

Though this provision will extend the idea of a licence involving a potential recall to prison (as opposed to just supervision) to all custodial sentences, and so impose additional protection where someone is clearly likely to remain dangerous for a period longer than the custodial sentence, it still fails to cope with the problem of the person who is first seen as being dangerous after the point of sentence.

23.4.2 SEX OFFENDER ORDERS

In order to cope with disquiet about sex offenders, particularly paedophiles, who are living in the community, the CDA 1998 contains the provision that a chief officer of police may apply to a magistrates' court for a sex offender order. The person must be a sex offender (meaning that he or she must have been convicted of or cautioned for a sex offence to which part I of the Sex Offenders Act 1997 applies, or been found not guilty by reason of insanity, or been punished by a court outside England and Wales for a similar offence) and must have acted in such a way as to give reasonable cause to believe that an order is necessary to protect the public from serious harm from him or her. Note the similar formulation of dangerousness to that used in restriction orders. The provisions of the order are not specified — they must merely be necessary to protect the public from serious harm and can last for up to five years. The penalty for breaching a sex offender order is up to five years in prison.

This is an extraordinary provision, in that the person concerned does not have to have committed any particular proscribed act in order to trigger the order, nor are the restrictions in any way specified. It means that anyone convicted of a sexual offence can become liable to constraints on their life at any time thereafter.

23.5 Basic Premises of the Criminal Justice System in Dealing with the Mentally Disordered

23.5.1 DIAGNOSING MENTAL DISORDER

The basic choice for any criminal justice system in dealing with the mentally disordered is between keeping the offender in the penal system and dealing with him or her in the same way as any other offender (which is seen by many as fair), and handing him or her over to the mental health professionals. For many years now, the system in England and Wales has taken the view that, in theory, an offender who has been found to be mentally disordered should receive special treatment which is relevant to his or her condition. A number of special sentences have been set up which have the effect of handing him or her over for medical treatment to the mental health services. The court does not retain any further stake. In practice, however, the position is very much more complicated. First he or she needs to be diagnosed as mentally disordered, not just according to the prevailing medical criteria, but, if he or she is to receive a specific sentence, according to the legal criteria laid down in the relevant Act.

23.5.2 THE LEGAL DEFINITIONS OF MENTAL DISORDERS

For most of the civil and criminal disposals in England and Wales, the legal definitions of the various forms of disorder are set out in the MHA 1983, s. 1. Four main groups of mental disorder are defined: mental illness, severe impairment, impairment, and psychopathic disorder. Very briefly, 'mental illness' includes those abnormalities considered to be illnesses, such as schizophrenia or manic depression, but it is not actually defined anywhere. 'Severe impairment' and 'impairment' are defects in intelligence, where 'severe impairment' means that the patient is incapable of living an independent life or of guarding himself against serious exploitation. 'Psychopathic disorder', the most controversial, means 'a persistent disorder or disability of mind (whether or not including significant impairment of intelligence) which results in abnormally aggressive or seriously irresponsible conduct on the part of the person concerned'. Note that, in the case of offenders, the addition of the behavioural part of the definition does not change anything — it was primarily included on humanitarian grounds in respect of civil patients.

There are two points to note from the presence of these legal definitions for diagnosis:

(a) If a person is not considered by a doctor to fall within the categories laid out in s. 1, then, however much that doctor or that court may think that that person is mentally disordered, he or she cannot be given any of the disposals which take their definition from s. 1.

(b) For all 'medical disposals', the courts are dependent upon one or more doctors (depending upon the sentence involved) stating that the person fits the legal category before any sentence can be imposed. In this way, one can see the doctor as the 'gateway' to medical disposals, just as the probation officer is the gateway to probation or supervision orders. Particularly in respect of mental illness, which is undefined, it is difficult for anyone, including lawyers, to challenge current medical opinion. This is exacerbated by the lack of recognised medical standards as regards the diagnosis and treatment of mental disorder, so that what happens in an individual case is difficult to match against any accepted standards of treatment practice.

The definitions above come from the MHA 1983, which governs the entry criteria for hospital orders and restriction orders — the only powers for compulsory detention in a mental hospital. Other definitions lie in other Acts. For example, the condition of mental treatment with a probation order comes under the PCC(S)A 2000. The court may make such a condition if it receives evidence from a medical practitioner and the court is satisfied that the offender's mental condition 'requires and may be susceptible to treatment; but is not such as to warrant the making of a hospital order or guardianship order' (sch. 2). Here there are no specific legal diagnoses and no attempt to define the nature of the treatment or the disorder. It is therefore a potentially much wider measure, but requires the expression of the defendant's willingness to comply with the requirement. It will, therefore, not be suitable for all.

Other provisions which often are used to deal with the mentally disordered fall under other legislation and rules: the M'Naghten Rules, manslaughter by reason of diminished responsibility, being found unfit to plead. Each has its own legal definition of the types of disorder which the defendant must satisfy. For each, medical evidence is often called, but its weight varies with the different provisions. These are all relatively rare matters, certainly when beginning practice, and all will require further preparation using the considerable literature which has accumulated on them.

23.6 Detection of Disorder

23.6.1 READING THE CLUES

The need for detection of disorder was mentioned in **23.5.1**, and must occur before any medical report can be requested. What will give a clue that such a report might be useful?

Any defendant will have been seen by the police and by his defence lawyer before he or she appears in court. If he or she seems to behave in a bizarre fashion, either while committing the crime or while talking to these people, someone may think of asking for a medical report to be prepared. Again, if the defendant mentions to the probation officer who is preparing a pre-sentence report or to his or her defence solicitor or counsel that he or she has previously had treatment for mental disorder, then someone may think of asking for a medical report to be prepared. It is all a bit hit and miss though — and it is important for counsel to be watching out for such signs.

Remands for psychiatric assessment may, therefore, occur on application by the prosecutor or defence or on the intiative of the court.

23.6.2 MEDICAL REPORTS AND THE NEW POWERS

Most reports are requested after conviction. This will usually require an adjournment, which may be in custody. Medical reports on bail, which will enable the doctor to see how the patient will adjust to the specific treatment regimen in his or her institution, will, however, be unlikely to be welcomed in the case of serious offences. This dilemma was particularly prevalent before the MHA 1983, which introduced three new possibilities which should always be borne in mind by counsel. Recent figures by the Department of Health indicate that they are being under-utilised, possibly because they are not widely known.

These provisions are not described in detail here, nor those for the disposals for the mentally disordered, since they are well set out in *Archbold* and other texts. Counsel should refresh their memories on the specific requirements whenever they think it likely that there may be a need to use such provisions, since each differs significantly, and since the conditions are relatively complex. The scope of the provisions is briefly:

(a) The ability to remand to hospital (under the MHA 1983, s. 35) for a report on the accused's mental condition (Crown Court and magistrates' court). This requires the evidence of one doctor and a place already organised, so does not help with the original diagnosis, but does allow the client and medical team to work together for a period in the relevant institution before sentence. Much better than a remand in custody, if a hospital order is being contemplated.

(b) The power to remand to hospital for treatment (s. 36). Primarily a humanitarian measure for those clearly disordered and in need of treatment but charged with very serious offences, prior to trial. Crown Court only, two doctors required. Extremely limited use so far (e.g. 32 cases in 1985).

(c) The power for the court to request of the regional health authority whether a place is available (s. 39). It does not, however, require the authority to produce places. Again used very rarely (the Home Office and Department of Health are trying to make it more useful).

23.6.3 THE REQUIREMENTS OF THE POWERS OF CRIMINAL COURTS (SENTENCING) ACT 2000

The PCC(S)A 2000 contains provisions for requesting medical reports where the 'offender is or appears to be mentally disordered' (s. 82(1)). If the court is obtaining a pre-sentence report then, for such offenders, the court should also obtain and consider a medical report before passing a custodial sentence. However, if the court is of the opinion that it is unnecessary to obtain a medical report, it does not have to obtain one.

Before passing a custodial sentence on an offender who is or who appears to be mentally disordered, the court should consider any information which relates to his or her mental condition (whether in a medical report, a pre-sentence report *or otherwise)* and should consider the likely effects of such a sentence on the offender's mental condition and on any available treatment for that condition. *R* v *Fawcett* (1995) 16 Cr App R (S) 55 indicates that the court should have a medical report before passing a sentence using s. 80(2)(b), if the danger posed by the defendant could be due to his or her medical condition or personality problem, in order to exclude the need for a medical disposal (such as a hospital order).

The purpose behind the provisions in the Act is clearly to encourage courts to obtain medical reports in most cases where the offender is mentally disordered. In recent years, several London magistrates' courts have had the facility of obtaining an immediate medical report through a duty psychiatrist attending the court and this is now spreading throughout the country. The probation officer preparing the pre-sentence report will often suggest that a medical report be prepared, but defence counsel must also bear those provisions in mind and request an adjournment for such a report where necessary. If the client is in danger of a custodial sentence, it is quite clear that such a report should be prepared, given that the court should consider the effect of the sentence on his or her mental condition and the possibility of obtaining treatment. It is necessary to consult the probation officer, etc. locally before preparing any mitigation, in order to be aware of the local facilities for remands for medical reports.

23.7 Powers of the Courts in Relation to Mentally Disordered Defendants

23.7.1 BEFORE SENTENCE

(a) The police may use their powers under s. 136 of the MHA 1983 to remove someone who is disordered, etc. in a public place to a place of safety.

(b) The police or CPS may decide not to prosecute because voluntary treatment is to be undertaken by the defendant. Always think of telling the prosecution if this is the case.

(c) Compulsory admission under the civil provisions of the MHA 1983 and dropping of prosecution: in an emergency (s. 4) for 72 hours, for assessment (s. 2) for up to 28 days, or for treatment (s. 3) for initially six months. Definitions of disorder as in s. 1.

(d) Use of the Criminal Procedure (Insanity) Act 1964, s. 4 (whether the defendant is unfit to plead). Only 30–40 cases per year, though new legislation has improved the results for the defendant and may make the use of this provision more likely.

(e) Under s. 37 of the MHA 1983, the magistrates' court may make a hospital order without proceeding to conviction if the defendant is suffering from mental illness or severe impairment (rare).

(f) Use of the diminished responsibility defence in charges of murder, which has largely replaced the insanity defence (again because of the consequences, but also because the scope of the definition of mental disorder under diminished responsibility is wider than the largely cognitive disorders permitted for insanity).

(g) A few cases taken under the M'Naghten rules pleading insanity.

23.7.2 AT SENTENCE

(a) Probation order with requirement as to mental treatment under the PCCA 1973. The definition of disorder is quite wide, but it only applies to 'treatment', though this may be inpatient, outpatient, or under the care of a named doctor. It requires the offender's expression of willingness to comply with the requirement and has the disadvantages that:

(i) the offender may subsequently not go for treatment (there is no compulsory element);

(ii) there may be problems of liaison between medical and probation personnel. It may be helpful to ensure the roles of each are thought about at the time of the reports.

(b) Probation order without requirement, suspended sentence, etc. There are no statistics on the use of these non-specific measures for the mentally disordered, but it is likely that they are much more numerous than specific 'medical disposals'.

(c) Hospital orders under s. 37 of the MHA 1983. Compulsory treatment, initially for six months, but extendable. Can be discharged by the doctor responsible for the patient (Responsible Medical Officer), by the health authority, or by the patient applying to a Mental Health Review Tribunal. This is not a secure order and the conditions of detention can be varied by the hospital.

(d) Restriction orders under s. 41 of the MHA 1983 — where the public needs to be protected from grave harm only. Crown Court only. Patient may be released through application to a Mental Health Review Tribunal, or the Home Secretary may release patients conditionally or absolutely. Only the Home Secretary may change the conditions of detention. The order is for compulsory detention under secure conditions.

Restriction orders have been dealt with by the Court of Appeal in *R* v *Birch* (1989) 11 Cr App R (S) 202. This stated that the court should go through the following questions in order in dealing with cases of mental disorder:

(i) Is a period of compulsory detention apposite?

(ii) If so, are the conditions for a hospital order satisfied?

(iii) If so, should the person be given a hospital order, or be sent to prison?

(iv) If it is decided he or she should receive a hospital order, are the conditions for making a restriction order satisfied (protecting the public from serious harm)?

(v) If they are, should he or she be given a restriction order, or a life sentence, or a determinate prison sentence?

(vi) If a restriction order, should it be one for an unlimited period (favoured in *R* v *Gardiner* [1967] 1 WLR 464) and commended again in *R* v *Birch*) or one for a fixed period?

The court was held not to be bound by any medical evidence that the person is not dangerous in reaching its decision. It was also confirmed that protecting the public from serious *harm* in the provisions for making a restriction order meant serious *harm* and not serious *risk*. In other words, a person who committed frequent offences but none of these involved danger to others should not receive a restriction order. *R* v *Birch* reiterates that prison may be used for those who are dangerous even though they are also mentally disordered, but states that a hospital disposal is to be preferred. Prison should really only be given if no hospital place is available, or if there is an element of culpability which requires punishment and hospital is felt to be really inappropriate.

(e) However, placement in a Special Hospital is not currently something decided by the courts, but by the Secretary of State for Health. The courts may request placement in a Special Hospital, but cannot demand it. There is a great shortage of places, because of the difficulty of obtaining places in ordinary hospitals for patients released from Special Hospitals. The C(S)A 1997 now allows courts to specify a particular hospital in relation to restriction orders.

(f) Life imprisonment (see below).

(g) Determinate prison sentences. Many disordered and most dangerous offenders almost certainly receive ordinary prison sentences. For the disordered, this may occur because no one has diagnosed their condition. It may occur because they do not fit the current medical ideas of the treatable, or the legal definition in the Acts. In a few instances, it may be under the provisions of s. 79(2)(b) though this is not intended for the disordered. More probably, it may occur because the facilities do not exist in their locality to permit their optimum treatment. One study of the South East prison population found that 31% of sentenced prisoners would benefit from psychiatric attention. The problem for both sentencers and counsel in dealing with the sentencing of mentally disordered offenders is a lack of suitable facilities. One clue as to why this might have happened may lie in the comment of the House of Commons Social Services Committee, which is still valid today:

> Any fool can close a long-stay hospital: it takes more time and trouble to do it properly and compassionately. The Minister must ensure that mental illness or mental handicap provision is not reduced without demonstrably adequate alternative services being provided beforehand both for those discharged from hospital and for those who would otherwise seek admission.

(h) A hospital and limitation direction under ss. 45A and 45B of the MHA 1983 is an order which enables the court to sentence an offender suffering from a treatable psychopathic disorder to a term of imprisonment, and in addition, to detention in hospital. The offender is treated in hospital for as long as it is necessary, and, at the end of the period of treatment, or if found to be untreatable, is returned to prison to serve any unexpired term of imprisonment. For a critique of this power, see Eastman, N., and Peay, J., 'Sentencing Psychopaths: Is the "Hospital and Limitation Direction" an Ill-Considered Hybrid?' [1998] Crim LR 93.

23.8 Life Imprisonment

The conditions for imposing life imprisonment have been set out in *R* v *Hodgson* (1967) 52 Cr App R 113 (judgment of Mackenna J) and *R* v *Wilkinson* (1983) 5 Cr App R (S) 105) judgment of Lord Lane CJ). In *R* v *Hodgson* it was stated that:

> When the following conditions are satisfied, a sentence of life imprisonment is in our opinion justified: (1) where the offence or offences are in themselves grave enough to require a very long sentence; (2) where it appears from the nature of the offences or from the defendant's history that he is a person of unstable character likely to commit such offences in the future; and (3) where if the offences are committed the consequences to others may be specially injurious, as in the case of sexual offences or crimes of violence.

The *Hodgson* criteria continue to be relevant after the enactment of CJA 1991, but part I of the Act, essentially, requires the offence to be a violent or sexual offence as defined by the Act (see *R* v *Robinson* [1997] Crim LR 365). This is only rarely a constraint.

R v *Wilkinson* showed that:

> It seems that the sentence of life imprisonment, other than for an offence where the sentence is obligatory, is really appropriate and must only be passed in the most exceptional circumstances. With a few exceptions it is reserved for offenders who for one reason or another cannot be dealt with under the provisions of the Mental Health Act, yet who are in a mental state which makes them dangerous to the life or limb of members of the public. It is sometimes impossible to say when that danger will subside, and therefore an indeterminate sentence is required, so that the prisoner's progress may be monitored by those who have him under their supervision in prison and so that he will be kept in custody only so long as public safety may be jeopardised by his being let loose at large.

However, in *R* v *Wilkinson*, it was also shown that just being a bad burglar or robber was insufficient – there needed to be the required mental element as well. The need for an element of mental disorder has been confirmed post the CJA 1991 in *R* v *Spear* (1995) 16 Cr App R (S) 242. This restriction on the use of the life sentence is welcome, but still the definition of disorder and dangerousness in such imprecise terms permits its use in a wide variety of circumstances.

R v *Wilkinson* shows that the second element set out in *R* v *Hodgson* requires some element of mental disorder – but that where a hospital order was indicated and a suitable place was available, the hospital order was to be preferred. The requirement for sentencers to use a hospital order (normally a restriction order) in cases of treatable mental disorder was confirmed by *R* v *Hutchinson* [1997] 2 Cr App R (S) 60, where the Court of Appeal varied a life sentence to one of a hospital order plus restriction order in a secure hospital (seen as sufficient to satisfy the element of public protection), in a case of a man with schizophrenia where the medical evidence said a hospital order was to be preferred.

The mental element for life imprisonment has never required medical evidence stating the mental element to be before the court, but three recent cases now cast doubt on the need for a mental disorder element (in psychiatric terms) at all.

R v *Hatch* [1996] Crim LR 679 was a case of persistent paedophilia, in which the psychiatric evidence showed that the appellant did not suffer from mental disorder within the MHA 1983, and, though the appellant was likely to continue to offend towards boys around 10–12 years of age, there was no prospect of effective medical treatment. The Court itself judged that the appellant did have a serious personality disorder (i.e. his sexual orientation) and would remain a real danger to young boys – the key aspect being that he would continue to offend against vulnerable youngsters.

Attorney-General's Reference (No. 76 of 1996) [1996] Crim LR 670 was a case of rape and false imprisonment of a woman aged 21, where the offender had previous convictions for ABH and rape, and was originally sentenced to a longer than normal sentence under s. 80(2)(b). A life sentence was given on appeal, though there was no medical evidence of any disorder. As the commentator in the *Criminal Law Review* indicates, both cases suggest that a persistent sexual offender committing aggressive acts may satisfy the conditions for life imprisonment irrespective of whether it is possible to explain his behaviour in psychiatric terms (justified by the Court in the latter case because there was no knowing how long the appellant would remain a danger to young women).

Attorney-General's Reference (No. 32 of 1996) (Steven Alan Whittaker) [1997] 1 Cr App R (S) 261 picks up the same theme. This was a case of GBH with intent, with a previous conviction for murder, so the defendant was on life licence. Within three days after being allowed home leave he committed this offence on a girl he met at a night club. The possibilities open to the sentencer were a determinate sentence, a s. 80(2)(b) sentence and a life sentence. It was agreed that a s. 80(2)(b) sentence was wrong – since the appellant was already subject to a life sentence, there was no need for an additional public protection element. The original sentencer had rejected a life sentence, because there was no medical evidence of any personality disorder. The Court of Appeal thought this was an unnecessarily narrow view – where there was a very serious offence (the *Hodgson* first criterion), then the sentencer needed to see whether there was evidence that the offender might remain a serious danger to the public for a period which could not reliably be estimated at the time of sentence (a serious danger often being sexual or physical violence). The grounds for such a belief might often lie in the offender's mental condition, but need not. In this case, the offender had behaved in a violent and highly dangerous manner during a short period of weekend release. Here then, we see a broader concept of dangerousness for a life sentence, now free from the necessity for clear mental instability.

23.9 New Proposals for Detention of Psychopaths

Recent high-profile cases have highlighted the concerns caused by offenders suffering from untreatable personality disorders who cannot be detained in hospital, and those who cannot be detained in prison after the expiry of their sentence, even though they may remain a danger to the public. The government has responded to these concerns by announcing proposals for the introduction of an indefinite, reviewable order for detention of persons suffering from untreatable personality disorders, whether or not they have been convicted of an offence. The proposals have led to a great deal of criticism on human rights grounds as it is feared that individuals would be detained, not for what they have done, but for what they might do in future. As a result, the reforms are likely to be challenged in the courts under the provisions of the Human Rights Act 1998, when they are brought into force in October 2000.

TWENTY-FOUR

YOUNG OFFENDERS

24.1 Introduction

In this chapter we will be concerned with the sentencing of two distinct age-groups, which can be grouped together as young offenders but which in legal terms constitute the two separate categories of 'juveniles' and 'young adults' (the category of juveniles may be further separated into 'children' (aged 10–13 inclusive) and 'young persons' (aged 14–17 inclusive)).

All young defendants under 18 are dealt with in 'youth courts', which are specially constituted magistrates' courts with special powers (some of which are discussed below). Young adults are those aged 18–20 inclusive: they are dealt with in the ordinary adult courts, but the range of powers available to those courts is different for this age group.

24.2 Juveniles

24.2.1 JUVENILES AND THE WELFARE PRINCIPLE

The last three decades have seen conflicts of approach to the problem of dealing with juveniles who offend. The legal principle has remained throughout that of welfare: a court 'shall have regard to the welfare of the child or young person' (CYPA 1933, s. 44(1)).

The CYPA 1969 was designed to revolutionise the approach to young offenders in at least three main ways — first, by diverting many of them away from the courts altogether; second, by giving considerable discretion to social workers in cases where the court made a 'care order'; and third, by initiating the containment and treatment of these children in trouble in the community rather than in institutions.

During the 1970s considerable dissatisfaction with the Act was voiced, even though the Act had not been fully implemented, and the magistracy in particular campaigned for greater powers to deal with the 'tougher' young offenders. The 1980s saw the grant of more powers to the juvenile courts by the CJA 1982, but also an initiative towards the development of 'intermediate treatment' schemes as substitutes for custody. Thus, although the courts obtained their greater powers, the decade saw a fall in the numbers of juveniles sentenced to custody.

24.2.2 DIVERTING JUVENILES FROM COURT

One of the policies behind the 1969 Act was to encourage the police and other agencies to deal with young offenders without bringing them before the court. The most common approach was to issue a formal caution to a juvenile offender: a youngster who was prepared to admit the offence would be required to attend a police station and would be cautioned by a senior officer in uniform. The Home Office circular to the police urged them to caution all juvenile first offenders unless there is a strong reason against, and cautioning has remained the most frequent response to youth offending throughout the 1990s accounting for some two-thirds of boys (with only one-third being prosecuted) and over 80% of girls. However, the CDA 1998 will introduce a new statutory framework. Sections 65 and 66 give statutory authority to 'reprimands' and 'warnings' for young offenders. Reprimands are for non-serious offences by first offenders. Warnings are for second-time offenders or for more serious forms of first offence, and they result in the young offender being referred to a 'youth offending team' for remedial treatment. A warning is intended to be a final warning, and for any subsequent offence the normal response would be to prosecute. When a youth who has already received a warning is convicted, the youth court will not be able to grant a conditional discharge. Since, as we shall see below, discharges have accounted for roughly one-third of sentences in the youth court in recent years, this will require a considerable change in sentencing practice. (See further, Fionda, J., 'New Labour, Old Hat: Youth Justice and the Crime and Disorder Act 1998' [1999] Crim LR 36.)

24.2.3 THE LEGISLATIVE FRAMEWORK

The legislative framework is complex, and the three principal statutes are the CYPA 1933, the CJA 1991 and the CDA 1998. The general principle in sentencing young offenders remains the 'welfare principle' established by CYPA 1933, s. 44. The main contribution of the CJA 1991 was to rank the various sentences in order of severity and to require courts to have primary regard to the seriousness of the offence; that Act also placed greater emphasis on parental responsibility for the misdeeds of the young. The main aims of the CDA 1998, apart from replacing the system of police cautioning, are to rationalise the scheme of custodial sentences for young offenders and to introduce measures aimed at reparation and rehabilitation.

The sentencing framework established by the CJA 1991 for adult offenders and consolidated in the PCC(S)A 2000 applies also to youth courts, but with some departures. For the least serious forms of offending the court should consider a discharge, bind-over, fine, or (if the offence is serious enough) one of the new reparation orders or action plan orders. On the next level up, if the offence is serious enough to warrant it, the court should consider a community sentence (and, where available, a reparation order or an action plan order). In the relatively few cases of great seriousness, the custody threshold in PCC(S)A 2000, s. 79 must be satisfied before a custodial sentence is imposed.

24.2.4 DISCHARGES, BIND-OVERS AND FINES

The power to order an absolute or conditional discharge is the same as that for adult offenders (see **18.2** and **18.3**) apart from the new restriction on granting a conditional discharge to a youth who has previously received a final warning (see **24.2.2**). But there are significant differences in respect of bind-overs and fines.

24.2.4.1 Binding over

A court has the same power to bind over a juvenile to keep the peace and be of good behaviour. The important difference in the youth court is the power to bind over the juvenile's parents. By s. 150 of the PCC(S)A 2000, the court has a duty to consider binding over the parents of a juvenile offender aged 10–15 inclusive, and a duty to give reasons in open court if it does not think it desirable to do so. The form of the bind-over is 'to order the parent or guardian to enter into a recognisance to take proper care of him and exercise proper control over him'. The sum may be no more than £1,000, and the maximum period is three years or until the juvenile's eighteenth birthday, whichever is the shorter. Where a youth court is dealing with an offender aged 16 or 17, it has the power to bind the parents over but no duties.

24.2.4.2 Fines

Where the juvenile is aged 10–15 inclusive, the parents must be ordered to pay the fine unless this would be unreasonable or they cannot be found. If the parents are paying their means are taken into account. If the child is paying, her or his means are taken into account. Where the juvenile is aged 16–17 inclusive, the parents may be ordered to pay: there are different rules where the juvenile is in the care of the local authority (s. 137 of the PCC(S)A 2000), and see *Bedfordshire CC* v *DPP* [1995] Crim LR 962.

24.2.4.3 Compensation orders

The same general principles apply in respect of compensation orders, which a court must consider making in every case involving injury, loss or damage (see **18.6**). The amount of the compensation must take account of the means of the person ordered to pay. Parents must pay if the child is under 16, and may be ordered to pay if the offender is aged 16 or 17.

24.2.4.4 Reparation orders

Section 73 of the PCC(S)A 2000 introduces reparation orders. A court may make such an order in respect of a young offender, requiring him or her to complete no more than 24 hours of work within three months, having considered a written report which indicates the type of work that is suitable for the offender and the attitude of the victim(s) to the requirement of the order. Courts may only make such an order if s. 73 is in force locally; they may not make such an order if the young offender is being sentenced to custody, or is being made the subject of a community service order, combination order or supervision order with an action plan order (see below). See M. Wasik, [1999] Crim LR 470 for discussion.

24.2.5 COMMUNITY SENTENCES

Before a court passes a community sentence, it must satisfy the threshold test in PCC(S)A 2000, s. 35(1), that the offence (or the combination of the offence and one or more offences associated with it) is serious enough to warrant a community sentence. If this test is satisfied, the court is then governed by s. 35(3): the order or orders made must be both proportionate to the seriousness of the offence(s) and the most suitable for the offender (see **19.4** for discussion). In view of the welfare principle which applies in the youth court, the latter requirement is especially important.

The court's powers differ according to the age of the juvenile. If the offender is aged 10–15 inclusive, there are only three community orders available to the court: the attendance centre order, action plan order and the supervision order. However, for offenders aged 16 or 17, sometimes referred to as 'near-adults', no fewer than seven forms of community orders may be available.

24.2.5.1 Attendance centre orders

There are over 100 junior attendance centres in England and Wales, their aim being to deprive young offenders of a few hours' leisure time at weekends (usually Saturday afternoons) and to involve them in various constructive activities and physical exercise during their attendance. The minimum number of hours which a court may order is 12 hours except where the juvenile is under 14, and the court is of the opinion that 12 hours would be excessive. The maximum number of hours which a court may order is 24 hours where the juvenile is under 16 and 36 hours where the young offender is 16 but under 21 (PCC(S)A 2000, s. 60).

The original idea behind attendance centres was that they would provide a 'short, sharp shock' to young offenders who were sent there, but it is doubtful whether this is now uppermost in the minds of those who run the centres, and it is not clear how attendance centres are viewed by members of youth courts.

24.2.5.2 Supervision orders

These are similar to the probation order, but they differ in certain ways. In particular, the supervision order does not require the consent of the juvenile unless certain additional requirements are made, and the supervision is usually carried out by the local social services department rather than by the probation service.

The order may run for up to three years, and sch. 6 to the PCC(S)A 2000 empowers the youth court to impose various requirements as part of an order. Requirements to refrain from certain specified activities may also be imposed, but courts have rarely done so. The power to impose supervised activity requirements has been used more widely: the court specifies the nature of the activity programme in which the juvenile must participate (from among those activities offered by the local authority), and also specifies the duration of the requirement, which may be up to 90 days.

Perhaps the most important of the requirements which may be added to a supervision order is the requirement of intermediate treatment (IT). The idea behind IT is that constructive and challenging programmes in the community can be devised for offenders who are regarded as 'tough' or 'difficult' and who might otherwise be sent into custody. The significant decline in the use of custody for juveniles during the 1980s was attributed to the new initiative to develop intermediate treatment in the early part of the decade. The IT programmes are run by the local social services departments, but magistrates have also been involved in the direction of the schemes. Before the court makes a supervision order with additional requirements, it must obtain and consider a pre-sentence report. Breach of a supervision order has the same consequences as breach of other community orders (see **19.10**).

24.2.5.3 Probation orders

We now move from the only two community orders available for offenders aged 10–15 inclusive, the attendance centre order and the supervision order, to the other four orders available for those aged 16 and 17. The CJA 1991 introduced probation orders into the youth court for the first time. The legal requirements are the same as for adults (see **19.5**). A court should use a probation order where it is of the opinion that this is more suitable for the offender than a supervision order. The difference lies in the additional requirements which may be inserted into each order, and in the different supervising agencies (the probation service for probation, and local authorities for the supervision order). Probation orders might be more appropriate for 16- and 17-year-olds who are thought to be relatively mature. The court must obtain and consider a pre-sentence report before making a probation order with additional requirements.

24.2.5.4 Community service orders

The maximum number of hours for 16- and 17-year-olds in the youth court is the same as for adults, i.e. 240 hours. For further discussion, see **19.6**.

24.2.5.5 Combination orders

This form of order is available for offenders aged 16 and 17 on the same principles as adult offenders (see **19.7**). The court must obtain and consider a pre-sentence report, and must be satisfied, as always, that the restrictions on liberty are commensurate with the seriousness of the offence(s). This is regarded as the most restrictive order short of custody.

24.2.5.6 Curfew orders

This new form of order, in those areas where it is available, may be used for offenders aged 16 and 17 on the same principles as adult offenders (see **19.8**). A pre-sentence report is not mandatory, and this order may be added to other orders so long as the whole community sentence remains commensurate with the seriousness of the offence(s).

24.2.5.7 Action plan orders

Section 69 of the PCC(S)A 2000 provides for action plan orders. The order requires the young offender to submit to supervision for three months, during which time he or she must participate in, or refrain from, certain specified activities. The purpose of the requirements is to secure the rehabilitation of the offender or to prevent the commission of further offences. The court must consider a written report indicating the benefits to the offender of the proposed requirements, and the attitude of the parents or guardians to those requirements. An action plan order may not be imposed on a young offender who is sentenced to custody or is subject to any community sentence other than a supervision order.

24.2.5.8 Community sentences for juveniles

To summarise, the youth court has a choice of three community orders for offenders under 16 (attendance centre, supervision, action plan order), and a choice among all seven orders when dealing with those aged 16 and 17. The powers for these 'near-adults' are similar to those of magistrates' courts when dealing with offenders aged 18–20, and the aim is to give courts greater flexibility to make orders which are suitable to the degree of maturity of the particular juvenile. The breach powers in respect of all community orders are the same as for adults (see **19.10**).

24.2.6 CUSTODIAL MEASURES FOR JUVENILES

It will be apparent that the emphasis in dealing with young offenders is, first, diversion from the courts altogether and, second, treatment in the community where possible.

In a few cases the court may take the view that only a custodial sentence can be justified, having considered the seriousness of the offence in relation to s. 79(2)(a) of the PCC(S)A 2000 and the importance of promoting the welfare of the child.

Where a child or young person is prosecuted for murder or manslaughter, the case must be heard in the Crown Court. If the conviction is for murder, the sentence fixed by law is detention during Her Majesty's pleasure. However, regard must now be had to the judgment of the European Court of Human Rights in *T* v *UK*; *V* v *UK* [2000] Crim LR 187, which found that the ECHR rights of the applicants had been breached in two major respects. First, the trial of boys aged 11 in the Crown Court, even with the modifications made by the judge, violated their right to a fair hearing (Article 6) because it was practically not possible for them to participate in the proceedings. The Government may decide that trial in some form of youth court, with a High Court judge presiding, should be introduced. Secondly, in relation to the sentence of detention during Her Majesty's pleasure, the fixing of the tariff by the Home Secretary violated Article 6, since he is a politician and not an 'independent and impartial tribunal' and the fixing of the tariff is essentially a sentencing decision. The Court also held that the absence of provisions for regular review of the need for the continued detention of HMP detainees violates Article 5(4). Legislative changes can therefore be expected.

24.2.6.1 Detention and training orders

Until the implementation of the CDA 1998 the courts could pass sentences of detention in a young offender institution on offenders aged 15 to 17 inclusive and, in limited circumstances specified by the CJPOA 1994, secure training orders on offenders aged 12 to 14 inclusive. The provisions were consolidated in the PCC(S)A 2000 and the effect of s. 100 of the 2000 Act is to combine those forms of custodial sentence into one, now named the detention and training order. This sentence not only becomes the standard form of custody for young offenders, but its availability is also extended down to offenders as young as 10. However, s. 100(1) and (2) requires certain conditions to be satisfied, according to the age of the offender:

(a) In the case of all young offenders, the court must be satisfied that s. 79(2) of the PCC(S)A 2000 is fulfilled; this will normally mean the condition in s. 79(2)(a), that the offence is so serious that only a custodial sentence can be justified (see **21.5.2.1**). The youth of the offender is generally treated as a strong mitigating factor, which may take a case below the custody threshold.

(b) In the case of young offenders aged 10–14 inclusive, the court must additionally be satisfied that the offender is a persistent offender.

(c) In the case of young offenders aged 10 or 11, the court must be satisfied that only a custodial sentence would be adequate to protect the public from further offending by him or her, and that the Home Secretary has brought this provision into force.

Once the appropriate requirements have been fulfilled, the court must determine the length of the detention and training order. Section 101(1) states that 'the term of a detention and training order made in respect of an offence (whether by a magistrates' court or otherwise) shall be 4, 6, 8, 10, 12, 18 or 24 months', imposing stringent and unprecedented restrictions on the courts which may prove difficult where it is desired to mark small but significant distinctions between co-offenders. Moreover, the provision appears to permit a youth court to impose a custodial sentence of up to two years, whereas in the past youth courts (being part of the magistrates' courts) have been restricted to six months for a single offence and 12 months for two or more offences. The effect of s. 101(1) in this respect has recently been considered by the Court of Appeal in *R* v *Medway Youth Court, ex parte A* [1999] Crim LR 915, where it was held that the youth court's sentencing powers have been increased by the recent Acts.

24.2.6.2 Detention under s. 91 of the PCC(S)A 2000

There is an extra power available to the courts when dealing with particularly serious offences by juveniles. It not only enables the court to exceed the limits on a 'detention and training order', just described, but is also available from the age of ten upwards (s. 91 of the PCC(S)A 2000). However, this power is only available to the Crown Court, and then only when the juvenile has been tried on indictment.

Section 91 empowers the Crown Court to order that a juvenile who has been convicted of an offence carrying a maximum of 14 years' imprisonment or more shall be detained for a specified number of years (within the statutory maximum for the offence) in a place approved by the Secretary of State. Although it is rarely necessary for courts to use this power there have been several appellate decisions. The Court of Appeal has now replaced the old guideline judgment in *R* v *Fairhurst* (1986) 8 Cr App R (S) 346 with a completely re-cast guideline judgment: *R* v *AM and Others* [1998] 1 WLR 363 (*sub nom. R* v *Mills* [1998] Cr App R (S) 128). The Court of Appeal affirmed the principle that no young offender should be given a custodial sentence unless this is necessary, and then for no longer than is necessary. The main point of the new judgment is that there is no longer any need to preserve a 'gap' above the normal two-year maximum sentence of detention and training: courts may, where appropriate, use the s. 91 power to impose a sentence between two and three years, as well as longer terms.

The effect of *R* v *AM* is also to confirm the decision in *R* v *Pinkney* [1997] Crim LR 527, which holds that a young offender who pleads guilty, and who does not receive a s. 91 sentence, may still be given the maximum two-year sentence if the court would have been justified in giving a longer, s. 91 sentence in the absence of a guilty plea.

It was widely anticipated that one consequence of extending the jurisdiction of youth courts to cover 17-year-olds would be a greater resort to s. 91. In fact the legislature has facilitated greater resort to s. 91 by extending the categories of offence that fall within it. Although all offences with a statutory maximum of 14 years qualify, statutes have now altered the boundaries somewhat. The reduction in the maximum penalty for non-residential burglary from 14 to ten years takes that offence outside the scope of s. 91 (see *R* v *Nagar* (1993) 15 Cr App R (S) 273); on the other hand, indecent assault by an offender aged 10–17 is within the scope of s. 91 even though its statutory maximum remains at ten years, and the offences of causing death by dangerous driving and causing death by careless driving while under the influence of drink or drugs by an offender aged 14–17 are also included. However, the kindred offence of causing death by aggravated vehicle taking remains outside s. 91 (*R* v *Ore* [1994] Crim LR 304).

In determining the length of s. 91 detention, the court will be bound by s. 80(2)(a) of the 2000 Act to ensure that the term is commensurate with the seriousness of the offence, unless there is a crime of violence or sexual offence which leads to the imposition of a longer 'public protection' sentence under s. 80(2)(b). As a matter of procedure, a court which intends to invoke the s. 91 power must state clearly that this is the section under which a sentence is imposed. Thus in *R* v *Egdell* [1994] Crim LR 137 the trial judge had imposed six years' detention in a young offender institution, without mentioning s. 91, and the Court of Appeal held that this was an unlawful sentence. The maximum for detention in a young offender institution was then one year (now raised to two years), and so the sentence had to take effect as a sentence of one year's detention (see also *R* v *Venison* [1994] Crim LR 298). The Court of Appeal emphasised that it is the duty of prosecuting counsel to point out errors or omissions of this kind, so that the judge may correct them promptly.

Section 91 also provides for the sentence of detention for life in appropriate cases, where the offence itself carries a life maximum. One example is *R* v *Bell* (1989) 11 Cr App R (S) 472. Before passing such a sentence the court must satisfy the requirements in ss. 80(2)(b) and 81 of the PCC(S)A 2000.

24.3 Young Adults

24.3.1 DEALING WITH YOUNG ADULT OFFENDERS

Offenders aged 18–20 are dealt with in the ordinary adult courts but under somewhat different sentencing provisions. The policy in dealing with young adult offenders is not expressly one of 'welfare', as with juveniles, but there remains the strong view that special measures are necessary to deal with young adults in the community rather than in custody and, when it is thought necessary to impose custody, to segregate young adults from older offenders. These policies show awareness that many young people cease offending in their lower twenties, and that as little as possible should be done which tends to confirm them as offenders and to classify them with more hardened, older offenders. Otherwise, sentences might have the effect of reinforcing criminal habits rather than allowing them to be broken.

The framework of the PCC(S)A 2000 applies to young adults no less than to adults and to juveniles. The powers in respect of discharges, fines and compensation orders are exactly the same as for adults. If the court regards the offence as serious enough to warrant a community sentence, then it is bound by s. 35(3) to make orders which are both commensurate with the seriousness of the offence(s) and most suitable for the offender. The choice of community orders is slightly wider for young adults than for adults, since there are five possibilities: probation, community service, combination order, curfew order (where available), and an attendance centre order. The requirements for the attendance centre order are the same as when dealing with offenders aged 16 and 17 (see **24.2.5.1**), but there are senior attendance centres for those aged 18–20. A court may only make an attendance centre order on a young adult if there is a senior centre in the locality.

24.3.2 CUSTODY FOR YOUNG ADULTS

Restrictions on the use of custody for this age group have been in force since the CJA 1982. Where custody is imposed, detention for offenders aged under 21 is in a 'young offender institution'. There the Prison Department endeavours to hold juvenile boys separately from older boys serving longer terms, but the institutions for females have insufficient numbers for any such separation. Young offender institutions have to deal mostly with boys and young men who have considerable criminal records. The aim is to make the regime more constructive and instructional than at adult prisons. The provisions in ss. 79 and 80 of the PCC(S)A 2000 apply to regulate the imposition of custodial sentences on young adults, as on offenders of all other ages. One of the leading cases on s. 79(2)(a) is *R* v *Cox* (see **21.5.2.1**), a case of a young adult. A review of the decisions in **21.5.2** revealed no clear criteria, but offenders in this age-group can expect some mitigation on account of youth. There is no suspended sentence for offenders under 21.

Statistics on the use of sentences for young adults convicted of indictable offences appear in **Figure 24.1**, although it should be borne in mind that until 1992 the category of young adult referred to all offenders aged 17–20 inclusive, whereas since 1993 it refers only to those aged 18–20.

Figure 24.1 Persons aged 18 and under 21 sentenced for indictable offences by sex and type of sentence or order

England and Wales — Number of persons (thousands) and percentage

Sex and year	Total number of persons sentenced	Absolute or conditional discharge	Fine	Probation order	Community service order	Attendance centre order	Combination order	Curfew order	Young offender institution	Otherwise dealt with	Total immediate custody	Total community sentence
					Number sentenced for indictable offences							
Males												
1987	75.4	7.1	30.6	8.9	10.4	1.2	*	*	16.4	0.8	16.4	20.5
1988	73.2	6.7	30.5	8.9	10.0	1.0	*	*	15.1	1.0	15.1	19.9
1989	63.5	7.1	27.2	7.9	8.3	0.9	*	*	11.0	1.1	11.0	17.0
1990	65.4	8.4	27.7	8.4	9.0	1.1	*	*	9.7	1.2	9.7	18.6
1991	64.7	9.8	24.0	8.7	9.6	1.3	*	*	10.1	1.2	10.1	19.6
1992	58.8	9.9	20.6	7.5	9.0	1.2	0.2	*	9.0	1.3	9.0	17.9
1993	53.1	9.0	18.0	6.2	7.4	0.8	1.6	*	9.0	1.2	9.0	15.9
1994	50.1	8.1	15.5	6.3	6.9	0.7	2.0	*	9.6	1.1	9.6	15.9
1995	47.3	7.1	14.1	5.7	6.3	0.5	2.2	–	10.4	0.9	10.4	14.7
1996	46.2	6.6	13.3	5.3	5.8	0.5	2.4	0.0	11.2	1.0	11.2	14.0
1997	48.1	6.9	14.0	5.4	5.8	0.5	2.7	0.0	11.8	1.1	11.8	14.4
Females												
1987	9.4	2.5	3.6	2.1	0.5	-	*	*	0.5	0.1	0.5	2.6
1988	8.8	2.4	3.3	2.0	0.5	0.0	*	*	0.5	0.1	0.5	2.5
1989	8.2	2.6	2.9	1.8	0.4	-	*	*	0.4	0.2	0.4	2.2
1990	8.3	2.9	2.8	1.8	0.5	-	*	*	0.3	0.2	0.3	2.3
1991	8.1	3.1	2.3	1.7	0.6	0.0	*	*	0.3	0.1	0.3	2.3
1992	7.3	2.9	2.1	1.4	0.5	0.0	0.0	*	0.3	0.1	0.3	1.9
1993	6.3	2.3	2.0	1.0	0.4	0.0	0.1	*	0.3	0.1	0.3	1.6
1994	6.2	2.3	1.7	1.2	0.4	0.0	0.1	*	0.3	0.1	0.3	1.8
1995	5.7	1.9	1.5	1.2	0.4	0.0	0.2	–	0.4	0.1	0.4	1.8
1996	5.6	1.8	1.3	1.3	0.4	0.0	0.2	0.0	0.5	0.1	0.5	1.9
1997	6.2	1.9	1.4	1.4	0.5	0.0	0.3	0.0	0.6	0.1	0.6	2.2

Figure 24.1 cont.

England and Wales | Number of persons (thousands) and percentage

Sex and year	Total number of persons sentenced	Absolute or conditional discharge	Fine	Probation order	Community service order	Attendance centre order	Combination order	Curfew order	Young offender institution	Otherwise dealt with	Total immediate custody	Total community sentence
Males					Percentage sentenced for indictable offences							
1987	100	9	41	12	14	2	*	*	22	1	22	27
1988	100	9	42	12	14	1	*	*	21	1	21	27
1989	100	11	43	12	13	1	*	*	17	2	17	27
1990	100	13	42	13	14	2	*	*	15	2	15	28
1991	100	15	37	13	15	2	*	*	16	2	16	30
1992	100	17	35	13	15	2	0	*	15	2	15	30
1993	100	17	34	12	14	1	3	*	17	2	17	30
1994	100	16	31	13	14	1	4	*	19	2	19	32
1995	100	15	30	12	13	1	5	–	22	2	22	31
1996	100	14	29	11	13	1	5	0	24	2	24	30
1997	100	14	29	11	12	1	6	0	25	2	25	30
Females												
1987	100	27	38	23	5	-	*	*	6	1	6	28
1988	100	27	37	23	6	0	*	*	5	1	5	29
1989	100	31	36	22	5	-	*	*	4	2	4	27
1990	100	34	33	21	6	-	*	*	3	2	3	27
1991	100	38	28	21	7	0	*	*	3	2	3	28
1992	100	40	29	19	7	0	0	*	3	2	3	26
1993	100	37	31	17	7	0	2	*	5	2	5	25
1994	100	36	27	20	7	0	2	*	5	2	5	29
1995	100	34	26	20	7	0	3	–	7	2	7	31
1996	100	32	23	22	8	0	4	0	9	2	9	34
1997	100	31	22	23	8	0	4	0	9	2	9	36

Figure 24.2 Persons aged 14 to 17 sentenced for indictable offences by sex and type of sentence or order

England and Wales | Number of persons (thousands) and percentage

Sex and year	Total number of persons sentenced	Absolute or conditional discharge	Fine	Probation order	Supervision order	Community service order	Attendance centre order	Combination order	Curfew order	Young offender institution	S. 53, C&YP Act 1933	Otherwise dealt with	Total immediate custody	Total community sentences
	Number sentenced for indictable offences													
Males														
1987	58.8	11.6	17.3	3.1	6.5	4.6	6.3	*	*	8.2	0.2	1.0	8.2	20.5
1988	53.6	10.5	15.7	3.3	5.6	4.4	5.5	*	*	7.3	0.2	0.9	7.3	18.9
1989	40.3	9.4	11.4	2.6	4.2	3.1	3.9	*	*	4.7	0.1	0.9	4.7	13.8
1990	38.2	9.7	10.0	2.7	4.0	3.2	3.9	*	*	3.6	0.1	0.9	3.6	13.9
1991	34.9	9.9	7.4	2.6	3.6	3.3	3.7	*	*	3.5	0.1	0.8	3.5	13.3
1992	31.4	9.6	5.5	2.1	3.6	3.0	3.5	0.1	*	3.3	0.1	0.7	3.3	12.2
1993	29.4	9.2	3.3	1.2	4.7	2.4	3.8	0.6	*	3.3	0.3	0.6	3.3	12.8
1994	32.6	9.9	3.9	1.3	5.9	2.4	4.1	0.7	*	3.6	0.4	0.5	3.6	14.3
1995	34.3	10.1	4.0	1.4	6.3	2.5	4.1	0.7	0.0	4.2	0.4	0.6	4.2	15.0
1996	36.5	10.4	4.1	1.6	6.8	2.6	4.1	1.0	0.0	4.8	0.6	0.6	4.8	16.1
1997	37.8	10.6	4.4	1.7	6.7	2.8	4.0	1.2	0.0	5.1	0.7	0.7	5.1	16.4
Females														
1987	5.9	2.2	1.8	0.6	0.6	0.2	0.2	*	*	0.1	0.0	0.1	0.1	1.6
1988	5.6	2.3	1.6	0.5	0.5	0.2	0.2	*	*	0.1	0.0	0.1	0.1	1.4
1989	4.8	2.2	1.2	0.5	0.4	0.1	0.1	*	*	0.1	0.0	0.1	0.1	1.2
1990	4.9	2.3	1.1	0.5	0.5	0.2	0.1	*	*	0.1	0.0	0.1	0.1	1.3
1991	4.4	2.3	0.8	0.4	0.4	0.1	0.2	*	*	0.1	0.0	0.1	0.1	1.2
1992	4.0	2.1	0.6	0.3	0.5	0.1	0.1	0.0	*	0.1	0.0	0.1	0.1	1.1
1993	3.6	1.8	0.4	0.2	0.7	0.1	0.2	0.0	*	0.1	0.0	0.0	0.1	1.2
1994	4.4	2.3	0.4	0.2	0.9	0.1	0.3	0.0	*	0.1	0.0	0.1	0.1	1.5
1995	4.7	2.3	0.5	0.2	0.9	0.1	0.3	0.0	–	0.1	0.0	0.0	0.1	1.7
1996	4.9	2.3	0.5	0.3	1.0	0.2	0.3	0.0	–	0.2	0.0	0.1	0.2	1.9
1997	5.3	2.3	0.5	0.3	1.1	0.2	0.4	0.1	0.0	0.2	0.0	0.1	0.2	2.1

Figure 24.2 cont.

England and Wales — Number of persons (thousands) and percentage

Sex and year	Total number of persons sentenced	Absolute or conditional discharge	Fine	Probation order	Supervision order	Community service order	Attendance centre order	Combination order	Curfew order	Young offender institution	PCC(S)A 2000, ss. 90 and 91	Otherwise dealt with	Total immediate custody	Total community sentences
	Percentage sentenced for indictable offences													
Males														
1987	100	20	29	5	11	8	11	*	*	14	0	2	14	35
1988	100	20	29	6	11	8	10	*	*	14	0	2	14	35
1989	100	23	28	6	10	8	10	*	*	12	0	2	12	34
1990	100	25	26	7	11	8	10	*	*	9	0	2	9	36
1991	100	28	21	8	10	9	11	*	*	10	0	2	10	38
1992	100	31	18	7	11	10	11	0	*	10	0	2	10	39
1993	100	31	11	4	16	8	13	2	*	11	1	2	11	44
1994	100	30	12	4	18	7	13	2	*	11	1	2	11	44
1995	100	29	12	4	18	7	12	2	0	12	1	2	12	44
1996	100	28	11	4	19	7	11	3	0	13	2	2	13	44
1997	100	28	12	4	18	7	11	3	0	14	2	2	14	43
Females														
1987	100	37	31	10	11	3	3	*	*	2	0	2	3	27
1988	100	42	28	9	10	4	3	*	*	3	0	2	3	25
1989	100	45	24	11	9	3	3	*	*	2	0	2	2	26
1990	100	48	22	11	10	3	2	*	*	2	0	2	2	26
1991	100	52	17	10	10	3	4	*	*	2	0	2	2	26
1992	100	53	15	8	12	4	3	0	*	2	0	2	2	27
1993	100	51	12	5	19	4	5	1	*	3	0	1	3	33
1994	100	52	9	5	20	3	6	1	*	3	0	1	3	34
1995	100	49	11	5	20	3	7	1	–	3	1	1	3	36
1996	100	47	9	6	21	4	7	1	–	3	1	1	3	39
1997	100	43	9	6	22	4	7	2	0	5	1	2	5	41

Figure 24.3 Sentencing table by age

AGE	10	11	12	13	14	15	16	17	18	19	20	21+
DISCHARGE (ABSOLUTE/CONDITIONAL)	✓	✓	✓	✓	✓	✓	✓	✓	✓	✓	✓	✓
BIND-OVER[1]	MAX. £250				MAX. £1,000				✓	✓	✓	✓
COMPENSATION ORDER[2]	✓	✓	✓	✓	✓	✓	✓	✓	✓	✓	✓	✓
FINE[2]	MAX. £250				MAX. £1,000				✓	✓	✓	✓
ATTENDANCE CENTRE ORDER[2][3]	MIN. 12 Hrs — MAX. 24 Hrs.						MAX. 36 Hrs.					×
SUPERVISION ORDER	✓	✓	✓	✓	✓	✓	✓	✓	×	×	×	×
PROBATION ORDER	×	×	×	×	×	×	✓	✓	✓	✓	✓	✓
COMMUNITY SERVICE ORDER	×	×	×	×	×	×	✓	✓	✓	✓	✓	✓
CURFEW ORDER	×	×	×	×	×	×	✓	✓	✓	✓	✓	✓
COMBINATION ORDER	×	×	×	×	×	×	✓	✓	✓	✓	✓	✓
REPARATION ORDER	✓	✓	✓	✓	✓	✓	✓	✓	×	×	×	×
ACTION PLAN ORDER	✓	✓	✓	✓	✓	✓	✓	✓	×	×	×	×
DETENTION AND TRAINING ORDER	✓	✓	✓	✓	✓	✓	✓	✓	×	×	×	×
DETENTION IN A YOUNG OFFENDER INSTITUTION	×	×	×	×	×	×	×	×	MIN. 21 DAYS			×
S. 91 DETENTION	✓	✓	✓	✓	✓	✓	✓	✓	×	×	×	×
DETENTION DURING H.M. PLEASURE	✓	✓	✓	✓	✓	✓	✓	✓	×	×	×	×
IMPRISONMENT	×	×	×	×	×	×	×	×	×	×	×	✓
SUSPENDED SENTENCE OF IMPRISONMENT	×	×	×	×	×	×	×	×	×	×	×	✓

(1) The Table refers only to binding over the offender. If the offender is under 16, the court *must* bind over the parents or give reasons; if the offender is aged 16 or 17, the court may bind over the parents.

(2) The Table refers only to compensation orders and fines imposed on offenders. If the offender is under 16, the court *must* order the parents to pay, using the adult scale; if the offender is aged 16 or 17, the court may order the parents to pay.

(3) The minimum number of hours is 12, except where the juvenile is aged under 14, and the court is of the opinion that 12 hours would be excessive. See **24.2.5.1**.

APPENDIX 1

TUTORIAL QUESTIONS

Tutorial 1

MULTIPLE-CHOICE QUESTIONS

1. The police have reasonable grounds for suspecting that Edward has committed an armed robbery in which £500,000 was stolen. On a Monday morning Edward is arrested, cautioned and taken to the police station. He arrives at the police station at 11.30 am. The custody officer is of the opinion that there is not sufficient evidence to charge Edward. The same officer also has reasonable grounds for believing that the detention of Edward is necessary to obtain such evidence by questioning him. Edward is interrogated on a number of occasions. At 11.30 pm on the next day, Tuesday, what action should be taken?

[A] Edward should be released or charged unless his continued detention without charge for a further nine hours is properly authorised by the station superintendent.
[B] Edward should be released or charged unless his continued detention for a further 12 hours is properly authorised by the station superintendent.
[C] Edward should be released or charged unless earlier on Tuesday a magistrates' court issued a warrant of further detention authorising the keeping of Edward in police detention.
[D] Edward should be released or charged unless the police intend to apply to a magistrates' court for a warrant of further detention (authorising the keeping of Edward in police detention), in which case they may hold Edward at the police station overnight and should apply for such a warrant at the next scheduled sitting of the magistrates' court (which will be at 10 am on the following morning, Wednesday).

2. Kelvin is charged with, and acquitted of, an offence of criminal damage. He was refused legal aid on the ground of means. He now makes an application for costs which the magistrates refuse because (a) Kelvin is a man of substantial means, and (b) Kelvin misled the prosecution into thinking that the case against him was stronger than it actually was. The basis of the magistrates' decision is:

[A] Correct as regards (a) but incorrect as regards (b).
[B] Correct as regards (b) but incorrect as regards (a).
[C] Incorrect on both points.
[D] Correct on both points.

3. Andrew has been convicted in the magistrates' court of criminal damage to a bus shelter. The value of the damage done was £800. The magistrates decide to adjourn prior to sentencing, to enable a medical examination and report to be made. A fully argued bail application is made on Andrew's behalf but he is remanded in custody. Which of the following possibilities most accurately describes what Andrew may now do with a view to obtaining bail?

[A] He may only apply for bail in the Crown Court.

[B] He may only apply for bail in the Crown Court and if unsuccessful may then apply for bail to a judge in chambers in the High Court.
[C] He may apply for bail to a judge in chambers in the High Court and if unsuccessful may then apply for bail in the Crown Court.
[D] He may apply for bail in the way described in [B] or in the way described in [C], the choice being his.

4. The Bail Act 1976, s. 4 provides that a person to whom it applies 'shall be granted bail except as provided in Schedule 1'. In which one of the following situations does s. 4 apply?

[A] When a person is convicted on indictment and his case is adjourned for reports prior to sentencing.
[B] When a person, convicted and sentenced by magistrates, is appealing against sentence.
[C] When a person, convicted and sentenced by magistrates, is appealing against conviction.
[D] When a person, convicted by magistrates, is committed by them to the Crown Court for sentence.

TUTORIAL QUESTIONS

1. You are briefed to appear at Casterbridge Magistrates' Court on 26 May to represent Amanda, who has been charged that, on 11 May, she stole from a department store a china figure worth £50. Amanda is aged 22, single, unemployed and in receipt of social security benefits. She has one previous conviction, that also being for shoplifting. She was given a conditional discharge by the Sanditon Magistrates' Court of which she will be in breach if convicted. Amanda has made one previous court appearance in connection with the present charge, that being on 12 May when she was unrepresented and was remanded for a fortnight on unconditional bail. Your solicitors state that Amanda did not instruct them until the morning of the 22nd and that it has not been possible in that time to make an application for legal aid. They therefore ask you to take whatever steps are necessary to obtain legal aid for Amanda.

(a) Describe what you would do to comply with your instructing solicitors' request and summarise the considerations which will be taken into account in deciding whether the legal aid application should be granted or not.

(b) Assuming that the application is refused, what further steps could the defence take to obtain legal aid?

2. *R* v *Bruce*

Aim: This case will be used in a Criminal Litigation class to illustrate the context and some of the issues involved in an application for bail. The accused is in custody, the case is to be remanded today by the magistrates, and the accused wishes to apply for bail.

Before the class, it will help if you look at **Chapter 36** in the ***Advocacy Manual***. Consider the order in which people will do things and what those things are. What ought to happen if the quiestion of bail arises? Plan what you should do as counsel, basing your plan upon the brief either for the prosecution or defence (you will be told before the class which party you represent; remember the opponent's instructions are confidential). Also, you may be called on to play any one of the roles in the hearing — perhaps a barrister, court clerk, or the accused. The more you have thought about how the hearing as a whole should be conducted and what everyone's part will be in it, the easier the class should be.

After the 'hearing' has taken place, there will be a class discussion on how the hearing went — maybe you would have decided the question of bail differently from the 'court', or you had different suggestions that could have been made in the application.

IN THE BLACKHEATH MAGISTRATES' COURT

R

— v —

Barry Bruce — Defendant

Instructions to Counsel for the Defence

Counsel has herewith:

1. Summary of the charges
2. Proof of evidence from the Defendant
3. Letter from the Defendant's father
4. Defendant's antecedents

Counsel is instructed to represent Mr Bruce at the next hearing of the case. He faces 2 charges — one of theft, the other handling stolen goods, both contrary to the Theft Act 1968. He will plead Not Guilty to both charges. His Proof of Evidence will fill in the details of the defence case.

He is currently on remand in custody, having elected summary trial, and counsel is requested to make an application for bail at the next appearance, next Thursday at 10.00 am. Counsel is advised that the court refused bail on the only other application, made last week by Instructing Solicitors, on the ground that Mr Bruce might interfere with the main Prosecution witness — Ashley Arthur — who is known to him.

Mr Bruce lives quite near to Mr Arthur in Blackheath. However, Mr Bruce's parents live in Ealing, some considerable distance away, and if he went to live there, there could be little chance of contact with the witness in the ordinary course of events.

Also, Mr Bruce (currently unemployed) now has the offer of a job from his uncle, Charlie Campbell, doing painting and decorating. It is unlikely that Mr Campbell will be able to attend the hearing as this is a busy time of year for him. Mr Bruce's father is in hospital but has given Instructing Solicitors a written assurance that his son may live with him, pending the outcome of these proceedings.

Counsel is asked to use his best endeavours in the circumstances and make a strong application. Mr Bruce is a regular client of Instructing Solicitors — our experience indicates that he 'does not suffer fools (or timidity) gladly'!

Copy of letter from Mr Bruce's father:

364B Buttermelt Tower,
Ealing, West London.

1st of September 2000

To whom it may concern,

I know that my son is in trouble with the law again. I am going into hospital on the 1st of October for an operation and will be in for about 2 weeks. Barry can come and stay but only until his trial comes up. He's always been a handful and as his mother and I get older, we can't control him. If he does not behave this time, he'll have to go back inside as we don't want the aggravation at our age. Still, he is our son and this will always be his home.

Yours faithfully,

(signed) J. Bruce

Details of charges (taken by Instructing Solicitors from charge sheet)

Charge 1: On a day unknown between the 3rd August 2000 and 10th August 2000, Barry Bruce dishonestly received stolen goods, namely a Sanyo hi-fi stereo music system, knowing or believing them to be stolen.

Charge 2: On the 9th of August 2000 Barry Bruce stole a video cassette, the property of AA Newsagents Limited.

Proof of Evidence

Mr Barry Bruce of 255, Hazlitt Gardens, Blackheath, who will say —

I have been falsely accused of two crimes. They are both supposed to have occurred when I was in the local newsagent's shop. The owner, Ashley Arthur, is someone I know from my local pub, The Red Herring. Occasionally, I have sold him some stuff that I had got from other friends — boxes of video tapes, jewellery and the like. It's all been no questions asked and went smoothly till the last time. I was promised by a friend that he was due to take delivery of some top quality hi-fi equipment. It was going to cost me a monkey but I managed to persuade Arthur to buy it from me (unseen) for a straight £1,000.

Unfortunately, after he took delivery of it Arthur's place got raided by the police. I think he was clean except for the hi-fi, which he persuaded them he come by innocently. The police took the hi-fi away and I think Arthur blamed me for tipping them off (which I did not do). Anyway, the next time I went into Arthur's shop we had a bit of a barney about the raid and his hi-fi. At one point he disappeared out the back of the shop for a couple of minutes. That must be when he rung the police because they turned up about 5 minutes later. The police came in the shop and spoke to Arthur. He said something like 'That's the man'. One of the police then grabbed hold of me and arrested me for handling.

At the police station, I was searched and they found a video tape. This was from a batch that I had sold on to Arthur a couple of weeks previous but I had kept about 12 for myself. I know Arthur has been knocking them out in his shop but there is no way that mine came from there. They already had price labels on when I got them. I got a bit violent in the shop and started swearing but this was because I had been fitted up. I said to Arthur that I would tear his head off and spit down his throat but it was in the heat of the moment. I have had time to reflect on matters in custody and am quite content to see that justice is done in the court.

I have spoken to my father on the telephone and understand I can live with him until my trial. Also, my mum told me on a visit that my uncle, Charlie Campbell, is holding a job open for me with his firm. Although the job is based in Blackheath, I won't be there much as we will be doing jobs all over London.

I badly want bail as I am very worried about leaving my girlfriend alone in the last few months of her pregnancy.

I can remember my last three convictions. Two were in Ealing Magistrates' Court in 1998 for burglary (I got Community Service, about 150 hours) and one in 1999 at Blackheath Magistrates. That was for a fight in a pub — I was done for simple GBH and got a 3-month suspended sentence.

Metropolitan Police

Antecedents of:	Barry BRUCE
Address:	255, Hazlitt Gardens, Blackheath, London
Age:	22
Date of Birth:	31.3.78
Place of Birth:	Paddington, West London
Date of 1st entry into UK:	N/A
Occupation:	Unemployed

Education: He attended Boyson Comprehensive School, leaving aged 16, with 3 GCSEs in English, General Studies and Art.

Main employments during last 5 years
Has had several jobs of short duration since leaving school. These include casual labour for market stallholders and delivering community (free) newspapers.

Home conditions and domestic circumstances
Lives with his girlfriend (who is expecting their child) in a 1 bedroom flat. Is not claiming Social Security as such, although the rent for the flat is paid by the DSS. No regular commitments. Girlfriend's parents sometimes help with shopping bills.

Outstanding matters
If convicted, will be in breach of a 3-month suspended sentence imposed by Blackheath Magistrates' Court on 2.12.99.

List of previous convictions attached: Yes/No
Date of arrest: 9.8.00 —/In custody

Officer in case: D. C. Duncan
Station: Blackheath East
Telephone number: Date: 6.9.00
Supervising Officer:

Convictions Recorded Against: Barry BRUCE — CRO No. 34567/95
Charged in name of Barry BRUCE — Date of Birth 31.3.78

Date	Court	Offences	Sentence
Total number of convictions 6. Has not previously served a custodial sentence.			
5.7.95	B'heath M/C	Theft	Fine £30
15.9.95	Greenwich M/C	1. Handling 2. Handling	Con. Dis. 1 year
1.5.98	Ealing M/C	1. Burglary 2. Burglary	Comm. Serv. 150 hours
2.12.99	B'heath M/C	Causing GBH	3 months' imprisonment suspended for 1 year

IN THE BLACKHEATH MAGISTRATES' COURT

R

— v —

Barry Bruce (Defendant)

Instructions to Prosecute

Herewith:

1. The charges against the accused
2. List of objections to bail
3. Antecedents/CRO form
4. Case summary

This case is due in court again next Thursday. The accused has elected summary trial and a date is likely to be fixed by the court at the next hearing. There are two civilian witnesses and two police officers. The time estimate is — half a day.

The accused is currently remanded in custody. On the last occasion that bail was actively considered by the court, it was denied due to possible interference with the chief prosecution witness, Mr Ashley ARTHUR.

Charges:—

1: On a day unknown between the 3rd August 2000 and 10th August 2000, Barry Bruce dishonestly received stolen goods, namely a Sanyo hi-fi stereo music system, knowing or believing them to be stolen.

2: On the 9th of August 2000 Barry Bruce stole a video cassette, the property of AA Newsagents Limited.

Objections to bail:—

1. Likely interference with prosecution witness — the accused knows him and lives nearby.

2. Likely to commit further offences — has a record of similar crimes in his record. No apparent income. See antecedents.

3. May abscond. If convicted of either charge, the accused will be in breach of a suspended sentence. See antecedents.

Case summary:—

In late July 2000, ARTHUR was offered by BRUCE (and agreed to buy) an expensive hi-fi system. On the 4th August, a Mr Smollett was the victim of a burglary at his flat. Among items taken was an expensive hi-fi. This was later sold by BRUCE to ARTHUR; it was recovered from ARTHUR on the 7th and identified by SMOLLETT as his.

ARTHUR owns a shop in Blackheath. On 9th August, BRUCE went in and ARTHUR called the police.

BRUCE was arrested in the shop and became very aggressive and abusive towards ARTHUR, threatening him with serious injury.

A video cassette was later found on BRUCE at the police station. This was identified by ARTHUR as coming from his shop. BRUCE had not bought it.

At the station, BRUCE made a full confession of both offences to D. C. Duncan and P. C. Ewart.

[Note: Antecedents and CRO form are not copied — see the Defence brief.]

Tutorial 2

MULTIPLE-CHOICE QUESTIONS

1. Colin is charged with criminal damage to David's Rolls Royce motor car. The value of the damage has been estimated by a Rolls Royce approved dealer at £5,579.86. Colin asks you about the appropriate court of trial. Which ONE of the following statements about this situation is correct?

[A] He must be tried summarily.
[B] He may be tried summarily but only if both he and the magistrates agree.
[C] He may only be tried on indictment if both he and the magistrates agree.
[D] He must be tried on indictment.

2. Brian is charged with theft. He appears before the magistrates to determine the mode of trial. Which of the following propositions is **false**?

[A] He may be tried on indictment if he so elects, despite the wishes of the magistrates.
[B] He must be tried on indictment if the magistrates so decide whatever his wishes are.
[C] He may only be tried summarily if both he and the magistrates agree.
[D] He may only be tried on indictment if the prosecution is brought by the DPP, Attorney General or Solicitor General.

TUTORIAL QUESTIONS

Mode of trial

Questions 1 and 2 deal with the procedure for determining the court in which the defendant will be tried.

1. Edward appears before Muggleton Magistrates' Court charged with:

(a) dangerous driving;

(b) taking a motor vehicle without the owner's consent; and

(c) driving while disqualified;

(d) assaulting a police officer in the execution of his duty.

The prosecution case is that officers in a marked police vehicle saw Edward driving a car on a public road. Knowing him to be disqualified, they signalled to him to stop but he accelerated, driving at speeds of 70 mph in a built-up area, going onto the wrong side of the road, causing oncoming traffic to brake sharply, and eventually crashing the car into a lamppost. He then escaped on foot but was later arrested at his home address. During the course of the arrest, he punched one of the police officers. Enquiries reveal that the car Edward was allegedly driving was taken without the owner's consent earlier that day. It is expected that Edward will plead not guilty to all charges and allege mistaken identification on the part of the police. Dangerous driving is an offence triable either way; driving while disqualified, taking a vehicle without the owner's consent and assaulting a police officer in the execution of his duty are summary offences.

(a) Describe the procedure by which the mode of trial for the dangerous driving charge will be determined.

(b) Advise Edward of the extent to which he is entitled to know the nature of the prosecution case in advance of trial (i) if he is tried on indictment and (ii) if he is tried summarily.

(c) Advise the prosecution on whether, if the dangerous driving charge is committed for trial, it will be possible for the other charges to be tried on indictment also.

2. David appears before Kingsport Magistrates' Court charged with two offences of criminal damage. The first charge alleges that, on 1 September, he intentionally damaged a motor vehicle; the second alleges that, on 3 September, he intentionally damaged a window. The prosecution case as regards the first offence is that, following an argument with a relative, he threw a stone at the windscreen of the relative's car as he was driving away from David's house. As regards the second offence, the case is that, after being told to leave a public house because he was the worse for drink, he threw a brick through a window of the pub. The value of the damage involved in the first charge was £50; the value of the damage in the second was £100. David wishes to be tried on indictment.

Advise him as to whether he has a right to be so tried.

Election

Questions 3 to 6 deal with the defendant's decision whether to elect Crown Court trial.

In each of these situations, you are defence counsel in the magistrates' court. Today the court will determine the mode of trial for the defendant. He or she may be asked to choose whether he or she wishes to be tried in the magistrates' court or Crown Court. The defendant is likely to want your advice on this matter. Consider what you could say.

3. Arnold (aged 32) appears at the magistrates' court on two charges. The first (theft) alleges that he stole two loaves of bread and a pint of milk from a milk float in the street. The second (making off without payment) alleges that, having ordered and consumed a fried breakfast, Arnold tried to leave a cafe without paying for his meal. According to prosecution witnesses, he was caught 'red-handed' on both occasions.

Arnold has no fixed address, staying in hostels when he can afford to do so. His employment record consists largely of casual jobs which were menial and low-paid. He has seven convictions, covering the last ten years. Offences involve dishonesty (of a minor nature) or violence/breaches of the peace. If convicted of either of the two latest offences, he will be in breach of a conditional discharge imposed five months ago by another court.

Instructions from the client: Arnold is in custody and would like to stay there for the winter months. He intends to plead Not Guilty, insisting he is innocent, but he has no witnesses. He says the prosecution eye witnesses are lying and have grudges against him.

4. Bertie has been charged with theft from his employer. The allegation is that he took stock (electrical components) from his employer's warehouse over a period of several months, with a total value of £4,300. No property has been recovered.

There are two main prosecution witnesses, the works supervisor and another colleague from Bertie's former place of work. Both say they saw him walk out of the warehouse with items, place them in the boot of his car in the car park and eventually drive home with the items at the end of his shift. Bertie made no admissions to police officers, and refused to be interviewed without his solicitor being present.

Bertie is aged 26 and has no previous convictions. He is married with two young children.

Instructions from the client: Bertie says he can call his ex-employer to testify that he was being considered for promotion at the time of his arrest. He says that he suspected the two prosecution witnesses of stealing the stock that he is charged with stealing.

5. Craig is aged 34. He is charged with stealing a car. The car was recovered from a multi-storey car park attached to a block of flats some 200 metres from Craig's house. Police arrested Craig inside the car. He has four previous convictions for theft (not of cars) and has been in prison on two occasions. He is alleged to have made a full confession on the way to the police station. There are no eye witnesses to the theft.

Instructions from the client: Craig will plead Not Guilty. He says that the car had been in the car park for three days before his arrest and that he thought it had been abandoned. He was thinking about using it for spares for his own car. He denies making the confession, saying that he has always maintained his innocence.

6. Dennis is charged with assault occasioning actual bodily harm. The incident occurred at a nightclub when an argument developed over who was going to drive a young lady home. The victim (and main prosecution witness) suffered a broken nose and lost two teeth. Dennis (aged 18) is a promising amateur boxer and was not marked.

The victim (aged 24) has several previous convictions for offences of violence. Dennis has no previous convictions. At the police station, Dennis expressed contrition for his part in the incident.

Instructions from the client: Dennis will plead Not Guilty, relying on self-defence. He has no witnesses. He says his 'admission' was an expression of regret for losing his self-control but was not meant to be an acceptance of guilt.

Now go through those situations again and think about how you, as prosecuting counsel, might address the court on the suitable location for the case to be dealt with. (Remember you should liaise with the staff of the Crown Prosecution Service if this is a CPS prosecution.)

Tutorial 3

MULTIPLE-CHOICE QUESTIONS

1. Which of the following groups is not allowed into a youth court room during a hearing?

[A] Probation officers concerned in the hearing.
[B] Journalists reporting the hearing.
[C] Witnesses, after they have testified in the hearing.
[D] Barristers waiting for their case to start.

2. Portia (aged 16) appeared with Quentin (aged 20) in the adult magistrates' court on a joint charge of theft. Quentin elected to be tried on indictment. The magistrates felt that it was not necessary in the interests of justice to commit Portia to the Crown Court for trial. Portia has now been tried and convicted by the adult magistrates' court. Which one of the following statements is correct?

[A] Portia must be sent to the youth court to be dealt with.
[B] Portia must be sent to the youth court to be dealt with if the magistrates do not think a custodial sentence is called for.
[C] Portia may be committed to the Crown Court for sentence if the magistrates think that a custodial sentence is called for.
[D] Portia may be dealt with in the magistrates' court or, if none of that court's sentences is appropriate, sent to the youth court to be dealt with.

TUTORIAL QUESTIONS

1. Fiona (aged 16), Gillian (aged 14) and her twin brother, George, are all found guilty in the youth court of three ofences of burglary and one of inflicting grievous bodily harm. On each occasion, they went to a house where an elderly person lived alone,

tricked their way in by asking to use the lavatory, after which two of them would search the premises while the third kept the victim occupied in conversation. Pension money, savings and jewellery were stolen to a total value of approximately £1,000. On the third occasion, the victim became suspicious and tried to stop them leaving. They knocked her to the ground, causing bruising and a head wound which required 20 stitches. Reports reveal that Gillian and George have a difficult background. Their mother admits that she cannot keep control of them. Moreover, their father and older siblings all have criminal records. George has previous findings of guilt for shoplifting and stealing a car radio, but Gillian has not been in trouble before. Fiona is also of previous good character. She comes from an excellent home, and the report can give no explanation for her involvement in the offences other than 'a desire for thrills'. She apparently met Gillian and George at a youth club where together they planned the offences.

(a) What are the magistrates' maximum custodial sentencing powers?

(b) What are their powers, if any, to commit for sentence?

(c) Was this an appropriate case to be tried in the youth court?

2. *R* v *Barley*

Aim: To familiarise yourself with both the procedure at a summary trial and the special rules relating to juveniles.

This is a simple case of theft in the youth court. You should prepare this as you would for any summary trial. There will not be role-play in the class but you should be ready to discuss all issues relevant to the case.

IN THE BLACKHEATH MAGISTRATES' COURT

R

— v —

Billy Barley

Instructions to Prosecute

Billy Barley is charged with theft. He is alleged to have stolen a leather jacket, the property of Newtrend Limited, on 3rd August 2000. He was stopped by a store detective, employed by the company, a short distance from their shop after a chase. The jacket was recovered from him. Police were called and Constable Field attended the scene. No admissions were made.

Both witnesses — the store detective, Ellis Farmer, and Constable Field — have been warned to attend court on the next hearing.

Billy Barley is in receipt of legal aid and has instructed Messrs Planter and Reaper of 22 Harvest Street, WC5.

Barley's date of birth is 1st of February 1987.

STATEMENT OF WITNESS

Statement of: Ellis FARMER
Age of witness: Over 18
Occupation of witness: Store detective

[Usual declaration omitted]

Signed: E. Farmer
Signature witnessed by: Drew Field, PC 202Y

I am employed as a store detective by Newtrend Limited. I have held this position for 3 years. For the last 6 months I have been at the Oxford Street Branch.

On the 3rd August 2000, I was on duty on the ground floor of the shop when my attention was caught by a youth who I now know to be Billy BARLEY. He was standing by a mirror and was wearing one of our new leather jackets. He seemed to be more interested in watching what was going on around him than looking in the mirror.

I moved to a different position, keeping him under observation the whole time. After I had been observing him for about thirty seconds, he suddenly ran towards the exit, still wearing the jacket. I was unable to stop him before he left as several customers were between us.

When I got outside, I saw him running through the mall and gave chase. I caught him just around the corner in Orchard Street, some 300 metres from the shop. He had taken the jacket off and appeared to be about to hide it. I took him by the arm and said, 'You're coming with me. The police will have to come. You've stolen this jacket and it's store policy always to prosecute.' He said, 'I don't know what you're talking about. A boy just gave this to me.' I replied, 'We'll let the police sort this out. Come with me'.

We returned to the shop where I called the police and eventually repeated my story to Constable Field in the presence of Billy Barley. The jacket was recovered intact and there is no claim for compensation.

Dated 4.8.00

Signed: E. Farmer
Signature witnessed by: D. Field

STATEMENT OF WITNESS

Statement of: Drew FIELD
Age of witness: Over 18
Occupation of witness: Police Constable 202Y

[Usual declaration omitted]

Signed: D. Field
Signature witnessed by: G. Fallow P. Sgt 545Z

On the 3rd August 2000 at 4.25 pm I was on duty in Oxford Street when, as a result of information received, I attended the premises of Newtrend Limited at 755 Oxford Street. There I spoke to an employee of the store, Ellis FARMER, and then I asked a youth, who I know to be Billy BARLEY, 'The store detective says you were seen trying the jacket on and then you ran out of the store without paying for it. What have you got to say?' He replied, 'It's a mistake. I was waiting for my bus when a boy came running around the corner, threw the coat down and kept running. I went to pick it up when this person came up and arrested me.'

The store detective said, 'I got a good look at him in the shop. I know it was him.' I said to BARLEY, 'I am not satisfied with your answer. I am arresting you for theft of this leather jacket from Newtrend.' I then cautioned BARLEY and he said 'Can I ring my Mum?' We then went to Paddington Green Police Station where, at 7.45 pm and in the presence of his parents, he was charged with theft of the jacket, cautioned and made no reply.

Dated 10.8.00

Signed: D. Field
Signature witnessed by: G. Fallow

Extract from Record of previous Findings of Guilt:

Billy BARLEY (d.o.b. 1.02.87) has 2 findings of guilt recorded against him, both in the Westminster Youth Court. Both offences were for burglary of dwelling houses. The first finding of guilt, recorded on 13.05.99, resulted in an order that there be a fine of £50. The second, dated 10.02.00, resulted in an order that he be conditionally discharged for 1 year.

WESTMINSTER YOUTH COURT

Sitting at Seymour Place, W1

R

— v —

Billy Barley

Instructions to Counsel for the Defence

Counsel is instructed to represent Billy Barley at Seymour Place Youth Court on his trial. He is charged with shoplifting — taking a leather jacket from a Newtrend shop in Oxford Street. No one else is alleged to be involved. He will plead *Not Guilty*.

Instructing solicitors understand that there are 2 Prosecution witnesses, a store detective and arresting officer.

The evidence seems quite weak, in the opinion of instructing solicitors, with the case turning on identification. Counsel is, of course, familiar with the guidelines for such cases, laid down by the Court of Appeal in *R* v *Turnbull* [1977] QB 224. Billy Barley was found in possession of the jacket, a fact which he does not deny, but he has an explanation which he told the arresting officer.

There are no defence witnesses, apart from Billy, although his parents have been told by instructing solicitors to attend Court with him. Counsel is asked to use his best endeavours to secure an acquittal.

Proof of Evidence

Billy Barley of 65 Plough Lane, London W9, who will say:

On the day in August when I was supposed to have stolen the jacket, I was in Oxford Street, looking around the shops. I had arrived there at about 2 p.m. and saw all that I wanted to by about 4.30. Then I went to catch the bus home. This is a number 85 which stops in Orchard Street, just off of Oxford Street.

I had just got to the stop when a boy came running around the corner from Oxford Street. He was running hard so I watched to see why. He had something in his hand and threw it to the ground as he went past the bus stop. He kept going, up towards Baker Street.

I was curious about what he had thrown away so I went and picked it up. It was a leather jacket, brand new. I saw it still had the price ticket in and was just looking to see the size when this person came up and told me I was under arrest for shoplifting. I said I did not know anything about it but I was taken to a shop, Newtrend, in Oxford Street.

I did not know what to do but eventually the police came. The store detective said that I had been under observation in the shop and had run out with the jacket. When the police officer asked me if that was true, I denied it and told them what happened. No one believed me and I was taken to the police station.

My Mum and Dad were called down to the station and got me. I have never admitted to stealing the jacket. I would not recognise the boy who had the jacket. I did not know him. There were some other people at the bus stop who must have seen it all but there is no way I could trace them.

I think the jacket is a size 40-inch chest. That is too big for me.

3. In the case of *R* v *Billy Barley* (see above), assume that Billy is alleged to have been acting in concert with his cousin Charlotte (aged 18). How would the procedure differ?

Tutorial 4

MULTIPLE-CHOICE QUESTIONS

1. Alphonse is convicted in the magistrates' court of theft. He wishes to appeal to the Crown Court against his conviction. Which of the following is the appropriate procedure:

[A] Alphonse notifies the magistrates' court and the prosecution of his intention to appeal.
[B] Alphonse notifies the magistrates and the prosecution of his intention to appeal, and sets out his full grounds of appeal.
[C] Alphonse applies to the magistrates for leave to appeal to the Crown Court.
[D] Alphonse applies to the Crown Court for leave to appeal to that court, stating brief grounds of appeal.

2. Graham is convicted of two offences of handling stolen goods in the magistrates' court, and sentenced to two months' imprisonment on each offence, to run consecutively. He wishes to appeal against sentence. In dealing with Graham the Crown Court may:

[A] Pass any sentence that it could have passed following a trial on indictment.
[B] Pass any sentence that the magistrates could have passed.
[C] Pass any sentence which is not greater than the sentence that the magistrates actually passed.
[D] Treat the case as if Graham had been committed to them for sentence.

TUTORIAL QUESTIONS

Appeals from the magistrates' court

1. Fiona is charged with driving without due care and attention, contrary to the Road Traffic Act 1991. She pleads not guilty. At the close of the prosecution case, her solicitor makes a submission of no case to answer. The chairman of the magistrates, upholding the submission and acquitting Fiona, says:

We take the view that your driving clearly fell below the standards of a reasonable prudent driver. However, we put that down to inexperience on your part. There is nothing in the prosecution evidence to suggest that you were not doing your best to drive properly. You did not mean to be careless. For that reason we find that there is no case to answer.

Advise the prosecution on whether, and if so, how, it can appeal against the magistrates' decision.

2. Christine is charged with stealing from Harridges, a large department store, an expensive box of chocolates. She is jointly charged with her husband, Harold. She agrees to summary trial. Christine pleads guilty and Harold not guilty. In view of her plea, the prosecution offers no evidence against Harold. Having learnt that Christine has previous convictions for shoplifting and considered a pre-sentence report, the magistrates pass a sentence of three months' imprisonment. When the defence solicitor goes to see Christine in the cells, she tells him for the first time that Harold made her steal the chocolates by threatening her with violence if she did not do so. Also, on the morning of her first appearance before the magistrates, he had said to her, 'You'd better not tell them I made you do it or it will be the worse for you when I get you home'.

Is it possible for Christine to appeal to the Crown Court against conviction? If so, how do you think the Crown Court would deal with the case?

3. Ben, aged 23, is charged with wounding Claude. The offence is alleged to have taken place in a public house shortly after a football match between 'United' and 'City'. Ben is a 'United' supporter whereas Claude supports 'City'. Ben intends to plead not guilty — he says he was acting in self-defence and that he was attacked by Claude and other 'City' supporters. Ben has two previous convictions for offences of violence. He appears at the Whitehaven Magistrates' Court and elects summary trial. Ben does not give evidence at his trial. After hearing all the evidence the magistrates convict Ben and sentence him to three months' imprisonment.

A week after the hearing Ben's solicitors discover that the police had taken a statement from Desmond, a witness whose evidence supported Ben's account. Neither Ben nor his solicitors knew about Desmond. Ben wishes to appeal against both conviction and sentence. Advise Ben as to his rights of appeal.

4. Francis appears at Blackacre Magistrates' Court charged with theft. The magistrates find the matter is suitable for summary trial and Francis elects summary trial. At the end of the prosecution evidence, his solicitor makes a submission that there is no case to answer. The magistrates retire to consider and when they return the chairman announces that they find Francis guilty. What steps can be taken to quash the conviction? Describe in brief outline the appropriate procedure.

5. Barry is charged with being found drunk in a public place. The prosecution alleges that he was found in the garden of a block of flats. Barry admits that he was drunk but says that the gardens are not a public place. He is convicted. Describe the procedure on an appeal against conviction by way of case stated to the High Court.

Committals for sentence

1. Sid is charged with assault occasioning actual bodily harm, to which he indicated that he wishes to plead guilty. The information is put to Sid and he pleads guilty. The prosecuting solicitor tells the magistrates that Sid is a police officer who committed the offence when off duty, as a result of the victim provoking him deliberately by making offensive remarks about the police. The magistrates were not previously aware that Sid was a police officer. Antecedent evidence shows Sid to have no previous convictions. No other offences are taken into consideration. Can the magistrates properly commit Sid to the Crown Court to be sentenced under s. 38 of the Magistrates' Courts Act 1980?

2. Lorna appears at Whiteacre Magistrates' Court and pleads guilty to an offence of criminal damage. She is in breach of a sentence of three months' imprisonment, suspended for two years, imposed by another magistrates' court. What action can be taken in respect of the suspended sentence?

3. Martin, aged 22, appears in Barchester Magistrates' Court charged with obtaining property by deception, contrary to s. 15 of the Theft Act 1968. At the plea before venue hearing, Martin indicates a plea of guilty. Martin is further charged with having (on another occasion) interfered with a motor vehicle, contrary to s. 9 of the Criminal Attempts Act 1981. This is a summary offence punishable with a maximum of three months' imprisonment. Martin again pleads guilty. He has previous convictions for dishonesty.

What powers to commit for sentence do the magistrates possess in respect of Martin and what powers of sentence will the Crown Court possess in the event of such committal?

Tutorial 5

MULTIPLE-CHOICE QUESTIONS

1. Astrid is charged alone with shoplifting. She elects jury trial and is committed for trial to the Crown Court. She wants to get maximum publicity for the case in order to encourage any defence witnesses to come forward. She asks for reporting restrictions to be lifted. The magistrates:

[A] must grant her application unless the prosecution opposes it;
[B] must refuse the application if they believe it will prejudice her right to a fair trial;
[C] must grant her application;
[D] must grant her application if it is in the interests of justice to do so.

2. Charles is charged in an indictment containing counts of causing grievous bodily harm with intent and forgery (the alleged offences relate to unrelated factual situations). At Charles' trial his counsel objects to the indictment on the ground that the counts are improperly joined. The trial judge (i) rules that the counts are improperly joined and (ii) orders that the indictment be severed.

The judge was:

[A] Right on point (i) and acting beyond his powers on point (ii).
[B] Right on point (i) and acting within his powers on point (ii).
[C] Wrong on point (i) and acting beyond his powers on point (ii).
[D] Wrong on point (i) and acting within his powers on point (ii).

TUTORIAL QUESTION

R v *Lewis and others*

Aim: To consider on behalf of the prosecution which counts can properly be included in one (or more) indictments against Lewis and the others. After reading the papers carefully, you should consider what counts should be included in the indictment(s). Once you have done this, try to draft your own indictment, setting the counts out properly (in terms both of form and content).

Disclosure

Case study A

Derek is charged with unlawful wounding contrary to s. 20 of the OAPA 1861. The prosecution case is that he 'glassed' Eric in a fight in a public house between supporters of rival football teams. Derek is committed for trial in the Crown Court by way of s. 6(2). The evidence served includes:

(i) a statement from Eric which says that he was attacked by Derek (whom he knows), who was wielding a glass which was used to cut him across the cheek;

(ii) a statement from Frank, who is a friend of Eric, in which he says that Eric was wounded in an unprovoked attack by a man fitting Derek's description.

(iii) a doctor's statement, dealing with Eric's injuries;

(iv) a statement from the inspector who ran the parade at which Frank and Eric identified Derek as the man who injured Eric.

1. As prosecutor, decide whether you should reveal any of the following by way of primary disclosure:

(a) a statement from Godfrey, a bystander who knows none of the other participants in the incident, who states that Eric was slashed with a broken glass by a man fitting Derek's description, but only after Eric had struck the first blow;

(b) Eric's spent previous conviction from 15 years ago for indecent assault on a teenage boy;

(c) Eric's previous conviction from seven years ago for assault occasioning actual bodily harm against his wife;

(d) Godfrey's previous conviction last year for shoplifting.

2. Derek tells you (his defence counsel) that he was in the pub when the 'glassing' took place, but he was an onlooker and took no active part in proceedings. He says that the witnesses are lying because of hostility between supporters of the two rival football teams (Eric and Frank support a different team from him). He has a doctor's report which tells of an examination on the morning after the incident, in which he was found to have bruising to the face and chest consistent with a series of punches. Derek says he cannot remember how he got this bruising, but admits that he does not remember much of the night in question, as he had drunk nine pints of lager and a few whiskies.

Draft Derek's defence statement assuming that you have received by way of primary disclosure whatever you have decided (in response to Question 1) the prosecution ought to disclose.

3. Assuming that you, as prosecutor, receive the defence statement issued in response to Question 2, is there anything further which you ought to disclose by way of secondary disclosure?

Case study B
Stanley has been committed to the Crown Court for theft. The allegation arises from his conduct while he operated a building society agency. Over the period in question, customers of the building society paid to the agency cheques and cash totalling approximately £132,000. £8,000 never reached the building society, but was spent by Stanley.

In the course of his interview under caution, Stanley stated that the building society did not require him to pay the actual cash or cheques straight into their account. He was perfectly entitled to pay the cheques into his own account, provided that he reimbursed the building society by writing appropriate cheques thereafter. He went on to claim that his partner, Harry, would confirm that the society had always accepted his cheques, even when it was clear that they reflected transactions with customers conducted up to a month earlier.

The chief prosecution witness at committal was Lois, an employee of the building society, who stated that the hard and fast rule was that all cheques had to be paid into the building society account within, at most, 48 hours.

1. As prosecutor, consider whether you should reveal any of the following by way of primary disclosure:

(a) A statement from the chief security officer of the building society, stating that Lois had asked him whether there was a reward for employees who helped to prevent fraud committed against the building society.

(b) A copy of a manual issued to agents of the building society, stating that 'cheques and cash should generally be paid into the building society account within seven days'.

(c) Harry's conviction four years ago for shoplifting.

2. Put yourself now in the position of defence solicitor. Stanley tells you that he told the truth in interview, but that he forgot to mention that he had been told by the Head

of Agency Operations that he could pay cheques and cash into his own account, provided that he made a cheque to cover the transaction 'within a reasonable time'.

Draft Stanley's defence statement on the assumption that the prosecution has sent you (a) above, but not (b) or (c).

3. Assume that you, as the prosecutor, receive the defence statement issued in response to Question 2. Is there anything further which you ought to disclose by way of secondary disclosure?

IN THE CROWN COURT SITTING AT LEWES

R

— v —

Lewis and others

Instructions to Counsel for the Prosecution

Counsel has herewith:

1. Bundle of depositions and witness statements
2. Antecedent history of the accused

Counsel is instructed

(i) to prosecute in this matter;
(ii) to settle the appropriate indictment; and
(iii) to advise on the procedure to be adopted in relation to any counts added to the indictment.

The four accused were committed to stand trial on a single charge of robbery, contrary to the Theft Act 1968, s. 8, by Brighton Magistrates' Court on 3.9.00.

Case Summary
On 17.4.00 a branch of the South Downs Building Society was held up at gunpoint by two masked men. One kept watch by the door, observing both the people inside the branch and passers-by. The other demanded money from a cashier. On obtaining a holdall containing £15,967, the two men fled on foot. They were pursued by a passer-by and one of the men stopped and shot the pursuer, a Mr Goodbody. They then made good their escape, using a car parked nearby.

The prosecution case at committal was that three of the accused, namely Lewis, Duke and Ella, were involved in the actual robbery with Ella as the driver of the escape vehicle, a stolen Ford Escort XR3i. The fourth accused, Peterson, stored the vehicle in his garage for several days prior to the robbery.

Committal charge
Against Finlay LEWIS, Arthur DUKE, Gerald ELLA and Leonard PETERSON

You are charged that, on the 17th day of April 2000, you did rob Mary Penny of £15,967, contrary to the Theft Act 1968, s. 8 (1).

STATEMENT OF WITNESS

Statement of: Mary Penny
Age: Over 18
Occupation: Building society cashier
[Usual declaration omitted]

Dated 3rd May 2000

I am a cashier for the South Downs Building Society. I work in the Churchill Square Branch. I have been there for about 4 years.

I remember the 17th of April 2000. I was at work that morning. At about 10 am two men entered the branch. Both were wearing dark-coloured donkey jackets which had orange fluorescent material on the top half. They had on dark balaclava helmets with 'Porky Pig' masks. They were both carrying what looked like sawn-off shotguns.

One of the men shouted for everyone to get on the floor. There was some screaming and the same man shouted to shut up.

He came to my window and said 'fill this with money and nobody will get hurt.'

He produced a nylon holdall and passed it through the window. I looked to the manager who indicated that I should do as the man asked.

I emptied the contents of the tills into the bag. This was both cash and cheques. Then I gave it back to the man at the counter.

All this time the other man had just stood by the entrance door, pointing his gun at the staff and customers.

The man with the holdall joined the other one by the door. One of them shouted 'Nobody move and you won't get hurt' and they both ran out. I think it was the man with the holdall who shouted.

I had pressed the silent alarm as the man approached my window and about two minutes after the men left, several police officers arrived.

I would describe the man with the holdall as about 6 feet tall and medium build. His voice was unusual. He had an accent. Irish is how I would describe it.

I saw his hands when he gave me the bag — they were white.

On the 26th of April I attended an identification parade at Brighton Police Station where I saw a number of men. They all looked about the same height and build as the man with the holdall.

They each said the words 'fill this with money and nobody will get hurt'. I picked out the 5th man. I am sure he was the man with the holdall.

I did not get a good look at the second man. I think he was about 2 inches shorter than the other one, again medium build. I would not recognise him again.

The whole incident lasted for about 5 minutes.

I did not see the face of either man. I did not see their hair, they were both wearing balaclava helmets.

Their jackets were not tight on them. They could have been slimmer than medium build.

I saw no distinctive features on either man. The voice was distinctive.

I would call it Irish. I have no Irish relations or friends. I have not been to Ireland on holiday. I have never been to Scotland.

I can recall the voice of the man with the holdall. I am sure that the man I picked out at the identification parade had the same voice. I am not mistaken. I am not an expert on voices or regional accents.

Signed: Mary Penny
Signature witnessed by: D. Law, DS

STATEMENT OF WITNESS

Statement of: Reginald Goodbody
Age: Over 18
Occupation: Retired grocer
[Usual declaration omitted]

Dated 3.5.00

(Witness sworn)

On the 17.4.00 I was in Brighton for some shopping. My wife was with me.

We started looking around the shops in Churchill Square. Just after 10 o'clock we were going past a small parade of shops when two men ran out of the South Downs Building Society premises there.

I was about 20 yards away from them. They ran towards me and my wife. They had a bag and guns. They were wearing balaclava helmets. They had workmen's jackets on — black I think, with orange patches.

I realised they had robbed the Building Society and I put up my arms to try and stop them. One got past me but I caught hold of the bag that the other one was carrying.

We got into a bit of a struggle over the bag. I think people were coming out of the Building Society by now.

The other man ran back and shouted at me to let go. When I said No, he shot me in the leg with his gun.

I fell over and let go of the bag. Both of them ran off.

The one I was struggling with was about my height and build. I am 6 feet tall and weigh about 13 stone. The other one was about the same. I can't recall him clearly.

I would not recognise either of them again. Their features were quite obscured by their helmets.

I went to hospital in an ambulance with my wife. The Royal Sussex Hospital in Brighton.

I was there for 8 days. My leg was badly damaged by the gun. It was a shotgun cartridge. I lost some blood and quite a bit of muscle and flesh in my calf.

I now have to walk with a stick. I find my mobility is very restricted. I attend the hospital physiotherapy department every week to build my leg up.

The one with the bag shot me. The gun did not go off in the struggle — I am quite sure.

I do not think it can have been an accident — he deliberately took aim and fired. There was nothing I could do.

The man who shot me shouted at me to let go of the bag. I cannot recall his exact words. He did not have an accent. I did not notice any accent.

The other one never spoke at all.

Signed: R. Goodbody

Signature witnessed by: D. Law, DS

STATEMENT OF WITNESS

Statement of:	Brenda BROWSE
Age:	Over 18
Occupation:	Housekeeper

[Usual declaration omitted]

Signed by: B. Browse
Signature witnessed by: D. Law, DS 494P

Dated 11.5.2000

On the 17th of April 2000 I left my home to meet a friend in Brighton. We had arranged to meet by the Oxfam shop, just along the road from Churchill Square. I got there early, at about 9.30 am. There were several cars parked around the area but I did not take any notice of them. I went to a cafe over the road for a cup of tea.

While I was in the cafe, I could see the road ahead — Mountfort Road. There was a dark blue Ford Escort parked there with a man sitting behind the wheel. The car was there the whole time I was in the cafe. At about 10 o'clock, as I was about to leave, two men came running along the road, shouting something. The man in the car started the engine and the two men leaped into the car. It tore off down the road, towards the junction by the cafe and straight over without waiting to see if anyone was crossing the road.

I was astonished by this behaviour and made a note of the car registration number. It was E838 JPO.

I would not recognise the two men who jumped into the car again but both were wearing workmen's jackets with orange fluorescent patches like Council workmen wear. I think they both had dark hair.

The man in the car was quite slim with dark wavy hair, fair-skinned and in his early twenties. I would recognise him again.

I am willing to attend court to give evidence.

Signed: B. Browse
Signature witnessed by: D. Law, DS

STATEMENT OF WITNESS

Statement of:	Brenda BROWSE
Age:	(Details as above)
Occupation:	
Address:	

Dated 15.5.00

Further to my statement of 11th May 2000, on the 15th of May 2000 I was asked to attend Brighton Police Station. I was met by Inspector Charger who explained that there was going to be a parade where the man I saw in the Ford Escort might be. He explained that the man might not be there and I was to look at all of the men very carefully. He said only if I was sure I saw the same man, I should stop and touch him on the shoulder.

I was escorted into a waiting room by a WPC and eventually taken to a large room with several men lined up against one wall. I went to one end of the line and walked along it. The seventh man was the one I had seen driving the Ford Escort on the 12th of April. I was quite sure and I touched him on the shoulder. He did not do anything. The Inspector asked me to leave the room as the parade was now over.

I was then brought to a room where I wrote this statement.

Signed: Brenda Browse
Signature witnessed by: D. Law, DS

STATEMENT OF WITNESS

Statement of:	David LAW
Age:	Over 18
Occupation:	Detective Sergeant 494P, Brighton C.I.D.

[Usual declaration omitted]

Signed: D. Law
Signature witnessed by: A. Libby, DC 675P

Dated 18.5.00

On 17th April 2000 at 12.10 pm, as a result of information received, I went to 33 Dials Lane in Brighton where I found a navy blue Ford Escort XR3i which appeared to have been abandoned in a hurry. The doors were wide open. Under the driver's seat were some shotgun cartridges. The registration number of the vehicle was E838 JPO.

I had reason to believe that this vehicle had been used in an armed robbery which had occurred earlier that day in Brighton and I requested that a Scenes of Crime Officer attend the location in Dials Lane.

On 11th May, I went to a private house at 72 Power Station Row, Southwick. The door was opened by a woman who identified herself as Sharon Ella. I asked her if I could speak to Gerald Ella — she replied that he was not in. Subsequently, I attended the rear of the house where colleagues had apprehended Gerald ELLA, while he was climbing over a fence in the garden of number 72.

I said to him, 'Are you Gerald Ella?' He replied, 'What if I am?' I said to him, 'I have reason to believe you were involved in an armed robbery on the South Downs Building Society in Brighton on the 17th of April, specifically as the driver of the getaway vehicle.' He replied, 'You've got a very good imagination for a copper'.

I then told him that his fingerprints had been identified on the getaway vehicle, the navy blue Ford Escort. He seemed to be about to fall down so I grabbed him and said, 'I am arresting you for your part in the South Downs robbery on the 17th of April 2000. You do not have to say anything. But it may harm your defence if you do not mention when questioned something which you later rely on in court. Anything you do say may be given in evidence'. He made no reply and was taken to Brighton Central Police Station under escort.

He was later seen by myself and DC Libby in an interview room at Brighton Central at 10.25 pm on the 11th. He was reminded of the caution and I then asked him if he was prepared to talk to us about the robbery. He indicated that he did not wish to talk to us and he was returned to his cell at 10.28 pm.

I was present at 7.35 am on the 12th of May when ELLA was charged with robbery, the charge was read over to him, he was cautioned and made no reply.

At 2.40 pm on the 12th of May I interviewed Arthur DUKE at Brighton Central Police Station where he was in custody. DC Libby took a contemporaneous note of what was said. At the end of the interview, DC Libby read the record to DUKE who signed each page as a correct record. The interview concluded at 3.02 pm.

At 6.00 am on the 13th of May I went to 22 Bramber Street, Brighton. There I saw a man I now know to be Finlay LEWIS. I said to him, 'Are you Finlay Lewis?' He said, 'Yes, why?' I told him that he had been implicated in the robbery of the South Downs Building Society in Brighton and he replied, 'Someone's a grass. I'm saying nothing till I see my solicitor.'

After a brief search of the premises, I told LEWIS that he was under arrest for robbery and cautioned him. He replied 'I'll be wanting a word with my solicitor.' He was then taken to Brighton Central Police Station and booked into a cell.

I saw LEWIS again at 2.10 pm that day in the interview room, together with DC Libby. The interview was recorded by DC Libby and ended at 2.25 pm. DC Libby read his contemporaneous notes over to LEWIS who then signed each page as correct.

At 4.45 pm on the 13th of May LEWIS was charged with robbery, the charge was read over to him, he was cautioned and made no reply.

Signed: D. Law
Signature witnessed by: A. Libby

STATEMENT OF WITNESS

Statement of: Alan LIBBY
Age: Over 18
Occupation: Detective Constable 675P, Brighton C.I.D.

[Usual declaration omitted]

Signed by: A. Libby
Signature witnessed by: V. Worthy, PS 111P

Dated 18.5.00

At 6.00 am on the 12th of May 2000, I went to a private flat at 344 Lewes Road, Brighton, together with several other officers. The door was answered by a man I now know as Arthur DUKE. I said to DUKE, 'I have reason to believe that you were involved in an armed robbery last month on a Brighton building society. Have you got anything to say?' He replied, 'You've got the wrong man this time.' I asked if we could look round his flat and he said 'Yes'.

On the floor of a wardrobe in the bedroom I found a balaclava helmet. A shoebox in the same wardrobe contained six shotgun cartridges. Hanging in the wardrobe was a navy blue donkey jacket with an orange fluorescent upper half. I said to DUKE, 'Where did you get this jacket?' He said, 'I've had it for a while now. I wear it if I get any building site work.' I then showed him the balaclava and cartridges and said, 'How do you explain these then?' He did not reply.

I said, 'I am arresting you for robbing the South Downs Building Society in Brighton on the 17th of April this year.' I cautioned him and he made no reply. He was taken to Brighton Central Police Station.

At 2.40 pm on the same day, I was present when DS Law interviewed DUKE at Brighton Central Police Station. I recorded the interview contemporaneously. At its conclusion I read the record over to DUKE who then signed each page as a correct record. The interview was terminated at 3.02 pm. I produce the record of interview, AL/1.

At 5.25 pm on the 12th of May DUKE was charged with robbery, the charge was read over, he was cautioned and made no reply.

On the 12th of May at 10.50 pm, I went to 65 Brighthelmstone Street where I saw a man I now know to be Leonard PETERSON. I said to him, 'Are you Lennie Peterson?' He said, 'That's right. Who are you?' I showed him my warrant card and explained that I was investigating the robbery of the South Downs Building Society.

I said, 'I have reason to believe that you garaged the car for the gang before the robbery. What have you got to say?' He said, 'I know nothing about it.' I said, 'It's right that you've got a lock-up garage at the back of the house, isn't it. That's where the car was kept.' He replied, 'Who's been talking out of turn?'

I said, 'The car was stolen on the 8th of April — that's a week before the robbery. It had to be kept somewhere, out of sight. I think you warehoused it for the gang. For all I know, you stole it, too.' He said, 'Look, I'm no car thief. Gerry ELLA asked me to keep it safe for him until he needed it. He brought it round on the 8th and took it away on the 17th. That's all I know.'

I told him he was being arrested for the robbery and cautioned him. He made no reply and was then taken to Brighton Central Police Station.

At 7.30 pm on the 13th of May at Brighton Central Police Station PETERSON was charged with robbery, the charge was read over to him, he was cautioned and replied, 'I've been very silly and it's all for nothing. What can I say.'

On the 13th of May at 2.10 pm, I attended an interview of Finlay LEWIS by DS Law in an interrogation room at Brighton Central Police Station. I recorded the interview contemporaneously and produce the record, AL/2.

Signed: A. Libby
Signature witnessed by: V. Worthy

Extracts from interview of Arthur Duke by DS Law, recorded by DC Libby (AL/1):-

Q. Do you want us to wait for your lawyer?

A. No, let's get it over.

Q. As I mentioned on the way here, we've found some fingerprints on the Escort and it looks like they are yours.

A. Oh yeah.

Q. I'm serious. Those prints place you in the car. Take them together with what we found in your home . . .

A. All right. It was never meant to end up the way it did.

Q. What do you mean?

A. The old man. Finlay's always been stupid but that tops the lot.

Q. So it was Finlay that shot Mr Goodbody?

A. Yes.

Q. Is that Finlay LEWIS?

A. Yes. I should never have agreed to take part in it. Finlay had it all set up before I got invited. His original partner had to drop out — he's on remand in Brixton at the moment.

. . .

A. Finlay had Gerry ELLA and Len PETERSON lined up. He knew Gerry from Wandsworth and Len was a friend of Gerry's.

. . .

A. I kept watch while Finlay played the hard man with the cashier. Everything went smooth as silk until the old man grabbed Finlay's bag. I couldn't believe what they were doing. Just as I went back to help, Finlay's gun went off and the old boy went down. I don't know whether it was an accident or not.

Extracts from interview of LEWIS by DS Law, recorded by DC Libby (AL/2):—

Q. I am refusing to delay this interview so that you can have your solicitor present because I believe that delay may prevent recovery of the stolen money.

A. No reply

. . .

Q. . . . remind you that you are under caution . . .

Q. This was a very serious offence. I tell you now — I'm more worried about the guy that got shot than the money. Have you got anything you want to say?

A. No reply

Q. Look I'll be straight with you. We've got a confession from Arthur and he's dropped you right in it.

A. I don't believe it.

Q. Have a look at this. (Hands piece of paper to Lewis)

A. Well, it seems like you know it all. Why bother talking to me?

Q. We need to get your side of things, to see how everything fits together.

A. There's no point in holding back now — so much for honour amongst thieves. It was Arthur's idea — he'd planned it for weeks before he spoke to me. We decided that we needed a driver and I knew Gerry from our time in Wandsworth.

Q. You mean Gerry ELLA and HMP Wandsworth in South London?

A. That's right.

. . .

Q. Who got the car?

A. That's down to Gerry. I don't know where it came from — he just got it for the day. The first time I saw it was when I got in it after the job.

Q. Who did what in the shop?

A. I asked for the cash while Arthur kept everyone calm.

Q. With a sawn-off?

A. You don't want heroes in a situation like that.

Q. Like Reg Goodbody?

A. Is he the old boy? He never should have interfered. He got what was coming to him.

Q. From you?

A. No way. That was Arthur. I could have got the bag away from the old man but Arthur got impatient with him.

. . .

Q. So where's the money now?

A. Money? That's rich. Lots of it was cheques. The rest, well, I'll need a nest egg for when I get out, eh?

Q. So you won't tell me where it is?

A. No reply

. . .

Summaries of the antecedent histories of the accused men:—

Finlay LEWIS (Age 40) Born Stornaway, Outer Hebrides.
18 previous convictions including 2 for wounding (s. 18 OAPA) and 3 for armed robbery. Last conviction was at Portsmouth Crown Court for robbery in May 1992. Sentenced to 10 years' imprisonment. Released June 1999.

Arthur DUKE (Age 43) Born Catford, London.
8 previous convictions, mainly for offences of dishonesty. 1 recorded for robbery. Last conviction was at Brighton Magistrates' Court in February 1994 for a fraud on the Department of Health and Social Security. On committal to the Crown Court, sentenced to 6 years' imprisonment. Released April 1998.

Gerald ELLA (Age 26) Born Worthing, West Sussex.
6 previous convictions, all for theft of cars, except the last one. In 1992 a 3-year term of imprisonment was imposed by Inner London Crown Court. In September last year, Brighton Magistrates' Court fined him £250 and banned him from driving for 1 year for driving whilst unfit through drink or drugs.

Leonard PETERSON (Age 55) Born Brighton.
16 previous convictions, all for petty offences of dishonesty. Imprisonment has been ordered in the past, but the last conviction was in 1983 and resulted in a conditional discharge.

If you would like to try your hand at drafting an indictment in a simpler case, try the following short problem.

R* v *Adams

Arthur ADAMS was charged with stealing from Jane BROWN a handbag containing a purse, lipstick and £20 in money. He elected for trial on indictment and he has recently been transferred for trial at Casterbridge Crown Court on that charge. The papers have been sent to you by the CPS and you have been asked to draft an appropriate indictment.

There is evidence to the effect that John SMITH was amongst the crowds in the area of Trafalgar Square at around 11 pm on New Year's Eve 1999 when he was suddenly jostled. He felt inside his jacket pocket, where he had been carrying his wallet, and found that it was missing. He reported the matter to the first police officer he saw. Jane BROWN's evidence is that at around 1 am on New Year's Day 2000 she was in Trafalgar Square when a youth violently wrenched her handbag away from her. Shortly after, she believed she saw amongst the crowds the person who had taken her handbag. She pointed him out to a police officer who arrested him. That person was Arthur ADAMS.

He was searched, and found to have £300 in cash on his person (none of which could be positively identified as having been stolen from either John SMITH or Jane BROWN) together with a wallet containing a cheque card personalised in the name of John SMITH. Subsequently SMITH confirmed that the wallet found in ADAMS' possession was the one which he (SMITH) had lost earlier that night.

ADAMS made a statement to the police in which he said that (i) he had found the wallet on the ground about half an hour before he was arrested and had been waiting for a suitable opportunity to hand it to the police (ii) the wallet was empty when he found it and (iii) he was not the person who had taken Jane BROWN's handbag, she being mistaken in her identification of him.

Having drafted the indictment, consider any objections which the defence might raise against it either on arraignment or at a pre-trial hearing.

Tutorial 6 Sentencing (1)

MULTIPLE-CHOICE QUESTIONS

1. Under the Criminal Justice Act 1991 a court may make a probation order if it is of the opinion that the supervision of the offender by a probation officer is desirable in the interests of:

[A] Securing the rehabilitation of the offender.
[B] Protecting the public from harm from the offender.
[C] Preventing the commission of further offences by the offender.
[D] Any of the above.

2. Johnny, aged 19, appears before the Narrowview Magistrates' Court charged with three offences of theft (triable either way). He pleads guilty and asks for 20 other offences of theft to be taken into consideration. Which one of the following is a correct statement of the law?

The magistrates:

[A] Must obtain a pre-sentence report before sentence.
[B] Must obtain, but need not consider, a pre-sentence report before sentence.
[C] Must obtain and consider a pre-sentence report and may only impose a sentence recommended by that report.
[D] Must obtain and consider a pre-sentence report unless they take the view that one is unnecessary.

TUTORIAL QUESTIONS

1. (a) David is aged 22. He is employed as a painter and decorator earning £150 per week net. He is charged with one offence of theft. It is alleged that on 1 October 2000 he stole various items valued at £85 from a building site. He has the following previous convictions:

(i) On 22 December 1999 at Greenacre magistrates' court he received a conditional discharge for two years for an offence of theft of paint and other materials.

(ii) On 2 September 2000 at the Blackacre magistrates' court he was placed on probation for two years for an offence of burglary.

David appears at the Blackacre magistrates' court and pleads guilty to the charge of theft. The pre-sentence report indicates that a financial penalty will be appropriate. What courses are open to the magistrates? What action can the court take relating to the conditional discharge or probation order?

(b) Edwina (aged 23) appears at Whiteacre magistrates' court and pleads guilty to an offence of assault occasioning actual bodily harm contrary to the Offences against the Person Act 1861, s. 47. She is subject to a community service order of 80 hours imposed by another magistrates' court. What action can be taken in respect of the community service order?

2. Ben, aged 32, pleaded guilty in the Brentvale Crown Court to causing death by dangerous driving. He was driving his car within the speed limit at about 8 p.m. last November. He approached traffic lights which were showing red against him, drove across them and collided with a motor cyclist who was killed. He had drunk a pint-and-a-half of lager at about 6 p.m. but it was not suggested that he was driving whilst unfit through drink.

Ben claims that he had failed to see the lights for some inexplicable reason and it was accepted by the prosecution that there was no evidence of bad driving before he had reached the traffic lights.

Ben is employed as a surveyor and earns £28,000 per annum. He has one previous driving conviction for careless driving two years earlier, when he was fined £200 and his licence was endorsed with 4 penalty points.

You appear on his behalf. His pre-sentence report is not of great assistance. What factors would you ask the judge to take into account when considering the appropriate sentence?

What sentence would you suggest to the judge?

Would your answer be any different if Ben had been over the prescribed alcohol limit?

3. Jimmy, aged 22, pleaded guilty to one count of burglary at Romchester Crown Court. He was concerned in four dwelling-house burglaries in which various items of personal property were stolen. He admitted that he had acted as a lookout while other accomplices entered the houses. The sole count was charged as a specimen count.

He has two previous findings of guilt as a juvenile for theft for which he was conditionally discharged on each occasion and one for burglary when an adult for which he was placed on probation for two years.

He is a self-employed window-cleaner and earns £250 per week take-home pay.

You appear on his behalf. His pre-sentence report confirms that he will consent to a community service order for which he is suitable. What factors would you ask the judge to take into account when considering the appropriate sentence?

What sentence would you suggest to the judge?

Would your answer be any different if Jimmy had been responsible for cleaning the windows of the houses concerned?

4. Edward (aged 22) and Frank (aged 21) both plead guilty at Casterbridge Crown Court to robbery. Prosecuting counsel, in summarising the facts of the offence, states that Edward and Frank stopped the victim (a Mr Brown) as he was walking along the street late at night. Edward held a knife to Mr Brown's throat while Frank searched Mr Brown's pockets, and took a wallet containing £100. They both then ran away. Defence counsel, in mitigation, denies that either of his clients had a knife or any other weapon, although he concedes that they threatened to 'beat Mr Brown's face in' if he struggled. The antecedents of the offenders disclose that Edward has two previous court appearances, one in March 1998 for taking a car without the owner's consent (conditionally discharged for one year) and the other in June 1999 for shoplifting (ordered to perform 80 hours' community service). Frank has not been in trouble before. A pre-sentence report on Frank indicates that he would respond to a probation order. In passing sentence the judge says:

> What I find most disturbing about this case is the use of a weapon. I listened most carefully to what learned Defence counsel had to say on the matter of the knife, but I read the statement of Mr Brown before I came into court, and I am quite satisfied that a knife was used to threaten him. Reluctant as I am to deprive young men of their liberty, I would be failing in my duty to the public if I did not pass a sentence which will serve as a warning to others that this kind of conduct will not be tolerated. You, Edward, had the knife and you will be sentenced to a term of 3 years' imprisonment. In your case, Frank, I thought about making a probation order. In some ways it is an attractive alternative to a custodial sentence, but I have to deal with you in a way which will be a deterrent and an example to others. I take into account your age and your not having committed any offences in the past, but even so the shortest sentence I consider appropriate is one of two years' imprisonment.

Advise Edward and Frank whether they have any grounds for appealing against sentence. How long will they actually spend in custody?

Tutorial 7 Sentencing (2)

MULTIPLE-CHOICE QUESTIONS

1. Spendthrift, aged 45, appears at the Rentacourt Crown Court on an indictment containing 45 counts of conspiracy to defraud, theft and false accounting. He pleads guilty to 15 counts and the remaining counts are left on the court file marked 'not to be proceeded with without leave of this court or of the Court of Appeal'. As a result, there has been considerable saving in time and cost of a lengthy and burdensome trial. In mitigation, you cite a Court of Appeal decision which indicates by way of general guidance that a certain proportion would be an appropriate discount from the sentence which would otherwise be imposed on a contested trial. What is that proportion?

[A] One-half.
[B] One-third.
[C] One-sixth.
[D] One-tenth.

2. Robin, aged 19, appears at the Dimview Crown Court where he pleads guilty to two counts of residential burglary. He asks for 12 other offences of residential burglary to be taken into consideration upon sentence. When sentencing, which of the following would the judge be required to consider when deciding whether or not the case is serious enough to reach the 'custody threshold':

[A] That one count and one 't.i.c.' are so serious that only a custodial sentence would be justified.
[B] That one count and two 't.i.c.' offences are so serious that only a custodial sentence would be justified.
[C] That the two counts and no more than one 't.i.c.' are so serious that only a custodial sentence would be justified.
[D] That the two counts and one or more of the 't.i.c.' offences are so serious that only a custodial sentence would be justified.

3. Harry, aged 17, appeared at the Camberden Youth Court on a charge of unlawful wounding contrary to s. 20 of the Offences Against the Person Act 1861. The maximum custodial sentence for the offence is five years. Harry pleaded guilty to the charge. What is the maximum custodial sentence which may be imposed on Harry by the youth court?

[A] Six months.
[B] 12 months.
[C] 24 months.
[D] Five years.

4. Oliver, aged 14, appears in the Newburgh Crown Court jointly charged with Ted, aged 15, and Charlie, aged 16, on an indictment containing three counts of burglary of dwelling houses (the maximum sentence for each offence being 14 years' imprisonment in the case of an adult). Oliver, Ted and Charlie are convicted of all three offences. Oliver is also subject to a supervision order for two previous findings of guilt for burglary. Ted and Charlie are given custodial sentences.

Which one of the following sentences will the judge **not** be empowered to impose on Oliver?

[A] A sentence of detention in a young offender institution.
[B] A supervision order.
[C] A detention and training order.
[D] A sentence of long-term detention under s. 53(2) and (3) of the Children and Young Persons Act 1933.

TUTORIAL QUESTIONS

1. Ray, aged 26 and unemployed, pleaded guilty at Knightsford Crown Court to wounding with intent contrary to s. 18 of the Offences Against the Person Act 1861. He picked a fight with a stranger in the street and slashed the victim's face with a razor causing severe injury. When this offence was committed, he was on licence after having served just under four years of a six-year sentence imposed when he was 21 for robbery of a betting shop with an imitation firearm (a cucumber in a plastic bag). His pre-sentence report discloses that he is a paranoid schizophrenic and that he is addicted to crack cocaine.

What factors will the judge take into account when determining the appropriate sentence to be passed on Ray? Would his condition of paranoid schizophrenia affect the imposition of sentence in any way?

2. On 20 November 2000 Rachel is convicted at Greenacre Crown Court of four offences of theft from shops. The offences took place on the same day and the total value of goods taken was £200. She has the following previous convictions.

Date	*Court*	*Offence*	*Sentence*
26 Feb 95	Magistrates' Court	Theft	Probation 2 years
5 April 97	Crown Court	Theft	Community Service 120 hrs
9 June 99	Crown Court	Criminal Deception	9 months' imprisonment suspended for 2 years

She was divorced in 1994 and is now 38 years old. Her two children aged 8 and 12 reside with her. Since her divorce she has suffered from bouts of depression. She has recently obtained employment as a nursing auxiliary and has formed a steady relationship with a man she hopes to marry. Her children are properly cared for and are doing well at school. According to her pre-sentence report she completed successfully and enjoyed the work she was required to do under the order for community service, and it is likely she would 'respond positively to some form of supervision'. What factors will the judge take into account in determining the appropriate sentence to be passed on Rachel?

3. Michael and Norman appear at Borough Green Crown Court jointly charged with theft of property valued at £1,600 from their employer. Both plead guilty. Michael is 35. He has three previous convictions for offences of dishonesty and is subject to a combination order imposed at the Doomchester Crown Court for handling stolen goods. When arrested he admitted the offence and gave the police information which led to the stolen property being recovered. Norman is 25. He has one previous conviction for common assault for which he received, and is now in breach of, a conditional discharge.

What sentence will the court consider in respect of both Michael and Norman and what factors will be taken into account in determining the appropriate sentence?

4. (a) Barney is aged 17. He appears at Doomchester Youth Court charged with an offence of aggravated burglary which he admits. His only previous court appearance was nine months ago when he was conditionally discharged for 12 months for an offence of theft. A pre-sentence report reveals that Barney's parents are unable to exercise any effective control over him, and that he has now left school with little prospect of obtaining employment. What factors will the magistrates take into account in deciding the appropriate sentence, and what options are open to them in passing sentence?

Would your answer be any different if Barney appeared in the Crown Court?

(b) Reggie, aged 19, pleaded guilty at Downtown Crown Court to supplying Ecstasy tablets in a nightclub. He has two previous convictions, one for being concerned in the supply of crack cocaine and the other for possession of heroin with intent to supply.

What factors will the judge take into account when determining the appropriate sentence?

5. Scott, aged 15, has pleaded guilty at Brixgreen Youth Court to assaulting a PC occasioning him actual bodily harm contrary to OAP Act 1861, s. 47. The facts were that when the officer stopped him in the street under the 'stop and search' provisions of PACE he picked up a piece of wood and struck the officer on the arm. Scott says that the officer made racist remarks and was just 'hassling me because I am black'. His pre-sentence report discloses that he has had a history of violence at school. His parents complain that he frequently stays out until the early hours of the morning. He has one previous finding of guilt when aged 13 for criminal damage, i.e. spraying graffiti on underground trains, for which he was made the subject of an attendance centre order.

What factors will the court take into account in determining the appropriate sentence to be imposed on Scott?

What would be the position if the prosecutor does not accept that the officer made racist remarks?

Would your answer be any different if Scott were aged 14? aged 17?

6. Marcina, aged 15, appears at the Toxtown Youth Court with two others, aged 15 and 16, charged with robbery. They attacked a 14-year-old girl at a bus stop and forced her to hand over £4.50. They are found guilty, and the evidence given indicates that Marcina played a minor role in the offence. She has no previous finding of guilt, but the pre-sentence report discloses that she was sexually abused by her stepfather some six months prior to the offence and lives in an area of high delinquency.

What options are open to the court in dealing with Marcina?

Would your answer be any different if the victim had been an elderly woman?

Tutorial 8

MULTIPLE-CHOICE QUESTIONS

1. Linzi appears before the Denton Crown Court to answer an indictment containing a single count of burglary, the particulars being that she entered the house of her next door neighbour and stole a hair-drier. Linzi says that the neighbour gave her permission to go into the house and borrow things whenever she wished, but admits that having borrowed the hair-drier she later decided not to return it. At her trial, her counsel asks the judge to direct the jury that it may acquit of burglary but convict of theft. Which one of the following statements correctly represents the law?

[A] The jury can only convict Linzi of theft if the indictment is amended so as to include a count alleging theft.
[B] The judge may direct the jury that it is entitled to acquit of burglary and convict of theft if he or she considers that it is in the interests of justice to do so.
[C] The judge must direct the jury that it may only consider the offence which appears on the indictment.
[D] The judge must direct the jury that it is entitled to acquit of burglary and convict of theft.

2. Edward is convicted in the Middlemarch Crown Court of burglary and sentenced to two years' imprisonment. He appeals against his conviction. Depending on the facts and evidence put before the Court of Appeal, which one of the following options is open to the Court of Appeal?

[A] Order a retrial.

[B] Make a direction for loss of time.
[C] Substitute a verdict of guilty of theft.
[D] Exercise any of the above powers.

TUTORIAL QUESTION

You have here the brief for an appeal to the Court of Appeal against conviction — *R* v *Lewis and Duke*. This is a continuation of the case used in Tutorial 5.

In the brief are the papers that would normally be available to counsel in order to advise on appeal and settle Grounds of Appeal.

For Lewis and Duke, prepare your appeal for the defence. Consider the arguments for and against the appeal.

Finally, consider ancillary points — e.g. whether Lewis or Duke should apply for bail pending the hearing; whether they can (or must) be produced in court for the hearing.

Lewis and Duke were convicted of the present offences on 5 January 2000. They received substantial terms of imprisonment.

R v *LEWIS AND DUKE*

Counsel has herewith extracts from notes supplied by N. B. Good, Esq. who was Defence counsel for the applicants at their trial.

Counsel is instructed

(i) to draft Grounds of Appeal against conviction for the applicants and

(ii) to advise on the merits.

Both applicants were convicted by a jury at Lewes Crown Court of robbery, contrary to s. 8(1) of the Theft Act 1968. Duke was also convicted of wounding with intent to cause grievous bodily harm; Lewis was convicted of this although not alleged to have actually committed the wounding.

Leave to appeal will undoubtedly be required from the single judge, no certificate having been granted by the trial judge.

As counsel was not instructed for the Defence at trial, instructing solicitors should make one or two points clear. First, the applicants were on trial for an armed robbery with two other men, Gerald Ella and Leonard Peterson, both of whom pleaded guilty to their parts in the incident. The applicants were separately accused of wounding Mr Goodbody with intent (OAPA, s. 18).

Ella turned Queen's evidence at trial and appeared as a witness for the Crown. His evidence was potentially very damaging for the applicants.

The judge allowed the Crown to adduce Duke's interview after a *voir dire*. The Defence made no objection to the Crown adducing Lewis's interview in evidence, subject to both interviews being edited to remove any references to the applicants having criminal records. The Crown agreed to this.

Duke did not testify in either his defence or on the *voir dire*. Lewis did testify in his own defence, alleging mistaken identity and fabrication.

Extracts from Defence counsel's notes of the trial follow.

Prosecution Case

1. *Cross-examination* of Gerald Ella (for Lewis and Duke)

I am not making the whole thing up.

Lewis and Duke planned the thing from start to finish.
I am not lying about this, they know it's true.
It is right that I have not been sentenced yet, but I am only doing this because I want to tell the truth.
I was a willing party to the plot but those two schemed it all, without them it would never have come off.

---

2. *Voir dire* (on Duke's interview)

Examination-in-chief of DS Law
I told Duke that we had his fingerprints from the Ford Escort.
At that time I thought there was a strong possibility that some of the prints we found might belong to Duke.
Some time after that interview occurred, I was informed by our forensic laboratory that none of the prints taken from the car matched Duke's fingerprints.

Cross-examination of DS Law (for Duke)
When I told Duke we had his prints, I genuinely thought that was the case.
It was not a deliberate lie.
I didn't need to lie, he knew what we'd found at his place.
I would describe it as unfortunate, that's all.

Judge's decision on voir dire:
. . . I am not satisfied that it has been demonstrated that DS Law lied to the defendant, Duke. It seems to me that there was a simple error of judgment. DS Law made an assumption which was very likely to be correct but later proved to be incorrect. I am not persuaded that the confession has been shown to be so unreliable that I should exclude it from the trial . . .
. . . I am bound to say, in any event, that there is no basis for the exercise of any discretion that I might have under s. 78 of the Police and Criminal Evidence Act to exclude the confession, as Mr Good argued.

---

3. *Cross-examination* of DS Law (for Lewis)

Lewis did take part in the interview, as recorded by DC Libby. DC Libby and I did not put our heads together and make up the interview.
Everything happened as recorded in the notes.
Lewis signed each page of the notes.

I don't agree that the signature looks 'nothing like' Lewis's.
Lewis actually spoke those words, they are not a figment of my imagination.

Defence Case

4. *Examination-in-chief* of Lewis

I know nothing about this robbery except what I've read in the newspapers.
I do know Gerald Ella but, until we were both arrested for this, I had not seen him for about 4 years.

5. *Judge's decision on an application by Crown to cross-examine Lewis under Criminal Evidence Act 1898, s. 1(f)*

I am satisfied that the cross-examination of both Gerald Ella and DS Law was such that no jury could be left with the thought that Lewis alleged them to be merely mistaken. Indeed, Mr Good has not sought to persuade me to the contrary. I have no hesitation in permitting the Crown to use Lewis's criminal record to show the jury his true character.

---

6. *Cross-examination* of Lewis

It is correct that I have several previous convictions.
About 18 altogether.
Some of them for robbery.
They were armed robberies.
Yes, they involved guns but no-one was ever hurt.
My last conviction was at Portsmouth Crown Court in 1992.
That was for an armed robbery.
I was sentenced to 10 years' imprisonment.

---

7. *Judge's Summing-up* (Extracts)

. . .

You may have heard something about the standard of proof, members of the jury. Well, the Court of Appeal has said there is no magic formula to help us judges to help you. But I can tell you that the defendants should only be convicted if you are persuaded in your own minds of their guilt. If in doubt, acquit.

. . .

As to Count 2, wounding with intent. You've heard Lewis testify that he was not there, and I shall be dealing with his testimony later. As to the law — the Crown do not say he was the man who pulled the trigger but they do say that Lewis must have agreed with Duke before the robbery that, in the event of trouble, they would use their guns. Or else, why carry them?

Even if there was no agreement, which you may think is so unlikely as to be fantastic, the Crown say that simply by standing by and watching Duke shoot Mr Goodbody, Lewis is as guilty as Duke. It's what we lawyers call aiding and abetting.

. . .

Miss Penny was quite clear that the masked man who spoke to her had an Irish accent. Whatever it was, she picked out Lewis as that masked man at a parade, having heard him utter that same phrase. You may think she is unlikely to forget the sound of that voice, members of the jury. Anyway, you had the benefit of hearing Lewis for yourselves. We know he comes from the Outer Hebrides originally and he hasn't lost his accent. Could you have thought he was Irish?

. . .

Ella's testimony was, you may think, quite persuasive. He is, on his own admission, an accomplice of the others. Until recently, I would have had to give you a complicated direction about his evidence. Now things are simpler. We can look more realistically at each witness's evidence on its own merits.

I caution you to take care when examining Ella's testimony — he is, after all, a self-confessed criminal but I need say no more about it.

. . .

DS Law told us about the frank admissions made by Lewis once he was incarcerated in Brighton Police Station and realised the game was up. You heard Mr Good suggest to DS Law that he'd made it all up with DC Libby — a suggestion hotly refuted by these two officers, who both have many years' experience in enforcing law and order. You may think, as I do, that Lewis's interview had the ring of truth about it. That's a matter for you.

A similar point was put to Gerald Ella — that he was lying to lighten his own sentence. I shall be dealing with Ella at the end of this trial, members of the jury, so don't worry about that.

As a result of this cross-examination of the Crown's witnesses, I allowed the Crown's application to cross-examine Lewis about his chequered past. What did that tell you about the sort of man Lewis really is? A man experienced in the ways of violence and armed robbery? There it is, I say no more about it.

. . .

Finally, you must consider the evidence against each man separately and on each count separately. You may recall that we heard the interviews of Lewis and Duke in which each clearly damned the other as well as himself. What they say about the other one outside the witness box is not evidence in the case and you must do your best to ignore it.

Note for Appeal. After the jury retired to deliberate (2.15 pm), the usher caught one of them slipping back into the jury room. The judge was informed and, in court, asked the juror where she had been. She said she had left to telephone her husband to say she might be late home (this was at 3.15 pm). No one saw her either leave the jury room or use the telephone. The judge rejected my suggestion to discharge her and allowed her back into the jury room.

The subsequent guilty verdicts (delivered at 3.45 pm) were unanimous.

APPENDIX 2

ANSWERS TO EXERCISES

(The exercises are set out in **Chapter 9**.)

(1)

INDICTMENT No.________

The Crown Court at Bluebridge

The Queen v MICHAEL MASTERS

MICHAEL MASTERS is charged as follows

Statement of Offence

ATTEMPTED THEFT contrary to Section 1(1) of the Criminal Attempts Act 1981.

Particulars of Offence

MICHAEL MASTERS on the 14th day of February 2000 attempted to steal a wallet belonging to Mary Martin.

Date:________________ An officer of the Crown Court________________

(2) Provided that the prosecution evidence upon which the transfer took place discloses a case to answer on a count of attempted theft, that count could stand. You could of course add a count of receiving.

(3)

INDICTMENT No.________

The Crown Court at Newton

The Queen v NOREEN NAYLOR

NOREEN NAYLOR is charged as follows

Statement of Offence

POSSESSING A CONTROLLED DRUG contrary to Section 5(2) of the Misuse of Drugs Act 1971.

Particulars of Offence

NOREEN NAYLOR, on the 15th day of March 2000, had in her possession a controlled drug, namely cocaine.

Date:______________ An officer of the Crown Court______________

(4) The defence should apply to have the indictment quashed, since it is bad for duplicity.

(5) The offences of burglary and going equipped should be included in one indictment. They are founded on the same facts. It is arguable whether the robbery should be charged on a separate indictment. It is *not* founded on the same facts. Does it form part of a series of offences of the same or similar character? All are offences of dishonesty. But they are committed two months apart. The venue of the alleged offences, and other material factors, would be taken into account in deciding whether the robbery should be separated.

(6) The presence of a co-defendant would not in itself settle the matter. The factors outlined in the previous answer would still have to be examined.

(7) Richard's counsel would no doubt wish to apply to sever the charges which Robert faces alone. The two are still likely be tried jointly on the robbery charge, however prejudicial Robert's interview is for Richard. The judge will have to remind the jury that what one defendant says in interview is not evidence against the co-defendant.

(8)

INDICTMENT No.__________

The Crown Court at Blackbridge

The Queen v SIMON SCHOFIELD

SIMON SCHOFIELD is charged as follows

COUNT ONE

Statement of Offence

BURGLARY contrary to Section 9(1)(b) of the Theft Act 1968.

Particulars of Offence

SIMON SCHOFIELD on the 19th day of June 2000, having entered as a trespasser a building known as 108 High Road, Blackbridge, stole therein six necklaces and four bracelets.

COUNT TWO

Statement of Offence

HANDLING stolen goods, contrary to section 22(1) of the Theft Act 1968.

Particulars of Offence

SIMON SCHOFIELD, on the 19th day of June 2000, dishonestly received certain stolen goods, namely a necklace and four bracelets belonging to Stanley Sutton, knowing or believing the same to be stolen goods.

Date:__________ An officer of the Crown Court__________________

Note: On the given facts, the prosecution would no doubt say that either Simon was the burglar or he received the goods from the burglar. Since burglary is the more serious charge, it comes first.

APPENDIX 3

THE VICTIM IN COURT

The purpose of this appendix is to alert you to the very particular and special problems faced by the victims of crime, especially those who appear as witnesses in any criminal proceedings. It is a large and complex area, and this section can do little more than draw your attention to the issues involved. While it is intended as background reading only, you should not underestimate its importance in the conduct of your professional life.

This appendix deals only with the Victim's Charter, a new edition of which was issued in June 1996. Other information may be obtained from the Home Office, The Crown Prosecution Service and Victim Support. A list of useful addresses is included at the end of the Victim's Charter. The Charter itself may be obtained from the Home Office.

Note that the word 'victim' is technically correct only after a verdict of guilt has been recorded. Until then, the word 'complainant' would probably be more accurate. However, for the sake of simplicity, the word 'victim' is used throughout this chapter.

Note also that much of what is said relates to all witnesses, and not just those who are the victims of crime, and the word 'victim' should be understood to include other witnesses where appropriate.

History and Background

Until the middle of the nineteenth century, the person primarily responsible for the prosecution of offences was the victim himself. Consequently, he played a central role in the criminal justice system. With the introduction of efficient police forces, which took over the prosecuting role, the victim was reduced to the status of a mere witness, and any rights he may have had came to be ignored by the system. Indeed, many victims have found that the criminal justice system has served them so badly as to be a greater trauma than the offence itself. Some say that they would never again report an offence and face the criminal justice process a second time.

In recent years, a number of steps have been taken to try and redress the balance:

(a) 1964 saw the introduction of the Criminal Injuries Compensation Board (CICB) which has power to make *ex gratia* payments to victims of crime following an application to them by the victim. However, many victims knew neither that the scheme existed, nor how to make the application.

(b) In 1972, the court was given, for the first time, a power to make compensation orders to benefit victims in suitable cases. Similar problems of ignorance existed as with the CICB. This power has recently been extended by the CJA 1988, and students should refer to the sentencing section of this Manual for details.

(c) In 1974, the first victim support scheme was established in Bristol. Since then, such groups have proliferated, with now some 350 groups throughout the UK.

They are nationally organised, under the title of Victim Support, a registered charity, with a detailed Code of Practice to ensure consistency. Victim Support gives assistance to victims of offences immediately after they have been committed, throughout any court proceedings, and thereafter for as long as such support is needed. Special projects have been organised to improve skills in dealing with the most sensitive cases, such as cases involving racial harassment, the families of murder victims and child victims of offences. Recent research, by Mike Maguire and Claire Corbett, entitled 'The Effects of Crime and the Work of Victim Support Schemes', established that those who had been visited by Victim Support made a better recovery than those who did not. The writer is indebted to Victim Support for their assistance in writing this section of the Manual.

(d) In 1988, a working party, under the chairmanship of Lady Ralphs, CBE, JP, DL examined how a court appearance could be made less of an ordeal for the victim, and reported its findings under the title *The Victim in Court*. Following this, in 1990, the Government introduced *The Victim's Charter: A Statement of the Rights of Victims of Crime*. A new edition of the Charter was issued in June 1996, entitled 'The Victim's Charter: A statement of service standards for victims of crime'.

RECENT CHANGES

A number of changes have taken place over recent years to improve the position of victims of crime. These changes include:

(a) Information for victims.

One of the major complaints made by victims of crime is the lack of information available to them. Many will have had little or no previous contact with the police, the courts etc., and have very little idea of how the system works; nor has it been explained in a way which the victim can understand. Further, information has rarely been forthcoming about the progress of the case itself — whether any one has been arrested, whether bail has been granted, when a trial is to be expected and so on.

In order to give victims more information, the Home Office has produced two leaflets entitled *Victims of Crime* and *The Witness in Court*. The first should be made available to all persons who report crime to the police. It explains how to obtain compensation (from both the CICB and the court) and how to obtain information about crime prevention and about the progress of their case. The second leaflet explains what is involved in being called as a witness and giving evidence in court.

See the Charter discussed below, and 'Projects' at the end of this **Appendix**.

(b) Rape victims.

Home Office Circular 69/1986 to chief police officers offers advice on the treatment of rape victims and victims of domestic violence. It includes suggestions for the provision of suitable facilities for the examination of witnesses, references to advice and counselling services and police training.

The CJA 1988 provides for the anonymity of the rape victim from the moment the allegation is made throughout her life, regardless of whether or not any proceedings follow.

(c) Compensation.

The CJA 1988 contains provisions to increase greatly the use of compensation by the court. Students should consult the Sentencing section of this Manual for details.

(d) Witnesses.

In February 1999, the National Witness Service was launched. This is designed to offer support to every witness in every court in England and Wales within the next three years.

The Victim's Charter

(1) AIMS

The Victim's Charter aims to explain what happens after an offence has been reported to the police, and the standards of service you should expect. It acknowledges that the way a victim is treated cannot make up for what has been suffered, but states as its aim to make sure that the unpleasant effects of crime are not made worse by what happens later. The aim of the Charter is to treat victims of crime fairly and courteously and to provide a good service.

It can be noted that the Charter omits a comment included in the earlier version, that while justice is dispensed openly, the media have a particular responsibility not to violate needlessly the victim's privacy by turning the proceedings into a public spectacle.

(2) WHAT THE VICTIM CAN EXPECT

The first part of the Charter sets out details of what the victim can expect when reporting a crime. These expectations are set out below:

(a) The victim can expect that a reported crime will be investigated and to receive information about what happens. There are several elements to this, including the fact that the police will respond quickly to the report, do their best to catch the person responsible and keep the victim informed of any significant developments in the case such as any decision to drop or alter charges, any trial date and the final result of any court proceedings. See 'Projects' at the end of this **Appendix** for a further discussion.

Victims of serious crimes, such as the family of a murder victim, or the victim of rape should expect to receive particular help.

(b) The victim can expect to have the chance to explain how the crime has affected him or her, and have his or her interests taken into account. To this end, the police will ask the victim about details of any loss, damage or injury, and about any fears of further victimisation. The victim's interests also include such matters as the likely release date of someone who has committed a serious crime. See 'Projects' below.

(c) The victim can expect to be treated with respect and sensitivity if he or she has to go to court. To make giving evidence easier, the victim may, among other things, ask to see the court room before the trial, have a friend or relative accompany him or her to court, and, if possible, wait separately from any other witnesses. Further, the Charter aims to make sure that witnesses do not have to wait more than two hours before giving evidence, and to pay expenses within five days. The Charter contains particular measures for dealing with child witnesses.

(d) The victim can expect to receive emotional and practical support. This will initially come from Victim Support, but the Charter also informs the victim of the Criminal Injuries Compensation Scheme and the power of the court to make a compensation order.

(3) INFORMATION AS TO WHAT WILL HAPPEN NEXT

This part of the Charter deals with different stages of the criminal process and outlines the work of Victim Support and the Witness Service, which Victim Support runs in every Crown Court to assist all witnesses. In particular, the Charter deals with the following issues:

(a) Help from the police. This reiterates that the police will investigate the crime as quickly as possible and are the main point of contact in relation to the case.

(b) Compensation. The power of the court to make compensation orders, and the work of the Criminal Injuries Compensation Scheme are outlined.

(c) When someone is caught. The decision of the police to caution the offender or to charge them with the offence is explained, as is the work of the Crown Prosecution Service.

(d) Being a witness. The difference between the Crown Court and the magistrates' court is briefly explained, and the fact that the victim should inform the police if there are any days on which he or she would be unable to attend.

(e) Help at court. This section reassures the victim that as much practical help will be given as possible in terms of finding the way round the court building, but points out that no-one will be able to discuss with the victim the details of the evidence he or she will give.

(f) Special cases. The Charter recognises the very special needs of some victims, such as children and the victims of sexual assault. Special provision is made for them.

(g) The trial. A victim who has to give evidence is reminded that they may be accompanied by a friend or a representative of Victim Support if they wish. Little is said about the trial process itself, perhaps because it is envisaged that the victim will visit a court before the trial and have some idea of what is involved. However, the sentencing process is briefly outlined, including the defence's plea in mitigation, pre-sentence reports and the power of the Attorney-General to refer unduly lenient sentences to the Court of Appeal.

(h) After the court case. This section relates to victims who are still worried about their safety, and refers them to the police for advice and practical assistance where necessary.

(i) Information about the release of offenders. Within two months of the passing of a life sentence or in other cases which involve a serious sexual or violent offence, the victim will be contacted by a member of the Probation Service to inform him or her about rules relating to the release of prisoners and to establish whether the victim wishes to be informed of any plans for the release of the offender. Any concerns that the victim expresses will be taken into account by the Probation Service in making plans for the supervision of released prisoners. See 'Projects' below.

(4) COMPLAINTS

The Charter concludes with a section on complaints, acknowledging that while all the agencies involved in the investigation and prosecution of crime aim to provide a high standard of service, things do sometimes go wrong. The Charter informs victims of the complaints procedure for any of the following agencies:

(a) The police.

(b) The Crown Prosecution Service.

(c) The Crown Court.

(d) A judge.

(e) A magistrates' court.

(f) A magistrate.

(g) The Probation Service.

(h) Victim Support or the Witness Service.

(i) The Criminal Injuries Compensation Authority.

Projects

A number of projects are under way to further investigate the effect of crime on victims and how they should best be treated. Two projects in particular may be mentioned:

(a) Keeping victims informed. The Victim's Charter states that victims should be kept informed of significant developments in their case, and in certain areas of the country, the system is in place and works well. The service is, however, patchy. A single point of contact is required and the police were recognised to be the logical agency. This has become known as the 'one-stop-shop'. A pilot study has been undertaken to test systems to ensure that relevant information is gathered and passed on to victims who wanted it at the right time and in the most appropriate way.

The 'one-stop-shop' has two elements:

(i) Victims seeking information about the case can contact the police, who will assist or put them in touch with someone else who can help.

(ii) The police will tell victims about certain key developments. Under the Charter, all victims will be told if a suspect is caught, cautioned or charged. The pilot schemes, however, only include some offences, and do not affect any existing arrangements there may be in any police area.

The pilot operates by asking the victim to 'opt-in' to the scheme if they wish to receive further information, and if they do, they will be informed of any substantial changes to the charges brought by the CPS, the date of any trial and the outcome. A letter asking if the victim wishes to opt in and a reply form will be sent to the victim after charge and before the papers are sent to the CPS. The form should be returned within two weeks.

This project has now been completed and evaluated, and a number of issues need to be resolved before the scheme is taken any further. The fact that some victims opted-in for a service while others did not tended to create a division which became complex, expensive and likely to fall into error. While there were some victims who did not wish to be contacted, these were rare. Suggestions have therefore been put forward that either a second opportunity to opt-in is given, or that the system is provided across the board, with victims being given the opportunity to opt-out.

Difficulties with the failure to provide the promised information, the provision of late information, and the lack of information about bail decisions was also highlighted. A perhaps surprising result of the project shows that some victims who opted-in were less satisfied at the end of the day than those who did not. The reason for this seems to be that expectations were raised which were not fulfilled for whatever reason, or that expectations were raised about matters which the project was never intended to fulfil, and were inevitably disappointed. For example, a victim may expect to be kept informed of *all* the developments in a case and not just the key ones, though this was never promised.

(b) Victim statements. The aim of a victim statement is to give victims the chance to tell all the agencies involved what effect the crime has had on them. Two different types of statement are being piloted:

(i) Victim's Own Statement. Accompanying the letter about receiving further information under the 'one-stop-shop' scheme, the victim will receive a letter asking them if they wish to make a statement. A pro-forma will be included, setting out a number of questions that the victim may wish to answer, though the victim may add anything else.

(ii) Victim/Police Statement. In this version no pro-forma will be included with the letter and the victim is simply asked whether he or she wishes to make a statement. If requested, the police will arrange to take the statement, asking similar questions to those included in the pro-forma.

This project has also been completed and evaluated, and is again subject to further consideration. The purpose of the victim statement needs to be clearly agreed and made clear to the victim and the agencies involved. In particular, no decision has yet been taken as to whether the victim statement would be taken into account in sentencing, and if so, in what way.

Neither type of victim statement has proved completely satisfactory, and an effective method needs to be found. The evaluation committee leaned towards the idea of a general form which victims can fill in unaided or assisted as they chose, rather than a completely form-free approach. There was also perceived to be a need to allow the statement to be updated and a system needs to be developed to permit this to happen.

Social Difficulties

Students should be aware that victims of crime sometimes face social difficulties as a result of the crime, in addition to the particular difficulties, for many victims, of the trial process itself. The main problem seems to be that most institutions and agencies with whom the victim will be dealing appear to expect that the effects of the crime are much more short-lived than they often are, leading to a '*Haven't you got over it yet?*' approach. While these difficulties are not the responsibility of the barrister, you should be aware of the possibility of them when dealing with the victims of crime from whichever point of view. Difficulties may be experienced in a number of areas, including:

(a) Some victims have found that their employers are unsympathetic, appearing to be more concerned with getting them back to work quickly rather than attempting to offer any support. This may be true wherever the offence has happened, but is clearly much more significant if the offence took place at work.

(b) A good number of victims of crime wish to move house following the crime, either because of on-going harassment, the fact that the crime happened in or near the home or that the offender knows where the victim lives. Though relationships between organisations such as Victim Support and housing agencies are improving in many areas, some victims find that they have been treated unsympathetically or suffered unnecessary delay, occasionally finding that they have been classified as having made themselves voluntarily homeless when they are unable to continue living in the accommodation where the offence took place. Victims who are home-owners may find that in order to move quickly, the property must be sold at less than the market value.

(c) Some victims may need more specialised help from counselling or psychiatric services that are available through organisations such as Victim Support. The adequacy of such services varies throughout the country and again the main problem seems to be delay in obtaining the help needed.

Reparation

Under the CDA 1998, the courts may pass two new sentences: the action plan order and the reparation order. The action plan order will require the offender to partake in specific activities, or to desist from specific activities, designed to achieve the offender's rehabilitation. The order may also specify that reparation is made to the victim of the offence (with their consent) or to the community.

The reparation order will require the offender to undertake certain work for the victim, provided the victim agrees. This will be a maximum of 24 hours work to be undertaken within a period of three months from the making of the order.

The existence of such order may be very beneficial to victims. Reparation may include writing a letter of apology to the victim or apologising in person, cleaning graffiti or repairing criminal damage. Any one of these may help the victim put the crime behind them. However, it is seen as very important that the reparation is something which is commensurate with the seriousness of the offence, is something to which the victim agrees and finally, is tailor-made for this offender, this crime and this victim, rather than a standard response to the type of crime.

See **24.2.4.4** and **24.2.4.5** of this Manual for a full discussion of these orders.

The Youth Justice and Criminal Evidence Act 1999

The aim of the YJCEA 1999 continues the reform of the youth justice system begun in the CDA 1998. It introduced a new order to the youth court, to ensure that offenders take greater responsibility for their offences.

The Act also contains some measures relating to vulnerable witnesses, the most important of which are:

(a) restrictions on the freedom of an unrepresented defendant to cross-examine the victim of rape and other serious sex offence cases;

(b) restrictions on the evidence which may be adduced about the previous sexual experience of the victim of a rape or other serious sexual offence;

(c) special measures to help certain classes of witnesses give evidence. Those classes of witnesses are children, those suffering from a physical or mental disorder, or those whom the court is satisfied are likely to suffer fear or distress in giving evidence, whether because of their own circumstances or the circumstances of the case.

INDEX